Sporting with the Gods

Sporting with the Gods

The Rhetoric of Play and Game in American Culture

MICHAEL ORIARD

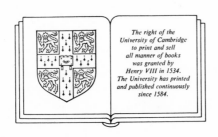

The right of the
University of Cambridge
to print and sell
all manner of books
was granted by
Henry VIII in 1534.
The University has printed
and published continuously
since 1584.

CAMBRIDGE UNIVERSITY PRESS

Cambridge
New York   Port Chester   Melbourne   Sydney

Published by the Press Syndicate of the University of Cambridge
The Pitt Building, Trumpington Street, Cambridge CB2 1RP
40 West 20th Street, New York, NY 10011, USA
10 Stamford Road, Oakleigh, Melbourne 3166, Australia

© Cambridge University Press 1991

First published 1991

Printed in the United States of America

Library of Congress Cataloging-in-Publication Data

Oriard, Michael, 1948–
Sporting with the gods : the rhetoric of play and game in American
culture / Michael Oriard.
p.   cm. – (Cambridge studies in American literature and culture)
Includes bibliographical references and index.
ISBN 0-521-39113-X
1. American literature – History and criticism. 2. Play in literature.
3. United States – Popular culture. 4. United States – Civilization.
5. Sports in literature. 6. Games in literature.
7. Metaphor.   I. Series.
PS169.P55075   1991
810.9′355–dc20
                                              90-44788
                                                   CIP

British Library Cataloguing in Publication Data

Oriard, Michael
Sporting with the gods : the rhetoric of play and game in American
culture – (Cambridge studies in American literature and culture)
1. American culture, history. Sociological perspectives
I. Title
306.0973

ISBN 0-521-39113-X hardback

Page 412: Cover illustration from *Playboy* Vol. 2, No. 9, published
by Johnson Reprint, Inc., reprinted by permission of Harcourt Brace
Jovanovich, Inc.

For Julie, Colin, and Alan
For my father
And in memory of Ronda O'Leary Oriard

We live in a skeptical age in which games are increasingly important. When life has no ontological meaning, it becomes a kind of game itself. Thus it's a metaphor for perception of the way the world works, and also something that almost everybody's doing – if not on the playing fields, then in politics or business or education. If you're cynical about it, you learn the rules and strategies, shut up about them, and get what you can out of it. If you're not inclined to be a manipulator, you might want to expose the game plan for your own protection and ask how it can be a better game than at present. And formal games reflect on the hidden games, more so in an age without a Final Arbiter. So it's an important metaphor to be explored.

Robert Coover (1983)

Contents

Preface

When the One Great Scorer comes to write against your name He marks
– not that you won or lost – but how you played the game.

Grantland Rice

This study explores the cultural history of a metaphor, a cliché, the trope
in a variety of forms that says life is a game. George Lakoff and Mark
Johnson have described how metaphorical language, even when it has
become utterly conventional, not only reveals human thought processes
and cultural values, it also creates the perceived reality.[1] The rhetoric of
"games" and "play," I argue throughout the book, has functioned in
just this way. Its presence early in the nineteenth century, its full flowering during the Progressive Era, and its continuing proliferation through
the 1980s obviously bear some relationship to the widely acknowledged
shift in America from a work–centered culture to one that has increasingly
privileged the values of play. If my subject is the metaphor, then, its
context is not just the history of sport and play but that larger cultural
transformation as well, with the result, as I discovered early on in my
writing, that what I was attempting to cover was potentially unman-
ageable. The more I pursued my simple metaphor in its many not-so-
simple incarnations, the more I realized how much was at stake: American
ideas not just about sport and play themselves, but about all of the things
for which sport and play have become emblems – heroism, success,
gender, race, class, the law, religion, salvation; the relations of Humankind, God, and Nature. A couple of sporting lexicographers in 1989 –
going well beyond my generic "sport," "game," and "play" – identified
more than seventeen hundred metaphors in common American usage
derived from sports, games, and recreations.[2] Several times, usually at

the moment of realizing that yet another potentially vast subject ought to be considered, I felt like the mother in a folk tale read to me as a child, who has been given a magic pot to make porridge for herself and her daughter so that they will never go hungry; but who one day, after setting the pot to cooking, forgets the magic words to turn it off and soon finds herself and her entire village shin-deep in mush.

All along I remained convinced that what was most valuable in my study was the pattern I was discovering. As I came to realize that my subject could easily fill several volumes, I persisted in clinging to a sense of the whole by maintaining a narrow focus on the metaphors themselves while attempting to ground them adequately in their cultural contexts. In the following chapters, then, the reader will find discussions of the explicit sporting rhetoric in a range of American texts and only secondarily a consideration of the many cultural phenomena clearly related to sport and play. This book is not an exploration of four centuries of American history *sub specie ludi;* it is not a study of actual sports and games – football and baseball, gambling and board games, children's play and adult recreation – that have their own rich histories; it is not a study of game*like* or play*like* behavior and values (an analysis, say, of rule-bound social structures *as* games; of sexual desire, the cultivation of style, or literature itself *as* play). Nor is it a study of the mass media or the popular arts marketed through those media, the numerous options for American recreation and leisure. Culture itself, as Huizinga first argued in 1938, is playlike in fundamental ways; modern "mass culture" or "consumer culture" is rooted in conspicuous playfulness of a kind that Huizinga considered not truly play at all. All of these topics appear here only sketchily as a general context for my specific subject.

That subject, to repeat, is not the play element in American culture but the specific rhetoric of sport, play, and game, and my sense of that rhetoric's most significant functions. The history of this rhetoric necessarily coincides with the social history of sport and play in America, which begins, ironically, at that very moment when, according to Huizinga, the play element began to disappear from Western civilization. The concurrent rise of capitalism, Puritanism, and industrialism in the sixteenth and seventeenth centuries – the historical moment when permanent European colonies were founded in the New World – separated play from work and assigned them to different spheres, to the disadvantage of play. Contrary to a prevailing stereotype, the Puritans in the New World did not ban all play, but they did indeed grant it decidedly minor importance. Colonial Americans, Puritan and otherwise, banned sports and games selectively: gambling always but recreational activities only when pursued to excess, at inappropriate times, or in a dangerous manner. By the eighteenth century, particularly in the South but also in

New England, assured economic survival and the consolidation of a prosperous leisure class led to greater tolerance for play generally, and to a range of specific sporting practices closely tied to the economic and social hierarchy. Frontier settlers sported in one way, merchants and wealthy planters in others; poor and rich, slave and free, rural and urban, male and female, Calvinist and Deist all found, or were allowed, different modes of play. The Revolution, however, followed by the responsibilities of new nationhood and the renewed asceticism of a second great religious awakening, reasserted the primacy of work and the frivolity of play.

Beginning in the 1830s, reformers began to call for a change. The Industrial Revolution completed the triumph of capitalism ironically by devaluing work through the total separation of capital from labor. With the Industrial Revolution came not just a new kind of leisure but the beginning of an uncomfortable awareness that perhaps leisure, not labor, offered the best opportunities for human fulfillment. By the 1860s a sporting revolution was underway throughout American society in a multiplicity of forms determined as before by gender, race, social or economic class, religion, occupation, and region. Over the next century and more, down to our own day, a work-centered culture increasingly granted play a vital place in human life. From the long view this transformation may seem a steady, gradual response to the shift from a producing to a consuming economy, but in the decade-to-decade, generation-to-generation working out of American culture, no such simple development appears. Cultural change in America has been a matter of fits and starts, gropings and hesitations, sudden advances and abrupt recoilings – all within the framework of overall transformation – and such is the cultural history of play in America. A wide range of documents suggests that the Progressive Era from the 1890s to the First World War was that moment when the opposing principles of work and play contested in more or less troubled equality within middle-class American culture, making this period a cusp between America's Century of Work and its Century of Play.

The rhetoric of sport and play that I examine records Americans' troubled accommodation to the changes that lie behind this social history. But it also reveals American attitudes toward many things – business, politics, religion, personal relations – not directly related to sport and play. Behind my account of specific rhetorical figures lies a cultural history not of play as physical activity, nor of play as an element within culture, but of play as a projection of the society's inner life, its understanding of human possibility.

As a window into that inner life, then, I trace the histories of a number of rhetorical figures – images, similes, metaphors, analogies – that express heroic codes, strategies of survival, states of being, life itself as "sport," "game," or "play." I am not responding to Huizinga's charge in *Homo Ludens* that modern civilization, judged from the perspective of a transcendent ideal of play, has been impoverished by a decline of the spirit of play. Rather, through historically specific and changing definitions I seek not to judge the quality of American culture according to timeless standards but to understand it as a complex system of responses to historical change.

The key terms of my inquiry – "play," "game," and "sport" – have in fact had shifting definitions over time. "Play" appears in this study also under the guise of "mirth," "frolic," "amusement," and other obvious cognates, the term "play" itself becoming common as the equivalent of those words only after the mid-nineteenth century. "Play" under all of these linguistic signs has connoted spontaneity, freedom, intuition, naturalness, release; but also disorder, anarchy, abandon, chaos – depending on both the historical moment and the specific writer's values. (The obvious use of "play" that I do not consider is its meaning as mimickry, pretending, or performance – a parallel universe of meanings whose history would double the size of an already large book.) Throughout the colonial period and into the nineteenth century, "game" was chiefly associated with gaming, or gambling, the most objectionable of all recreational vices. "Sport" referred to hunting and fishing or was used in the context, to "make sport" of someone's infirmity, or to "sport with" one's moral duties, that is, to mock or belittle. Over the course of the nineteenth century, the largely negative or narrow connotations of "game" and "sport" began to compete with altogether positive and broader ones, as sport itself became an increasingly prominent fact in American life. A "game" most simply became a playful contest between opponents (or against "the house"), according to agreed upon rules, for a particular stake. The "games" important in American culture overwhelmingly fell into two classes: competitive contests and games of chance (*agôn* and *alea* in Roger Caillois's well-known typology). But "game" also could mean plot or scheme, evasion or trivialization (as in "playing games" in the contemporary pejorative sense). The linguistic confusion created by a "game" that could either affirm or defy social values reflects not only the flexibility of American usage but also a divided culture. "Sport" during this period came to refer almost exclusively to the newly popular athletic contests, as usages such as "dead game sport," a favorite in dime novels, disappeared by the twentieth century.

At the limits of abstraction, "work" and "play" in this country have always defined a fundamental antinomy: "work" as action for the sake of some exterior goal, "play" as action for its own sake. Work is concerned with ends, play with means: product and process. If "work" and "play" are imagined, then, as absolutes defining the boundaries of a continuum (rather than as activities that can exist in a pure state), "games" are activities on that continuum embodying in varying degrees both "work" and "play." While play is always defined in opposition to work (to effort, striving, earnestness), a "game" marks the meeting of "play" and "work" in the social world. A game is paradoxically a workful expression of the play spirit, or a playful kind of work. The "games" described in American writing are thus wonderfully revealing as expressions of conflicting values. The "game" of business, for example, a pervasive metaphor from the late nineteenth century to the present, celebrates work by casting it as play with the tension between work and play in the metaphor often unacknowledged. For the student of American culture such metaphors can become specific and discrete prisms through which to examine large-scale and highly complicated responses to shifting economic, social, and political realities.

In its largest ambition this book thus seeks to develop resonant contexts for examining the relationship of work and play as a cultural dichotomy whose importance is as fundamental as the more widely studied conflicts between nature and civilization, individual and society, self and other. As these terms have been embedded in written narratives, the results have included representations of Western and Southern sporting myths; the "games" of love, business, politics, and life itself; and the "play" of holy children, childlike blacks, and other popular icons (often racist or sexist) of countercultural freedom. In the following chapters, I will develop the well-known concepts of sportsmanship and gamesmanship in what I hope are unfamiliar ways: not just as fair or unfair tactics in games but as contrasting worldviews, incompatible yet interwoven into the basic fabric of American culture (Part I); I will examine the theologically grounded rhetorical figures of the "game of life" and the "sport of the gods" by which an increasingly secularized culture clung to belief in the transcendent possibilities rooted in its religious past (Part II); I will trace the development of these various figures of the "game" in the twentieth century, as structural continuity accommodating profound change (Part III); and finally, both in contrast to these "games" and in summation of their underlying impulse, I will consider the idea of "play" itself as a fundamental expression of both countercultural rebellion and middle-class desire from the 1830s to the 1980s (Part IV). The history of what "play" and "game" successively represent and what they oppose provides a concrete record of cultural transformation. Throughout these chapters, by tracing a handful of specific tropes through a detailed cultural history, I have attempted to negotiate between the alternatives of grand synthesis and microhistory, between pattern and particularity.

No theoretical model but my material itself has governed my interpretation of America's sporting rhetoric. Whatever claims I make on the reader's attention lie not in any original contribution to cultural theory but in the mass of details I have assembled. I wish, however, to acknowledge here the basic assumptions that lie behind my study. The "American culture" I examine has been variously called the "dominant," "hegemonic," or "mainstream" culture. In preferring the more neutral term "middle-class," I am well aware of the implications. I take the double challenge of cultural studies to lie in recognizing cultural diversity without ignoring the relationship of culture to political power. The sporting rhetoric I examine is predominantly the language of white middle-class males. In discussing that language I attempt to give proper attention to the significance of gender, race, and class, but also to avoid reducing the so-called mainstream culture to a single voice of consensus. At the same time, while rejecting the notion of "dominance" that is sometimes too simply attributed to this culture, I attempt to explore the more complex relationship of cultural forms to political power. Middle-class American culture has not been uniform but diverse, not coherent but contested, not simply coercive but frequently at odds with itself. White middle-class males and females share common bonds of race and class but not of gender; white and black males share common bonds of gender and sometimes class, but not of race. The intersections of gender, race, and class are frequently inscribed in the various tropes I consider; but in addition, the white middle-class male "mainstream" has itself always been contested.

Using fiction to represent this heterogeneous middle class might seem to risk reducing its diversity; after all, those who write and read novels represent a narrow slice of the populace. Moreover, my study pays considerable attention to that same small group of white male writers who not too long ago were assumed to comprise *the* American literary tradition. Yet I emphatically do not want to present here another "melodrama of beset manhood," deaf to all the voices that lie on the periphery or altogether outside Anglo-masculine angst. In four specific ways I have attempted to counter the potential limitations in my approach. First, as suggested above, I wish to challenge the too often overstated claims for the uniformity of the white male literary tradition. Second, I wish to consider the canonical male writers *in,* not against, the American grain. The definition of the "dominant" American literary tradition as an "adversarial," one which has been the custom since the 1920s when high modernism triumphed at the same time that professional study of American literature began, is one of the more curious paradoxes of our literary history. Third, in order to describe a heterogeneous and contested cultural center, I attempt to take into account the broad range of writing of which canonical texts comprise only a small part. And fourth, by emphasizing conflict rather than consensus, I at least leave room for the many voices that remain unheard, although I by no means account for every one.

In giving more extended treatment, then, to the writings of Emerson and Thoreau, Hawthorne and Melville, Twain and James, Hemingway and Faulkner, I intend these writers to be more representative than exceptional. Set within my overviews of cultural attitudes as expressed by dozens of other novelists, popular preachers, success prophets, and the like, these writers are meant to illustrate the complex interplay between the individual author and the culture. I use these novelists, that is, not to represent the artist as prescient seer whose understanding cuts through the confusion of lesser mortals, but to represent the individual consciousness within American society. At times these "major" authors have in fact cut through the confusions of their day; at other times they have succumbed to them.

If my long labors on this book have taught me anything, it is the difficulty and risk of generalization; but I would identify one overriding tendency in the rhetorical traditions I trace in these chapters. My ultimate subject, less by design than discovery, is a popular American "metaphysics" and its complex interplay with "politics" in the broadest sense. The rhetorical figures of "sport," "game," and "play" are abstract renderings of concrete social behavior; and this process of abstraction itself, this cultural impulse toward metaphysics or transcendence, has political implications. When western expansion and Indian warfare are explained by analogy to a "game," the real human cost can be forgotten as the workings of brute force are transformed into "fair play." When business is explained metaphorically as the great "game of life," the actual impact of economic competition or monopolistic practices may become lost in the celebration of the successful businessman's sporting success. When readers are urged to "play" in the world rather than to work in it or conform to its demands, assumptions about the leisure and abundance necessary for life to be play may be left unexamined.

The popular rhetoric of "play" and "games," in other words, is profoundly ideological, yet its relationship to political power is not at all straightforward. The function of rhetoric is to persuade. The rhetorical figures I discuss are sometimes popular fantasies of an idealized past or future, sometimes more ambivalent wrestling with an intransigent present; they express values, hopes, fears, desires, anxieties, even entire social philosophies or worldviews. Ultimately, the linguistic construction of life as game or play has served to reinforce existing power relations, but that generalization does not adequately account for the messier relations of language and power. Sometimes the sporting rhetoric overtly resists the prevailing political power of the day; sometimes it endorses, promotes, and enhances it; sometimes it seems to resist but tacitly augments the power arrangements through its evasions. And sometimes, though not all that often, it is evoked by those in power in ways meant to consolidate that power. The resulting ambiguity and confusion reveal a culture often at odds with itself.

In the following chapters I offer mostly brief readings or summaries of a large number of texts, restricted to discussion of the rhetorical figures that are the subject of this book. The result, I fear, is that some readers may be frustrated by the absence of longer, more fully developed discussions of individual novels or stories. I feel there is no choice in this matter, that no claim for pattern can be convincing without quantity of evidence. In lieu of detailed analyses of the numerous relevant texts, I hope to have developed persuasive and meaningful contexts within which any number of texts can be read. But I also discuss a handful of texts and writers in greater detail to explore the ways in which the rhetorical figures have sometimes structured entire worlds, both "real" and fictional. And although I trace each specific rhetorical figure separately, I intend that all of them be seen as the many strands in a single complex pattern whose shape will be complete only with the final chapter. It is only in the coexistence of multiple meanings of "play," "game," and "sport" – all within the rhetorical performances of a single American middle class – that the diversity and complexity of that middle class's values and beliefs will fully emerge.

The question of play's role in human experience has engaged a number of famous thinkers: from Friedrich Schiller in the eighteenth century to Fourier, Marx, and Nietzsche in the nineteenth; to Huizinga, Ortega, Heidegger, Sartre, and Derrida in the twentieth. The pattern I construct does not record that grand ongoing intellectual debate but the homelier history of ordinary as well as extraordinary Americans' groping, uncertain, often confused efforts to come to terms with the meaning of play, and the meanings of the many things represented as "sport" and "game" and "play," in their socially grounded lives.

Acknowledgments

Although this payment will be inadequate, I would like to thank the people and institutions who assisted me over the dozen years of research and writing that lie behind this volume. Research grants from Oregon State University's College of Liberal Arts and Research Council provided release-time to begin my study. A year-long fellowship from the National Endowment for the Humanities provided the large chunk of time that made completion of a long draft possible. In its final stages, a grant from the Edward Smith Memorial Endowment in the English Department at OSU provided funds for the illustrations.

On a more personal level, several scholars responded with extraordinary generosity to queries from a stranger. David Reynolds and Frances Cogan allowed me to read works in progress; Daryl Jones sent a photocopy of a hard-to-find dime novel; Richard Etulain, Ronald Bosco, and the late Henry Nash Smith pointed me in directions that led to important sources of information; Merton Sealts, Jr., read an early chapter on Melville and sustained me with his encouragement. Closer to home, my deepest gratitude goes to three good friends – my long-time mentor Eric Solomon and my current colleagues David Robinson and Kerry Ahearn – who read a very long manuscript, sharing not just precious time but invaluable criticism. At Cambridge University Press, the manuscript's two anonymous readers, Albert Gelpi as series editor, Carolyn Viola-John as copy editor, and Julie Greenblatt as editor each contributed good will as well as professional knowledge toward bringing the book into print. To all I say thank you.

For help in locating, acquiring, and reproducing illustrations I thank Erika Wilson, Michael Lofaro, Herbert Siegel, Andrea Lunsford, Scott Leonard, Robert Weis, Robert Cenedella, and Wayne Tonack. I am grateful to several colleagues at Oregon State University for a variety of services, large and small: to Robert Frank, chair of the English Department, for many acts of support, both administrative and financial; to Doris Tilles and her staff in the interlibrary loan office of Kerr Library, who in effect created my own research collection; to Diane Slywczuk, Anterra Bereyl, Anne Wilson, and Lois Gangle, who provided secretarial and administrative assistance. And thanks, finally, to the editors of *Modern Fiction Studies, The Southern Literary Journal,* and *Studies in American Fiction* for permission to reprint material that originally appeared in those journals.

The elephantine gestation of this book spanned the birth of my two sons and the death of my mother. I have thus indulged myself in a small break from convention, multiple dedications to those who matter most.

Prologue
"The Game and the Nation"

To borrow a simile from the foot-ball field, we believe that men must play fair, but that there must be no shirking, and that success can come only to the player who "hits the line hard."

Theodore Roosevelt, *American Ideals* (1897)

Boys, you've heard the new rules read. Now the question is: what can we do to beat them?

Buck Ewing, baseball manager (c. 1900)

In 1902, American readers opened a novel (often enough to make it the number-one best seller of the year) on a scene of frontier sport. A group of cowboys is trying to lasso a seemingly uncatchable wild pony, an animal as adept at avoiding the rope as a "skilful boxer" at ducking opponents' hard rights and lefts. To entertainment-starved passengers from the East, belatedly entering the dusty Western town in which this drama is set, the whirling, plunging horses and the laughing, cursing cowboys make for grand "sport," with the wild ponies clearly the reigning champs. But someone, the Easterner on the train who reports the tale, suddenly notices a smoothly tigerish, well-muscled young man on the outskirts of the melee, who now enters the contest. With a barely perceptible motion he flicks his rope once, the noose snaking out straight and falling true. Just like that, "the thing was done." The pony abruptly tame as a choir boy, a fellow passenger marvels, "That man knows his business."

Thus was introduced to American readers a figure who would become the prototype for the nation's most popular fictional hero over the next

1

half-century. The novel, of course, was Owen Wister's *The Virginian*, whose story was already familiar to many readers in 1902, as it had appeared in several installments of *Harper's* magazine over the previous decade. Woven into a novel now, Wister's western sketches offered readers an episodic narrative that follows the adventures of the "slim young giant" of this opening scene through a series of performances that make Western life seem joyously unending sport. "Cowboys at their play" in the local saloon nearly come to violence over poker, but they more innocently also compete in verbal contests in which wit wins respect without threatening physical harm. At the center of this frolicsome company stands the hero of the pony-roping. The several sportive incidents of this opening sequence culminate in the young man's bet with a "rollicking" friend that he can trick a salesman out of his bed in the overcrowded boarding house. The saloon empties, as the rest of the cowboys pour out to witness the outcome of the Virginian's little "game," bursting into hilarity and applauding with appreciation when the half-dressed city man bolts into their midst with terror in his eyes and a triumphant Virginian in his bed. The cowboys explode in a whirling, raucous dance through the streets, "prancing and roaring" and sweeping the entire male community into varied "gambols," muting their merriment only when they learn that a local woman is sick. Even the laconic Virginian, whose "internal mirth" has not cracked his deadpan performance, at last lets loose in "wildly disporting himself." "What world am I in?" the narrator wonders as he drops to sleep several hours later at the end of his first eventful day in the West. A "great playground of young men," he answers himself when he has begun to understand.[1]

With the morning sun the cowboys return to work, but their spirits never wander far from play. The Virginian remains a boy among boys as well as a man among men in this Western playground. As a cowboy, the Virginian is a ranch worker who rises to foreman and by novel's end to owner and entrepreneur. But to abandon this hero altogether to a world of labor would have dulled his aura irreparably. A fundamental tension between work and play lies at the heart of the novel, together with the more obvious conflicts between East and West, civilization and nature, male and female definitions of society. Wister found his solution in an elaborate exposition of cowboy life as a "game" – play, but play with a purpose – out of which he developed a full-scale political and moral philosophy. Although the Virginian enjoys his boyish pranks, in his serious moods life to him is more truly a hard game of chance and skill, in which *quality* will win out. "Equality is a great big bluff," the Virginian tells the schoolteacher Molly; life is full of winners and losers, born unequal and remaining unequal in their ability to play the hands they're dealt (144). Wister dramatized this theme most conspicuously midway through the novel in three chapters titled "The Game and the Nation," Acts First, Second, and Last (the entire episode appeared initially as a single story in *Harper's* in May 1900). At the center of these chapters is an elaborate contest between the Virginian and his archenemy Trampas; at stake is the loyalty of the men for whom the Virginian, as ranch foreman, has responsibility on a cattle drive and their return by train. Trampas plays against his hated rival by attempting to lure the men to the Montana goldfields. But the deeper stake is human worth and national ideals. In the perennial conflict between "the quality and the equality," Wister's narrator declares that the American way is summed up in the phrase, "Let the best man win." The Virginian and Trampas compete both to determine the "best man" and to validate America's commitment to meritocracy.

On the train taking the steers east, while the cowboys play a "harmless game of poker," the Virginian elucidates this deeper game. Having read Sir Walter Scott's *Kenilworth* as part of his program of self-education under Molly's guidance, he explains to his Eastern friend, our guide throughout the narrative, that the great men and women of English history and literature all played a kind of political poker, their relative achievements measurable as skill at this game. "Victoria'd get pretty nigh slain sliding chips out agaynst Elizabeth," the Virginian declares; then in describing Shakespeare's Prince Hal he makes his point more explicit:

> Now cyards are only one o' the manifestations of poker in this hyeh world. . . . If a man is built like that Prince boy was built (and it's away down deep beyond brains), he'll play winnin' poker with whatever hand he's holdin' when the trouble begins. Maybe it will be a mean triflin' army, or an empty six-shooter, or a lame hawss, or maybe just nothin' but his natural countenance. Most any old thing will do for a fello' like that Prince boy to play poker with. (154–6)

Although the narrator is only puzzled, the reader knows that the Virginian and Trampas are engaged in such a game of poker themselves.

The narrator in fact, representing an effete Eastern upper class whose values the Virginian repeatedly challenges, becomes an unwitting chip in this contest. When the poker becomes verbal, the Virginian scores a point then loses several more when his tenderfoot friend falls for one of the cowboys' tall tales. But he recoups all his losses, sweeping the table in effect and winning the loyalty of his entire crew, when his last, most elaborate play leaves Trampas soundly beaten. As the men await their train, whether to Billings with the Virginian or to Rawhide with Trampas, the Virginian forages for enough frog legs to feed the hungry passengers. Before a partly knowing, partly uncomprehending audience of townsfolk, Eastern travelers, Indians, and his own men, the Virginian plays his hand. The meal eaten, he spins a tale of frog-ranching in Tulare County where wages are high but the work risky: The frogs not only threaten to break through their fence, they also prove extremely difficult to brand. With Trampas hanging on every word, the Virginian draws out the story with increasingly preposterous details, then concludes his melodrama of greed and revenge, "Frawgs are dead, Trampas, and so are you." A friend jumps in, "Rise up liars, and salute your king!" The men are his and Trampas is beaten "at his own game" (200–6).

Defeat in a liars' contest would seem of little consequence to men who live a hard physical life, but "the game" has potent connotations in this Western world. Most simply, it is but another name for the Western code that governs the Virginian's actions toward Trampas throughout the novel. Clashing first with his enemy over an actual poker game in the opening chapters, then in the liars' contest for the loyalty of the other cowboys, the Virginian settles the matter at last in the novel's climactic shootout. Following a series of "move[s] in a game" in which the Virginian's friends assure "no foul play" (456, 479) – and against the wishes of Molly, whose wedding to the hero must await the outcome of this manly business – the final contest is waged as the code demands. Man to man and by the rules, the Virginian faces his enemy and beats him fairly, while Molly waits for him after all.

That "the game" serves in *The Virginian* as the fundamental metaphor for life is obvious; what must be more carefully noted is the heterogeneous nature of this game and its specific and deep connections to Progressive Era American culture. The central contest between hero and villain is set explicitly against the rule of law: a higher code rooted in "the ancient eternal way between man and man," as opposed to the way of "the great mediocrity" that "goes to law in these personal matters" (463). The woman, naturally, fails to comprehend this manly game. Molly plays her own little "games": the evasive and hypocritical games of love (132–3) that contrast sharply to the open contests of the Virginian and the other cowboys, even the scoundrel Trampas. The masculine and feminine worlds are utterly separate, colliding most painfully when Molly learns that her lover has lynched a man as the code requires (we'll return to this crucial scene) and when he must choose to meet Trampas, man to man, before he can meet her, man to woman, for their wedding. The Virginian would be no man to marry her should he violate these priorities.

A second individual outside the forthright masculine world of the game is a traveling "missionary to us pore cowboys," as the Virginian calls Reverend MacBride, a bigoted Calvinist who preaches innate depravity and predestination to men whose simple virtues dwarf his own claim to sanctity. The Virginian's sporting code amounts to a natural religion,

presided over by an umpire God who "plays a square game with us if
He plays at all" (220). When the bishop who is to marry Molly and the
Virginian acknowledges that the groom's meeting with Trampas must
take precedence over the church's sacraments, the novel suggests that
true religion and the cowboy's game are entirely compatible. In fact, "the
game" amounts finally to a man's calling in both the theological and the
secular senses of that word. Late in the novel, the hero describes to Molly
someone returning "afteh he had played some more of the game." Molly,
as a woman, is puzzled. "The game?" she asks. "Life, ma'am," the
Virginian translates. "Whatever he was a-doin' in the world of men"
(349–50).

Our hero's own "game" in this sense becomes clear only at the end
of the novel. In what seems almost an afterthought, an answer to curious
readers who might wonder what happens to the cowboy after marrying
the schoolteacher, the narrator reports that over the years he has traded
his cattle for a coal mine and other "various enterprises," and has become
"an important man" in the newly prospering West. This anticlimactic
telescoping of the Virginian's mature years actually amounts to the most
significant element in the novel's relationship to its culture. In the cowboy's metamorphosis into an entrepreneur, his values and elaborately
worked out code come to represent not the loftier ethic of a vanished
pastoral West but the morality of American capitalism in the era of
Rockefeller and Carnegie. They also represent work transformed into
play. In the novel's final pages, the Virginian honeymoons with Molly
in a Western Eden, where the man becomes a boy again, at play with
his bride in their earthly paradise, then after this rejuvenation returns to
work and duty. Molly worries "that his work would kill him," but the
narrator doubts it. The man who plays at his work by the rules of the
game is no mere drudge on a treadmill. In *The Virginian*'s last chapter,
the cowboy hero has become a sporting entrepreneur, his game the
energizing spirit of a commercial age.

The triumph of "the game" in the Progressive Era

The Virginian became a number-one best seller in 1902 (and
continued to sell well enough to rank fifth the following year) not by
formulating an original worldview but by incorporating commonly held
ideas into a compelling narrative formula. This novel, then, not only
became the *ur*-text for the most popular literary and film genre for the
next six decades, it also expresses the *Zeitgeist* of its own age in a particularly effective way. To speak casually of "the game" of business, or
politics, or social relations, or what have you, has become so commonplace today as to seem an unconscious use of our vernacular language.

But such usages have a history, and the turn of the century marks the period when this metaphor first became both conspicuous and pervasive. Those who wrote about "the game" in the Progressive Era did it self-consciously, with a sense of expressing serious ideas through the metaphor, not just of echoing a familiar colloquialism. And what they expressed touched many of the deepest beliefs and anxieties of the age.

A taxonomy of "the game" in the Progressive Era yields at least four different types, each of them present in Wister's novel. In the first place there is the "game" as a social/political philosophy: the game played by the Virginian against Trampas for position and power. This is the game of the Western code, of men in nature, but it is also the game of the hero's personal honor, its other roots lying implicitly in his Southern heritage. An altogether different kind of "game" – an anti-game really – appears in the Virginian's courtship of Molly: a contest between a man and a woman with love at stake, in which "winning" is possible only when the game is abandoned. And finally, there are two "games" in which some sort of "salvation" (rather than merely secular reward) is at stake: on the one hand, the "game" of a man's calling, as the hero describes it to Molly; on the other, a more desperate "game" barely hinted at in *The Virginian* but suggested by the unequal dealing of hands by Chance or Fate for the poker game of life. These last two games represent two perspectives on the same metaphysical issue: "liberal" and "conservative" accounts of human possibility. In the first, winning is assured for the deserving and persevering – the "quality," as the Virginian puts it, but in a more obviously transcendent sense now; in the second, losing is inevitable, but a sort of tragic victory is possible for those who fail heroically by not backing down.

An astonishing range of writers in the 1890s and early years of the twentieth century explored these "games" in a variety of contexts. The new generation of male novelists, including Richard Harding Davis, Stephen Crane, Frank Norris, Theodore Dreiser, and Jack London, as well as numerous lesser known figures, seems to have been obsessed with imagining life in terms of these various games. Davis, Crane, Norris, and London all wrote about actual sports in their journalism and fiction, but they more revealingly used conspicuous sporting metaphors in their writing about war, business, and survival. Crane claimed that football taught him all he needed to know about war in order to write *The Red Badge of Courage;* however dubious, the claim itself is revealing, and the novel does in fact use sporting metaphors in striking ways.[2] More typically, Crane's short fiction reveals an obsession with chance, sometimes with characters who are actual gamblers, at other times through metaphor. Dreiser and London shared this preoccupation with chance, and they also shared with Frank Norris a deeper fascination with a sort of Nietzchean sportsman who engaged the powers of the universe in a cosmic contest. In Dreiser's Cowperwood novels, Norris's unfinished trilogy of the wheat, and much of London's work, the gods and their nearly godlike adversaries quarrel in the heavens while punier mortals merely watch, dumbstruck with awe and their own mediocrity.

The least read of these writers today was the most popular and influential in his own time. Richard Harding Davis was the beau ideal of "manliness" in the 1890s and early 1900s: handsome enough to model for Charles Gibson; like Crane, Norris, and London, an athlete himself and a writer of sports journalism; with Crane and London, among the most famous war correspondents of the age. Davis's fiction is full of "soldiers of fortune" who are governed by ethical codes derived from the athletic field, but it is his war correspondence that most strikingly suggests the power of "the game" as a metaphor of masculine heroism. Davis's account of the Greco-Turkish War opens with a description of the opposing armies as "two football teams lined up for a scrimmage." He compared scenes in the Boer War to a "crowd on the bleaching boards at a base-ball match" and to Derby day at Epson Downs, the muddy uniforms of French soldiers in World War I to "those of football players on a rainy day at the end of the first half," the Rough Riders in Cuba to gridiron heroes "moving in obedience to the captain's signals." For Davis, there seems to have been no difference between the heroism of the football field and the heroism of the battlefield, and no irony in describing the one in terms of the other.[3]

To these major figures of America's literary "strenuous age" can be added dozens of others. In addition to the Western fiction that quickly settled into popular formulas, stories about politics and business in particular became vehicles for elaborating on "the game." "Frontrunners" and "dark horses," "holding all the cards" and daring "bluffs" peppered the political lexicon of both the smoke-filled rooms and the fictional renderings of them, usually to expose a corrupt politician as a game-playing villain. An old Irish pol in Alfred Henry Lewis's *The Boss* (1903) explains to his protege, "City Government is but a game; so's all government." A crusading reformer in I. K. Friedman's *The Radical* (1907) denounces the game's basic unfairness by describing life as "a game of blindman's buff through which the poor stumble, blindfolded, exploited by wealth, mocked at by law, abandoned by justice."[4] The businessman, on the other hand, evoked more ambivalence. Not only Norris, London, and Dreiser, but such writers as Will Payne, Frederic C. Howe, and Henry Kitchell Webster routinely portrayed speculation as gambling, business transactions as competitive games played less for the monetary stake than for the exhilaration of the play itself. Their attitudes were deeply divided over the consequences of such contests. In their novels, compassion for the powerless majority, for whom dollars meant survival rather than sport, competed with fascination for the titanic player who often loomed grandest in heroic defeat.

"The game," in short, expressed deeply felt American beliefs at the turn of the century, part worldview, part fantasy. Americans had no monopoly on this metaphor, but at least within the Anglo-American world there were significant national differences. The English version of "the game" – in Kipling's fiction, in Henry Newbolt's "Vitaï Lampada" (with its endlessly quoted refrain, "Play up! Play up! and play the game"), in the patriotic rhetoric of World War I – seems to have been more consistent and uniform: an expression of the gentleman's code of conduct that dates from the Renaissance and was reconstituted in the nineteenth century as the public-school ethos. This "games-ethic," as one of its historians has termed it, served in late-Victorian and Edwardian England as virtually an official creed for the ruling classes at home, at war, and throughout a far-flung empire.[5] In America, on the other hand, in a society whose class divisions were considerably less stable, "the game" was more diffuse, contested, and contradictory. At times the characterization of power and powerlessness, wealth and poverty, success and failure as the stakes in a game exposed the immorality of the winners or the amorality of a system that recognized no higher values; at other times it celebrated this system – implying an open contest and a fair field, each player with an equal chance to win, the winners deserving their good fortune and the losers having no one to blame but themselves.

I will not presume to account fully for the ubiquitous sporting rhetoric of the age, but it is possible to identify some of its most important sources and uses. Race was a factor: Celebrations of combative sportiveness in much Progressive Era writing were directly tied to Anglo-Saxon racial destiny and were motivated primarily by the perceived dangers of dilution, even eclipse, by hordes of European, Asian, and Southern black emigrants to Eastern cities. Class was also a factor: in this case, not a comparable fear of the rising underclass, but in some cases a justification of the power and privilege already held by the ruling classes, more often the ambivalence of a privileged, but not fully empowered, middle class. Denunciations of these games voiced the complaints of the powerless and their advocates.

And gender was a factor, too, particularly for the male novelists I have been using as examples. Among those who most celebrated "the game," many were motivated by fear that American culture had become dangerously "feminized." Essays in leading journals with titles like "The Effeminisation of Man," "The 'Effeminization' of the United States," and "Feminization in School and Home" sounded the alarm that America needed to regird its loins to assure preeminence in a world of mechanistic force and Darwinian struggle.[6] For writers the crisis seemed most acute. The dominance of women as both readers and authors, particularly since the 1850s, had by the 1890s created deep anxiety in a new generation of male novelists. In an age characterized by the nearly total estrangement of genteel literary culture from the world of masculine power in business and politics, literature and authorship themselves had become culturally defined as feminine. Norris, London, Upton Sinclair, and other writers promoted writing as *work*, not the aesthetic byproduct of leisure, and actively championed a "masculine" literature to counteract acculturated femininity.[7] Wister's Virginian speaks out for this literary program when he plays critic of the books that Molly gives him to read. He has no use for George Eliot and the "frillery" of Jane Austin's *Emma* and *Pride and Prejudice;* Browning seems false and silly to him – "a smarty" (320, 349). Among Shakespeare's characters, he prefers Mercutio to Romeo ("no man") and finds the subject of *Othello* too shameful to write down; but the first part of *Henry IV* has the stuff of life.

The Virginian sounds here like Frank Norris, who attacked the effeminacy of recent American fiction on similar terms and called for a new "virile" literature, concerned with "that great, grim complication of men's doings that we call life." Fiction "is not an affair of women and aesthetes," Norris insisted in 1901:

> The muse of American fiction is no chaste, delicate, super-refined mademoiselle of delicate roses and "elegant" attitudinizings, but a robust, red-armed *bonne femme* who rough-shoulders her way among men and among affairs, who finds a healthy pleasure in the jostlings of the mob and hearty delight in the honest, rough-and-tumble, Anglo-Saxon give-and-take knockabout that for us means life.

Norris's literary champions were Wister and Stephen Crane, Richard Harding Davis and above all Kipling (the foremost among the Anglo-American spokesmen for the "Great Game" of life).[8] "The game" in its manifold versions – with its connotations of activism, adventure, strenuousness, risk, aggression, competition, all leavened by fair play – became the favorite metaphor of a generation of male writers obsessed with manliness.

The gender imprint on "the game" was clear to women writers as well. In Edith Wharton's *The House of Mirth* (1905), Lily Bart as a woman cannot play the "game" of business and speculation but is expected to play by the rules of a very different "game": attracting a husband or trading sexual favors for financial assistance. Money and power lie at the root of both kinds of games, but women are banned from the one and victimized by the other.[9] The game thus reflected the unequal gender arrangements within American society, but also the peculiar relationship of belles lettres to those arrangements, by which powerlessness could become a major concern of any writer, male or female.

Those who embraced the image of "the game" fantasized or celebrated a way of living whose appeal had to be greatest for those in position to win life's prizes. Those who dissented from this affirmative view reminded their readers that games had losers, too, some of whom had little chance from the start due to gender, race, or class; while even the winners might gain their victories through less than admirable traits. The game seemed truly sporting to some, merely devious to others; and to others yet, it simply disguised brute force. But all of these writers agreed that life in Progressive-Era America was in some striking way a "game."

Sport and American values

In the metaphors I am describing, each element reflects on the other. The fact that business, say, was characterized as a game, rather than a battle, a calling, a duty, or a burden, tells us something important about cultural attitudes toward business during this period. From the other direction, that business could be celebrated by characterizing it as a game tells us something about games as well: that they were sufficiently important, or at least prominent, in the culture to be available as metaphors. This situation did not exist just a generation earlier. In the 1830s, Alexis de Tocqueville declared Americans "the most serious-minded people on earth," a judgment echoing Frances Trollope's belief, after traveling through the American West in the same period, that she "never saw any people who lived so much without amusement."[10] For the English statesman James Bryce to be astonished in 1905 by Americans' "passion for looking on at and reading about athletic sports," the culture had to have undergone a dramatic transformation.[11]

Trollope's and Bryce's countrymen had much to do with that change. Victorian England was, quite simply, "the world's game-master";[12] Americans looked to the mother country for leadership in athletic matters as surely as they imitated British art, literature, and other cultural expressions. In the nineteenth century, as sport became highly organized in England and was imprinted with the ideology of the British ruling class, Americans read Thomas Carlyle, Herbert Spencer, Thomas Hughes, and Charles Kingsley on the values of sport as keenly as they read Dickens and Thackeray. Compressing a complex subject to a handful of key ideas, I would emphasize that the Victorian cult of athleticism began with a concern for physical health in the 1830s, gained momentum as sport was increasingly seen to be an agent for both the social control of the working classes (as "rational recreation") and the character-molding of their future rulers, and reached its jingoistic extreme with the notion that cricket and rugby were ideal preparation for military and imperial responsibilities in ruling a colonial empire. The British officer in World War I who kicked a football toward enemy lines, then led his men in a mad dash after it, was only the most extreme exemplar of a faith widely held by those in his class.[13]

The pattern of health, discipline, morals, and military preparedness was replayed in discussions of sport on this side of the Atlantic, as Americans both followed the lead of British intellectuals and addressed their own similar concerns.[14] A new tolerance for play itself as necessary to human life – most conveniently dated from Horace Bushnell's 1848 Phi Beta Kappa address, "Work and Play" – contributed to the rising interest in sport, but no belief in play's value for its own sake ever superseded other factors in the public debate. Sport embodied playfulness less than it expressed the values of a work-centered culture accommodating itself to the newly discovered importance of play. Or rather, sport accommodated participants' desire to play, while at the same time enabling the advocates of sport to harness the play impulse to the new industrial order. Initially, sport in America was perceived as simple physical activity; by century's end it had become the carrier of a potent ideology.

The tenets of muscular Christianity, imported from England by way of Charles Kingsley and Thomas Hughes (*Tom Brown's School-Days* in particular), played a key role in promoting athletic sports and games. An American athletic movement *had* to have a religious impetus. In the face of Calvinist antagonism to games and amusements that continued well into the nineteenth century, Unitarians, Transcendentalists, and other liberal Christians in the 1830s began breaking away to espouse the values of play. A host of tracts with titles like *A Plea for Amusements, Public Amusements for Poor and Rich,* and *Christian Amusements* made the case for sport and play as essential activities for the morally as well as physically healthy Christian.[15] With the Calvinist notion of innate depravity ultimately at stake, resistance came from expected quarters. The conservative *New Englander,* reviewing a number of such books in 1851, warned readers to remember "that we were sent into this world, not for sport and amusement, but for *labor;* not to enjoy and please ourselves, but to serve and glorify God, and be useful to our fellow men."[16] No clearer sign of the shift toward liberalism can be found than the essay in the same *New Englander* sixteen years later under the identical title, "Amusements." This time, the writer warned that Christian literature on amusements had "made little allowance for recreation" and had "given such undue prominence to the sober side of life as to prejudice many against religion, as if it required a surrender of all entertainment."[17] The foundation for a new attitude remained the Bible, but the writer's interpretation now shifted from banning all activities not specifically allowed by scripture, to banning only those expressly forbidden. Given the inevitability of public amusements, the writer conceded, the believer must now distinguish Christian amusements from immoral ones.

Such acceptance by conservative Protestantism was a reluctant response to both the triumph of liberalism in religious matters and the conspicuous beginnings of a new leisure culture. Chief among the American muscular Christians who made sport in particular morally acceptable were such liberal ministers as Henry Ward Beecher, Thomas Wentworth Higginson, Moses Coit Tyler, and William H. H. Murray. Beecher's sermons from his Brooklyn pulpit and editorials in the *New York Ledger,* the *Independent,* and the *Christian Union;* Higginson's series of essays in the *Atlantic* from 1858 to 1862, beginning with "Saints and Their Bodies," from which the rationale for supporting organized college sport is sometimes dated; Tyler's lectures on the gymnastic system of Dio Lewis and his own serial novel *The Brawnville Papers* (1869); and Murray's sermons and several volumes of wilderness sketches made possible not just tolerating but proselytizing for sport in the second half of the century.[18]

That muscular Christians beginning in the 1850s arranged the marriage of sport and morality within the YMCA and other religious organizations makes obvious sense, but they also laid the foundation for what on the surface seems merely secular sport, including what became the major source of an American sporting ethic: intercollegiate athletics. The university enjoyed no clear preeminence in defining sport's social role in America, as the public school did in England; professional baseball and boxing, for example, received as much public attention as college rowing and football during the half-century of burgeoning athleticism. But because baseball and boxing were the sports of the lower class and the masses, they did not receive the same scrutiny and analysis that genteel moralizers directed at intercollegiate football, or a comparable legitimacy in middle-class culture.

In considering the emergence of a sporting ethic rooted in college athletics, it is most important to recognize that no single interpretation of sport's place in American life ever achieved consensus. The value of the games was debated from the outset and never resolved. The major contributors to the discussion, initially health reformers, then clergymen, became journalists and university faculty and presidents. Their chief subject was football, which by 1880 had supplanted crew and baseball as the major college sport. And the major vehicle for the debate was the periodical press, the primary source of information on all subjects for the American middle classes in the nineteenth century.

After two decades of more modest claims for football's physical and moral benefits, the full-blown rhetoric of national self-interest was unleashed in the 1880s, when distinguished spokesmen like Nathaniel S. Shaler, a professor of geology on the Harvard faculty for three decades, began to change the terms of discussion. Keywords in Shaler's 1889 essay in the *Atlantic* – "command," "cooperation," "the success of the race" – announced that the context for discussion had moved well beyond mere physical health; football was coming to be seen as both a moral training ground and a mirror of American industrial capitalism.[19] In the same years in which Frederick Taylor began the time-and-motion studies that revolutionized the American factory system, enthusiasts of college football began to call the game "scientific": a contest of strategies and technical innovations to accompany the prevailing mood of the technological revolution, and to prepare future technocrats.[20] The chief spokesman for scientific efficiency in football was Walter Camp, the man who introduced coaching to the game, who oversaw virtually all the rule changes by which the modern sport was created, and who, through frequent columns in *Harper's Weekly* and other popular journals in the late 1880s and 1890s, played a key role in shaping the attitudes of his fellow enthusiasts. "If ever a sport offered inducements to the man of executive ability," Camp wrote in 1892, "to the man who can plan, foresee, and manage, it is certainly the modern American foot-ball." Science, perfectibility through hard work, hierarchical control and corporate cooperation, an aristocracy of merit based on absolute equality of opportunity – these defined football to Camp.[21] In the writings of Camp and others, as economic and civic virtue replaced muscular morality in their rationales, the secular case nonetheless implicitly retained the teleological claims of the earlier moralizers. Football, that is, became an expression of late nineteenth-century secular religion.

Although both football and the case for football were well established by the waning years of the nineteenth century, the game nearly destroyed itself in the 1890s and early 1900s.[22] "Professionalism," overemphasis, distorted educational priorities, and above all the brutality of the game led to a crisis that resulted in President Roosevelt's demand in 1905 for an organization to regulate the sport. The columns of Caspar Whitney in *Harper's Weekly* in the 1890s and Harvard president Charles Eliot's annual reports to the alumni during this same period equally reveal the profound ambivalence many felt over what just a few decades before had been a simple schoolboys' game.[23] Football had come to express a cultural contradiction: the competing and incompatible values of what might be described, in cultural shorthand, as social Darwinism on the one hand and the older Christian and humanist traditions on the other.

This contradiction is no better expressed than in the concept of "fair play," which has obvious bearing on the meaning of "the game" in Owen Wister's America. The term appeared in English at least by 1595

The brutality in college football, vividly depicted in this drawing by W. A. Rogers for *Harper's Weekly* (October 31, 1891), raised a public outcry in the 1890s, when the game seemed to have little to do with "fair play." (Courtesy of Arizona State University Library)

in Shakespeare's *King John*, where Philip the Bastard refers to the chivalric code as a "fair-play order" and as "the fair-play of the world."[24] The modern notion of fair play, in other words, derived directly from the Renaissance ideal of the gentleman, as expressed in Castiglione's *Book of the Courtier* (1528), Thomas Elyot's *The Boke of the Governour* (1531), and the numerous other sixteenth- and seventeenth-century treatises on the subject.[25] Athletic exercises were prescribed in these books, with the primary emphasis on how the gentleman competed and against whom. For the gentleman, who had already "won" in life by the very fact of his class, winning or losing athletic contests mattered much less than the manner and style of competing; such contests not only sharpened his martial skills, they groomed him for administering the power that was his birthright. The courtly tradition broke down in the seventeenth century but was reconstituted in the nineteenth on British public-school football fields and cricket pitches, where class distinctions continued to demand that the manner of competing was more important than the outcome. And the terminology of the playing field became the language of ethics throughout English society.

Americans imported this aristocratic sense of fair play both in sport and in social/political ethics more generally. Playing fairly, winning or losing graciously, conducting oneself as a sportsman were widely admired, whether on the playing field or in life's larger "games."[26] This avowed commitment to fair play was complicated, however, by the salient facts of intercollegiate sport in the last decades of the nineteenth century (not to mention the facts of American political, economic, and social life): The fundamental reality of American sport, apparent to everyone, was the importance of winning. But the obsession with winning took two quite different forms on the football field. American sport was rife with the outright cheating and brutality that led to outcries from journalists and educators that the so-called sport should be abolished, but its participants and advocates also openly celebrated a kind of fair play that was antithetical to the gentleman's ideal.

The crucial difference lay in the way that British and American sporting communities tended to view rules. American admirers of sport, it is true, continually preached the values of fair play as practiced by the English sporting gentleman. But others – and sometimes the same ones – also applauded the "brainy" coach or player who could dream up tricks for winning by circumventing the rules. Such strategems constituted the essence of "scientific" football. While American sports fans disapproved of outright cheating, to many, bending the rules or finding loopholes in the rules that would give one side the advantage was smart play. The extraordinarily detailed and extensive rules of American football – compared to the few rules governing soccer and rugby, the games from which our football developed – resulted in large part from a continual need to create new rules for preventing unintended evasions of the old ones.

No less a paragon of sporting virtue than Amos Alonzo Stagg, who took the job as football coach at the University of Chicago because he believed that he "could influence others to Christian ideals more effectively on the field than in the pulpit," celebrated the American genius for outwitting the rule makers as one of the chief virtues of native sport. "The British play a game for the game's sake," Stagg acknowledged, while Americans "play to win." But that fact did not mean that Americans were less sporting. "I should prefer to lose every game rather than win one unfairly," Stagg wrote in his autobiography; "but there is a finer distinction than this between the British and the Yankee points of view." He explained:

> The British, in general, regard both the letter and the spirit [of the rules]. We, in general, regard the letter only. Our prevailing viewpoint might be expressed something like this: Here are the rules made and provided for. They affect each side alike. If we are smart enough to

detect a joker or loophole first, then we are entitled not only in law but in ethics to take advantage of it.[27]

While Stagg was preaching grace through football and bending the rules, his colleague at Chicago, Thorstein Veblen, was describing adult interest in sport as a sign of "arrested spiritual development" within the leisure class. In what Stagg called sportsmanship, Veblen found exploitation and the desire to inflict damage on others. Veblen recognized football as the chief sport promoted as "a means of physical or moral salvation" but found only "ferocity and cunning" in the game. What Stagg called fair play Veblen termed chicanery, browbeating, falsehood, and fraud. The necessity for umpires and the detailed rules, Veblen wrote, were evidence of widespread "fraudulent practices and attempts to overreach one's opponents."[28]

Who spoke for America, Stagg or Veblen? Both did, from different vantage points. To Veblen, football was but a dramatization of brute force and knavery; to Stagg, it was the arena for "fair play," but a dialectical fair play that valued absolute fairness between opponents while at the same time honoring the competitor who played successfully not just against the other fellow or team but against the rules as well. The poles of this dialectic can be described as "sportsmanship" and "gamesmanship," as those terms have been defined by historian John Dizikes. Sportsmanship implies acceptance of "both the explicit rules of the game and the code of conduct"; gamesmanship "acknowledge[s] the rules but refuse[s] to recognize the existence of any code."[29] Dizikes has argued that gamesmanship dominated American sporting ethics in the nineteenth century. I agree only in part: Gamesmanship *and* sportsmanship defined American fair play, which itself bore a complex relationship to the unadorned realities of brute force.

Theodore Roosevelt and imperial sport

What I would call a sort of double dialectic – force and fair play, but fair play in the form of both sportsmanship and gamesmanship – infuses the pervasive metaphors of "the game" in the Progressive Era. The actual game behind the American metaphor could be either gentlemen's sport or poker, both of whose values became incorporated into the popular sports of the age, which in turn became the chief source for sporting metaphors in the larger culture. Appeals to sportsmanship implied the importance of tradition, timeless values of right and wrong, a stable social order – the world as imagined or desired by the privileged classes. Appeals to gamesmanship celebrated fluidity and flux, the opportunity of the moment, the possibility of the underdog winning the finest prizes – the world as imagined or desired by those for whom position and power were not assured. Both sportsmanship and gamesmanship stood against mere force: the first sometimes disguising and justifying force by those who used it, the second denying force any absolute power.

These ideas can be recognized in the ubiquitous sporting rhetoric of Progressive Era fiction. The Virginian's "game" is rooted in a gentleman's code of sportsmanship, as is the game of Richard Harding Davis's novels and war correspondence. The wily gamesman typically appeared in the less respectable forms of popular fiction, during this period in the dime novel in its dying moments for example, but the Nietzschean gamblers of Norris, London, and Dreiser are also gamesmen of a more exalted sort, for the force they oppose is the deterministic power of fate or chance. From a wholly negative perspective, the muckraking novelists who exposed corruption at the heart of politics or business portrayed the "games" of their villains as mere masquerades for the workings of force and fraud.

These metaphors and their double dialectic were by no means limited to the era's fiction. Crusading journalists like Ida Tarbell, Alfred Henry Lewis, and Bolton Hall exposed politics and business as amoral gamesmanship; and Thorstein Veblen, as we've seen, declared the sporting temperament at the heart of America's business and leisure classes but a mask for predatory power. On the affirmative side, when prophets of success, prominent liberal ministers, popularizers of mind-cure therapies, and even America's foremost philosopher and psychologist, William James, celebrated what James in 1891 called "the game of existence," they implied that life was a *fair* game without explaining very clearly what sort of "fairness" they had in mind.[30]

No one better represents both the sportive view of life in all its variety and the ideological uses of the game metaphor in the Progressive Era than Theodore Roosevelt, the living American who stamped his personality and outlook on the era far more profoundly than Wister's fictional hero did. Roosevelt, said one commentator, "is not an American, you know, he *is* America."[31] And America in human shape was essentially a sporting man: In the words of Roosevelt's contemporaries, he was the embodiment of "the spirit of clean, manly sport," a man who goes "to his life work rejoicing as a strong man to run a race," "a fighter trained to the minute" for "the political game."[32] William Allen White remembered him as a man who loved to "combine danger with a frolicking intrigue" – a fight-or-frolic formula with a rich history in Western and Southern fiction by this time. Charles and Mary Beard wrote in 1927 that Roosevelt challenged the plutocrats in the 1912 election "in the name of 'decent government and fair play.' " A later historian used the same

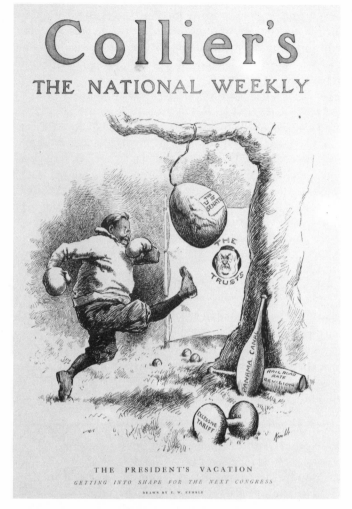

Cartoonists also portrayed Roosevelt as a sportsman – usually, as in this drawing by E. W. Kemble for *Collier's* (August 12, 1905), to celebrate, not burlesque, the president's athletic image.

language: "He thought of government not so much as having the character of a judge above and remote from the conflict as that of an umpire down on the field, prepared to interfere when the playing got too rough, and ready to send offenders to the bench."[33]

As a true sportsman, proclaiming a "Square Deal" for everyone, Roosevelt invoked the Sherman Anti-Trust Act against too-powerful corporations, settled a coal miners' strike, and preserved a wilderness playground for the nation's citizens from those who would exploit it for commercial gain. On the other hand, he virtually stole the Isthmus of Panama from Colombia, dismissed three companies of black soldiers from the army over a murder in which no guilt was established, and in general rode roughshod over his political enemies. The sportsman/umpire was not above bending the rules when expedient. Roosevelt was a strong believer in caste, in militarism and imperialism, in racial destiny – all seemingly at odds with the spirit of fair play he elsewhere avowed. "Without force," he wrote in one of his essays, "fair dealing usually amounts to nothing."[34] This tension between force and fair dealing, compounded by the contradictions in what Americans considered "fair," lay at the heart of the Progressive Era mentality so thoroughly represented in its representative man. And "the game" was a major rhetorical device through which Roosevelt and his age reconciled these contradictions – by denying them.

No one appropriated and trumpeted the sporting ethics of college athletics more conspicuously than Teddy Roosevelt. He was an athlete of sorts himself, initially to compensate for his frail physique and continual sickliness, later to proclaim a philosophy of robust Darwinism. In numerous essays before, during, and after his presidency, Roosevelt preached the virtues of all sports, but particularly football. In "The Value of an Athletic Training" (1893), his earliest pronouncement on these matters, he applauded the combination of "manliness and fair play," cultivated particularly by rugged physical sports, that raised up the nation's natural aristocrats, developed "good American citizens," and assured the preeminence of the Anglo-Saxon race. In "The American Boy" (1900), he responded to the growing concern over football's brutality by noting that the passion for athletics was "fraught with danger, if it becomes one sided and unhealthy," but assured his young readers that it "has beyond all question had an excellent effect on increased manliness."[35] To more mature audiences the message remained the same. Writing in the *Outlook* on "Character and Success" (1900), and addressing collegians at the Harvard Union on "Athletics, Scholarship, and Public Service" (1907), TR advocated a balance among athletic, artistic, scientific, and moral training; with sport essential because it was "essentially democratic" and developed the physical and moral courage necessary to a republic.[36]

"The American Boy" appeared in *St. Nicholas,* a juvenile magazine, the other essays in publications for adults, yet the rhetoric in all of them was surprisingly consistent. To his young readers Roosevelt comfortably assumed the language of Frank Merriwell, saying of the American boy, "He must not be a coward or a weakling, a bully, a shirk, or a prig. He must work hard and play hard." To a college audience he expressed his aversion to seeing "Harvard or any other college turn out molly coddles instead of vigorous men," a danger he foresaw if football were banned for its excessive roughness.[37] Roosevelt did, in fact, respond to college football's critics when the brutality of the game threatened to overwhelm its possible benefits. An ultimatum from the White House to college presidents in 1905 led to the creation of the National Collegiate Athletic Association, and to reforms crucial to the emergence of the modern game. But even as critic, Roosevelt remained football's best friend.

In TR's ranking of the most useful and valuable sports, athletic games such as football, baseball, and rowing actually came out second-best. Ahead of them Roosevelt placed what he considered the more naturally athletic activities: big-game hunting, mountaineering, chasing with horse and hound. These happen to have been the sports in which Roosevelt himself participated, but through them he also sought a connection to America's heroic past, awareness of which he felt essential to the nation's present and future. Roosevelt endorsed athletic sports because they offered opportunities to the vast majority of urban Americans for whom frontier sports were no longer possible. "In the old days," he wrote in the *North American Review* in 1900, "when we ourselves were still a people of backwoodsmen, at every merry-making there were sure to be trials of skill and strength, at running, wrestling, and rifle-shooting, among the young men. We should encourage by every method the spirit which makes such trials popular."[38]

By connecting modern athletics to frontier sport Roosevelt did more than defend embattled football programs against their critics. He also consolidated the elements of the Western sporting myth that came to literary fruition in Wister's *The Virginian*. Wister's cowboy hero, in fact, was intended by the author to be essentially TR in buckskin. Wister dedicated his novel to Roosevelt and in a rededication to a new edition nine years later called TR "the greatest benefactor we people have known since Lincoln." Classmates at Harvard, where Wister remembered first glimpsing the future president's gutty manliness at a boxing match, both men later traveled to the West to repair ill-health, then out of those similar experiences created their most enduring writing. (Their experiences and narratives followed the examples of Richard Henry Dana and Francis Parkman, whose rites of passage to patrician manhood in the 1840s in turn fell in a long tradition of gentlemen's adventuring.) And equally central to each man's writing was the explanation of masculine identity and national destiny in terms of a game.[39]

Roosevelt's own Western experience reads like a popular novel: the tenderfoot transformed into gun-toting hero. He went West wearing glasses, carrying the social baggage of a class and breeding far different from that of the men he encountered there. In roughly two years he reputedly earned respect for pluck and courage in hunting and for toughness on the roundup, whipped a bully and managed a challenge to a duel with both honor and bravery, and became a "minor folk hero" by tracking and capturing the notorious Redhead Finnegan, a local desperado who had stolen Teddy's boat. Roosevelt came west as "Four Eyes," "that dude Rosenfelder," and "Old Hasten Forward Quickly There" (after an unfortunate order he yelled to some cowboys). He earned not just his spurs but his good name. To his fellow Westerners, Roosevelt became "one of our own crowd"; "not a purty rider, but a hell of a *good* rider"; and, most glorious accolade of all, "a fearless bugger."[40]

But the legend of Roosevelt's Western life is less important in itself than as an enhancement of the legend he placed at the center of American history. In three books about Western sport drawing on his own experiences, and in a four-volume history of the "winning of the West," Roosevelt formulated the ideas that Wister would later explore in *The Virginian,* developing in the process the fullest expression of the sporting ethic that we have been considering. In *Hunting Trips of a Ranchman* (1885), *Ranch Life and the Hunting Trail* (1888), and *The Wilderness Hunter* (1893), Roosevelt developed a sporting code whose significance lay not merely in the ethics of hunting but in the achievement of America's destiny. Out of the simple opposition between those who killed for sport or meat and those "game butchers" who hunted only for the animals' hides – "for the sake of the few dollars they are too lazy to earn in any other and more honest way" – Roosevelt defined an essential American heroic tradition in terms of sporting fair play. In the American mainstream Roosevelt placed both the old-time mountain men and the cowboys of his own day, all of whom were contemptuous of shotguns, fire-hunting, and other tactics that gave the hunter an unfair advantage. But more significantly, Roosevelt gave a privileged place to the cattlemen of his own class, the owners of ranches rather than their workers, because these men were not only "keenly devoted to sport," which was proof of their descent from the original hunters, but they also had "a stake in the welfare of the country" and "a regular business carried on in it."[41]

Roosevelt's celebration of frontier sport thus had a clear agenda: a legitimating myth of national origins and future destiny in which an Anglo-Saxon elite plays a primary role. And myth became history in Roosevelt's multi-volumed chronicle of race expansion, *The Winning of the West* (1889–96). In his overall strategy as Western historian, Roosevelt first established the American frontiersmen as athletes and hunters, then portrayed their warfare with the Indians as a sporting contest. The sporting myth, that is, transformed force into fair play, morally justifying the conquest of the Indians and the continent. "Every true backwoodsman was a hunter,"[42] Roosevelt wrote in *The Winning of the West,* the best among them the same kind of hunters as the sportsmen in the ranching memoirs. Economic motives are strikingly absent from Roosevelt's account of the settling of the wilderness. Daniel Boone and his kind were, above all, exuberant competitors "impelled mainly by sheer love of adventures," consequently drawn "into the remote forest hunting-grounds where the perilous pleasures of the chase and of war could be best enjoyed" (I, 120). Words like "contest," "win," "fair," and "game" abound throughout the narrative, contributing to a later historian's judgment of "the insufficiency of a vocabulary strictly moral and athletic."[43] To make the first hunters progenitors not just of a triumphant but of a morally superior race, Roosevelt portrayed them as sportsmen rather than mere game-butchers. Although they occasionally used "methods we do not now consider legitimate" (bleating or shooting deer at salt-licks from a scaffold), the early wilderness hunters killed the majority of their game "by fair still-hunting," while "most of [them] did not approve of 'crusting' the game" (I, 121). Somehow, the modern reader imagines these men in 1769 less concerned with fair play than Theodore Roosevelt was a century later.

In the settlements these first hunters founded, the young men "were always eager to contend against one another in athletic games such as wrestling, racing, jumping, and lifting flour barrels; and they also sought distinction in vying with one another at their work" (I, 127). If their fights were sometimes brutal, at least they were always fair, and the same was true of their tactics in warfare. For the most part, Indians and whites played the "game" of war in different ways: Indians trusting "to wiles and feints," whites excelling in marksmanship and hand-to-hand struggles (I, 280, 380). In Roosevelt's historical archetypes, that is, sportsmanship – traditionally the code of gentlemen (however ironically attributed to hunters who defined the lowest class of all the whites) – is superior to gamesmanship, the code of a classless society. A motif runs through the entire history: a series of one-on-one and two-on-two skirmishes between white and Indian that stand metonymically for the clash of entire races, and that are consistently represented as gamelike contests between athletic competitors. An old Kentucky hunter named Castleman foils the Indians' "favorite strategem" of imitating animal sounds to lure hunters to their death. Another hunter named Mansker outraces an Indian to camp to reach a weapon. The famous Simon Kenton once has to run a "race" through an Indian gauntlet, dodging and speeding to safety until caught by mere chance (I, 123, 125, 292). In the most marvelous yet representative anecdote, Andrew Poe, another Kentuckian, rolls into a river grappling with his Indian foe. As the Indian reaches shore first and grabs a rifle, Poe's brother appears on the other side. "Both had empty guns," Roosevelt wrote, "and the contest became one as to who could beat the other in loading." As the Indian puts it, "Who load first, shoot first!" But the unluckly chief drops his ramrod in the river. "Seeing that it was all over, he instantly faced his foe, pulled open the bosom of his shirt, and the next moment received the ball fair in his breast" (I, 378). Was ever a contest fairer or the opponents more memorable? Sporting individuals, not overwhelming hordes, decided the outcome.

The net result of such incidents reveals the stake in Roosevelt's sporting rhetoric. Throughout *The Winning of the West* Roosevelt was intent on casting force as fairness: to demonstrate that the conquest of the red man by the white was not just the inevitability of large historical forces but the triumph of a superior race; that whites were not just more numerous and powerful but somehow just; ultimately that, despite the bloodshed, the winning of the West was "for the benefit of civilization and the interests of mankind" (II, 56). "The game" and its sporting code were crucial to this vision. Where forces were well matched and fairness was preserved in the contest, the outcome was earned and became a personal tribute to the victors. Not just the strong or more numerous but the "best" people prevailed. Roosevelt also insisted that the land fairly won became fairly administered. Once settled, the frontier knew few courts and little law, yet the pioneers "contrived to preserve order and morality with rough effectiveness." "Stern but fair justice" and "a dogged determination to be fair" characterized the frontiersmen's treatment of each other (I, 104, 105). In the Cumberland Settlement of 1779–80, a self-governing commonwealth based on an absolute democracy in which freemen elected and dismissed delegates, the leaders' "good sense and a feeling of fair play could be depended upon to protect the rights of the minority" (I, 552).[44] The West was won, and the United States became a great nation, because Americans not only were best at playing the game, they played it fairly.

"The game" and power

Roosevelt was a curious exemplar of his own ideals. Because he presented himself in his ranching and hunting memoirs as the descendent of the Daniel Boones and Simon Kentons who won a foothold in the wilderness (even using personal experience to footnote ideas in *The Winning of the West*), Roosevelt's own hunting behavior casts a revealing light on the myth he created. In *Hunting Trips of a Ranchman* and elsewhere, Roosevelt aimed his bitterest scorn at the "game butchers" who slaughtered their prey for purposes other than sport or meat. And in *The Wilderness Hunter,* he expressed his opposing personal credo: "I have never sought to make large bags, for a hunter should not be a game butcher. It is always lawful to kill dangerous or noxious animals, like the bear, cougar, and wolf, but other game should only be shot when there is need of the meat, or for the sake of an unusually fine trophy."[45] Many readers might have questioned the superior virtue of killing for head and horns rather than pelt, and Roosevelt's explanation why the early fur trappers were justified – because the element of danger was always present – while the later "game butchers" were not, rings false. But even granting Roosevelt all his premises, a reader might still wonder about TR's hunting morality. His own tally from his diary is revealing: between August 19 and September 16 on one hunting trip in 1884, Roosevelt's "bag" included sixty-four birds of various kinds, seven deer, two rabbits, six elk, fifty trout, two grizzlies, and one bear cub. On September 8, he spared a doe and two fawns, "as we have more than enough meat," but killed twelve grouse instead. On the return home, he killed another forty birds and animals of various kinds.[46] Roosevelt disparaged hunting birds, yet he killed them by the dozens. He was understandably proud of the nine-foot, twelve-hundred-pound grizzly he shot between the eyes; could he have been equally proud of the yearling white-tail deer also included in his "bag"? Could the trophy of a black-tail doe have been "unusually fine"?

This fundamental contradiction was evident in Roosevelt's public life as well. As president he espoused fair play and offered everyone a "Square Deal" but ran roughshod over the powerless when it served his purposes, most notably in the building of the Panama Canal. An opportunist, a sometimes unscrupulous tactician, a president obsessed with power, Roosevelt did not always practice his own platitudes.

My point is not to expose Roosevelt's hypocrisy but to uncover the contradiction in the culturally potent rhetorical figure of "the game." In a review of Benjamin Kidd's *Social Evolution* for the *North American Review* in 1895, TR revealed the dilemma in his own social philosophy most clearly. Roosevelt, like most public spokesmen of his class, did not simply subscribe to social Darwinism. In life "there must undoubtedly be a certain amount of competition," he wrote, "a certain amount of stress and strain, but it is equally undoubted that if this competition becomes too severe the race goes down and not up." Both progress and individual happiness flourish best in societies "where the grinding competition and the struggle for mere existence is least severe," and group survival depends on individuals' "tendency to work for the ultimate benefit of the community as a whole." Competition is essential, but cooperation equally so.

The question arose, then, how competition could be controlled. Roosevelt's answer: fair play.

> We wish the best men; and though we pity the man that falls or lags behind in the race, we do not on that account crown him with the

victor's wreath. We insist that the race shall be run on fairer terms than before, because we remove all handicaps. We thus tend to make it more than ever a test of the real merits of the victor, and this means that the victor must strive heart and soul for success.

Roosevelt's wish, in other words, was "to bring all people into the rivalry of life on equal conditions of social opportunities." The Virginian's "quality" and "equality" will emerge in their rightful places.[47]

For Roosevelt, if the game of life could be made fair, then life would be valuable and the best individuals and nations would rule and succeed. But what was fair? Campaigning for William Howard Taft as his successor in 1908, Roosevelt undermined a rival candidate's widely advertised address on national issues by releasing "the most sensational of all his messages to Congress" on the same day. "If Hughes is going to play the game," the President told reporters, "he must learn the tricks."[48] Roosevelt could play the gamesman as well as the sportsman and still be true to American ideals of fair play. But underlying both his outward sportsmanship and his less open gamesmanship lay the unadorned workings of political power. To avoid judging Roosevelt merely a ruthless fraud, it seems wiser to recognize a more complex relationship between potent cultural myths of sporting heroism and the manipulations of power that they sometimes transformed and disguised.

This relationship between "the game" and political power is revealed most concretely in Owen Wister's best seller. The rules of the Virginian's game create a moral dilemma when he is forced to lynch Steve, his "rollicking" partner in the boyish pranks with which the novel opens. Months later now, having captured two rustlers and discovered one of them to be Steve, the Virginian realizes that by the code of the West he must hang his best friend. Once again sporting rhetoric structures the scene: Captors and captives banter as friendly competitors about losing and winning points in a games (384–7). But the outcome of this seemingly friendly contest is a multiple hanging. Steve dies well the next morning, accepting his fate silently – too silently for the Virginian, who is haunted afterwards by his friend's refusal to forgive him. The normally stoical cowboy defensively insists that Steve "knowed the customs of the country, and he played the game. No call to blame me for the customs of the country" (410–11). But doubt lingers, evident in the Virginian's downcast manner, until he finds a note scrawled on a scrap of newspaper: "Good-by, Jeff [Steve's name for the nameless Virginian]. I could not have spoke to you without playing the baby" (420). Fairness is recognized; the game is validated.

But while the game's harsh rules are acknowledged by winners and losers alike, to an outsider they seem merely barbarous: Molly is horrified when she learns of the lynching. The Virginian's employer, Judge Henry, explains to the young woman the difference between lynching cattle thieves in the West and lynching blacks in the South – the one a moral, the other an abominable act – but Molly is unpersuaded. "Both defy law and order," she insists, but the Judge claims, no, that one act is *defiance,* the other *assertion,* of the law. "I want you to play fair," he tells her. Law derives from the people. When Westerners lynch, they hang the guilty who have remained unpunished by the community's incompetent or corrupt legal representatives – merely taking "back what they once gave." In the South, on the other hand, "they take a Negro from jail where he was waiting to be duly hung" (434–5).

The flaw in the argument is transparent, particularly in an age in which lynching for the most trivial offenses had become virtually a pastime in parts of the South. To justify frontier lynching, Judge Henry invokes fair play and the transcendent justice of the rules of the game. But he fails to address the unanswerable questions: Who makes the rules? Whose interest is served by the game? Who plays umpire? Steve's gesture of absolution is essential not just to the Virginian's peace of mind but to the novel's main theme; without it there is no game, only the arbitrary power of those who lynch him. Steve's hanging is justified by his guilt and by the rules of the game. But what if he were wrongly accused? And what if he refused to acknowledge the legitimacy of the rules? The Virginian's appeal to the game would merely euphemize his use of superior force.

Sportsmanship is the code of those who have power, for whom winning and losing will not disturb power arrangements, and playing well in itself confirms the legitimacy of power. Gamesmanship is the code for those to whom winning matters most, and for whom the outcome is in doubt. In one sense, "fair play" in the form of sportsmanship was preeminently the rhetorical sign of Progressivism, a political movement that was equally opposed to the large corporation, the organized working classes (especially socialists and labor unions), and local political machines. The admirable intentions and the inherent limitations – as well as the class bias – of the Progressives as a group are neatly summed up in this concept of fair play. To state the case bluntly, Progressive belief in fair play drew on the moral authority of gentlemen's agreements to declare justice for all while declining force as an instrument of justice. For all their energy, Progressives altered power arrangements very little. The function of fair play was more ideological than practical, for in weighing its enemies the Progressive movement feared the chaos of the mob more than the control of the corporation.

But if "fair play" is revealing as a rhetorical sign of Progressive conservatism, Roosevelt's own term for fair play – the "Square Deal" – is revealing in a different way. The Square Deal promised by Roosevelt, and presumably welcomed by the electorate, alluded not to gentlemen's sport but to the poker table, where the arts of gamesmanship, not the disinterested honor of sportsmanship, held sway. It is not the consistency but the contradiction in the era's sporting rhetoric that finally asserts itself. The conflicting definitions of "fair play" in the Progressive Era reflected some of the most troubling questions within the larger culture. Who had power, and by what right? Was America's destiny shaped by a providential hand or mere chance, or perhaps by brute force? In global terms, Anglo-Saxon destiny was at stake in a contest among races and nations for leadership in the world. Chest-thumping nationalism and revitalized imperialism marked the age, buttressed by a pervasive racism given new life by the science and pseudoscience of the period. At the same time, and contradictorily, many Americans were deeply concerned that traditional values had become eroded at home by an age of business enterprise in which the fittest might survive but at the sacrifice of all humane virtues. America and Americans in 1900 were deeply divided, collectively and individually, by the wrenching transformations that had taken place since the Civil War. The new Darwinian worldview clashed with the older providential Protestant one, faith in progress with knowledge of acute social problems, belief in democratic ideals with an awareness of growing class differences. At the most deeply personal level, the Protestant ethos of salvation through self-denial was challenged by a new economic order that was beginning to dangle pleasures and demand consumption. On the socio-political level, while few Americans openly endorsed social Darwinism, the apparent facts of a Darwinian world demanded a profound reexamination of traditional belief in social responsibility and Christian charity.

"The game" served to alleviate these tensions – not to alter the facts of American life, but to ease middle-class anxieties about them. I do *not* want to suggest that it was a tool consciously used by the powerful to subdue the powerless, but that it was a rhetorical device used much less intentionally by a wide range of writers and speakers to express a fantasy in which cultural dilemmas dissolved. In personal terms it contributed importantly to the construction of a white, middle-class, masculine ideal; in social terms it projected a political philosophy that reconciled force and fairness in the necessary competition of human existence. The game accepted competition as the norm but made it meaningful and conducive to both national progress and individual well-being. As a paradigm for human conflict, the game implied a rule-governed contest in which the better man won through superior merit, affirming a meritocracy that exalted the winners without altogether diminishing the losers (to be willing to play – to "get in the game," as a popular expression put it – was itself ennobling). Christian duty and Darwinian struggle met in the game, as did opportunity and equality, rugged individualism and social responsibility, entrepreneurial enterprise and the common good. To imagine an America shaped by the fair contests of competing individuals offered assurance that those who had power deserved it, those who did not had had their fair chance.

"The game," as we have seen, was actually many games: besides the sportsmanship and gamesmanship defining the Western (and Southern) code, love games, the game of a man's calling, and the more fatalistic game of playing whatever hand of cards one is dealt in life. Together, these variations off a single trope expressed many of the age's deepest fears and desires, as well as its capacity to reconcile cultural divisions under a guise of rhetorical consensus. In the chapters that follow I will attempt to anatomize the game's several parts. In Part I, my subject will be the emergence in the nineteenth century of the sporting myths and the love games that became commonplace in American fiction and American vernacular. Part II will trace the emergence of game metaphors to express contests for a "salvation" that transforms worldly into spiritual success. Part III will follow these "games" into the twentieth century, as they have become thoroughly, almost invisibly, absorbed into popular speech and belief. And Part IV, finally, will set against this entire discussion the opposing tradition of play itself: the recurring fantasy of life beyond games and power that has defined the spirit of the American counterculture for a century and a half.

Part I

Sportsmen and Gamesmen in the Nineteenth Century

In the days of the pioneer. . . . life was a desperate game of engrossing interest.

Henry Stoddard Curtis,
Play and Recreation for the Open Country (1914)

War is a rough game.

Basil L. Gildersleeve, *The Creed of the Old South* (1915)

Girls cant play ball.

Margaret Fuller, "The Great Lawsuit" (1843)

The Western and Southern sporting myths that Owen Wister collapsed into a single code of manly behavior developed separately in the nineteenth century but ultimately had a single source: the original dream that led many of the earliest European explorers and the readers of their accounts to imagine the Americas as the "terrestrial paradise." As the historian Edmundo O'Gorman has pointed out, Europeans could not discover a "New World" that they did not know existed; they invented it out of their own understanding.[1] From the outset "America" was as much a symbol or myth as a landmass in the Western Hemisphere, source and object of both European desires and European fears. One of those desires was for the earthly garden whose image had been kept alive from classical times to the Renaissance by poets and philosophers.[2] Within that garden, in many versions, humankind would frolic again in endless play.

New World realities clashed with Old World dreams from the begin-

29

ning, but the myth of the garden persisted as one vision among many. While the temperate climate and natural abundance of the West Indies and Carolinas hinted at an earthly paradise, the key to European attitudes lay in the natives. In the contrasting images of naked savage and natural nobleman that competed for more than two centuries after Columbus's voyages, the spirit of play infused many of the idyllic portraits. Peter Martyr, Columbus's chronicler and the first historian of the New World, described the natives of Hispaniola as being "used to live at libertie, in play and pastime" and accustomed to spending their days between planting and harvest in "tennis, dancing, hunting, and fishing."[3] Arthur Barlow, one of the founders of the initial unsuccessful English settlement on Roanoke Island in 1584, reported that the natives lived "after the manner of the Golden Age. . . . bring[ing] forth all things in abundance as in the first creation, without toil or labor," language echoed in Thomas Hariot's account in 1588 of the second abortive colony. In the same spirit once more, the poet Michael Drayton celebrated the 1606 expedition by proclaiming Virginia to be indeed "Earth's onely Paradise," where "the Fruitfull'st Soyle" would yield three harvests "Without your Toyle."[4]

The image of a labor-free garden of playful ease marked promotional tracts, not historical records, the literature of salesmanship and dreams not of actual experience. John Smith's history of the third and finally successful colony at Jamestown told a different tale from Barlow's or Hariot's: a story of slothful rather than playful Indian men, whose women labored in their place; and of "an idle, improvident, scattered" band of Englishmen who nearly perished through their idleness. In describing New England, where he never actually attempted to live, Smith more easily played the promoter, reporting that the settlers there lived a life of comparative leisure, needing to work only three days in seven to catch enough fish for trade and sustenance, their work more truly sport than toil. What a different place William Bradford described just four years later, gazing from shipdeck on what was to be his new home: a "hidious and desolate wilderness, full of wild beasts and wild men."[5]

Conflicting portraits of New World play and degenerate laziness continued throughout the colonial period and into the nineteenth century. Robert Beverley's *History and Present State of Virginia* (1705), for example, reads partly as promotional tract, partly as jeremiad. On the one hand, Beverley's *History* repeats the early accounts of the Indians as playful inhabitants of a paradisiacal garden: living "without the Curse of Industry, their Diversions alone, and not their Labour, supplying their Necessities." On the other hand, Beverley's report on his own European countrymen damns them for their "slothful Indolence" and unpardonable laziness, traits described as an unfortunate consequence of the same natural fecundity that supposedly enabled the Indians to play in edenic

This illustration of the New World as a sportsman's paradise accompanied a
Latin translation of John Smith's *Description of New England*, in the tenth part of
Theodor de Bry's *America* (1619). (Courtesy of the Library of Congress)

harmony.[6] The desires projected onto the cultural other were very different from the values required for successful colonization. In general,
New England writers were less susceptible to the pastoral image of idyllic
play; the wilderness, to the Puritan imagination, was Satan's domain, a
place in the words of the arch-Puritan Michael Wigglesworth, "Where
none inhabited / But hellish fiends and brutish men / That devils wor-
shipped."[7] In the South, on the other hand, competing images of play
and indolence defined a cultural dialectic that continued into the twentieth
century.[8]

   Play was also more simply what colonial Americans did for recreation
and amusement. During the seventeenth and eighteenth centuries, sporting pastimes were generally viewed as normal social behavior, subject
to constraints that were determined by gender, class, nationality, region,
and religious belief. Children played more than adults, Southerners more
than Northerners, the Dutch in New York more than the English in
Massachusetts, liberal Anglicans more than conservative Calvinists. Men
and women, slave and free, Southern planters and Southern backwoods
folk played in different ways. But all played. Puritans from William

Bradford to Increase Mather railed against play that violated the Sabbath, that smacked of pagan or Romish customs, that led to gambling, or that was immoderate or untimely; but they tolerated, even advocated, play in its proper place and uses. And whether praised or reviled, play was deemed natural; it was distrust of *nature,* in fact, that led to the restrictions on play. Revilers in the South of backwoods laziness and savage sport, no less than their more theologically minded cousins in New England, were concerned not with play itself but with the kind of play that arose in the semi-savage state. No effort was made during the colonial period to articulate a special relationship between sport or play and a distinctive culture (or cultures) emerging in the New World. The play, games, and sports of white Europeans, as opposed to the Indian "others" of European fantasy, were not tied to national or regional myths until the nineteenth century.

The antebellum beginnings of the sporting myths

Beginning in the 1820s, sport and play in effect lost their cultural innocence, and American fiction has left a rich record of that transformation. Descriptions of sport and games had appeared in native fiction virtually from its beginnings in the late eighteenth century. But the frontier sports in Hugh Henry Brackenridge's *Modern Chivalry* (1792–1815) and Royall Tyler's *The Algerine Captive* (1797), as well as the Southern sport in William Craft's poem "The Raciad," were merely objects of social satire, rendered in forms that reveal their British literary roots. In their scenes of horse races, horse swaps, and rough-and-tumble frontier brawling, Brackenridge's and Tyler's picaresque novels in the manner of Defoe and Fielding expressed an uneasiness over the capacity of common men for self-rule that was felt by many privileged Americans in the early national period. Craft's "Raciad," similarly, mocked the distorted values of Southern sportsmen, borrowing a literary model most obviously from Pope's "Dunciad." In his *Letters of a British Spy* (1803), another early novel, William Wirt more positively reiterated the conventional account of aboriginal New World play and its destruction by Europeans, but still without tying this event to a Southern foundation myth.

In the 1820s, however, literary images of sport began to bear the weight of national and regional myth. Not sport in itself but *how* one played became the crucial matter. The savagery of rough-and-tumble physical contests had long been used metonymically by shocked travelers to represent general social conditions on the frontier (one historian of frontier rough-and-tumble brawling has commented that "saving face" was literally necessary, when noses, ears, and eyes were routinely bitten off or gouged out during the fray).[9] Now sport began to be understood met-aphorically as well: as an emblem of American, or Southern, identity and destiny. The major literary figure to bring about this change was James Fenimore Cooper, whose portrait of the wilderness hunter as a noble sportsman became the prototype for generations of subsequent frontier mythologizers beginning with such writers as James Kirke Paul-ding, Charles Fenno Hoffman, and particularly Washington Irving, whose rambunctious fur trappers established another heroic sporting figure. In tandem with the Cooperian legacy, a group of Southern (and some Northern) journalists and professional men, writing in male sport-ing periodicals in the mid-1830s, transformed the frontier humor first expressed by Brackenridge and Tyler into a distinctive genre. This South-western humor retained the bawdiness and satiric edge of *Modern Chivalry* and *The Algerine Captive,* as well as the moral ambiguity of a vernacular "game" whose popular association with the gaming table identified it with the age's most reviled vice. And "blood-and-thunder" melodramas (some of them anti-Cooperian tales of frontier violence) were full of villains' unsporting "games." But during the "flush times" of Jacksonian America, the shiftiness of backwoods gamesmen also became an odd sort of triumphant genius in the tales of the frontier humorists. South-western humor, in other words, paradoxically celebrated what it sati-rized, while all the time verging on moral anarchy. The sportsmanship of Cooper's Natty Bumppo, the gamesmanship of Johnson Jones Hoo-per's Simon Suggs, and the villainy of William Gilmore Simms's Guy Rivers seem to have little in common, yet all three indirectly addressed several of the most troubling consequences of national expansion and the era's social changes.

While Cooper, Irving, and the Southwestern humorists were creating a number of paradigms of heroic frontier sport that would eventually produce a myth of national destiny, other writers were creating a com-parable myth to serve the South's peculiar needs. Beginning with John Pendleton Kennedy's *Swallow Barn* in 1832, the plantation romance be-came a major vehicle for promoting Southern superiority in both personal and societal terms, and images of sport played a crucial role from the outset in that Southern mythologizing. The South had always been more hospitable to sport than Puritan New England.[10] In Virginia as well as New England, economic necessity discouraged sport initially and for obvious reasons: Work, not play, assured survival. But economic security reduced the need for steady industry, while the fertile soil and temperate climate that had promised a New Eden to many of the early explorers did in fact make life much easier in the South than in New England. Religious objections to play and sport, moreover, were mild in colonial Virginia, where moderates held the upper hand against an ascetic Puritan minority. Most generally, Virginians felt stronger ties to England than the Puritans did. With the exception of the brief episode of Cromwell's ascendancy, Virginians identified with the official, tolerant religion and dominant political power in England throughout the colonial period. As unambivalent Englishmen living in rural conditions, Virginians continued the sporting practices of the Old World in the New. They raced and wrestled, hunted and fished, staged cockfights and gambled as they had done before emigration, or, in later generations, as their fathers and grandfathers had continued to do. Sport in Virginia was the sport of the English countryside, pervasive throughout all classes, with specific forms usually restricted to each class. Rich or poor, given their disposition to play, Southerners lived by the rhythms of agricultural life, which made them frequently seem to visitors, and in self-critical moments to themselves, excessively lazy. Alternating periods of intense labor and equally intense leisure, following the seasons of planting and harvesting, created a way of life very different from that in the more steadily industrious colonies of New England.

Southerners' eagerness to play, it must be remembered, was the norm, Puritan resistance the aberration. The South merely continued the sporting ways of the premodern Old World, while in New England a radical redefinition of life in terms of work was breaking ties with the Renaissance worldview.[11] Southerners played more or less unself-consciously until the 1830s, when the threat to their way of life and to its economic foundation in chattel slavery forced an elaborate defense and a reciprocal attack on the threatening North. At that point Southerners began to define themselves more narrowly in terms of sport and play, and to damn the dollar-chasing North for its antagonism to humane pleasure. But in the seventeenth and eighteenth centuries Southerners' life needed no defense, their fondness for sport no justification as a social philosophy. Work was work and play was play: The first assured survival; the second, pleasure.

Only in the 1830s did Southern sport become crucial to a regional myth that repressed racial, class, and gender antagonisms and celebrated the superiority of Southern life. The earlier revulsion against brutal sporting practices did not disappear altogether from antebellum plantation romances; not until the Civil War and the subsequent reimagining of the Old South as a Paradise Lost did images of sport become an unambiguously heroic element in a full-blown Southern myth. But in the novels of John Pendleton Kennedy, William Caruthers, John Esten Cooke, Nathaniel Beverley Tucker, and above all William Gilmore Simms, one can follow the emergence of this sporting myth that became for generations of Southern writers the enduring legacy of the defeated South, and for

American culture as a whole both an heroic ideal and a critique of the economic order that emerged victorious at Appomattox.

In laying out the contours of the sporting myths as they emerged in antebellum America, I have named only male contributors. In part this exclusion of women is justified, because the major spokesmen for the sporting myths quite simply were men; moreover, these myths for many reasons, most of them obvious, addressed matters of particular concern to American males. But men and women sharing the same race and class will necessarily have common interests, and gender divisions themselves in America are much more complicated than absolute separation would imply. Thus, to understand adequately the sporting myths of the West and South as expressions of middle-class hopes and fears, one must consider Caroline Kirkland alongside Fenimore Cooper, Caroline Gilman alongside J. P. Kennedy.

In general, Kirkland, Gilman, and the many other women writers who followed them rejected the sporting myths that I am examining, substituting more pacific images for the glorified competition and violence in men's writing. But it is essential not to overstate this difference. While women writing about the West tended to substitute a garden of play for a wilderness of violent sport at the center of their fantasy, male writers also envisioned this Western garden and were ambivalent about the bloody alternative. So, too, with the writers of plantation romances: Women most often rejected sport for play, but men responded to the violent exercises of sporting honor with their own ambivalence as well. In general, the Western and Southern sporting myths belong to a male tradition, but there are points of contact that must also be recognized.

Late nineteenth-century culminations

In the decades following the Civil War, while the sporting heroes of the West and South continued to develop in separate literary traditions, they also became parts of the same national middle-class culture. By the end of the century, the sportsmen and gamesmen and playful boy-men of the various strains in Western fiction had been collapsed into the single figure of the cowboy, who with the closing of the frontier became increasingly identified as *the* type of the collective American past. The Southern sportsman, on the other hand, became the object of a completely unfettered, wholly reactionary nostalgia for the Old South among the sons and daughters of the defeated Confederacy, but he also came to embody a national longing. To Northerners, the idealized sporting planter came to represent not the former grandeur of a defeated enemy but a lost alternative to the rampant materialism and debilitating competition in their own triumphant industrial system.

In the cases of both the Western and Southern sporting myths, the ambiguities and ambivalences of their original creators virtually disappeared in this period. Whereas Natty Bumppo in large part represented what had to be sacrificed to assure the necessary course of history, Cooper's heirs made the hunter-sportsman the embodiment of American destiny. Whereas Irving vacillated between the primitivist and anti-primitivist images of his Western archetypes, his heirs embraced the romantic trappers of *Captain Bonneville*, not the degraded ones of *Astoria*. Whereas the Southwestern humorists placed their crude backwoodsmen beyond the pale of civilization, their heirs softened the portraits, smoothing the rough edges to render them entirely suitable for sentimentalizing. And whereas antebellum plantation romancers did not altogether ignore the harsher possibilities in sportive masculinity, their postbellum followers completed the domestication of the cavalier sportsman begun more haltingly before the war.

Not the Civil War but the 1890s marks the comparable shift in Western mythmaking, as Americans became openly conscious that the frontier had disappeared. In both cases, nostalgia figured importantly, but a nostalgia that served also as social criticism. The sporting myths of both regions in the last decades of the nineteenth century addressed, albeit obliquely, the many-sided angst of Gilded Age America: the anxieties raised by economic competition; the consolidation of wealth and power; the widening gaps between rich and poor, owners and workers, the powerful and the powerless under whatever names. As the country rushed headlong into an industrial and technological future, committed to work and material prosperity, social Darwinism collided with the social gospel, and human worth seemed diminished in palpable ways. To tie the sporting myths more precisely to specific issues would oversimplify their cultural functions, but their general relevance to the pressing issues of the day seems undeniable.

Specific literary vehicles played the principal role in the continuing development of the two sporting myths. The Southern plantation legend, in which images of sport retained their central place, continued to be developed, more extravagantly now, in both fiction and nonfiction. History and fiction became nearly indistinguishable in their accounts of the Old South, while to the sporting gentleman was added another figure, the desperate sportsman of the Lost Cause, who epitomized what had been tragically forfeited in the sectional war. As race also began to occupy the foreground of the plantation legend, images of playful equality between black and white before emancipation expressed the culture's unwillingness to confront either its racism or the major social and political problems that followed the freeing of black slaves.

Western fiction after 1860 flowed in a divided mainstream: on one side dime novels, in which various images of "the game" became most thoroughly conventionalized; on the other, the magazine fiction in which the sporting cowboy emerged more slowly as an heroic ideal. Sportsmanship and gamesmanship figured in both literary forms, but the gamesman dominated dime novels, while the sportsman emerged as the sporting hero of magazine fiction. Dime novelists were not simply the heirs of the frontier humorists and blood–and–thunder romancers, however, or the magazinists the exclusive descendents of Cooper and Irving. As Cooper's stature fell in the new genteel literary culture, the Leatherstocking figure appeared more often in Beadle's publications than in *Harper's* or the *Atlantic*. Cruder versions of Irving's violently rambunctious trappers joined him there, equally shunned by the writers and readers of polite fiction. But the world of the dime Western tended more toward anarchy than order after the late 1870s, and only a gamesman could thrive amidst chaos. With the audiences for dime novels and magazine fiction to some degree divided along class lines, the gamesman was more clearly becoming a heroic paradigm for the political, socially, and economically marginal, the sportsman for those more assured of a secure place in society.

But gamesmanship also became domesticated by the end of the nineteenth century, as we saw in Amos Alonzo Stagg's celebration of American sporting ethics. To view our key terms from a slightly different perspective, I would point out that sportsmanship is fundamentally *transcendent,* in the sense that it appeals for validation to a timeless realm of absolutes (known through tradition); while gamesmanship appeals to no authority outside itself – the rules of the game are self-justifying (the presence of spectators, witnesses, is therefore essential to provide confirmation). Ultimately at stake in sportsmanship, then, is the player's standing in that transcendent realm; at stake in gamesmanship are only the spoils of the contest and the player's standing in the world of the onlooking community. This distinction between sportsmanship and gamesmanship is clear in the fiction, say, of Cooper and the Southwestern humorists, but by the end of the nineteenth century it was sometimes becoming blurred. "The game" itself came to acquire transcendent authority, by which the gamesman as well as the sportsman could be an unambiguous moral exemplar.

In Chapters 1 and 2, then, I will trace the Western and Southern sporting myths in popular fiction from Cooper to Wister, Kennedy to Thomas Nelson Page. Women writers in the second half of the century responded in a variety of ways. In general, while those who wrote of the West continued to distance themselves from the masculine myths, Southern women's writing became less distinguishable from men's in its handling of sport in the plantation legend. One plausible explanation would be that while the Western myth chiefly confronted issues of law and violence whose cultural definitions retained a deep gender imprint, the Southern myth chiefly criticized a kind of ruthless competition that alienated genteel males and females more or less equally. In any case, women writers celebrated and debunked but mostly ignored the Western sporting myth; they ignored and debunked but mostly celebrated the Southern sporting myth – though a thoroughly domesticated sporting myth now, to which the male writers also subscribed.

In Chapter 3, finally, I will consider the relationship of gender to "the game" in a larger cultural context. If, for the most part, women did not play the "games" at the center of Western and Southern mythmaking, they most certainly played the "game of love," a rhetorical figure that dates from classical antiquity but that also derived specific connotations from the meanings of "game" in the nineteenth-century American contexts discussed in these chapters. The "game" of love and the "games" of frontiersmen and Southern sportsmen, in other words, addressed the gender-inflected consequences of the same cultural values. An ideal of masculinity defined in terms of a sporting contest against other men, or perhaps against certain social forces, necessarily affected gender relations as well. Women writers' responses to the Western and Southern sporting myths bear testimony to this fact; women's accounts of the "game of love" address it more directly. A crucial distinction between these different games lies in the fact that the sporting myths presumed a contest of equals (or at least the illusion of equality), despite the fact that in nineteenth-century America the love games of men and women involved decidedly mismatched players. Moreover, the masculine games openly embraced competition as the fundamental fact of life, from which losers as well as winners would emerge. The point of "the game," as opposed to the operations of crude power, was that the winners earned their victories rather than received them as the prerogative of birth or class. Love games, on the other hand, denied their own competitive nature. The man and woman were to be not opponents but partners; the desired outcome, marriage, was assumed to be equally a victory for both. But the contextualized "game" in nineteenth-century American culture betrayed its deeper meaning: that sexual relations were in fact sometimes contests, with losers as well as winners. Women risked more because they had more to lose.

Women writers, then, in writing about love *games,* directly confronted the privileged powerlessness that nineteenth-century American gender arrangements conferred on them. But as with the Western and Southern sporting myths, it is important not to draw too rigid a line between men's and women's relationships to these "games" with all their cultural implications. In the second half of the century, as the widening gap between a "masculinized" political and commercial order and a "feminized" culture became more and more alarming to the genteel middle class, male writers found themselves increasingly troubled by their own "feminine" positions within American society. We can see the consequence of this anxiety in their domestication of the Western and Southern sporting myths. We can see it as well in men's and women's handling of the game-of-love motif in nineteenth-century fiction (I will use Henry James here as my representative male writer). Most generally, the "game" in various contexts was a gender-marked trope that elicited no simple consensus among women writers, but that became a rhetorical sign by which they declared a range of attitudes toward the male-dominated society.

In these first three chapters, then, I will trace the main contours of the Western and Southern sporting traditions and what might be considered an alternative tradition: both the heroic games of masculine prowess and these more varied games that embodied no comparably potent cultural myth, but that addressed the intimate consequences of the public issues with which the sporting myths wrestled.

1

Play, Sport, and
Western Mythmaking

The language of sport and play came naturally to Western writing, most simply because a number of distinctive – and picturesque – games were endemic to frontier life. By one definition, virtually every adult male along the frontier was a sportsman in the sense that he hunted for subsistence, his "game" not the contest but the animals he hunted. Other frontier sports included contests of individual physical prowess – shooting at a mark, foot and horse races, wrestling, pitching the bar, and so on – and such social contests as corn huskings, barn raisings, stump clearings, and the like. The first created sport out of the physical qualities necessary for survival, the second out of the collective efforts that built frontier communities. Specific groups had their own distinctive games: Trappers wrestled and fought, miners had drilling contests, cowboys competed at riding and roping. Finally, indigenous frontier sport included both the "frolics" of dances, weddings, and Fourth-of-July celebrations, and the pervasive gambling of the trappers' rendezvous, the mining camp, and the cattle town. In all of these cases sport was more than pastime; it conferred status, made play of essential skills, and ritualized the relationship of individuals to a physically demanding and risky existence.[1]

Visitors to the West were invariably struck – whether delighted or horrified – by these exotic frontier recreations. Reports on backwoods rough-and-tumble brawling and trappers' brutal roistering at the annual rendezvous confirmed the civilized world's deepest fears about the effects of the wilderness environment on personal restraint and social order.[2] Eyewitness accounts of the extravagant gambling of trappers, miners, and trail-weary cowboys invariably reveal a combination of fascination and outrage, conventional disgust for the hated vice strangely coupled to a sense of wonder at vice on so grand a scale.[3] In contrast, Washington

Irving's and Francis Parkman's delight in the pastimes of young rangers in their frontier camps implied that life in the wilderness brought out the innocence, not depravity, of human nature.

If frontier sport has a history, then, so do the culture's attitudes toward frontier sport. From the time the first Europeans projected onto New World natives their own deepest fears and desires, until well into the nineteenth century (and beyond), accounts of the wilderness and its inhabitants have revealed more about the perceiver than the perceived. Frontier sport in this context was but part of the larger social world being weighed in the balance: To celebrate or denigrate backwoods sport was to declare the relative values of nature and civilization. The colonial traveler's disgust with back country brawling, the Southwestern humorist's detached, ambivalent amusement, and Walt Disney's sanitized saga of Davy Crockett and Mike Fink wrestling on a Mississippi flatboat mark distinct moments in a long and complex cultural history.

My interest here lies in neither the history of actual frontier sport nor the history of popular attitudes toward it, but in the history of its metaphorical uses in the larger culture. When Crevecoeur, in the famous third of his *Letters from an American Farmer* (1782), denounced the wilderness hunter as the most degenerate of human types, he both passed judgment on actual hunters and advanced his argument about the relative merits of the natural and the civilized states. When Cooper in *The Pioneers* transformed this wilderness hunter into a cultural hero, he was saying less about hunters, whether as individuals or as a social type, than about abstract principles of law and justice. For material, then, I look to nineteenth-century imaginative writing rather than, say, to travel narratives – to a handful of familiar sources (Cooper, Irving, the Southwestern humorists, Bret Harte, the dime novelists, Owen Wister) as well as a number of less known ones – in order to trace the development of frontier sporting rhetoric into a full-blown social philosophy.

Antebellum beginnings I: Cooper and the frontier sportsman

James Fenimore Cooper created the prototypical sportsman hero in the Western literary tradition, the Southwestern humorists the prototypical gamesman. Washington Irving added the specific figure of the violently sportive fur trapper to this pantheon, but more generally was a major popularizer of the image of the Western wilderness as a violent playground. Caroline Kirkland, on the other hand, was the most prominent of a number of women writers who celebrated wilderness play of a considerably more peaceful sort. All of these writers made important contributions to developing Western myths rooted in large measure in images of sport and play; none of them, however, wholly ignored the

many contradictions that these myths entailed. Such a fundamental evasion would become the norm in later generations.

Cooper more or less stumbled onto the figure who would become the
foremost frontier hero in American fiction. Natty Bumppo, the old
hunter of *The Pioneers* (1823), appears initially as a garrulous, boasting
old coot who once slaughtered thirteen deer (plus fawns) from his door-
step. But as the novel progresses, Natty increasingly becomes identified
with a personal sporting code fundamentally at odds with the laws that
govern the nascent frontier community of Templeton. While the necessity of laws is never doubted, his countermorality exerts a powerful
resistance to them, calling into question the relationship of man-made
law to absolute justice. The hunter's sporting code thus becomes tied to
a transcendent moral order that, strangely but inevitably, must be sys-
tematically violated in even the most just of actual societies.

The figure of the wilderness hunter available to Cooper was a recently
transformed one. Crevecoeur's description of the hunter as a "ferocious,
gloomy, and unsocial" individual who lived "a licentious idle life" expressed the dominant attitude throughout the colonial period.[4] But the
mythologizing of Daniel Boone, that began with John Filson's *Discovery,
Settlement, and Present State of Kentucke* (1784) just two years after Crevecoeur's book appeared, and that was given new impetus by the celebration of frontier riflemen in the aftermath of the Battle of New Orleans
in 1814, produced a competing image in the popular imagination when
Cooper began writing.[5] By the time Boone died in 1820 the "Kentucky
hunter" was well established as a national type, a figure of rude manners
but superior gifts – the gifts of the wilderness environment that most
distinguished the new American nation from overcivilized Europe.

Images of the noble and the savage hunter continued to compete more
or less evenly until midcentury, after which the positive image increasingly overwhelmed the negative. In considering Cooper's contribution
to this contest of popular images it is important to realize that he did
not intend that Natty Bumppo be seen as a type of the wilderness hunter.
"Thou art an exception, Leatherstocking," Judge Temple tells Natty
during one of their disputes, "for thou hast a temperance unusual in thy
class."[6] Cooper, a patrician novelist, attributed to an unlettered backwoodsman of the lowest social class an English gentleman's code that
descended directly from the Renaissance courtly tradition. Natty stands
for "fair play," Judge Temple for the rule of law. "The law alone removes
us from the condition of the savages" (383), the Judge insists, and Cooper
clearly agreed. Sporting ethics are aristocratic, the law democratic; yet
by a different configuration law is also the power of the new elite,
resistance to law the futile effort of the disenfranchised. Thus, the tension
in the novel between law and fair play reflects both Cooper's own con-

flicting loyalties to democracy and landed interests, as well as the more widespread anxiety during this period about the place of law in a democratic society.

The Pioneers establishes this conflict in its opening episode, a dispute between Leatherstocking and Judge Temple over a slain deer, and then in a series of subsequent ones: a Christmas turkey shoot, parallel scenes of slaughtering pigeons and bass, and finally a sequence of more direct confrontations between the sportsman and the law. The scenes of actual frontier sport are part of the larger portrait of the rural New York in which Cooper spent his youth, picturesque recreations of a newly settled region's social customs. But Cooper also used these scenes of local color to explore both the necessity and the limitations of law. The development of the law in America from the Revolution to the Civil War was marked by a codification of statutes, the growing power of judges and lawyers, the court's increasing identification with commercial interests, a deepening awareness that America had only law, not tradition, to draw on for governing its citizens, and a continuing anxiety over the law's intrusions on personal liberty.[7] Americans of course responded to these developments with a variety of feelings, but collectively, as Daniel Boorstin has put it, they tended to be respectful of Law in the abstract but resentful of laws. The nation's dominant religious traditions contributed to this anti-legalism; with the exception of the Anglican Church, American colonial Protestantism defined individuals' spiritual responsibilities in opposition to the world's demands, as an absolute law superseding mere earthly ones. The separation of church and state under the constitution confirmed a belief that political laws and the laws of personal conscience might often be at odds; in these conflicts, conscience would take precedence. Law also meant different things to different classes. In such episodes as Shay's Rebellion in 1786 and the Whisky Rebellion in 1794, the lower classes struggled against the oppressions of the law; in the constitutional debates between Federalists and Republicans the more privileged classes questioned the capacity of the common man for self-governance. No consensus was possible in a country avowedly classless in which class nonetheless remained a certainty of life.

Cooper used frontier sport in *The Pioneers* to address this general conflict in specific ways. In the Christmas turkey shoot and the paired scenes of gargantuan slaughter that follow, Natty Bumppo's code of sportsmanship seems clearly superior to rule by law. At the turkey shoot, when Natty's flint snaps without firing on his first shot, Natty and Billy Kirby (the local champion at all manner of sporting contests, a figure who will become familiar in Western writing) attempt to determine whether "fair play" demands the old hunter be given another chance. "Fair play's a jewel," Billy says, his view on this matter consistent with

Leatherstocking's. But the law, in the person of sheriff Richard Jones, intrudes to resolve the dispute by fiat. Fair play functions through custom and consensus, the law through statutes and their interpretation. Sheriff Jones declares the misfire a miss; Natty wins the prize anyway on his second shot, but the basic conflict of the novel is now established. Natty is governed by his hunter's code, the new settlement by institutional law. Which will prevail, and which ought to prevail, become the crucial questions developed throughout the rest of the novel.

The scenes of pigeon shooting and bass fishing bring the consequences of rule by law and rule by sportsman's code into clearer focus. At the pigeon shooting Natty is initially a spectator, appalled by the "wasteful and unsportsmanlike" slaughter of birds by butchering methods (245). Richard Jones is the most ingenious of the killers, filling a small cannon with duck shot and then sitting patiently on a tree stump until a flock "worthy of his notice" comes into range to receive his "one 'fell swoop' of destruction." What the sheriff calls "princely sport" Natty terms wicked waste, and the hunter demonstrates the proper way to kill when he brings down a lone bird with a single shot from his rifle. Applause and astonishment reward him, but they place no check on Sheriff Jones. To Natty the pigeons are company; to the farmers who have come into the region they are pests. A wilderness and a settlement demand different rules. An identical drama is played out in the following two chapters, when Jones leads the villagers in dragging the lake for thousands of bass, while Natty pursues a single magnificent trout, taking it at last with a spear. An earlier similar dragging preserved the young settlement at a precarious time; unnecessary now, fishing in this way seems to Natty merely a perversion of sport. "The flesh is sweeter when the creater has some chance for its life," the hunter says (266). The sheriff's method of mass butchery and excess is "sinful and wasty" to the true sportsman (266).

Cooper orchestrated these scenes with care, placing each of the main characters conspicuously, having each reveal a distinctive attitude toward the events. Natty and Richard Jones define the extremes of pure sport and pure law. The sheriff is a prototypical wasteful American, restrained only by law, driven by quantitative rather than qualitative measures of success. Natty stands not for the free use of nature but for the restraint of a higher law, a moral code (adopted intact by Hemingway a century later) that demands fair play between individuals and three commandments for the hunter: 1) that he not be wasteful, 2) that he kill cleanly and humanely, and 3) that he not take unfair advantage.[8] Billy Kirby, Natty's partner in fair play on other occasions, joyfully participates in the carnage this time. Oliver, Elizabeth, and Louisa – the propertied class's second generation – betray themselves by sharing in the common frenzy over mass slaughter. And Judge Temple vacillates between the two positions. Caught up in the initial excitement on both occasions, he later recoils, agreeing with Natty's disgust over the waste. The two incidents have the quality of tableaux. In the second, Natty appears to the fishermen in the faint gleam of a campfire across the lake, "a small and uncertain light" (263) penetrating the obscurity of both the darkness and civilized minds. With spear in hand, standing erect in a fragile canoe, Natty is described as having "the *grace* of an experienced boatman" (265; my emphasis), wording whose connotations cannot be accidental.

In these two scenes of sport and waste Cooper seems to have placed himself firmly in Leatherstocking's camp. But in its climactic sequence of events *The Pioneers* assigns the future to Judge Temple, with some regret but no uncertainty. The sudden appearance of a magnificent buck provokes Natty to kill the animal in a sporting manner but out of season. Shortly after, he kills again, this time a panther about to mangle Judge Temple's daughter. By law, the two acts are altogether different: For the one, Natty is liable to fine and imprisonment; for the other, he earns a bounty and the Judge's gratitude. Natty, however, recognizes no distinction. After shooting the panther, he criticizes his own performance as if it had been the Christmas turkey shoot. Earlier he speared a drowning man with the same care he took to spear his single trout. To the hunter, sport and rescue are identical acts, more aesthetic than practical. The law judges ends, the hunter's code means.

When Squire Doolittle, Jotham Riddell, and Billy Kirby subsequently come to arrest Natty for killing the buck, law meets sportsman's code head-on. Cheered on by Billy Kirby, who urges them to "take it out like men, while . . . I see fair play" (337), Natty tries to fight for his rights, while the squire refuses, declaring the absolute preeminence of law. Law prevails. Natty is arrested and tried, acquitted for the personal assault on Squire Doolittle, who trespassed on Natty's property, but convicted for defying the law that Doolittle represents. And the law is above sentiment: Judge Temple must sacrifice his feelings as a grateful father to the demands of impartial law. In the novel's concluding scenes, after Natty escapes, rescues Elizabeth once again, then takes refuge in his secret cave, the law confronts him one last time, with Billy Kirby again present to plead for a sporting compromise. Cooper was unable to resolve the conflict. Unwilling to let the old hunter go to prison, but committed to Judge Temple's view of the necessity of laws, Cooper let the issue collapse in burlesque: a slapstick assault on Leatherstocking's fortress, with Billy guffawing as Captain Hollister, the leader of the attack, is sent tumbling down the hillside, and Squire Doolittle receives buckshot in "his posteerum," as Natty would say. Natty is pardoned by the governor and allowed to light out for the West at the novel's conclusion (a series of events, including the *deus ex machina* pardon, ironically anticipating his critic Mark Twain's burlesque resolution of *Huckleberry Finn*).

In *The Pioneers*, Natty's morality is both superior to Judge Temple's statutes and utterly irrelevant to the foundation of a workable society. Whether he fully intended the implications or not, Cooper in his first Leatherstocking tale exposed a fundamental contradiction at the center of American democratic ideals. Natty ironically represents an aristocratic code that must be superseded by laws. But Natty also represents the disenfranchised lower classes, subject to laws formulated by a propertied elite. Cooper's own divided allegiances – to Judge Temple's laws and Natty Bumppo's code – were ultimately consistent in valuing the rights (voiced by the Judge) and the values (voiced by Natty) of the traditional dominant class. By projecting these values onto an unlettered hunter, however, Cooper created an unresolvable conflict which obscures the aristocratic bias at the center of America's most potent supposedly egalitarian myth. An odd bit of history provides an interesting perspective on Cooper's view. Roughly contemporaneous with the period about which Cooper wrote, between 1769 and 1784 a community of one hundred to one hundred and fifty families in Western Pennsylvania governed themselves according to what they called a "Fair Play System," under which elected "fair play men" settled all civil and legal disputes. Historians of these fair play settlers have described them as proto-democrats, their system – "popular sovereignty, political equality, popular consultation, majority rule, religious freedom, an open class structure, free land, free labor, and a value system whose dominating feature was mutual helpfulness" – as, in essence, "the fair play of democracy."[9] *The Pioneers* claims otherwise. A "fair play system" could only work if all members of the community agreed on what constituted "fair play." For the different classes of Templeton no such consensus was possible.

In the subsequent Leatherstocking tales, with the exception of *The Prairie* (1827), Cooper continued to use the language of frontier sport to articulate conflicts between history and a transcendent ideal. In *The Last of the Mohicans* (1826), *The Pathfinder* (1840), and *The Deerslayer* (1841), the issue at stake is not law but the violent taking of a land inhabited for centuries by a darker race. Beginning in the seventeenth century, the frontier had forced upon Europeans a brutal mode of warfare to which they had been largely unaccustomed. General Henry Bouquet, a Swiss who served with the British army against Pontiac's Rebellion in 1764, had characterized American warfare, in language that looks forward to the later sporting rhetoric, as "a rigid contest where all is at stake, and mutual destruction the object. . . . In an American campaign everything is terrible. . . . victories are not decisive but defeats are ruinous; and simple death is the least misfortune which can happen."[10] Genocidal war continued intermittently for more than a century, not without strain on the national conscience. By the 1820s, Americans had long been accustomed to scalping and mutilating, but also to the guilt such acts aroused. In formulating a foundation myth for an America superior among nations, Cooper (like Roosevelt later) had to confront inescapable but unpleasant facts.

Whereas *The Last of the Mohicans, The Pathfinder,* and *The Deerslayer* all concern the relationship of personal morality to the necessities of brutal warfare, the first two novels seem but rehearsals for the unrestrained mythmaking of the final Leatherstocking tale. Natty's advice to Duncan Heyward in *The Last of the Mohicans* sums up the reality of wartime ethics (and the moral dilemma facing an epic romancer of American history): "Remember that to outwit the knaves it is lawful to practice things that may not be naturally the gift of a white skin."[11] Cooper's solution to the implicit amorality of war had been forecast in *The Pioneers;* contrary to his own advice, Natty deals with human foes by the same sporting code that governs his hunting. In both this novel and *The Pathfinder* Cooper used metaphors of sport to contrast Leatherstocking's wartime ethics to behavior others deem acceptable. As Natty says of killing Indians in the latter novel, "I pull no trigger on one of the miscreants, unless it be plain that his death will lead to some good ind. The deer never leaped, that fell by my hand wantonly."[12]

This equation of sport and war lies at the center of *The Deerslayer,* the novel in which Leatherstocking became most explicitly a transcendent figure. Particularly in the episode of Natty's rite of passage through the killing of his first human foe – one of the most famous scenes in nineteenth-century American fiction – the novice hunter becomes a mythic hero through rituals rendered as code-governed sport. In this scene Cooper reduced the entire European–Indian conflict with all its cultural resonance to a single confrontation between one red man and one white, as if he distilled *The Last of the Mohicans* and *The Pathfinder* to their irreducible essence, to get at what Philip Fisher has called the "hard fact" of the matter once and for all.

The presentation of the events is extraordinary. Retrieving two canoes that have drifted from their mooring, Natty is shot at from ambush but unhit. Spotting his Indian assailant hurrying to reload, Leatherstocking refuses to take "unfair advantage" by firing at an unarmed enemy. Instead, dropping his rifle "to the usual position of a sportsman in readiness to catch his aim," and resolving to "take it out like men" and trust to Providence for the outcome, Natty *talks.* In dialogue never heard on any frontier, the young hunter invites the Iroquois warrior to settle their dispute amicably, or, if blows must be struck, to accept his assurance of a "fair fight." In words that anticipate the thorough divorce of transcendent mythmaking from material facts, Natty insists that the stake is not mere property. "I wish it to be done in fair fight," he tells the Indian, "and not in a quarrel about the ownership of a miserable canoe." The language of sport in particular becomes the language of transcendence. When the wily Indian attempts another ambush – the Indian as gamesman, not sportsman, and an unsuccessful one at that – "then, indeed, the long practice of Deerslayer as a hunter, did him good service." Natty whirls and shoots instinctively (the fatal shot is not actually willed), then hovering over his dying foe assures him that he can keep his scalp, the material prize that less honorable white men would claim. Gazing up at his slayer ("as the fallen bird regards the fowler"), the puzzled but grateful native of the forest confers on the white intruder a new name and new identity: "No Deerslayer – Hawkeye – Hawkeye – Hawkeye. Shake hand."[13] With this astonishing initiation in the forest, Natty Bumppo becomes most fully the archetypal sportsman of Western myth. In *The Pioneers,* Natty insisted on killing game unwastefully, humanely, and fairly. Eighteen years later, in *The Deerslayer,* he most explicitly applies the same code to killing human enemies, under God's benediction.

Even in Leatherstocking's apotheosis, however, it is crucial to realize that Cooper did not cast the hunter as the representative white man in a symbolic history of American beginnings. Denied a mate, Natty Bumppo founds no line; endlessly praised for his unique moral excellence, Natty is not even typical of his class of hunters. Wantonly destructive Hurry Harry is more representative. Nor are red–white relations finally governed by Leatherstocking's sporting code, as Roosevelt and others would later insist. Besides Natty's first sporting kill, the novel describes several other conflicts between white and red in the language of sporting contests: a wrestling match between Hurry Harry and his captors, a canoe race between the Hutter sisters and their pursuers, the tortures inflicted by the Indians on Natty that are presented as contests to defeat his spirit. The final solution to the racial conflict, however, is no "game" but a massacre by British soldiers. Not Leatherstocking but Captain Warley comes to represent the white race in dealing with the red, slaughtering the Iroquois at the end of the novel in what Philip Fisher has called a "systematic, legal, and impersonal manner."[14] Natty, whose initial human killing required an entire chapter, is described in a single sentence as joining in the final slaughter. In view of the later bloodthirstiness of the popular Western formula, Cooper's serious attention to the morality of violence in the first 90 percent of the novel is one of its most striking features. Yet in the end, killing becomes general and casual, performed offstage, on women and children as well as warriors.

Force, not fairness, decides the outcome in Cooper's epic of white conquest, then, but the earlier exploits of Leatherstocking endured in the popular imagination. Cooper's model of the sportsman/hunter was copied down to specific details by such writers as James Kirke Paulding in *Westward Ho!* (1832), Washington Irving in *A Tour of the Prairies* (1835), and Charles Fenno Hoffman in *Wild Scenes in the Forest and Prairie* (1839).[15] William Gilmore Simms most copiously furnished his fiction with reincarnations of Cooper's sporting hero, such figures as Thumbscrew Wetherspoon and "Supple Jack" Bannister in the Revolutionary romances who teach the headstrong sons of Southern planters the necessity of "fair play." There was an anti-Leatherstocking voice as well: such writers as James Hall in *The Harpe's Head* (1832), Robert Montgomery Bird in *Nick of the Woods* (1837), and H. R. Howard in *The Life and Adventures of John Murell, the Great Western Land Pirate* (1847), who insisted that brutal force, not sportsmanship, governed life on the frontier and red-white conflicts.

Cooper actually agreed. Natty Bumppo represents a transcendent realm of romance against which the facts of history can be judged. But the ambiguities and ambivalences in Cooper's account of winning the frontier disappeared from the version that was eventually made official by historians like Roosevelt, and popular by Wister and his countless followers. Cooper's legacy to subsequent writers was a frontier hero whose moral code, rooted in sportsmanship (traditional fair play), transcended institutional law but was unable to supersede it. Cooper provided the hero for a powerful myth; subsequent writers moved that hero from the periphery to the center of American experience and dissolved the conflict between myth and history.

Antebellum beginnings II: Southwestern humorists and the backwoods gamesman

In the decade following Natty Bumppo's debut, the group of writers collectively known as Southwestern humorists began to develop the sportsman's companion in the myths of the West: the shifty gamesman. The "games" of Simon Suggs, Sut Lovingood, and their backwoods brethren were altogether different from Natty Bumppo's sporting contests. Like Cooper, the Southwestern humorists wrote about law, but as a shifting, unreliable affair, a "game" whose object has nothing to do with justice. Joseph G. Baldwin's chronicle of the "flush times" in the 1830s describes the confrontations of lawyers as contests not for legal justice but for status in the social order, with bets all around. Countless stories set various "games" against the law, as Cooper did, but with more emphasis on the relativity of a game-governed world than on the game's transcendent justice. Like Cooper, the Southwestern humorists wrote about violence governed by codes of fair play; but "fair play" here meant no-holds-barred: eyes gouged, noses bitten off, limbs broken. Like Cooper, in other words, the Southwestern humorists wrote about "games," but games that seemed a parody of chaos.

The humorous tales written by Baldwin, A. B. Longstreet, Johnson Jones Hooper, George Washington Harris and others exposed a crude, chaotic frontier world – the Crevecoeurian nightmare in its most outlandish form. But in their exotic barbarity these tales also reflected a turbulent era for the nation at large. Southwestern humor appeared at a time of dramatic change and growth: a booming economy, the breakup of families as young men were thrust into the competitive marketplace outside the home, mass exodus to the West or the cities, a widespread sense of restlessness and change that threatened traditional social groupings.[16] In the era's abundant advice literature, the gamesman as urban con man loomed large as a threat to public and private virtue. In unsettled conditions Americans' greatest fear was that *everyone* would ultimately resort to the gamesman's strategems.[17] In this context, by making the backwoods gamesman a figure of both barbarity and triumphant wit, the Southwestern humorists created a composite hero for a democratic epic while toying with pure anarchy.

Cooper was the most popular early American novelist. Southwestern humor, on the other hand, represents the subterranean strain in Western mythmaking. Published in *Crockett Almanacs,* William T. Porter's *Spirit of the Times,* and other sporting journals – male periodicals for a male audience – this fiction belongs to the tradition of what David Reynolds has termed "subversive" writing, which also included "blood-and-thunder" adventure fiction published in penny newspapers and cheap paperbacks. The "game" in this fiction, its reference not to sport but to the gaming table, was most often a rhetorical sign for vice: the plot or scheme of a ruthless villain (though sometimes a noble outlaw) operating entirely beyond the pale of respectable society. Reynolds's favorite example of this subversive tradition, George Lippard's lurid bestseller, *The Quaker City* (1844), is full of devilish "games" whose object most often is to defraud, deflower, or destroy an innocent victim.[18] Frontier fiction offers its own abundant examples: the bloodthirsty anti-Cooper novels mentioned earlier, the melodramas of Charles Webber and Emerson Bennett, the border romances of William Gilmore Simms. In *Guy Rivers* (1835), for example, Simms distinguished his aristocratic hero, his frontiersman hero, and his villain by rhetorical signatures that bear directly on my discussion. Ralph Colleton, the planter, speaks for the law; Mark Forester, a cross between Natty Bumppo and Billy Kirby, for sport and "fair play." And Guy Rivers, the bloodthirsty, demonic outlaw, engages in and gloats over his villainous "games."[19]

The Southwestern humorists, then, placed at the center of their stories a rhetorical figure whose connotations for contemporary readers were largely negative. They did not simply reverse these connotations, but neither did they subscribe to convention. Rather, through the framing of their tales they ambiguously condemned, satirized, and celebrated a kind of barbarous backwoods behavior that mirrored the recklessly competitive ethos of Jacksonian America. The relationship between tale and frame worked in both directions: The genteel frame exposed the backwoods barbarity in the tale; the vernacular tale mocked the gentility of the narrator. And anarchic humor laid bare the chaos of the frontier world while signaling the qualities (of gamesmanship) necessary to create order from the chaos. The *humor* of Southwestern humor enabled readers to laugh with both disgust and admiration at behavior that grotesquely mimicked their own economic, political, and social world, without separating the disgust from the admiration.

The primary subject of Southwestern humor is competition: the mad scramble for place and power in antebellum America. Virtually every activity in this writing becomes a contest: not just horse races, cockfights, gander pullings, and poker games; but horse swaps and camp meetings, dances and weddings, pranks and steamboat trips. Everything is up for grabs: wealth and status to be won by enterprise not birth, an entire social order to be determined by wit and opportunism. The "flush times" in Alabama and Mississippi are the flush times of the nation:

> And where can a man get this self-reliance so well as in a new country, where he is thrown upon his own resources; where his only friends are his talents; where he sees energy leap at once into prominence; where those only are above him whose talents are above his; where there is no *prestige* of rank, or ancestry, or wealth, or past reputation – and no family influence or dependents, or patrons; where the stranger of yesterday is the man of to-day; where a single speech may win position, to be lost by a failure the day following; and where amidst a host of competitors in an open field of rivalry, every man of the same profession enters the course with a race-horse emulation, to win the prize which is glittering within sight of the rivals.[20]

In this no-holds-barred world, to the winners go the spoils. Physical prowess is important: One of the staples of Southwestern humor is the contest between solitary man and gargantuan beast – T. B. Thorpe's "The Big Bear of Arkansas," for example, as well as numerous less known stories. *Davy Crockett's Almanac,* appearing annually between 1835 and 1856, wallowed in such sketches.[21] In one of the best of the less familiar tales, a backwoods hunter named Chunkey finds himself with powder for only one shot but two panthers in front of him. Killing one with his last bullet, he takes on the other in a "fair fight," hand to paw, "sometimes one, and then yother on top." Chunkey describes the entire deadly affair as sport, with himself as contestant, play-by-play announcer, and bookmaker all in one. "[I] had sich confidence in whippin' the fight," he reports, "that *I offered two to one on Chunkey,* but no takers!" Having won, he crows, "Oh, you ain't dead yet, Chunkey . . . if you are sorta wusted, and have whipped a panter in a fair fight, and *no* gougin'."[22] The "*no* gougin'" is the wonderfully comic fillip, the eccentric touch of the amusing though ignorant backwoodsman, but it also marks a distinctive courage and signals a significant triumph. By whipping the panthers in a "fair" fight Chunkey proves not just an ability to survive but his mastery over a threatening natural world. He embodies the joyful spirit of rugged individualism, however refracted his experiences through the humorous backwoodsy flavor and the distancing of a narrative frame.

Chunkey, Crockett, and their kin parodied traditional modes of sportsmanship in their "*no* gougin' " and "fair fights"; the gamesman, not the sportsman, was the hero for flush times. Physical prowess was less necessary than cunning, adaptability, coolness in bluffing, agility in sidestepping the stronger or more powerful; these were the traits necessary for survival in a competitive world without fixed moral values. One of the most distinctive tales of the Southwestern humorists is the story of outcheating the cheater. Many involve horse trading or similar transactions; in the most famous one, Longstreet's "The Horse-Swap" in his *Georgia Scenes* (1835), a wily trader unloads a horse with a great sore on its back, after a carefully orchestrated public ritual of moves and countermoves before a knowing audience, only to get a blind and deaf one in return.[23] The horse-swap was just a variety of poker, as were virtually all the games of the Southwestern humorists. The tales of actual poker and other gambling games only made the nature of the contest more explicit. In some, an innocent frontiersman is duped of all his money, but in the superior tales, the ones most representative of the genre, the trickster himself is tricked. In a typical sketch, Elijah Shaddock, the winner in a poker game, gives a disgruntled stranger one last chance to recoup his losses. The sore loser bets fifty dollars that he can turn a Jack on the first trial, then throws the entire deck on the table face up. "No you don't," says Elijah. "Yes I do," says the gambler, "it was fairly done." Shaddock responds, *"If there is a Jack in THAT pack, I'll be d—d!"* – and of course there is none: Shaddock has "promiscuously" removed all four.[24] Numerous other sketches play out the same pattern, with Johnson Jones Hooper's *Adventures of Captain Simon Suggs* (1845) offering an uninterrupted series of similar tales: Simon outwitting his hardshell Baptist father, a greedy land speculator, an old Indian woman, bettors at a lacrosse match, and the congregation at a camp meeting (a

Vol. 2.]   "GO AHEAD!!"   [No. 3.

THE CROCKETT ALMANAC
1841.

Tussel with a Bear. See page 9.

**Containing Adventures, Exploits, Sprees
& Scrapes in the West, &
Life and Manners in the Backwoods.**

Nashville, Tennessee. Published by Ben Harding.

The mortal contest between man and beast was a staple of Southwestern
humor, as in this cover from a Crockett Almanac in 1841. (Courtesy,
American Antiquarian Society)

tale that Mark Twain drew on for *Huckleberry Finn*).[25] In all cases, cheating creates a superior game in which the luck of the deal plays a reduced
role, the players' genius a greater one. As Simon Suggs puts it in the
genre's most memorable line, "It is good to be shifty in a new country."

But if gamesmanship represented a kind of genius, it also implied that life was ultimately amoral. On the surface of frontier gamesmanship was an ironic code of fair play, but beneath this surface growled the simpler beast of anarchy. This dark underside that is everywhere implicit in Southwestern humor is exposed to the full light of day in the Sut Lovingood sketches of George Washington Harris. Harris, like the other writers, was a humorist, not a moralist, but his humor was blacker, deriving from the amorality at the center of frontier gamesmanship and, by extension, from the ruthless anarchy that social critics found driving competitive American life. Sut Lovingood's gamesmanship is totally unprincipled, his motivations simply revenge, jealousy, or just plain orneriness. His "races" are merely escapes from outraged victims; his bets are wagers on others' miseries. In a typical episode, when Sut discovers an adulterous love note to his enemy the sheriff, he sees it as a mean advantage in their personal contest: "Now, I jis know'd es long es I hed that paper, I hilt four aces ontu that sheriff, an' I ment tu bet on the han." When his father's dog Boze attacks a stranger on another occasion, Sut only comments, "I put up the game at about six an' six an' Boze's deal, an' sorter hope that he mout turn Jack."[26]

The moral and cultural vacuum implied by Sut's games is most hilariously exemplified by an incident of his childhood. According to Sut's daddy, a "powerful sharp boy" once bet Sut a dozen "marvils" that he couldn't jump four feet on a course the other boy selects. Hoss Lovingood describes the outcome:

> Well! Smarty tuck "my son" within three feat ove a frame house an' told him to jump toards the house, an' at hit he went – you bet. The licks could be hearn a mile, but, arter a while, the weatherboards give way; so did the laths, an' plarster – "my son" Sut *won them marvils.* When he come home his head was as big as a bushell, an' his brains were churned as thin as water, an' when he shook his head, they sloshed. They slosh yet." (305)

In this wonderful parody of the future hero proving his mettle as a youth, the futility of victory reflects on the larger culture Sut represents. The games he plays throughout his career suggest "univarsal onregenerit human nater," not the beginnings of a new social order on the lawless frontier and the peculiarly democratic ethical code sometimes suggested by other Southwestern humorists. In ritual fights, status is conferred on both winners and losers; the "game" proves superior to law in settling disputes. But sometimes the "game" grows nasty. We should view the dialectic of antebellum frontier humor not as realistic debunking versus romantic mythologizing, but as a tension within the fiction generally. The framing of eccentric behavior within the voice of a conventional or pedantic narrator creates a tension that the anticultural behavior within the tale plays out. Barbarism and the superiority of the natural life, destructive anarchy and a higher code, compete for dominance in the characters' gamesmanship. Like Cooper, the Southwestern humorists developed a rhetorical figure of frontier sport that would later become central to a full-blown Western myth; but also like Cooper, their own treatment of this figure was much more skeptical than their literary heirs' would be.

Antebellum beginnings III: Washington Irving, Caroline Kirkland, and the garden of play

The literary origins of the frontier sporting myth that emerged fully developed in Owen Wister's *The Virginian* lay in no simple formula but in a cluster of contested, often contradictory images. I would like to add a third set of images: contrasting versions of the Western playground. On the one hand, we have Washington Irving's Rabelaisian playground of rambunctious fur trappers, on the other Caroline Kirkland's pastoral image of the Western garden. Gender becomes an important issue now, although I want to avoid the simple dichotomies that can too easily result from this sort of inquiry.

Irving revealed an interest in the cultural implications of play from early in his writing career. In "Rip Van Winkle" (1819), he set Rip's penchant for play against society's, particularly Dame Van Winkle's, insistence on work, in order to mock both the Franklinian work ethic and American gender relations. And in a more revealing work, his biography of Christopher Columbus ((1828), Irving addressed the original New World myth with a profoundly divided consciousness. Irving's Columbus on his first voyage discovers the idealized natives of European fantasy: men and women who live an "easy and idle existence," exempt from labor, wholly given to play. On the second voyage, however, a different group of natives are described as mired "in vacant inactivity" "*destitute* of powerful motives of toil" (my emphasis); while the Europeans, though vicious and licentious, also bring "the blessings of civilized life which [they] would widely dispense through barbarous and uncultivated regions." The conflict here between the values of civilization and the values of nature and play is finally resolved in an extraordinary conclusion that damns the Europeans for brutally ending "the pleasant life of the island." With the European invasion the natives lost "the dream in the shade by day; the slumber during the sultry noontide heat by the fountain or the stream, or under the spreading palm tree; and the song, the dance, and the game in the mellow evening, when summoned to their simple amusements by the rude Indian drum." The innocent savages were wrenched from play and forced to labor for their white conquerors, made to grope in riverbeds for the gold demanded in tribute. While the brutality of the Spanish conquest betrayed Columbus's more humane vision, even Columbus was guilty of ignoring the natives' natural rights as human beings. His Christian bigotry blinded him to the nobility of a people who lived by play.[27]

Irving's biography of Columbus suggests the degree to which the romantic imagination was drawn to images of play. And the hunters and trappers of Irving's Western writings in the 1830s are more problematic versions of these doomed playfellows. On returning to the United States in 1832 after seventeen years in Europe, Irving reassured his American readers of his true native spirit by writing three books about that most self-consciously American of subjects, the Western frontier. But he wrote them out of the divided consciousness apparent in his biography of Columbus (and in American culture as well). *A Tour of the Prairies* (1835) is the most ambivalent book of the three; its Cooperesque elements and delight in frontier sport are part of an overall structure of venturing into the wilderness then returning, gratefully, to civilization. *Astoria* (1836) and *Captain Bonneville* (1837) both concern the fur trade but from radically different perspectives. *Astoria* is a history of the American Fur Company, its hero not the trappers but their employer, John Jacob Astor, whose entrepreneurial genius is undermined by his degraded workers. *Captain Bonneville,* on the other hand, is a *romance* of the trapper's life, rich in the language and imagery of wilderness sport. For the most part, the mountain man or fur trapper was the lowest being on the human scale in the popular imagination of the 1830s. If the hunter was half-savage, half-civilized in typical accounts, the trapper seemed more truly half-Indian, half-animal, his "sport" at the annual rendezvous the clearest sign of his barbarity.[28] The trappers in both of Irving's volumes engage in this same riotous sport, but what degrades in one book redeems in the other.

It is important to acknowledge the complexity – contradictions would perhaps be more accurate – of Irving's attitudes, but I will restrict my discussion to *Captain Bonneville,* his book that most helped shape the Western sporting myth. Its essential strategy, repeated throughout the narrative, is to transform unconstrained, often brutal competition into strangely innocent sport. In a representative sequence of passages the narrator criticizes the trappers for their "virulent and sordid competitions" in which they sometimes seem "more intent upon injuring their rivals than benefitting themselves."[29] Then a few pages later, at the annual rendezvous, these same fierce competitors, whose "games" while trapping beaver have sometimes proved fatal, meet in joyful sport:

> The hunting season over, all tricks and manoeuvers are forgotten, all
> feuds and bickerings buried in oblivion. . . . This, then, is the trapper's
> holiday, when he is all for fun and frolic, and ready for a saturnalia
> among the mountains. . . . They drank together, they sang, they
> laughed, they whooped; they tried to out brag and out lie each other
> in stories of their adventures and achievements. . . . Now and then fa-
> miliarity was pushed too far, and would effervesce into a brawl, and a
> "rough and tumble" fight; but it all ended in cordial reconciliation and
> maudlin endearment. (111–12)

The trapper's sporting temperament at the rendezvous does not merely
heal old wounds, it transforms the earlier destructive competition of the
hunt into something positive. In the midst of the account of revelry, in
fact, the narrator reports that hunting rivalry "quickened their wits,
roused their energies, and made them turn every favorable chance to best
advantage." The result is a "rich stock of peltries" (111). It is worth
noting that Bonneville himself, on whose accounts Irving based his book,
described the annual rendezvous in a letter in 1833 as a scene of "the
most extreme debauchery and dissipation."[30] Irving took incidents from
the centuries-old wilderness nightmare, and from the contemporary
blood-and-thunder school of penny-paper fiction, and transformed them
into a popular fantasy acceptable to respectable, cultured readers. The
rendezvous that scandalized civilized observers becomes in *Captain Bonneville* the centerpiece of a playfully brutal life – with all the brutality
alleviated by the play. What most appealed to Irving's imagination was
"the mad carouse in the midst of danger" (269), a fight-or-frolic motif
later appropriated most conspicuously by Southern mythologizers of the
Confederacy. Here it implicitly romanticizes the rampant competitiveness of an expanding nation. At a time when social reformers were
recommending periodic amusement for the sake of more efficient labor,
Irving's trappers seem a grotesque case in point.

Irving's blending of revelry and rivalry was distinctly "masculine," a
fantasy of wilderness sport that threatened Victorian propriety, though
without going quite as far as the blood-and-thunder romances or Southwestern humor. An altogether different image of frontier play appears
in the Western writings of antebellum women, for whom Caroline Kirkland can stand as the female Cooper. In *A New Home – Who'll Follow?*
(1839), a memoir/novel of her life in the West, and in *Western Clearings*
(1845), a collection of sketches, Kirkland repeatedly confronted familiar
motifs from the masculine sporting myths with a woman's skepticism.
A typical scene appears early in *A New Home*. When the men from her
party of newcomers to the West return from a land hunt, they are clearly

no company of Boones and Kentons but ordinary men "tired and dirty, cross and hungry," bearing "no word of adventures, no boasting of achievements, not even a breath of the talismanic word 'land.' " One of the men, a self-proclaimed sportsman who seems but an "idler" to Mrs. Kirkland, plays a major role in ruining the expedition. According to one disgruntled member of the party, "It would have been as well if Mr.—— (the sportsman) had not taken quite so long to ascertain whether the white moving thing he had seen in the woods was a deer's tail or not." When the men find themselves far from home as night sets in, "not a word was said of 'camping out,' so manfully planned in the morning." Instead, they gratefully accept the hospitality of local settlers: Home, not adventure or sport, becomes the goal and climax of the expedition. Later, as the entire party resumes its journey to the new country, Kirkland reports with muted irony that "the sportsman came very near shooting a fat buck, and this miss kept him in talk for all day."[31]

Although this entire episode rings with the simple factual truth for which *A New Home* is known, Kirkland must have intended its larger implications as well. A woman who moved to the West in the 1830s could scarcely have been unaware of Boone's history, or of Cooper's and Irving's writings on the West, in which men in identical situations performed very differently. Elsewhere in the book Kirkland describes the chief obstacle on her Westward journey not as rampaging Indians but as a simple mudhole in which the wagon becomes stuck. She pays considerable attention to the children and furniture, even plants, that accompany the pioneers, and she dwells on domestic details: setting a table in a wilderness outpost, baking bread without the facilities of the modern kitchen, providing meals day after day under primitive conditions. The westward migration, in her telling, is emphatically an effort to bring civilization to the wilderness, with none of Cooper's regret for what is lost in the transformation. "As women feel sensibly the deficiencies of the 'salvage' state," Kirkland wrote, "so they are the first to attempt the refining process, the introduction of those important things on which so much depends." She speaks here of decorative additions to the home, a garden outside, a neat little gate in the fence. Kirkland's rhetoric strains the limits of straight narrative only in rapturous word-portraits of flowers and gardens, the chief effusion of this sort a description of the "magnificent *pleasance*" of grass and wildflowers in the natural garden of the woods near her home:

> We lacked not carpets, for there was the velvet sward, embroidered with blossoms, whose gemmy tints can never be equalled in Brussels or in Persia; nor canopy, for an emerald dome was over us, full of trembling light, and festooned and taselled with the starry eglantine,

> the pride of our Western woods; nor pillows, nor arches; for, oh! be-
> loved forests of my country, when can your far-sounding aisles be
> matched for grandeur, your "alleys green" for beauty? We had music
> too, fairy music, "gushes of wild song."... and withall the sound of
> a babbling stream which was ever and anon sweetly distinct amid the
> delicate harmony. (191)

Nowhere else in the book does the reader encounter such florid prose.
The "velvet sward" and "starry eglantine," exclamatory "oh!" and archaic "ever and anon," are evidence of the "colorings" she confessed in
her preface to have added to her simple story. The point is not that such
overwrought prose weakens the narrative, but that Kirkland strained the
language in service of a fantasy very different from the one for which
Cooper and Irving sacrificed literary restraint.

If Kirkland's *A New Home* is the nonfictional counter to the Boone
legends, her *Western Clearings* (1845) can stand opposed to Cooper's
Leatherstocking tales and Irving's romances as a touchstone in an alternative women's tradition in fiction. Against the violent sport celebrated
by Irving in particular, Kirkland consistently placed innocent play in a
wooded garden. Of the sketches in *Western Clearings,* "Ball at Thrum's
Huddle" and "A Forest Fête" deal with frontier festivities, while "Harvest Musings," "Idle People," and "Old Thoughts on the New Year"
are meditations on the place of play in pioneers' lives. Underlying all of
these sketches is an endorsement of play as necessary to human existence
generally, and to frontier life particularly, but a mode of play suitable
for the Garden not the untamed Wilderness. In every case, a pointed
difference or significant omission distinguishes Kirkland's writings from
the mythic prototypes already becoming established. "A Forest Fête"
concerns a Fourth of July celebration in which the girls lure the boys to
a picnic, away from their typical masculine amusements of "drinking,
scrub-racing; firing salutes from hollow logs, or blacksmith's anvils;
playing 'fox-and-geese' for sixpences; or shooting a turkey tied to a post,
at a shilling the chance."[32] The narrators of "Harvest Musings," "Idle
People," and "Old Thoughts on the New Year" do not celebrate the
playfulness of frontier life but rather mourn its excessive workfulness
(the criticism no less than the celebrations elsewhere confirming the
importance of play). In "Harvest Musings," the narrator laments the
absence of any festivities to celebrate the end of harvest, regretting that

> we have no days consecrated to innocent hilarity; no days of the feast
> of in-gathering, over which harmless Sport may preside, gladdening at
> once the heart of young and old, and strengthening the links of human
> sympathy. But this is a work-a-day world, and we are a working people.
> Granted; yet we should work no whit the less for an occasional interval
> of gayety. (64)

In "Old Thoughts on the New Year," brutally masculine and agreeably feminine versions of frontier sport are clearly distinguished. "We will not describe that vile form of the shooting-match," Kirkland wrote,

> wherein a poor turkey is tied to a post, to be mangled in cold blood by the boobies of the neighborhood. . . . This is a cruel, unmanly, un-western sport, and should be scorned by the forester. He has been driven to it by the unnatural lack of all decent amusement. The true shooting-match when conducted on the large scale, affords famous sport. (149–50)

Recall that Natty Bumppo was the "boobie" who hit the turkey in the Christmas shooting-match in *The Pioneers*. In contrast to the sportive cruelty of turkey shoots, a New Year's dance offers idyllic sport of a variety unique to the frontier, where physical freedom produces both superior health and abundant pleasure (150–1).

Kirkland was inconsistent in claiming whether or not frontier life was playful, but not in preferring "feminine" play over "masculine" sport, and not in championing the rural West over the urban East in terms of a feminized ideal. In two other sketches, "Bitter Fruits from Chance-Sewn Seeds" and "Ambuscades," she also more directly took on the two most cherished figures in the heroic male tradition. In the first, an old trapper of the type Washington Irving romanticized appears merely degraded and murderous. In the other, the noble hunter that Cooper celebrated is domesticated to make a proper husband. The West is a playground in Kirkland's writing, but heroic sportsmanship and gamesmanship have no place in it.

If Kirkland was not as influential as Cooper, she nonetheless spoke for a large number of other women writers. Mary Austin Holley's *Texas: Observations, Historical, Geographical and Descriptive* (1833) and Eliza W. Farnham's *Life in Prairie Land* (1846) debunk elements of the sporting myth in similar ways to *A New Home*. And domestic Western fiction of the 1850s – Alice Cary's *Clovernook* sketches, Ann S. Stephens's *Mary Derwent* (1858), Maria S. Cummins's *Mabel Vaughan* (1858), and Caroline A. Soule's *A Pet of the Settlement* (1860) – consistently celebrate edenic play but reject the violent sport honored, however ambiguously, by Cooper and Irving. From her study of these books, Annette Kolodny has concluded that antebellum male and female fantasies of the West were altogether distinct. Men and women shared economic motives for emigrating westward, "but the emphasis was different." Whereas men fantasized exploitation and mastery, women "dreamed more modestly, of locating a home and a familial human relation within a cultivated garden." Idealized domesticity lay at the root of this female fantasy. The published writings by women included no legendary heroes, no wilder-

ness Adams, not even a "recovered myth of a female Daniel Boone."
Instead, their frontier Eve was "a distinctly middle-class invention: a
vehicle for projecting the Victorian values of a genteel east onto an
imagined bourgeois west."[33]

In attempting to assess the relationship of gender to the Western sporting myth, I subscribe to Kolodny's thesis but with a qualification. Certainly the women's writing repeatedly debunks many of the most
cherished elements in the male fiction I have discussed. Holley described
the local hunters of the "Leather Stocking type" as workers and domestic
pets, not heroic sportsmen. Farnham reported that when the men from
her frontier community went hunting, "the whole mass of female nerves
in the village was in a flutter till they returned. Because it had been found
that in the absence of game they shot each other." A later description of
"the unmitigated barbarity of these merciless hunters" who club deer to
death in the deep snow is considerably more outraged and less ironical.[34]
And in *Mabel Vaughan* and *The Pet of the Settlement,* the authors pointedly
contrast womanly play (or productive labor) to manly sport, with an
obvious moral. In *The Pet of the Settlement,* for example, when a brother
and sister go hunting and berrypicking with their father, the girl romps
"ankle-deep in roses and cluster pinks," while the young man shoots
two birds. Uncle Billy, an aged hunter of the Leatherstocking type,
commends young Harrie on his marksmanship and forecasts braver sport
in Indian warfare. Margaret responds quite differently: "Too bad, too
bad, Harrie. They were so happy a moment since, – now their music-
tunes are hushed forever. Mother-birds, too, perhaps, and now their
little fledglings are so friendless." Worse, Uncle Billy proves too good
a prophet when Harrie indeed shoots an Indian, only to discover himself
the near-murderer of a young boy.[35]

All of this evidence notwithstanding, caution is needed in assigning
men's and women's Western writing to completely separate traditions.
It is essential to remember that Cooper, Irving, and the other writers in
this formative period consistently, if in different ways, revealed ambivalent feelings about the sporting myth. Cooper set Natty Bumppo
against society's laws without in any way abandoning his ultimate commitment to civilization. Like Cooper's sporting hunter, Irving's rambunctious trappers represented an heroic age that must give way to the
ordinary for the sake of social order – with the consequent nostalgia not
challenging the necessity or desirability of that process.

Against a supposedly consistent male fantasy of violent exploitation
Kolodny has opposed the myth of the garden in women's writing as its
exclusive gender imprint. But Charles Fenno Hoffman's *Wild Scenes in
the Forest and Prairies* (1839) contains more of the sublimity of nature than
of the violent incursions of heroic men. In his account of an "excursion"

to the Western frontier by a gentleman sportsman, Hoffman paid homage
to the Leatherstocking figure as a vanishing type whose passing was
necessary. As the forests are cleared for farms, "the old race of hunters
already begin to find a new employment in acting as guides to the owners
of lands, and projecting roads for them through districts where an ordinary surveyor could hardly be paid for the exercise of his profession."[36]
The anecdotes Hoffman told of a remaining hunter – now a guide for
excursionists and sportsmen – contributed to the masculine sporting
myth that was still in the process of formation (it is important to note
that Hoffman's conventional portrait domesticates the hunter). His more
numerous Indian legends and tales of "misplaced affection" in border
courtships could have come from the pen of either a man or a woman.

So, too, with the fiction of James Hall. Hall is remembered today only
for a tale of Indian-hating that Melville appropriated for *The Confidence-
Man*. But he was more typically the author of Indian legends and romantic
incidents of all kinds, of tragic love stories more often than tales of Indian
warfare. "The French Village" describes a courtship and the playful
society in an idyllic community of borderers. "The Pioneer" tells the
story of an Indian hater who gives up his vengeance for productive
farming after discovering that his long-kidnapped sister is content as the
wife of an Indian warrior. The significance of frontier existence is announced early in the narrative: The first whites dreamed that "Kentucky,
then the paradise of hunters, should be the garden of Western America."[37]
The pioneers, not the hunters, according to Hall's story, created such a
garden.

My qualification, then, is not of Kolodny's emphasis on the domestic
garden in women's Western writing but of her too narrow construction
of the masculine paradigm to which the garden stands opposed. The
centrality of the agrarian garden in Western mythmaking has been insisted
on since the ground-breaking studies of Henry Nash Smith, R. W. B.
Lewis, and Leo Marx. It is misleading to polarize either male and female
responses to frontier experience or male and female imaginings of it.
Most simply, male and female writers were equally committed to civilization, whatever that commitment might entail. But it is also essential,
as Kolodny has compellingly demonstrated, to recognize where gender
did make a difference in Western writing and mythmaking. The sporting
myth has belonged primarily, though not exclusively as we shall see in
considering later Western writing, to the male imagination, where it has
contended with a more social and domestic ideal. Excluded from the
arenas where heroic self-assertion was possible, and culturally defined as
the caretakers of order and propriety, women writers of the West subscribed more consistently to a domestic ideal in which innocent play,
but not violent sport, figured prominently.

The dime novel and the frontier gamesman

By the Civil War, eleven American towns bore the name Fair Play, often through a local legend. The novelist Helen Hunt Jackson described one such legend for readers of the *Atlantic Monthly* in 1879, the naming of Fair Play, Colorado, from a quarrel between two miners over a woman. When one of the miners was about to shoot the other, the man cried out, "Fair play! Give me fair play!" It was granted: Allowed to go find his own rifle, the miner returned and was properly shot dead.[38]

I assume that the *Atlantic*'s readers were both horrified and amused by this anecdote of frontier honor. By midcentury, frontier sportsmen and gamesmen were becoming Western stereotypes, but they were by no means yet the primary actors in a widely cherished Western myth. Through the closing decades of the nineteenth century, the diversity of popular Western writing continued, with genteel magazine fiction and dime novels maintaining to some degree the distinctions between antebellum conventional and "subversive" literary genres. Sportsmen and gamesmen appeared in both kinds of writing, but in different ways. Both figures flourished in dime novels from their initial appearance in 1860, but the gamesman came to dominate, and gamesmanship continued to represent an uneasy tension between order and chaos. The genteel magazines, the *Atlantic, Harper's, Scribner's,* and the like, did not consistently embrace any sort of Western hero until the 1890s. While the hero of this respectable fiction had to be a sportsman, the gamesman underwent a metamorphosis that blurred the distinction between the two. An officially sanctioned Western myth could emerge only from this magazine fiction; what is most interesting about the myth that did emerge is its embrace of gamesmanship as well as sportsmanship, and its reconstruction of the gamesman as a transcendent hero.

When Irwin P. Beadle introduced the first dime-novel series in 1860, he developed no new popular genre but new production and marketing techniques for the story-paper fiction and sensational potboilers that had been appearing for a generation. As Beadle's writers, and soon numerous competitors, began churning out series "novels" almost weekly under a variety of names and pseudonyms, the rhetoric of "games" became a part of their formulas from the beginning, growing increasingly conspicuous and pervasive as the plots grew wilder and woollier. The frontier sportsman, often explicitly modeled on Cooper's Leatherstocking but sometimes more closely resembling Billy Kirby, appeared more frequently in the early, tamer years. "The Hunter's Vow" (1864), for example, opens with a shooting match won by a young trapper with formulaic gifts: "the best wrestler, best shot, best woodsman, best worker and handsomest fellow in the settlement." Pete Wilkins of "The

Mustang-Hunters" (1871) engages in "a fair race" to capture an elusive Black Mustang. The scout Jehiel Filkens in "Old Bear-Paw, the Trapper King" (1873) fights an Indian chief with knives, after agreeing to "fair play." The hero of "Old Sib Cone, the Mountain Trapper" (1876) by Ned Buntline, one of the most popular and prolific of the dime novelists, prepares his men for an Indian fight much as Leatherstocking did in *The Last of the Mohicans*: "Now fellers!... we are going to have a game of ball. Keep cool and shoot straight; make every ball hit its mark. It's not the first time I've fought the Comanches, and at greater odds than this!" When Daniel Boone himself appears in Frederick Whittaker's "Boone, the Hunter" (1873), the author's debt to Cooper is particularly obvious. With a shooting match out of *The Pioneers,* a sporting code scrupulously observed by Daniel and his younger brother but repeatedly violated by the villain (an arrogant Englishman), and much talk of red and white "gifts," Whittaker's narrative shows its debts at every turn. Cooper's transformation of the historical Kentuckian became the model for a newly fictionalized Boone, the mythmaking circle completed.[39]

In Whittaker's story, however, the Boone-Bumppo figure becomes fully domesticated, his code not set against legal authority but made the basis of honest law. We can take a late dime-novel sportsman hero, Ted Strong, to complete the genre's connection among Boone, Cooper, and the man who made the wilderness hunter the prototypical builder of the American nation, Theodore Roosevelt. Strong's exploits appeared in a magazine titled *The Young Rough Riders Weekly* expressly to capitalize on Roosevelt's popularity by idealizing for juvenile readers the familiar virtues of the athlete-hunter-president. In one episode, when the hands from a rival ranch propose a tournament of cowboy sports, Ted instructs his lads, "We'll have to do the best we can, and do it in an honest, sportsman-like way. Never give in till your [sic] beaten and then acknowledge the defeat like a gentleman."[40] When they do in fact lose – because of tampered cartridges, burrs planted under saddles, a vicious unropable steer, and emphatically "professional" opponents – Ted and his young Rough Riders maintain the gracious demeanor of plucky amateurs bested at wholesome sport. Their *moral* victory wins them the admiration of the refined young ladies who witness the events, and, one can assume, of young readers everywhere.

Sportsmanship, then, did figure in the dime novels, which incorporated both the conventional and the subversive into their formulas. But gamesmanship predominated, particularly as the stories became more sensational and melodramatic. As early as the 1866 story "Big Foot, the Guide," the Falstaffian hero Jared Tomlinson expresses the gamesman's code as something much less reverent than the hunter's ideal of gentlemanly fair play. Having lured a turkey to its death by unsportingly imitating its call, Jared waxes philosophical in mock-heroic vein:

> This is the game of life .... Thus do we lay snares for unwary feet. I shall feast, to-night, upon the flesh of the bird I have betrayed through his love for his kind. But shall I like it less from this fact? No, I shall rather enjoy it. I should never have gained my present fair proportions, had I not preyed upon inferior animals. Such is life.[41]

Tomlinson speaks here as a less crude Sut Lovingood, his sentiments by now conventional but reflecting a more ambiguous morality than Leatherstocking-style sportsmanship. One also hears here the author in dialogue with his culture: mocking the gentleman's code of sportsmanship, but also mocking the mockers – the clearest sign that such ideas have become commonplace. The more typical meaning of "game" in dime novels was not the fair contest of Whittaker's Boone but the plot or scheme of William Gilmore Simms's Guy Rivers. When the hunter/trapper gave way to the plainsman and the noble outlaw as the dominant dime-novel heroes in the 1870s, embodied most popularly in Buffalo Bill and Deadwood Dick, both of these figures played "games" – the *same* games: Robbers' plots and heroes' plans for dealing with villains are rhetorically identical.[42] The metaphor became extremely protean. Murder, killing buffalo, being chased by a bear, a reward for a thief's capture, an attack by robbers, fights with Indians, and the practice of banditry are all termed "games" in a series of tales.[43] It is possible, I suppose, to dismiss the moral ambiguity of the dime-novel "game" as an accidental consequence of vernacular diffusion. It is also possible, however, to read it as a rhetorical sign of cultural ambivalence toward American social realities.

At a time in America when gambling was still reviled by respectable society, poker provided the most elaborate metaphors and incidents in Western dime novels. When Buffalo Bill is drawn into "A Game for Life and Death," as a chapter title expresses it, he plays poker for that mortal stake, the loser to stand ten paces away and be shot. When Frank James confronts a villain with his treachery, he tells the varmint, "I'm fly to it all, and your little game too[.] But you haven't won the trick yet, my laddie. No, you've got a little performance to go through before them cards turn up trumps." "Playing my cards" and "playing trumps" became common idioms.[44] The cast of gambling heroes in dime-novel stories of the 1880s and 1890s includes Flush Fred, Faro Saul, Monte Jim, The Lone Hand, Bluff Burke, Short-Card Charlie, Faro Frank, Bluff Bill, Keno Kit, Lone-Hand Joe, Ace High, Poker Jack, Poker Pete, and You-Bet Bob. They play cards fairly when possible but out-cheat their

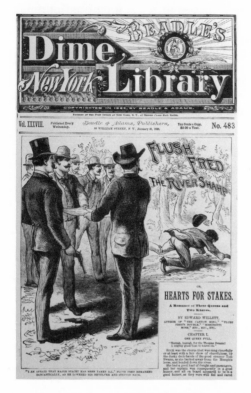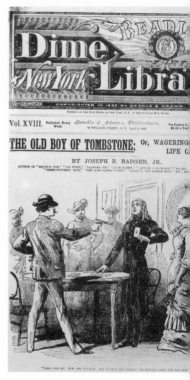

Four dime-novel covers from the 1880s and 1890s. (Reproduced by permission of The Huntington Library, San Marino, California)

rivals when necessary. And so with life. The scenes of their exploits include such aptly named places as Doubledeck, Hard Luck, Pokerville, Keno Camp, Poker City, Faro Flats, You Bet, Keno Bar, and Jack Pot. The titles of their tales sometimes compound the basic metaphor in dizzying alliterative effusions:

> "Flush Fred, the River Sharp; or, Hearts for Stakes. A Romance of Three Queens and Two Knaves"
> "Gentle Jack, the High Roller of Humbug; or, The Dark Deal at Doubledeck"
> "Deadwood Dick, Jr.'s, Big Play; or, The Bluff Game at Gold Ledge City"

And so on. In two dime-novel series alone, *Beadle's Dime Library* (1878–1905) and *Beadle's Half-Dime Library* (1877–1905), 146 titles with gambling terms or metaphors appear. One hundred forty-seven (with some

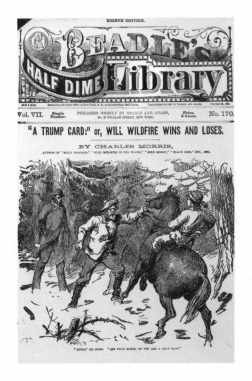

overlapping) are stories of "sports," the colloquial term for a gambler, dandy, and usually expert gunman given to playfully desperate, devil-may-care fatalism. "Sports" came in a variety of shapes and sizes: the Giant Sport, the Preacher Sport, the Parson Sport, the Dandy Sport, the Ventriloquist Sport, the Round-About-Town Sport, a Sport in Spectacles, the Bullet-Proof Sport, the Hayseed Sport, and even several Girl Sports. These characters could be either good or evil, though usually they helped the weak and thwarted the villains while remaining themselves ambiguously related to polite society. A "sport" could be either a frontiersman or an urban detective: The figure linked East and West in the two most popular dime-novel subjects. Dime novels appear to have been a primary vehicle for popularizing the idioms of the poker table throughout the culture. If the language of "busted flushes," "freeze outs," "calls," "raises," "bluffs," and "antes" originated with Western cowboys, as has been claimed, it still required a vernacular medium.[45] Dime novels seem likely to have established these poker metaphors in colloquial idiom, from which the terms would have penetrated "upward" into those social realms where gambling was most (officially) disparaged, until proper gentlemen like Theodore Roosevelt could use the language of gamesters as readily as did frontier "sports."

The Boone-Bumppo sportsman was never fully removed from the dime-novel pantheon, however. In such stories as Colonel Prentiss Ingraham's "Buck Taylor, King of the Cowboys" (1887), which introduced the cowboy to dime-novel readers, the antithetical traditions of sportsmanship and gamesmanship are tossed together by authors apparently unaware of their contradictory assumptions.[46] Dime novels, not more respectable literary forms, were the melting pot of late-nineteenth-century literary and rhetorical culture. Pat Garrett's *The Authentic Life of Billy, the Kid* (1882) – not itself a dime novel but a response by the Kid's killer to what he claimed were the libels of dime novelists – offers a particularly suggestive glimpse into the competing notions of "fair play" and mere ruthlessness in the popular imagination. In the book's first eight chapters, apparently written by a journalist named Ash Upson with whom Garrett shared authorship, Billy's viciousness is repeatedly redeemed by a kind of triumphant gamesmanship that makes him a noble outlaw in the dime-novel tradition of Deadwood Dick. In the next seven chapters, coauthored by Upson and Garrett, the Kid is more randomly "fair" and merely ruthless. Then in the final fifteen chapters Garrett writing alone offered a dry, matter-of-fact, unembellished account of his tracking and killing a thoroughly demythologized Kid for murdering Sheriff Brady.

But in one last twist of history and myth, in the "Addenda" (attributed to Upson) following the final chapter, the narrative returns to the archetypal realm where actions define cultural attitudes. In a long passage rich in stated and unstated conflicts over frontier ethics, Garrett claims that he was no cowardly bushwhacker in killing the Kid, but that in any case he would have taken whatever advantage he could:

> If there is any one simple enough to imagine that I did, or will ever, put my life squarely in the balance against that of the Kid, or any of his ilk, let him divest his mind of that absurd fallacy. It is said that Garrett did not give the Kid a fair show – did not fight him "on the square," etc. Whenever I take a contract to fight a man "on the square," as they put it . . . that man must bear the reputation . . . of an honorable man and respectable citizen; or, at least, he must be my equal in social standing.
>   . . . . I, at no time, contemplated taking any chances which I could avoid by caution or cunning. The only circumstances under which we could have met on equal terms, would have been accidental, and to which I would have been an unwilling party. Had we met unexpectedly, face to face, I have no idea that either one of us would have run away, and there is where the "square fight" would, doubtlessly, have come

off. With one question I will dismiss the subject of taking unfair advantage, etc. What sort of "square fight," or "even show," would I have got, had one of the Kid's friends in Fort Sumner chanced to see me and informed him of my presence there and at Pete Maxwell's room on that fatal night?[47]

Whoever is speaking here, Upson or Garrett, this passage wonderfully encapsulates the ambiguities of competing frontier sporting codes. The earnestness and prolixity of the argument reveal a very defensive writer aware of widespread belief in a code of fair play, not just in Garrett's critics but in the readers of the book, on which grounds the killer is expected to justify himself. The authors insisted on an absence of fair play in the actual West, and on the justice of capitalizing on one's "advantage." Less directly, they connected the code of sportsmanship to class consciousness (fair play owed only to "my equal in social standing"). But behind the defensiveness, they also seem to have acknowledged that fair play *ought* to prevail.

This passage and the entire book, with its idealized Robin Hood outlaw at the beginning and its vicious killer at the end, mix sportsmanship and gamesmanship, plus simple lawlessness, in a manner that does not obscure but exposes the diversity of cultural attitudes concerning force and fairness. Dime novels are most revealing in these contradictions. In the context of the business civilization emerging in the last decades of the nineteenth century, when the ruthless competition of financiers and captains of industry both fascinated and appalled largely powerless citizens, dime novels appear as morality plays grappling with the ambiguous values of the age.

"Magazinists" and the frontier sportsman

Dime novels, then, and the larger fictional tradition to which they contributed, account importantly for the proliferation of game idioms as metaphors for ethical codes or value systems that reflect the moral ambiguities within the developing industrial culture. Although determining the audience for dime novels resists full certainty, Michael Denning has argued persuasivly that in the relatively unstable class structure of mid- and late-nineteenth-century America, dime novels were the reading of the "producing classes," which included professionals, clerks, shopkeepers, and small farmers in addition to laborers. Genteel magazines, on the other hand, published the popular fiction of the middle and upper-middle classes, which included those same clerks, farmers, shopkeepers, and professionals, but manufacturers, bankers, and large merchants as well.[48] Thus the readership of dime novels and genteel magazines overlapped in a varied, yet common literary culture.

The "magazinists," as they were known, who wrote for genteel periodicals dealt with conventional Western materials much more self-consciously than the dime novelists, seemingly to address, if only indirectly, their class's longing for a stable social order. In the magazine fiction one senses an estrangement from contemporary America that is absent from the dime novels. Or perhaps more accurately, writers and readers of dime novels confronted their fears and angers more directly for they were embodied in melodramatic villains extravagantly portrayed. The magazinists on the other hand deflected or disguised their anxieties to a degree that suggests greater uncertainty. The dime novelists dealt with the present, the West of the Colorado mining camps in the 1870s, say, while such camps still existed. The magazinists wrote most typically of a West that had recently disappeared, waxing nostalgic over a vanished world whose realities they did not have to confront. The dime novelists wrestled in the muck of unsavory life, so to speak, while the genteel writers fled from the present to the past, to celebrate a hero related to their own world only by stark contrast. At the same time, as with Cooper and Irving before them, the genteel writers' commitment to the world of the East, of civilization, of elite culture, made the Western hero a problematic ideal. The result, through the end of the century, was a consistent portrayal of the Western hero as a noble sportsman whose values implicitly criticized the moral shortcomings of the readers' own world, but were presented with a certain detachment through a humorous or patronizing tone. The ambiguity of the magazine fiction derived not from any moral uncertainty but from the writer's (and presumably many readers') estrangement from both the contemporary commercial, industrial world, and the primitive alternative most effectively opposed to it in popular mythology.[49]

The Western hero of magazine fiction emerged in the 1860s, as the bemused patronizing of writers such as J. Ross Browne in "A Peep at Washoe" (Harper's, 1860) gave way to more romantic portraiture.[50] In 1867, the mythic Western hero debuted in Harper's in G. W. Nichols's account of Wild Bill Hickok, "the famous Scout of the Plains," that cast him in the mold of classical heroes, from his physical beauty to his courage and faultless honor. The author imbued him with all the frontier virtues of Cooper's Leatherstocking: astonishing marksmanship, skill with horses, knowledge of woodcraft, coolness and bravery. Wild Bill is a man of violence, the writer admits, but violence governed by a sporting code.[51] Harper's version can be set alongside responses by contemporary Western newspapers to both the events described and the descriptions of them in the influential Eastern magazine, as well as next to accounts of Hickok's life in dime novels. In dime novels Wild Bill appears as a gamesman, in newspaper reports merely a vicious killer; for respectable journals like *Harper's,* only a sportsman would do.[52]

The chief creator of this frontier sportsman in genteel periodicals was Bret Harte, whose major contribution to the frontier myth was the figure of the heroic gambler risking his life as readily as his fortune on the turn of a card. Harte's early stories, with their prostitutes and gamblers and other crude citizens of the gold-country mining camps, shocked readers but also appeared to capture the authentic West. What seemed disturbingly earthy in 1868 seems extravagantly sentimental today: prostitutes with hearts of gold and gamblers as noble as Lincoln himself. These figures were new to America in 1868, but through Harte and his imitators they became conventionalized in the sentimental realism that emerged as the dominant approach to Western materials. Harte in effect took a morally suspect figure from frontier humor and the dime novel and transformed him into Cooper's Leatherstocking.

I emphasize this cross-fertilization of genres as yet another confirmation of a diverse but common literary culture. Just as many of the early dime novelists modeled their heroes to a considerable degree on Cooper's Leatherstocking, Harte drew on the tradition of frontier humor but made it more palatable for genteel readers. What most distinguishes the stories that gained Harte both critical acclaim and a wide audience is their narrative voice. In effect Harte collapsed the contrasting voices of the frame and vernacular tale of Southwestern humor into a single complex voice that is simultaneously cultured and blasphemous, romantic and mock-heroic, sentimental and ironic. This voice is sustained throughout the best tales, as in this altogether typical passage from "The Luck of Roaring Camp," describing a crusty miner's first encounter with the camp's newborn babe:

> As Kentuck bent over the candle-box half curiously, the child turned, and, in a spasm of pain, caught at his groping finger, and held it fast for a moment. Kentuck looked foolish and embarrassed. Something like a blush tried to assert itself in his weather-beaten cheek. "The d——d little cuss!" he said, as he extricated his finger, with perhaps more tenderness and care than he might have been deemed capable of showing. He held that finger a little apart from its fellows as he went out, and examined it curiously. The examination provoked the same original remark in regard to the child. In fact, he seemed to enjoy repeating it. "He rastled with my finger," he remarked to Tipton, holding up the member, "the d——d little cuss!"[53]

The collision of crude miner and innocent baby, the tender and wondrous curse, the simultaneous mocking and sentimentalizing of unsavory characters who live sometimes nobly in an edenic, yet murderous, landscape

– this complexity created a narrative space for disparate readers: for Mark Twain, say, Harte's then friend and fellow irreverent Western bohemian, and for the editors and readers of the *Atlantic Monthly*, where Harte's stories quickly generated interest in local-color fiction from all regions.

The major sporting figure in Harte's fiction, the frontier gambler, juxtaposed nobility and moral outrage in a similar way. In Harte's three most famous tales – "The Luck of Roaring Camp" (*Overland Monthly*, August 1868), "Tennessee's Partner" (*Overland Monthly*, October 1869), and "The Outcasts of Poker Flat" (*Overland Monthly*, January 1869) – the professional gambler emerges as a gamesman by trade but a transcendent sportsman by instinct and action. He is a fatalist in a world dominated by chance, but his absolute commitment to honor and fair play lead to an ambiguous sentimental salvation. In "The Luck of Roaring Camp," rough miners bet on the outcome of a prostitute's pregnancy, then adopt the baby after the mother dies in childbirth. The gambler John Oakhurst christens him "Luck," in order to give him "a fresh deal all around," a fair start at life. The "luck," in fact, proves to be the camp's, whose regeneration is interrupted only by a catastrophic flood. In "Tennessee's Partner," robbery, betrayal, and lynching become mere cards played by stoical miners in a game of frontier euchre, through which outlawry and vengeance are transformed into public ritual.[54]

The quintessential emblem of sporting fatalism in these stories is the death of John Oakhurst, which concludes "The Outcasts of Poker Flat." Having been banished from Poker Flat, together with two prostitutes and a thief, Oakhurst "was too much of a gambler not to accept Fate. With him life was at best an uncertain game, and he recognized the usual percentage in favor of the dealer." When the four exiles and an innocent young couple that joins them are trapped in a snowstorm, Oakhurst coolly surveys "the losing game before him" then slips away to play out his hand his own way. On a deuce of clubs pinned to a tree with a bowie knife, the rescuers who arrive too late discover his scrawled epitaph:

BENEATH THIS TREE

LIES THE BODY

OF

JOHN OAKHURST

WHO STRUCK A STREAK OF BAD LUCK

ON THE 23D OF NOVEMBER, 1850,

AND

HANDED IN HIS CHECKS

ON THE 7TH DECEMBER, 1850

In the story's final line the narrator calls Oakhurst "at once the strongest and yet the weakest of the outcasts of Poker Flat."[55] This self-conscious ambivalence – the gambler as self-sacrificing hero, the gambler as blind fatalist – both typifies Harte's narrative strategy and signals the uneasiness with which genteel culture came to terms with this figure. Readers could be charmed or shocked by Bret Harte's stories, assured of the capacity for goodness in even the least likely souls, left uncertain whether proper values had in fact been affirmed after all, or convulsed with laughter at the moralism his fiction might have seemed to puncture.

Harte's literary legacy reflects this range of responses. One line of his influence leads to Mark Twain, and after him to Stephen Crane and Ambrose Bierce: to ironic Western fiction purged of all sentiment.[56] The other leads eventually to the fiction of Owen Wister and his countless followers, where romance is purged of all irony. But romance did not triumph immediately. Magazine writing about the West in the 1870s and early 1880s, both fiction and nonfiction, reveals a nagging ambivalence about its heroic or barbaric reality. A minister's accounts of frontier violence, "The Red Hand" and "Red Reminiscences of the Southwest," for example, reveal only moral outrage. Another writer in *Lippincott's Magazine* in 1881 viewed the West as the scene of a Darwinian struggle for survival, not of gentlemanly fair play.[57]

The genteel magazinists' inability to decide whether the West was a garden of innocence or the heart of darkness is most striking in the essays of specific authors who could not themselves decide. This confusion is nicely illustrated in an account of Leadville, Colorado, in 1879, in which factual narrative competes with both romantic fantasy and unmitigated revulsion. The sociology, geology, and economic history of Leadville are juxtaposed to accounts of sportive miners as playful as Irving's trappers, as gentlemanly as Cooper's Leatherstocking, as stoical as Harte's philosophical gamblers. In the essay's last few pages, the prose soars to romantic heights when the author describes Leadville at night as "a scene of wild hilarity, and yet of remarkable order" – a phrase that neatly sums up what becomes a very contradictory conclusion to a strangely bifurcated essay. The "shoot-out-the-lights ruffianism" of the old days has disappeared, the writer claims, though "wildness and wickedness . . . to satisfy the most insatiate seeker of excitement" remain. Gambling and other vices are but "picturesque phases of human nature," not to be condemned by the morally upright. The well-behaved gambler "loses and wins, or smiles benignantly across the table as the dealer divides a 'split.' " Respectable people stay away from the tables, of course, though the author recounts the "romantic history" of one deeply Christian citizen who repeatedly won and lost thousands on the turn of a single card.

Having reported all of this with obvious affection for the town, however, the author comments strangely:

> The streets of Leadville at night are not safe places for the unwary, or for men known to have wealth upon their persons. Shooting and stabbing and garroting are of daily occurrence, both by enticing careless men into dens where the deed may be secret, and by open attack.

But the author is not finished yet. He reverses field one more time, to offer one last dollop of confection to readers hungry for a romantic West: "Yet, I repeat, for a Western camp of its character and size, this is a safe and law-abiding community." Perhaps the key to the writer's paradoxical desire for a wild but gentle West lies in the volumes of Bret Harte he reports seeing on an assayer's desk. Here, however, the contradictory values sustained within Harte's single narrative voice are fragmented into cacophany.[58]

What such essays reveal is less literary complexity than confusion. The cultured East demanded that the Western frontier be both romantic and barbaric, both an escape from an overcivilized world and a confirmation of civilization's superiority. Bret Harte had fashioned a formula to satisfy both desires, but the formula (without Harte's irony) did not take firm hold until the 1890s. It is important to point out that while one could pick up virtually any Western dime novel from the 1870s or 1880s and find a sporting metaphor or two, quite likely an abundance of them, in the magazine fiction they remained scarce. The magazine fiction of these decades also suggests no clear "man's" West and "woman's" West at odds with each other. Women's voices are almost wholly absent from the Western dime novels of the era: Although women wrote twenty-seven of the first seventy in Beadle's initial series, they produced only six of the next eighty and fewer yet as years passed (of the 1103 stories in *Beadle's Dime Library* [1878–1905] and 1168 in *Beadle's Half-Dime Library* [1877–1905], where the West was woolliest and the rhetoric most sportive, not one was written by a woman – or at least under a woman's name, an important qualification, given the pseudonymous authorship of much of this fiction). In the early dime novels that women did write, the authors tended to undermine the sporting myths that had emerged during the antebellum period: through openly rejecting, more subtly inverting, or simply ignoring them. To cite just one example: In Mrs. Orrin James's "Rob Ruskin" (1868), the heroine, not the hero, runs the "race" from Indians for "stakes ... as high as ever were raced for – a human life"; while the frontiersman of the story is an utterly degraded, brutal, and ignorant outlaw, Crevecoeur's worst nightmare rather than Cooper's fantasy.[59]

Though no dime novel itself, *The River of the West* (1870) by the dime novelist Frances Fuller Victor, celebrates the violent but sportive life of the trapper Joe Meek in a manner identical to Irving's *Captain Bonneville*.[60] Generalizations must be cautious. For their part, male dime novelists granted female characters a surprising degree of freedom. By the late 1870s, as Henry Nash Smith has shown, rip-roaring Amazons, in the tradition of what David Reynolds has called "adventure feminists," became indistinguishable from male heroes (and villains) except by the physical fact of their sex.[61] Hurricane Nell can "outrun, out-ride, out-shoot, out-lasso, and out-yell" any man in town; she even wins a shooting match (with the hero betting on her skill) in the hallowed Leatherstocking fashion. Phantom Moll speaks of the "jolly life we outlawed sinners lead." 'Shian Sal smokes, gambles, swears, drinks, "and sometimes . . . pop[s] over a rough, jest to keep my hand in and let 'em know Sal is old bizness." Calamity Jane, the queen of the "softhearted Amazons," "kin drink whisky, shute, play keerds, or sw'ar, ef et comes ter it," as one of her admirers puts it. By the 1890s one finds a number of "Girl Sports" and "Card Queens," as well as a "Masked Faro Queen," a "Poker Queen," a "Sport-Queen," and a "Gambler Queen" gracing the pages of Beadle's productions.

It is difficult to know precisely what to make of all this. If only the physical fact of sex distinguished females from males in many of these stories, that fact alone would have seemed crucial to most readers in a society with decided views on feminine and masculine behavior, at a time when the liberated New Woman was becoming a conspicuous social phenomenon. The actual West did, in fact, have its famous/notorious women gamblers and frontierswomen: such figures as Doña Gertrudis Barcelo, Eleanor Dumont ("Madame Moustache"), Lottie Demo, and Alice Ivers ("Poker Alice"),[62] as well as sharpshooting Annie Oakley and Calamity Jane. But the dime novelists in other matters revealed no scrupulous regard for fact; it is unlikely that the existence of such women demanded their inclusion in the stories. Perhaps something so simple as a desire to attract female as well as male readers lay behind these representations. But since the readers of Western dime novels were predominantly male, these Amazons must have fascinated male readers in some way. In the pointed *unnaturalness* of gun-toting heroines and gambling villainesses one senses an anxiety over women's infringement on male terrain: a possible reflection, that is, of male uneasiness over the increasing freedom of women in the larger culture. In general, dime novels reveal a fundamental uncertainty about women: uneasiness over their stepping outside traditional roles, insistence on dealing with them at least partly in relation to those roles (always commenting on their beauty and marital status, for example), both admiration for and fear of their abilities.

In any case, while dime novels were distinctly, if ambiguously, gender-marked, magazine fiction by men and women in the 1870s and 1880s is nearly indistinguishable. Not until the 1890s, when male writers at last embraced a sporting myth long popular in less respectable forms, did the men's and women's images of an ideal West become fully distinct in genteel fiction. Women contributed almost nothing to the romance of honorable gamblers and courageous sheriffs facing down villains by the rules of fair play. The heroine of Alice McGowan's "A Successful Round-Up" (1902), who joins in cowboy sports early in the story, gives them up to lay her cheek on the Johnny's manly shoulder at the end.[63] Among stories by women that touch on the Western code at least obliquely, several reveal similar feminine revision: the entanglements of violence or honor with love, as in *The Virginian,* but with different results in the women's fiction. In stories from the 1890s by Mary A. Denison, Elia W. Pettie, Bessie B. Croffut, Nellie Mackubin, Anna Fuller, and Olive F. Canby, a distinct pattern emerges: Romantic love confronts Western violence as in *The Virginian,* but in every case the women writers placed love first.[64] Another group of stories portrays male honor not *opposed to* female needs, as in the popular masculine paradigm, but wed to love and feminine desires. In Mackubin's "A Coward," a typical case, a soldier redeems his honor by dying to save the fiancée of the woman he vainly loves. Other stories offer variations of this sentimental theme.[65]

The heroic "game" simply does not appear in women's Western fiction of the late nineteenth century.[66] The magazine fiction by men in the 1890s and early years of the twentieth century, on the other hand, at last embraced the heroic images of code-governed violence that were firmly embedded in the less respectable popular tradition. As part of the masculinist revolt against gentility and "effeminization" that was strangely irrelevant to the truly masculine world of business and politics, the magazinists began to write earthier Western stories in which the rhetoric of "games" and a sporting code played important roles. They also began to set the masculine West against an encroaching femininity. Again Bret Harte had created the pattern a generation earlier. Cooper's Leatherstocking had remained decidedly celibate. The Southwestern humorists had created an emphatically masculine humor; their portraits of women, often bawdy and disrespectful, were the very antithesis of Victorian propriety. But Harte created more active sexual antagonism in many of his stories. In "Brown of Calaveras" and "A Passage in the Life of John Oakhurst," for example, the gambler confronts a fundamental conflict between a deceitful woman and his honest game. No such conflict appears in the magazine writing of the seventies and eighties, but beginning in the 1890s it became a major theme in many stories. O. Henry placed it at the center of his light-hearted renderings of Western courtship. In

Alfred Henry Lewis's "The Man from Red Dog," Sam Enright concludes a tale of sexual misunderstanding with the observation that "hist'ry never shows a game yet, an' a woman in it, which is on the squar'." A character in a story by Frederic Remington says the same thing: "When a squar' woman gets in a game, I don't advise any bets."[67]

At their most extreme, men's and women's Western fiction from this period expresses a cycle of estrangement: men recoiling from their feared emasculation, women recoiling from the masculine fantasies created out of that fear. But it is important to note that male fiction did not reject the cultural feminine altogether. The Western formula concocted by Owen Wister and numerous imitators did not simply glorify violence, even when governed by a code, but set that violence in conflict with a sentimental and domestic world whose needs it ultimately served. Unless the Virginian takes care of Trampas first, Wister's novel tells us, marriage and domestic peace are not possible. Even in their aggressively masculinist voices, the men who created the formulas of Western sporting violence shared with the women who rejected them an ultimate commitment to a domestic ideal.

Beginning actually in the late 1880s, the Western hero of the men's magazine fiction, whether frontier gambler or, increasingly, six-gun-toting cowboy, became a highly romanticized figure. If a gambler, he was a strikingly domesticated one. Whereas dime-novel gamesmanship approached amoral anarchy, genteel magazinists consistently qualified the hero's recklessness with sentiment. In one tale, gamblers offer their entire holdings to a young woman whose new-born baby has died. In another, a nondescript clerk gambles wildly on mining stocks in order to bring a famed symphony orchestra to his frontier town. In yet another, a visiting man of the cloth – "green as well as black" – cleans out the town's fortunes on a single hand of poker, then identifies himself as an undercover Secret Service agent who gets his man and returns his winnings to the poor fools he has duped.[68] Gambling is made to serve charity, high culture, and law. Although the rowdier gamesman of Southwestern humor and dime novels makes an occasional appearance in stories of the trickster tricked, for the most part gamesmanship is either transformed into sportsmanship or rendered unobjectionable by serving sentimental ends.[69]

The more straightforward frontier sportsman, the heir to Daniel Boone and Natty Bumppo, was the cowboy, whose heyday in the genteel magazines began at that moment when historian Frederick Jackson Turner announced that the old West had vanished.[70] And the figure who emerged in the stories of numerous authors, both famous and forgotten, played the Virginian's "games."[71] In this fiction the sportsman's code served the law rather than opposed it; from an essentially countercultural origin in Cooper's Leatherstocking tales, growing out of the author's ambivalence toward democratic society, the sporting myth became in respectable fiction at the end of the century the basis for effective law. From another perspective, the sporting code retained its function as cultural criticism: The frontier sportsman, these writers implied (and sometimes stated more openly), embodied a mode of heroism antithetical to the values of contemporary commercial America. Western fiction satisfied readers' desire for the exotic and reconstructed an heroic past for the nation. But it also served as an implicit critique of the anti-pastoral present.

The chief writers of Western magazine fiction and nonfiction in the 1890s were Owen Wister and Frederic Remington: Wister, the creator of the formula that dominated popular Westerns for much of the next century; Remington, a representative of the road not taken in this fiction. The artist whose illustrations did most to shape the nation's visual image of the heroic West, Remington also wrote prolifically in *Harper's, Harper's Weekly,* the *Century,* and other popular magazines (about two-thirds of his 111 pieces between 1887 and 1906 deal with the West). His many reports on frontier sporting life among cowboys and military men reinforced Theodore Roosevelt's connection of national destiny to sporting heroism and the winning of the West. The manners demanded by civilization, Remington observed in one sketch about cowboy contests at a roundup, count "very little in the game these men play in their lonely range life."[72] But Remington stopped short of Wister's extravagant mythmaking, and with *Sundown Leflare* (1899), *John Ermine of the Yellowstone* (1902), and *The Way of an Indian* (1906), he abandoned his earlier ethnocentrism for a sympathetic treatment of Indian life. In this he joined such women writers as Helen Hunt Jackson in *Ramona* (1880), Gertrude Atherton in *Los Cerritos* (1890) and *The Californians* (1898), and later Mary Austin in *The Land of Little Rain* (1903) and *Lost Borders* (1909), who wrote from the perspective of the West's non-Anglo victims. The women's identification with the oppressed or supplanted races may have been a covert stategy for dramatizing, if only obliquely, their own subordinate position in society. With no comparable gender-specific need Remington similarly portrayed an elegiac, often tragic, romance of the vanished West.

The road very much taken by later writers was marked out most clearly in the 1890s by Owen Wister. Besides the tales that became *The Virginian,* Wister published numerous other Western stories in *Harper's,* including those collected in *Lin McLean* in 1898. The dominant theme of this volume is the cowboy's childlike playfulness, a quality essential to the romantic image of the West since Irving's frolicking trappers in the 1830s. Twenty-two-year-old Lin McLean is just a boy-man, perfectly in tune with the childhood of the region he inhabits, "in the old days, the happy days, when Wyoming was a Territory with a future instead of a state with a past."[73] Lin wins and loses at cards with equal complacency ("How Lin McLean Went East"). He engages in a contest for the affections of a slightly used woman, less for the prize than for the honor of the contest ("The Winning of the Biscuit-Shooter"). He joins with his fellow citizens in betting on the efforts of a rainmaker, losing "fair and square" with no regrets, only delight in the entertainment ("Lin McLean's Honey-Moon"). Cowboys shooting up the town for "jollification" are merely "playful, howling horsemen" and "large, headlong children" at play ("Separ's Vigilante") – a description reiterated at length in the book's final sketch. The town of Drybone, which "had known a wholesome adventurous youth, where manly lives and deaths were plenty," remains a playground for the young:

> The happy cow-punchers on ranches far and near still earned and in-stantly spent the high wages still paid them. With their bodies full of youth and their pockets full of gold, they rode into town by twenties and fifties, and out again next morning, penniless always and happy. And then the Four-ace Johnstons would sit card-playing with each other till the innocents should come to town again. ("Destiny at Drybone")

"Boys will be boys," as one character says in this final story. Writing elsewhere as historian, Wister drew the same picture. In "The Evolution of the Cow-Puncher" (1895), Wister described the West as "the cow-puncher's playground," a strange playground perhaps, where "battle and murder and sudden death [were] every-day matters," but a playground nonetheless.[74]

Although Wister's fiction became the acknowledged wellspring of Western writing in the twentieth century, it is in the Wolfville stories of Alfred Henry Lewis that we can most clearly see frontier gamesmanship transformed into a transcendent code indistinguishable from sportsman-ship – a crucial change in cultural mythmaking, given the potential an-archy in the gamesman's code. Though primarily a political journalist, Lewis under the pen name "Dan Quin" wrote seven collections of stories between 1897 and 1913 set in Wolfville, Arizona, a town roughly mod-eled after Tombstone.[75] The Wolfville stories are the sum of the many parts I have been discussing: Cooper's heroic sportsmanship, South-western humorists' comic gamesmanship; the earthy surface of frontier life in dime novels, the underlying sentimentality in magazine fiction. Lewis's Westerners are as playful as Irving's trappers and Wister's cow-boys, as abashed by the mystery of femininity as O. Henry's boy-men. But Lewis's mentor was most clearly Bret Harte, from whom he seems to have derived the combinations of crude speech and behavior with lofty sentiment, of fatalism with redemption. His major theme was Harte's as well: In the West, men played the hands they were dealt as honestly and courageously as they could. Lewis redefined Bret Harte's synthesis of sentiment and earthy detail for later readers whose sense of propriety had expanded to accommodate increasingly exaggerated ideas about the Western frontier.

All of the Wolfville tales are narrated by a character known as the Old Cattleman, a garrulous old raconteur unable to string together a half-dozen words without referring to the poker table. Nor can anyone else in Wolfville. The initial story in the earliest volume of the series, an account of "Wolfville's First Funeral," strikes the characteristic note in a graveside eulogy delivered by the keeper of the local dance hall:

> Mister King . . . has his weaknesses, as do we all. A disp'sition to make new rooles as he plays along for sech games of chance as enjoys his notice is perhaps his greatest failin'. His givin' way to this habit is primar'ly the cause of his bein' garnered in. I hopes he'll get along thar, an' offers a side bet, even money, up to five hundred dollars, he will. He may alter his system an' stand way up with the angels an' seraphs, an' if words from me could fix it, I'd shorely stack 'em in.

On the man's tombstone the townsmen erect this epitaph:

JaCK KInG

LIfE AiN'T

IN

holding A Good Hand

BUT

In plAying a PorE Hand

weLL.[76]

The sentiments are Bret Harte's, the voice Scotty Briggs's out of Twain's *Roughing It,* but this is not simple parody. The voice – whether the Old Cattleman's or another's – continues in story after story for seven volumes. It becomes familiar, less a parody of Western vernacular than the native speech of this Western community. And embedded in the language is an ethical system stricter and less forgiving than any merely legal code. What seems parody becomes the substance of myth. The model is poker, but the emphasis is on fairness, not trickery. As Cherokee Hall says in one of the tales in *Wolfville Days* (1902):

> Life is like stud-poker; an' Destiny's got an ace buried every time. It either out-lucks you or out-plays you when it's so inclined; an' it seems allers so inclined, Destiny does, jest as you're flatterin' yourself you've got a shore thing. A gent's bound to play fa'r with Destiny; he can put

a bet down on that. You can't hold six kyards; you can't deal double; you can't play no cold hands; you can't bluff Destiny. All you-all can do is humbly an' meekly pick up the five kyards that belongs to you, an' in a sperit of thankfulness an' praise, an' frankly admittin' that you're lucky to be allowed to play at all, do your lowly best tharwith.[77]

To speak of "Life" and "Destiny" in the language of poker is to invoke the eternal verities of a transcendent moral order. In a fate-ridden world, the citizens of Wolfville not only reveal their innocence through their playfulness; they *redeem* their lives through scrupulous adherence to the code of fair play.

The sentimental synthesis of sportsmanship and gamesmanship in the Wolfville tales, in a setting bearing almost no relation to either the contemporary scene or any historical epoch, marked the course that popular Western fiction would take in the twentieth century. Even at their wildest and woolliest, dime novels reflected at least some of the gritty reality of morally ambiguous frontier life. With the Wolfville tales, as well as *The Virginian* and the abundant formulaic Western fiction to follow, the West disappeared as a real place to become entirely a state of mind. In that fantasy world sportsmanship and gamesmanship, despite their contradictory assumptions and implications, merged into a single sporting code that reconciled individualism with community interests, personal liberty with law, competition with fairness, violence with moral stability. By the beginning of the twentieth century, the rhetoric of sport and play in Western writing had become both protean and powerful.

2

Play, Sport, and Southern Honor

Although Wister collapsed the popular images of the South and the West into a single heroic cowboy from Virginia, the traditions on which he drew developed independently in the nineteenth century. Sharing a common tie to the original fantasy of a New World garden, the Western myth emerged in the antebellum period to address fundamental issues raised by democracy and expansion, the Southern myth to justify a quasifeudal agrarian order. After the Civil War, as the Southern celebration of organic and gracious leisure became less a defense of an agrarian economic and social order whose era had passed than an implicit critique of triumphant Northern capitalism, the two sporting myths met again on common ground. Whether the hero was a code-governed cowboy or a fox-hunting Southern gentleman, the unnamed context was an industrial order that diminished individual worth and ran roughshod over traditional ethics. But from the 1830s through the 1850s, when the actual traditions of sport and leisure in the South first became the basis of an idealized regional self-portrait, the sporting myth that emerged in plantation romances served different cultural needs from Cooper's and Irving's.

Sport and antebellum southern honor

The key to antebellum Southern character in the popular image was an all-embracing code of honor, the essence of a myth that was rooted in fact. A sense of honor was not peculiar to the South, of course, but as numerous historians have demonstrated, it took a distinctive form there. In America, while Northern honor by the nineteenth century had become equivalent to respectability, the Southern code emphasized appearances, valor, and proofs of masculinity through risk and violence.[1]

Though it pervaded all classes – witness the grotesque code that governed even the most brutal eye-gouging contests in the back country – its function as the moral system of the aristocracy dominated the popular consciousness. Whether slavery exaggerated the Southerner's sense of honor or was itself a product of it has been a matter of dispute among specialists, but either as cause or reinforcement slavery played a key role in the transformation of Southern honor beginning in the 1830s.[2] As slavery became more necessary to the Southern economy, and at the same time Northern critics grew more strident, Southerners worked out a justification for their "peculiar system" based on the superiority of a moral code rooted not in laws but in gentlemen's understandings – parallel, in other words, to Cooper's frontier myth, but in a very different context and with very different purposes.

The three primary social rituals in which honor found expression – hospitality, sport, and the duel – all contributed to a sporting myth. The first involved an essential element of Southern leisure, the second was literally sport, and the third was rooted in an oddly sportive approach to personal violence. Again myth transformed fact. While New England culture was officially committed to steady industry, from which sport offered occasional respite, Southerners more readily engaged in the sports of the English countryside from which they originally emigrated, as part of the natural rhythm of their lives.

But sport in the South was "natural" in culturally determined ways: Most significantly, from at least the late seventeenth century it bore the deep imprint of class. By barring competition among different social classes, preserving most hunting and fishing rights for landowners, and banning a variety of sports from the lower but not the upper ranks, Southern laws retained a fundamental element from the Old World sporting heritage.[3] But in the relative instability of New World conditions, the planters' identification of themselves as a leisure class led inevitably to a persistent ambivalence about work and play. Having assigned labor to the lower classes, leisure to the upper, the planters defined themselves by their play but had to earn it by their work. Men like Robert Beverley and William Byrd praised the fruitfulness of their land yet issued periodic jeremiads against those who lived too easily on it. While the actual life of white Southerners, rich *and* poor, was marked by the alternating periods of labor and leisure endemic to agricultural societies, the gentry had to justify itself in contradictory ways: one set of needs insisting it appear more industrious than it was, another set demanding it appear more leisurely. In effect, Southerners were caught between the medieval and the modern worlds: between the earlier assumptions of aristocratic leisure and the work-centered demands of an emerging commercial order. In this transitional stage, leisure and laziness, as C. Vann Woodward has put it most succinctly, were unresolvably the Janus faces of the South. Puritan New England for a variety of reasons more readily embraced modernity.[4]

When Southern partisans in the 1830s, then, began to proclaim the superiority of Southern life in large part through the region's traditions of leisure and sporting honor, they had to transform a cultural contradiction into an unambiguously heroic image. And the actual sports of colonial planters confronted these apologists with an additional challenge. Far from the sporting gentleman of later myth, the colonial planter was an often ruthlessly competitive, even brutal combatant in "sports" that sometimes seemed closer to mayhem. "Gentlemen" by class often fought as savagely as backwoods brawlers; even horse races, the chief sport of the gentry, were less sporting events than "violent duel[s] that tested not only the speed of the horses but also the daring and combative skill of the riders."[5] Horse races were also occasions for the pervasive gambling that touched the very heart of the planters' worldview. The diaries of such prominent planters as William Byrd, Landon Carter, Robert Carter, and George Washington reveal the extent of a passion for gambling that often shocked observers and in some cases proved ruinous to the planters themselves.[6] According to T. H. Breen, racing and gambling expressed not just the "competitiveness, individualism, and materialism" of gentry culture; they were also what Clifford Geertz has termed "deep play," that ritualized the planters' sense of life itself as violent and risky.[7]

As sectional rivalry exaggerated the importance to Southern apologists of the code of honor, such sporting traditions became matters of intensely self-conscious scrutiny. Race week in Fredericksburg, Williamsburg, or Charleston – traditional events so important that schools, shops, and courts closed down – became occasions less for fierce rivalry than for public display of Southern honor. Outright cheating in such public sporting contests would have meant disgrace; to win shabbily would have been far more harmful to one's honor than to lose. Bets had to be paid without argument; as a gentleman from South Carolina put it in 1853, "A gambling debt is a debt of honour, but a debt due a tradesman is not."[8]

Hunting, too, became increasingly important as a ritual expression of Southern honor. Traditionally, European hunting had always been associated with class distinctions; early game laws prescribed who could hunt, and where and when. Southern honor more narrowly prescribed *how*. The necessities of being well-equipped and of making the hunt the focal point of a larger social affair that concluded with a festive dinner were part of the code. But the manner of the hunt itself was also crucial. The chase was more important than the mere killing of the game; the "spice of chivalry" separated true sportsmen from disreputable "pot-hunters." The hunter was to be like Castiglione's courtier, maintaining his composure in the excited pleasure of the hunt. The prey was to provide a "fair test" and be given a fair chance. As one writer declared, unfair methods made the sportsman's blood "boil over with contemptuous indignation." Fire hunting was taboo for the strictest gentlemen; a contest was fair only when the quarry was skillful and given, as an avid fox hunter put it, "the advantage of considerable 'law.' " The inherent unfairness of man's superiority to the brutes was to be offset, within reason, by the hunter's placing limits on himself. Although this sportsman's hunting code was less closely adhered to than other, more essential, elements of the code of honor, it was widely acknowledged in sporting periodicals such as the *American Turf Register and Sporting Magazine* from its founding in 1829. Cooper's Leatherstocking followed a similar code; Southerners foregrounded its aristocratic assumptions.[9]

Sport, together with hospitality, were the elements of Southern honor that lent themselves most easily to regional myth. As Bertram Wyatt-Brown has argued, the obligation both to extend and to accept hospitality in lavish style sometimes led to a competition among hosts that proved as ruinous as extravagant betting.[10] In the popular stereotype, Southern hospitality seemed more simply an expression of the gracious leisure of Southern life, its whole-hearted commitment to innocent play. The duel, on the other hand – Southern honor's "ultimate sanction" – was least amenable to romantic mythmaking in antebellum America.[11] Repugnant to both Christian morality and Victorian social virtues, the duel represented the prebourgeois secular worldview at its most dangerous. Sport, in a sense, occupied the middle ground between hospitality and the duel: more clearly an arena for heroic display than the hospitable sideboard, less a threat to conventional morality than the duel. Dueling itself was tolerable to an officially disapproving Southern society only through its sportive elements: its rituals, rules, and formal structures, as well as its fundamental requirement of fair play. John Hyde Wilson's transcription of the *code duello* in 1838 with its meticulous details of dueling propriety, as well as the frequency of bloodless duels that elevated public ritual over personal vengeance, made the similarity of the duel to a sporting event more striking yet. Whether pursuing a deer or facing an affronted rival at twenty paces, the Southern gentleman of the antebellum period had to be a sportsman, because to be any other kind of competitor would have surrendered all status.

The honorable Southern sportsman, then, was not just a figure of regional fantasy; even the most iconoclastic revisionist historians acknowledge his reality. In debunking the myth of the South, they demonstrate that the sources of and reasons for the code of honor lay to a large degree in a harshly demanding and doomed commitment to slavery and class privilege. Although historians insist that slavery either engendered or exaggerated the Southern obsession with honor, the myth of the Old South placed honor first: Slavery did not necessitate a code of honor; Southern honor created a benevolent slavery superior to the treatment of the Northern working class.

Novelists contributed much to this idea. Like the popularizers of the Western myth, the romancers of the South denied any economic motive in their region's social system. The plantation of fiction was primarily an arena for display of the Southern gentleman's manly virtues. Slavery was maintained through a system of benign paternalism and *noblesse oblige,* the planter reluctantly keeping his slaves until a better solution became possible. In the fiction before the Civil War, slavery was given an accidental role in the plantation world; after 1865, benevolent slavery became the retrospective key to the perfection of antebellum Southern life, a life based on the mutual love of master and servant. What mattered most in the earlier fictional planter's life was the style of his leisure activities. In his play and sport the Southern gentleman's high cultivation signaled the superiority of his region and class and the stability of a social order that correctly gauged the inequality of men.

Kennedy and the plantation romance

By the consensus of literary historians, the tradition of the plantation romance proper can be traced to John Pendleton Kennedy's *Swallow Barn,* but its essential features began to appear in the 1820s.[12] Isaac Holmes's *Recreations of George Taletell* (1822) celebrated the sporting leisure of country life in Carolina, particularly at Christmastime when slave as well as owner enjoyed "holiday frolics." More ambivalently, George Tucker's *The Valley of Shenandoah* (1824) embraced Southern play but rejected honorific sport; the social habits that give Virginia gentlemen the "polished and easy grace which is possessed by the highest classes in Europe" also lead in the novel to dissolute gambling and a tragic affair of honor.[13] In Holmes's and Tucker's novels the South is a different region from the country's other half, but its distinctive way of life and economic order were not yet the objects of intense outside criticism. As both the criticism and the defense intensified from the nullification crisis to the attack on Fort Sumter, plantation romances from *Swallow Barn* (1832) to James Hungerford's *The Old Plantation* (1859) became a major voice in the war over cultural images.

In the same year that John Calhoun raised the disturbing possibility of nullification, and a year after Nat Turner's scourge of the Virginia countryside, *Swallow Barn* began the delineation of Southern customs and characters that hardened into stereotype within a generation. A

Unionist and social progressive, Kennedy portrayed planter life and values with some ambivalence, an ambivalence that marks antebellum plantation romances more generally. But Kennedy's final allegiance is never in doubt. Existence on a Southern plantation, he implied, was rooted in the spirit of play, sometimes with ridiculous consequences but at bottom as a testament to the superiority of Southern life. In narrating the novel through the viewpoint of a Northern visitor who is repeatedly surprised by what he finds on the Southern plantation, Kennedy suggested a contrast between his own region and that of Benjamin Franklin's heirs in the commercial North that in the end was clearly flattering to the South.

When the Yankee Mark Littleton arrives at Swallow Barn, he finds playful children, playful animals, and equally playful adults. His first impression on arrival is of "a troop of children, white and black, [who] trundled hoops across the court-yard, followed by a pack of companionable curs who seemed a part of the game; whilst a piano within the house served as an orchestra to the players." Later in the evening, the children drag their favorite uncle into their sport until exhaustion drives them to bed. The adults are no less playful. Games of whist, discussions of hunting and horsemanship, all-night card games, and day-long hunting expeditions take up a good deal of this Southern household's time. The frequent visits from plantation to plantation are always marked by "that noisy, mirthful play of frolic spirits" that characterizes Southern life generally.[14]

Within this world, the planter Frank Meriwether, his nephew Ned Hazard, and their various neighbors conduct their affairs in the manner of Southern sportsmen. In two of the three major scenes of sport, Kennedy played the satirist, looking with bemusement on the innocent follies of his sportive Southern males. The first involves a land dispute between the tenants of Swallow Barn and those of The Brakes, a neighboring plantation. Although Isaac Tracy of The Brakes doesn't want the land in question, honor demands that he bring a lawsuit for it. For his part, Frank Meriwether of Swallow Barn wants neither the land nor victory in the suit, but simply to cede the property to Tracy would insult him. A settlement is finally reached in a comic scene presented metaphorically as a fox hunt. As the litigants leave the plantation house to view the disputed property, they look like "a party setting out to beat a cover, with the principle huntsman in advance" (197). After they accidentally raise an actual fox, one of the participants reports the outcome:

> About forty years ago, the law suit began with the quest of a wild-goose, and, having exercised the ingenuity of all the low-country lawyers in succession, during this time, it has now turned into a fox-chase, and ended by earthing a poor little harmless quadruped, precisely at the place of beginning. (211)

A settlement is reached when Meriwether, through a double-talking lawyer, persuades Tracy to take the land, his honor intact.

A second satiric episode involves the sporting honor of the lower classes: a fantastic tale told by a vagabond minstrel about a blacksmith, Mike Brown, who loses an affair of honor with the devil. A heavy drinker with a violent temper, Brown encounters Old Nick several times in a neighborhood swamp, in each instance falling victim to his devilish pranks. When at last Mike vows vengeance, he resolves to treat the affair "like a gentleman, and to give his adversary fair play." He demands satisfaction; the devil agrees. Mike tells him, "Remember, as you set up for a gentleman, I expect fair play." "Honor bright!" the devil answers. When they set the terms, however, Mike leaves unfortunate loopholes. After Satan chooses the swamp as the dueling ground, Mike becomes so mired he cannot move, while the devil walks away laughing. "You are no gentleman," cries Mike. "Granted," says the devil; "I never set up for one" (283–92).

In these two scenes, Kennedy poked fun at Southern honor and Southern sportsmanship. Frank Meriwether is an honorable man, but Isaac Tracy merely a likeable fool. Mike Brown is a barbarian pretending to gentlemanliness, the devil a wily gamesman, not a sportsman. The humor is genial, in the manner of neoclassical wit and, more specifically, Washington Irving's *Knickerbocker History of New York,* Kennedy's declared model. Like Irving, Kennedy poked gentle fun at his own region: The honor of the Southern sportsman seems a childish masquerade. Such is not the case with the third scene, however, a fight between Ned Hazard and Miles Rutherford, a lower-class drunkard and bully. Hazard, the aptly named hero, is the book's premier sportsman. In this scene, he properly ignores Rutherford's taunts until the man slurs the good name of old Isaac Tracy, father of his beloved Bel. The matter is a delicate one. A gentleman does not brawl with commoners, particularly drunken ones, but the insult to his prospective father-in-law demands reprisal.

The manner of Ned's response is the crucial thing. Having told the assembled spectators, "I want you to see fair play, and on no account to interfere with me as long as I have it," Ned sets to with his fists. To thrash a ruffian, as Castiglione wrote three centuries earlier, is obviously more honorable than to be beaten, particularly since Rutherford has the advantage in size and strength. But Ned does more than win. As a planter's son he has been trained in "the principles of pugilism," whereas Rutherford is a brawler. Like his kind since Castiglione, he displays the *style* of a gentleman even in this less-than-exemplary contest. "He had the entire command of the game," striking "his blows with a countenance of so much gayety, that a spectator would have imagined he buffeted his adversary in mere sport." In the manner of the idyllic opening of the novel, a playful spirit redeems planter character from any hint of baseness. When he drops Rutherford to the ground, Hazard announces, "I will not strike him whilst he is down." When Rutherford rises, Ned pledges "a fair field, and as much of this game as you have relish for." After Rutherford declines, to the cheers of the spectators, Ned and his friend Littleton return to Swallow Barn, as the well-impressed Yankee puts it, "like knights to a bannered castle from a successful inroad, – flushed with heat and victory, – covered with dust and glory; our enemies subdued and our lady's pledge redeemed" (359–68).

There is nothing patronizing or humorous in this scene. Ned Hazard is the sporting gentleman *par excellence,* Kennedy's portrait an entirely admiring one. Ned jeopardizes his courtship of Bel Tracy by fighting, but only until she understands the honorable motive that led him into that "vulgar ring of clowns" to soil his hands "in a rough-and-tumble struggle with a strolling bully" (370). Sporting virility, that is, offends the feminine temperament (more on that shortly), but even paragons of maidenly virtue recognize the legitimate demands of male honor.

Even in his ambivalence, then, his blending of satire with sentiment, Kennedy left no final doubt about the virtues of Southern life. What is ultimately at stake becomes clear only in the final chapters, when a tour of the slave quarters at Swallow Barn opens into a defense of slavery on the grounds that the system, though morally wrong, is preferable to turning helpless blacks loose to fend for themselves. The planter has an obligation to his slaves; kind treatment has to suffice until the ultimate solution can be found. In these chapters also, Kennedy implicitly linked the honor of Ned Hazard's bout of fisticuffs to the honor of Frank Meriwether's proprietorship, and bathed them both in the sentiment of a pervasive play spirit. Just as black children play with white in mutual affection, Ned Hazard sports with adult slaves on a possum hunt (where the white man's sense of fair play, lacking in the blacks, saves their prey from annihilation, to be chased another day). The code that Ned follows here, and that leads him to grant even a lower-class bully fair play in a potentially brutal fight, is the same code that creates in Frank Meriwether a sense of obligation to his dependent slaves. Unintentionally no doubt, Kennedy implied what later critics of slavery would argue: that the master's sense of honor derived in large part from the dependence, even degradation, of his slaves.[15] Quite intentionally, on the other hand, Kennedy declared the superiority of Southern life to be rooted in its essential playfulness.

In the three decades following the publication of *Swallow Barn,* literary renderings of sport and play became a locus for sectional polemics in a wide range of Southern writing. Frontier humorists, sporting authors like William Elliott and Charles Whitehead, and plantation romancers from Kennedy, William Caruthers, and Nathaniel Beverley Tucker to John Esten Cooke and William Gilmore Simms increasingly wrote out of a self-conscious concern with both the South's social problems and its relationship to the North. In many cases, the two were at odds: The South's own follies, worthy of the satirist's caricature or the critic's censure, were rooted in the very qualities that made Southerners different from Yankees and therefore needful of defense under growing sectional antagonism. In response, these antebellum writers tended to celebrate the playful leisure of Southern life with no misgivings, while the Southern gentleman with his code of honor remained a problematic figure.

Tales of the Southwestern humorists considered in Chapter 1 in a different context appear here as the grotesque renderings of sporting Southern honor among the back country lower classes. The writers for the most part were neither planter aristocrats nor lower-class farmers but professional men whose social standing fell somewhere between. Their collective attitude was neither positive nor negative but the more complex response of men confronting not the follies of outsiders but an outrageously exaggerated version of values they partially shared. The oafish countryman practicing his eye-gouging techniques in Longstreet's "The Fight" and boasting bumpkins challenging each other to no-holds-barred brawls aped the more refined manners of dueling politicians and lawyers. The code of honor rested uneasily on the Southern conscience, but the Southern social order without a code of honor would have been nearly indefensible. If the honor of ruffians was slightly appalling, it remained somehow the same sort of honor on which Southern men "of the better sort" also shaped their lives.

The sporting sketches of writers like William Elliott in *Carolina Sports by Land and Water* (1846) and Charles E. Whitehead in *Wild Sports in the South* (1860) dealt with safer matters: the hunting and fishing that became essential to the cultural ideal of the Southern sportsman. For these writers, field sports were both joyful play and moral exercises. On the eve of the Civil War, Whitehead took a partisan glance northward when he commented on the frequency of hunts in the Southern states, "where time is not regarded with the monetary eye to value with which it is measured in Doctor Franklin's proverbs."[16] Elliott more fulsomely celebrated fox hunting in particular, the traditional sport of the Southern gentry, as the most glorious kind of play. In Elliott's telling, the gambols of the animals and the frolics of their pursuers make the chase the most intoxicating of innocent pleasures. In one sketch he breaks into the wildest exclamation:

> Huntsmen, is it not charming? Does it not made [sic] your pulse quicken? Is there not a thrill of pleasure shooting through your frame?

Can you tell your name? Have you a wife? a child? *Have you a neck?* If
you can, at such a moment, answer such questions, you do not feel
your position, and are but half a sportsman!!![17]

Elliott and Whitehead emphasized *fair* play as well: Natty Bumppo's
hunting code served a distinctive function in the context of Southern
sport. To Elliott, fire hunting was "nearer akin to poaching, than to
legitimate hunting" (149). When the hunting becomes too easy in one
of Whitehead's sketches, the narrator laments, "Dear me! this is like
shooting deer in a park!" (128). In Elliott's words, hunting and fishing
properly done were not only "innocent and manly" but "promotive of
good morals." Whitehead made a complementary case for the superiority
of gentlemen's hunting techniques to those of the backwoodsman. For
both writers, the ruling class knew how to hunt, and hunting trained
the best ruling class.

In his concern over game laws that were eroding the traditional privileges of the landowning class, Elliott asserted the superiority of a hierarchical society at a time when such issues were arousing heated political
debate. Although sport, not the South, was Elliott's and Whitehead's
subject, by implying certain attitudes toward sport as the distinctive
beliefs of Southern gentlemen they obliquely entered the controversy
over competing ways of life that would soon erupt in Civil War. Both
play and fair play were essential to their account of Southern sport because
the two supposedly embodied the principles on which Southern life more
generally was lived.

Frontier humor and sporting sketches occupied the periphery of antebellum Southern writing, plantation romances its center. In addressing
most directly the matter of honorific sport in its larger social context,
these novels collectively reveal the ambivalence but ultimate partisanship
that marked the antebellum period. The form of the novels (domestic
romance with its necessary love story) was in basic ways at odds with
its other subject (masculine sporting behavior). Writers of hunting
sketches in periodicals like the *Spirit of the Times* had a more narrowly
masculine subject and readership. Moreover, writers of plantation romances also dealt with the sporting gentleman in a social world bound
to reflect the tensions of the actual society, but sectional loyalty made
its own demands. These factors contributed to a body of fiction that
wrestled with these issues rather than merely asserted them. Most of the
plantation romances celebrated the play element in Southern culture,
though even in this not without dissent: The hero in Nathaniel Beverley
Tucker's *George Balcombe* (1836) claims himself at one point to be grateful
that economic hardship has prevented him from "drowsing his existence
on the banks of the Potomac, a lazy, luxurious country gentleman."[18]
At the opposite extreme, James Hungerford in *The Old Plantation* (1859)

nostalgically evoked an uncle's plantation in 1832, with its juleps and cobblers, cotillions and frolics, pleasant rambles and local legends, as the earthly paradise fully realized.

But the most characteristic voice in antebellum Southern fiction was to some degree divided in its assessment of the region's distinctive culture. Tucker himself in another novel published the same year as *George Balcombe* countered his criticism in one book with praise in the other for Southern "fair dealing," so unlike the Northern way of "wolf eat wolf, and Yankee cheat Yankee." Equally important to the Southern myth that would grow increasingly glorious through the century, Tucker in *The Partisan Leader* accounted for the love of master and slave by describing the fair play of sporting children on the plantation:

> You have the equal friendship of those with whom you ran races, and played at bandy, and wrestled in your boyhood. If sometimes a dry blow passed between you, they love you none the less for that; because, unless you were differently trained from what is common among our boys you were taught not to claim any privilege, in a fight, over those you treated as equals in play.

Equality in sport somehow implied that slavery itself was rooted in fair play.[19]

William Caruthers and John Esten Cooke also contributed important elements to the Southern version of the sporting myth. In *The Cavaliers of Virginia* (1834–5), Caruthers turned away from the more problematic Southern present to write of its heroic past, specifically of Nathaniel Bacon's rebellion in the seventeenth century that becomes a foundation myth for an embattled region in the nineteenth. Caruthers identified the earliest cavaliers as "the first founders of the aristocracy which prevails in Virginia to this day": "that generous, fox-hunting, wine-drinking, duelling, and reckless race of men, which gives so distinct a character to Virginians wherever they may be found."[20] In *The Virginia Comedians* (1854), Cooke endorsed the same foundation myth but gave it a complicated resonance in the contemporary world. He also gave the plantation mansion its classic description as a shrine to sport: Effingham Hall is furnished with deer antlers, fishing rods, guns, and pictures of celebrated race horses – emblems of the major activities of its tenants. But Cooke was no simple sentimentalist. The most ambivalent of all these antebellum romances, *The Virginia Comedians* celebrates Southern leisure and satirizes its excesses, offers sporting heroes and sporting fanatics, and centers its convoluted narrative on a figure who represents both the best and the worst of the sporting gentry. Reckless, hot-blooded, arrogant, and foppish, Champ Effingham is the South's wayward but beloved son, his sins too potent to be simply damned or forgiven.

Champ's lascivious designs on a young actress and his fatalistic gambler's approach to life are finally chastened by a soldier of the yeoman class whose sense of fair play and easy tolerance tempers his own gambling instincts. Through Captain Ralph's mentorship, young Effingham recovers from his dangerous obsessions to marry the angelic playmate of his youth.[21]

However tidy its ending, *The Virginia Comedians* never resolves the conflicts it raises. Champ's marriage at the end cannot erase the earlier portrayal of Southern females as the prey of cruelly sportive males; his relationship to an exemplary sportsman of the yeoman class does not convince the reader that republican values actually flourish in the quasifeudal South; black slaves remain the unacknowledged obstacle to any claim for a Southern political and social ideal. But the persistence of these contradictions seems due less to defective literary skill than to Cooke's willingness to engage Southern life and culture in a serious way. If he could not resolve these issues, he nonetheless raised them. The domestic romance was simply an inadequate vehicle for such an inquiry. Although its conventions demanded a sentimental worldview, its subject of Southern honor, with roots in masculine sport, resisted the power of the sentimental. The resulting tension is typical of antebellum plantation fiction as a whole, its central sporting myth not yet fully realized.

Caroline Gilman and the woman's south

The tension between sentimental convention and masculine subject in plantation romances reflects the comparable tension between sentimental culture and masculine honor in the antebellum South itself – a problem about which Southern women writers inevitably had much to say. Southern honor, as scholars have shown, depended almost as much on female submissiveness as on Negro slavery.[22] Patriarchy reigned more fully in the antebellum South than in the North; the Grimké sisters notwithstanding, no fledgling women's movement emerged in Dixie before the war. Fathers, not mothers, held the preeminent right to name offspring, and Southern fathers played a more assertive role in their daughters' courtships and marriages than did their Northern counterparts. Women had little legal protection and less education or occupational freedom. Men enjoyed a sexual double standard and a license within marriage (for drinking, gambling, and the freedom to come and go, as well as for sexual relations with slaves) that was utterly denied women. As Bertram Wyatt-Brown has written, male honor "required that women be burdened with a multitude of negatives, a not very subtle way to preserve male initiative in the never-ending battle of the sexes." Women could not express their passions; their role as ornaments was nearly as important as their managerial ability in the household. Strong women in the antebellum South held their power "by virtue of willfulness, not prescriptive right."[23]

As part of this fundamental inequality Southern women were cut off from the sporting traditions central to the Southern male myth. The virility of the Southern male required dependent females, but the chief customs of his manly display – hospitality, sport, and dueling – too easily flourished at the expense of domestic stability. Women, together with ministers, were the chief opponents of gambling and dueling. A typical antebellum tract "by a Lady of Mississippi" denounced "the fallacious principles of the modern code of honour" and claimed that women must assert themselves to produce a "revulsion in public feeling" against the practice of dueling.[24] Aside from whatever moral objections they aroused, gambling, the keeping of horses and hounds, and the demands of extravagant hospitality were costly. Hunting kept men away from home for long peiods, while duels obviously risked their permanent removal. Kennedy implicitly, perhaps unwittingly, acknowledged a potential gender conflict in *Swallow Barn* when he defined the Southern planter entirely in terms of his leisure activities, the plantation mistress entirely in terms of her labors. In Southern fiction by women the conflict is more than implicit or potential. The crisis in Eliza A. Dupuy's *The Planter's Daughter* (1858), for example, is brought about first by a father's "style of princely hospitality, such as has ruined nearly all the old families in his native state," then by the "spirit of the gambler" that leads him into ruinous speculations.[25] Most pervasively if only indirectly, the sporting habits required of the Southern gentleman were potentially objectionable to women as concrete expressions of that more comprehensive system of patriarchy and honor that required submissiveness, self-sacrifice, and narrowly circumscribed actions and feelings.

Not surprisingly, then, plantation romances written by women bear an interesting relationship to those by men. The divided attitudes of Kennedy and company suggest the ambivalence of males from within the world of masculine honor. Women wrote from without that world, yet from within the larger Southern world from which both genders faced those outside their region. An antebellum female writer, particularly in the 1850s when sectional antagonism grew more extreme, faced a similar dilemma to the one that confronted feminists in the 1960s, who resolved it by subordinating gender concerns to the cause of racial solidarity or anti-war protest. In celebrating Southern life, as the Southern woman invariably wished to do, the most potent available image glorified the very Southern masculinity that threatened her in many ways. As a consequence, women writers in this period consistently embraced the emerging Southern myth but subverted it in two fundamental ways:

One, they separated the spirit of play crucial to Southern identity from
the sporting traditions through which many male writers celebrated it;
and two, they domesticated the cavalier sportsman to create a more
feminized ideal.

Against Kennedy's *Swallow Barn*, Caroline Howard Gilman's *Recollections of a Southern Matron* (1837) can stand at the beginning of a tradition
of plantation romances by women. Through her narrator Cornelia, a
young girl who grows to womanhood on the plantation, Gilman expressed more piety and paid more attention to domestic scenes on the
plantation than did the male authors. She described housekeeping, gardening, music, the deficiencies of schools, a matron dealing with a peddlar. But she also more revealingly dealt with conventional masculine
activities from an outsider's perspective. Racing, hunting, and dueling
lie on the periphery, not at the center, of the narrative. Gilman described
horse racing but to emphasize the splendor of the horses not the skill of
the riders, even apologizing to readers "who doubt the morality of a
horse-race." Nothing about honor, competition, betting.

In Gilman's account the men hunt, while the women persuade them
not to kill the beautiful birds. When father goes hunting, Cornelia says
nothing of his valor or marksmanship but describes at length his outrage
over a favorite old hunting jacket having been traded to a peddlar. When
Cornelia herself accompanies the men on a hunt, she thrills to the "sympathy of the hounds, their diligence and docility," but not to the killing.
A duel receives the most impassioned feminine criticism. When her
brother is insulted, Cornelia reacts instinctively to the prevailing male
ethos by telling him, "I can bear anything better than your disgrace,
brother." But afterwards, she rues her "preconceived views of physical
courage" that "overbalanced the claim of high moral duty." Through
Cornelia, Gilman interjected her authorial voice to clarify the responsible
woman's position:

> It is not my object here to argue for or against duelling; that is the
> province of abler minds; but I may venture to show how *female* influence
> may "ride on the whirlwind and direct the storm" of masculine feeling
> for good or for evil; how the genius of Christianity, or even worldly
> philosophy, quietly exhibited in woman's gentle tones, may come with
> their enlightening power, not for the avoidance of mere physical pain,
> but with a serious regard to man's true dignity and ultimate destiny.

The duel is not shown, only the sister and mother rushing too late to
prevent it, arriving just in time to bear their wounded loved one away.
Randolph, his antagonist, exclaims, "Would to God that society required
not this sacrifice!" The young man nearly dies, but recovers under feminine care.[26]

Gilman's South was Kennedy's South but with a marked difference. Seen from the perspective of those who wait at home, sport, dueling, and the lesser requirements of the code of honor take on a different cast. While female objections to duels make obvious sense, Gilman's extended treatment of a deer hunt offers a more telling commentary on Southern women's possible alienation from their husbands', sons', and brothers' social customs. Cornelia's account begins as if it will describe a female rite of passage through immersion in the masculine mysteries of the hunt. "Often in childhood," she begins, "when I had heard the stir and preparation for the chase, I had longed to take a part. . . . As I advanced in years, and felt perfect confidence in my own skill in horsemanship, I frequently urged papa to allow me to accompany him; but he objected on the score of the dangerous character of our woods for one in female attire on horseback" (241). One hears here the voice of young Ike McCaslin a century later, watching the men depart for their annual hunt, awaiting the day when he will be old enough to join them. Cornelia's handicap is not her age, however, but neither is it simply her sex. Female attire, not femininity, keeps her from the hunt. When she finally wins her father's consent, the reader expects to discover that petticoats and a long skirt have nothing to do with spirit and ability; that Cornelia will prove herself as fitting a companion to father, brothers, and male friends, in the woods as in the parlor.

Something very different happens. When one of her brothers shoots a buck but fails to bring it down, Cornelia rallies to the wounded deer, not to the disappointed hunter. "My sympathies were stirred for the noble animal," she reports, "and, as I saw him bound on, I uttered a shout of joy" (244). As the scene continues, a different "hunt" temporarily takes over the foreground. When Cornelia's horse bolts at an accidental flick of the whip, "the sport was forgotten" as her beau races after to bring her animal under control, then blushingly gazes into her eyes, trembling to ask the question of questions. Only the buck's reappearance prevents a proposal. Rejoining the hunters, Cornelia now pleads for the deer, "Oh, let him go, pray, let him go . . . he has won his life. I cannot bear to have him killed." The men reluctantly lowering their guns, Cornelia and a female companion "waved our handkerchiefs in triumph, and shouted our congratulations as the noble animal sprang, apparently unhurt, from the water, and was lost in the thickets on the opposite bank" (247–8). Even now the episode is not quite over. On the hunters' return, Mamma runs from the house "in an agony of trepidation," because their hounds have trampled through her carnations, one of them making a bed in the wallflowers. Sportsmen join with matron to shoo the pesky dogs away.

This entire scene is rich in the unstated implications of the plantation romance written by women. The Southern lady of popular legend was as known for her feminine beauty, tender sensibilities, and domestic artistry as the gentleman for his sporting valor. But Gilman created more than a portrait of what women did while their men were away. Male and female clash in little ways: over the honoring of a favorite hunting jacket, over the killing or sparing of a hunter's prize, over the prior right of mistress or master's hounds to the garden plot. Gilman wrote an idyl, however blemished by the near fatality of a duel and the deaths of Cornelia's mother and two children after she becomes a Southern matron. But that idyl exists separately from, and partly at odds with, the entire tradition of masculine honor that engaged Kennedy, Cooke, and other male writers. Gilman's romance of Southern womanhood is rooted in play, but not in the aggressive competitive sports of Southern honor.

Gilman's *Recollections* can be seen as the first in a series of plantation romances by women, parallel to those by men – not separate literary lines but gender-marked versions within a single genre. And in those novels by women, the pattern of antagonism to the forms of masculine sporting honor consistently appear, offering less a woman's view of the same world than a partial revision of the male myth. Male and female versions are not simply pro- or con-; male writers, after all, responded to "masculine" sporting practices with their own ambivalence. Rather, the women writers tended most often to share the male celebration of play, even to exaggerate it, but more consistently than the men they balked at endorsing the code of honor, going further in rejecting its violent forms.

Both strategies are apparent in such novels as Caroline Lee Hentz's *Marcus Warland* (1852) and *The Planter's Northern Bride* (1854), Marion Harland's *Alone* (1854), and Eliza Ann Dupuy's *The Planter's Daughter*. All of these novels include detailed scenes of Southern play: Christmas revels, whites dancing to black music and blacks to white, frolics and amusements and parlor games (at which "nothing was staked," as Dupuy assured readers). In this the women shared a vision with the men who wrote plantation romances: The play element in Southern culture was its most distinctive feature and the one that most pointedly made the South superior to the North.

In addressing the traditional masculine forms of play and display, however, the women disagreed significantly with male writers. Harland and Dupuy opposed them more directly than Hentz did. Besides the ruinous hospitality that Dupuy criticized, she returned repeatedly to the speculations and criminal "games" that the villain, Mr. Malcolm, plays at the susceptible planter's expense. Malcolm is "a gambler on a magnificent scale" who plays "subtle game[s]," with "human hopes and fears" as the "counters." Mr. Harrington, the planter of the title, is duped and swindled in business, while his son Victor falls to the temptation of the simpler gambling with cards, bringing disgrace on himself and ultimately his own death.[27] Harland took on horse racing and dueling in the same spirit. On one occasion, a character in *Alone* notes that "men squander thousands for the intellectual gratification of a horse-race; an exhibition in which, I allow, the brute is generally the nobler animal."[28]

Hentz's treatment, particularly in *Marcus Warland,* was subtler, more in the manner of Gilman's account of the deer hunt. As one of many "anti-Tom" novels written as rejoinders to *Uncle Tom's Cabin, The Planter's Northern Bride* focuses primarily on the relations of master and slave, eulogizing the Southern system in part for its foundation in play but paying little attention to the myth of the sporting gentleman except to claim he was *not* indolent and self-indulgent, contrary to Northern assumptions. (*Uncle Tom's Cabin* itself, the *bête noir* of all Southern partisans in the 1850s, actually expressed the same antagonism to masculine sporting practices that aroused Southern women. Augustine St. Clare, Stowe's humane slave master, dies the accidental victim of a rencontre between two intoxicated Southern gentlemen; and another planter sells his quadroon mistress, Cassy, whom he claims to love, in order to pay a gambling debt. In these two cases the gendered views of sporting honor from North and South were identical, however different the writers' sectional loyalties.)

In *Marcus Warland,* Hentz thoroughly undermined the oppressive virility of the Southern sportsman. The hero as a boy is "quite a Nimrod in the woods," until one day, having killed a deer, "he felt that he was a cruel murderer, and would have given the best blood of his own heart to have restored life to the stiffening limbs of the bleeding animal."[29] Shortly afterward, Marcus springs to his rifle to drive off a brutal slave driver – the *proper* use of a sportsman's gun, the novel implies. Several years later, now adopted by a kindly planter and his kindlier wife, and restored to the station his own drunken father had forfeited, Marcus bursts into the house one day calling to his foster mother and sister: "Victory, dear Mrs. Bellamy! Victory, Katy! I've won the prize, the golden badge of merit, and I come to lay it at the feet of my benefactors" (62). Readers familiar with the plantation romance would expect the young man to flourish a fox's tail or some other sporting trophy. Instead, bending one knee with cavalier grace, Marcus lays a blue ribbon on Mrs. Bellamy's lap: a prize for the best essay in his high school. "I only cared to obtain this because I thought it would gratify you," Marcus adds, as if the contrast to masculine competitiveness were not already sufficiently striking. This scene is echoed later in the novel when Marcus wins first honors at his college graduation.

All of these scenes depend for their full effect on the reader's familiarity with the masculine myth. By the 1850s, Kennedy, Caruthers, Cooke, and others had clarified actual sporting behavior into a cluster of images and rhetorical figures that had become identified with a unique and superior Southern character. Hentz, Harland, and Dupuy ignored this Southern male myth or more directly undermined its more offensive assumptions. To call the women who wrote these novels "feminists" would distort the reality. Nor can they be considered realists working against a romantic tradition. But to claim they simply wrote fantasies more congenial to the feminine imagination would not adequately account for their pointed handling of the well-established stereotype of the sporting Southern gentleman. The *fact* that Southern men engaged in sports virtually required some allusion, but not the subtle undercutting of the myth that accompanied the fact. If not quite feminists, these female authors were self-consciously women writing out of the experience of living in a patriarchal society. Yet they were Southern loyalists, too, and members of the privileged classes who found security within the system that circumscribed their lives. Their version of the Southern myth did not assault it directly, but sought to redefine its most troubling features.

Simms and the Southern foundation myth

The fullest development of the antebellum sporting myth appears in the fiction of William Gilmore Simms, where the ambivalence I traced earlier is not diminished but is more successfully resolved within its embodying literary form. In *The Virginia Comedians,* when Cooke created Captain Ralph to serve as Champ Effingham's mentor in fair play, he adopted a strategy that had become common by the 1850s. Kennedy in *Horse-Shoe Robinson* (1835) and Caruthers in *The Knights of the Golden Horseshoe* (1845) also made backwoods hunters, not tidewater gentlemen, the chief spokesmen for the sporting code.[30] But it was chiefly Simms, the most popular and influential of all these novelists, who fashioned these characters and their relationships into a fully developed Southern foundation myth. What Simms did in effect was to wed Southern character to one of the most potent myths in the larger culture: Cooper's frontier myth embodied in the Leatherstocking tales. Simms repressed the problems raised by gender and race but confronted most ingeniously the issue of class. His noble frontiersmen join with the sons of the planter elite to create a social order rooted in class but also merit: a hierarchy that recognizes natural as well as hereditary aristocracy. Duty and ability, leadership without arrogance, a sense of *noblesse oblige,* and a willingness to recognize the virtues of exceptional members of the lower classes – all were essential to Simms's sense of the ideal ruling class. And underlying his ideal of personal conduct, differentiating those who contributed positively to the new society from those who threatened it, was the most elaborately worked out sporting code in antebellum Southern fiction.

Simms developed this foundation myth primarily in his seven romances of the Revolutionary War.[31] Beginning with *The Partisan* in 1835 and concluding with *Eutaw* in 1856, Simms portrayed the role of South Carolina's rebel patriots in the final years of the Revolution through a series of volumes in which fictional characters played out emblematic roles within the context of historical events. The cast of essential characters remained fairly consistent.[32] From the upper class: a young planter-hero, whose elder kinsman (father or uncle) must be won over to the partisan side; a Briton or Tory (usually an unscrupulous climber from the lower class) who is both politically and personally antagonistic to the hero; and the patriotic daughter of a Tory father, who loves the hero and is desired by the villain. At the other pole, besides the black slaves, lies a class of outlaws and misfits aligned with the loyalist cause while the British are ascendant but more truly committed to their own greed and vices. And between these extremes lie the frontiersmen, merchants, innkeepers, farmers – the varied middle class, either partisan or loyalist, that provides most of Simms's more original characters. In portraying the partnership of the best of this class with the best of the planters, the novels fall easily into two groups: an early trio: *The Partisan* (1835), *Mellichampe* (1836), and *The Scout* (originally *The Kinsmen* [1841]); followed by a late quartet: *Katharine Walton* (1851), *Woodcraft* (1852), *The Forayers* (1855), and *Eutaw* (1856). Although certain concerns tie all seven together, a significant shift in the relationship between the scout and his aristocratic leader in the late novels reveals the impact of sectional antagonism on the evolution of the Southern sporting myth.

In the early triad, the chief spokesmen for fair play are a series of frontiersmen and commoners who sometimes serve as mentors to reckless young planter heroes. Thumbscrew Wetherspoon and John Davis in *The Partisan*, Thumbscrew again (Witherspoon now, due to careless editing) and Bill Humphries in *Mellichampe*, and "Supple Jack" Bannister in *The Scout* are avatars of Cooper's Leatherstocking; not at odds with oncoming civilization, however, but the guarantors of its moral grounding. Although Robert Singleton of *The Partisan* is an exemplary planter hero who requires no tutoring, in the next two novels it is the scout who teaches his headstrong young leader the lessons of fair play necessary for a true ruling class.[33] In all three of these early novels, the scout also most conspicuously exemplifies the sporting code in a series of striking set pieces. In *The Partisan*, a simple soldier, John Davis, proposes a fair-play contest to a wholly dishonorable British Sergeant who has fallen into his hands. "I'm for fair play," Davis tells him as he proposes to release him for "a fair fight with broadswords" – a weapon with which the Sergeant in fact will have a decided advantage. "You shall have as fair play as ever you had in all your born days before."[34] This scene is replayed in *Mellichampe,* when Bill Humphries, an innkeeper's son, offers "fair play" and a chance for freedom to a captured Tory spy; and in *The Scout,* when Jack Bannister declares similar terms to settle matters with a traitor. "A good gripe about the ribs" with "the blessing of Providence upon the argyment," as Supple Jack puts it, will determine not just the better man but the better side in the war (144–54).

In these successive incarnations the backwoodsmen grew increasingly heroic, increasingly identified with the ideal values that triumphed with the partisan side in the Revolutionary War. Their sporting code elevates them within the existing social hierarchy to a place just below that of the planter class, though never equal to or above it. Political and social authority belongs to the planters, not the scouts, but the frontiersmen's morality becomes incorporated into the emerging social order. Whereas Cooper's hero remains at odds with triumphant civilization, in Simms's South no such problem exists. By linking the Leatherstocking figure to the aristocracy in this way, Simms suggested that the South, however much it seemed rooted in class privilege, embraced in truth a democratic meritocracy. His aristocrats earn their standing rather than assume it, with the Leatherstocking-like frontiersmen sometimes showing them the way.

All seven novels embrace the same sporting code in most respects, tied to a central myth that persists largely unchanged. Sporting characteristics distributed among the various classes reveal a moral hierarchy transcending any social one. The partisan bands exemplify Simms's model for class relations, their leaders maintaining both easy comradeship with and proper distance from their various subordinates. Most pointedly, a series of scenes of sportive play in the partisan camps – seemingly drawn directly from Irving's Western writing – roots these relations in the same values that infuse the plantation romances. In *The Partisan,* the "lively chat, the hearty glee, the uncouth but pleasant jest" of Francis Marion's men at their ease recall the carefree hospitality of Swallow Barn and its like (II, 163–4). Much more extensively, first in *Mellichampe* then in *Katharine Walton* and *The Forayers,* nearly identical scenes of sports and card-playing in Marion's camps elaborate on this image. In *Mellichampe,* "the men playfully gambolled about among the forest avenues"; in *Katharine Walton,* their "famous frolicking" allows Marion's soldiers to unloosen "their livelier impulses and recompense themselves for the restraints of the past in a cheerful hilarity and play"; and in *The Forayers,* Marion's men are the "chief sinners" at cards and dice during a brief respite from war – "sinners" only ironically of course, in a scene in which such "sinning" is in fact the most innocent play.[35]

The counterforce to these playful partisans is represented by the bands of outlaws and scoundrels who revel in very different "sports." Simms divided into two sets the various sporting practices that aroused ambivalence among his fellow antebellum writers, assigning the admirable ones to his noble characters, all unsavory ones to their enemies. Whereas Marion's men *play* at cards and dice, the rogues and scoundrels in the novels gamble viciously and unfairly, and the language that describes them is drawn from blood-and-thunder literary conventions rather than from wilderness romance. On the one hand, that is, "fight-or-frolic" sportiveness characterizes Jack Bannister's match with his traitor captive. As Jack prepares to fight, he changes his "intense earnestness of air and tone" for a manner "even playful and sportive . . . with all the buoyancy of a boy traversing the playground with 'leap-frog' and 'hop o' my thumb" (149). "Mad Archy" Campbell of *Katharine Walton,* on the other hand, reveals a reckless excess of this spirit, in his headlong rush to live beyond the bounds of respectability by bet and duel. Villains are the chief players of "games," that ubiquitous term throughout the seven novels for a variety of plots and strategems. Although heroes can resort to gamesmanship when necessary (Major Singleton can even offer advice in *Katharine Walton* on "How to Play with Knaves" on their own terms, as a chapter title puts it), their more characteristic mode is sportsmanship. In *The Partisan,* Singleton tells a young aide, "War is not a sport, but a duty, and we should not love it" (II, 147). But this and all the subsequent stories demonstrate that to fight in a sporting manner, *à la* Natty Bumppo, does in fact redeem battle from mere murderousness.

The essential sporting code remains consistent throughout the Revolutionary romances, then, but a crucial shift occurs in the last four novels in the 1850s, when the scout disappears as spokesman for fair play and mentor to the headstrong planter, who himself steps forward to become the chief exemplar of the code. Through the seven tales Simms developed a consistent foundation myth for the South, combining class and democratic meritocracy into an ideal social order rooted in a sporting code. But in the 1850s, believing sectional war inevitable and imminent, Simms subtly shifted the balance toward the planters. Although his sense of the ideal relations among the classes never changed, in the 1850s he attributed the source of Southern values more exclusively to the aristocracy. The frontier myth out of which his scouts emerged was a national legacy, the sporting planter a sectional one. Southern virtues, Simms implied more strongly in the 1850s, were distinctively, even uniquely, Southern.

No scout figures prominently at all in *Katharine Walton* or *Woodcraft.* Then in *The Forayers* and *Eutaw,* two halves of the single narrative with which the Revolutionary romances conclude, Jim Ballou appears in the role of Thumbscrew Witherspoon and Jack Bannister before him. This time, however, the planter hero, Willie Sinclair, chastens and teaches the scout, rather than the other way around – not in the requirements of fair play but in the necessity of temperance. And Sinclair, not Jim Ballou, becomes Simms's representative Southern patriot, the foil to the villain Robert Inglehardt, a low-born American Tory risen in the British army by cunning and avarice. In a two-page digression beginning a chapter in *The Forayers,* the narrator describes the two "players at this game of war in our humble legend," Sinclair and Inglehardt, as types for contrasting codes of conduct. While Inglehardt "is, to the last, a creature full of strategem," Sinclair "prefers the open to the sly game – the manly to the merely cunning." Sportsmanship has explicitly become the code of the planter hero, gamesmanship the recourse of the lower-class upstart. Sinclair risks more in the game than Inglehardt: Whereas the turncoat is driven by personal gain, Sinclair "stakes, on the issue, other purposes than those which simply affect himself" (382–3). Those "other purposes," of course, are the outcome of the war and the fate of a new nation striving to be born. But in 1855, at stake for Simms also was the moral basis of Southern society. In the face of a new political and ideological enemy, soon to be an actual one on battlefields, South Carolinians' preference for the "open" and "manly" game in the Revolutionary War implied much more than it stated. A long scene in *Eutaw* reinforces the reader's sense of Inglehardt's villainy: an exchange between the Tory and a prisoner in which Inglehardt speaks at length in the language of gambling, declaring life a game in which individual lives are staked for no higher purpose than to test the whims of Fortune.[36] Willie Sinclair, in stark contrast, plays for the future of his region and country.

Simms's novels are the richest in all antebellum fiction for both the quantity and range of their sporting rhetoric. His preeminence among Southern writers also gave his version of the sporting myth particular power, but once again I return to ambivalence as the prevailing attitude before the Civil War. And unlike the women writers who were a minor voice in Western mythmaking, Southern women had an important role in shaping their region's sporting myth in ways that downplayed the violence and anarchy that remained less repressed in the developing Western myth until much later. It was a thoroughly domesticated cavalier who reigned over the legend of the Old South in the late nineteenth century, in fiction by both women and men. But arousing ambivalence or not, the sporting myth even before the War had become a potent cultural narrative.

This fact is evident in the more overt sectional debate waged in the years immediately preceding the Civil War. Daniel Hundley, for example, in his *Social Relations in Our Southern States* (1860), included a chapter on "The Southern Gentleman" that rooted his subject's character in his enjoyment of "rollicking out-door sports and amusements," wholly different from the grimmer pleasures of dollar-chasing Yankees. The glories of the fox hunt, Hundley claimed in an extravagant celebration indistinguishable from William Elliott's, are "so imperfectly understood in the Free States, wherein every species of pastime which hinders the making of money is regarded as sinful."[37] In setting the South above the North through his own region's play spirit, Hundley echoed the sentiments of Henry Wise, Edmund Ruffin, and the many contributors to *DeBow's Review* who were primarily concerned about the South's economic dependence on the North, but who frequently strove in their essays to strike a balance between the need for industrial progress and the retention of leisure habits.[38] Even William Fitzhugh, the most hardheaded of Southern apologists, attributed to free societies a debasing and unscrupulous "war of competition" that made each man the enemy of every other.[39] Fitzhugh made a case for Southern leisure by implicit contrast.

Southern polemicists in the end shared the novelists' ambivalence. The South needed industrial progress as well as traditional leisure habits; the Southern sportsman both promoted and undermined his society's needs. All of these writers confronted an emerging Southern myth in the context of their own awareness of the actual South. But the destruction of the Old South in the Civil War removed all obstacles to wholehearted mythologizing. The disappearance of the antebellum plantation and its sporting master assured their apotheosis in the last decades of the nineteenth century as a fantasized counterforce to the prevailing values of industrial America. Ambivalence died at Appomattox, not to rise again until the Southern Renaissance in the twentieth century.

Sport, the Old South, and the lost cause

Although it is a truism by now that the antebellum South was romanticized more extravagantly after the Civil War than before, we must note the qualitative as well as quantitative change in the Southern sporting myth during this period. Dueling and gambling nearly disappeared altogether from the heroic model of the sporting gentleman, while field sports, particularly fox hunting, emerged more prominently as an arena for exalting Southern character. Links to medieval chivalry, often through detailed accounts of ring tournaments, became more explicit, and the spirit of play received greater emphasis as a quality that distinguished life in the Old South from the grinding regimen in the materialistic, work-centered North. Most generally, in all of this postwar celebration of Southern play and sport, the image of the Old South was largely purged of its earlier, sometimes problematic, virility in favor of a more sentimental, domesticated ideal.

After the war the impulse behind the fiction changed. Writers still wished to justify the South, of course, but defending a world that no longer existed had to be less important to these writers than criticizing the unwelcome world that had triumphed: the competitive capitalist North and the New South that emulated it. The writers of Southern romances after the war were not businessmen and politicians but men and women of letters, loyal to their region certainly but alienated from the prevailing commercial values as well. And the problem of unassimilated free blacks was part of this new order. Images of playful equality between the races before emancipation, and the larger context of sport and play in the planter's life, became conventional expressions of sentimental genteel culture. That culture itself coexisted uneasily with the political and economic values of the age.

The Civil War had somewhat different consequences for women's writing in the South than for men's. The war and its aftermath affected the lives of women specifically as profoundly as they did the South more generally. On the one hand, the death of a quarter-million men necessarily placed more responsibility on women, together with both the freedom and the power entailed. The census of 1870 revealed 25,000 fewer men than women in North Carolina, 36,000 fewer in Georgia, 15,000 in Virginia, 8,000 in South Carolina. Southern women gained greater occupational freedom as well as educational opportunities; they took active roles for the first time in missionary work and temperance societies.[40] To the male descendants of the planter class, the Old South represented an ideal place now horribly changed. To women, the loss was compensated by definite gains.

Women generally joined their male counterparts in glorifying the *ancien regime,* then, but they also seem to have been freed to explore more varied possibilities than were available to them before the war. The antebellum plantation romance by women consistently portrayed a domestic ideal; in the postwar period this version held the middle ground within a wider range of treatments of the sporting myth. No woman writing before the war was as contemptuous of the sporting gentleman as Augusta Jane Evans in *St. Elmo* (1866); no woman writing before the war so celebrated this figure as did Mary Johnston in *The Long Roll* (1911). As the sporting planter became an historical anachronism, he was both praised and damned more extravagantly as a cultural symbol than when the symbol bore a closer relation to fact; and in both their praising and their damning, women writers announced at least a partial freedom from gender and political constraints that had been more oppressive in the antebellum period.

In the middle ground, occupied by both male and female writers, play was supreme but sporting honor was carefully circumscribed. The domestication of the Southern myth through genteel sentimentalism is no more apparent than in the work of the most respected and popular of the late-nineteenth-century male writers Thomas Nelson Page. I offer as an index to the postbellum perspective the essays Page collected in *The Old South* in 1892. As was so often done by Southern writers after the war, Page announced his intention at the outset to dispel certain misapprehensions concerning the lost civilization, to present instead a "true history" of the region.[41] The real agenda behind his history, however, emerges quite clearly in the essays.

Early in "Glimpses of Life in Colonial Virginia," Page quotes a sharply critical English traveler observing the Virginia gentry: "They are all excessively attached to every species of sport, gaming, and dissipation, particularly horse-racing, and that most barbarous of all diversions, that peculiar species of cruelty, cock-fighting" (135). Page makes no comment at all here – neither assent nor defense – but, five pages later, when he returns to the topic, his own words are very different: "The planters lived in a style patterned on that of the landed gentry in England... engaging in horse-racing and other *gentle* diversions" (139–40; my emphasis). Page acknowledged the horse-racing but not the betting that accompanied it. He made no mention of cock-fighting or anything "barbarous" at all. By a few rhetorical omissions he transformed criticism to celebration. In summarizing the habits of the colonial gentry later in the essay, Page restored some of the virility that "gentle diversions" would deny, when he described

> their sons going to William and Mary or across to Oxford or Cambridge, and growing up like their sires, gay, pleasure-loving, winning or losing garters on wagers, jealous of privilege, proud, assertive of their rights, ready to fight and stake all on a point of principle, and forming that society which was the virile soil from which sprang this nation. (154)

The young men gambled after all, but for nothing more costly than garters. "Gay, pleasure-loving men" were not ones to resort to the "dissipation" that the eighteenth-century Englishman noted. They fought, but only for honor. In short, Page defined a masculine ideal wholly inoffensive to a sentimental culture.

A second essay, "Social Life in Old Virginia Before the War," portrays the descendants of these colonial planters in a manner that confirms this image. In interpreting the South to the North at a time when rampant Yankee materialism was fair target for any critic, Page found in Southern sport a potent device. Images of play abound in this essay. White and black children of the Old South are said to have played together in idyllic harmony, "forming the associations which tempered slavery and made the relation one of friendship" (178). Harvest time on the plantation meant not work but a "festival": "The severest toil of the year was a frolic. Every 'hand' was eager for it. It was the test of the men's prowess and the women's skill" (180). Plantation life was more work than ease, Page claimed and as prevailing attitudes still demanded, but the planter transformed work into play, consistent with a growing tendency among progressive-minded Americans to challenge the primacy of work. The master of the plantation was a grave patriarch presiding over the play of less responsible dependents, but at appropriate times he too could be "jovial, even gay." His sons were "given to self-indulgence," "wasteful of time and energy beyond belief," "addicted to the pursuit of pleasure" – the customary failings of an aristocratic character. But they also shared the "corresponding virtues": the generosity and high-spirit that made these same "languid, philandering young gentlemen of Virginia . . . the most dashing and indomitable soldiery of modern times" (191–3). Their prewar "life was gay": It included Christmas revels and tournaments, "*scientific* horse-racing" (my emphasis), and preeminently fox hunting among their sports. Hunts were not displays of masculine prowess but "great frolics." The young men pursued the fox for the honor of claiming the tail as an offering to a favored beauty; even small boys had sweethearts for whom they rode (203–4).

The chief fault of the South, Page readily admitted, lay in its commitment to pleasure, but in his telling this apparent hedonism becomes a virtue disguised as a vice. The Old South was guilty only of having "fallen short in material development in its narrow sense" (221). Surely this was praise by faint damning in America of the 1890s. And in compensation, the South "abounded in spiritual development" – a trade-off Page's readers would have surely applauded. The adjectives with which Page expressed the general quality of Southern life, "gay" and "charming," evoke play without criticism. Although the men and women of the Old South were indeed "a careless and pleasure-loving people," as their critics claimed, "their festivities were free from dissipation" (200).

The rhetorical strategy of his portrait of the antebellum South clearly reveals a complex intention dictated by the times. Opening with a romantic portrait of an edenic land of play (to counteract the prevailing materialism and exploitation of the age), the essay turns to an assertion of the hard work and gravity of plantation life for the masters (to counteract any implication of frivolity in the earlier section), then reasserts the Old South's essential play spirit (not as the lesser of two evils but as the greater of two goods). The result is a reactionary vision of the past that is simultaneously an implicit critique of the present, but that also abets the status quo by failing to address contemporary social and economic problems directly.

In these essays Page characterized his region for an entire nation and era in a manner seemingly lifted directly from Kennedy's *Swallow Barn*. And a chorus of voices joined his. In his final book, *Virginia: A History of the People* (1883), John Esten Cooke turned from fiction to the history of the Old Dominion, drawing on the most reliable sources available for a factual account. But in a few interpretive passages interspersed throughout his narrative, Cooke also more subjectively characterized the quality of life in colonial Virginia as imbued with a "spirit of mirth" that led to ubiquitous balls and dances, horse races and cock fights, footraces and wrestling contests.[42] In "The Old Virginia Gentleman," a popular platform lecture first delivered in 1877 and frequently reprinted, George W. Bagby evoked the myriad sports and carefree diversions that animated plantation life. In *Plantation Life Before Emancipation* (1892), the Reverend R. Q. Mallard not only devoted a chapter to the pastimes of children as the source of proper and friendly race relations, he also tapped the growing emphasis on athletic sports as essential to robust manhood in order to proclaim the South's superiority in this regard as well (as Daniel Hundley had done three decades earlier). Walter Hines Page, one of the chief spokesmen for the New South and a major publisher of the era, worried in the *Atlantic* in 1902 how to retain the old regime's traditional "qualities of fellowship and leisure" in the face of "the march of industrialism." The scholar Philip Alexander Bruce judged the social life of seventeenth-century Virginia worthy of an entire volume in his series on the institutions of the Old Dominion, emphasizing Southerners' hearty enjoyment of their diversions, freed from "the gloomy influence of the austere fanaticism of the Puritans."[43] Although none of these writers pointed out that the celebrated qualities of Southern life were widely assumed to be lacking in the commercial North, contemporary readers would have had no difficulty making the connection. Nor did the writers have to manufacture their facts; what was crucial was simply what they chose to emphasize (or ignore) and the manner in which they portrayed it. And with each retelling, the portrait of the sporting gentleman of the Old South became more firmly embedded in the popular consciousness.

History and fiction are indistinguishable in creating this portrait. Although there were variations, even pointed disagreements among the novelists, the basic narrative was more consistent for the half-century following the Civil War than it had been earlier. It began with a foundation myth: Novelists who described the first ancestors of Southern families invariably resurrected the cavalier sportsmen of the seventeenth century – the cavalier not, of course, as a member of an historically specific political party but as a type for Southern chivalry. The founder of a noble Southern family in John Esten Cooke's romance of the Civil War, *Surry of Eagle's Nest* (1866), is typical: a cavalier who fled England after the beheading of Charles I and settled in Virginia because "land was cheap and foxes abounded." This first Surry quickly acquired "a number of thorough-breds, and a pack of hounds, married and settled down," dedicating "his energies to fox-hunting and raising blood horses for the remainder of his life."[44] Just as the hunters in the frontier myth invaded the wilderness in search of game, not gain, the first Southern planters, according to the Southern myth, emigrated from England to find freedom and sport.

Other writers claimed medieval chivalry as the ultimate source of Southern life, literally in some cases by extending family lineage to medieval Europe, more often figuratively by giving characters names such as Perceval St. George or referring repeatedly to Southern gentlemen as "knights." The ring tournament, both in fact and in fiction, became the most visible symbol of Southern gentlemen's ties to sporting knighthood.[45] In Francis Fontaine's *Etowah* (1887), mounted knights bearing the colors of their ladies compete for the rings as their forebears jousted and pursued the Holy Grail in happier times, before anyone conceived so bizarre a notion as equality. In *His Second Campaign* (1883), Maurice Thompson described how medieval "jousts and tournaments took the form of social contests for superiority," and how in the same spirit the old Southern aristocracy "loved the chase" and preserved "the pomp and lavish hospitality, the dangerous rivalry and deadly feuds, the clash of weapons in honorable fray, and all the stately formalities of a long-buried age." John Fox, Jr. treated the same theme with more irony in *A Knight of the Cumberland*.[46]

In the fictional reconstruction of the Old South, then, sport became a key link between Southern life and medieval chivalry. The nearly total disavowal of gambling and dueling in this fiction (except in the extreme necessity of defending a lady's honor) is matched by a greater attention to hunting, but hunting of an extremely sentimentalized sort.[47] Astride his horse, bounding through brake and meadow at breakneck speed after an elusive fox, the Southern male appears at his manliest, but this manliness is placed in the service of Southern womanhood. In George Cary Eggleston's *A Man of Honor* (1873), John W. Moore's *The Heirs of St. Kilda* (1881), and Page's " 'Unc' Edinburg's Drowndin' " (1887), the heroes compete with their rivals for the fox's tail only as the prize to be won for a lady's favor. Masculine prowess dissolves into sentimental gesture in what may be taken as the archetypal tableau in this late-nineteenth-century fiction.

The most extravagant celebrations of Southern sporting heroism are found in novels like Moore's *St. Kilda* and Fontaine's *Etowah* that were printed in Southern cities and presumably read only by Southern readers for whom partisanship was an undisguised virtue. The overt intention of most postwar Southern writers, for all their romanticizing of the old regime, was to reconcile sectional differences. Truly felt or not, this theme was required by Northern publishers and editors.[48] Although novels like Eggleston's *A Rebel's Recollections* (1875), William Baker's *Colonel Dunwoddie, Millionaire* (1878), and Page's *Red Rock* (1898) contrast Southern sporting honor to Yankee unscrupulousness,[49] more typically this fiction assumes an even-handed perspective. But criticism of the ruthlessly competitive North was nonetheless powerful for being implicit. *The Heirs of St. Kilda* and *Etowah* do not even pretend to disinterest. The centerpiece of Fontaine's novel is an extended account of a ring tournament linking Southern sportsmen to medieval knights in order to celebrate the glories of aristocracy. In Moore's novel, a fox hunt and a horse race replace the tournament in revealing Southern character untouched by the ruthless competitiveness that outsiders sometimes demonstrate. In the hunt the hero wins his manhood but also a trophy for his lady; in the horse race the young man upholds the fame of St. Kilda stock against both an English import and the rivalry of ruthless social climbers new to the valley, preserves the principle of sport for sport's sake against those who advocate purses and side bets for the races, and gains glory for himself but only by winning through fair play.[50]

The sporting hero who emerges from all of this fiction by male writers is thoroughly domesticated, and in this he differs little from the image in many Southern women's novels from the same period. For a touchstone woman's text I would nominate Constance Cary Harrison's *Flower de Hundred* (1890), with its Throckmorton cousins, Miles and Dick, as the central figures for examining Southern sport. Miles, true to his martial name, is "madcap Miles," who "learned to handle a rod, to swim, to shoot, to wrestle, to climb trees after mistletoe and hawks' nests, to row, to sail a cat-boat" before he outgrew the nursery. "Dashing, aggressive, and troublesome," Miles is the object of everyone's love but also of their worry, a pale descendant of Cooke's Champ Effingham. Dick, in contrast, has "a gentle nature, and a deprecating, almost timid appeal in his manner for the good-will of his friends" – the antithesis of rollicking Miles. During the course of the novel, the virile and effeminate cousins are drawn toward a golden mean: While Dick makes the effort "to keep up with Miles in athletic exercises," Miles astonishes the household with his quiet reserve and interest in books. Miles reforms his life to please his beloved Bonnibel, who has told him that "she might fancy, but would never choose for a comrade in life, a mere idler and ignorant roisterer." In the manner of Caroline Gilman's *Recollections of a Southern Matron,*

In popular iconography George Washington was a fox-hunting sportsman as well as the Father of His Country – a testament to the power of this cultural myth well into the twentieth century. The painting is John Ward Dunsmore's *First Gentleman of Virginia* (1909). (Collection of Fraunces Tavern Museum, Gift of George A. Zabriskie Memorial)

Harrison's novel describes a fox hunt with more attention to the luncheon afterward than to the kill itself, another hunt in which Bonnibel confides to Miles her sympathy for the "poor little wretches" who are hunted. Eventually, Dick is killed in the Civil War, while Miles returns safely, to marry and take up farming, not the chase.[51]

Harrison reworked her basic strategy in *A Son of the Old Dominion* (1897), set on the eve of the American Revolution, in which she initially celebrates sport then criticizes it later as a distraction from more pressing matters.[52] In this middle ground of postbellum women's plantation fiction I would also place Mary Tucker Magill's *The Holcombes* (1871) and Mary G. McClelland's *Broadoaks* (1893), which celebrate without qualification the Christmas revels and "frolicing" endemic to Southern life but pointedly domesticate masculine sport.[53] Whether to emphasize the common sentimental vision that McClelland, Magill, and Harrison shared with the male writers, or to insist on the difference in degree of sentimentalization between the male and female versions, is a matter of perspective. If the main subject is gender, the women writers' more extreme softening of the sportsman's image is important; if the subject is a sentimental ideal that became conspicuous in middle-class American culture in the last part of the nineteenth century, the difference is negligible. Portraits of the sentimental sportsman, whether Harrison's or John Moore's, served as a covert protest against an economic order in which neither sentiment nor sportsmanship seemed to matter very much.

Men and women who rejected the masculine sporting myth altogether, however, in notable instances did so on very different grounds. At the sentimental extreme, such novels as James Lane Allen's *Two Gentlemen of Kentucky* (1899) and *A Kentucky Cardinal* (1902) and Margaret Preston's *Aunt Dorothy: An Old Plantation Story* (1890) equally ignore sport, honor, and their trappings altogether. But among the outright debunkers, male and female perspectives can be distinguished. In Mark Twain's *Huckleberry Finn* (1885) and George Washington Cable's *The Grandissimes* (1880), the sporting myth is indiscriminantly destructive, without preference for male or female. The early chapters of *Huck Finn* poke fun at the pretension of Southern honor through Pap Finn's racist declamation on the affronts to his white dignity; then burlesque turns to outrage in the Shepherdson–Grangerford feud, in which irrational violence is rendered as a grotesque parody of Southern sportsmanship: Acknowledging "rules" and keeping score only point most tellingly to the insanity of mayhem masquerading as sport.[54] In like spirit, Cable's foundation myth for the prideful Creole families in his novel begins ironically with a roll of the dice, by which a Fusilier-Grandissime wins both a bride and the eternal enmity of the DeGrapions. Another game of chance, a poker game this time, results in an insult to Grandissime honor that can only be avenged in a fatal duel. Not only does the sporting honor of these aristocratic Creoles lead to violence, much of their violence is done by unruly mobs, not honorable individuals. Pride and violence are the twin curses of Creole society in Cable's novel; underlying both are caste and racism, the abominations that extend familial rivalry into cultural suicide.[55]

Gender is not an explicit issue in either of these novels. In *Huckleberry Finn*, women stand outside the world of male violence; in *The Grandissimes*, men and women equally share the fatal Creole pride, displaying it in ways appropriate to their culturally defined gender roles. On the other hand, gender lies at the heart of women writers' most radical breaks from the plantation legend. In a single passage in *The Battle-Ground* (1902), for example, Ellen Glasgow laid bare the gendered inequality underlying Southern sport and hospitality:

> The master might live with lavish disregard of the morrow, not the
> master's wife. For him were the open house, the shining table, the well-

stocked wine cellar and the morning rides over the dewy fields; for her care of her home and children, and of the souls and bodies of black people that had been given into her hands.[56]

Two of the period's greatest best sellers, Augusta Jane Evans's *St. Elmo* (1866) and E. D. E. N. Southworth's *The Hidden Hand* (serialized in 1859 then frequently reprinted before finally appearing as a novel in 1888), take considerably greater license with sacred conventions. St. Elmo Murray is a "tall, athletic man"; cynical, fierce, and passionate; given to "midnight orgies and habitual excesses," and to hunting, billiards, horse races, and ten-pins.[57] Edna Earl is repulsed by this monster of sporting excess, until St. Elmo renounces his masculine prowess and grovels through several hundred pages to prove his worthiness to wed her. Southworth's heroine Capitola, on the other hand, usurps the male's sporting role for herself. She rides recklessly, joins enthusiastically in the annual shooting over her uncle's plantation, and even challenges the aptly named villain, Craven LeNoir, to a duel. In one of the great set pieces from one of the century's most popular stories, Capitola first claims for herself the most extreme rights of the male, then reduces masculine honor and its public display to nonsense, when, after giving LeNoir an apparently fatal wound in a duel, she announces that her gun was loaded only with sweet peas. Humiliated as well as bloodied, the villain slinks away while onlookers laugh uproariously. Capitola claims that religious principles prevented her taking more fatal vengeance; her rollicking glee over the prank suggests a less pious motive.[58]

Thorough debunkers like Twain, Cable, Evans, and Southworth represent the minority among postbellum Southern writers. Gender alone did not determine who rejected and who celebrated the sporting myth, and both sexes contributed to making the domesticated sportsman the dominant hero of the plantation legend. He was rivaled only by one other figure (whose creators again were both male and female): the Southern soldier in the Civil War who viewed battle as a grand chase or hunt and who fought as if sporting in the jaws of death. John Esten Cooke established the pattern in *Surry of Eagle's Nest* (1866) and *Mohun* (1869), a pair of novels based in part on Cooke's own service under J. E. B. Stuart, who became the paradigm of this doomed sporting hero. Stuart has much company in *Surry*, where several great Southern warriors – Pelham, Farley, Jackson, Ashby – are consistently described as playful, sportive, reckless cavaliers.[59] But Stuart is the grandest of them all, the sum of all Southern soldiery (as well as a man whom a later historian would judge a genius at self-promotion[60]). In *Surry* Cooke gave readers a Stuart who "could march all night, fight all day, and then ride a dozen miles and dance until sunrise" (83). A Stuart to whom "war seemed mirth" and who "delivered his blows with laughter" (396); who infected his men with his own "genius of mirth," leaving them "crazy with delight, singing and dancing" as they rode to battle (86, 130). The rhetorical figure that sums up Stuart's career is the same one that Irving and Simms tied to their rambunctious frontiersmen: In war and in life, Stuart wants "nothing better than 'a fight or a frolic' " (82).

The sportiveness of *Surry* becomes tragic grandeur in *Mohun*. When Stuart attends a ball the night before one battle early in the war, the narrator describes the attitude of the young men and women there, some of whom would be dead in hours, as a kind of doomed playfulness: "All went merry as a marriage-bell, and they danced to the joyous music. Soon the cannon would begin to roll, and the youths would charge to that stormy music as they danced to this." This motif dominates the second novel. After a defeat Stuart leads his men not in mourning but in a night "of uproar, and mirth, and dance." In a series of chapters titled "The Opening of the Hunt," "The Game A-Foot," and "The Chase," war becomes a "strange mingl[ing]" of "blood, jests, laughter, mourning." During the bitter winter of 1863–4, while Stuart's men establish a merry bivouac despite their hardships, Surry muses about the enemy:

> I wonder if our friends across the Rapidan who were going to crush us, were as gay as the folk about to be crushed? The future looked stormy, but we laughed – and we did right, did we not, friend? That mirth was not unseemly – not unworthy of approval. It is evidence at least of "game."[61]

Cooke's images of Southern sportsmen and their tragic sportiveness reappeared again and again in postbellum fiction, including Cooke's own nonfiction account of the war, in which Stuart appears as the same "gay cavalier," his raids the same mix of "the fun, the frolic, the romance – and the peril too" that he portrayed in his novels.[62] The figure of Stuart has fascinated Southern writers to this day. Eggleston's portrait of him in *A Rebel's Recollections* is identical to Cooke's;[63] William Faulkner had him partly in mind in creating Col. Sartoris; Barry Hannah resurrected him for two stories in *Airships* as recently as 1978. But Stuart also became a type for all Southern soldiery. Eggleston characterized ordinary rebel soldiers as "hardy lovers of field sports, accustomed to out-door life, and in all physical respects excellent material to make an army" (70). In *Etowah,* Fontaine wrote that war is "exciting to the true soldier as is the spirit of speed to the race-horse about to enter the arena" (237). In "Marse Chan," Page's hero dies in battle in the only proper way for a Southern sportsman to die (the description belongs to black Sam): "I seen 'im when he went, de sorrel four good lengths ahead o' ev'y urr hoss, jes' like he use' to be in a fox-hunt" (33). In *The Clansman,* Thomas Dixon described confederate soldiers' famous rebel yell as "the cry of the hunter from the hill-top at the sight of his game!"[64] In novel after novel, writers transformed war into desperate play, their Southerners fighting not for hate, revenge, or even survival, but for the joy of fighting.

One would expect women writers to be less susceptible than men to the romance of sporting death. In Glasgow's *The Battle-Ground,* for example, the "game of war" in which John Esten Cooke and many others found Southern manhood at its best expresses only brutal instincts, as when the narrator describes the young hero early in the strife:

> As he bent to fire, the fury of the game swept over him. All the primeval instincts, throttled by the restraint of centuries – the instincts of blood-guiltiness, of hot pursuit, of the fierce exhilaration of the chase, of the death grapple with a resisting foe – these awoke suddenly to life and turned the battle scarlet to his eyes. (312)

Afterwards he feels nauseous as if after a debauch. But Glasgow did not speak for a female consensus. Among postbellum women writers one also finds what was nearly unthinkable before the war: a number who celebrated sporting honor as vigorously as any man did, even when its outcome was tragic.

Grace King's nostalgic history of New Orleans, in which, contrary to Cable's assertion in *The Grandissimes,* dueling under the Oaks epitomizes the romance, the gallantry, and the exquisite honor of the Creole male, is particularly striking in this context. Another memoir, Susan Dabney Smedes' biography of her father, renders the potentially troubling privileges of the sporting male as sentimental virtues.[65] In fiction, the major figure in celebrating the masculine sporting myth was Mary Johnston, a popular novelist whose own father and cousin had been heroes in the war. In *The Long Roll* (1911), Johnston's treatment of the desperate cavalier sportsman is indistinguishable from John Esten Cooke's (except for *The Long Roll*'s more impressive historical authenticity). An earlier novel, the bestselling *To Have and to Hold* (1900), is more sentimentally romantic – but in the manner of Caruthers' *Cavaliers of Virginia* not of Gilman's *Recollections,* rich in the rhetoric of sportive honor.[66] Likewise, nothing in *The Long Roll* suggests the gender of its author. Insofar as Johnston romanticized Confederate soldiery in an otherwise realistic novel, she did so in the manner of John Esten Cooke, with references to war as a "tourney," a "fox hunt," and a "deer drive" that root the conflict in the Southern myth.[67] Johnston's distinctive signature, in both *The Long Roll* and *To Have and To Hold,* was her emphasis on the spirit of desperate play, again as Cooke had done before her with Jeb Stuart. At the height of the war in the later novel, when the heroine and her family come to the President's mansion for seemingly inappropriate festivities, the Confederate vice-president assures her:

> Ah, Miss Cary, when you are as old as I am, and have read as much, you will notice how emphatic is the testimony to song and dance and gaiety on the eve of events which are to change the world! The flower grows where in an hour the volcano will burst forth; the bird sings in the tree which the earthquake will presently uproot; the pearly shell gleams where will pass the tidal wave. (431)

Jeb Stuart makes similar speeches in Cooke's novels. In Johnston's retelling, this gallantry and heroic bravado characterize all of her Southern soldiers, their desperate playfulness signaling their triumph in defeat.

Mary Johnston as well as John Esten Cooke, Constance Cary Harrison as well as Thomas Nelson Page, developed the figures of the domesticated sportsman and the fight-or-frolic rebel soldier in late-nineteenth-century Southern writing. By the end of the century, the mere mention of a hero's Southern origins – Wister's cowboy from Virginia, Frank Norris's Magnus Derrick from North Carolina in *The Octopus* – imputed to the character a set of beliefs and manners that readers instantly recognized. Gamesmanship had nothing to do with this Southern world; sportsmanship prevailed. But it was no longer simply a Southern world that was evoked. The Southern sportsman became a national hero not because sectional antagonism diminished after Reconstruction, but because he represented a longing that middle-class Americans north and south shared. He was the spirit of the antimodern, not only of the South's Lost Cause but also of the nation's Lost Chance.

By the end of the nineteenth century, the Western and Southern sporting myths had emerged from a complex interplay of cultural and countercultural impulses. Initially, Natty Bumppo's hunting code had defied the legal statutes of Templeton, and the Southern planter's aristocratic code of honor had challenged egalitarian laws. But through the course of the nineteenth century the sporting codes in various reformulations came to stand for the culture's most openly professed values. The Leatherstocking figure became the founder of civilization, not its chief critic; the gambler and the cowboy were domesticated by sentimental writers to make them defenders of the status quo. Yet the idealized sportsmen of the South and the West also continued to serve, at least implicitly, as a critique of not-so-ideal social and political realities. To portray life as an honorable game was to deny it was often a mere struggle of forces, with power as the object. The sporting myths, then, could be cultural celebration, escapist fantasy, and accommodation with *realpolitik,* perhaps all at the same time.

3

Gender and the Game

The Southern sporting gentleman took his place with the New England spinster, the midwestern farmer, and numerous other figures to define the cultural mythography of late-nineteenth-century regional writing. Henry James's novel *The Bostonians* (1886) was one of many novels by non-Southerners to explore this terrain, offering a detailed contrast of New England and Southern characters and consciences. Olive Chancellor's earnest commitment to equal rights stands against Basil Ransom's reactionary assumptions of class privilege, though in James's complication of the stereotypes, Olive's earnestness verges on pathology and Basil's class arrogance includes a healthy contempt for shallowness and sham. But Olive Chancellor and Basil Ransom also represent more than their regions; among other things, they express extreme views on the gender issues of the day. In *The Bostonians,* the heroic language of masculine sport openly confronts the altogether different language of New England feminism, as Basil and Olive contest for control over Verena Tarrant, the young clairvoyant whose abundant beauty is matched by an utter lack of self-possession. One result of this conflict is an elaborate rhetorical pattern of the sort for which James is particularly noted. Basil is described initially as a Mississippi planter impoverished by the Civil War, who has ventured north to find success as a lawyer: "Here he would enter the game and here he would win it." Established at the outset as the code word of Basil's ambition, this game motif is developed in a succession of identical images. In his bewilderment over Olive's initially inviting him to Boston, Basil wonders "what game was being played with him" but is not unduly worried; whatever might arise, "he was good for any game." Basil's early return to New York yields the novel's center stage to Olive and Verena, but when the narrative next looks in on him at the beginning of Book Second, Basil is immediately identified by his rhetorical signature. Depressingly unsuccessful so far in both his legal career and his first attempts at a literary one, Basil wonders whether "the game was to be won in New York."[1]

In part, the figure of "the game" declares Basil's Southernness; in part, it links him to another rhetorical tradition to be examined in the following chapter: the "game" of business or a man's calling as hinted at by Owen Wister's Virginian. But in part this "game" also signifies Basil's gender. Another male in the novel, the journalist Matthias Pardon, characteristically uses a different version of this sporting idiom. Desiring to promote rather than possess Verena, Pardon thinks of her as a "great card" to be played in a national tour of paying exhibitions – as does Verena's first promoter, her own father (140, 143, 102). The novel's women have altogether different rhetorical markers; in particular, while the superficial Verena is consistently described in theatrical images, Basil's antagonist Olive over and over appears not as a player in the "game" but as a soldier in the *battle* of life.

This battle is both political and sacred; Olive is described in, and herself uses, the language of both a religious crusade (in which her role is to be a martyr) and a military conflict. In addition to the numerous literal references to "battle," an ancillary cluster of images characterizes Olive as "earnest" (while Basil is "sportive"), "hard" (while Basil is "chivalrous"), entirely committed to "work" (while Basil also seeks "fun"). "We must be hard if we wish to triumph," Olive tells Verena in a characteristic mood (132). About her, the narrator makes a refrain of a few key words, as in this comment: "She seemed to see the glow of dawning success; the battle had begun, and something of the ecstasy of the martyr" (144).

It is through the collision of these rhetorical patterns that James subtly worked out the personal, regional, and gender conflicts at the center of the novel. I am particularly interested in gender here. For Basil, the contest with Olive to possess not just the body but the soul of Verena Tarrant is grand sport. In one scene, prevented from listening to Verena lecture on women's plight in the next room, Basil (most unchivalrously) tells Olive's sister Mrs. Luna, "I haven't the least idea of losing any of the sport in there, you know." Later, when Verena declares her unwillingness to give up lecturing on women's rights should they marry, Basil answers with a "sportive reply" (256, 389). For Olive, on the other hand, the contest is a "war to the knife" (383). Olive thinks of both her personal conflict and the normal relations of the sexes in terms of a "fight," of "stab after stab," of "torture," of "weapons" – most inclusively of "battle" (373–7). Basil speaks of and to Olive in *mocking* martial images; their contest is just sport to him because he doesn't believe women have any real power. Basil's "chivalry" is Olive's "persecution"

(391). Olive is engaged in a "fight . . . to the death"; Basil responds in a "jocose spirit" (391–2).

The contest between a warrior and a sportsman ought to go to the warrior, but Basil of course wins. Neither Basil nor Olive qualifies as a hero(ine) in James's novel; the sometimes devious gentleman and the too selfish martyr equally fail as exemplars of Southern and New England codes of honor. The outcome, rather, seems to say something about the unequal chances for success in gender conflict. Near the end, when defeat seems inevitable, Olive reflects that "women had from the beginning of time been the sport of men's selfishness and avidity" (408). The novel does not endorse so extreme a view; but earlier, when Verena tells Olive that she hopes to persuade Basil on two or three points of the feminist agenda, Olive warns her against "a contest that isn't equal." Yes, the novel suggests, contests between men and women cannot simply be "fair." In the final scene, having vanquished Olive and her entire sisterhood and won Verena as an ornament for his dubious future, Basil comes closest to seeming the monster Olive has considered him, laughing at Verena's agitation and "palpitating with his victory."

The game of love

The Bostonians can serve as a touchstone text for this chapter in a number of ways. Through its rhetorical patterns it suggests two extremely different kinds of masculine sportiveness: the "game" men play – against other males, presumably equals – in the public arena with success as the prize; and the game men play in the private realm of sexual relationships, in which the "opponent" and the "prize" are strangely identical, and the "loser," a woman who is both superior (in goodness and beauty) and inferior (in intellect and physical power) to the male, is presumed to win by her losing. James's use of identical language for such different contests produces in The Bostonians a rich sense of the conflicts in the "normal" roles and relations of men and women in nineteenth-century America. The fact that James was a male, writing skeptically about the domestic consequences of masculine sporting codes and behavior, is also important to our understanding of the relationship of gender to the rhetoric of game playing.

In my discussions of the Western and Southern sporting myths I argued that their largely masculine orientation should not obscure their more complex relationship to gender. Women writers as well as men developed the figures of the domesticated sportsman and the fight-or-frolic rebel soldier in late-nineteenth-century Southern writing. The Western sporting myth, on the other hand, was more thoroughly the creation of male writers. Most generally, Western and Southern fiction reveals both major differences between men's and women's writing and significant points of contact. In his study of the diaries of men and women who traveled the overland trail to find new homes in the West, historian John Mack Faragher has observed that more than two-thirds of the content concerned the same "three broad themes – practical matters, health and safety, and natural beauty" – while sharp differences appear in the remaining third:

> Women were concerned with family and relational values – the happiness and health of the children, family affection, home and hearth, getting along with the traveling group, and friendship especially with other women. Men were concerned with violence and aggression – fights, conflicts, and competition, and most of all hunting.[2]

In these differences, that is, the personal writings of nineteenth-century frontierswomen examined by Faragher and the many other historians who have been recovering the history of the woman's West mirror the differences in men's and women's Western fiction.[3]

The diaries and memoirs of the women (both their less conscious and more crafted writings) reveal a feminine sensibility at odds with masculine displays of prowess. On the one hand, there are simply the omissions: Women had no stake in testing their own powers against others; their triumph lay in holding the family together, not against Indians and outlaws, but against disease and accident.[4] When they celebrated their experience, women identified different pleasures from men's: the beauty of nature rather than the bounty of game, entertainments and social amusement rather than sporting contests, female companionship rather than male rivalry.[5] Occasionally the women diarists more directly assaulted the elements of the masculine myth, as in several accounts of frontier hunting. "Our men are well-armed," noted one wife in a representative passage. "William carries a brace of pistols and a bowie knife. Aint that blood-curdling? I hope he won't hurt himself."[6]

Faragher's assigning of sport to the one-third of difference in men's and women's diaries, against two-thirds of shared concerns, can serve loosely as a metaphor for all the fiction I have been discussing: The sporting myths in general belong to a male tradition, but that difference must be seen within a larger context that includes considerable commonality. Philip Fisher has discussed *adventure* and *sentimental* plots as basic paradigms in nineteenth-century American fiction, but not as exclusively male and female genres. Cooper's *The Deerslayer,* in Fisher's most revealing example, sets the adventure plot (Indian warfare) against the sentimental plot (the potential unions of the marriageable characters) in a narrative in which murderous adventure eventually overwhelms sentiment.[7] Adventure and sentiment coexist in male writing, that is, and not always with adventure ascendant. The American novel in the nineteenth century, *The Deerslayer* included, was fundamentally a love story, whether set within a wilderness epic, a melodrama of high finance, or a domestic tale. The Western story typically involved a conflict between adventure and sentiment; the Southern story typically softened adventure with sentiment; the business novel, as we will see in Part II of this study, was closer to the Western than to the plantation romance in its typical plot.

As the previous discussions have demonstrated, several versions of the adventure plot develop a "game" in which the central male becomes a hero through his sporting prowess. There is a particular "game" endemic to the sentimental plot as well, but a significantly different one. The love story generated no cultural myths to compare with the Western and Southern ones; it concerned what was considered ordinary rather than extraordinary in men's and women's experiences. The sporting myths of the West and South chiefly addressed behavior in the political and economic realms (defined most broadly), the worlds where nineteenth-century males competed for survival, status, honor, position, power. These myths expressed a fantasy in which the disturbing competition of American public life was transformed into ennobling contest. The game of love, in contrast to the sporting myths, turned inward to address the intimate relations of men and women, sometimes to celebrate but more often to criticize the basis on which they were played out. The two kinds of "sport," in other words, were related as the outward and inward expressions of a single worldview that placed competition at the center of life.

The Southern and Western sporting myths generated several richly detailed narrative formulas; the love-game most often was more narrowly a motif, a recurring conventional image of love and courtship as sport. Both men and women used this motif in their fiction. We saw earlier that Owen Wister contrasted the little denials and evasions of Molly's "game," by which she keeps her cowboy suitor at a distance until she is ready to accept him, with the more forthright Virginian's contests with his fellow males. In Wister's telling, this love game is false by definition: a game of lies rather than frank agreement, of undeclared rather than open competition; a game that the woman plays while the man refuses, and that can be won only when the woman decides at last to quit playing. The competition of males in a public arena is very different from the competition of men and women in the private realm. Here, *The Virginian* tells us, there should be respite from the hard rivalries of men. Here, the world-wearied male ought to be able to let down his constant guard, to find in a home and a loving woman a gentle, and gentling, counterbalance to the necessarily fierce competition that is constant outside. Love ought to be no game but more innocent play.

The love game in *The Virginian* is an interlude between weightier contests; from Molly's perspective, however, it would appear more central. In Edith Wharton's *The House of Mirth,* a woman's novel from the same period, this game is no distraction from the main business of life but the only business in which Lily Bart is allowed to engage. Although both men and women wrote about the love game, it addressed women's culturally defined gender role more directly than men's. For men, it touched their private but not their public lives; for women in the nineteenth century, the private defined the officially sanctioned limits of female experience.

The context for this "game" of love, then, was not simply the sexual relations of men and women but the social, political, and economic conditions that determined the boundaries of women's lives. The hierarchical gender arrangements that have marked all of Western history in varying ways assumed particularly complex forms in nineteenth-century America, when extraordinary gains in social freedom for women were matched by the closest circumscription of their political identities. The relative economic power women enjoyed during colonial times disappeared under the new industrialism. During the transitional period from 1780 to 1830, the place of the middle-class home in American society changed as well: from a source of family manufacture to domestic sanctuary from the competitive, individualistic world of business, industry, and politics. For lower-class women, the factory replaced the home altogether as the source of economic security.[8]

The consequences for women's lives were profound and complex, and have only in the last two decades begun to receive serious attention from historians, chiefly feminists. One result was the so-called cult of True Womanhood that was not the single consensual ideology that Barbara Welter originally claimed, but that was indeed a powerful conservative ideology that competed with more progressive views of the women's role in antebellum America.[9] True Womanhood defined women as the caretakers of morality, culture in the narrow sense, and all the civilizing virtues necessary to soften the harshness of men's public lives. Against culturally sanctioned aggressive and domineering manhood, it required a quartet of contrasting virtues: not industry, thrift, and the rest of the Franklinian litany, but piety, purity, submissiveness, and domesticity. Women were to assure that gentleness and beauty would not disappear from civilization, but without interfering in the competitive marketplace where gentleness was weakness, and beauty a luxury that had to be earned first by wealth. True Womanhood elevated women as never before through a grand hypocrisy that exalted the virtues least useful in the marketplace.[10]

On the other hand, the progressive ideal as embodied in such books as Catharine Beecher's *A Treatise on Domestic Economy* (1841) emphasized a much more material existence for women. A woman's genius lay not in her detachment from this world but in her competence within it, a competence circumscribed by the limits of woman's sphere but empowering within those limits. The champions of female competence promoted the older values of the "Age of Homespun" by viewing the wife/mother/woman as a strong, self-reliant, highly capable person – able both to shingle a roof and earn a family-supporting income when necessary. Rather than delicacy and submission, they urged physical fitness, rigorous education (as appropriate for women's role), *prudent* marriage, and productive employment.[11]

The rhetorical figure of the game of love most directly touched the dilemmas raised by the cult of True Womanhood, in particular the central place in women's lives it gave to courtship and marriage. But it reflected the concerns of middle- and upper-class women generally in a society that made them politically and economically dependent on men (working girls were potential victims of a very different "game" – the sporting seduction of conscienceless upper-class rakes). Although progressive thinkers declared a bad marriage worse than no marriage and pleaded for the spinster a legitimate social position, the more conservative champions of True Womanhood acknowledged no status for a woman outside her role as wife and mother. Whose view predominated in antebellum America can be suggested by Catharine Sedgwick's extraordinary preface to her late novel, *Married or Single?* (1857). Presenting herself as a writer with perhaps an unwelcome theme, Sedgwick promised readers that, consistent with both "the ancient laws of romance" and "the great law of Nature," her hero and heroine will be husband and wife; but her story's moral will be less conventional. "We raise our voice with all our might," she wrote, "against the miserable cant that matrimony is essential to the feebler sex – that a woman's single life must be useless or undignified – that she is but an adjunct of man – in her best estate a helm merely to guide the nobler vessel."[12] In a society in which such earnest pleading on the spinster's behalf could be necessary, the "game" of love had to be invested with profoundly serious implications.

We can take *Godey's Lady's Book,* the bible of True Womanhood, as a key to the meaning of the love game in antebellum America. What we find are contradictory images. On the one hand, we can look to the frontispiece of the June 1831 issue, which illustrates most clearly the sentimental ideal. Around a central tableau showing a cupid courted by a supplicant maiden are arranged four smaller portraits of cupids fishing, swimming, picking fruit, and playing with a winged heart. The accompanying text explains these images to be representative of "love under the various forms in which poetry and painting have embodied that

PUBLISHED FOR THE LADY'S BOOK — JUNE 1831.

Philadelphia — L. A. Godey & Co. No. 112 Chesnut Street op. Post office

Ornaments for Ladies fancy Works.

"The Sports of Love," frontispiece to *Godey's Lady's Book*, June 1831. (The Beinecke Rare Book and Manuscript Library, Yale University)

changeful and capricious deity," all of them together "illustrative of the Sports of Love."[13] A few months earlier, *Godey's* editorialized less enthusiastically about erotic games. Under the title "Sporting with Female Affections," the writer pleaded that a man of honor and integrity would never think "of sporting with the affections of the fair sex, nor even of paying his addresses to any one, till he is perfectly convinced his own are fixed on just principles."[14]

These contradictory meanings already had a long literary and artistic tradition by the 1830s. Love in the Western world had been characterized as a sport since Greek and Roman poets first conceived Cupid, the god of love, as a mischievous, often blindfolded boy, letting fly the shafts from his bow with sportive indifference. From Ovid's *Ars Amatoria* to *The Art of Courtly Love* by Andreas Capellanus in the twelfth century; to Shakespeare's love-game comedies, Middleton's *Women Beware Women,* Pope's "Rape of the Lock," and Marivaux's *Le Jeu de l'amour et du hasard* in the seventeenth and eighteenth centuries; the conceit that lovers engaged in what was essentially a sporting contest, whether a delightful or duplicitous one, became conventional. The specific metaphor of the hunt – the "love chase" – that emerged from classical mythology and such writers as Aeschylus, Euripides, Horace, Virgil, and particularly Ovid, became widespread in the Middle Ages in works by Chaucer, Chrétien de Troyes, Gottfried, and numerous others, and continued to be a commonplace in Renaissance poetry.[15] Both conflict and playfulness are embedded in this rich tradition; in appropriating the literary models of sportive love nineteenth-century America adapted them to its own sexual politics. When *Godey's* referred sentimentally to the sports of love, it invoked a tradition in which female superiority was assumed, male deference and devotion presumed to complement it. But in its attack on men who "sport with female affections," *Godey's* implied that in nineteenth-century America female power was largely a fiction. The sports of love might prove very unsporting when the players were unevenly matched.

The dominant image of the love game in early American fiction was the negative one: the Ovidian game of seduction, with the woman as frantic prey. The chief literary model for this plot was Samuel Richardson's *Clarissa* (1748), whose villain, Lovelace, became the type for later sporting scoundrels. In his single-minded assault on Clarissa's virtue, Lovelace speaks of his "game" with her, of "the joys of the chase, and in pursuing a winding game," of his sexual freedoms with her as "a *frolic* only, a *romping-bout*," and of his own "sportive cruelty" as somehow natural.[16] Richardson's ablest American imitator, Hannah Foster, recreated Lovelace almost identically in Peter Sanford, Eliza Wharton's seducer in *The Coquette* (1797), a novel whose regular reprinting throughout the nineteenth century suggests its continuing power to articulate women's concerns. Sanford combines sportive with more martial language when he describes himself with Eliza "play[ing] off her own artillery by using a little unmeaning gallantry." And on another occasion, "If she will play with a lion, let her beware of his paw." And yet again, writing to a friend: "If a lady will consent to enter the lists against the antagonist of her honor, she may be sure of losing the prize." Sanford, of course, wins his game, while Eliza – pregnant, abandoned, banished, and finally dead – pays the loser's penalty.[17]

Novels such as *The Coquette* were cautionary tales for young ladies, warning less against the predatory male than against feminine susceptibility, and portraying the wages of sin, or even of imprudence, as shameful death. Since the game of love was fraught with peril, virtuous women did not play at all. *The Coquette,* however, dramatized not just conflict between the sexes but a powerful resistance to American society's prescribed role for women: a tension between the official insistence on a woman's moderation, restraint, and passionless prudence, and Eliza's desires for "festive mirth" and "the busy scenes and active pleasures of life" (135, 187). The official culture in Foster's novel says, "Restrain thyself," but Eliza's heart longs for at least a measure of playful freedom. In paragraphs and even individual sentences, *The Coquette* moves dialectically between two clusters of opposed code words: "regulation," "reason," "moderation," "duty," "sobriety," "decorum," "domestic tranquility," and so on; and against these, "amusement," "frivolity," "mirth," "levity," "hilarity," "gayety," and "pleasure." The first set identifies society's expectations of a woman; the second, Eliza's desires. A woman's *proper* course is never in doubt, and Eliza clearly errs in dallying with the rakish Sanford rather than accepting the marriage proposal of sober-minded Reverend Boyer. But Eliza's conflict and the novel's continuing appeal to female readers suggest that those readers lived in a society in which duty and desire could be fundamentally at odds. The "game" dramatized most concretely both the attractions and the dangers of erotic love: In its preliminary rounds it seems to offer Eliza innocent pleasure, but when the stakes grow serious, the woman who has agreed to play becomes a victim of her own dangerous desires as much as of the sporting male. The pathetic power of Foster's narrative lies in the fact that Eliza has no acceptable options, only dreary marriage or a kind of licentiousness that entails no real freedom. The novel suggests that Eliza, a representative young American woman, is caught in a double bind of her culture's manufacture that assures her misery.

The Coquette marks the beginning of a fictional tradition in which representations of sexual love as a "game" provide an index to middle-class women's feelings about their social position. By the 1830s, as seduction and betrayal disappeared from respectable American fiction as a major theme (while continuing with amazing energy in the lurid potboilers of George Lippard and other writers, women included, in the penny papers), more conventional courtship became the arena for the game of love.[18] In less melodramatic form the issue remained the same: To play the game of love risked losing what society insisted was most important in a woman's life – marriage.

For women who depended on marriage for status and on men for economic security, courtship became a crucial prelude to that all-important event. In a culture that still glorified work and denigrated play, the *game* of love could trivialize more easily than romanticize that process. But more to the point, the flirtation game ritualized inequality, with feminine allure, weakness, evasiveness, and supposed innocence of passion becoming "moves" in the game. In particular the conservative ideal of nineteenth-century womanhood placed American women between not easily reconciled expectations: to be femininely provocative to males seeking marriage, yet to be themselves restrained and passive, virtually immune to passion.[19] Only through evasive, manipulative "games" could such a balancing act succeed. Modern feminists have described how, when "confined to powerlessness and dependence, the woman glories in subservience, manipulates from beneath, and calculates a dominion of submission, sacrifice, and acceptance."[20] Plays games, that is. If court-

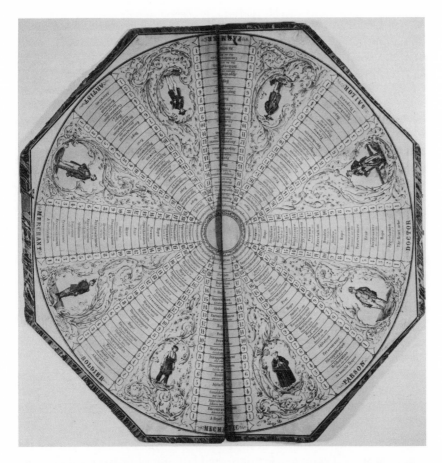

Given the didactic purposes of most nineteenth-century board games, "The Game of Coquette and Her Suitors," published in Boston in 1858, might seem strangely anomalous: The first player (Parson, Doctor, Sailor, Farmer, Artist, Merchant, Soldier, or Mechanic) to reach the center of the board wins the hand of the Coquette. The "game of love" appears considerably more positive here than in most of the sentimental fiction of the day. (Courtesy, the Essex Institute)

ship was that period when women traded the relative freedom but powerlessness of the single life for the relative security but constraint of marriage, then the "game" concerned an event of crucial, but also crucially ambiguous, importance.

Numerous women writers throughout the nineteenth century and beyond rejected these games outright. From the 1830s through the 1850s, *Godey's* is full of stories about coquettes, both male and female, who squander their opportunities for love and marriage by unwisely playing games.[21] The dime-novel *Waverly Library* (one of several series for women readers, the counterpart to the adventure series for men) included a handful of stories – "A Fateful Game; or, Wedded and Parted," "A Thorny Path; or, Playing to Win," and "A Desperate Game; or, For Love's Own Sake" – that focus on courtship and marriage troubled by complications.[22] In perhaps the paradigmatic American text in this tradition, Sedgwick's *Married or Single?*, the metaphors of sporting love consistently signify faithlessness or erotic threat. A young bachelor described as "the first prize in the matrimonial lottery of fashionable life" (I, 54) turns out to have seduced several servant girls and compromised a married woman. The heroine's stepsister, a too worldly young woman, thinks Grace Herbert herself secretly has designs on this "king of trumps"; Grace "keeps her cards to herself" and "plays them well," in the stepsister's words (II, 65–6). The "king of trumps" himself wagers with a friend on his prospective marriage to Grace, and at the moment when he feels at last that she will be his, he declares, "The game is mine!" (II, 36). In all of these instances Sedgwick clearly intended the language of the lottery and the whist table to signify the dangers that can befall women who take a gamester's view of marriage.

Grace discovers the truth about her suitor in time, then after several years of productive spinsterhood is rewarded with a good marriage. As Nina Baym has argued, such marriages in domestic fiction were as much symbolic as literal: the sign of the heroine's achievement of a "feminine ego."[23] The "game," then, in which marriage was the stake was marked with comparably grave importance. Another feminist critic, Mary Kelley, has also reminded us that the ideal of love in domestic fiction had nothing to do with physical passion. "What love is," wrote one domestic novelist, Maria McIntosh, in the language of the love game, is "not the sport of an exuberant fancy, not the wild tumult of a passion," but rather selfless devotion and duty.[24] In short, while the "game of love" was already a literary trope with a long history, in nineteenth-century America it was much more than a grace note in women's writing. In domestic fiction particularly, the "game" as the sign of masculine oppression or erotic passion often confronts the language of duty, selflessness, devotion, and the hearth in a collision of gender-marked rhetorics. In stories in which the "game" functions in this way, women who play, lose.

A cultural conversation about "games"

The dime-novel romances mentioned above were reprints of stories by Englishwomen; Lovelace and Clarissa also had their offspring in nineteenth-century British fiction, of course. Without having examined the English literary tradition with any thoroughness, I consider it likely that a comparable interest in "games" would be found there, given the importance of the public-school sporting ethic and its rhetoric in England's larger political and cultural life.[25] I would also expect the rhetorical patterns to differ in some ways from ours, in part because of the differences in the two cultures' sporting philosophies; in part because, as commentators have pointed out, women in nineteenth-century American fiction tended to be stronger and more independent than comparable heroines in British fiction.[26] In nineteenth-century American fiction, in any case, the "game" is not *always* dangerous, or women always losers.

As I mentioned earlier, the game of love became the basis of no mythic narrative but persisted as a motif embedded in a wide range of texts. A pair of novels from early in the twentieth century, Ruth Weiman's *Playing the Game* (1910) and Ruth Comfort Mitchell's *Play the Game* (1921), are exceptions in that they are structured entirely around the love-game trope. Interestingly and appropriately, the two books take opposing sides on the politics of the love game. In Weiman's novel – with chapters titled "The First Move," "The Game Is On," "The Sporting Chance," and so on – the mood is light but the theme is nonetheless critical: Playing the game evades true emotions; the heroine "wins" only by giving up the game to marry the man who truly loves her. Mitchell's version, on the other hand, portrays marriage as the woman's parallel to male sport, both of which can, and should, be governed by fair play.[27]

The lack of agreement in these two longer works illustrates the impossibility of generalizing in any simple way about gender and the "game." Whereas *Godey's,* the bible of American womanhood in the middle decades of the nineteenth century, repeatedly warned against the dangers of *playing* at love, Mary Jane Holmes in her domestic bestseller, *Tempest and Sunshine* (1854), reversed Thomas Middleton's Jacobean tragedy by having her heroine win a husband in a game of chess (a motif replayed in a later story in the *Atlantic,* titled "A Game of Solitaire").[28] The rich variety of fiction by nineteenth-century American women is only beginning to be appreciated; David Reynolds, for example, in his study of popular writing in the antebellum period, has demonstrated how reductive any claim for a single "women's literary tradition" must be. Reynolds has excavated the popular fiction both of women's rights (including quite radical stories in feminist newspapers) and of women's wrongs (including the literature of the temperance and abolitionist movements, in addition to anti-seduction and anti-prostitution fiction), and classifies a wide range of heroines, from "moral exemplars," "adventure feminists," and "women victims," to "working women," "feminist criminals," "sensual women," and "feminist exemplars." Having traced these figures and themes not just in the canonical literature of the "American Renaissance" and the domestic best sellers of the "Other Renaissance," but also in the immensely popular novels first serialized in the penny newspapers then in some cases republished in book form by reprint houses, Reynolds has properly complicated all efforts at literary and cultural history.[29]

Rather than claim any single narrative pattern as representing the "dominant" woman's perspective on the "game," then, I would emphasize as a start toward fuller understanding a many-voiced, variously motivated conversation both within and against a sporting rhetoric that was culturally defined as masculine. Women writers' general tendency to reject "games" is complicated by several telling examples of female characters who play them successfully. A general tendency to restrict women's game-playing to the sphere of sexual love is likewise complicated by instances of women stepping well beyond the bounds of female propriety to take on the male "at his own game." It is important to note the tendencies; it is equally necessary to acknowledge the complications.

This cultural conversation can be illustrated by a range of voices in late-nineteenth-century novels and stories by prominent writers. I begin with Harriet Beecher Stowe, whose "society novels" of the 1870s – *Pink and White Tyranny* (1871), *My Wife and I* (1871), and *We and Our Neighbors* (1873) – chiefly offer a series of pointed lessons on men's and women's proper roles in marriage and in society. In all three novels Stowe's chief concern was to counteract the age's dangerous tendency to make women of the prosperous classes into useless ornaments and frivolous pleasure-seekers. In *My Wife and I* and *We and Our Neighbors*, Eva Van Arsdel learns to forego the superficial pleasures of the society belle for the more profound satisfactions of wifehood, motherhood, and domestic economy. The game in these two novels – what Stowe termed "the race for fashionable leadership" and "races that are run between families" – chiefly signifies specious social rivalry.[30]

In *Pink and White Tyranny,* the most overtly didactic of these novels, the "game" is the conventional sport of love illustrated by *Godey's*. The story of a misbegotten marriage, *Pink and White Tyranny* centers on the relationship of John and Lillie Seymour, a conscientious and public-serving wealthy man and his heartless, selfish, materialistic wife. Lillie, before her marriage, is introduced as "the most adroit 'fisher of men' that has been seen in our days" – a sporting motif that appears several times in the opening chapter. "A belle by profession," Lillie is adept at the "little games" of "smiles and wiles, advices and devices," by which she "hooks" John Seymour, who for once in his life acts the fool in not seeing through Lillie's superficial manners to her true character. If Lillie in her intellectual and spiritual impoverishment is a monster of selfishness, however, she is in large part a victim of the many males who taught her from her girlhood, by look and action, "You don't need to be or do anything. Your business in life is to look pretty, and amuse us." As a "pet woman of society" Lillie in fact becomes less the successful player of her little games than "everybody's toy." In the climactic chapter titled "Checkmate," in which the chess image is elaborately developed, John Seymour finally realizes the disaster of his marriage, but he rejects divorce to accept the duty of his marriage bond. In the chapter's final paragraphs Stowe's narrator steps forward to make this theme explicit.[31]

In her society novels Stowe was unsparing in her criticism of women who devote their lives to frivolous "games." But generalizing even about this one writer is risky. In *Uncle Tom's Cabin* (1852), Stowe also wrote about an altogether different game and female player: Simon Legree's discarded mistress Cassy, who beats her vicious master at his own "game" through an ingenious escape plan.[32] More interesting yet is a scene from *My Wife and I* in which the heroine plays croquet as part of a foursome of rival belles and their rival suitors, with the game of croquet serving as an elaborate emblem of competing ideals and ambitions. The tournament is hosted by Wat Sydney, a wealthy owner of Western mines and suitor to the heroine, Eve Van Arsdel. Sydney is described as "a man, heart, soul, and strength, interested in that mighty game of chance and skill by which, in America, money is made." Opposed to this ruthless, game-playing businessman (a familiar figure in the era's novels about finance) in courting Eva is Harry Henderson, the novel's gentle and genteel narrator. Eva's counterpart is Sophie Elmore, who wishes to marry Sydney as much as Sydney wants Eva.

The players' badinage that accompanies their sport reveals their attitudes toward marriage and life. When Eva suggests that "croquet is the game of life," Sydney declares his guiding philosophy: "It teaches you just how to manage, use your friends to help yourself along, and then croquet them into good positions; use your enemies as long as you want them, and then send them to—" "The Devil," mumbles Harry's cynical friend who is watching the contest. For his part, Harry describes a game that perfectly mirrors his own passivity, even helplessness, in the public arena. "Some go on with a steady aim and true stroke," he says, "and make wickets, and hit balls, yet are croqueted back ingloriously or hopelessly wired and lose the game, while others blunder advantageously and are croqueted along by skillful partners into all the best places." Sydney desires Eva as an ornament for his public success; Harry longs for a partner who will direct his life toward the highest good. Eva and her mother offer feminine views on this matter. "There are few of us girls that make our own wickets in life," Eva says. "We are all croqueted along by papas and mamas." Sydney responds, disingenuously, "And many a man is croqueted along by a smart wife." But Mrs. Van Arsdel has the final word, also perhaps disingenuously: "But more women by smart husbands."[33]

This playful exchange, with its masked hints of sexual interest, touches on a most unplayful subject: the power arrangements in personal relationships. Stowe allowed the characters to speak for themselves, without authorial comment, but in determining the outcome of the croquet match she made her point about this more significant game as well. Eva wins, then offers her prize to a grateful Sophie, the runner-up: suggesting women's superiority to the men in the sport, but also Eva's superiority to Sophie in ultimately renouncing competition. Afterward, describing the event to a friend, Eva gives Stowe's sporting symbol explicitly political meaning when she observes, "I can imagine the excitement we women would make of an election if we should ever get into politics. Would we not croquet our adversaries' balls, and make stunning split-shots in parties, and wire ourselves artfully behind wickets, and do all sorts of perplexing things? I confess if the excitement should get to be half as great as in playing croquet, I should tremble to think of it" (352–3). In this same spirit of female independence, by choosing passive, earnest Harry Henderson over Wat Sydney, Eva takes a mate who will be her partner, not her master, in a life of selfless duty, modest material success, and deep contentment. Sophie Elmore "wins" both the offensively aggressive, competitive suitor and the frivolous life that she unwisely desires.

Stowe's croquet match is both a skillfully "literary" appropriation of a conventional trope and a representation of her long-standing commitment to a woman-centered domestic ideal. A more intriguing, because less conventionally restrained, voice is Louisa May Alcott's, whose story "The King of Clubs and the Queen of Hearts" (1862) offers a textbook example of the woman's cautionary tale, while her blood-and-thunder thrillers challenge Victorian values as Stowe never did. Subtitled "A Story for Young America," "The King of Clubs" outwardly makes light of the calisthenics mania that temporarily seized Alcott's home town in the heyday of Dio Lewis and the first stirrings of muscular Christianity (Alcott herself was a superb athlete). But overriding that local interest is a narrative that follows in the tradition, now thoroughly sentimentalized, of The Coquette. The "king of clubs" is a German teacher of gymnastics, the "queen of hearts" his favorite pupil and the local belle. Their love is nearly frustrated by "the new game" of captivation that is sweeping their New England village. At first this sportiveness seems delightful; the older generation, the narrator says, could learn a lesson from these young people:

for here all was honest, sincere, and fresh; the old world had not taught them falsehood, self-interest, or mean ambitions. When they lost or won, they frankly grieved or rejoiced, and wore no masks except in play, and then got them off as soon as possible.

"If blue-eyed Lizzie frowned, or went home with Joe," she continues, "Ned, with a wisdom older lovers would do well to imitate, went in for another game of foot-ball, gave the rejected apple to little Sally, and whistled 'Glory Hallelujah,' instead of 'Annie Laurie,' which was better than blowing a rival's brains out, or glowering at woman-kind forever after."

To play at love rather than engage in serious rivalry removes the sting of rejection and downplays the import of the stakes (while the youthfulness of the players emphasizes the game's essential unseriousness). But immediately following this passage appears another on Dolly, the erstwhile "queen" of the story. Having declared to her twin brother Dick, as the rules dictate, that she does not like August Bopp, the gymnast, Dolly discovers that in fact she does – for the truth of the matter is that "for all her coquetry and seeming coldness, Dolly had a right womanly heart of her own." Alcott set this "womanly heart" against the "game," their objects entirely different: marriage versus play for its own sake. Playing the game ultimately leads to misery for all parties. Only when Dolly finally declares to Bopp the secret of her heart does the confusion dissolve and true love conquer.[34]

This slight tale, seemingly worth noting only because it develops the game-of-love motif so fully, becomes more interesting when set alongside two of Alcott's so-called "thrillers" from the same period. During the years in which she wrote the wholly unobjectionable "King of Clubs," Alcott was also selling stories to editors of less respectable story papers, in which writers were granted considerably more license. In two of these stories, "Pauline's Passion and Punishment" (1863) and "Behind a Mask, or A Woman's Power" (1866), Alcott wrote about "games" a woman might play in ways that complicate any sense of her sentimental conventionality.

"Pauline's Passion and Punishment," winner of a one-hundred dollar prize and publication in *Frank Leslie's Illustrated Newspaper,* restates the theme of "The King of Clubs," only in more daring terms. In a melodramatic story of a scorned woman's vengeance against her duplicitous lover, the "game" Pauline plays carries heavily erotic and even violent overtones; yet it is fundamentally the same game Dolly learns not to play, and the consequences of playing are but a more violent version of Dolly's averted fate. In her wrath over her abandonment Pauline declares that "two can play at the game of hearts," and in a familiar mingling of martial and sportive imagery she accepts her faithless lover's challenge "to the tournament so often held between man and woman – a tournament where the keen tongue is the lance, pride the shield, passion the fiery steed, and the hardest heart the winner of the prize." Having lured Gilbert to "stake his last throw and lose it," Pauline eventually triumphs over her foe, but at the moment of her victory she must watch in horror as Gilbert exacts his own revenge by murdering their innocent spouses.[35]

Beneath its violent and passionate surface, "Pauline's Passion and Punishment" does nothing to undermine the moral lesson of Alcott's juvenile tale. But the same cannot be said of "Behind a Mask," published in *The Flag of Our Union*. The heroine of this story, Jean Muir – a scheming, lying, disreputable divorcée and former actress – successfully plays her "game" at the expense of a wealthy family, by tricking the family's patriarch into a marriage that gives her not just wealth but a position of unassailable power. The pattern of game-idioms is carefully constructed. Gerald, the heir to Coventry Hall, first speaks of "the game" to his brother Ned, when he suggests that the new governess may have designs on marrying Ned. The term is used next by a loyal maid who accuses Jean of coming between Gerald and his fiancée but admits her inability to stop her: "I saw your game and did my best to spoil it, but you are too quick for me." Only at the end of the story does Jean herself use the word, and only then does she reveal the true object of her game. Threatened with exposure but "resolving to win the game in defiance of everything," Jean rushes old Sir John into marriage then openly confronts her now helpless adversaries. The last paragraph states simply that "the game was won."[36] In this succession of images Jean appropriates the rhetoric of the wealthy and powerful males; she transforms a conventional love game into a contest whose openly avowed stake is not love at all but power; and, most significantly, she remains unpunished and unremorseful in her success. At the end of the story she is a proud, defiant, lower-class woman who has usurped the power and privileges of the wealthy.

Alcott's fantasy of female power will seem uncharacteristic if her more famous didactic fiction is assumed to represent her true literary voice. But such an interpretation would be inappropriate. *Frank Leslie's Illustrated Newspaper* and *The Flag of Our Union* were but two of the numerous story papers that thrived in the middle decades of the nineteenth century. "The King of Clubs and the Queen of Hearts" was serialized in another of these papers, Ripley Bartlett's *Monitor,* which differed from *Leslie's* and *The Flag of Our Union* by being published in Concord with all the respectability of Concord behind it. "The King of Clubs," which was later published in a volume of Alcott's stories, was directed chiefly toward a genteel audience of middle- and upper-middle-class young women. "Pauline's Passion" and "Behind a Mask" were directed toward the emerging "mass" audience that included a wide range of the lower and middling classes. The important thing to remember is that *The Monitor* was not Alcott's "normal" literary outlet, her fiction in *Leslie's* and *The Flag of Our Union* the aberrations in an otherwise respectable career. Rather, *The Monitor* and *Leslie's* represented different options for the professional writer at midcentury, male or female; Alcott published in both of them for the same reason: money. Once she became famous, Alcott abandoned the story papers for more "respectable" publishers, but in simple terms of numbers of readers the story papers actually represent the literary "mainstream" during this period. More important, "Behind a Mask" ought not necessarily to be considered atypical of Alcott's views. The anonymous or pseudonymous publication of these stories indicates the author's realization that blood and thunder might not play well in her native Concord. But Alcott once told a friend that her "natural ambition is for the lurid style," particularly enjoyable because it ran counter "to the respectable traditions of Concord." After publishing one last anonymous potboiler in 1877, Alcott wrote in her journal, "It has been simmering ever since I read Faust last year. Enjoyed doing it, being tired of providing moral pap for the young."[37] Although Alcott turned almost exclusively to "moral pap" after 1868 because of the great success of *Little Women* in that year, an understanding of her attitudes toward the "game" that women sometimes played or were forced to play must take her blood-and-thunder tales at least as seriously as her conventionally moralistic ones. Likewise, Alcott's "lurid" tales must be taken at least as seriously as her "moral pap" as evidence of nineteenth-century American middle-class women's response to the "game."

The chief of the story papers was Robert Bonner's *New York Ledger,* and Bonner's chief author for nearly four decades was E. D. E. N. Southworth. Southworth cannot be simply linked to the best selling domestic novelists who also emerged in the 1850s, as is sometimes done. Her fiction appeared first, in serialized form, in the *Ledger,* then was republished in hardcover over and over by the cheap reprint houses. While her total readership is literally incalculable, by all accounts she was read by more Americans than any other writer in the second half of the nineteenth century. Despite (or because of) this, her writing sat at the boundary of respectability; in 1881, the American Library Association Cooperation Committee included Southworth in a list of sixteen popular writers whose works were considered "injurious" by many librarians.[38] Yet she was the most popular writer of the age.

In one novel, *Fair Play* (1868), Southworth used the sporting image in the title both to refer, conventionally, to what the heroine owes her honorable and pious lover, and to champion, more radically, her demand for women's rights.[39] But the most revealing text for my purposes here is the most popular of all Southworth's novels, *The Hidden Hand*, serialized in Bonner's *New York Ledger* in 1859, then reprinted by Bonner twice more before appearing as a book in 1888.[40] A different episode from the one I discussed in the last chapter can serve as my paradigm here. In Chapter XVI, having defied her uncle and guardian by riding alone into the nearby forest, Capitola finds herself pursued apparently by a member of the nefarious Black Donald's desperado band. Though Cap had earlier longed for a chance to capture Black Donald himself – "by strategem, I mean, not by force" – she now seems more likely to become a victim. But as the ruffian rides beside her, cunningly inviting her to stop and sit with him a while, Cap *more* cleverly puts him off by claiming to be willing but pettishly demanding that they must wait until they find a suitable place. At last, within sight of her uncle's estate, Cap agrees to stop, if her companion will first spread his horse blanket on the ground. As the scoundrel (implicitly a would-be rapist) complies, Cap whips her horse across the river to safety; "the baffled villain turned and saw that his game was lost! He had been outwitted by a child!" Cap's response? In Southworth's words: "Turning, as she wheeled out of sight, Capitola – I'm sorry to say – put her thumb to the side of her nose, and whirled her fingers into a semi-circle, in a gesture more expressive than elegant."[41]

The pattern is a familiar one – the trickster tricked – but the "stake" involved and the gender of the contestants (not to mention Cap's most unlady-like gesture) produce very different implications. Capitola reminds us of Stowe's Cassy, whose own plight and triumph are scarcely less melodramatic despite appearing in a more respectable novel. Nina Baym claims *The Hidden Hand* for the tradition of "woman's fiction"; Elaine Showalter, on the other hand, identifies Southworth as a subverter of the "feminine novel."[42] As a novel *The Hidden Hand* was offered as another tale of pious love triumphant, (the cover and frontispiece of the 1888 first hardcover edition shows the portrait of a late-nineteenth-century society belle). But as a serial it promised rip-roaring action and a consistent flirting with respectability. In short, *The Hidden Hand* served multiple audiences in seemingly conflicting ways.

This cross-breeding is apparent everywhere in the novel, much like Cooper's wedding of frontier epic to the conventional love story. The story of Capitola's escapades with a violent-tempered uncle and wild bandits alternates, sometimes chapter-by-chapter, with a simpering love plot involving an extremely docile blonde, blue-eyed heroine from the sentimental tradition, Clara Day. When Capitola commands the stage, the "woman's role" receives some violent shocks. The reader first meets

Cap as an impudent but scrupulously honest Bowery orphan (a fore-shadowing of Horatio Alger's Ragged Dick and countless clones), dressed in boy's clothes because as a girl she has been unable to find odd jobs. Removed to Major Ira Warfield's Virginia estate where she is outfitted as a Southern belle, Capitola retains her saucy impudence; the adjectives that describe her most frequently are "capricious," "untamable," "be-witching," and "mischievous." In the interplay of plots and chapters the rhetoric of the sentimental love story – "duty," "devotion," "piety," and the rest – collides with the rhetoric of blood-curdling melodrama: place names like Hurricane Hall, Devil's Hoof, Devil's Run; personal names like Stealthy Steve, Headlong Hal, and Demon Dick. The nar-rative voice openly claims not to approve of "poor Cap," only to offer her story to readers' "charitable interpretation" (148); but narrative in-terest in Capitola overwhelms the conventional love story as decisively as Natty Bumppo pushes aside the genteel lovers in *The Pioneers*. As Cap thumbs her nose at the outwitted villain, Southworth thumbs her own at the conventions of proper sentimental fiction.

The "game" belongs to the rhetoric of the novel's adventure plot. Those who use the word (with one exception), or about whom it is used, are rascally schemers: Major Warfield in his plots against Cap and his own enemies; Black Donald and his gang in their general lawlessness (see 38, 199, 221, 269). The exception, of course, is Capitola, whose cross-dressing behavior is complemented by her cross-traditional ver-nacular. Capitola is the novel's figure of "fair play" (320, 592) and fight-or-frolic sportiveness (326, 370, 387). Cap joins enthusiastically in the traditional sports of the plantation, fights a duel, rails against the un-manliness of males, and chafes at the constrictions placed on females. Cap wins contest after contest from would-be abductors, in scenes rhe-torically graced by the conventional language of masculine sport (see 262, 389, 475). In a late scene echoing the episode from Chapter XVI described earlier, Cap outwits Gabriel LeNoir and his son Craven, then gleefully proclaims what her strategem means:

> It means, your worships' excellencies, that-you-can't-come-it! it's no go! this chicken won't fight. It means the fat's in the fire, and the cat's out of the bag. It means confusion! distraction! perdition! and a tearing off of our wigs! It means the game's up, the plays [sic] over, villainy is about to be hanged, and virtue about to be rewarded, and the curtain is going to drop, and the principle performer – that's I – is going to be called out amid the applause of the audience. (389)

As she did earlier, Cap punctuates this triumph by thumbing her nose at the bewildered villains.

In *The Hidden Hand,* the melodramatic convention of elaborately and preposterously drawn out secret identities, whose unraveling reveals nearly every major lower-class character to be the lost wife or nephew of a wealthy landowner, creates a social world of extraordinary fluidity. Commoners are granted the opportunities normally reserved for the privileged, only to be revealed at last to belong rightfully to the privileged classes by birth as well as merit. In this world of social flux, the additional masking of sexual identity blurs the boundary of gender in such a way as virtually to deny separate men's and women's spheres. The narrative, on the level of disguise, plays with the possibilities of a classless, gender-free society, while on the level of "true" identity it asserts conventional distinctions. Within this ordered/chaotic environment, Capitola's mastery of the masculine "game" of power counters the female acquiescence fundamental to the sentimental love plot involving Clara Day and her courtly lover, Traverse Rocke. Cap's "game" becomes a major sign of gender mobility, Southworth's creation of a sportive heroine her declaration of female power and independence.

The conventional order seemingly prevails in the end, as Capitola marries her earnest lover, Herbert Greyson, is reunited with her mother, and claims her inherited estate. But Cap never undergoes the process of tempering and chastening that was central to the "woman's novel" as described by Nina Baym. Her final act in the novel, on the eve of her wedding, is to free Black Donald from prison, in order to prevent his hanging the next day. Donald has proven to be a noble outlaw of the type increasingly popular in blood-and-thunder writing. Donald's tribute to Cap's victory in "a fair contest" (592) is the true thematic climax of the novel – not the wedding that takes place the following day.

With two more voices, these from the turn of the century, I will conclude this discussion of women's varied uses of sporting rhetoric. Writing at a time when the "New Woman" was becoming a conspicuous and, to many, a disturbing challenge to traditional gender roles, Kate Chopin and Edith Wharton wrote novels about society's fatal indifference or antagonism to independent women's desires. In both Chopin's *The Awakening* (1899) and Wharton's *The House of Mirth* (1905), the rhetoric of games again serves as a marker of the masculine world – for Chopin, defined in terms of freedom and possibility; for Wharton, of sportive manipulation – from which women are excluded or by which women are crushed. The heroines in both novels die from complex causes, some of which are represented through the rhetoric of games.

In the early chapters of *The Awakening*, Edna Pointellier appears to the reader as doubly alienated. Not just a woman in a male-dominated world, Edna is an American, work-oriented Protestant in a distinctively Creole, play-oriented Catholic society. Unlike her husband Leonce, who has his socially approved outlets for both work and play, the office and the billiard room, Edna finds opportunities to work denied her and the play of the Creole leisure class pointless or oppressive. Inclined to seriousness by her upbringing, she is incapable of playing the conventional game of flirtation that amuses her Creole friends (and which a contemporary journalist described as "a game played on top of the table between evenly matched players" that "ends in a draw").[43] As an inveterate moralist Edna cannot play "on top of the table"; as a wife and mother she has too much at stake to be "evenly matched" in love with the barely post-adolescent Robert Lebrun; as a sensual yet unfulfilled woman she cannot be satisfied by a "draw." Unsuited for sanctioned Creole play, Edna is also denied any opportunity for meaningful work.

In two sporting motifs Chopin represented Edna's unconventional desires as neither simply for work nor simply for play. The first is gambling – betting on horses – a passion she picked up from her father, an arrogant Kentucky planter. At the racetrack where she, not her male companion, is the high-stakes gambler, Edna plays out her desire for risk and adventure that is denied outlets in her domestic life. What Patricia Meyer Spacks has written of Gwendolen Harleth in George Eliot's *Daniel Deronda* could be said of Edna Pontellier as well: "Gwendolen [Edna] gambles in the same spirit with money or with herself, her own highest stake."[44] Edna's second sport is swimming, not as the summering Creoles conceive it but as Hemingway would say a half-century later of Santiago's fishing in *The Old Man and the Sea*: "far out." Swimming for Edna is neither recreation nor immersion in the feminine element, but mastery of her body and its environment, an expression of her longing to experience the "masculine" *agôn* that wrestles with the world and achieves a sense of power despite its obstacles. "A feeling of exultation overtook her," the narrator says in describing Edna's initial success at swimming, "as if some power of significant import had been given her to control the working of her body and her soul. She grew daring and reckless, overestimating her strength. She wanted to swim far out, where no woman had swum before." Swimming "intoxicates" her; it *em*powers but also threatens to *over*power her. She swims *alone,* "reaching out for the unlimited in which to lose herself." But just a fledgling swimmer, Edna in this initial trial quickly reaches her limit and in "a flash of terror" envisions her death.[45]

This extraordinary scene prefigures the novel's conclusion, when Edna, completely blocked by conflicting desires that she cannot even formulate and a sense of duty to her children, does indeed swim too "far out" in an ambiguous act of suicide/liberation. The description this time is more sensuous than agonistic, her body naked, the sea enfolding her "in its soft, close embrace" (113). Edna also, in the novel's last lines, recalls the most charmed moment of her girlhood, seemingly a sign of futile romanticism. But the connotations of her swimming from the earlier scene complicate the impression of romantic surrender in this final one. Both defiance and exhaustion are evoked when the "old terror" of exceeding her limits "flamed up for an instant, then sank again" (114). Swimming remains a complex sign of both potential feminine ability in a masculine world and the frustration of that potential through the world's sexual politics.

In *The House of Mirth,* whose heroine confronts the world represented by sporting rhetoric wholly from the outside, Edith Wharton did not even acknowledge this potential. Wharton, in effect, reconsidered the world of Stowe's society novels with an emphasis on the relations of sex, economics, and power. One scene in particular can serve as our touchstone. Midway through the novel, Gus Trenor, the married head of one of New York's first families, suggests to Lily Bart that she owes him a little affection. A beautiful, socially ambitious woman without capital, Lily has earlier accepted Trenor's offer to speculate on Wall Street with her small savings. Now, having returned $9,000 to her, supposedly the profits from a series of ventures, Trenor expects a return on *his* investment. "A man's got his feelings," Trenor tells Lily, " – and you've played with mine too long. . . . by gad, that ain't playing fair: that's dodging the rules of the game. Of course I know now what you wanted – it wasn't my beautiful eyes you were after – but I tell you what, Miss Lily, you've got to pay up for making me think so." A moment later Trenor adds, "Oh, I'm not asking for payment in kind. But there's such a thing as fair play – and interest on one's money."[46]

The conjunction of sportive and economic language here adds a new dimension to the cultural conversation I have been examining. As a woman without independent means, Lily Bart, like Edna Pontellier but in different ways, is doubly disadvantaged for a game whose players define their positions by both class and gender. In the passage just cited, Gus Trenor appears to be yet another ruthless male of the Lovelace sort, appropriately recast in turn-of-the-century America as a wealthy Wall Street speculator. But Wharton's rendering of the "game" is much more subtle and complex than this stereotype would allow. Earlier, when Trenor responded to Lily's distress by offering his financial services, Lily had provoked his proposal with a little calculated flirtation, as "part of the game to make him feel that her appeal had been an uncalculated impulse" (136). Trenor's demand for "fair play" is in many ways a reasonable expectation of his due, yet Lily Bart is no more the stereotyped coquette than Trenor is the conventional rake. Although Lily willingly entered the game, only deluding herself that she would not have to play as well as he – or deluding herself about the nature of the stake – her decision to play was determined by factors over which she had little control. The only way Lily Bart can succeed, even survive, in the upper levels of the New York social set is by playing such "games." But lacking a fortune, the only way she can play is by risking her public respectability and private self-esteem.

This scene is prefigured by a literal rather than metaphorical game Lily plays earlier in the novel. The Trenors' circle plays bridge for high stakes; Lily cannot afford to play, but she cannot afford to dull her chances for social success by not playing. "In the Trenor set," Lily realizes, "if one played at all one must either play high or be set down as priggish or stingy" (41). Having started reluctantly, however, after a small taste of winning Lily develops a passion for the game and a gambler's recklessness for playing it, with the result that she accumulates debts she has no resources to pay. Having begun as an innocent victim, she becomes an accomplice in her own undoing. Yet before assigning guilt entirely to Lily now, it is necessary to return to the original conditions of the game. The Trenors and their kind play bridge for amusement; the monetary stakes are meaningful only as the markers of victory and defeat in the game. Lily plays out of desperation, for stakes that amount to either happiness or misery. In the later "game" with Gus Trenor the stakes have this same fundamental difference: for Gus, challenge and amusement; for Lily, her sense of self and standing in society, wagered against the material security only wealth can bring. Millionaire Gus Trenor can play a "game" of profits-for-favors with Lily as unconcernedly as he plays bridge for dollars a point. It turns out, in fact, that Gus did not speculate with Lily's money at all but simply gave her his own. For Lily Bart the stakes in both games are higher than she can afford to lose.

Of the five writers I have been considering, Wharton alone called attention to the material base of the real social arrangements masked by the rhetorical figure of the "game." Herself a product of the Gus Trenors' world, Wharton understood that "a society of irresponsible pleasure-seekers," as she called the characters in her novel, could live in a house of mirth only if they could pay the rent.[47] A sporting event recalled in Wharton's autobiography resonates interestingly with the metaphor of the "game" in the novel. At "picturesque archery club meetings" a young Edith had watched "lovely archeresses in floating silks or muslins, with their wide leghorn hats, and heavy veils flung back only at the moment of aiming." The veils, clearly, were a hindrance to the sportswomen – their wearers "could hardly see or breathe" – but they were essential to maintaining the "shell-like transparence" of perfect complexions, more important attributes than the mere winning of games.[48] To the young girl the fair "archeresses" seemed fairytale goddesses; seeing them heightened her youthful desire to tell romantic stories. To a reader of *The House of Mirth,* on the other hand, the sport of these privileged women seems less a contest of marksmanship than a display of goods for the marriage marketplace. Veils help win husbands, not archery contests. As we saw in considering America's distinctive understanding of "fair play," winning is important only if you have not already won by virtue of class or wealth.

In the terms of Wharton's remembered archery contest, Lily Bart has both to win the match and to preserve her moral complexion; but it is impossible to do both. In a later Wharton novel, *The Custom of the Country* (1913), Undine Spragg indeed wins the "game" that Lily Bart is also forced to play, but Undine sacrifices her "complexion" entirely, becoming monstrous in her success.[49] Wharton took the title of her earlier book from Ecclesiastes – "the heart of fools is in the house of mirth" – which elsewhere declares that the race is *not* to the swift. Lily Bart is destroyed as a loser in the "game"; Undine Spragg is differently destroyed by winning it. In both novels sporting and economic language converge: In her "game" to win a husband Lily must wager the "assets" of her physical beauty and irreproachable reputation. In an early attempt to snare Percy Gryce, an exceedingly dull man with an exceedingly attractive income of $800,000 per year, Lily thinks of Gryce as a catch to be "landed," a "reward" or "victory" to be won; while everyone in the Trenor set "play[s] fair" in not obstructing her chances (75, 53, 119). Lily loses Gryce because, finally, she cannot bear the thought of winning him.

As her later efforts become increasingly desperate, Wharton never lets Lily become a mere victim. Rather, as in the bridge game, Lily is always a willing/unwilling player. In staking herself, she can find pleasure in contemplating her worth; but her moral growth is signaled when she realizes at last that she is worth too much to be staked so cheaply. Having resolved finally not to play any longer, however, Lily discovers that she is unfitted for living outside the world of the sportive rich. "It was easy to despise the world," the narrator says of her, "but decidedly difficult to find any other habitable region" (421). In an ironic accolade to her resolve, a *nouveau-riche* admirer calls her "a dead game sport" (413), the term from dime novels for a reckless adventurer willing to risk all on a card, unmoved by the results. To praise Lily in the same abstract language of competition that masks the very social and economic forces that destroy her only accentuates her tragedy.

Money and its attendant power are palpable realities in *The House of Mirth,* the "game" an abstraction that denies its material grounding. The "game," that is, becomes a sign of the *void* at the center of ambition and desire. Those who render their aspirations in terms of a game reveal the nothingness for which they strive. The rich make the rules; they are "that portion of society which, while contributing least to its amusement, has assumed the right to decide what forms that amusement shall take" (209). Having tried to play their games, Lily comes to feel "herself of no more account among them than an expensive toy in the hands of a spoiled child" (389). Her final act, before taking poison, is to redeem her spiritual worth by paying her material debt to Gus Trenor – not a move in the game but a final renunciation of it. At the end of the novel, while Lily is indeed dead, she is neither "game" nor a "sport."

Although it is impossible to generalize on the basis of a few texts, the darker vision in the novels of Chopin and Wharton, compared to those of Stowe, Alcott, and Southworth in the previous generation, confirm historians' view that gender conflict deepened as the nineteenth century gave way to the twentieth. But against that overview of gender relations, women writers' "conversation" with masculine sporting rhetoric can also remind us of the messy details that generalizations to some degree always repress.

Nineteenth-century American women's responses to the "game" could have been motivated by numerous factors besides the writers' gender. The five writers I have singled out were all white and, except for Wharton, middle-class, but their intimate experiences with men and economic relations with society varied considerably. Stowe had powerful male figures in her life, chiefly in her father and famous brother, and had a troubled relationship with her own husband, whose sexual needs disturbed and taxed her. Stowe, Alcott, and Southworth supported themselves and their families through their professional writing – Stowe, because her husband earned too little as a minister; Alcott, who never married, because her "genius" father was incapable of bearing the economic burden; Southworth, because her husband deserted her under mysterious circumstances. Chopin was early a widow; Wharton shed a husband after years of a bad marriage. In short, the five writers lived in varying relations to men and the marketplace; as a marker of such relations and of that world, the "game" should be expected to suggest some of that variety. The collision of domestic and sporting rhetoric, and the various constructions of this sporting language, reveal several ways in which nineteenth-century American women could come to terms with their place in a deeply gendered society.

Henry James and the sexual contest

Having begun this chapter by insisting there are no absolute and separate male and female versions of the "game," I will conclude by inserting male writers into the discussion of love games, in order to reinforce that basic point. Owen Wister spoke for many male writers in placing women outside the world of the "games" that test men in the public arena but assigning them a full role in this sentimental "game." In relation to the rugged games that men have to play, women sometimes represent obstacles, as Molly does in *The Virginian;* they sometimes offer relief to game-wearied males; and they sometimes are incidental victims of men's competitive obsessions in their professional lives (this last possibility appears frequently in the business novels to be discussed in Part II). In relation to the love games, women are sometimes victimizers, sometimes victims; but in both cases game playing inhibits the possibilities of genuine love. In *The Virginian,* Wister sided with the man against the woman who plays her little games. In *Blix* (1899), Frank Norris took the woman's side; the heroine tells the man that his protestations of love are only "part of the game" that she could play too, "but it's playing with something that's quite too serious to be played with." In *A Hazard of New Fortunes* (1890), William Dean Howells described both insincere lovers as players of a deceitful "game." In *Sister Carrie* (1900), Theodore Dreiser also assigned blame evenly, as well as more broadly: Personal relationships in that novel are uniformly contests for power in which one or the other partner is dominant at any given moment, and in which "romantic" love is not even conceivable. In *The Bostonians,* as we saw earlier, James developed this same theme more obliquely, while numerous other male writers worked with these various possibilities.[50] (In a pair of classic cases from the next generation, Fitzgerald's Amory Blaine in *This Side of Paradise* is the victim of a game-playing flapper, while Hemingway's Frederic Henry of *A Farewell to Arms* is the player of trivializing love games at the expense of Catherine Barkley.) Despite these differences, all of these writers agreed on one thing: that love should be no game.

The game of love, then, although I present it here chiefly as the "feminine" counterpart to the masculine sporting myths, tied to a domestic drama rather than to outdoor adventures, has not been the exclusive concern of women. The major male writer to explore the game of love, of course, was Henry James, the great exception in every literary history that defines the American mainstream in terms of solitary males and violent adventure. James more accurately represents his generation as the "great feminine novelist of a feminine age of letters," in F. W. Dupee's words.[51] James was the chief writer within that entire school of late nineteenth-century "sissies," to use Alfred Habegger's term,[52] who rejected the competitive worlds of business and politics, and against whom in turn the masculinists at the turn of the century rebelled. James wrote approvingly, if briefly, of masculine game playing in *The American* (1877), where he portrayed Christopher Newman as a man for whom "life had been . . . an open game" in which "he had played for high stakes."[53] And in *The Portrait of a Lady* (1881), Caspar Goodwood reveals a similar manly sense of fair play, developed, one would assume, in managing his cotton mills in America. But these were early novels, and such characters disappear from the later ones. James more consistently wrote about sexual games, the "games" of Alcott and Wharton rather than Harte and Wister – games in which innocent women are bartered and sold as mere coinage in a grotesque marketplace.[54] Like Wharton in particular among the women writers, James placed power, not passion, at the center of the game of love, and viewed it from the perspective of the powerless.

There is no major Jamesian sporting text; rather, his fiction as a body of writing reveals several common themes and patterns. At the center of several novels is a contest to determine the fate of a sensitive female. Sometimes this game involves competition to possess the woman: not just Basil Ransom versus Olive Chancellor for Verena Tarrant in *The Bostonians,* but also Christopher Newman versus the Bellegardes for Claire de Cintré in *The American,* Morris Townsend versus Dr. Sloper for Catherine in *Washington Square* (1880). Sometimes the contest is a conspiracy to marry the victim to one of the conspirators: Madame Merle and Gilbert Osmond engineering Osmond's marriage to Isabel Archer in *The Portrait of a Lady,* Kate Croy and Merton Densher plotting a similar future for Milly Theale in *The Wings of the Dove* (1902). And sometimes – as in "The Aspern Papers" (1888), *What Maisie Knew* (1897), *The Spoils of Poynton* (1897), *The Awkward Age* (1899), and *The Golden Bowl* (1904) – a young woman's happiness is at stake in a more general and elaborate scheme of moves and countermoves among a variety of characters. In every case, James portrayed these situations explicitly as "games" of power masquerading as something more benign.

James differed from the women writers in most often portraying his female characters as stake or plaything, rather than active, if unwilling, contestant in the game. One exception, Eugenia in *The Europeans* (1878), unsuccessfully plays a "deep game" to secure a husband;[55] another, Fleda Vetch of *The Spoils of Poynton,* is drawn into a "double game" which she can win only by losing what would most make her happy: marriage to Owen Gareth.[56] But Claire de Cintré, Catherine Sloper, Isabel Archer, Verena Tarrant, Tina Bordereau, Maisie Farange, Nanda Brookenham, Madame de Vionnet, and Milly Theale are remarkable for their non-participation in the games that place what is most important in their lives at stake. *Washington Square* offers the most straightforward contest between male antagonists with a passive woman as the "prize." Catherine Sloper, in fact, openly accepts this role, only to discover that her father's money is the real stake in Morris Townsend's eyes; while Dr. Sloper has played only out of arrogance, and her Aunt Penniman has assisted Morris for her own selfish pleasure. Catherine is the prize no one particularly cares to win. Maisie Farange plays a similar role in *What Maisie Knew,* in which she serves merely as "football" or "the little feathered shuttle-cock" in a vicious game played by her divorced parents and their new mates.[57]

In these two novels, the sexual antagonism is most blatant, the games men and women play most obviously destructive. It is important to note that while females are always the victims, males are not exclusively the victimizers in the Jamesian world. Mrs. Penniman's culpability is nearly as great as Morris Townsend's or Dr. Sloper's, her motives, if anything, less defensible because more foolish. In *What Maisie Knew,* men and women are equally vicious, while Sir Claude alone elicits some sympathy for his role. In "The Aspern Papers," a young man and an old woman play a "game" for control of some valuable papers, while a young woman's happiness hangs in the balance.[58] In *The American,* Christopher Newman plays fairly in his contest for a wife, while the old marquise, Madame de Bellegarde, violates their agreed-upon rules.

A psychoanalytic reading of James's fiction would emphasize not the criticism of gender arrangements but the author's apparent revulsion directed at sexuality itself. Unlike the popular genteel writers who simply removed sex from their portraits of human experience, James, however discreetly, acknowledged the full powers of eroticism. But he seems to have recoiled from them. The "secret" to be discovered in many of James's novels is a sexual act: "sex seen as something low, furtive, and manipulative."[59] Thus, in *The Portrait of Lady,* Isabel fully realizes her own plight only when she comes to understand the full intimacy of Osmond and Madame Merle; in *What Maisie Knew,* the chief question throughout the novel is always, what, if anything, Maisie comes to understand about her various parents' sexual entanglements; in *The Ambassadors,* Lambert Strether must discover the intimate nature of Chad Newsome's relationship to Madame de Vionnet; in *The Wings of the Dove* and *The Golden Bowl,* it is Milly's knowledge of Kate and Densher, and Maggie's of Amerigo and Charlotte, that provide the narrative and moral climaxes.

But these novels can reveal more than their author's sexual squeamishness. From a political or sociological perspective rather than a psychoanalytic one, James probed the power arrangements underlying sexuality with unblinking clear-sightedness. In all these novels, the "games" of the sexually initiated are meant to deceive and subjugate innocent victims. When Osmond accuses Isabel of having "played a very deep game" by blocking his plan to marry Pansy to Lord Warburton, he only calls attention to his own mode of sexual manipulation. In *The Ambassadors,* when Strether asks himself, "What game under the sun is [Chad] playing?" he begins to discover not just the young man's relationship to the French woman but whether Chad has merely used her. In *The Wings of the Dove*, Kate's and Densher's first "game" is to deceive Aunt Maud into thinking they have given up any hope of marriage; their second, determined early by Kate and understood only much later by Densher, is to marry Densher to Milly Theale for the fortune that will come to him on her early death.[60] James seemingly recoiled from sexual passion, but he also understood that sexuality in the economic and political world is a form of power.

Such games of power disguised as eroticism predominate in a ludic world of exceptional diversity.[61] In the late novels particularly, the "game" comes to represent not just sexual intrigue but three more general things: the variety of interactions among the characters, the process of seeing or understanding by which the characters come to know, and the art of fiction itself. In his preface to *The Awkward Age*, James called his method of constructing the story "my game," and described having "all the pieces of the game on the table together" in a particular scene – implying both the relations of the characters and the relations of the pieces of the narration. In the prefaces to *The Wings of the Dove* and *The Golden Bowl*, he similarly mentioned "my game . . . of driving portents home" and "the entertainment of the great game" in which the characters are engaged – this latter reference also emphasizing his detachment from their situation.[62] These different purposes complement each other as various forms of indirection. Throughout James's fiction, characters play a variety of exploitative and manipulative "games." But the image of an intricate game also expresses James's view of social relations themselves as subtle moves and countermoves, nuances of inflection and posture, "manners" as Lionel Trilling defined them in his famous essay. And finally, the characters' revealing themselves to each other through hints and evasions mirrors James's own aesthetic game with his readers, a game of subtle signals and obliquities rather than straightforward revelation. For James, art and reality were both most interesting when revealed, as Emily Dickinson would say, "at a slant."

To see all of these strategies at work in one scene, we can consider the climactic chapter of *The Golden Bowl*, in which Maggie decides on a course of action while watching the others play bridge. The symmetrical square of natural and unnatural relationships developed in the novel – Maggie and Amerigo, Charlotte and Adam Verver on the one hand; Maggie and her father, Charlotte and Amerigo on the other – is like a multilayered game of chess governed by elaborate rules. Fanny Assingham's "favourite game" is the manipulation of these pieces (her husband accuses her at one point of acting "as if you were playing some game with its rules drawn up").[63] But the more important game, for Maggie, involves discovering the truth about Charlotte and Amerigo; and, for

the reader, of discovering with Maggie the subtle clues to that relationship. Through pointed game images, James portrayed Maggie as an
uneasy player. In her first uncertain awareness of infidelity earlier in the
novel, Maggie realizes she cannot express her jealousy to her father
without a reason. But Maggie has no reason, and she fears to disrupt the
game in any case:

> There was a card she could play, but there was only one, and to play
> it would be to end the game. She felt herself – as at the small green
> table, between the tall old candlesticks and the neatly arranged counters
> – her father's playmate and partner; and what it consistently came back
> to, in her mind, was that for her to ask a question, to raise a doubt, to
> reflect in any degree on the play of the others, would be to break the
> charm. The charm she had to call it, since it kept her companion so
> constantly engaged, so perpetually seated and so contentedly occupied.
> To say anything at all would be, in fine, to say *why* she was jealous;
> and she could, in her private hours, but stare long, with suffused eyes,
> at that impossibility. (XXIV, 34).

Maggie decides to withhold her "hideous card" (XXIV, 107), until
the revelation of Amerigo and Charlotte's intimacy explodes the charm
of their little *ménage à quatre*. Now, in the remarkable scene of the bridge
game, Maggie decides to withhold her card permanently, stepping outside the game so that her father can retain the illusion that it continues.
In the most extended game image in James's fiction, echoing Middleton
and Pope most noticeably, Verver and Fanny play partners at bridge
against Charlotte and the Prince, while Maggie observes from a distance,
meditating on the tableau before her. Though inept at cards, Maggie in
watching the foursome feels herself "holding them in her hand." As she
realizes that "she might sound out their doom in a single sentence,"
Maggie instead smiles gently on each player, then signals her renunciation
by moving out to the terrace. Sensing a mute appeal from the others to
preserve the illusion that all is well, Maggie forgoes "the straight vin-
dictive view, the rights of resentment, the rages of jealousy, the protests
of passion"; sealing her decision, after Charlotte has joined her on the
terrace, with a dramatic embrace and kiss under the searching eyes of
the other three players (XXIV, 232–51).

Here is all of James in miniature: the elaborate formal game, the victim
discovering the truth then renouncing the game, all executed for the
attentive reader by carefully orchestrated indirection. In this late novel,
James also created in Maggie Verver his most ironically triumphant victim. Several innocents in the earlier books – Catherine Sloper, Isabel
Archer, Maisie Farange, Milly Theale – triumph by not playing the
corrupt game of wayward passion. In *The Golden Bowl* more ironically,
Maggie's renunciation of the game becomes her most brilliant move in

it, making herself master of the now pitiable Charlotte and the cringing Amerigo, at the personal cost only of her father's companionship as he returns to America with Charlotte as his wife. Maggie seems slightly monstrous here: her moral superiority not entirely deserved, Charlotte and Amerigo's passion for each other much more honest than her own for her father. Both Maggie and Charlotte play the evasive "games" forced on women by a society that grants their gender no power. But like Kate Densher in *The Wings of the Dove,* Charlotte achieves dignity as a kind of desperate player, dependent on bravado, or "bluff," because she lacks the wealth that others can assume. Maggie simply retreats behind the power of her class. To picture Maggie and Amerigo together in the coming years brings no pleasure; Verver and Charlotte, little more. What price victory? the reader wonders. Whereas Milly Theale in *The Wings of the Dove* more simply triumphs over her victimizers by submitting to their game, in *The Golden Bowl* "feminine" power defeats passion. But renunciation or inhuman conquest make grim alternatives. In this late novel, the premier "sissy" writer penetrated most shrewdly to the hard nut of power at the center of sexual relations. By assigning Maggie and Charlotte to their respective fates James offered a subtle and penetrating critique of a society ruled by social class and rigid gender roles. And whether as feminist or sissy, James gave his primary sympathies, in his last novels as well as his first, to the innocent rather than the sexually knowledgeable, to the victims rather than the initiators of the "game."

In his extensive, highly self-conscious use of sporting rhetoric, James appears not to have been the great exception among American novelists after all. The protean figure of the "game" at the turn of the century attracted James as well as Owen Wister, Edith Wharton as well as Richard Harding Davis. In all its variations this "game" was concerned with the nature of power, both the desire to attain it and the consequences of having or not having it. Sporting myths and love games simply addressed a fundamental issue in different ways: the hard facts of power in the public and private realms.

Concerned with power, the ubiquitous "game" of popular rhetoric was necessarily, and deeply, gender-marked. Men and women bore different relations both to the actual sports and games that were becoming an American obsession by the end of the century, and to the historical processes and social actions for which these contests provided ideologically charged metaphors. But tracing the figure of the "game" also reveals in highly concrete ways the complexity of gender relations and of the relations of gender to class and power. Against the gross differences in the ways male and female writers used sporting rhetoric appear the many subtler gradations of similarity and difference. It is essential to note the kinship of Washington Irving and Frances Fuller Victor, of John Esten Cooke and Mary Johnston, of Edith Wharton and Henry James. It is equally essential to note the general tendency of women writers to subvert, transform, or simply ignore both the popular icons of masculine sporting prowess and their metaphorical representations. The "game" was "masculine" in nineteenth-century American culture, but as a cultural construct "masculinity" itself was neither the exclusive property nor the inevitable birthright of men. For the historian of gender, then, the "game" can serve most usefully not to establish boundaries between male and female literary or social traditions, but to mark a site of conflict where "masculinity" and "femininity" meet in a variety of revealing ways.

Part II

Raising the Stakes

Know ye not that they which run in a race run all, but one receiveth the prize? So run, that ye may obtain.

I Corinthians 9: 24

Life for him had been an open game, and he had played for high stakes.

Henry James, *The American* (1877)

And there was one that wrestled with him until daybreak who, seeing that he could not master him, struck him in the socket of his hip, and Jacob's hip was dislocated as he wrestled with him. He said, "Let me go, for day is breaking." But Jacob answered, "I will not let you go unless you bless me." . . . And he blessed him there.

Genesis 32: 26–30

Talk not to me of blasphemy, man, I'd strike the sun if it insulted me. For could the sun do that, then I could do the other; since there is ever a sort of fair play therein.

Herman Melville, *Moby-Dick* (1851)

My survey of "the game" in nineteenth-century American culture is not yet complete. Midway through *The Virginian* the stakes are suddenly raised when the hero refers in passing to a God who "plays a square game with us if he plays at all." Wister left the point barely implicit but nonetheless clear: The cowboy's contests win him not just status in a frontier community but the benediction of an approving Providence.

151

Wister's novel embodied a motif that had been developing since frontier fiction was first written: Natty Bumppo's ritualistic sporting behavior signifies a sort of natural holiness; the hunter of Southwestern humor – McNutt's Chunky, say – stalks not just a wild animal but a Great Spirit, with something transcendent implicitly at stake (roughly, man's relationship with nature itself); Bret Harte's frontier gambler plays one game against his opponent, another against Fate or Chance, gambling not just for a few dollars but for his place in the cosmos as well.

"The game," in other words, sometimes had a theological dimension, suggesting a contest in life not for mere survival or power but for "salvation" in its many guises. In the sporting myths discussed in Part I that dimension, when present, was only implicit, a metaphysical extension of the more earthly contest. But there has been another strain in American culture, rooted not in frontier contest and Southern honor but in Protestant theology. Nineteenth-century religious liberalism, with its emphasis on human free agency, repeatedly found expression in an image of "the game of life," drawing on a long rhetorical tradition going back to St. Paul that cast Christian striving as a "race" or "contest" against temptation, with immortal life the "prize" for victors. Religious conservatism, on the other hand, always less receptive to the ascendance of play and sport in the nation's life, nonetheless found occasional expression in very different sporting motifs. Conservative insistence on God's absolute sovereignty lay behind an image of humanity as the "sport of God" (or in its secular forms, "sport of the gods," "sport of fate," and "sport of chance"). In contrast, resistance to this forbidding deity led to literary portrayals of life as a *desperate* game in which salvation was not to be earned but wrested from God, the all-powerful Opponent. Lying behind both liberal and conservative images were the age-old questions of fate, chance, and will in human life. The "game of life" implied all will, the "sport of the gods" all fate; the desperate "game" placed fate and will in opposition. The "sport of chance," finally, envisioned the will subject not to powerful forces but to random events. At stake, then, in each case was a fundamental understanding of human existence, in language that also reflected the culture's growing acknowledgement of play's place in human life. And each of these rhetorical figures bridged religious and secular ideas, accommodating religious tradition to an increasingly secularized world. The Puritans' dual calling – duty to God and duty in the world – collapsed in the nineteenth-century success ethic into a materialistic view of "salvation." When the "sport of God" became the "sport of chance" in naturalistic fiction, conservative theology met contemporary secular pessimism in a way that confirmed human helplessness but without a compensating belief in Providential design. The patterns of sporting rhetoric in nineteenth-century fiction and popular success literature thus provide a particularly concrete record of middle-class Americans' conflicting responses to the radical transformation of their most fundamental sense of the human condition.

As a simile in a religious context, the "game of life" in various forms had its roots in St. Paul's letters, in four primary texts. Paul wrote to the Philippians of "press[ing] toward the mark, for the prize of the high calling of God in Christ Jesus" (Phil. 3: 14); to the Corinthians of running a race "that ye may obtain [the prize]" (I Cor. 9: 24); to the Ephesians of "wrestl[ing] not against flesh and blood, but against principalities, against powers, against the rulers of the darkness of the world" (Eph. 6: 12); to Timothy of having "fought a good fight" and "finished my course," for which a crown of righteousness awaited him in heaven (II Tim. 4: 7–8). These four passages provided texts for Christian sermons and treatises for centuries before the Puritans settled in Massachusetts Bay. The notion of life as a contest against the powers of darkness would seem to suggest the importance of the human will in spiritual struggle, but for the Puritans this was dangerous territory where heresy lurked. St. Augustine, together with Paul a major influence on Puritan theology, cited I Cor. 9: 24, in fact, to caution Christians against false confidence in their own powers to win salvation. "We must both will and run," he acknowledged. "But it is not of him that willeth, nor of him that runneth, but of God that hath mercy, that we obtain what we wish and reach what we desire." God alone could give mankind both the power to will and the object willed. Other teachers, from Origen and Nemesius of Emesa in the third and fourth centuries to Bernard of Clairvaux in the twelfth and Martin Luther in the sixteenth, cited the same Pauline passages in sermons and treatises on the Christian life. For the later Puritans, Augustine's cautionary interpretation defined the orthodox position.[1]

The conservative sporting metaphors can be traced to different sources. The secular version reaches back to Greek and Roman antiquity, where Fate and Chance were embedded in deities: Moira and Tyche for the Greeks, Fata and Fortuna for the Romans. The workings of chance were typically imagined as the roll of dice or the turning of Fortune's wheel by a carelessly sportive goddess. In Book X of Plato's *Republic,* Socrates speaks of a man's duty to order his affairs as rationally as possible, once "the dice have been thrown." In Boethius's *Consolation of Philosophy* from the sixth century, the capricious goddess tells the philosopher, "Here is the source of my power, the game I always play: I spin my wheel and find pleasure in raising the low to a high place and lowering those who are on top. Go up, if you like, but only on the condition that you will not feel abused when my sport requires your fall."[2] These images appear regularly in medieval literature, where Fortune plays her games with human beings: dice in Chaucer's "Knight's Tale" and "Monk's Tale,"

chess in his *Book of the Duchess,* shuttlecock in the *Roman de la Rose,*
bowls in a poem by Deschamps – in which the mortal players "either
win or lose according to their fortune." Shakespeare invoked the same
deity in *King Lear,* when he had the blinded Gloucester cry out to Edgar,
"As flies to wanton boys are we to th' gods; / They kill us for their
sport."[3]

The Christian version of this trope – human destiny as if governed by
the roll of dice – derives ultimately from the doctrine of the lot. In the
Old Testament, the Promised Land was divided among the twelve tribes
by lot, priests and kings were chosen by lot, Moses selected among
proferred goats for sacrifice by lot. In the New Testament, the eleven
remaining Apostles chose Matthias as Judas's replacement by lot.[4] In a
world governed in even the smallest detail by all-powerful, all-knowing
gods or God, casting lots simply left the decision to the deity. Consequently, to consult God for frivolous reasons was blasphemous, but in
crucial matters of polity or religion this course most honored God's
wisdom. Belief in the efficacy of the lot implied no acknowledgment of
chance but its opposite: God's providential control of human affairs. This
theological dogma in fact, more than moral and social concern, lay behind
the conservative Protestant abhorrence of gambling ("gaming") well into
the nineteenth century. As John Cotton wrote in 1656 about cards and
dice, "We may not make a pastime of them, if they bee lots, it is an
ordinance of God, and therefore not to bee made a pastime of." Contrary
to the claims of the more worldly that "there are some religious lots,
some indifferent" (and therefore suitable for amusement), Cotton responded simply, "I say all lots are religious. In all kinds of lottery,
whatsoever it bee about, wee appeal to God, who is disposer of all
things." To gamble, in other words, would make a pastime of sin, would
"play with the Judgements of God."[5] In a series of sermons and tracts
over the next two hundred years, John Cotton's position was reaffirmed
by Increase Mather later in the seventeenth century, by Cotton Mather
in the eighteenth, by Eli Hyde early in the nineteenth, by John Richards
as late as 1852. In all of these cases, gambling, or *"Lusory* Lots" in the
elder Mather's term, was forbidden not just as vice but as blasphemy.
God controlled the dice that governed human fates and was not to be
invoked for frivolous purposes.[6]

The Christian version of fate – God's sovereignty, man's helplessness
– appeared in other ludic metaphors. The contest between the forces of
darkness and light with man's soul at stake was likened in Renaissance
emblems, for example, to a tennis match between God and Satan.[7] Christian and pagan concepts of divine sovereignty and fate, Providence and
chance, coexisted through the Middle Ages, leaving a rich legacy of
conventional tropes to later centuries. But there was also another Chris-

Hen we obferve the *Ball*, how to and fro
The *Gamefters* force-it ; we may ponder thus :
That whil'ft we live we fhall be playd with fo,
And that the *World* will make her *Game* of us.
Adverfities, one while our hearts conftraine
To ftoope, and knock the Pavements of *Defpaire* ;
Hope, like a Whirle-wind mounts us up againe,
Till oft it lofe us in the empty ayre.
Sometimes, above the *Battlements* we looke ;
Sometimes, we quite below the *Line* are toft :
Another-while, againft the *Hazard* ftrooke,
We, but a little want, of being loft.
　　Detraction, *Envie*, *Mifchief*, and *Defpight*,
One Partie make, and watchfully attend
To catch us when we rife to any *Height* ;
Left we above their hatred fhould afcend.
Good-Fortune, *Praifes*, *Hopes*, and *Induftries*,
Doe fide-together, and make *Play* to pleafe us ;
But, when by them we thinke more high to rife,
More great they make our *Fall*, and more difeafe us.
Yea, they that feeke our *Loffe*, advance our *Gaine* ;
And to our *Wifhes*, bring us oft the nigher :
For, we that elfe upon the Ground had laine,
Are, by their ftriking of us lifted higher.
When *Balls* againft the Stones are hardeft throwne,
Then higheft up into the Aire they fly ;
So, when men hurle us (with moft fury) downe,
Wee hopefull are to be advanc'd thereby :
　　And, when they fmite us quite unto the Ground,
　　Then, up to Heav'n, we truft, we fhall rebound.

A Renaissance emblem by George Wither (1635), with man as the tennis ball, played with by the world. (Courtesy, The Newberry Library) tian rhetorical convention, beginning with that enigmatic story from Genesis in which Jacob wrestles with God and wins a blessing from him, that toyed with the idea that mortal man could pit his puny strength against an omnipotent God and somehow win. "This passage is regarded by all as among the most obscure passages of the whole Old Testament," Martin Luther wrote in his commentary on this text. "That is a horrible battle," Luther observed, "when God Himself fights and in a horrible fashion opposes His opponent as though on the point of taking away life." Worse, Jacob's opposing God and winning might seem to have questioned God's sovereign power and man's submission to His will. Luther addressed these problems by emphasizing that the contest was a *game.* "God at times is accustomed to play with His saints," he explained. Through this play – this "excellent and very salutary exercise" – God disciplined the saints, tempting them to despair so as to strengthen their faith, but without tempting them beyond their endurance. Jacob "was completely unequal to this great struggle and yet remained unconquered."[8]

For the American Puritans, Jacob's wrestling served as a figure for·the power of prayer in its most agonistic form. Samuel Mather, in one of the Puritans' basic texts on biblical typology, identified Jacob as a type of Christ *"in regard to his wrestling and prevailing with the Lord,"* and this "wrestling" was a commonplace in Puritan writing.[9] Thomas Shepard described in his autobiography "the spirit of God wrastling with me"; John Williams, a minister held captive by Indians for two-and-a-half years, invoked the biblical story of Jacob's wrestling as analogous to his own situation.[10] That gloomiest of Puritans, Michael Wigglesworth, seems to have been particularly attracted to the figure of Jacob the wrestler. Wigglesworth's diary records three different incidents of "wrestl[ing] with the Lord" in prayer for himself or his pupils at Harvard.[11] Increase Mather described in his autobiography an experience of wrestling with God that is worth quoting in full. In April 1689, Mather had been in England for some time, pleading the colony's case before the new king, when he wrote in his diary:

> This day God helped me to wrestle with him in prayer. The blessing which I especially begged for, was, That I might return to New England with good Tidings. I sayed before the Lord with Tears and great meltings of soul, That I would not let him go, nor rise from my knees except Hee would grant me that blessing. And I was perswaded and did firmly believe that it would be so. I promised God that I would be his servant, and endeavor to live an holy life to his glory all my dayes; and that when Hee should bring me again to New England I would endeavor that all his people throughout that land should joyn together in offering solemn prayses to his glorious Name for his goodness in restoring them to former mercyes and enjoyments.

Throughout his autobiography Mather frequently bargains with God in this manner, praying with a conditional "if You do this, I'll do that." In one sense, he simply called on God to honor His covenant, but he also pushed the covenant closer to an agonistic contest, the invocation of Jacob's wrestling in the quoted passage making this tendency most clear.[12]

Artillery election sermons, in their typical characterization of the Christian life as a spiritual contest, gave this motif its most conspicuous rhetorical expression during the colonial period, but in conjunction with the liberal version as well, the Pauline metaphors of life as a race for God's prizes. Rather than assigning these different tropes to separate literary and cultural traditions, in fact, it is important to recognize them as two sides of the Puritan *agôn*. The dominant image of the spiritual contest in these sermons was the one Christians waged against Satan and sin, and this contest could be described in terms suggesting either *battle* or *sport*. The distinction between the two was not so clear as in a later world when athletic games had become prominent. Beginning with the earliest published artillery sermons – Urian Oakes' *The Unconquerable, All-Conquering & More-Than-Conquering Souldier* and Joshua Moodey's *Souldiery Spiritualized*, both printed in 1674 – the primary motif is the martial metaphor: Christians as soldiers in God's army, engaged in unceasing spiritual warfare against Satan. But the sportive language of Eph. 6: 11–12, 2 Tim. 4: 7–8, and 1 Cor. 9: 24 occasionally became entangled with the martial imagery, suggesting different but overlapping versions of the spiritual contest. When Oakes preached that the true believer "runs and Wrestles, and . . . strives, *and fights the good fight of Faith*," and when Moodey declared that sin "must be fought by those that will *run the Race set Before them*, who must therefore *Fight* as well as *Run*," the martial and the sportive language became nearly indistinguishable ways of describing the Church militant. The same mixing of images appears in Joseph Belcher's *The Worst Enemy Conquered* (1698) and Samuel Danforth's *The Duty of Believers* (1708), while the martial analogy alone prevailed in others – for example, Samuel Nowell's *Abraham in Arms* (1678), Cotton Mather's *Military Duties* (1687), Peter Thatcher's *The Saints' Victory* (1696), Samuel Willard's *The Man of War* (1699), and Grindal Rawdon's *Miles Christianus* (1703).[13]

At the same time, some of these sermons mixed in references to wrestling with God as well as with Satan. In *Souldiery Spiritualized* and *The Duty of Believers*, Moodey and Danforth wrote of this sort of wrestling as if it were a commonplace among their listeners. "Those must *Fight* as well as *pray, wrestle in prayer, pray and wrestle*," Moodey urged, "and that not with God only (as *Gen.32.24*) but with Satan too, *Eph.6.12*." The "not . . . only" takes a Christian's wrestling with God for granted. In similar spirit, Danforth in *The Duty of Believers* wrote of the saints that "*by the Prayer of Faith, they wrestle with God day and night, that the growing Vices of the times may be reformed,*" and in another sermon urged his listeners to "wrestle with God in prayer; [to] take no denial at his hand."[14]

The Pauline contest was more pervasive, however. As the artillery sermons continued up to the Revolution, Enlightenment rationalism and topical concerns about French papists and colonial independence increasingly replaced the older theme of Christian soldiery. But spiritual warfare remained a casual motif at midcentury in many sermons. And Nathaniel Walter's sermon *The Character of a Christian Hero* (1746) offers a particularly revealing perspective on the mingling of sportive with martial language. Although the earlier writers did not clearly distinguish sport from warfare, Walter portrayed St. Paul as the model of the Christian hero in three distinct roles: soldier, racer, and steward. In the writings of Protestant liberals over the next two centuries, soldiery increasingly gave way to athletic contest as the proper metaphor for Christian endeavor – a more appealing image for liberal Christians in an age when organized sport began to assume an important place in American life. Walter's sermon thus suggests an intermediate stage in the evolution of the metaphor.[15]

Nineteenth-century metaphors of life as a game with salvation at stake had varied roots and took varied forms, then, as Protestant theology adapted to changing times. The "game" or "race" of life came to express the liberal faith that men and women were the agents of their own salvation. But in an increasingly secular world, and one in which liberal Protestantism aligned itself with the emerging business classes, the matter of "salvation" itself became blurred. The distinction between spiritual and earthly striving all but disappeared, with the game of life becoming, as Wister's Virginian put it, whatever a man did in the world of men. The object of his game, whether wealth or power or the traditional Christian afterlife, became the player's own version of salvation. "The game" in this context preserved the forms and deep structure of Puritan theology while radically transforming its content and values. In the game, church met marketplace on equal terms; players of the game pursued salvation in ways both obviously different from and strangely similar to those of their Puritan forebears.

The "sport of God" (or of the gods, of chance, of fate) through similar transformations came to represent the tenacious conservative insistence on man's weakness in a world governed by inexorable forces, even as that world became wholly secularized and Chance replaced Providence as the ruling principle. And whereas the liberal "game of life" rejected Calvinism altogether, the image of Jacob's wrestling – of man contesting *against* God – appeared in certain writers' fiction as a challenge to Calvinist pessimism from within its own tradition. For the player who refused to accept his own weakness, but whose God was more tyrannical than benevolent, salvation became the stake in a contest with God or Chance on the omnipotent Opponent's terms. In this desperate contest loss was inevitable, but in tragic defeat lay ironic victory; God-bullied man could only lose the game, but in playing defiantly he seemed to transcend his human frailty if only in a profoundly ambiguous way. Beginning with Melville's *Moby-Dick,* the figure of this desperate game came to represent a distinctive American tragic sense. The "sport of the gods" and this contest or gamble against the gods can be viewed as metaphysical games-manship and sportsmanship – the popular social philosophies discussed in Part I given a transcendent spiritual dimension. As literary motifs, these sporting images created strange bedfellows, linking Calvinists at the beginning of the nineteenth century to naturalists at the end, and both to existentialists several decades into the next. The worldview in each instance remained strangely constant in fundamental ways.

The following three chapters will trace the development of these several ludic motifs in nineteenth-century fiction and nonfiction. In the "game" of a man's calling, as it appeared in secular success literature and in popular preaching, the traditional dual callings of spiritual and worldly duty became virtually equivalent, their common language revealing how sep-arate ideas became blurred in cultural assumptions. Also, the transfor-mation from a predominantly moral to a psychological definition of success, represented by successive versions of this extraordinarily protean "game," marks in highly concrete ways the secularization of liberal Prot-estantism into what Jackson Lears and others have called a "therapeutic ethos."

Nineteenth-century business novels contextualized this "game" in a variety of ways. Actually, not one but two fundamentally distinct "games" appear over and over in this fiction: the despised game of speculation (or "business gambling"), with ties to the blood-and-thunder convention of vicious gamesmanship; and the honorific game of pro-ductive business enterprise played by financial sportsmen. The first game was most often condemned as wholly self-serving and materialistic, the second often celebrated as both public-spirited and personally transcen-dent. In contrast to the traditions of sportsmanship discussed in Part I, however, the transcendent authority of the grand "game" of business and life was more openly theological. Unlike the Southern sportsman whose behavior evoked the values of traditional aristocracy, the hon-orable player of business games was an exemplar of Christian virtue. His game won him not just honor but "salvation." Late nineteenth-century business novels are thus an invaluable record of deeply significant cultural assumptions about the relationship of business to personal worth and the common good. And of changes in that relationship. For the other story these novels tell is of the transformation of the speculator from a social blight to a transcendent superman. In the novels of Frank Norris, Theodore Dreiser, and other creators of fictional business Titans at the turn of the century, gamesmanship came to represent not the threat of chaos but the personal force of the cosmic gambler. It would be difficult to overstate the significance of that transformation.

Chance thus underwent a radical cultural redefinition around 1900: from a blasphemy against Providence or an obstacle to self-determination, to a guarantor of limited individual freedom in a universe of force. The naturalists can be viewed in this context against the novelists at the beginning of the nineteenth century, whose underlying conservative theology was represented in images of the gods' sport. The other side of the conservative *agôn* – the desperate game of Jacob's wrestling with God – was given its classic expression in Melville's *Moby-Dick,* then informed certain naturalistic novels, but without generating its own distinct literary tradition until the 1920s, the decade of Melville's rediscovery. In the contrasting motifs of the gods' sport with man and man's contest against the gods, students of American culture can observe Americans' grappling with philosophical abstractions in concrete social contexts. Driving toward abstraction and metaphysics, all of these "games," both liberal and conservative, tended to downplay the social, political, and economic realities in which power had palpable consequences. Yet the process of abstraction itself reveals a great deal about the ways in which middle-class Americans attempted to cope with desire for power and feelings of powerlessness. The games of spiritual contest are not an opposing tradition to the simpler games of prowess discussed in Part I, but their complement. Power and powerlessness are the issue in every case. With these next three chapters, then, my overview of "the game" in nineteenth-century American culture will at last be complete.

4

Playing the Game of Life

Washington Gladden, a minister and chief spokesman for the Social Gospel in America, began an essay on "Learning to Win" (1914) with these words:

> Life is a contest. There is a prize to win. What is the prize?
> It is manhood, or womanhood. To become what we are meant to be, to fulfill our destiny – that is what we are here for. Matthew Arnold said that God, according to science, is the stream of tendency by which all things fulfill the law of their being. His will, therefore, is that we should be perfect men and women. That is the prize that he has set before us.[1]

Four years later, one Zebediah Flint began a different book with a seemingly skewed echo of Gladden's message:

> The jolliest, the most fascinating game in the world. The source of pride, pleasure and satisfaction. And anybody can play it; with a little effort can play it well. And the harder you try the better you play and the better you play the more there is in it. It is the game of life, or rather the game of getting on and prospering and really living life.[2]

The book was called *Playing the Game,* its publisher the Fiscal Service Corporation, its purpose to teach readers how to accumulate wealth through wise investing. Gladden's and Flint's versions of "the game" seem altogether different yet strangely similar; they move from opposite directions toward a common middle ground. Flint's game seems to have a crudely material object, yet he insisted that players would be "happier, better off financially, physically, morally and mentally for the playing of it" (52). Gladden's stake was spiritual but only in a highly rational, modern, even secular way. Gladden jumbled together God, science, and Matthew Arnold in explaining life's "prize." "Perfect men and women"

161

could mean ideal citizens as easily as saints, successful individuals in business rather than in personal virtue. Flint spoke in the voice of Gilded Age prophets of success, Gladden of Protestant liberals; both with the accents of early twentieth-century progressivism. The longer one considers these two passages, the more Zebediah Flint's "game" seems a highly concrete instance of Washington Gladden's: not secular and religious versions of the same motif but different understandings of human purpose, of what ultimately amounts to "salvation." The "game of life," in other words, was the rhetorical meeting point of liberal Protestantism and an age of business in a single gospel of success.

Of Puritans, covenants, and contests

The Pauline metaphor of the "race" for God's "prizes" provides the rhetorical link between America's Puritan past and "the game" of Washington Gladden and Zebediah Flint. To sketch out the rough contours, if not the detailed process, by which Protestant theology could be transformed into a barely spiritual "game" for whatever a person desires, we must begin with the original Puritan dilemma over God's sovereignty and man's duty. The ablest Puritan divines endlessly wrestled with this problem, always wary of the dangers on either side. To overemphasize moral responsibility risked Arminianism; to underemphasize it risked Antinomianism. But the Antinomian Controversy of 1636–8, which resulted in the banishing of Anne Hutchinson to Rhode Island, thrust the Boston Puritans along a path of inevitable Arminianism. From the first generation's notion of "preparation" that declared the necessity of disposing oneself to respond to God's call, to the Half-Way Covenant of 1662 that granted partial church membership to the children of the saints despite their not having yet demonstrated evidence of election, to the eventual extending of church membership to all professing Christians, in a series of stages the theology of the first Massachusetts Bay colonists became progressively more liberal with each generation.

No Puritan consensus drove out all other contenders, of course. Separatists and Non-Separatists; Episcopalians, Presbyterians, and Congregationalists all fought for their own versions of orthodoxy. In the eighteenth century, the divisions grew wider, particularly after the Great Awakening of the 1740s that permanently split the Christian community into rational and evangelical factions. Liberal, moderate, and conservative theological traditions continued into the nineteenth century and beyond, but the entire theological spectrum shifted leftward as well, while the definitions of "liberal" and "conservative" theologies underwent major changes. The triumph of liberalism in the late nineteenth century resulted not from the growth of traditionally liberal denominations – Unitarians and Universalists, who never thrived beyond eastern Massachusetts – but from the liberalization of the great evangelical mainstream. "Liberal" and "conservative" came to define not separate sects but factions within Congregationalism, Presbyterianism, and the other major denominations; those terms now signifying not beliefs about human agency, which almost all Protestants came to accept, but modernist and fundamentalist responses to a changing world. "Liberals" in this sense wrote the books, dominated the media (such major religious periodicals as the *Independent* and the *Christian Union*), and in other ways gained cultural power (in part through their congregations of prosperous merchants). Although the majority of Americans remained theologically conservative, liberalism achieved social and cultural preeminence.[3]

The "game of life" belongs to this socially dominant liberalism, specifically to the conjunction of moral and material striving that defined its place in American culture. In his classic study of the relationship of capitalism to Protestantism, Max Weber wrote that in the United States, where this connection was most evident, "the pursuit of wealth, stripped of its religious and ethical meanings, tends to become associated with purely mundane passions, which actually often give it the character of sport."[4] I am suggesting that religious meanings were not "stripped" but transformed, that the sportiveness of business redefined its "ethics" – that business enterprise, in short, remained a transcendent calling even when its object seemed to have become mere material gain. For my purposes, the popular metaphor of "the game" provides a record of the disappearance of the distinctions between the material and the spiritual. Sporting rhetoric did not invest business with spiritual consequences in the nineteenth century but the other way around: Its association with business raised "the game" to quasi-religious importance. But once invested, the metaphor of the game facilitated the cultural transformation of business from a partially spiritual to a wholly secular activity while preserving its transcendent status. In seventeenth-century Protestant doctrine, business was considered more valuable as a regenerative process than as a means of producing goods and wealth. The nineteenth-century success ethic retained this emphasis: In a nation obsessed with wealth, perhaps the most striking fact about the public discourse on American acquisitiveness is that wealth itself was never declared more important than the acquiring of it. "The game" inscribed the preeminence of process in its fundamental assumption that "winning" lay in playing itself.

To a seventeenth-century Puritan, Washington Gladden's "game of life" would have seemed outrageous blasphemy. In what seems a preternaturally prescient observation, Benjamin Colman early in the eighteenth century warned his congregation, "Let it be never nam'd among us, nor said that God and things Sacred are our Game."[5] To have con-

ceived the most important matter of all – one's own spiritual state – as
the stake in a game would have trivialized the very essence of God's
design for the world. To Colman early in 1707, "game" connoted frivolity; to Gladden in 1914, after some fifty years of a growing popular
enthusiasm for a variety of sports, "game" connoted competition and
striving in its most serious yet joyful form. The inversion of religious
orthodoxy over two centuries was equally thorough. Gladden's assumptions that the players in the game of life freely chose to compete
and earned the prizes they won would have appalled Colman's fundamental beliefs in divine sovereignty and human depravity. But the seeds
of Gladden's game were nonetheless present in Puritan theology from
the beginning; the nineteenth-century "game of life" preserved both the
outward forms and the underlying structures of Puritan orthodoxy while
radically altering its content.

Specifically, sporting rhetoric facilitated the cultural transformation of
the Three C's: Puritan ideas about calling, covenant, and conversion.
The Puritan notion of the calling has been the subject of so much discussion since Weber's *The Protestant Ethic and the Spirit of Capitalism* that
little comment is needed here. Puritan theology taught that every Christian had two callings: as Cotton Mather put it, one a general calling "to
Serve the Lord Jesus Christ, and Save his own Soul, in the Service of
Religion"; the other "a Personal Calling" or "a certain *Particular Employment,* by which his Usefulness in his Neighborhood is distinguished."[6]
The Christian served God through both callings, rendering strict account
for every moment of his time. Business was pursued not for personal
gain but for God's glory; only God could reward worldly labor with
success, but He promised such success to those he had saved. In "the
game" of nineteenth-century liberal preaching and success writing, the
distinct religious and secular callings collapsed into one, offering material
prizes that were virtually equivalent to spiritual salvation.

The structure of that game was a transmutation of covenant theology.
Puritan divines identified a series of covenants that governed every aspect
of the saints' lives. In the initial Covenant of Works that God contracted
with Adam, the Creator promised eternal life if men and women would
fulfill certain commitments. After Adam, by sinning, violated the Covenant of Works, God in his goodness contracted a new Covenant of
Grace with Abraham, through which those numbered among the elect
would be saved despite their unworthiness. The key element in this
account of salvation was that the Covenant of Grace was understood as
a genuine contract of *mutual* obligation. Despite his absolute sovereignty,
God freely bound Himself to fulfill the conditions of his compact (Perry
Miller has described the Covenant as essentially identical to a business
contract, a metaphor common among the Puritans themselves).[7] The

Covenant of Grace marked only the beginning of man's contractual relationship with God. Congregational organization was based on a church covenant governing membership and prescribed practices. Civil government in Puritan communities drew its legitimacy and authority from a social covenant, by which an individual's or community's worldly fate was tied not to contingency or chance but to contractual accountability.

The Puritans' God who bound Himself to these covenants became the nineteenth-century liberals' God who implicitly agreed to the rules of a "game." And the manner of playing that game, finally, or rather the form the rules took, was a reconstituted "morphology of conversion." As articulated by William Perkins, William Ames, and numerous other Puritan teachers, the morphology of conversion described the stages through which God took the souls of individuals He had chosen to be saved. Because "proof" of the soul's election was required for church membership – and by extension for the benefits of full citizenship within Puritan communities – the morphology of conversion had a central place in Puritan theology. God's saving grace would produce recognizable signs that would be consistent among those who had been saved. A morphology of conversion in clear stages – Effectual Calling, Justification, Sanctification, and Glorification, all of these further broken down into smaller steps – could thus be described as a standard against which anxious Puritans could measure their own spiritual experience, and against which prospective church members could be tested.[8]

For a single model of this morphology we can take William Perkins's treatise *A Golden Chaine* (1592), which included the diagram reproduced here, clearly marking out each step toward salvation or damnation. Notice that Perkins identified the steps by which man was acted upon, not by which he earned election. Yet in his theological writings Perkins also identified the means to weaken the flesh and strengthen the spirit through prayer and fasting, deeds of mercy, holy meditations, reading of scriptures, and so on. The Puritan orthodoxy that emerged from the Antinomian Controversy insisted on God's sovereignty but also on individual responsibility; this paradox eventually collapsed into unambiguous affirmation of human agency.

The pattern embedded in the morphology of conversion appeared in the transcripts of public confessions recorded by ministers, in the ministers' own spiritual autobiographies, even in narratives of Indian captivity, which in their formulaic telling became allegories of spiritual redemption. The pattern was always the same: sinfulness followed by a first awakening, followed by backsliding into sin, followed by true conviction and the soul's transfiguration.[9] Interestingly, this pattern follows the model of the hero's career described by scholars such as Joseph Camp-

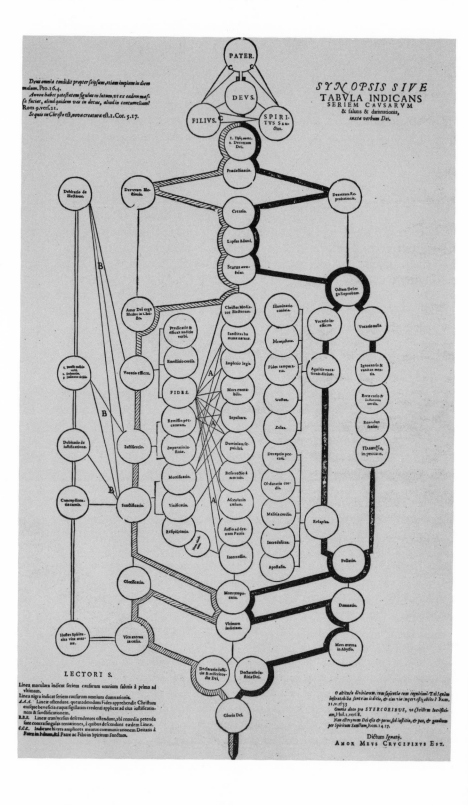

bell as a transhistorical, transnational paradigm of psychological matu-ration.[10] It seems quite possible that the Puritans developed their model for salvation out of the same psychological needs that had generated heroic myths in diverse cultures for centuries. Their distinctive contri-bution to this cross-cultural tradition was to ground the archetype in the forms of their Protestant theology. And they bequeathed to future gen-erations a paradigm of heroic striving with spiritual, not just psycho-logical, implications.

For our interests here, the striking resemblance of Perkins's mor-phology of conversion to a modern board game is particularly notable. It is coincidence only, no doubt, but a curious coincidence nonetheless, that the *Game of Goose,* which became the prototype for most English and American board games over the next four centuries, was first pub-lished in England in 1597, just five years after *A Golden Chaine.* The *Game of Goose* was a simple race game, its ancestors at least four thousand years old, in which the object was to be first to traverse the board and gain the goal. Success depended on pure chance (the roll of the dice), as Perkins's Christian depended on God's predestinating will. By the nine-teenth century a pattern that seemingly merged the morphology of con-version with the *Game of Goose* appeared in board games of moral improvement, with titles like *The Game of Human Life* (1790), *Mansion of Happiness* (1800), *The Reward of Merit* (1801), *Virtue Rewarded and Vice Punished* (1818), and so on – games intended to instruct young people in proper Christian living.[11] Along these same lines, the most popular nar-rative formulation of the Puritans' morphology of conversion, John Bun-yan's *Pilgrim's Progress,* was in fact reimagined in nineteenth-century America as a game (Part One of Louisa May Alcott's *Little Women* [1868] draws on this Pilgrim's Progress game from Alcott's own childhood). These various games suggest how children's play came to mirror popular notions of the successful Christian life. Our question concerns how the successful Christian life came to be viewed as a game. The morphology of conversion posited an analogous way of thinking about salvation as the reward for those who followed a set of rules in overcoming a series of obstacles. With acknowledgment of human agency, a more secular spirit, and a new enthusiasm for competitive sports, that morphology of conversion would become transposed into a "game."

Liberal Protestantism, then, by the middle of the nineteenth century assumed the individual's power to earn salvation. It blurred the distinc-tion between religious and secular callings, allowing mere wealth to

The "morphology of conversion" as illustrated by William Perkins in *The Golden Chaine*, from the Latin edition of 1590. (By permission of the Folger Shakespeare Library)

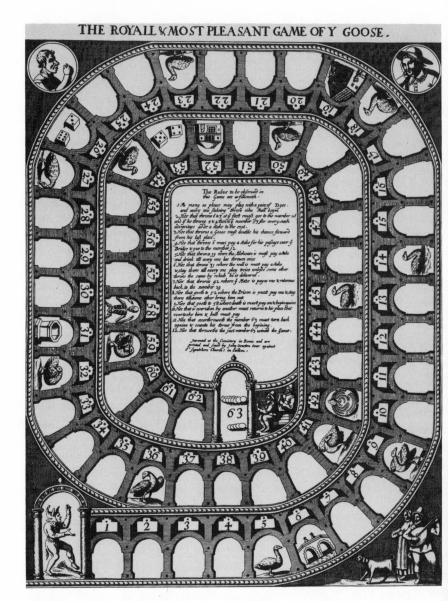

The prototype of modern "race" games: *The Royal and Most Pleasant Game of Goose* (1597). This is a reproduction of a 1670 edition. (Reprinted with the permission of the Colonial Williamsburg Foundation)

become not God's reward for holiness but holiness itself in the secular religion of nineteenth-century business. It retained from covenant theology, even after its virtual disappearance in the eighteenth century, the conception of a God who would bargain with his creatures, binding himself reciprocally to the agreed-upon rules. And it preserved an implicit morphology of conversion, a pattern of advance and retreat in striving against obstacles toward an ultimate reward, that persisted even when the conversion experience ceased to be important in the liberal Christian's religious life. The nineteenth-century "game of life" embodied all of these transformed theological principles. The deep structure of Puritan thinking persisted, as the worldview it supported became radically secularized into a gospel of wealth.

That the potential for transformation was present long before it took place is apparent in the person and writings of Benjamin Franklin, who can take his place in our story as the great "game's" First Player – before personal success was fully articulated as a game. Franklin's role in secularizing the Protestant ethic has long been recognized; he also seems to have been the first American writer to declare explicitly the correspondence of life to a game. Puritan ministers who preached on Paul's letters to Ephesians or Corinthians presented the "race" of Greek athletes as a simile or type for the saint's spiritual contest. Franklin both secularized this contest and took the further step in transforming simile into metaphor. The descendant of good Nonconformists on both sides of his family and reared, as he reported in his *Autobiography* (1771–90), on *Pilgrim's Progress* and Cotton Mather's *Essays to Do Good,* Franklin had the superficial habits of a Puritan without their substance. Always desirous of more time in his youth for reading and self-improvement, but limited to evenings after work or Sundays for these pursuits, Franklin consistently missed church services so that he could pursue his more worldly "salvation." In the *Autobiography* he made explicit the nature of this salvation when he described his method of writing Poor Richard's Almanac – filling the spaces "that occur'd between the Remarkable Days in the Calendar, with Proverbial Sentences, chiefly such as inculcated Industry and Frugality, *as the Means of procuring Wealth and thereby securing Virtue,* it being more difficult for a Man in Want to act always honestly" (my emphasis).[12] Here is one of those crucial moments in American intellectual history, signaled only by a slight semantic reordering of a basic Protestant tenet. Puritans from John Cotton to Cotton Mather had believed that virtue would be rewarded with prosperity; here, Franklin inverted the process, making wealth the means of achieving virtue.

Franklin's famous "Project of arriving at moral Perfection" in the *Autobiography* foretells the fate of the morphology of conversion as well.

Form of the Pages

		S	M	T	W	T	F	S
TEMPERANCE. *Eat not to Dulness. Drink not to Elevation.*								
T								
S		••	•		•		•	
O		•	•	•		•	•	•
R			•			•		
F			•			•		
I				•				
S								
J								
M								
Cl.								
T								
Ch.								
H								

Figure 1

His scheme to master one of thirteen essential virtues each week, completing four courses in a year, assumed that man, not God, controlled the soul's destiny. If Perkins's morphology only looked forward to modern board games, Franklin's "Project," while still not termed at any time a game, reveals gamelike qualities much more fully (and his thirteen virtues overlapped considerably with those on the actual board games that began to appear around the time he was writing). Franklin devised a sort of score card by which he could measure his success at virtue-getting, a "little Book" in which he marked his faults against each of the virtues for every day of the week (see Figure 1). In addition to keeping boxscores, he developed a program for the useful employment of each of the twenty-four hours in a day (see Figure 2). Franklin thus set his course on a sort of Parker Brothers road to his own kind of "salvation," explicitly ascribing his worldly triumphs to his progress through the squares on the board:

> And it may be well my Posterity should be informed, that to this little Artifice, with the Blessing of God [a token acknowledgment], their Ancestor ow'd the constant Felicity of his life down to his 79th Year in which this is written. . . . To *Temperance* he ascribes his long-continu'd Health, and what is still left to him of good Constitution.

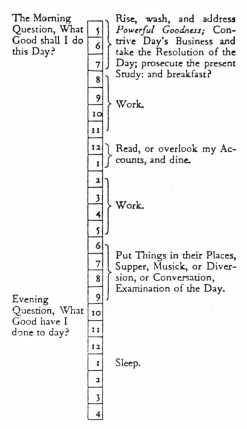

Figure 2

To *Industry* and *Frugality* the early Easiness of his Circumstances, and Acquisition of his Fortune.... (157)

And so on. The saints' covenant with God became Franklin's pact with himself, the rewards for proper behavior guaranteed now not by God but by natural laws. Playing the game well was amply rewarded, and the game could be played, and won, by many. Contrary to the Puritans' belief that only a small number would be saved, the American success myth has from the beginning been fundamentally democratic. One of Franklin's more grandiose schemes for human improvement was a "Party for Virtue," whose members would practice his thirteen virtues for their own and others' benefit. Although the sly humor of the *Autobiography* causes the modern reader to wonder how seriously to take Franklin's grandiloquent earnestness, certainly in the nineteenth century he was widely read as a wise man, not an ironist.

The morphology in Franklin's *Autobiography* is not of conversion but of worldly success: the "salvation" of an eighteenth-century rationalist, which included a necessary portion of moral goodness. Insofar as Franklin represents his age, his scheme reveals most clearly the degree to which the forms of covenant theology could persist as the substance changed dramatically. Franklin professed a distinctly puritanical aversion to spending time frivolously. "Reading was the only Amusement I allow'd my self," he wrote of his youth. "I spent no time in Taverns, Games, or Frolicks of any kind" (143). When Franklin did play, he played with a purpose, as in his swimming for health. But life itself was a sort of game to Franklin, as it could be to no Puritan. In addition to his scheme for attaining the thirteen virtues, Franklin also marked out the major faults of his youth as "Errata": like the Puritan's backslidings, the player's false moves in his game of life, which he had to rectify in order to proceed satisfactorily. And transforming play into work, he simultaneously made a sport of self-improvement, as when he taught himself foreign languages:

> An Acquaintance who was also learning [Italian], us'd often to tempt me to play Chess with him. Finding this took up too much of the Time I had to spare for Study, I at length refus'd to play any more, unless on this Condition, that the Victor in every Game, should have a Right to impose a Task, either in Parts of the Grammar to be got by heart, or in Translations, etc., which Tasks the Vanquish'd was to perform upon Honour before our next Meeting. As we play'd pretty equally we thus beat one another into that Language. (168)

Compare this game of self-improvement to the morally instructive games devised for his children by Cotton Mather, Franklin's Puritan alter ego. In his diary Mather wrote:

> There is an Ingenuity, which I may use, to insinuate the Maxims and Lessons of Piety, into the Minds of my younger Children. I would observe what Games and Sports they are upon, when the Hours of Recreation recur unto them. And I would by way of occasional Reflections, as plainly as tis possible, mind them of those pious Instructions, which the Circumstances of their play may lead them to think upon. Hereby their Minds will insensibly improve, and be drawn on to higher Matters; and perhaps the Maxims and Lessons thus convey'd unto them, will be of use to them, and abide by 'em all their dayes.[13]

The man of the world and the man of God used actual games in similar ways for different purposes: success and salvation. These distinctions would collapse in "the game" of the Progressive Era.

Actually, Franklin was less than candid in the *Autobiography* about his reluctance to play chess; he played it passionately. And in his famous essay on the "Morals of Chess" (1779), written between installments of the *Autobiography*, Franklin made explicit what his *Autobiography* only implied. In the essay he described the utility of chess, through which the players could acquire foresight, circumspection, caution, and perseverance. Chess prepared one for life, according to Franklin; it also more directly was itself like life: "For life is a kind of chess, in which we have often points to gain, and competitors or adversaries to contend with, and in which there is a vast variety of good and evil events, that are in some degree the effects of prudence or the want of it."[14] The Pauline "race" in Puritan sermons situated the contest in the spiritual realm; here Franklin placed it squarely in the world. In Franklin we see how easily covenant theology evolved into a sort of salvation game, "salvation" implying now whatever ultimate good life offered. It is striking that in this essay Franklin downplayed competition, even recommending that a more skillful player help his opponent avoid mistakes for the sake of maintaining a challenging equality. For Franklin, the opponent whether in chess or in life was not a rival but oneself—in life, one's own inclination to err. The game of life that would evolve in the nineteenth century became rooted in this doctrine.

Franklin stands, then, at the head of that long line of his countrymen who would speak or write over the next two centuries of "playing the game" or engaging in the "race" for life's "prizes." Franklin transformed Puritan theology into a secular success ethic and wrote the first major statement about the "game of life." As Sacvan Bercovitch has written, "Early New England rhetoric provided a ready framework for inviting later secular values – human perfectibility, technological progress, democracy, Christian Socialism, or simply (and comprehensively) the American Way – into the mold of sacred theology."[15] Franklin stands behind both Zebediah Flint's "game" of moneymaking and Washington Gladden's more spiritual one. In his rhetoric, the pattern of his thinking, and his underlying spirit of play, Franklin was the first American to reconstruct Protestant theology as a secular but salvific game of life.

The secularizing of salvation . . .

Franklin's version of the game of an individual's calling did not become a commonplace until the last decades of the nineteenth century. Although Franklin became one of the endlessly cited and quoted sources for American success writing, he serves in our story more to prefigure than to bequeath the sporting rhetoric of later generations. To trace the emergence of this rhetoric we must follow the literary tradition of advice manuals and conduct-of-life books from the antebellum period into the writings of popular preachers and lay prophets of success in the last decades of the century. What emerges most obviously is a sense that the notion of life as struggle persists through the century, but that the nature of that struggle changes significantly: from battle, more and more to sporting contest. With the advent of modern technological warfare – experienced by Americans in the Civil War – and the concomitant rise of organized sport, the two forms of contest became considerably less similar. Together with the image of Jacob's wrestling, as we saw, the Pauline metaphors of contest that mixed sportive with martial rhetoric had expressed the agonistic element in Puritan theology (as opposed to such other elements as submission and pietism). The shift from battle to sport as the dominant metaphor, within shifting social contexts in which the connotations of a spiritual "race" or "game" changed significantly, illustrates most concretely how liberal Protestantism came to deny its agonistic heritage. In the seventeenth century, the "race" in Paul's epistles was a simile drawn from the games of pagan Greece. In the late nineteenth century, the "race" alluded to the athletic sports that were becoming a popular passion – sports now tied to a loudly trumpeted ethic of fair play. To strive for spiritual victory as if at sport under these conditions was altogether different from the Puritans' view of spiritual life as a hard contest – and from spiritual contest as warfare in an age that knew the destructiveness of total war. Sporting metaphors, in fact, may have done more than reflect changing fashion and values; to some degree they may have subtly helped to transform American beliefs and values while seeming to express rhetorical, and theological, continuity.

Conduct-of-life writing in America goes back to the Puritans, who read the moral treatises of Richard Baxter, Lewis Bayly, John Bunyan, Cotton Mather and numerous others as guides to living out God's commandments in the social world. Such tracts and lectures proliferated in the 1830s, as a direct response to the social upheavals of beginning industrialism.[16] As young men left home for city, farm for factory, concerned ministers and lay preachers published books and lectures to offer spiritual guidance for these uprooted young people. Most striking in these books, the writers advised not how to succeed but how not to be corrupted by success; their distrust of wealth is everywhere apparent. Even Freeman Hunt, an influential spokesman for the business community as editor of *Hunt's Merchant's Magazine,* over and over in a popular collection of his writings, *Worth and Wealth* (1857), warned that all value lies in the process of properly pursuing success, not in the prosperity attained. And with few exceptions, these antebellum advice manuals simply do not include the metaphors of life's game. A revealing case: The first edition of Reverend Daniel Eddy's *The Young Man's Friend* in 1855 emphasized character-building and contained no sporting metaphors; the revised second edition, ten years later, paid more attention to worldly success and compared life, approvingly, to "a race-course in which a countless number of persons are contending for the prize."[17]

Such metaphors were not altogether absent from antebellum conduct books, but they were rare. In *The Foundations of Success* (1844), Reverend John Todd quotes St. Paul and refers to "the strong race which you must run with your generation"; and in *Worth and Wealth* Hunt mentions, only in passing really, "the great game of life" that men must play, but he more insistently and repetitiously warns his readers against very different "games": "the unhappy race of avarice and aggrandizement" and "the race of worldly advancement."[18] A Scottish minister's *The Race for Riches,* published in America in 1853, uses the sporting image of the title only in its negative connotations, the theme from Ecclesiastes that the race does not go to the swift.

Recall from Part I that the word "game" itself in this period usually meant "gaming" (gambling), a vice that received particular attention in advice literature for the young. Karen Haltunnen has identified the confidence man, in certain guises a gambler/speculator, as an archetypal villain in this writing. Urban gamblers lured country youths to their moral ruin; business gamblers taught them a perversion of economic striving. "In the spectre of the gambler/speculator," Haltunnen has written, antebellum moralists "embodied their fears of the economic forces shaping the young American republic: the rapid expansion of the national market and of speculative economic activity."[19] Spokesmen for the business community were no less insistent on the evils of speculation than the moralists. Freeman Hunt denounced "the licensed gambling of the stock exchange" and the "deep game" of financiering. He described the good merchant as one who "gets rich by industry and forecast, not by sleight of hand and shuffling his cards to another's loss," and who is unwilling "to risk everything . . . on the hazard of a single throw." The "fast" man of business, in contrast, was one to whom life was "very much like a Mississippi voyage to those on the lookout for a race, consoling themselves with the reflections that the chances of their rival's boiler bursting and blowing them to atoms would be as great as their own."[20] Edwin Freedley included in his *Practical Treatise on Business* (1853) an essay by a merchant of Boston on "How to Get Rich by Speculation." But even in this apparent endorsement, the author distinguished practical, enlightened, and nonhazardous speculation from wildly sportive risk taking. In this writing generally, to see life or business as sport is to misapprehend its true purposes.

To measure the distance from Jacksonian America to the Gilded Age, consider an 1883 volume with Hunt's same title and entire passages lifted from Freedley. A gilt-embossed, 704-page tome, illustrated with steel engravings and scroll-worked text, T. L. Haines' *Worth and Wealth* enjoyed "high favor during the eighties" when many employers gave it to their workers in lieu of Christmas bonuses.[21] Throughout the book Haines recast Hunt's distrust as celebration. To Haines, life is "a race, a contest, not of whistling locomotives, not of white-winged ships, but of toiling men, on foot, shoulder to shoulder, on the same dusty road to riches, struggling for success." "Race," "prize," "victory," "winning" are endlessly repeated keywords in 104 brief essays, suggesting the exhilaration of pursuing success. St. Paul is the guide to life's contest, but a St. Paul paraphrased for a secular age:

> Human life may well be compared to a race-course, in which a countless number of persons are contending for a prize. The aged have nearly finished; the young have just commenced. The prize set before them is success, which most persons suppose to be a competent support, an unsullied reputation, and a useful life. These are the chief elements of prosperity, which it is the duty as well as the right of the young man to secure if possible. . . . It is a race in which hundreds and thousands are disappointed at every trail; and where one succeeds, and receives the wreath of victory, many others tire and faint ere half the course is finished.[22]

Writing a single generation after Freeman Hunt, Haines emphasized the duty to be prosperous rather than the dangers that could result from wealth. But strangely, Haines also lifted a long account of the "Testimony of Millionaires" from Freedley's 1853 volume that directly contradicts the major themes of his own book. Echoing one millionaire's insistence on the value of prayer, the author (Haines, Freedley – someone else who Freedley quoted?) comments, "Prayer prepares the mind for great undertakings; it gives an earnestness and seriousness to the character; it curbs that levity and frivolity which trifle with important concerns, viewing everything as a game."[23] Simple editorial carelessness may account for this inconsistency; many of these success manuals are patchworks of quotations and anecdotes from numerous and wide-ranging sources. But the inconsistency can also represent a culture in transition. In any case, in the bulk of Haines' book, the "game" is ennobling, not heretical. Haines appears as a modern St. Paul urging new Corinthians toward a kind of salvation in which the worldly and otherworldly became joined.

It is useful to chart two paths through the sort of writing that Haines' volume represents: the published sermons and lectures of such popular liberal ministers as Horace Bushnell, Henry Ward Beecher, and Lyman Abbott, and the more avowedly secular writings of the lay prophets of success and an occasional outspoken business tycoon such as Andrew Carnegie. What emerges from the writings of these various men is evidence that, even as the secular and sacred realms became wholly separate

– a decisive rupture with the colonial Protestant worldview – a popular rhetoric developed that concealed the rupture while investing the secularized economic forces with sacral language and ideas. The Liberal ministers in the half-century after the Civil War used the language of secular success – "power," "win," "race," "game" – to express their view of the religious calling. Secular writers used the language of religion – "morality," "character," "service" – to describe the stakes in the game of success. As American culture and society grew more secular during this period, the ministers' preachings became not an alternative to the success ethic but a religious gloss on it. In other words, the secularization of salvation accompanied the sanctification of success, with the "game of life" providing a rhetorical meeting point.

The uneasiness with which liberal ministers reconciled Christian religion to the prevailing secular and commercial values is reflected in their resistance to a whole-hearted embrace of sporting language. The rhetoric of life's contest in the sermons of the so-called father of religious liberalism, Horace Bushnell, reveal the ambivalence of a serious theologian who wrestled with the dilemmas posed by the liberalism he preached. In some sermons Bushnell urged his listeners and readers to get in the contest; in others he warned them against the illusory rewards of what the world called "the game of life."[24] Henry Ward Beecher, Bushnell's heir as the preeminent liberal spokesman of the following generation, addressed with comparable inconsistency the sportive or martial nature of life's struggle. That the image of spiritual life as a game was not yet a commonplace in 1872 is strikingly suggested in one of Beecher's sermons from that year, when he refers to St. Paul's figure of the race in Phil. 3 as "a living one then" but "merely a classical illustration now." But despite his embrace of Spencer and Darwin, Beecher felt little affinity to the opposing image of life as a battle. In two sermons delivered in 1869 and 1872, Beecher used Paul's letter to the Ephesians to describe life as hard struggle but ultimately to undercut the agonistic connotations of this view. Men and women are unequally equipped for life's "race," Beecher acknowledged, but since victory is inward, not outward, all can win through the struggle itself.[25] Although the extraordinary flexibility (some would claim flaccidity) of Beecher's mind produced an incoherent and self-contradictory body of writing, one of his more consistent themes was a muscular Christian emphasis on "winning" life's promised rewards.[26]

Lyman Abbott, Beecher's more learned successor at Brooklyn's Plymouth Church, as well as Beecher's chief heir to liberal leadership in the larger culture, also continued to mix his metaphors. In sections of a treatise on "Christ's Secret of Happiness," in successive issues of the *Outlook* (1906), for example, Abbott declared life first a battle then a

Pauline race, concluding in the second issue that "the pursuit of life is itself life's highest prize."[27] This blend of the martial and the sportive, with the sportive ultimately ascendant, marks Abbott's published sermons throughout his career. The image of a "race" as a perpetual striving for perfection, with victory ultimately assured by God's promise, perfectly illustrated Abbott's central principle of spiritual evolution.[28] Abbott was a quintessential late-nineteenth-century liberal in accommodating both the sportive and the martial, the agonistic and the consolatory, human power and dependence. For Abbott, II Tim: 7–8 summed up not just Paul's theology but his own, as well as the competing desires of late-nineteenth-century liberalism: "Life is a battle – fight it bravely; life a course – run it eagerly; life a faith-keeping – hold it firmly; but do not think to win the righteousness by your battle, by your race, or by your faith-keeping: God will give it to you; it is his true gift, if you simply love him and wish to see him." Struggle, assured victory, and God's ultimate power are all affirmed in the face of the manifest tensions among them. In another sermon drawn from the same text, Abbott again declared Christian life both battle and sport, but this time he distinguished their relative importance. "We fight the battle," Abbott wrote, "that we may get liberty to run the race."[29]

Given the ambivalence of his predecessors, Washington Gladden's wholehearted, unqualified embrace of the "game of life" in his 1914 essay might seem merely idiosyncratic. Gladden's essay, in fact, reiterated a view he had expressed a half-century earlier in his first collection of lectures on the conduct of life: that even in a society utterly committed to competition for advancement, the success that truly mattered was available to everyone who made the effort. Writing in 1868 on "Success," Gladden pointed out that "in the old Grecian races there was only one prize for the multitude of competitors." "In the races of life," on the other hand, "all who run well are crowned." Rejecting the fratricidal competition of American capitalism for the exhilarating, guilt-free challenge of an opponent-less game, Gladden assured his readers that in these races "men are matched, not against men, but against difficulties and hindrances." The success Gladden wrote of was not wealth at the cost of nobler impulses, nor fame and power without principle, but those same worldly objectives gained by "rectitude and benevolence," in other words, material success along "the straight road of Christian integrity." Success was surer the honest way. As for the nature of that success, Gladden concluded with a caution: "It is your duty to succeed in your calling, but it is not your first duty. The great business of life is to get for yourselves wisdom, grace, and manliness. These are the highest prizes offered you in the race of life. So run that ye may obtain them."[30]

"Success" was addressed to young readers, as was Gladden's *Straight*

Shots at Young Men (1900) three decades later. In such volumes liberal ministers were more liable to blur the distinctions between spiritual and material striving than in their sermons for adults.[31] Gladden's 1914 essay, describing character and selfhood as "prizes" to be won by confronting obstacles and adversaries "in fair fighting," simply echoed the advice he had been offering young readers throughout his ministry. The consistency of Gladden's sporting rhetoric from 1868 to 1914 clearly reflects a personal style different from, say, Bushnell's or Beecher's. But over this half-century there was also a general shift from martial to sportive rhetoric in liberal preaching throughout the culture. Gladden's late essay seems to address an audience that takes for granted the idea that life is a game; the metaphor seems more a convention now than an erudite gloss on Paul's epistles.

Other influential liberal preachers contributed to this convention: William H. H. Murray, pastor of Park Street Church in Boston, who preached that the Christian should have no less determination than the worldly man who "plays the game of life boldly, asking no odds"; Wilbur Crafts, whose *Successful Men of To-Day and What They Say of Success* (1883) promoted hard work as "the winning horse in the race of life"; Phillips Brooks, Episcopal bishop of Massachusetts, whose published sermons returned insistently to the spiritual contest, both the martial and the sportive; and Brooks' successor as bishop, William Lawrence, whose famous essay, "The Relation of Wealth to Morals" (1901), declared that "godliness is in league with riches" and, contra Ecclesiastes, that "the race is to the strong."[32] The image of life as a game for either spiritual or material prizes received widespread ministerial sanction. Although none of these ministers lost sight of what were higher and lower callings, their language nonetheless contributed to blurring the distinction.

... And the sanctifying of success

This blurring occurred in large part because the sermons and essays of liberal ministers reached an audience inundated by popular success writing considerably less concerned with this-world/other-world distinctions. The lay preachers of success were not systematic philosophers but purveyors of platitudes, all of which carried a single message: *Everyone* can succeed. They quoted St. Paul, Benjamin Franklin, and Ralph Waldo Emerson, as well as captains of industry, merchant princes, financiers, artists, and anyone else who could lend authority to their preachings. Their rhetoric continually returned to a handful of keywords and catch phrases: "running the race," "winning the prizes of life," "wresting victory from defeat" – "winning," "winning," "winning." Their titles were sometimes no more than these phrases: *Win Who Will;*

or, The Young Man's Key to Fortune (A. C. McCurdy), *Winning Out* (Orison Swett Marden), *Men Who Win* and *Women Who Win* (both by William M. Thayer). They offered assurance to their readers that despite the apparent rootlessness, confusion, and powerlessness inherent in modern life, they could in fact be masters of self and surroundings, winners in the "game."

Parallel to the apotheosis of the sporting cowboy in the 1890s, success writing from the Gilded Age to the Progressive Era changed, not through any sudden break or step-by-step progression but in a shift of emphasis and context. I single out William Makepeace Thayer and Orison Swett Marden to represent the change, but they were joined by a host of others. In Thayer's *Tact, Push, and Principle* (1880) – as well as Haines' *Worth and Wealth*, William Matthews' *Getting on in the World* (1872), James D. Mills' *The Art of Money Making* (1874), even John T. Dale's later *The Secret of Success* (1889) – persistent religious rhetoric and traditional values continually look back to a pre-industrial world. As Richard Weiss has pointed out, "success" was not defined by an American dictionary as "the gaining of money" until 1891.[33] In general, Gilded Age sporting rhetoric is less conspicuous and more restrained than it would soon become; an earnest tone and theme of moral duty predominate. Like Haines, William Matthews (a professor of rhetoric and English literature at the University of Chicago) used metaphors of the "game" extravagantly, yet his emphasis on distinguishing true from false success, his scorn for Gilded Age greed and excess, his confusion of martial with sportive rhetoric, and his reminder from Ecclesiastes that "the race is not always to the swift" distinguish *Getting on in the World* from later unfettered celebrations of the grand game of personal fulfillment. In the volume's concluding essay Matthews asks, "Is life a scrub-race, where, at every hazard, though you have to blind the man on your right and trip the one on your left, you must struggle to come out ahead?" His own answer is clear; the alternative "race" he championed is more scriptural than economic.[34]

The particular value of Thayer's *Tact, Push, and Principle* for my narrative lies in its direct rhetorical links to the Puritan sermon and spiritual biography. A Congregationalist minister forced to give up preaching because of throat trouble, Thayer turned to magazine editing and then the writing of self-help books and biographies of successful men as an alternative form of preaching. After some introductory remarks in his *magnum opus,* Thayer states his text, not from St. Paul but from Samuel Budgett: "THE CONDITIONS OF SUCCESS ARE TACT, PUSH, AND PRINCIPLE." A series of explications of those three key terms follow, then applications of them to everyday life. At the center of the book lies a morphology of success as formulaic as the Puritan conversion narrative, based here

on the biographies of famous men: unpromising beginnings, early in-
dications of remarkable ability or determination, early setbacks and obstacles overcome, a major breakthrough followed by a rapid rise to
preeminence in a chosen field – all achieved through a familiar cluster of
virtues: industry, thrift, frugality, perseverance, honesty, punctuality,
order, and so on (Franklin's thirteen, plus others demanded by the contemporary marketplace). Those who would follow this course would
win "the prizes of life" in the "mighty contest going on now among
forty-five millions."[35]

What prizes? In a later volume, *Success and Its Achievers* (1893), after
numerous references to the "race of life" and winning the prizes, Thayer
wrote, "A business run by industry, tact, honesty, perseverance and
philanthropy, will make a noble man of the proprietor in any age and
anywhere."[36] The implications are not altogether clear: Does virtue lead
to success or success to virtue? The Puritans had initially viewed success
as God's material reward for the elect; Franklin had altered the equation
so that wealth became nearly a prerequisite for virtue. For Thayer, success
could not be had without virtue, but virtue seemingly could not be had
without success. Later in the same book, Thayer answers his own implied
question: "The acquisition of money becomes a valuable school of discipline when conducted upon Christian principles. It calls into exercise
the best qualities of mind and heart" (279). Success *is* virtue, then, and
here lay the central doctrine of the game of life, the completion of Franklin's transformation of covenant theology.

The collapsing of secular and spiritual definitions of success might
seem predictable in the writings of a former minister such as Thayer,
but the version of success promoted in the more thoroughly secular
writing of the late nineteenth century does not fundamentally differ. The
millionaire captains of industry, whose success was to be emulated, had
little to say about these matters. Although their countrymen often viewed
them as heroic or despicable players of "games," the robber barons
themselves remained silent or promoted a more modest and cautious
self-image.[37] To take an extreme but far from unique case, Philip Armour, the meat packer who made his fortune by cornering pork in
anticipation of the Civil War, declared in an interview in 1898 (written
by Theodore Dreiser for Orison Swett Marden's *Success* magazine) that
happiness consisted in doing for others.[38]

The major exception, in both his compulsion to speak publicly and
his willingness to endorse a view of life as a sporting contest, was Andrew
Carnegie. In an early essay, Carnegie described the young men from the
country who seek success in the city as "athletes trained for the contest,
with sinews braced, indomitable wills, resolved to do or die."[39] In like
spirit, the essays in *The Empire of Business* (1902) repeatedly refer to "the

race" and the prizes to be won in it. The essay "Business" in particular, presented first as a lecture at Cornell University in 1896, reads like Carnegie's answer to Perkins and Franklin, offering his own morphology of success as a game. Addressing young men bent on careers in business, Carnegie marked each turning point on the game board: Choice of a Career, Start in Life, Openings to Success, Second Step Upward, Where to Look for Opportunities, and so on. Just as Perkins charted the road to damnation as well as election, Carnegie, describing the best strategies for success in "the long race," also warned against the erring path of speculation and weighed college education as a possible help or hindrance. Near the end of the essay he described in detail the "Rewards of a Business Career" – his own version of the "mansion of happiness" awaiting the victors in the race. The successful businessman acquires a kind of wealth that transcends mere money:

> I believe the career of the great merchant, or banker, or captain of industry, to be favourable to the development of the powers of the mind, and to the ripening of the judgment upon a wide range of general subjects: to freedom from prejudice, and the keeping of an open mind. And I do know that permanent success is not obtainable except by fair and honourable dealing, by irreproachable habits and correct living, by the display of good sense and rare judgment in all the relations of human life.

What could the agnostic Carnegie be describing here but his own version of "salvation"?[40]

Whereas the Puritans said that virtue would be rewarded with prosperity, and Franklin that wealth made virtue more easily attainable, Carnegie joined Thayer, as well as Bishop Lawrence, in saying that the pursuit of success necessarily entailed the acquisition of virtue. Then, in the final stage of transformation, the grounds for success shifted from the moral to the psychological. In this context, the "game" became redefined under the influence of the New Thought movement to become a rhetorical sign of the new (desperate) faith in the power of the mind to master the material world – a contribution to what Jackson Lears and others have called the "therapeutic ethos" that accompanied and accommodated the emerging consumer economy. As Lears has described the process, with technological change, the new corporate economy, and the softening of Protestant theology, a "production ethos persisted" but in a very different form: "Success began to occur in a moral and spiritual void," and self-realization rather than public duty became the chief aim of life.[41] By shifting the conditions of success from morality to psychology, New Thought – the various mind-cure programs of Mary Baker Eddy, Ralph Waldo Trine, and others that led in the twentieth century to Emile Coué, Dale Carnegie, Norman Vincent Peale, and, eventually, the New Age self-actualizers of the 1970s and 1980s – was a major element of this therapeutic ethos. "Mind power" became a compensation for lack of control over material conditions.[42] And "the game" in its grand abstractness and autotelic nature was easily adapted to the new philosophy of positive thinking.

With the field of contest relocated from the social world to the individual psyche, winning "the game" of success became truly possible for all – or at least for all who felt alienated from the economic and political power centers yet who were materially comfortable within the world controlled from those centers. Earlier success writers insisted that in the face of self-evident material limitations everyone could win a *modest* prosperity (and that for moral reasons such moderate success was preferable to spectacular wealth). Later success writers set no limits on the success available to everyone, because material conditions became strangely irrelevant (or could be assumed to be adequate), and because "success" meant whatever the individual wanted it to mean. The proliferation of sporting metaphors under the new dispensation cast the dilemmas of the industrial order in increasingly abstract, metaphysical terms, where reconciliation was possible that was no longer conceivable in the material world.

Elbert Hubbard's *The Book of Business* (1913) offers a striking model of this cultural shift. In response to a hypothetical employee's desire to remain neutral in his firm's rivalries, Hubbard declares that "business is a fight – a continual struggle – just as life is. Man has reached his present degree of development through struggle." But Hubbard goes on: "The struggle began as purely physical. As man evolved it shifted ground to the mental, the psychic and the spiritual, with a few dashes of caveman proclivities still left." And after a few more lines: "The neutral in this game of life is a dead one."[43] In bracketing this passage, "struggle" and "game" are rhetorically made equivalent here, yet the sudden switch in terms, with "the mental, the psychic and the spiritual" mediating between them, marks a decisive shift in the rhetoric of success.

This shift is deeply ironic – paradoxical, contradictory – in many ways. To opt finally for "game" over "struggle" is to declare life a joyful contest that all can win, rather than a grim battle notable as much for its casualties as its victors. To abandon earnest striving for exuberant play would seem to suggest that the world has become a more hospitable place. In 1853, Edwin Freedley observed that "he who has an abiding confidence in his good fortune . . . has the most happy disposition; but it is not a temperament that fits him for great deeds." In 1896, in *The Art of Rising in the World,* Henry Hardwicke asked whether modesty and diffidence or self-praise and confidence were "surer cards in the game of life." Contrary to Freedley, he decided for self-confidence.[44] Yet Hardwicke, as well as other contemporary writers such as Erastus Wiman (*Chances of Success,* 1893) openly confronted the fact that worldly success was now harder to achieve. Not the ignorant business man but "the athlete in knowledge" will win "the race of the future for fortunes," according to Wiman. Hardwicke offered a comparable analogy: "As he who in a lottery possesses most tickets has the best chance of the prize, so he who has the greatest variety and extent of attainment has assuredly the greatest reason to expect success."[45] How, the reader might ask, could one feel joyful and self-confident in the face of diminished chances of success? One answer – the rhetorical solution to the troubling material facts of the age – lay in the reconstituted "game." Psychological success could compensate for obstructions in the material world.

The influence of New Thought on the success ethic is no more apparent than in the writings of Orison Swett Marden. Marden himself made and lost and made again a fortune, the last through *Success* magazine (1898–1911) and dozens of volumes of advice to aspiring young men and women culled from interviews with the great and near-great. His first and most popular book, *Pushing to the Front* (1894), went through 250 editions, while sales of all his books reached three million worldwide in twenty-five languages. Among the prophets of success Orison Swett Marden was the most spectacularly successful. "The race of life" is a refrain in Marden's prose; "winners" of "prizes" enter "the contest" and get "victory out of defeat." All of these phrases are invoked in *Pushing to the Front* in a variety of contexts.[46] In his collections of interviews – *How They Succeeded: Life Stories of Successful Men Told by Themselves* (1901), *Little Visits with Great Americans* (1903; enlarged 1905), and numerous others – Marden, like Thayer earlier in his popular biographies, used the actually successful as models for the hoping-to-be-successful: "spiritual biographies" for an age in which the spirit created itself in office and board room. The pattern in all of Marden's books is consistent. The rapacious monopolist John D. Rockefeller appears no different from the pious shopkeeper Amos Lawrence (father of Bishop Lawrence). Each man wins his race through Christian virtues and sound business principles, which are the same thing.

But if Marden and Thayer seem to have shared a common worldview in many respects, in others Marden struck a significantly different note. In *Tact, Push, and Principle,* Thayer expressed the faith of all success writers when he assured his readers that every one of them could win in life's contests. "Willingness to begin in a small way, advance slowly, and bend all the energies to the controlling purpose of life" produces "winners in this race." Thayer spoke to a world in which opportunity was assumed; inequality of talent was perceived to be the chief obstacle.

Marden, speaking to a world in which the prospects for worldly success had diminished, compensated with even more comforting assurance in *Pushing to the Front*: "Our reward is in the race we run, not in the prize" (235). Simply to play the game was to win it – as enthusiasts of athletic sports were also claiming in order to downplay mere victory (although the evidence of the actual contests emphatically claimed otherwise).

Two classic juvenile novels spanning our period mirror this psychologizing of success. In the opening chapters of Louisa May Alcott's *Little Women* (1868–9), Mrs. March sets her daughters a task in the form of a game: a week-long Pilgrim's Progress game in which each child will play the pilgrim, bearing her own particular burden as she strives to develop sound moral habits. (This motif is mirrored in such popular nineteenth-century American board games as Milton Bradley's *Checkered Game of Life* [1860] and Parker Brothers's *Game of Christian Endeavor* [1896]). A half-century later, in Eleanor Porter's *Pollyanna* (1913) the structure of the instructional game persists but in altered terms. Pollyanna persuades her entire town to play the "Glad Game," whose object is contentment with oneself and with everyone and everything in the world. Moral striving has been replaced by feeling good. Even the minister, who has despaired over the backbiting and contention rife in the village, is visited by Pollyanna in his dark night of the soul and won over to the game through a reminder of the Bible's "rejoicing texts." Human perfection is the game's object in both novels, but the definition of perfection and the way to achieve it are utterly transformed.

All games fall on a continuum between pure play at one extreme, pure striving at the other. The "game" of success, from the Gilded Age to the Progressive Era, slid markedly toward play. In his preface to the enlarged 1905 edition of *Little Visits with Great Americans,* Marden signaled this shift most explicitly. Claiming to summarize the chief lesson taught by the lives of the successful, Marden wrote:

> The far-away goal of success, with its reward of fame, wealth, and all that money can procure, appears to fade from the worker's sight as he advances toward it, and the incitement to labor for material reward is lost in the joy of congenial labor for its own sake. The player loses sight of the hope of victory in the mere zest of the game. This note appears again and again in the life stories of the great workers as revealed by themselves, and accounts for the spectacle, so puzzling to many, of the master of millions apparently grasping for more millions in his declining years. There can be no content with present achievement, however great, because all who have achieved great things have discovered that the ends sought are lost in the value of the faculties developed by the search, and they hence seek, not additional reward of toil, but rather the pleasurable exercise of the chase.[47]

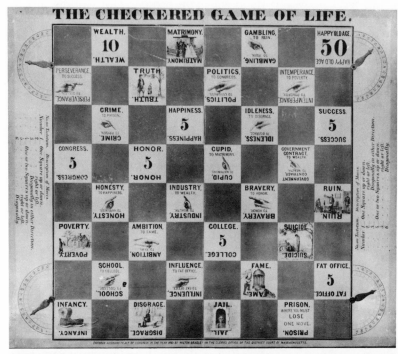

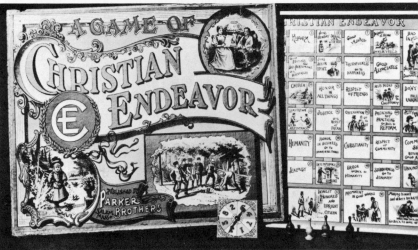

Nineteenth-century games of moral improvement, by the foremost manufacturers of American board games. Milton Bradley, *The Checkered Game of Life* (1860). (Used with permission of Milton Bradley Company, Subsidiary of Hasbro, Inc.) Parker Brothers, *The Game of Christian Endeavor®* (1896). (Used with permission from Parker Brothers © 1986)

The unsatisfied millionaire had long been a theme in success literature, usually to make the point that modest wealth, put to use for the public good, was preferable to great riches. In contrast, Marden transformed obsessive acquisitiveness into joyous sport. The millionaire plutocrat becomes not an exploiter of the people but an exemplar of the sportive pleasure everyone can enjoy. But in fact the interviews that follow this preface (several of them written by Theodore Dreiser and included without attribution) don't bear out Marden's interpretation. The plutocrats invariably cast their careers in conventional terms of Christian striving; to the curious public they insist that business is no game but earnest work. By reinterpreting their success as play, Marden both invoked the *Zeitgeist* of a new age and dissolved the distance between the millionaire and the clerk. If the point was simply to play, everyone could truly win.

"The game" and the crises of capitalism

Sporting rhetoric in the success literature of both liberal ministers and lay prophets addressed the dilemmas of the emerging consumer culture more directly than did the Western and Southern sporting myths. As the fierce competition of industrializing America increasingly gave way to monopoly by the end of the century, the consequences of competition were not at all obvious. The age of millionaires and consolidation was also an age of unprecedented corruption, of labor unrest, of a business cycle in which periodic panics toppled giants as well as pigmies (according to a contemporary estimate, 95 percent of businesses during this age of business failed).[48] It was an era of profound disruptions and wrenching transformations: of changes that once took centuries now occurring within a generation.[49] And the effects of these transformations were felt in individual psyches as well as large-scale demographics.[50] The new economic order defied the Protestant ethic that had long served as a fundamental faith. The traditional idea of a "calling" was incompatible with both the sudden and spectacular wealth of the plutocrats and the tedious labor of the factory workers; the beginning of a shift by the end of the period from a production- to a consumer-based economy began to challenge the primacy of work itself. The social Darwinism popularized by Herbert Spencer and his followers, with its belief in natural selection and the survival of the fittest, clashed with older traditions rooted in the Bible and Christian precepts that required service and altruism. Faith in progress competed with despair over the loss of traditional values: the forces of modernism and antimodernism hopelessly at odds. The various efforts by social workers to deal with urban poverty, the new concern with leisure (both its abundance for some and its lack for others), the handicraft movement of the late 1890s, the popular mind-cure movements preaching self-fulfillment were all attempts to come to terms not just with a new economic and social order but also with its psychological impact on ordinary citizens.

The "game" – of business, of success, of life – addressed these anxieties. Historian Robert C. Bannister has insisted that Spencer's ideas were not openly adopted by prophets of success and captains of industry to justify the age's business practices (Carnegie was an exception); rather, America's Spencerians were capitalism's critics – men like Henry George, Henry Demarest Lloyd, and Edward Bellamy – who made "the charge, usually unsubstantiated or quite out of proportion to the evidence, that Darwinism was widely and wantonly abused by forces of reaction."[51] Social Darwinism was important less as a practical philosophy than as an interpretation of contemporary events. As such, social Darwinism made life a battle. The success ethic made it a game. The martial metaphor, as we have seen, had coexisted in America with the sportive one since Puritan times, but by the beginning of the twentieth century the image of the game was at last overriding the image of battle in popular rhetoric. The liberal ministers who preached from the text of the 'game of life were in many cases the same ones who provided a justification for intercollegiate athletics in its formative period by elevating the sporting contest from pastime to character-building enterprise. The "game of life" was related to college sport in the late nineteenth century as theory to educational practice: On football fields young men were training themselves for that larger game of business and life where secular "salvation" was at stake. The "battle of life" would have implied victory to the merely powerful in this contest; the "game of life" suggested fairness and equality, and something more besides: the spirit of play itself. If one played rather than warred at life, then the contest was not so grim, the prospect of defeat not so terrifying. One could celebrate the game of life more easily than the battle.

I am tentatively proposing that "the game," rather than social Darwinism, was the foremost popular social philosophy at the turn of the century. The protean image of an abstract "game" could serve seemingly contradictory purposes. In an age of fierce laissez-faire competition, the "game" could imply that the contest was fair, just as in a later age of giantism and incorporation, the "game" could imply that fair competition continued. Above all, the "game" internalized the contest: It was rooted in competition against one's own weaknesses, not against any individual (a crucial difference from the Southern and Western sporting myths). Not only did the champions of the game preach that everyone could *play* it (contrary to the realities of lower-class conditions), they came to insist that everyone could *win* (every white male, that is; the success ethic was preached only to young men, and white superiority was assumed). Victory lay not in matching Rockefeller's millions but in realizing one's own potential. In *The Exceptional Employee* (1913), Marden acknowledged that the young men for whom he wrote were no longer likely to be country youths come to a city of vast possibilities, but "employees," ciphers in a corporate organization facing limited opportunities for advancement. The message is the same, but it takes on a new urgency in the context of drastically circumscribed corporate opportunities: "It has ever been men of ordinary ability and common virtues, with uncommon application, with supreme determination and persistence, who have won the great prizes of life."[52]

It is important to remember that the full-blown cult of the self-made man emerged after the age of self-made success had passed, and that the 1880s and 1890s were a period of deep labor unrest. As one historian has noted, "In the two decades after the Centennial Exhibition of 1876, with its grand celebration of American industry and progress, there were more strikes and more people wounded in labor demonstrations in the United States than in any other country in the world."[53] The success ethic was less a blueprint for success than a reassurance that traditional values still prevailed, proclaimed at a time when observable facts told a different story. This reactionary quality of the success literature is true of the Western and Southern sporting myths as well (and of popular myth generally?), whose function was to consolidate beliefs in times of crisis when the underpinnings for those beliefs were being kicked away.

In its abstractness and adaptability, the "game" rhetorically solved dilemmas it never explicitly addressed. It is possible to read late-nineteenth-century success literature today unaware that labor unrest, the consolidation of capital, and the constriction of opportunity were pressing problems (there were exceptions: In *Chances of Success,* for example, published in 1893, Erastus Wiman addressed the recent business panic and resulting economic depression by calling for a new fiscal policy). Most often the sporting metaphor suppressed political, social, and economic realities, offering metaphysical solutions to thoroughly material problems. The game denied its materiality altogether; whether early or late, in the writings of a minister or a promoter of investments like Zebediah Flint, acquisition of wealth was always subordinated to the process: to the development of character, the realization of individual potential, or the joy of the contest.

At every stage of its metamorphosis, the game's players were said to control their own destinies. For Thayer and company, conditions of birth and environmental factors presented no insurmountable obstacles to the boy or man who entered the race with determination and perseverance. For exponents of the New Thought like Elbert Hubbard, success was "a result of mental attitude."[54] Furthermore, luck or chance played no part whatsoever – a striking feature in conceptions of the game of life in all of the success literature I have been describing (Progressive Era novelists dramatically inverted this doctrine, as we will see in the next two chapters). Captains of industry and prophets of success spoke with one voice here. Although the boom-and-bust cycle taught hard lessons about the chanciness of success, the official philosophy declared otherwise. And while great fortunes in fact were made (and lost) on Wall Street and in other kinds of speculation, the spokesmen for the success ethic roundly denounced any such gambling on chance. On this point Ford and Carnegie were as adamant (in their public stances anyway) as Thayer and Marden. The industrialists most explicitly opposed actual speculation; the preachers of success denied the reality of chance more generally in human destiny, in terms that echoed Puritans' theological objections to gambling.[55] "There is no such experience as *luck* among men," Thayer insisted in *Tact, Push, and Principle*. "There cannot be in a world of law and order. If there were no God and no Divine government, and chance and chaos ruled the hour, there might be a place for luck somewhere in the universe" (58). To these men of the nineteenth century, luck denied both divine Providence and the spirit of democracy that guaranteed equal opportunity to all (a century later, as we shall see in Chapter 9, champions of capitalism embraced chance as the very source of democratic justice). To believe in luck was to accept disorder as the underlying principle of human life. When the time comes that virtue is punished and vice rewarded, Thayer wrote in *Success and Its Achievers*, then "can a sensible man embrace the popular delusion about luck" (18). Marden made the same point in *Pushing to the Front*: "Has God abdicated? Is the universe an infinite chaos, in which order has no throne? . . . Then is there such a game of chance as men call luck" (333). Professed faith in the character-building powers of earning wealth masked the traditional distrust of wealth itself, particularly unearned wealth. But belief in chance was the ultimate threat to character.

By downplaying competition, consolidation, and chance – the elements of what might be considered capitalism's own painful *agôn* – "the game" expressed an official faith in fairness, in the face of a reality anything but fair in the sense intended, while mediating between "work" and "play" at a time when the values expressed by those terms were in upheaval. The rhetoric of sporting success seems progressive, imbued with the spirit of a "strenuous" age, yet it was politically conservative in counseling acquiescence rather than resistance to "natural" forces. The game metaphor contributed to what Jackson Lears has called the pattern of "evasive banality" in the official doctrines of progress that ignored the profound uneasiness throughout the culture. More positively, it offered anxious citizens assurance of cultural continuity (its consolations, of course, were available only to those who were troubled but not materially crushed by the economic order). As Daniel T. Rodgers has observed of the late-nineteenth-century success literature, "The striking phenomenon of the age was not change but persistence amid change. Or, to be precise, it was the endurance of the outer husk of the work ethic as an increasingly abstract ideal, more and more independent from work itself."[56] The game of life was just such an abstraction: retaining the structure of traditional covenants, calling, and conversion, but utterly transforming them. The Puritans assumed a final end beyond the mere striving for it. The idea of a "game," on the other hand, assumed that in a fundamental way the playing was for its own sake. Thus, although the game reconciled moneymaking to spiritual values and perhaps alleviated other tensions within the culture, it also jeopardized that entire process by denying its ultimate purposefulness. In the "game of life" one sees American capitalism in uneasy transition. The metaphor expressed the values of a new order in ways that clung to older beliefs, masking in its vagueness the culture's growing uncertainty over individual and social ends. In the twentieth century, that sportive metaphor would prove equally adaptable, an echo of continuity amidst perplexing and disturbing change.

5

"The Game" in Business Fiction

Liberal ministers and success prophets articulated an abstract game; novelists grounded it in social contexts. As the fictional paradigm of the sporting business hero I would propose, perhaps surprisingly, not the collective protagonist of Horatio Alger's 120-odd novels but Gilbert Patten's Frank Merriwell. The rhetoric of "race" and "game" are really not parts of Alger's worldview.[1] Alger's heroes prove their worthiness through demonstrating traditional virtues in their lowly lives as bootblacks or newsboys, then "win" success through a lucky accident, perhaps by rescuing the son of a future benefactor. Despite such titles as *Work and Win,* life in Alger's fiction is neither a game nor a battle; it is no contest at all. Alger, an ordained minister, endorsed the values of an older world *against* the competitive spirit that was rationalized, domesticated, and celebrated by the rhetoric of "games." "Luck and pluck" are the keys to success in Alger's world, yet they have no causal relation either to each other or to success. Luck is not blind chance on which one can gamble, but the workings of Providence. Pluck – shorthand for the values of the Protestant ethic – is a sort of "preparation" for the Providential act, as preparation was understood by seventeenth-century Puritan ministers (the individual was responsible for disposing himself for salvation, but only God could grant saving grace). Although Alger's novels always implied that the deserving would be blessed by luck, he made no attempt to demonstrate that success would necessarily follow upon virtue. In the "game," on the other hand, the victors always won life's prizes.

Patten's Frank Merriwell, not Alger's Ragged Dick, is the paradigmatic juvenile hero of the "game of life." All-around champion of virtually every popular sport during the period of his regular appearances in the *Tip Top Weekly* (1896–1913), the era when sporting rhetoric became fully normalized, Frank Merriwell (and his brother Dick) applied their sporting spirit to off-the-field ventures that ranged from staging dramas to running a railroad to investing on Wall Street. Contest was the essence of Frank Merriwell's world, but contest governed by an unbending code of sportsmanship. The dramatic conflict underlying most Merriwell stories was a simple contest between Frank and a villain who didn't "play fair." On the baseball field it was a crooked umpire or an unscrupulous opponent who presented the obstacle to Frank's victory; on Wall Street it was a ruthless speculator. The playing field was thus an actual arena at times but more often the dominant metaphor for an entire universe. In Russel Nye's words, "The Merriwells equated virtue with the discipline of sport. . . . Using the athletic contest as his central device, Patten stressed success as self-improvement, self-realization, self-control, self-conquest."[2]

In this Manichean moral universe, the specific "game" of business is structured around the simple opposition of the gamesman's material contests to the sportsman's transcendent one. Two episodes from Merriwell's long career illustrate this conflict. In the first story, from 1898, Frank explains why leaving college for work has been no hardship, why he in fact prefers work to playing baseball:

> Work is the greatest sport in the world, for it is a game at which one plays to win the prize of his life. . . . It draws out the best qualities in a man, it tests him as nothing else can. Oh, yes, work is the champion sport, and success is the prize for which all earnest workers strive.[3]

In the later story, in 1907, Frank encounters the "Wolves of Wall Street," uncovering a swindle of the sort perpetrated by Gould and Fisk with the Erie Railroad. The chief swindler repeatedly speaks of "the game" he plays, with altogether different implications from Frank's own grand game of work. As arrogant and sanguinary as his name, J. Bradbury Blood plays a no-holds-barred gambling game of schemes and manipulations. Frank thwarts him, saves an unwary but honest loser from bankruptcy, and preserves his own fortune (several millions) from the clutches of Blood and "the System." And he makes an important distinction: "The margin operator is merely a gambler. There's a legitimate method of dealing in stocks, and the man who buys good securities outright usually comes *out right* in the end."[4]

In the Merriwell stories we see the direct connection between the socioeconomic world and those amateur sports that were the chief referents for the "games" of popular speech and thinking about success. The use of the metaphor of the "game" to designate both the reprehensible behavior of speculating scoundrels and the honorable acts of the productive businessman indicates a fundamental ambiguity in the culture's attitudes toward economic enterprise. The compatibility of Protestantism with capitalism in its early stages, about which Max Weber developed his famous thesis, broke down as capitalism followed the logic of profits. As we saw in Chapter 4, success writers drew a clear distinction between production and speculation, a distinction that was considerably less clear in the actual marketplace. No railroad, for example, could have been built without speculators' capital. Moreover, with industrial expansion, surplus profits not only devalued labor but made profit an end in itself. Contrary to the success myth, speculation was less a crime against capitalist productivity than a logical extension of the profit motive. Thus the celebration of the "game" of business enterprise but the denunciation of the "game" of speculation in the success literature unintentionally represents the close relationship of these supposedly contradictory economic acts.

Whereas the juvenile Merriwell stories maintain a simple distinction between contrasting "games," adult novels between the Civil War and World War I naturally address the issue more complexly. Paralleling but also complicating the success literature, these novels contextualize the issues underlying the various versions of "the game" by placing the sportive businessman in a world of economic and social relations in which his game playing has concrete results. In this fiction, then, the student of American culture can observe the genteel middle class's wrestling with issues that success writers could more easily ignore. As has often been the case in the various genres I have discussed, the 1890s marked a turning point. For virtually all the novelists of the Gilded Age, the differences between legitimate and illegitimate games had moral significance. Many writers in the Progressive Era, on the other hand, overrode this distinction in order to fantasize a human hero equal to the appalling forces of an indifferent universe.

Between two worlds

In 1877, when a recently expatriated Henry James wished to create a prototypical American, he made him both a businessman and, more generally, a player of the game of life. In *The American* we do not see Christopher Newman at work – by the novel's opening he has already made his fortune and left America for Europe to find culture and a wife – but the narrator offers this summary of his career:

> Christopher Newman's sole aim in life had been to make money; what he had been placed in the world for was, to his own perception, simply to wrest a fortune, the bigger the better, from defiant opportunity. . . . Upon the uses of money, upon what one might do with a life into which one had succeeded in injecting the golden stream, he had up to

his thirty-fifth year very scantily reflected. Life had been for him an open game, and he had played for high stakes. He had won at last and carried off his winnings; and now what was he to do with them?[5]

What, indeed? In America Newman won in wash tubs; now in Europe he seeks grander prizes. The earlier game turned a little sour: Waking up to the pettiness of his rivalry with another stock gambler led to his decision to see Europe. "As soon as I could get out of the game," he tells his friend Tristram, "I sailed for Europe." But Newman is too shrewd a player not to cover his bets for the future: "I have made over my hand to a friend; when I feel disposed, I can take up the cards again" (33).

Having laid one hand down, however, Newman cannot avoid playing another – James gave readers an "American" whose understanding of life was limited by the rules of his game. "The sense of great risks and great prizes" in Europe appeals to Newman's sporting instincts. Chiefly at stake now is a beautiful wife, "the greatest victory over circumstances" he can imagine (48). His resources are tact, push, and principle as Thayer would soon define them. Newman believes in neither luck nor fate; his destiny lies in his own hands. In his courtship of Claire de Cintré, he thinks of her as his "prize" or his "triumph" (247, 264), their betrothal as his "victory" (282).

But Christopher Newman confronts in Europe a people who do not see life as a game, or in any case play by his rules. Not all of the novel's Americans play games, nor its Europeans deny them, but in Claire's family Newman confronts the antithesis of all he stands for. Urbain de Bellegarde and his mother quite simply do not "play"; they scheme, in deadly, humorless earnest. At stake for them is not victory for its own sake but family pride with a long and complicated history. Having to Newman's mind agreed to the rules and the specific stake (Claire in marriage), the Bellegardes simply withdraw their permission when they determine that the marriage will not serve their interests. When Newman suspects some "foul play" in their past, he chooses a particularly apt term: implying not just the possibility of family scandal but the denial of Newman's own sense of *fair* play in their interference with his proposed marriage. The naive Newman poignantly remains a sportsman throughout the conflict: appealing first to the Bellegardes' "sense of fairness" (372) and ultimately rejecting mere vindictiveness. When he recognizes his defeat at last but decides to forgo revenge, Newman realizes that "they had hurt him, but such things were really not his game" (469). In the novel's final scene, after Newman has watched his evidence against the old marquise and her son turn to ash in the fireplace, Mrs. Tristram suggests to Newman that his magnanimity has been less his triumph than his defeat; the Bellegardes had presumed upon it all along. Although they have felt no obligation to play "fairly," they knew that the American would.

In his portrait of the American, James mixed affection with bemusement. On the one hand, the novel suggests, how naive it is of Newman to believe that life can be played as an honorable game. On the other hand, how admirable. And above all, James implied, how American. James spoke for a generation of late-nineteenth-century realists, most of whom could muster little of James's comedic detachment. From Europe, the American businessman could perhaps more easily appear to James a *naïf;* within America he was a considerably more troubling figure. If a dominant view can be described, it distinguished between honorable and dishonorable players at the game of life and business. The honest businessman in this fiction typically plays at the success writers' victimless game of life, while his unscrupulous alter ego competes in a more ruthless gamesman's contest, closer to the schemes of dime-novel Western villains, at the expense of innocent victims. A study of the period's popular magazines discovered a shift around 1903 from approval to criticism in the general attitude toward the businessman, but a double vision actually characterizes a divided sensibility throughout the half-century following the Civil War.[6] In contrast to success prophets, abetted with greater ambivalence by liberal ministers, who promoted an untroubled game of life that everyone could win, and to triumphant capitalists, who pursued expediency while remaining largely silent about their ethics, genteel writers of Gilded Age fiction revealed a deeply divided consciousness. They typically expressed horror at an economic order dominated by unscrupulous robber barons, while clinging to a faith that traditional values had not been altogether lost.

What might be termed the larger genre of economic fiction looks back to the tales of working girls in antebellum story papers described by David Reynolds in *Beneath the American Renaissance;* in the genteel literary tradition, to such works as Rebecca Harding Davis's "Life in the Iron Mills" (1861) and Elizabeth Stuart Phelps's *The Silent Partner* (1871), where criticism of industrial exploitation is not tied specifically to the career of a game-playing businessman. Phelps did use a chess image in the context of business: Her heroine, Perley Kelso, is "checkmated" in her desire to become an active partner in the mill when her manufacturer father dies. More interesting in retrospect, Phelps's presentation of a millworkers' strike as an unskilled, futile boxing match, in which the strikers bash "each other principally in the contest" rather than their oppressors, anticipates Ralph Ellison's elaboration of both theme and image in *Invisible Man* eight decades later.[7] But Phelps did not finally characterize either business or life as essentially a game.

These early novels of economic exploitation were written by women: those marginalized by gender empathizing with those marginalized by class. But business fiction by men and women in the 1870s and 1880s does not address "the game" in any clearly distinguishable way. The context for this fiction is invariably a conflict between honor and avarice in business practice; the game of business does not become transcendent until around 1900. In Mark Twain and Charles Dudley Warner's *The Gilded Age* (1873), the novel that named the era, the images of the businessman and his ethics rest on a distinction between the industry, perseverance, common sense, and hard work of Philip Sterling in struggling for "victory" in life; and the little "games" and wagers of Colonel Sellers, corrupt congressmen, and other speculators seeking wealth through chicanery.[8] In such less remembered novels as Josiah Holland's *Sevenoaks* (1875), Robert Grant's *An Average Man* (1884), Maurice Thompson's *A Banker of Bankersville* (1886), Rebecca Harding Davis's *John Andross* (1874), Mary Abigail Roe's *Free, Yet Forging Their Own Chains* (1876), Amanda Douglas's *Hope Mills* (1879), and Ellen Warner's *Queen Money* (1888), the same distinction is maintained, regardless of the author's gender. All of these novels denounce the "stock-gambler," the laissez-faire "race" for wealth, and the "games" played by ruthless financiers at the expense of the powerless and the principled. And all of them implicitly or explicitly set the business game against home, the transactions of the marketplace against the transactions of lovers. Refusing to enter the "race for wealth" or to play the game of "acquisition at all hazards and by any means," the heroes of Grant's and Thompson's novels turn instead to the love of good women, a theme that appears in the fiction by women as well. Douglas's *Hope Mills* reveals a distinctive female touch in having the great benefactor of an experiment in cooperative manufacture be a woman who desires "to see a small party of men trained to honesty and fair play." But otherwise there is no clear difference in these novels between male and female portraits of the businessman. Although gender is significant in this fiction in a variety of ways, in the specific treatment of "the game" it leaves no clear imprint. As we saw in Part I, in the nineteenth century, gender intersected with race and class, and with the conflicts between culture and economics, in ways that resulted in no completely separate male and female literary traditions.[9]

All of these novels implicitly or explicitly bridge two worlds. Their essentially preindustrial values, the values of the traditional Protestant ethic, conflict with a newer laissez-faire economic order, with tradition usually triumphant. In resisting social and economic change, if only through nostalgia, this business fiction confronted the problem of power and powerlessness more directly than Western fiction did. The wily gamesman of Southwestern humor is no hero in this fiction. As we saw in Chapter 1, the gamesman without power, only superior wit, became a sort of democratic hero in the tales of frontier humorists. The gamesman *with* power in the novels of business, on the other hand, is a ruthless exploiter. As this distinction became blurred, beginning with the novels of the business titan at the turn of the century, the relationship of the powerful to the powerless became deeply ambiguous.

Of all the earlier novels, Josiah Holland's *Sevenoaks* bridges the preindustrial and industrial worlds most schematically. At the novel's center lies the first great fictional monster in the "game" of business, Robert Belcher. As proprietor of both the mill and the sole mansion of Sevenoaks, a small town in the Northeast, Belcher victimizes his fellow citizens in a series of "games" in which he is determined that "he would sweep the board, fairly or foully, or he would not play." Having exhausted Sevenoaks' resources, Belcher moves on to the larger arena of New York's stock market, where he finds himself "playing for two stakes – present profit and future power and glory" in a series of schemes. Speculation is the mark of Belcher's villainy. Even as a mill owner he is unsatisfied with the steady, modest profits of industrial production (while the profits he does make derive chiefly from a stolen patent). Belcher's move to New York and involvement in stock gambling offer a lesson right out of the most moralistic success literature. The unsatisfied millionaire is a warning against mistaking wealth for true success. Even at his most triumphant, Belcher's victories bring no lasting pleasure, and his disregard for fair play brands him a scoundrel in the financial community.

Set against the self-defeating player of the swindler's game are Paul Benedict, Belcher's former employee whose invention he stole to make his initial fortune, and Jim Fenton, a spiritual descendant of Cooper's Natty Bumppo, who lives in the forest surrounding Sevenoaks. More obviously than any of these other novels, *Sevenoaks* through these characters sets the game in a context of cultural transformation. Against Belcher's amoral games of commercial scheming, Fenton represents the hunter's code of an older, pastoral order, the two moral systems clashing directly when Fenton helps Benedict sue Belcher over the mill owner's false patent claims. "The magnitude of the stake for which the defendant had played his desperate game" astonishes judge and jury, who award it all to Benedict. After Belcher flees arrest, whimpering like a sick boy, "Played out! played out!" Benedict assumes ownership of the mill at Sevenoaks, bringing prosperity to the entire town. And in the most intriguing aspect of the plot's resolution, Jim Fenton and his new wife are rewarded with a hotel to operate. The man of nature, that is, does not disappear back into the wilderness, in the immemorial manner of

Daniel Boone and Natty Bumppo, but leaves the woods to enter honest business: the prize of legitimate wealth "won slowly, by honest industry," as the novel puts it (and as a host of writers from Freeman Hunt to William Thayer preached). Belcher is consigned to only the first circle of the speculator's inferno, tending bar on a steamboat while he mindlessly mumbles about new corners in commodities. Belcher's happy idiocy denies him even the dignity of a tragic fall.[10]

Sevenoaks and the rest of these early novels established a pattern that prevailed to the end of the century: the distinction between the gamester and either the honest player or the nonplayer, the downplaying of mere wealth as the object of the true game, the opposition between woman/ family and the game in many of its forms, and the rejection of speculation as a path to success. What most distinguishes these early novels from later ones is their desire to straddle two epochs – to cling to older, simpler virtues in the face of a rapacious new economic order. The taming of a capitalist monster in Sevenoaks by a near-cousin of Leatherstocking, who is then rewarded with a small business, only expresses this longing for continuity most openly. Nature in Sevenoaks is not valued over civilization, as in Romantic myth; rather, the novel wants readers to believe that modern civilization need not progress at the expense of older values. The same combination of social criticism and quiescent nostalgia that we saw in Western and Southern writing operates here as well.

William Dean Howells's two business novels in the 1880s signal a turning point in the fictional portrayal of the game: a greater unease over business itself, unresolvable by simply distinguishing sportsmen from gamesters. In the differences between The Rise of Silas Lapham (1885) and A Hazard of New Fortunes (1889) the reader feels a deepening awareness that economic realities have irrevocably changed the nation. Although the differences in the novels most directly reflect Howells's changing personal views, to a great extent in response to the unjust conviction of eight anarchists following the Haymarket riot of 1886, they can also represent a more general shift in American novelists' treatment of business.

The Rise of Silas Lapham, for all its praise as the pioneering novel of business, is yet another narrative that views modern business from the vantage point of a vanishing preindustrial order. Like Holland, Grant, Roe, and others, Howells also stopped short of serious confrontation with the social and moral disruptions of the Gilded Age. And "the game" served the same function in Howells's novel that it did in Sevenoaks and The Average Man. When Silas Lapham boasts to a journalist in the novel's opening scene that "I've played it alone," he speaks in the voice of the success prophets and Andrew Carnegie who preached the advantage of rural background and childhood poverty. In the same spirit he later brags to Bromfield Corey that his toughness in the struggle to succeed in business is "just like exercising your muscles in a gymnasium. You can lift twice or three times as much after you've been in training a month as you could before." Silas, however, did not *win* but fell into success: inheriting his family's unwanted farm only to find a paint mine under it. Silas is more a farmer or miner of paint than a manufacturer of it, more a Jeffersonian anachronism than a captain of industry.

Silas Lapham doesn't truly become a full-blooded businessman until he makes what Walter Benn Michaels has called "the quintessentially capitalist gesture": He speculates.[11] Convinced of his own shrewdness in the game of business, Silas indulges heavily in stock trading, despite his wife's incessant warnings that speculation is no "better than gambling," that it is simply "like betting on the turn of a card." Once in the game, however, Silas is carried along by its logic. When his losses mount and bankruptcy threatens, Silas attempts to buy out his chief competitors in the paint business, so that he "would have the whole game in his own hand." But he fails in that, too. His salvation comes finally not by playing the game well but by refusing his former partner's fraudulent "games" altogether – victory through withdrawal as in the novels by Grant and Thompson.[12]

The "game" in *Silas Lapham* is Howells's rhetorical sign for capitalist amorality. But by retreating to his farm at the end of the novel, metaphorically as well as literally, where he will continue to thrive on a more modest scale, Silas signals the possibility of maintaining premodern values in the face of modern capitalism. Moreover, through Silas's business arrangement with Tom Corey, Howells unconvincingly created a concluding model of an economic order rooted in an alliance of aristocratic and yeoman values just as Holland did in *Sevenoaks*. That other world where Silas blundered into and lost the "game" still exists, but it can be ignored.

Four years later, in *A Hazard of New Fortunes* (1889), Howells rejected such evasions by probing more directly the economic conditions that the "game" represents. Compared to *Silas Lapham,* this novel offers a more palpable sense of the city as a place that shapes people's lives and of business as an enterprise with far-reaching consequences, and it exposes the implications of financial sport with subtler insight. In a novel built around a collection of regional and social types, each of whom expresses a distinctive political, social, and moral outlook, the capitalist Dryfoos and his publisher Fulkerson both represent the man of business and his philosophy. To link them in this way may seem inappropriate, as irascible Dryfoos and amiable Fulkerson are men of contrary temperaments; moreover, the wealthy capitalist and the more modestly successful publisher would seem to represent equally contrary kinds of businessmen.

But Howells's use of sporting rhetoric suggests a commonality between Dryfoos and Fulkerson, through which business enterprise itself, not just its perversion by speculators, is called into question.

Fulkerson speaks incessantly in the language of games: of being "bound to win," of "little games," of "playing it alone."[13] Fulkerson's sportive vernacular expresses the cheerful, strangely innocent amorality that characterizes him throughout the novel, that victimizes no one but leaves him incapable of perceiving the deeper issues at stake in the novel's drama. Unlike Basil March, who balks at Dryfoos's intrusions into editorial decision making, Fulkerson is willing to adapt to any set of rules whatsoever. Rather than a particular kind of businessman, Fulkerson is the businessman as a pure type: For him business is indeed a game, governed by self-validating rules and separated from any larger social context. But because Fulkerson has no real economic power, his gamesmanship results in distress for no one.

Rather than Fulkerson's inverse, Dryfoos is the same sporting businessman, but the considerable power of his wealth leads to consequences not possible in Fulkerson's life. Like Silas Lapham, Dryfoos is a beneficiary of fortuitous wealth; contrary to the success literature, he likewise stumbles on his wealth by accident. And like Silas again, Dryfoos gambles passionately in the stock market, a perversion of true enterprise in all of the fiction I have been discussing. But Dryfoos is not simply a man of good intentions who surrenders to temptation. He is Silas Lapham transformed by living in a world of real forces, and Howells expressed this difference through the novel's sporting rhetoric. Unlike Silas, Dryfoos understands the consequences of the game he plays so ruthlessly. To his son Conrad's idealistic claim that when the magazine makes money no one loses it, Dryfoos responds in a way that refutes a fundamental assumption in the success prophets' game of life: "Can you prove that? . . . Whatever is won is lost. It's all a game; it don't make any difference what you bet on. Business is business, and a business man takes his risks with his eyes open" (222). Dryfoos not only subscribes readily to the social Darwinism unacknowledged by almost all writers on business success, he himself becomes a victim of it – not by losing but by winning. Howells himself explained the two meanings of "hazard" in his title: Civilization had become, he wrote in a letter, "a state of warfare and a game of chance, in which each man fights and bets against the odds."[14] Dryfoos wins a fortune in his games of chance but at the same time falls victim to fortune's dangers. When mere moneymaking first became his sole object, the narrator explains, Dryfoos lost "the hard working, wholesome life" of his rural youth. "He began to honor money, especially money that had been won suddenly and in large sums" (263). Dryfoos developed the "gambler's admiration of wonderful luck" (264) – that *bête noir* of the success cult – "betting" on stocks, following "the game" on Wall Street, the "winning and losing" of great sums (415). In his commitment to business as a game, Dryfoos is no monster of the Belcher type, only a destructive, and self-destructive, *naïf*. When his "luck" turns bad at last with Conrad's random death during a street-railway strike, Dryfoos can still think of life only in terms of the game he's played, telling someone afterward, "All I want is to be fair and square with everybody" (460). There is something pathetic in so sincere but simple a response to events and circumstances so complex.

Basil March, Howells's spokesman in the novel, glimpses with horror the far-reaching implications if life is just the sort of game Dryfoos assumes it is: a zero-sum contest for base survival. At his most despairing, Basil tells his wife (in a familiar mix of martial and sportive language):

> Someone always has you by the throat, unless you have someone else in *your* grip. I wonder if that's the attitude the Almighty intended his respectable creatures to take toward one another! I wonder if He meant our civilization, the battle we fight in, the game we trick in! I wonder if he considers it final, and if the kingdom of Heaven on earth, which we pray for– (436)

Basil's statement goes unfinished, Isabel interrupting him before he can voice the ultimate blasphemy. In this powerful scene, Howells probed beneath the surface of the popular sporting rhetoric to glimpse into an abyss it too often concealed.

But Howells, like Basil March, did not voice the ultimate blasphemy. Having penetrated to the potential cynicism and amorality of the "game" of business that defined its own ethical system and left the players accountable to no one outside its boundaries, Howells stopped short of indicting contemporary American society for committing itself to that game. In *Sevenoaks,* Paul Benedict and Jim Fenton represent an alternative manner of business enterprise to Belcher's; in *A Hazard of New Fortunes,* Fulkerson is an alternative to Dryfoos, his darker double, only in lacking great wealth and the power that comes from it. But Howells refused finally to accept his own narrative logic, settling instead on a note of Christian hope that is validated nowhere in the novel. Unlike Silas Lapham, who finally was not changed by playing the game, Dryfoos and his family are profoundly altered by their sudden and enormous wealth and his commitment to the ethics of the game. In blocking Conrad's desire to be a minister, Dryfoos symbolically turns against those traditional values that sustain Silas Lapham. Silas returns to Vermont at the end of his novel, but there can be no return to Moffitt for Dryfoos. The concluding gesture toward Christian acceptance simply cannot offset all of these facts. The novel itself denies its own ending and remains a moving attempt to come to terms with a profoundly altered economic order.

From trickster to titan

Howells's darker vision contributed to a metamorphosis of the fictional businessman in the 1890s and early years of the new century. Although the older convention of pitting a traditional moralist against a game-playing monster of the new Business Age survived in novels like Robert Herrick's *The Man Who Wins* (1897) and Charles Dudley Warner's *That Fortune* (1899), new patterns emerged around the turn of the century as the tycoon became an ubiquitous figure in popular fiction.[15] By 1893, in Herbert Gutman's chronology of industrialization, the United States was not just a mature industrial nation but the leading industrial producer in the world.[16] It is appropriate, then, that in the business fiction of the Progressive Era, the financial or manufacturing tycoon is now a given rather than a possibility. In describing this age of muckraking it is important not to oversimplify middle-class attitudes toward this millionaire gamesman. Having examined the popular magazines of the 1890s and early twentieth century, Theodore Greene concluded that the portrait of the American businessman was overwhelmingly positive until 1903, after which it became more critical.[17] But muckrakers did not hold the floor unchallenged in the aftermath of exposés by Ida Tarbell, Lincoln Steffens, and Ray Stannard Baker in *McClure's* in 1903. The *Saturday Evening Post,* the most popular and most emphatically middle-class of the mass-circulation weeklies in the era, remained "dedicated to 'the romance of business,'" as Greene put it. The *Post* criticized the trusts and the wealthy elite for adversely affecting the middle class, but also in part for making possible a backlash that might lead to socialism.[18] In the agitation for reform, fear of mob rule outweighed fear of the trusts.

If the *Post* is an accurate index, much of America was obsessed with the business tycoon in these years. In the last half of 1902 alone, it serialized its editor George Horace Lorimer's own "Letters from a Self-Made Merchant to His Son," Henry Kitchell Webster's "The Copper King: The Romance of a Trust," Will Payne's "The Plant at High Grove," and Frank Norris's "The Pit." A typical single issue (August 23) included installments by Payne and Webster, plus an essay on "The Millionaires" by David Graham Phillips and the advice of a railroad executive on "Beginning in the Railroad Business." This half-year also saw the following articles: "The Captains of the Farming Industry," "How Millions Are Lost and Won," "Sons of American Millionaires," "The Making of a Billionaire" (about Rockefeller, by Phillips), "The Trust Builders," "The Money Kings of the New Dynasty," "Conscience

and Corporations," and more of the same. Interestingly, primarily frontier romances by Owen Wister, William Allen White, Emerson Hough,
and lesser known writers competed for space in the *Post*'s pages – seeming
to express an alternative fantasy rooted in pastoral nostalgia, but really,
as I have argued in regards to *The Virginian,* offering another version of
the success myth.

The *Post*'s writers reached no consensus. An Editor's Column in 1906
declared business "The Great Game" of unrivaled fascination, only to
introduce a new series by Will Payne, "Modern Business Practice," that
was highly critical of its subject. At the end of 1904, another writer in
the *Post* described inside information as the "loaded dice" used by bankers
and executives in "the Wall Street Game," but he admitted that such
practices were neither illegal nor probably immoral, only "unsportsmanlike." And in discussing J. P. Morgan as a case in point, the writer
restrained his criticism, regretting only that Morgan was not a greater,
that is, more public-serving, banker and man.[19]

The published novels of the era, many of them originally serialized in
the *Post, Everybody's, Cosmopolitan,* and other mass-circulation magazines, reveal continuity with the earlier fiction but important new elements as well. The conflict between honorable and dishonorable
businessmen largely gives way to that between weaker and stronger
players of the game. More strikingly, whereas the earlier novelists unan-
imously endorsed gentlemanly sportsmanship in business practice, their
successors in the Progressive Era sometimes admired the gargantuan
gamesmanship of financial giants. In this blurring of distinctions between
sportsmanship and gamesmanship, production and speculation, the business titan became a transcendent figure, not by appeal to either social or
religious tradition, but by invocation of the cosmic forces – Chance,
Fortune, Force itself – that were his imagined opponents in the game.
The titan was thus cast as a Nietzschean superman, yet in his larger-
than-life stature he was paradoxically also an emblem of common human
desire and possibility. Ordinary readers could see in the self-made robber
barons men of modest backgrounds, like their own, who amassed fortunes not through privilege but through personal power (at the expense
of the masses notwithstanding). All of the novels of business in the
Progressive Era were anti-corporate, even when they romanticized business. They insisted on giving business a name, and a body, at a time
when Peter Finley Dunne was describing the uneasiness created by the
new "uncanny race of incorporeal but corporate persons" that now ran
the economy.[20] Reform-minded novelists exposed the titan as a monster
of corruption; in many other novels he embodied a fantasy of autonomous selfhood. In both cases he was a human person, undiminished by
the new impersonal economic order.

A preoccupation with power, then, more than wealth, or even morals, dominates this fiction. The writers still valued honesty, but the forces of fair play prove increasingly powerless to check the scheming robber barons. Only a titan can defeat another titan. The loser's downfall makes a thunderous crash, its enormity conferring almost tragic dignity on the fallen giant. More challenging to tradition, the ruthless gamesman sometimes thrives, unpunished altogether, an object not of admiration certainly but of fascination: the man of will and power mastering a world that belittles the efforts of ordinary mortals. Even in defeat, the greatest of these speculator titans seem less object lessons in traditional morality than wondrous exemplars of the defiant human will, losers not of petty contests with opponents in the stock exchange but of defiant contests with Chance or Fate. Gambling, the vice denounced by every moralist in the nineteenth century, including the most ardent champions of the success ethic, came to define for some the heroic spirit of the modern age; but gambling now on a cosmic scale. In an article in *Harper's Weekly* in 1903, Edwin Lefevre, one of the many popular writers about business and businessmen in the Progressive Era, identified the speculator, that bane of past ages, as the soul of American enterprise (in a self-conscious manner, I should add, suggesting that Lefevre clearly understood his iconoclasm). Denying the conventional contrast between speculators and honest businessmen, Lefevre claimed that "every business man speculates, not occasionally, but all the time." Without speculators willing to take risks, no railroad would be built, no factory erected, no industry consolidated for America "to become a world power." Lefevre sidestepped the question of ethics altogether to insist that "the American gambling spirit," not the conservatism of its critics, was what made the United States an economic force in the world.[21] In such contexts, the magnitude of loss would be overwhelmed by the loser's audacity in entering the contest at all. The businessman transcended his petty world of trade or speculation to become both the most troubling and the most enticing hero/villain of the age.

For many reasons, then, the novels of business in the Progressive Era followed a logic of excess. The shift from a universal revulsion against excess in the novels of Holland, Howells, and the other Gilded Age writers, to a glorification of excess in many of the novels after 1900, bears out Jackson Lears's account of a shift from the older "scarcity therapy" (hoarding a limited supply of personal energy) as the key to personal happiness, to an "abundance therapy": the paradoxical insistence on unlimited psychic resources in the face of the constrictions of an increasingly organized and rationalized society.[22] At a time when outdoor exercise and lived experience were becoming cultic obsessions, the epic contests of Great Bulls and Bears in Wall Street or the wheat pit of the

Chicago Board of Trade embodied a fantasy to ameliorate readers' own thwarted desires.

These novels' excesses were rhetorical as well as thematic: in their self-conscious epic descriptions, in their typography (most conspicuously, a plethora of capitalized nouns that cast the stories in archetypal terms), and not least in their abundance of strikingly repetitive references to "the game." To characterize this fiction generally: The metaphor of the "game" encapsulated a profound cultural ambivalence, a longing for personal power accompanied by a deep anger against those who most obviously had power in the real social and political world. While the cowboy was also a popular figure of power, he existed in a fantasy world where his power bore only an abstract relationship to the world of his readers. The millionaire financier or captain of industry, on the other hand, represented power whose actuality could be everywhere felt.

As expressions of this ambivalence, two metanarratives, often in combination, dominate this fiction. The first is the traditional plot of the gamesman with power exploiting those without it. Novels like Frederic Howe's *The Monopolist* (1906) and Upton Sinclair's *The Moneychangers* (1908) embody this plot most explicitly by focussing on the victims of the titan's games. As a typical muckraker, Sinclair was chiefly concerned with what a character in his novel calls "the vast public which furnished all the money for the game – the people to whom dollars were not simply gamblers' chips, but to whom they stood for the necessities of life."[23] The moral bankruptcy and/or fall of a buccaneering capitalist was a second version of this basic plot. In several novels – David Graham Phillips' *The Master-Rogue* (1903), Robert Herrick's *The Memoirs of an American Citizen* (1905), Thomas W. Lawson's *Friday, the 13th* (1907), William Allen White's *A Certain Rich Man* (1909) – a giant is toppled, to illustrate the ancient warning of Ecclesiastes against the vanity of riches. The downfall is sometimes as spectacular as the rise: bankruptcy, madness, physical deterioration, loss of loved ones, miserable death. White's "certain rich man" undergoes an astonishing reformation out of his deep remorse; Herrick, the subtlest of these writers, more conventionally portrayed the emptiness of even the greatest victories in the game.[24]

Although all of the novelists overtly retained the traditional values of earlier generations, in many instances, wittingly or not, they portrayed monsters so potent and resourceful that readers could not help admiring them even in the face of overt disapproval. In a number of Will Payne's stories in *On Fortune's Road* (1902), for example – "A Day in Wheat," "The Salt Crowd's Trade," and "The End of the Deal" – as the game of business threatens home and femininity in conventional ways, the mighty player dwarfs his weaker victims in narrative interest.[25] The second narrative, then, nonexistent before the 1890s, celebrated the titanic gamesman as a figure of transcendent power. Often this plot centered on a contest between rival titans, in many cases the "two kinds of business men" described by the narrator of Samuel Merwin's *The Short-Line War* (1898):

> those who make their business at once work and play, a means of acquiring wealth and a most exciting game whose charms make all other games seem flat and unprofitable; and another class who, though they may enjoy work, turn for recreation to whist or philanthropy or golf.[26]

In preferring the player at business and life to his less daring fellows, Merwin expressed a desire inadmissible a generation earlier.

Merwin's novel, like Payne's "The End of the Deal" and *The Money Captain* (1898), Henry Kitchell Webster's *The Banker and the Bear* (1900), and Harold Bell Wright's major best seller, *The Winning of Barbara Worth* (1911), present the era's most telling morality play. Centered on a clash of speculators, these narratives work out an Olympian contest waged by the descendants of the original Titans, warring in the heavens unmindful of the poor creatures cowering below. The squeaks of opposition from earnest clerks have no effect on the financial gods who heave their thunderbolts at equal adversaries. Traditional moral values are not ignored. Merwin's Jim Weeks plays by the rules, whereas his opponent for control of a railroad line bribes politicians and recognizes no ethical boundaries; in *The Banker and the Bear*, "The End of the Deal," *The Money Captain,* and *The Winning of Barbara Worth* others take these contrasting roles. But in these novels playing itself on so grand a scale ultimately supersedes moral quibbles over the manner of playing.

In the first metanarrative, the gamesman who thrives at ordinary citizens' expense is an exploiter. In the second, the gamesman who triumphs over near-equals emerges as a larger-than-life hero strangely kin to the frontier trickster; that is, ironically, as a sort of *democratic* hero. The ambivalence that derives from a simultaneous longing for power and fear of power marks this fiction in conspicuous ways. The celebration of the financial gamesman depends on ignoring or suppressing the existence of "the people" as accidental victims of the titanic contest. All attention goes to the game itself and its mighty players. The business titans are players of the game, within or against the rules, playing for the love of play and victory itself as much as for the rewards to be won. A corner on some commodity is the typical stake, a source of boundless wealth for the winner but more important a symbol of complete mastery: control of *all* the wheat or *all* the lard – Olympian power in its most concrete form. As Webster's narrator says of the players in one contest,

"It is not the stake but the play that interests them." The enormity of the stake – not just a fortune for the winner but loss of everything for the loser – only heightens the players' zest in playing. When the great bear of Webster's novel finally loses, more through circumstance than a superior opponent, the narrator declares that "it was Nemesis that had overtaken him; or, to phrase it more modernly, the reflex action of the very force that had contributed so largely to his former success."[27]

Here is the most distinctive new voice in Progressive-Era fiction, announcing the metamorphosis of the businessman into a demigod unlike anything imagined by the more conservative success prophets. In his contest with Nemesis, or with Force or Chance as others termed it, the monopolist or overreaching speculator comes to embody neither an ideal for young men to emulate as they embark on careers in business, nor a moral lesson about the road not to be taken, but the fantasy of an individual's unbridled will defying the gods themselves, his inevitable destruction diminishing only slightly the grandeur of his assault. And by abstracting his opponent as Force or Chance, the novels simply ignore the actual consequences of financial manipulations in the material world.

The male writers of these novels were seemingly less sanguine about modern business practices than disturbed by the enervation, the "effeminacy," of the culture. With the exception of Edith Wharton's *The Custom of the Country* (1913), business novels by women from this period – Margaret Deland's *The Iron Woman* (1911), for example, and Edna Ferber's three volumes about businesswoman Emma McChesney – reveal no interest at all in the mighty titan I have been describing. Although Wharton's Undine Spragg is superficially a counterpart to the financial gamesmen in the fiction by men, Wharton made no attempt to make her larger-than-life. Sarah Maitland of Deland's novel is no monster at all but a conscientious, misguided woman who sacrifices everything, including her maternal and feminine instincts, to *work* hard for her children; and the "iron woman" of the title actually turns out to be seemingly fragile Helena Ritchie, whose iron lies in her commitment not to economic struggle but to Christian duty. Ferber's *Roast Beef, Medium* (1913), *Personality Plus* (1914), and *Emma McChesney & Co.* (1915) bristle with sporting imagery, but in order to celebrate the joyful competition of honest business on a small scale, particularly as played by a woman in a "man's game."[28]

The sometimes uneasy partnership of male and female writers under the banner of gentility that marked the fiction of the 1870s and 1880s broke down by the turn of the century, when a number of the men became fascinated by the aggressively virile, sky-assaulting tycoon. The male novelists who were drawn to this figure usually held conventional views about business morality, and in addition had to write for a primarily female readership. Like the fiction of the previous generation, their novels invariably set business against domesticity, with the titan's financial obsessions causing hardship for his wife and family. And the resolution of the conflict, again as was conventional, usually lay in affirming the values of home against the marketplace. Yet the business plot in many of these novels overshadows the domestic plot, dramatic interest in the titan's career dwarfing its hurtful consequences for wives and families. These are novels at odds with themselves; an irresolvable conflict between gargantuan desire and traditional morality consistently subverts their conventional narrative patterns.

Norris and Dreiser

This fundamental conflict, or contradiction, is played out in intriguing ways in the fiction of Frank Norris and Theodore Dreiser, two writers who conceived major trilogies centered on the tycoon. Having presented only fragmentary discussions of individual novels to this point, I have had to ignore the circuitous, conflicted routes by which specific novels arrive at their untidy resolutions. As a conclusion to this chapter, Norris in particular can serve as a representative as well as individual writer; Dreiser's view was more completely his own.

Norris's unfinished Epic of the Wheat epitomizes the upper-case rhetorical extravagance of the era's business fiction. In *The Octopus* (1901), not just the Wheat and the Railroad, but Love, the People, the Song of the West, the Vision, the Answer, and countless other entities are given archetypal meaning in an epic romance whose ultimate protagonists are implacable natural Forces. And in *The Pit* (1903) there is no let up. Sporting rhetoric has a conspicuous place in both novels' hyperthyroidal prose. Norris used it in *The Octopus* to develop the contest between the ranchers and the railroad in the San Joaquin valley and in *The Pit* to characterize the dealing in commodities on Chicago's Board of Trade. Moreover, the upper-case rhetoric of games and gambles raises Magnus Derrick and Curtis Jadwin, the overreaching heroes of the two novels, to Olympian heights, from which their falls can seem nearly tragic. In both novels, however, the drive toward metaphysical abstraction, in which sporting rhetoric plays a major part, is at odds with the felt life of the human protagonists and their acts. A fundamental confusion arises when Norris attempts to combine the two dominant plots of exploitation and titanic contest. Additional confusion is created when Norris attempts to resolve all conflict in a benign philosophy of force. The contest of large-F Forces initially seems to exalt the human players, only to render their grandest acts inconsequential in the end. These contradictions and confusions, which result from Norris's own muddled thinking, also typ-ify many of the other novels I have discussed.

The Octopus is chiefly a novel of epic contest, with contradictory ges-tures toward social criticism and philosophical fatalism. Adapting the actual historical conflict between small farmers and the Southern Pacific Railroad at Mussel Slough in 1880, Norris made the farmers mighty ranchers, presiding not over a few hundred acres but over kingdoms of wheat, and then made the leader of the ranchers, Magnus Derrick, neither a victim nor a simple opportunist but a gambler against Chance itself. The characterization of Derrick illustrates well the era's obsession with personal magnetism as an inner force to which others will defer. Magnus never demonstrates in his actions any reason for everyone to regard him as their natural leader, an indubitably great man, yet he never appears in the novel without mention of this personal power. And in a novel in which every major character has a distinctive rhetorical signature, a Ho-meric epithet, Magnus is ever and repetitiously the gambler: "the most redoubtable poker player of Calaveras County" in his early years, "the great gambler" always.[29] A gambler in the gold mines during the days of the '49'ers, Magnus becomes a gambler in wheat and then a gambler of his entire fortune and his honor in the contest with the railroad. Above all, in pursuing his usually capitalized "Chance," Magnus becomes a *cosmic* gambler, pitting his human powers against the indifferent forces of the universe.

Magnus's transcendent "game" is always distinguished from the ubiq-uitous petty "games" of lesser mortals. Magnus is introduced as a gam-bler in the second chapter when the ranchers first gather to plot a strategy for the "game" the railroad plays with shipping rates (68). The other ranchers readily accede to the need to play a "game" of bribery in re-taliation (105, 107); only Magnus balks, his reputation for honesty es-sential to him. But his fellow ranchers know how to entice him. "You are not the sort to shrink from taking chances," Osterman tells him. "To play for big stakes is just your game – to stake a fortune on the turn of a card. You didn't get the reputation of being the strongest poker player in El Dorado County for nothing [a bit of narrative confusion about the scene of Derrick's early exploits]. Now, here's the biggest gamble that ever came your way" (110). Magnus's "game" in practical terms is the same one played by Osterman, Annixter, Harran, and the other ranchers, yet the narrator insists that the consequences are im-measurably greater for the redoubtable gambler. Magnus's game is tran-scendent simply because of who he is: "the Master," "the Leader." The greater the man, the greater the risk, the greater the game.

The novel repeatedly makes this distinction. After Annixter tells Der-rick that "everybody plays the game now as we are playing it," in the next paragraph Magnus wonders "if this were his chance, after all, come at last after all these years. His chance! The instincts of the old-time gambler, the most redoubtable poker player of El Dorado County, stirred at the word. Chance! To know it when it came, to recognise it as it passed fleet as a wind-flurry, grip at it, catch at it, blind, reckless, staking all upon the hazard of the issue, that was genius" (185). Annixter, Osterman, Dyke, Genslinger, all speak of petty, material "games"; only in Magnus Derrick's contest is anything transcendent at stake. And having staked more, Magnus loses more. All of the ranchers lose the "game" with the railroad over freight rates and the grading of their property. Magnus also loses his beloved son Harran in the shootout, as well as home, reputation, dignity, and sanity. Although Magnus's fall recalls the exemplary defeats of dishonest gamesmen in earlier business novels, it differs because of Norris's obvious attempt to evoke tragic awe at his downfall. Magnus's flaw is not greed but hubris, his presumption to stand not just above his fellow mortals but eye-to-eye, toe-to-toe, with Chance and Force.

In the profusion of sporting metaphors Norris invested "the game" with many of his deepest values. It is gender-marked, as when Annie Derrick repeatedly shrinks before the players' masculine aggressiveness, and when the ranchers' contest with the railroad is contrasted to the frivolous social games of San Francisco as it is turned into what the manufacturer Cedarquist contemptuously calls a "Midway Plaisance" (303). It is also class- and race-marked, most notably in the remarkable scene of the jack-rabbit drive. Having organized the drive and herded the rabbits into a corral, the Anglo-Saxon ranchers withdraw in disgust as the "hot, degenerated" Portuguese, Mexicans, and mixed-blood Spaniards indulge in the cruel sport of clubbing the poor brutes (502). The managerial elite is absolved of all responsibility for the slaughter. Instead, the ranchers and their families turn to alternative sport: after a great barbecue, to the footraces and wrestling that traditionally follow Homeric feasting, characterized by "an honest Anglo-Saxon mirth and innocence" (505). The contrast between different "sports" is anything but subtle.

In the novel's wide canvas of such games Magnus Derrick's portrait is finally more contradictory than tragic. Derrick's great gamble is repeatedly declared heroic, yet the means of playing the game are merely shameful – the result, a jumble of moral comeuppance and self-created human grandeur. By attempting to have the same "game" stand for tragic overreaching and petty exploitation, Norris created only confusion. The rhetorical extravagance of the paeans to Derrick's contest with Chance seem imposed on a plot whose fundamental fact is exploitation. The ranchers exploit the land (raping it with their plows in gorgeously overwritten primeval encounters of nature and machine) and dream of forming their own trust to oppose the railroad's. When a worker, Dyke, becomes a landowner, he too immediately follows the fundamental drive to exploit. In a single conversation Dyke first attributes his success in hops to his "daisy" of a foreman, then, in virtually the next breath, declares that with his good fortune he can now fire the foreman before the next crop ("I've learned the game myself" [344]). The ranchers are exploiters, yet at the same time the novel casts them as "the People," victims of the octopuslike railroad and its minions' exploitative "games."

The true "people" are simply unrepresented by the major actors in *The Octopus,* and their inappropriate identification with the ranchers reminds readers that somewhere in this world are actual persons who must pay the consequences no matter who wins the great "game." *The Octopus,* in fact, offers a case study in the tendency toward abstraction that particularly marks turn-of-the-century masculinist fiction, but that is also more generally present throughout the traditions of sporting rhetoric I have been examining. The railroad's and ranchers' wholly material "games" have bitter economic consequences; as cosmic gamble, on the other hand, Magnus Derrick's personal "game" transcends its roots in mere bribery. Norris did not resolve this contradiction but added another: Both the material and the material/transcendent games are rendered meaningless by the novel's final vision of life as purely abstract force. In the concluding scenes that have generated most of the critical controversy over the novel, Shelgrim, the president of the railroad, tells the distraught poet Presley, "The Wheat is one force, the Railroad another, and there is the law that governs them – supply and demand. Men have only little to do in the whole business." The Wheat grows itself, the Railroad runs itself; farmers and capitalists are powerless to direct either (576). Presley is unpersuaded until his mystic friend Vanamee affirms this view, recasting it according to the benign evolutionary theism that Norris learned from Joseph Le Conte at the University of California. While some critics wish to dissociate Norris from Presley, in order to exonerate the author of the character's determinism, the novel ends not in Presley's but in the third-person narrator's voice: "Greed, cruelty, selfishness, and inhumanity are short-lived; the individual suffers, but the race goes on." The wheat continues inexorably to market, to feed the world's hungry, "and all things, surely, inevitably, resistlessly work together for good" (651–2). When the railroad is redefined as a natural Force instead of a powerful oligarchy, the novel becomes a decidedly ironic epic in which the heroes and villains are inconsequential. Presley – and Norris – absolve Shelgrim in the same way that the Anglo-Saxons were earlier absolved of killing the jack rabbits despite managing the drive. Wrestling with the fundamental theme of naturalistic fiction, the question of human power and

powerlessness, Norris transformed an historical incident of brutal violence into an epic contest of powerful gamesmen, then denied the players
any power at all in a world of self-generating forces.

The Pit repeats less interestingly both the gesture toward epic and the
contradictory denial of this move in the name of impersonal force. The
scene in which the broker Gretry draws Curtis Jadwin into speculating
on the commodities market is typical. Till now content with his fortune
in real estate, Jadwin is attracted not by the money to be made but by
"the fun of playing the game," and even more by what his "strange sixth
sense" tells him is his "Chance":

> Every now and then during the course of his business career, this in-
> tuition came to him, this *flair*, this intangible, vague premonition, this
> presentiment that he must seize Opportunity or else Fortune, that so
> long had stayed at his elbow, would desert him. In the air about him
> he seemed to feel an influence, a sudden new element, the presence of
> a new force. It was Luck, the great power, the great goddess, and all
> at once it had stooped from out the invisible, and just over his head
> passed swiftly in a rush of glittering wings.[30]

As this passage makes clear, against conventional moral objections to
speculation Norris cast his great speculator as both a spirited sportsman
and a cosmic gambler, twin markers of one of the most popular fantasies
in the age of Teddy Roosevelt. But as in The Octopus, Norris mixed the
narratives of exploitation and cosmic contest in a way that only accentuates the contradiction implicit in this fantasy. The novel offers conflicting ways to read Jadwin's career. From one perspective, his obsession
with gambling in commodities nearly ruins his marriage, and every
move he makes in the wheat pit reverberates outward in often troubling
ways. His "luck" comes from crop failures throughout the world; his
successful corner literally takes food from the mouths of starving babes,
as bread prices soar. His defeat, then, becomes personal salvation like
that given Silas Lapham: He is restored to his wife and to a life of work
and modest striving. From the novel's other perspective, Jadwin pits
himself not only against Crookes, the Great Bear, but against the capitalized Wheat, even "the earth itself " (347), in a contest that at least for
a time elevates him above ordinary humanity. When Jadwin is defeated
at last, after descending into the pit to "play [his] hand alone" in his "last
move in the great game" (390), no puny mortal undoes him. As the little
men in the pit cheer the great man's fall, Crookes pays his rival his due:
"They can cheer now, all they want. *They* didn't do it. It was the wheat
itself that beat him; no combination of men could have done it – go on,
cheer, you damn fools! He was a bigger man than the best of us" (396).
Chastened mortal, fallen titan, Jadwin becomes finally just a human

cipher if the reader takes seriously the notion that the wheat cornered itself and now, released, flows on to its predetermined destinations. In both volumes of Norris's unfinished trilogy, social criticism, a fantasy of human power, and a philosophy of evolutionary theism confront each other irreconcilably. Exploitative "games," the Great Game, and finally no game at all inscribe this thematic confusion in the novel's rhetoric.

As Norris's novels make clear, the financier as symbol of overreaching human will proved an uneasy fit with the financier as a fact of American economic life. Norris's artistic failure is more usefully seen as a sign of the cultural confusion that has persisted into the 1980s in various ways. The one Progressive-Era novelist who succeeded in creating a convincingly Olympian business titan without blinking at the social and economic consequences of his career was Theodore Dreiser. As a poor boy who became obsessed with his own success, Dreiser had greater personal stake than the upper-middle-class Norris in the possibilities of self-creation. As a contributor to Orison Swett Marden's *Success* magazine (interviewing men like Carnegie, Edison, Armour, and Field), Dreiser also had first-hand acquaintance with personalities who had won in business. What is most striking about *The Financier* (1912) and *The Titan* (1914) in this context is how little Dreiser's portrait of Frank Cowperwood resembles the writings he did for Marden and *Success*.[31] In describing Cowperwood's struggle to "win" life's "prizes," his "race for wealth and fame," Dreiser used the language of the success prophets to portray a brutal, amoral universe in which losers far outnumber winners and the keys to winning are chance and ruthlessness.

Although readers of just *The Titan* would never suspect it, Cowperwood has to learn to be ruthless. From the opening of *The Titan* to its final page, the great financier coolly, *unreflectively* bribes whoever needs bribing and works whatever trick is necessary to defeat his rivals. I emphasize "unreflectively," because Cowperwood does not always act this way. Next to *The Titan*, its predecessor *The Financier* seems nearly a Jamesian novel of consciousness (however un-Jamesian the subject), revealing the consciousness of a "money-genius" as he learns to conduct his affairs without moral scruple. The famous episode in Chapter I of *The Financier*, in which a lobster's devouring a squid teaches young Frank how life is organized, is preceded by a rarely discussed one in which Frank (an avid player of baseball and football) beats up a local bully with his fists while the admiring gang leader assures "fair play." The narrator reports that Frank learned from this incident, as well as the other, that winning brings rewards (in this case the patronage of Red Gilligan), but the contrast between the "fair play" of Frank's fight and the Darwinian struggle in the fish tank also establishes a dual perspective through which

Frank Cowperwood continues for some time to view the world. Through the initial phase of his career as a financier Frank maintains a basic instinct for fair play despite his increasing awareness that the triumph of the strong is the rule of life. At the point when Cowperwood has achieved his first great success and is on the verge of becoming a major figure in political and financial manipulations, Dreiser describes him not as a tiger in the jungle, or even as a competitor in some fierce sport, but as a master chess player:

> Imagine yourself by nature versed in the arts of finance, capable of playing with sums of money in the form of stocks, certificates, bonds, and cash, as the ordinary man plays with checkers or chess. Or, better yet, imagine yourself one of those subtle masters of the mysteries of the higher forms of chess – the type of mind so well illustrated by the famous and historic chess-players, who could sit with their backs to a group of rivals playing fourteen men at once, calling out all the moves in turn, remembering all the positions of all the men on all the boards, and winning. This, of course, would be an overstatement of the subtlety of Cowperwood at this time, and yet it would not be wholly out of key.[32]

Chess is a rule-governed game, as nearly a test of pure intellect as a game can be. Cowperwood is not *overly* scrupulous in his financial dealings, to be sure. In that foreshadowing episode in the first chapter, the narrator pointedly observes that Frank fought fairly, except in the small matter of not removing a ring from his finger. Although the ring is not mentioned later in the fight, it undoubtedly contributes to Frank's bloody slashing of "Spat" McGlathery's face. As a financier, Cowperwood maintains this same sort of ambiguous "fair play": While participating in the misuse of city funds and other "games" (the term is a refrain), he avoids outright illegality, and he treats his colleagues and subordinates fairly. But he does all of this without ever jeopardizing his self-interest.

The experience that teaches Cowperwood to trust only force, not fairness, is his massively detailed financial fall, precipitated by the great Chicago fire of 1871, and in its aftermath, the ruthless machinations against him by the major political brokers in Philadelphia that result in a bitter thirteen-month prison term. Cowperwood at last decides that "life was a dark, insoluble mystery; but, whatever it was, strength and weakness were its two constituents. Strength would win; weakness lose" (476). From this point through *The Titan,* the detailed attention to Cowperwood's interior life yields to a sometimes numbing documentary of his financial and political strategems. After nearly 700 pages describing the gain and loss of his initial fortune, in a single final chapter of *The Financier* Cowperwood makes a bigger one when the great panic of 1873 presents him an opportunity; then in *The Titan* he plays a dizzying series

of "games" (social and sexual as well as financial), fairly when convenient, more often not, all of them singlemindedly pursued for power
and pleasure in service of his simple motto, "I satisfy myself."[33] In *The
Financier,* one of the politicians who engineers Cowperwood's conviction
is described as a man who "was willing to play fair when fair was the
game. When it was not, the reach of his cunning was not easily measured"
(317). Frank is surprised when he finds himself a victim of this cunning;
in *The Titan* the passage could easily describe his own philosophy.

The *Financier* is chiefly concerned with Cowperwood's fall; *The Titan*
ends in another defeat, his failure to win a fifty-year franchise for his
street-railway company. The second novel also concludes with an authorial explanation of the Spencerian "equation" that assures an ultimate
balance between the individual and the mass; between the strong, lest
they be too strong, and the weak, lest they be too weak. From this
account, the two novels might seem to follow the pattern of such contemporary ones as Phillips' *The Master-Rogue* and Lawson's *Friday the
13th* in chronicling the fall or moral bankruptcy of a mighty capitalist.
But Dreiser was no conventional moralist. Cowperwood is indeed an
exploiter, but he is also a mighty player of the "game." Like Norris,
Dreiser incorporated both of the era's principal narratives of business
into his novels, but unlike in *The Octopus* and *The Pit,* the result is not
inconsistency and confusion. Even as he becomes utterly ruthless, Cowperwood remains believably, impressively powerful – without the narrative denying the consequences of his machinations. Although "the
people" are not actors in the two novels, their existence is repeatedly
acknowledged, both in Cowperwood's reflections on those who are born
to be weak and in the narrator's periodic expressions of compassion for
those who endure their weakness with dignity. There is no inconsistency
here. The master player of financial games *is* an exploiter, these novels
say, but the exploitation of the weak by the strong is the law of life.
One can feel compassion for the weak, one can wish for honest politics
and finance, but the strong will prevail.

The Cowperwood novels, in other words, solve the cultural dilemma
expressed in the "game" of business fiction in the simplest possible way:
They renounce morality. As we have seen, ambivalent longing for power
and fear of power's real effects are central to the era's business novels
both individually and collectively, often resulting in narrative confusion.
Exposés of the exploiter typically undermine their own intentions as the
ruthless gamesman emerges as far more interesting – appalling yet fascinating – than his earnest moral critic. Celebrations of the sportive titan,
on the other hand, undercut themselves when they fail to acknowledge
the material consequences of his acts. When the two narratives compete

within single novels, as in *The Octopus* and *The Pit,* the contradiction inherent in the era's definition of the "game" becomes most obvious.

Dreiser cut through the cultural and narrative ambivalence by recasting it as dialectic: The gamesman with vast power is also an exploiter, the exploiter also a creator of wealth and a builder of cities. *The Financier*'s opening description of Philadelphia in the 1830s, a city nearly two hundred years old and with 250,000 inhabitants, ironically emphasizes *lack*. "Many of the things that we and he [Cowperwood] knew later were not then in existence," the narrator comments, then begins listing them: "the telegraph, telephone, express company, ocean steamer, or city delivery of mails. There were no postage-stamps or registered letters. The street-car had not arrived, and in its place were hosts of omnibuses, and for longer travel, the slowly developing railroad system still largely connected with canals" (1). The city first seen by the wide-eyed small-town girl at the opening of Dreiser's *Sister Carrie* is a hive of energy and a cornucopia of objects to be desired. The very different city into which Frank Cowperwood is born is an unmade place to be created by those who are strong enough to seize the opportunity. Philadelphia, and Chicago afterward (a different, less finished Chicago than Carrie encounters), are built by Frank Cowperwood and his kind, the ruthless financiers, meatpackers, gas developers, and street-railway magnates who accumulate wealth and power at the expense of weaker citizens but in the process create great metropolises. Dreiser offered no resolution or amelioration between ambition and exploitation, simply declaring them as facts of American life.

Dreiser's "solution" to the cultural dilemma was a troubling one, to be sure. The majority of reviewers were offended by both the amorality and the sexuality of *The Financier* and *The Titan*.[34] And his view did not lead to a dominant tradition of naturalistic representations of the "game" of business. Rather, from the 1920s to the 1980s, the "game" continued to embody cultural uncertainty and conflicting values, the desire for transcendent personal power continuing to confront the often disturbing consequences of power in the material world.

6

Desperate Players and the Sport of the Gods

By casting the player of the game of life as a cosmic gambler, Norris and Dreiser joined two traditions that had remained separate through the nineteenth century. The entrepreneurial hero of success literature labored to fulfill the divine plan, becoming an agent of both Progress and Providence. The naturalists' gamesmen and gamblers, on the other hand, lived by *defiance* of whatever Forces ruled the universe and held lesser men to a paltry existence. In defiance they towered over grubbing mankind; in defiance they were destroyed by the Forces they blasphemed. Whether design or randomness finally governed the universe was uncertain, but in either scheme individuals mattered little, and only so far as they resisted their fate. By transforming grim struggle into a sporting contest, the spirit of play at least made defeat meaningful.

The sporting Titan transformed the "game of life," then, into a more desperate game, with "God" as Opponent rather than Umpire and Rulemaker, the stake not to be bestowed by God but wrested from him. The Titan's kin were the gambling frontiersmen who wagered not just gold against a faro dealer but their lives and livelihoods against Fate or Chance, in a world in which losers outnumbered winners many times over. His ultimate spiritual kin were the most conservative colonial Puritans and their Edwardsean offspring: the believers in human helplessness and an all-powerful predestinating God. The success prophets' game of life promoted a popular version of Protestant liberalism; this other game resided in the Calvinist tradition, whether to endorse or to defy it. In images of mankind as the sport of the gods (or of Chance or Fortune) and of individuals contesting against whatever power controlled their lives, a number of writers denied the rosy assurances of the liberals to portray life as a more desperate affair.

This deeply agonistic sporting rhetoric had its roots in the doctrine of the lot and in Jacob's wrestling with God as a type for spiritual struggle. But whereas the Puritans "wrestled" with their God as an essential aspect of their religious experience, this motif virtually disappeared from the popular religious culture by the end of the nineteenth century. The obvious incompatibility of such wrestling with religious liberalism can be neatly illustrated in an 1869 sermon by Henry Ward Beecher, with Gen. 32 as his text. Beecher acknowledged that the description of Jacob's wrestling was "one of the most remarkable narratives of the intercourse of the divine with the human that is contained in literature." But Beecher made no effort to comprehend this narrative. "As to what this wrestling was – the whole mode of it; we know nothing," he confessed. The lesson he drew from it was the transformation of Jacob's character from craftiness to nobility of purpose. About the crux of the text – the implications of a man *wrestling* with God – Beecher had nothing to say; *could* have nothing to say, given his commitment to a religion of love and moral duty.[1]

For more conservative Protestants Jacob's wrestle at Peniel remained an important type in the revivalism of the religious Awakening during the century's early decades; Cynthia Griffin Wolff has claimed in this regard that Jacob was "the prototypical hero for the men and women who were New England's final Puritans."[2] Even here, Jacob's story was reinterpreted in such a way as to soften the Puritan *agôn*: Wrestling with a God of justice became imploring a God of mercy. For example, Charles Grandison Finney, the most famous preacher of the Awakening, cast Jacob the wrestler as a supplicant to a benevolent God, demonstrating the power of "prevailing prayer" for Christian emulation. Other less renowned revival ministers shared this view: one describing "fervor" in prayer as that quality "which wrestles with God"; another attributing his own conversion during a revival to "the direct work of the Holy Spirit in answer to the wrestling, agonizing prayers of my dear mother"; a third counseling his fellow ministers to rekindle languishing fervor during revivals by "wrestl[ing] as Jacob did" to keep the Lord among them.[3] Absent from all of these metaphors is the mysterious, terrifying, enigmatic sense of the passage in Genesis, the possibility that God in some real way might be an opponent to his paltry creatures, resisting their pleadings.

Even in this softened version, the image of Jacob's wrestle disappeared altogether. As Protestant evangelicalism underwent a transformation, in Richard Rabinowitz's terms, from "doctrinalism" to "moralism" to "devotionalism" (from Edwards to Finney to Dwight L. Moody, as representative figures), Jacob and what he represented ceased to speak meaningfully to succeeding generations.[4] The disturbing power of Gen. 32 depended on an acute consciousness of the immeasurable distance between God's divinity and Jacob's humanity. But over the first half of the nineteenth century, the religious sensibility of evangelicals increas-

ingly shortened the distance between God and His human creatures –
God now perceived as a loving Father, men and women as his beloved
children – until the notion of "wrestling" with God became unimagin-
able. For Charles G. Finney, as I noted, "wrestle" signified "prevailing
prayer." In a book with that very title in 1884, Dwight L. Moody
identified Jacob, along with Abraham, Hannah, and Elijah, as a figure
of prevailing prayer in the Old Testament. But no mention of Jacob's
story follows this brief mention, and Moody proceeds to describe the
qualities of love, faith, and *submission* essential in the one who prays,
assuring readers that a sincere cry for help will be answered.[5] In other
sermons Moody spoke more strenuously of the "battle" of life, but as
a liberal would. Liberals and evangelicals, in fact, were not doctrinally
very distinct in the late nineteenth century. Liberals pursued salvation *in*
the world, evangelicals against it; liberals worked for salvation, evangelicals worked to deserve the salvation that God freely gave them;
evangelicals wanted more enthusiasm than rationalism in their religion.
But on the benevolence of God and the availability of grace liberals and
evangelicals differed little.[6]

It seems to have been Billy Sunday, one of Moody's chief revivalist successors and, significantly, a former professional baseball player, who
introduced sporting rhetoric into evangelical preaching. Sunday's enjoin-
ders to "get in the game" sound not unlike Washington Gladden's, only
shouted with more fervor.[7] There was, in fact, an *agôn* in Sunday's preaching, but men and women were to wrestle with Satan, not with God.

In the second half of the nineteenth century, then, as the God of justice
became a God of love, "wrestling" with God lost all significance for
evangelical spirituality. Beginning with Herman Melville, however, it
became a central image in a literary tradition that eventually included a
number of the most acclaimed American male novelists. For Melville,
who could neither believe nor be comfortable in his unbelief, as Hawthorne noted, the *distance* between humanity and divinity – whether the
divinity of a Supreme Being or the divinity to which humankind could
aspire – remained a searing fact. "Salvation" for Melville, however conceived, was no free gift but the prize to be won only in the most desperate
of contests.

Melville and the sport of the gods

EXTRACTS from EXTRACTS

There go the ships; there is that Leviathan
whom thou hast made to play therein.
Psalms.

> Soon to the sport of death the crews repair:
> Rodmond unerring o'er his head suspends
> The barbed steel, and every turn attends.
> *Falconer's Shipwreck.*

Sport-of-the-gods imagery appears in American fiction from the beginning. The earliest American novels explored a narrow range of ideas and situations, most of them copied from the work of such popular English novelists as Samuel Richardson, Laurence Sterne, and Anne Radcliffe.[8] One of the most common plots involved a series of physical or moral travails inflicted on the protagonist, who either prevails or succumbs. Whether explicitly religious or not, these early novels were overwhelmingly conservative in their implicit theology, stressing the virtuous individual's submission to God's will and confidence in His Providence. But just as Puritan divines had done in the seventeenth century, the authors of such novels as *Fidelity Rewarded* (1796), *Ferdinand & Elmira* (1804), *The Asylum* (1811), and *Henry and Julietta, or Virtue Rewarded* (1818), balanced avowals of mankind's dependence on God, the "Eternal Disposer of events" as Isaac Mitchell called him in *The Asylum,* against declarations of the necessity of moral virtue.[9] The novel by its nature, given its dependence on character and action, cannot easily sustain an arch-conservative theology. In any case, God's sovereignty in this early fiction increasingly yielded to human agency, as the transformation of American popular fiction by the Civil War both followed and fed the triumph of liberalism in the culture more generally.[10]

James Butler's *Fortune's Foot-ball; or, The Adventures of Mercutio* (1797–8) can serve as the exemplary novel at the beginning of the sport-of-the-gods tradition. In *Fortune's Foot-ball,* Mercutio is a young man of brilliant prospects who undergoes an extraordinarily improbable series of rescues, captures, and escapes before attaining final happiness. Nearly married or actually married to three different women; captured by pirates, a press gang, Spanish sailors, and pirates again; and roving by will or under duress from London to Italy, Marseilles, Quebec, Spain, Persia, Constantinople, Moscow, Amsterdam, and ultimately back to England; Mercutio is truly "fortune's football." Midway through the first of the novel's two volumes, in a lull between crises, the narrator interjects: "But alas! Fortune, that fickle goddess, had raised her foot with a design to give him another kick."[11] Fortune continues to kick until the end of the novel.

What a later generation would consider inept plotting serves a theological design. The bizarre coincidences wrought by Fortune's kicks of the ball suggest both the pagan goddess and the inscrutable Providence of the Calvinist God – their interchangeable presence in the novel echoing the Medieval conjunction of antithetical Christian and pagan traditions, but also signaling the imminent breakdown of religious orthodoxy. Butler's motif appears in several other novels of the day. In William Hill Brown's *The Power of Sympathy* (1789), a remorseful seducer confesses that he has been "like a ship without a rudder, buffeted on the bosom of the ocean, the sport of winds and waves." In the anonymous *History of Constantius and Pulchera; or Virtue Rewarded* (1796), the heroine writes to her domineering father to plead for compassion on one who has "been the sport of fortune." In *Edgar Huntly* (1799) and *Arthur Mervyn* (1799–1800), Charles Brockden Brown wrote of "the sport of chance" and of a character bemoaning "that demon of whose malice a mysterious destiny" made him "the sport and the prey." These writers continued the long tradition of using a pagan trope to express a Christian view of Providence. Brown alone among them challenged the assumptions underlying the trope, exposing the self-delusions of characters who refuse accountability. And in *The Algerine Captive* (1797), Royall Tyler parodied the entire "fortune's football" school when the hero's mother dreams in her pregnancy of Indians kidnapping her son and "playing at football" with his head. "She was sure Updike was born to be the sport of fortune," the narrator reports. Parody can succeed only when the object parodied is well known to readers. Tyler's burlesque offers the best evidence of all that the trope was a conventional one.[12]

Versions of this rhetorical figure recur in a wide range of fiction in the nineteenth century: in the semi-pornographic, gothic potboiler, *The Quaker City* (1844), by George Lippard, in which the perversely godlike sorcerer, Ravoni, makes "playthings" of lesser mortals; in Bret Harte's stories about stoical gamblers like John Oakhurst, who viewed life as "at best an uncertain game" with "the usual percentage in favor of the dealer"; in A. D. T. Whitney's domestic tale, *Odd or Even?* (1881), in which a clergyman likens Providence to a game of solitaire played by God; in Maurice Thompson's *The Banker of Bankersville* (1886), in which a wastrel calls himself "a foot-ball of luck" and life a "lottery" in which he has been fortunate.[13] I would be reluctant to claim a very precise pattern of development, but in the large movement from Butler at the beginning of the century to Dreiser at the end, the context of meaning shifted from providential theology to deterministic naturalism to reflect an emerging scientific worldview where religious doctrine had formerly commanded a consensus. Moreover, by the end of the nineteenth century, chance was officially granted a role in human affairs after generations of denial. Through this intellectual revolution, the sport of fortune or the gods persisted as a surprisingly flexible image, accommodating fatalists at one extreme and sentimentalists at the other. In addition, images of sporting chance and cosmic gambles recast the heroic agonistic

Christian life in a new form but with remarkably similar substance. A sense of man's equivocal place in the cosmos survived in a different guise. The nineteenth-century novelist whose sense of life most deeply engaged the sporting, agonistic God was Herman Melville. Brought up in both the Unitarianism of his father's family and the Calvinism of his mother's, Melville came to rebel against the tyrannical Patriarch who predetermined human actions and predestinated men and women for heaven or hell; but he could not embrace his opposite, the Kindly Father who gathered children to his bosom and smiled benignly on the pious souls who did his bidding. In the decade more typically represented by domestic best sellers with angelic heroines protected by a divine Benevolence, Melville wrote novels that brood over the presence of evil in life and the constraints on human freedom, over the possibilities of human grandeur in light of mankind's observable pettiness, over the nature of a God who could have created such an ungodlike species as humans. In Melville's fiction men and women repeatedly appear as the sport of the gods, but out of that basic condition emerges contrary possibilities: Either humankind as a whole is so inconsequential as to be laughable, or individuals achieve their greatest dignity through defying their unfair fate.

In *Moby-Dick* (1851), the chief spokesman for man as "the sport of the gods" is Stubb, the good-humored, careless second mate who is indifferent to peril and responds to the "shocking sharkish business" of life with a laugh: "Because a laugh's the wisest, easiest answer to all that's queer; and come what will, one comfort's always left – that unfailing comfort is, it's all predestined."[14] Stubb acknowledges God's power here but alludes more truly to circumstance. In Melville's parable of fate, chance, and will in human life, Stubb is the one who believes in the absolute sovereignty of chance. As we shall see later, Ahab makes no such concession and plays a different game, but for Stubb the game of human existence can only be an absurd affair presided over by a Practical Joker. If indeed human acts are predestinated, then life is *mere* play: pretending that one's actions and strivings matter when in fact they make no difference whatever in the scheme of things. In the chapter appropriately titled "The Hyena," Ishmael describes those "certain queer times and occasions in this strange mixed affair we call life when a man takes this whole universe for a vast practical joke." To grow despondent or to rebel would be equally foolish; hardships and even death seem "only sly, good-natured hits, and jolly punches in the side bestowed by the unseen and unaccountable old joker." To a man who so views life, the greater the trial, the larger the joke. According to Ishmael, "There is nothing like the perils of whaling to breed this free and easy sort of genial, desperado philosophy" (226). To men such as Stubb, the perils of the whale-boat – with the crew all entangled in out-rushing ropes – warrant only laughter. "Gayer sallies," says Ishmael, "more merry mirth, better jokes, and brighter repartees, you never heard over your mahogany, than you will over the half-inch white cedar of the whale-boat, when thus hung in hangman's nooses" (280).

Ishmael himself shares this "desperado philosophy" at "certain queer times and occasions." For Stubb, it sums up life. When a typhoon disables the *Pequod*'s masts and stoves in Ahab's whale-boat for "sport," Stubb responds with a song:

> Oh! jolly is the gale,
> And a joker is the whale,
> A' flourishin' his tail,–
> Such a funny, sporty, gamy, jest, joky, hoky-poky lad, is the Ocean,
> oh! (504)

Having overheard Ahab's response to this event, Stubb reports to Starbuck: "Well, well; I heard Ahab mutter, 'Here some one thrusts these cards into these old hands of mine; swears that I must play them and no others' " (502). To Stubb no philosophy could be truer: "And damn me, Ahab, but thou actest right; live in the game and die in it!"

We might describe Stubb's attitude as sportive nihilism; his laughter – his sense of the *sport* of life despite its grimness – alone redeems human existence from despair. Competing views and voices appear in *Moby-Dick,* but before attending to mad Ahab as a tragic wrestler we can follow the sport-of-the-gods motif in Melville's writing into his later fiction: fate imagined as a row of billiard balls in *Pierre* (1852), for example, and as a cat "sporting" with its trapped prey in "The Encantadas" (1856).[15] In these stories, as in *Moby-Dick,* sportive fatalism explains only part of a more complex metaphor, but in *The Confidence-Man* (1857) it expresses the solitary truth. Melville's increasing sense of alienation from his audience and culture in the 1850s transformed Stubb's laughter of stoical, good-humored resignation into something darker and more pervasive. To *Moby-Dick*'s human view of the gods, *The Confidence-Man* appends a divine view of humanity: a look through the wrong end of the telescope at human creatures smaller than life. Such creatures can evoke only laughter when seen from God's perspective. The reader watching them sees not the pain of human struggle and misery but a pageant of human folly.

As author, Melville was as much a god sporting with his readers as his Confidence Man was a god sporting with his victims; the novel has spawned a myriad of contradictory interpretations, each defiantly plausible. The Confidence Man himself has been identified by some as God, by others as Satan – Melville's apparent point precisely: The Supreme Being of his universe is a shape-shifting satanic God or divine Demon,

a Practical Joker who plays many roles, from Christ to Satan, for the
sake of his game. The events of the novel take place between dawn and
dusk on April 1, the Feast of All Fools. The Confidence Man appears in
a series of seven or eight avatars, duping a variety of victims of trivial
sums of money, but more importantly exposing their worst defects of
character. It is important to note that these victims never lose anything
of genuine value. No pauper gives his last mite, no rich man is impoverished, no trusting soul is disabused of his or her belief. Those who
give a few dollars toward fraudulent schemes and those who resist the
Confidence Man's entreaties are equally "victims": not bilked of valu-
ables but exposed as fools or knaves. The mystery of the Confidence
Man's identity and purpose deepens when his ultimate avatar, Frank
Goodman the cosmopolitan, appears on board to transact the novel's
most enigmatic games. But critics who find apocalypse and damnation
in the final chapters grant too much significance to what literally happens.
Goodman fails to move the distrustful Missourian Pitch, exposes Charlie
Noble as a hypocrite, reveals Mark Winsome and Egbert to be intellectual
frauds and transcendental misanthropes, buys an inexpensive tract from
a crazy beggar, and tricks the barber out of a free shave before myste-
riously leading a "clean comely old man" into darkness. None of this
matters much. The last scene in particular has proved the crux of interpretations that find suggestion of apocalypse. But the comic novel "in-
creases in seriousness" not because the old man is led by Satan to
damnation, but because the foolishness and knavery of humankind are
shown to be general, not isolated, and to be due ultimately to the un-
trustworthiness of God.

By the time the pageant of All Fools Day has been completed, readers
have been overwhelmed by evidence of human insignificance. Only fools
and knaves have paraded before them: from knavish tossers of pennies
at Black Guinea's mouth and foolish dupes for charitable scams, to the
knavish Charlie Noble, Mark Winsome, and Egbert, and the foolish old
man with his Bible, his money belt, and his toilet-stool life preserver.
The benevolent Episcopal clergyman is no hero, only a fool; Colonel
John Moredock is no hero, only a knave. *The Confidence-Man* is not
genial satire, because it offers no contrasting worldview, no alternative
to the unpleasant image of humanity a reader must find in the novel. If
humankind's noblest acts are no more than "the result of some chance
tips of Fate's elbow in throwing her dice," as Charlie Noble implies,
then human existence is a sorry prospect indeed. In a different sporting
image, one of the avatars of the Confidence Man declares life a card
game "in which every player plays fair, and not a player but shall win."[16]
Anyone who would believe this bromide of American optimism, Melville's novel says, is a fool. By extinguishing the solar lamp in the novel's

last scene, the Confidence Man signifies that humanity has truly proven itself in the previous forty-four chapters a benighted race. The act is his "*Fiat nox*."

The sportive nihilism of *The Confidence-Man* is but one of the philosophical possibilities in *Moby-Dick*, the novel in which the multiple facets of Melville's understanding of human existence, from radical skepticism to grandiose aspiration, are held in the most fruitful tension. In *Moby-Dick*, the sportive nihilist Stubb is a single character, a minor one; Melville's masterpiece comprehends *The Confidence-Man*'s understanding of comic absurdity within a context of overriding tragic (but ambiguous) heroism. Put simply, Ahab refuses to submit to being the gods' sport, insisting that he can enter the contest against them. For him, transcendence remains possible, not as a reward tendered by a sovereign deity to those who play well at the game of life, but as the stake in a contest *against* God to be won only by relentless opposition.

In *Moby-Dick*, Melville embraced the parable of Jacob the wrestler without equivocation.[17] As revivalists were softening the implications of that enigmatic story, Melville in Ahab recreated Jacob the wrestler not as supplicant but as defier, his Opponent not the benevolent deity of Finney but the stern Lord of Michael Wigglesworth. The most popular American poem at midcentury, Henry Wadsworth Longfellow's "Song of Hiawatha" (1855), provides an interesting contrast. During a long fast the Indian hero wrestles four times with a messenger from the Master of Life, winning at last the victory that brings fertility to his people.[18] In other words, the exotic world of Indian folklife could be used to convey the conventional beliefs of Anglo-American readers. Longfellow's popular epic is obviously closer in spirit to the revivalism of Finney than to the defiance of Melville. Embodied in the White Whale, Melville's God is awesome and forbidding, perhaps malicious, at best indifferent. He is not the Dispenser of rewards and punishments so much as the Obstructor of man's desires. He is the Creator of man's limitations, the Constraint on man's will. He gives man a soul that can aspire to divinity but traps it in a shell of clay. But as a sporting God, He also agrees to a rule-bound contest in which mortals might test Him in fair play, and therein lies the possibility of redemption. By extending his covenant to man, the Calvinist God made human existence meaningful. By transforming the covenant into a game, Melville blasphemously declared that man might become a god. As God's opponent in the game, man shares in his Adversary's divinity, for only equals can engage in sporting contest. Moby Dick dwarfs the mere mortals in the whaling crews he encounters, but Ahab rises to the White Whale's stature by welcoming a one-on-one confrontation of strength against strength. By playing alone, Ahab declares himself equal to the Opponent God.

The other possibility, of course, is that Ahab is mad. To imagine oneself able to engage God in an equal contest according to the rules of fair play is not only blasphemy but insanity. From the perspective of the normative world represented by his crew, Ahab is indeed mad, but in conceiving the game and playing it out to its tragic conclusion, Ahab was the first of several major figures in American fiction to create his own ordered, salvific universe in defiance of mere sanity, and perhaps of objective fact. Melville's contemporary, Søren Kierkegaard, defined religious faith in *Fear and Trembling* (1843) as virtually a kind of madness. Melville portrayed a more ambiguous madness in Ahab's contest with God, but Ahab's madness is also his transcendence. In one of his famous letters to Hawthorne during the writing of *Moby-Dick,* Melville praised the man of "sovereign nature" who "may perish; but so long as he exists he insists upon treating with all Powers upon an equal basis."[19] He was creating such a figure in Ahab.

The sailor Jack Chase of *White-Jacket* (1850), the novel that preceded *Moby-Dick,* is an earlier version of the god-defying sportsman. In one scene, as a squall off Cape Horn tosses the ship's flying jib about "like a foot-ball," and cannon balls careening about the gun deck convert it into "an immense bowling alley," Jack Chase countermands his captain's order by running the ship into the face of the storm. "As with ships, so with men," White-Jacket comments; "he who turns his back to his foe gives him an advantage. Whereas, our ribbed chests, like the ribbed bows of a frigate, are as bulkheads to dam off an onset."[20] In *Pierre* (1852), the novel that followed *Moby-Dick,* Melville imagined another hero who defies the powers of the universe in a similar contest. But Pierre Glendinning only shakes his fist at the sky; Ahab flings a harpoon at a more concrete embodiment of the powerful Opponent.[21] *Moby-Dick,* that is, translates the natural contest of *White-Jacket* into a metaphysical one, in which the confrontation of mortal and immortal foes is more compelling than in *Pierre*.

The sporting rhetoric that expresses Melville's theology of defiance is centered in three major scenes: Ahab's pledging of the crew to the destruction of Moby Dick in "The Quarter-Deck" and five succeeding chapters; Ahab's defiance of nature in the eight chapters from "The "Quadrant" to "The Log and the Line"; and finally the three days of "The Chase." The first sequence establishes the terms of the contest – its players, rules, and stakes. In "The Quarter-Deck," in one of the novel's most quoted passages, after declaring Moby Dick a mask of inscrutability and malice through which he must break, Ahab announces to Starbuck and the crew the terms that govern his contest with the Whale: "Talk not to me of blasphemy, man; I'd strike the sun if it insulted me. For could the sun do that, then could I do the other; since there is ever a sort of fair play herein, jealousy [jealously?] presiding over all creations. But not my master, man, is even that fair play" (164). The White Whale here is identified not as a specific "god" but as that inexplicable force in the universe that each individual confronts, that wall beyond which lies truth but also chaos, that insists on human finitude and the unknowableness of life. Unwilling to accept the limitation of his own being, Ahab will contest with the personification of that inscrutability in "fair play." Whether the universe observes principles of fair play in a sense does not matter. By declaring it so Ahab makes it so; he creates the game by which he can strike the sun if it insults him, can make himself equal to the greatest powers in the universe. "True wit and madness" are "near allied," Dryden wrote in the late seventeenth century. Genius *is* madness, Melville answered. But the question remains: Is Ahab's Promethean act of creation meaningful or delusive? The essence of Ahab's game is that by contesting with God he becomes godlike himself; his "fair play" insists that the opponents are evenly matched. "God hunt us all, if we do not hunt Moby Dick to his death!" (166), cries Ahab at the end of the scene, and godlike Moby Dick will indeed hunt Ahab even as Ahab hunts him. Transcendence and self-immolation seem equally possible in the outcome.

Alone in his cabin after this scene, Ahab mocks the gods as "cricket players" and "pugilists" (168); in an age of bare-knuckle prizefighting Ahab challenges these pugilist gods to a no-holds-barred contest, winner take all. The gods would sport with men, as Stubb also recognizes, but Ahab refuses to be a mere plaything. When the gods seemingly respond to Ahab's challenge with a squall, mirrored on the *Pequod*'s deck by a fight among the drunken sailors, Tashtego makes the connection: "A row a'low, and a row aloft – Gods and men – both brawlers!" (178). Mere land-tied mortals like Starbuck are incapable of echoing Ahab's challenge. In his soliloquy following Ahab's, Starbuck understands his captain's mad aspirations – Ahab, he says, "would be a democrat to all above" (169) – but Starbuck cannot approve this "heaven-insulting purpose." When Ahab asked him earlier, "Art not game for Moby Dick?" Starbuck replied, "I am game for his crooked jaw, and for the jaws of Death too, Captain Ahab, if it fairly comes in the way of the business we follow; but I came here to hunt whales, not my commander's vengeance" (163). Nothing so paltry as business can engage the godly, god-defying player, Ahab.

In the final chapter of this section, Ishmael's meditation on Moby Dick, the stake in the contest is developed fully. Compared to an "Arkansas duellist" on his previous meeting with Moby Dick, when he blindly tried to end the White Whale's life with a six-inch blade, Ahab contests not for survival like the Davy Crocketts and Chunkeys of frontier storytelling, but for "salvation." To Ahab, the white whale embodies "not only all his bodily woes, but all his intellectual and spiritual exasperations." Moby Dick is the "monomaniac incarnation of all those malicious agencies which some deep men feel eating in them," "all the subtle demonisms of life and thought," "all the general rage and hate felt by his whole race from Adam down" (184). To defeat such an opponent would free the world from evil.

The second key sequence in which sporting rhetoric structures the events begins at Chapter 118, where Ahab and his as yet unseen Opponent make their first moves in the contest. Ahab initiates the action by crushing the quadrant, calling it a "foolish toy! babies' plaything of haughty Admirals, and Commodores, and Captains" (501). To contest with God one must be equal to God, relying on no mere plaything such as a quadrant. The Opponent counters this defiant move with a typhoon, disabling the *Pequod*'s masts and stoving Ahab's whale boat in his "sport" (503). Stubb reacts in character with a playful song, while Starbuck sees only the gods' intentional punishment of the blasphemous captain. Ahab combines the perspectives of both mates. Like Starbuck, he perceives a willful malignity in the God he has insulted, but like Stubb he declares that God to be a sporting one. When Starbuck cries out to have the lightning rods affixed to the masts, Ahab refuses: "Let's have fair play here, though we be the weaker side" (505). The weaker side can be equal to the divine Opponent only if it plays on the Opponent's terms. "God, God is against thee, old man," Starbuck warns, and so He is, but what the mate cannot accept is that to oppose God is the only way to become godlike oneself. As Ahab blows out the flame on his burning harpoon point, he signifies his equality as a player.

The events that follow this chapter are further moves and countermoves in the contest. A severe gale makes of the ship "but a tossed shuttlecock to the blast," and when the winds abate, Starbuck puns off Ahab's earlier insistence on fair play: "I came to report a fair wind that's only fair for that accursed fish." The fair wind was only "juggling" the *Pequod,* however, for the thunder turned the ship's compasses, tricking the steersman to sail in the wrong direction. Ahab responds by fashioning his own compass, triumphantly declaring himself "lord of the level loadstone." The Opponent moves again, snapping the line and sinking the log, but Ahab recovers from this loss as well. To each move by the Power of the universe, Ahab makes a countermove: "I crush the quadrant, the thunder turns the needles, and now the mad sea parts the logline. But Ahab can mend all" (513–21).

All of these incidents are preliminaries to the main event, the actual three-day chase for Moby Dick with which the novel concludes. Ahab, as the solitary player against God, is appropriately the first to see the

White Whale. Moby Dick is described not only as a "grand god" but in language suggestive of sport:

> Before [the whale's head] far out on the soft Turkish-rugged waters went the glistening white shadow from his broad, milky forehead, a musical rippling playfully accompanying the shade; and behind, the blue waters interchangeably flowed over into the moving valley of his steady wake; and on either hand bright bubbles arose and danced by his side. (548)

Having launched his own boat to the chase, Ahab attempts a maneuver to gain the advantage, but Moby Dick, "as if perceiving this strategem," counters the move, crushes the boat in his jaws, shakes it "as a wildly cruel cat with her mouse," then bites it completely in two, spilling Ahab and his crew into the sea (549–50).

On the second day, Moby Dick makes the initial move, breaching in an "act of defiance." Ahab decides to take his foe "head-and-head, – that is, pull straight up to his forehead," a tactic Ishmael calls "not uncommon" but certainly the only strategy appropriate for the player against God. Moby Dick responds by rushing upon the whalers with open jaws, diving deep, then surging upward to stove Ahab's boat from the bottom, carrying off Fedallah entangled in the whale lines (558).

The third day dawns fair and fresh, only for Ahab to discover that the hunter is the hunted: "He's chasing *me* now; not I, *him*." Ahab reverses his course to confront his foe *mano-a-mano* once again, crying as he approaches, "Forehead to forehead I meet thee, this third time, Moby Dick!" The whale charges, dashing the other two boats but leaving Ahab's unmarked, then turns his fury on the ship. The "god-bullied hull" is stoved, but even yet Ahab neither submits nor despairs: "To the last I grapple with thee," he cries in his final defiant sally before Moby Dick drags him in perverse embrace to his death (564, 571).

In his dying cry of defiance Ahab calls Moby Dick "thou all-destroying but unconquering whale" (571); these paradoxical words contain the key to Ahab's possible triumph. There can only be ambiguity in this matter, given the nature of the opponent and the stakes, but the terms of that ambiguity can be laid out with some assurance. In *Moby-Dick* Melville wed the traditional Christian, specifically Calvinist *agôn* to the frontier tall tale (the book's use of Western materials has been well documented).[22] In that deeply ironic juxtaposition lies one of the novel's fundamental indeterminacies. When Chunkey in the Southwestern humor tale whoops his pleasure in having whipped a panther in a "fair fight," he does not consciously transform his foe into a transcendent Opponent. Ahab demands "fair play" in his contest with the gods, wholly conscious of the implications. The reader must ask, whose allegory is this, Melville's

or Ahab's? One perspective on the novel sees Ahab as Melville's embodiment of the Calvinist tradition in a critique of Western theology.[23]
In this reading, Ahab possesses Western man's habit of mind by which
he sees contest as the essence of both spiritual and physical life. He is
doomed because he is an obsessive allegorist who insists on spiritual
struggle. From another perspective the allegory is Melville's: the contest,
not Ahab's delusion but his heroic response to the only God Melville
knew. In this reading, a mere mortal must be destroyed in any contest
with the Almighty, but victory can be gained even in defeat. If Ahab is
mad to contest with God, it is with the madness of genius, for though
he fails in his vengeance and cannot expunge evil from the world, he
succeeds in wresting "immortality" for himself.

Melville's achievement in *Moby-Dick* was to make such self-created
grandeur seem possible: to hold futile destructiveness and defiant transcendence in a compelling dialectic, confronting readers with a sense of
mystery, not certitude, at the root of human existence. As the novel
moves from repeated assertions of Ahab's dominant will to greater emphasis on his internal compulsions, Melville seems to have leaned toward
an overriding fate as the chief determinant in human life. Early on Ahab
cries out, "What I've dared, I've willed; and what I've willed, I'll do!"
(168). But in the final calm before the three-day chase for Moby Dick,
Ahab confesses his will overwhelmed by some "nameless, inscrutable,
unearthly thing" that drives him toward destruction contrary to his "own
natural heart" (545). This late groan of despair, however, cannot be taken
to signify the final dominance of Fate. When Stubb sees in Ahab a kindred
soul playing the cards dealt him, he distorts their similarity. Stubb submits to Fate's dealing of the cards; Ahab accepts the hand but actively
plays it – a crucial difference. Mediating between predestination and free
will, numerous theologians from Augustine on expressed the paradox
of "conditional necessity" as a willing of one's fate. Ahab embodies a
similar position. Stubb does not take the fateful dealer seriously; Ahab
does but claims that his "right worship is defiance" (507). In the novel's
most moving lines Ahab concedes the gods' "speechless, placeless
power" but vows that "to the last gasp of my earthquake life [I] will
dispute its unconditional, unintegral mastery in me. . . . Thou canst blind;
but I can then grope. Thou canst consume; but I can then be ashes"
(507). In the final disaster then, while Starbuck futilely prays, "My God
stand by me now!" and Stubb grins at the grinning whale in a morally
meaningless death, and the harpooners remain "fixed by infatuation, or
fidelity, or fate" to the masts awaiting their doom, Ahab alone plays out
the full mystery of fate, chance, and will. Ishmael survives but more by
chance than justice. Ishmael's many identities as school teacher, raconteur, bumpkin, trickster, pedant, mystic render him as the sum of com

mon humanity rather than as a specific self. His survival signifies the perpetuation of humankind, witness to mysteries and daunting struggles it only partially understands, before which it stands in awe but to which it cannot or will not commit itself. This noncommitment is the basic act of survival – part choice, part chance, part necessity – by which everyday reality continues largely unengaged with the ultimacies of Good and Evil, self-creation and self-annihilation. Ishmael survives, but by grappling with the "all-destroying but unconquering whale" to the end of the contest, Ahab creates himself as a god.

This is the crucial paradox at the center of the contest against God that Melville first articulated and that Hemingway and Faulkner most notably reiterated in the next century. Defeat in life is inevitable, Melville suggested, but when willed and embraced as if the outcome of a sporting contest, defeat possibly becomes tragic victory. The essential ambiguity is inherent in the sporting metaphor. Once again we see the consequences of the shift from martial to sportive rhetoric in a new cultural context. Spiritual *warfare* against God would imply inevitable destruction; a *game,* on the other hand, drawing on the nineteenth century's discovery of the values of sport, can imply the possibility of victory beyond defeat. By invoking fair play Ahab not only calls on the gods to deal justly with him, he pledges his own commitment to honorable means in contesting against them and thus creates a universe in which he can become godlike.

Ahab, however, also causes his own death and the deaths of all his crew, save one. Creation is murder, self-creation is self-annihilation, redemption is loss. A deeper indeterminacy in *Moby-Dick* derives from the sporting rhetoric itself. If the image of a game confers potential meaning on Ahab's acts that warfare could not imply, it also calls into question the meaning of the struggle in a more fundamental way. By presenting Ahab's contest both from within, from Ahab's perspective, and from without, from Ishmael's, Melville exposed the essential indeterminacy underlying the desperate sport against the gods. A game by its nature is at once meaningless and meaningful: its meaning self-created in the rules, without reference to the external world. Within the boundaries of the game, Ahab creates an ordered, meaningful relationship between gods and men, stakes that can be won, terms by which actions can be meaningful. From outside, from the perspective of an Ishmael, the game is madness, an illusion imposed upon an altogether different reality. Only from within, on the game's own terms, is Ahab's struggle heroic. Outside the game, individuals are of little consequence except collectively, as partners in a "joint-stock world" that demands brotherhood as a check against the universal cannibalism of life. While reason demands accommodation to the joint-stock world, mankind is cursed by infinite aspirations. Writing in the middle of the nineteenth century, at a time when Calvinism was yielding to a scientific-humanist world-view in America, Melville seems to have been unwilling to commit himself simply to Ahab's existential vision, but neither did he simply denounce it. As Hawthorne later wrote of him, Melville could "neither believe nor be comfortable in his unbelief." The image of the sporting contest creates a compelling dialectic out of this irresolution.

The naturalists and chance

Melville's agonistic vision defied both Calvinist orthodoxy, which insisted on submission, and the ascendant sentimental liberalism that promised salvation without struggle. Little read and often reviled, *Moby-Dick* can scarcely be said to speak for its era, but although Melville's impact on other writers was postponed until his rediscovery in the 1920s, it is nonetheless possible to identify Melvillean traditions, writers not who were influenced by Melville but who shared his vision.[24] The naturalists at the end of the century in various ways expressed a secularized version of Melville's ambiguously tragic *agôn;* the chief successor to his dark comic vision, on the other hand, was Mark Twain.

From the beginning, Twain's fiction included images of a manipulative, sportive "god" toying with his petty creatures. Power and powerlessness virtually obsessed Twain all his life; abused innocents, cowardly weaklings, and superior men contemptuous of these others appear throughout his fiction.[25] Although no literal sporting god appears until late in Twain's career, implicit versions abound in his earlier writings. I am thinking here not of a victim like Laura Hawkins in *The Gilded Age* (1873), described by her lawyer as "the sport of fate and circumstances," but of Hank Morgan and his predecessors and successors: Twain's "transcendent figures," as they have been called, who sport with weaker mortals.[26] Tom Sawyer, who draws the entire adult population of St. Petersburg into his imaginative play, is a benign version of this superior being who sports with the inferior. The King and Duke play this role for a time in *Huckleberry Finn* (though not Colonel Sherburn, who is transcendent without being sportive). In both of these novels the superior player's potential for destruction is held in check, barely so in the case of the King and Duke. With Hank Morgan of *A Connecticut Yankee* (1889), however, the gulf between the now fully empowered player and his playthings becomes frankly disturbing, particularly because his language and the language that describes him imply innocent sport. Speaking continually in the slang of poker and athletics, Hank Morgan plays against Merlin and other opponents with the advantage of thirteen centuries of technical knowledge, making the contest completely one-sided. "Step to the bat, it's your innings," he tells Merlin, just before blowing up his tower by igniting gunpowder with a lightning bolt. In a later confrontation, boxing metaphors take over – "the magician was hit hard," "that jab made this fellow squirm," "*that* was a noble shot" – as Hank "prophesies" with the aid of long-distance telephoning. In routing Dowley the blacksmith in yet another scene, the Yankee strikes "below the belt" by using nineteenth-century intelligence to expose sixth-century fraud:

> Well, when I make up my mind to hit a man, I don't plan out a love-tap; no, that isn't my way; as long as I'm going to hit him at all, I'm going to hit him a lifter. And I don't jump at him all of a sudden, and risk making a blundering half-way business of it; no, I get away off yonder to one side, and work up on him gradually, so that he never suspects that I'm going to hit him at all; and by and by, all in a flash, he's flat on his back, and he can't tell for the life of him how it all happened.

That is Hank's style: gamesmanship rather than sportsmanship, but exploitative gamesmanship by the one with power, not subversive gamesmanship by the trickster who circumvents power. When in the novel's climax Hank challenges the entire chivalry of England, he calls his move a "bluff," declaring it "sound judgment to put on a bold face and play your hand for a hundred times what it is worth; forty-nine times out of fifty nobody dares to 'call,' and you rake in the chips." As always, the Yankee plays with a stacked deck and no real risk or gamble. Hank uses the language of fair play to describe his most unfair sporting with virtually helpless opponents. His final "game" is the "fair hand" of poker he plays with fifty-two young boys as the cards in his deck against twenty-five thousand knights, killing everyone on both sides.[27]

With Hank Morgan, as with the other transcendent figures that recur in his fiction, Twain dreamed of a man becoming a god, but as power inevitably grew brutal the dream became a nightmare. The cultural ambivalence over power and its effects that I discussed in relation to business novels was also basic to Twain's most fundamental view of life. In his fiction after *A Connecticut Yankee,* Twain's dark-comic mode became darker, less comic, as the powerful player became more godlike and remote, the victims of his sport more pathetic and helpless (Twain's antithetical playful humanism will be discussed in Chapter 10). In "The Man That Corrupted Hadleyburg" (1899), a stranger makes a "square bet" with himself that the best citizens of the town are all corruptible, then tempts them to corruption; in "The $30,000 Bequest" (1904), a misanthropic old relative corrupts an ordinary, reasonably decent couple with a cruel hoax perpetrated from long distance. Twain had loved hoaxes all his life, practicing them himself as a young reporter in Virginia

City and incorporating them frequently into his fiction. But in these two
late stories, the stranger as hoaxer becomes a solitaire-playing god contemptuous of the insignificant mortals whose lives he disrupts. In one
of Twain's late manuscripts, "Three Thousand Years Among the Mi-
crobes" (1905), humankind is reduced to microscopic insignificance. In
another, "The Chronicle of Young Satan," one of the fragments spliced
together by Albert Bigelow Paine to create *The Mysterious Stranger* (1916),
the omnipotent jokester literally becomes God at last, but a God ironically
named Satan who sports with mere humans for careless pleasure. In this
unfinished novel, Twain most explicitly adopted the gods'-eye view of
paltry humanity found in Melville's *Confidence-Man*. Satan creates and
destroys human figures, brings joy or pain to the boys of Eseldorf, with
equal indifference. In the story's central image, Satan explains to Theodor
that the events of human history are but a row of dominoes toppling
one after another in an unchangeable course toward pointlessness:

> Among you boys you have a game: you stand a row of bricks on end
> a few inches apart; you push a brick, it knocks its neighbor over, the
> neighbor knocks over the next brick – and so on till all the row is
> prostrate. That is human life. A child's first act knocks over the initial
> brick, and the rest will follow inexorably. If you could see into the
> future, as I can, you would see everything that was ever going to happen
> to that creation; for nothing can change the order of its life after the
> first event has determined it.[28]

This analogy echoes Melville's row of billiard balls in *Pierre*. In Twain's
version, any attempt to alter the succession of events in a person's life
merely redistributes the pain and misery in the world without reducing
human unhappiness.

The idea of an indifferent or malicious deity governing human affairs
ties Twain, if only ironically, to an age of belief; his image of human
destiny as the outcome of an immutable sequence of toppling dominoes
links him also to the new generation of writers who read the latest social
science and reinterpreted philosophical determinism in wholly secular
terms. Although the specific influences on Norris, Crane, Dreiser, and
London varied to a considerable degree, they shared a common view of
man as, in the words of Robert Frost's "Oven Bird," a "diminished
thing." Yet they also rebelled against the evidence of his diminishment,
attempting to reassert some measure of his past heroic grandeur. One
result was a version of Melville's desperate game, but the "salvation" at
stake now became more ambiguous than ever. Unlike Melville, who
wrote from within a still largely theistic culture, the naturalists wrote
from within a more fully secular one. Their clinging to transcendence,
then, necessarily produced more problematic texts.

In the classical configuration of fate, chance, and will, the naturalists emphasized fate (recast now as scientific determinism) and chance, while refusing to surrender entirely the possibility of human freedom. They viewed the world in part in terms of what Ronald Martin has called "the universe of force," an idea that originated in scientific literature in the 1840s and became "widely popular and influential in America around the turn of the century."[29] As the laws of mechanics generated a cosmic philosophy, writers such as Norris and Dreiser, as we saw in the previous chapter, redefined man himself as a force. One result was the epic contests of buccaneering capitalists by which solitary men proved themselves commensurate to the impersonal forces that would determine their lives. Although those forces ultimately prevailed, human force, or will, could resist heroically.

In this chapter I want to focus more closely on the second term in the naturalists' equation of human possibility: on the element of chance as represented by their sporting metaphors. In that still astonishingly prescient book of the 1830s, *Democracy in America,* Alexis de Tocqueville observed that "chance is an element always present to the mind of those who live in the unstable conditions of a democracy." Tocqueville was specifically interested in explaining why Americans were more drawn to trade than to farming: to careers in which success was uncertain but the rewards potentially immense, as opposed to agricultural pursuits that offered "an almost certain reward . . . but a slow one."[30] The answer, he felt, lay in democratic classlessness. Where wealth alone admitted one to the social aristocracy, slow but certain rewards could have but limited appeal. In the absence of traditional aristocracy, only the rich could claim the privileges of nobility; merchants, industrialists, and financiers had the greatest opportunities for wealth. Thus, although commerce, manufacturing, and finance were risky, with stakes so high and not impossibly beyond reach, the risk was worth taking.

Sixty years later, James Bryce in *The American Commonwealth* (1893–4), the other great nineteenth-century document on the civilization of the United States written by a European, confirmed Tocqueville's observation. Describing the prevalence of speculation among the people at large, Bryce noted "the pre-existing tendency to encounter risks" that is "inborn in Americans, and fostered by the circumstances of their country." "The habit of speculation" among Americans, Bryce concluded, was not a peculiarity that would disappear in more settled times, but was "a part of their character."[31] The naturalists' fascination with chance raises intriguing questions in relation to Bryce's and Tocqueville's insight. Frank Norris' portrait of Magnus Derrick as a cosmic gambler – not just the most redoubtable poker player in El Dorado country as a young man, but a gambler in minerals during the gold rush, then a gambler in wheat, ultimately a gambler in the contest of transcendent Forces – would seem to confirm a view of success in America more than a half-century old. The opposite is in fact the case. Although, as Tocqueville pointed out, America was quintessentially a nation of gamblers, this fact was not celebrated, or even openly acknowledged, until the end of the nineteenth century when Western gamblers and gambling capitalists became ambiguously sanctioned cultural heroes.

Americans always gambled; the multitude of tracts and sermons against gambling are themselves sufficient evidence. While Puritan ministers were preaching their restrictive doctrine of the lot, colonial citizens were conducting lotteries to finance a variety of public projects.[32] Gambling in many forms infused the nation's social life, its political life, and its economic life. Nineteenth-century Washington became famous as the nation's poker capital as well as political capital; several presidents were avid players, and its politics reeked of inside deals. Banks in Jacksonian America gambled on the future by issuing notes unbacked by specie; railroad developers risked fortunes against the chance of immeasurably greater fortunes; a committee investigating the Black Friday panic of 1869 reported with dismay that "gambling is the very life-blood of the nation."[33] We have seen in other chapters the importance of gambling to colonial Southern planters and to frontier adventurers of all kinds – individuals within "chance cultures" who acknowledged the precariousness of existence. But no official approval of gambling preceded the Progressive Era. Although Bret Harte made stoical gamblers the heroes of several stories (with touches of irony) in the 1860s and 1870s, this part of his formula was not widely imitated by genteel writers until the 1890s. Dime novelists filled their narratives with gambling and gambling metaphors, but dime novels, though read also by respectable citizens, were considered fiction for the lower classes and were not openly accepted by the "better" sort of people until well into the twentieth century when they became objects of nostalgia. The attacks on speculation in the success literature ignored not only the fact that speculation was rampant but that it sometimes met with popular approval. Whereas Charles Francis Adams, Jr., and his younger brother Henry denounced Jay Gould as a gambling rascal, a popular biography following close on Gould's death expressed admiration for "the greatest Wall Street gambler," for a man whose "life was a continual game of chance."[34] With the gambling titans of Norris and Dreiser, then, the cultural mainstream at last openly celebrated what it had long feared or ignored, but what had its own long life in American popular culture.

Science and philosophy discovered chance in the nineteenth century. Although probability theory since its formulations by Pascal and Huygens in the seventeenth century had been fundamentally deterministic,

mathematicians and physicists in the nineteenth began developing the
concepts of indeterminacy that in the twentieth century would lead to
quantum theory, wave mechanics, uncertainty principles, even a science
of "chaos." In American philosophy Charles Peirce in particular, later
to be echoed by William James and John Dewey, claimed a more crucial
role for chance in human experience than had been acknowledged before.
Peirce's "tychism," positing an evolutionary universe rooted in both
reason and chaos, ever moving from randomness to increasing order,
foretold the growing acceptance of chance in twentieth-century philosophy.[35]

But the naturalists did not read Peirce along with Herbert Spencer.
Although they may have found ideas about the role of chance in human
affairs in the novels of Balzac and Zola, they also absorbed them from
their own culture. Gambling was by no means an exclusively American
vice, of course, but its popular images in the nineteenth century – as
opposed to its pervasive practices – had distinctive national characteristics. The European gambler was invariably portrayed as a decadent aristocrat who squandered his wealth at elegant spas. The stereotypical
American gambler was altogether different: in his primary guises either
an urban confidence man tempting unwary youth, or a financial speculator wagering a fortune on the stock market or in "bucket shops."
The gambling dandy revealed the moral bankruptcy of aristocracies; the
shrewd operator exposed the particular evils to which democracy and a
market economy were prone. The corruption of youth threatened the
moral health of the body politic; speculation – "business gambling" as
it was typically termed – threatened both economic stability and traditional belief in the values of work and merit. The American versions of
gambling, as Tocqueville first suggested, were the snares to which citizens were particularly susceptible in a highly mobile, unstable society.

But chance as an element of a secular metaphysics was more deeply
threatening than as a mere social vice. The philosophers' questions about
fate, will, and chance were translated into sociopolitical terms in
nineteenth-century America as fixed social classes, self-reliance, and circumstance. Chance, that is, echoing Tocqueville now in a slightly different way, was inherent in American democratic assumptions as a
counterforce to human freedom. Americans insisted on their classlessness; according to the liberal faith in progress, fate had no role in determining success. Officially, those who dominated the dissemination of
ideas insisted on every man's ability to shape his own future, but they
acknowledged chance's role to a considerably greater degree than the
success prophets' absolute denial of luck would seem to allow. If deterministic forces (whether material or spiritual) are denied, failure must be
interpreted either as weakness or as chance. Both factors figure in nine-

teenth-century views of success. Among the many reasons why ante-bellum writers of conduct-of-life literature preached the values of modest material achievement was an awareness of the riskiness Tocqueville iden-tified as endemic to careers in trade. Postbellum success writers' nearly frantic denials of chance can only imply a growing fear that success and failure were more random than rational. Through the entire period, belief in self-determination was accompanied by acknowledgment of the need for opportunity. One major issue underlying all of the popular tracts on success concerned the availability of opportunity – of chances – to achieve success. "Luck and pluck," chance and self-determination, were deemed equally necessary.

But the equation, luck + pluck = success, was not constant in popular belief. I can only generalize broadly here, rather than document a step-by-step transformation, but luck was granted a considerably greater role in human lives at the end of the century, after several decades of industrial consolidation, than in the preceding era. That is, luck was vehemently denied in the period when markets were least stable and the role of luck most obvious, then openly acknowledged in the period when the control of markets in fewer hands reduced luck's importance. Belief in chance was inversely proportional to actual opportunities. In *The Theory of the Leisure Class* (1899), Thorstein Veblen described belief in luck as "an archaic trait," incompatible with and a hindrance to "the modern in-dustrial process."[36] How ironic that at the very time he was writing, chance was beginning to be proclaimed not just as an inevitable element of economic life but as a validating principle of twentieth-century Amer-ican capitalism. Individuals in the late nineteenth century felt severely limited by the "incorporation" of economic and social forces, to use Alan Trachtenberg's term, and science and philosophy contributed to this pervasive feeling of diminishment with various determinisms. Thus, the essential meaning of chance underwent a radical change. At midcentury, chance was widely perceived to be a check on self-determination, both the arbitrary obstacles wrought by business cycles (the panics of 1837 and 1857, say), and the more normal problems of unpredictable markets and natural catastrophes. However, the classical and medieval belief in the goddess Fortuna persisted: the fatalism by which the lowly were raised and the great brought low by the arbitrary turnings of Fortune's wheel. By the end of the century, as is most evident in the writings of the naturalists, chance was redefined as a check not on personal agency but on the consolidation of political and economic power, and on the deterministic forces of heredity and environment. The "main chance" defined chance as opportunity, not as uncaused event.

The naturalists thus embraced the American speculative spirit that Tocqueville recognized in the 1830s but that had been denied by the caretakers of the nation's moral health, in order to confront their own age's most fundamental material and philosophical dilemmas. Their sporting rhetoric gave precedence to metaphysics. While the liberalization of American Protestantism was replacing a deterministic with a benevolent deity, science and the social sciences were countering with a wholly secular and more absolute (because more comprehensible) determinism. In this more thoroughly fated secular world, sportive chance no longer represented the limits on self-determination in an unfated universe, but guaranteed a measure of individual freedom in a universe of force.

Progressive-Era sporting rhetoric addressed the universe of chance and force in various ways. In his *Education,* Henry Adams expressed his pessimistic determinism by describing history as a "game" of uncontrollable forces. In contrast, William James characterized man's relationship to God in a famous essay as a chess game between novice and master, asserting human free will in a determined but providential universe (although God will necessarily win the game, man can nonetheless play as well as he is able).[37] Death dices with Life for the fates of a young Poet and a Dancer seeking love in Louise Bryant's *The Game,* an avant-garde one-act "morality play" staged in 1915 by the Provincetown Players. Life wins this time, but the fates of these lovers, and of all mankind, remain the whim of repeated dice rolls.[38] The sky-assaulting tycoons of business fiction, Twain's omnipotent hoaxers, and Alfred Henry Lewis's comic frontier fatalists assert yet other views on the question of human will in a world of circumscribed freedom. In the context of this varied yet consistent impulse to view chance in metaphysical terms, Paul Laurence Dunbar's novel, *The Sport of the Gods* (1902), is strikingly different. Despite his title that would seem to place the novel squarely in the tradition of transcendent contest, Dunbar took a position that later black writers would consistently follow, opting for politics over metaphysics. The "gods" of which Berry Hamilton and his family are the helpless sport are no abstraction but rather the powerful white people in a racist society.

The major literary naturalists – Crane, Norris, Dreiser, and London – wrestled incessantly with chance and freedom, materialism and transcendence, often in the language of gambling and sport. Chance and contest were equally important to the naturalists' worldview. Pure contest dominates much of London's boxing fiction and his tales of wilderness survival; pure chance dominates such stories as Norris's *McTeague* (1899), in which a lottery precipitates the central action, and the main characters are described as utterly and irredeemably "the sport of chance."[39] The naturalists' fiction is most interesting when chance and contest interact, when chance in fact makes contest possible. This is the case in Norris's and Dreiser's business fiction, where chance grants Magnus Derrick, Curtis Jadwin, and Frank Cowperwood opportunities to contest for great wealth and power, yet also assures their ultimate defeat.

Among the naturalists, Norris and London were the compulsive abstractionists in their treatment of chance – or Chance. In this they also shared a profound intellectual confusion which, more than an artistic shortcoming, must be acknowledged as one of the distinctive literary voices of the age. We have already seen these tendencies in Norris's Epic of the Wheat; they are pervasive in London's fiction as well. Competition and Chance are always writ large in London's fictional world. When he emphasized Competition, he created Nietzschean supermen; when he emphasized Chance, he presented life as either a grand adventure or a losing gamble. When he mixed the two, as he frequently did, his human playthings flirt at least for a time with becoming godlike. But at the same time, London's social conscience raged against the exploiting of the powerless. London never successfully reconciled his fantasies of personal power to his passion for social justice, and the resulting confusion is reflected in his sporting rhetoric.

"Competition [is] the secret of creation," London wrote in his first novel.[40] Life is a high-risk gamble, he declared in numerous stories of poker and other games of chance with vast wealth or even life itself as the stake.[41] London's boxing stories proclaim the preeminence of either fate ("A Piece of Steak"), chance (*The Game*), or will (*The Abysmal Brute*). His tales of sled dogs in the Yukon are pure pop-Darwin: In *The Call of the Wild* (1903), when Buck is kidnapped and taken to the Yukon, he discovers that the "law of club and fang" has replaced the "fairplay" he learned to expect as a "sated aristocrat" in California.[42] When the protagonists are human, sport replaces battle as the dominant metaphor. "Man is a natural gambler," says Wolf Larsen in London's most famous novel, *The Sea-Wolf* (1904), "and life is the biggest stake he can lay. The greater the odds the greater the thrill."[43] But from sporting with the lives of others, Wolf Larsen's own life becomes the sport of a greater force, as he deteriorates physically until his defiant will is hopelessly trapped in a powerless body. In a novel fundamentally at odds with itself, Wolf Larsen is both a fascinating *Uebermensch* and a cruel oppressor – a diminished Ahab, with no meaningful object for his mad quest.

Any representation of London's fiction through a single novel risks reduction, but for mapping the twists and turns through naturalism's intellectual landscape *Burning Daylight* (1910) is particularly valuable. The novel begins as another Yukon tale of Darwinian adventure in which the fittest to survive is Elam Harnish, also known as "Burning Daylight." The initial setting is appropriately a saloon and casino. "In all lands where life is a hazard lightly played with and lightly turned aside," the narrator comments, "men turn, almost automatically, to gambling for diversion and relaxation. In the Yukon men gambled their lives for gold, and those that won gold from the ground gambled for it with one another."[44] Burning Daylight is the chief among these gamblers, an archetypal player of cosmic sport:

> He was a man's man primarily, and the instinct in him to play the game of life was strong. . . . He had known nothing but hard knocks for big stakes. Pluck and endurance counted in the game, but the great god Chance dealt the cards. Honest work for sure but meagre returns did not count. A man played big. He risked everything for everything, and anything less than everything meant that he was a loser. (6)

The echoes of Tocqueville are surely unintentional, but *Burning Daylight,* like *The Octopus* and *The Pit,* reads like an archetypal rendering of the Frenchman's thesis. Elam loses his entire fortune, forty thousand dollars, without regret on a single poker hand, then wins an insignificant amount on a bet that he can cover two thousand frozen miles in sixty days to deliver the mail, then follows a "hunch" to an eleven-million-dollar fortune. Like Magnus Derrick and Curtis Jadwin, he is driven not by greed but by the joy of contest:

> Desire for mastery was strong in him, and it was all one whether wrestling with the elements themselves, with men, or with luck in a gambling game. It was all a game, life and its affairs. And he was a gambler to the core. Risk and chance were meat and drink. True, it was not altogether blind, for he applied wit and skill and strength; but behind it all was everlasting Luck, the thing that at times turned on its votaries and crushed the wise while it blessed the fools – Luck, the thing all men sought and dreamed to conquer. And so he. (61)

Turn-of-the-century American writers celebrated risk because adventure seemed nearly driven from the world, leaving as options mostly submission or defeat. *Burning Daylight* is full of such rhetorically overblown extrapolations of the cosmic game, as it follows its hero's career through a series of bizarre turns. Having played his hunch and competed with other men by the sportsman's code of "square dealing and right playing" (82), Daylight leaves Alaska as King of the Klondike, looking now for bigger games to play. But here the socialist in London suddenly begins to compete with the Nietzschean romantic. The game Elam discovers in San Francisco and New York is the exploitative game of big business as portrayed by muckrakers. Fleeced once, he learns the new rules well enough to become the most successful and ruthless gamesman on the West Coast, though preying on the robbers rather than the working class they robbed: a capitalist with a socialist's conscience, but a social Darwinist as well. The "game" he won so heroically in the Yukon now seems no different from this version played by financiers and captains of industry at the expense of the poor. "He saw the game played out according to the everlasting rules, and he played a hand himself. The gigantic futility of humanity organized and befuddled by the bandits did not shock him. It was the natural order" (161).

The romantic hero of Alaskan fortune hunting has become first a successful robber-baron gamesman and now a disillusioned nihilist. But London's narrative takes yet another turn. When Elam falls in love with Dede Mason, he throws away his entire fortune – now thirty million – to marry and live in idyllic primitiveness in the Sonoma Valley. At first, Dede seems to him "the most remarkable card" in Luck's deck (299), but when she proposes to flip a coin to resolve her indecision about marrying, Elam refuses. "I'll be everlastingly damned if I'll gamble on love," he tells her. "Love's too big for me to take a chance on" (300). The gambler has given up gambling and decided to worship Love, not Chance, but in one final turn London reconciles the game to the woman. Elam's life with Dede is a "new game" in which he finds "in little things all the intensities of gratification and desire that he had found in the frenzied big things when he was a power and rocked half a continent with the fury of the blows he struck. . . . And this new table on which he played the game was clean. Neither lying, nor cheating, nor hypocrisy was here" (352). When Elam finds traces of gold on his property, he nearly reverts to his old sporting ways, until sight of Dede recalls him from temporary frenzy. He decides to plant the hillside through which the vein runs with hundreds of eucalyptus trees.

Ronald Martin has argued that such novels as *Burning Daylight* and *The Sea-Wolf* are essentially socialist. The act of renouncing capitalist individualism, Martin points out, would be meaningless were not London's protagonists heroically, gloriously, powerfully individual.[45] If so, London did his work too well in *Burning Daylight*. The "game" and its master player seem utterly heroic at every moment in the novel, despite the irreconcilable conflicts between the different versions of it. It is in these contradictions in fact, embodied in the competing definitions of the single metaphor of the "game," that *Burning Daylight* most fully represents the conflicting desires of its age.

In the fiction of London and Norris, the naturalists' longing to assert human grandeur in the face of constricting forces seems to result too easily in gorgeously silly, big-chested posturing. But naturalism's more subtle possibilities can be found in Crane and Dreiser. While Norris and London often became lost in clouds of abstraction, Crane and Dreiser more thoroughly addressed similar issues of force, chance, and freedom in the everyday world. Dreiser's own rhetorical excesses are only too obvious, particularly in his authorial digressions into cosmic philosophy in *Sister Carrie*. But the massive weight of Dreiser's documentary realism gives the operations of force and chance credible concreteness in his fiction. At one point in *The Financier,* the narrator comments that in a largely deterministic world, pity appears "in odd crannies and chance flaws between forces."[46] If we substitute "individual freedom" for "pity," we have an apt description of Dreiser's general worldview. The Civil War, the Chicago fire, and the panic of 1873 are the major factors in Frank Cowperwood's successes and failures, each from Cowperwood's perspective a "chance flaw between forces" that enables him to exercise his own personal strength. That strength is itself a gift, not a simple matter of choice, but if the ability to seize opportunity is given, the will – the desire – to do so is not. Desire is not a universal instinct in Dreiser's world but rather his term for human will and freedom.[47] Cowperwood's desires set him apart from his cautious father; Carrie's desires set her apart from Hurstwood. Those incapable of desiring merely drift, as if in the state of "weightlessness" that Jackson Lears has described as a pervasive feeling at the turn of the century.

And chance mediates between force and desire. If a world of pure will is unthinkable in 1900, a world of pure force is intolerable. Near the end of *Jennie Gerhardt* (1911), Lester Kane tells Jennie that "all of us are more or less pawns. . . . moved about like chessmen by circumstance over which we have no control."[48] "More or less" is the key to Dreiser's worldview, the narrow opening to limited freedom. Lester himself insists on fairness in all of his affairs and is incapable of "snaky deeds." In all of Dreiser's novels chance events both disrupt the sway of force and create opportunities for individuals to either act or not act. Belief in chance, which traditionally was renounced as both a blasphemy against providence and a negation of human effort, becomes for Dreiser a more desperate faith in limited individual autonomy. June Howard has written of Carrie, as if echoing the passage from *The Financier* quoted above, "The forces of chance – not really laws of causality, but rather the interstices between those laws – open the possibility for her success."[49] In *Sister Carrie,* a motif of fortune's dice and two strategically placed card games reinforce the importance of chance in the characters' lives. Carrie playing euchre for dimes with Drouet and Hurstwood early in the novel is all desire; Hurstwood losing at poker near the end is all doubt and fear. Each of the characters is to some degree subject to what the narrator calls "the forces which sweep and play through the universe," and their capacities to desire are affected by age; yet chance and desire nonetheless assure at least minimal human freedom.[50] Chance creates opportunities; those who are alive in their desires seize them.

Of all the writers I have been discussing, Stephen Crane most finely

anatomized the relationship of chance to freedom, most thoroughly es-
chewed apotheosizing chance as a cosmic force rather than an intimate
experience of everyday life. In his pervasive irony and pared-down prose
Crane seems the most modern of these writers, yet in another way he
seems a son of the nineteenth century. Where Dreiser struggled to rescue
human freedom from an amoral universe of force, Crane struggled to
retain human responsibility. Walter Benn Michaels has gone so far as to
insist on Crane's kinship with the era's moralists, who denied any role
for chance in a providential universe.[51] But this kinship describes Crane's
view of chance only partially. Rather, in Crane's fiction chance continually dissolves into causation, causation into randomness, with a resulting
moral ambiguity; yet at some point in the sequence moral responsibility
enters. Crane's moralism was not an echo of convention but a reconstruction that acknowledged a new complexity in moral judgments.

   Although he participated in the era's sporting rhetoric, Crane differed
from the other writers in important ways. Crane shared Norris's and
London's fascination with sport, but with a marked difference. Whereas
Norris (like Richard Harding Davis) was drawn to the manly romance
of football, and London to the atavism of boxing and blood sport, Crane
was more subtly interested in the psychology of risk and fear that athletes
shared with other physical adventurers. Crane's own "gritty" style of
playing baseball in college reappeared in his nonchalant bravado as a war
correspondent. As Edwin Cady first emphasized in 1962, Crane's experience in sports taught him "the cosmic gambler's stoic outlook: de-
spising the petty, safe, and comfortable; prizing the chance-taking, the
enterprising, the seeking, aggressive and tough." Cady also first suggested the possibility that "the trope basic to Crane's vision was that of
the game."[52] Crane's was not the simply heroic game of Owen Wister,
or even Frank Norris, but a complex, deeply ironic one. Several of
Crane's stories either parody or more subtly invert several of the heroic
sporting emblems whose history I have been tracing. In "The Bride
Comes to Yellow Sky" (1898), the Western gunman's code romantically
celebrated in the Wister school of 1890s magazine fiction becomes the
destructive foolishness of overgrown boys, easily overridden by the first
meager elements of oncoming civilization. In the opening chapter of
Maggie (1893), the vicious game of "King of the Hill" played by bowery
urchins with rocks for missiles parodies the contest for success in the
Darwinian jungle. And Crane's Whilomville stories parody yet another
figure, the playful child, to be discussed in Chapter 10. Whereas these
essentially parodic fictions attack popular sporting myths directly, the
intricate ironies of "The Open Boat" (1897) and *The Red Badge of Courage*
(1895) transform conventional narratives of heroic adventure into complex parables of human existence. In "The Open Boat," the "race" is

most surely not to the swift, the able oiler, but by chance and mutual
assistance to the more ordinary survivors of the capsized boat. In *The
Red Badge,* varied sporting motifs – analogies to football, boxing, and
footraces – serve not to collapse war into sport in the manner of Southern
romance, but to open up a chasm between the bloody actualities of war
and the heroic sporting language by which war had become conventionally represented.[53]

Crane consistently undercut popular heroic figures of sporting prowess
in all of these examples, but with no loss of admiration for a more
precarious and ambiguous sort of physical and moral courage. Crane's
fiction in effect takes the masculinist fantasy of writers like Norris and
Davis and reimagines it through a sense of life, shared with Dreiser, as
the intricate interplay of chance, force, and human agency. His chief
sporting figure for this vision is the gambler. He appears briefly as the
fire chief in *The Monster* (1899), described as a man "who viewed a fire
with the same steadiness that he viewed a raise in a large jack-pot."[54] He
is more fully represented in several of Crane's Western sketches – "The
Five White Mice," "A Man and Some Others," "Moonlight on the
Snow," and of course "The Blue Hotel" (all published in 1898) – in
which Bret Harte's romantic fatalism is transformed into parables of
chance and responsibility. In "The Five White Mice," for example, two
narratives intersect: In the first, the New York Kid's loss of a dice game
sets in motion a sequence of causation that ultimately prevents a murder;
in the second, the Kid experiences an epiphany when he suddenly recognizes that the Mexicans he is about to kill are human beings rather
than markers in his "new game." This is not a simple moralist's story
about apparent chance actually being providential design, but a subtler
tale of chance events having causal consequences and of the dangers that
follow from believing that chance negates moral responsibility.[55]

This theme is played out in various ways in the other stories about
gamblers, most intricately in the most famous of them, "The Blue
Hotel." The plot of "The Blue Hotel" is structured around three successive and very different contests: a game of cards, a fight, and a murder.
The setting, Fort *Romper,* suggests innocent playfulness; the opening
paragraphs, in contrast, which describe Scully working his "seductions"
upon visitors and "catching" customers – "practically [making] them
prisoners" – imply coercion.[56] The entire story, in both its narrative and
imagery, turns on such ironic juxtapositions that necessarily raise questions about human freedom and responsibility. Johnnie's game of High-
Five with a local farmer ends in a quarrel (play become conflict); when
a new game is formed, with Johnnie and the cowboy as partners against
the Swede and the Easterner, the cowboy's "board-whacking" manner
transforms a game of chance – the luck of the draw – into a contest of

"prowess and pride" (145). When a third hand is played, with the Swede now acting the board-whacker, his sudden outburst, "You are cheatin'!" pushes play all the way to violence. A striking image captures the strangeness of this unstable moral universe. In the brief scuffle following the Swede's accusation, "the boots of the men trampled the fat and painted kings and queens as they gazed with their silly eyes at the war that was waging above them" (156). "What's the good of a fight over a game of cards?" the Easterner asks (157). Play/contest, chance/prowess, "silly eyes"/"war," "fight"/"game": The underlying game undergoes repeated metamorphoses.

Behind this instability lies the issue explicitly raised by the Easterner only at the end of the story: the question of accountability. Both the imagery and the narrative itself constantly twist chance and causation in ways that blur responsibility for the ultimately fatal sequence of events. The fight between the Swede and Johnnie – "players" having become "contestants," in the story's rhetoric – would seem to be an encounter between free agents to settle their dispute through proof of physical superiority. But Johnnie's words after being accused of cheating – "We must fight" – suggest powerlessness before some unspoken code. Scully "permits" and "arranges" the match, serves as "master of the ceremony," gives the signal "Now!" for the fight to commence. Throughout the story, in other words, Scully plays the godlike role of creator and destroyer, a man who controls his little world, only to find himself helpless at last to prevent his son's defeat. The fight itself is described as "a perplexity of flying arms" in the dark; the two combatants are said to "breathe like men on the rack" (160) – images of first chaos, then powerlessness. The Swede is first "demoniac" then "berserk," yet at the same time "agiley" in control (157, 161). The description of the outcome – "Johnnie's body again swung away and fell" (161) – identifies no human agent. In such language agency and helplessness continuously fold into each other. When Johnny falls the first time, the cowboy and Scully insist on fair play, the Westerners answering the Swede's fear and suspicion with impeccable honor. Yet this code is not freely followed. "If we only could—" moans the cowboy after the fight has ended, hungering for the revenge that the code denies him (164).

To the cowboy and the Easterner, the Swede's actions seem meaningless and random, yet they set in motion a sequence of cause and effect. To the Swede, on the other hand, the others seem in dark conspiracy against him, yet he experiences their actions as random, when they run counter to all his expectations. This confusion of order and randomness takes a final turn in the story's second act. Demanding that someone drink to his victory in the saloon after the fight, the Swede mistakes a professional gambler for a "little dude," "by chance" laying his hand on the shoulder of the one man who in fact represents the threat of violence he has all along feared (168). Crane seems to have been particularly fascinated by the professional gambler (he is the protagonist of "A Man and Some Others" and "Moonlight on the Snow" as well). The professional gambler is a manipulator of chance through skill, yet also a stoic who accepts whatever chance dictates despite his efforts. Most important and contrary to the image popularized by Bret Harte, Crane's gambler is not a fatalist; rather, in making a profession from chance he accepts accountability for outcomes over which he has imperfect control. As a "square" gambler, the figure in "The Blue Hotel" is a man of honor and moral responsibility; in fact, more than his fellow townspeople, who hypocritically allow him to prey on "reckless and senile farmers" but not on themselves (166–7). The city fathers trust and respect the gambler, and admire his domestic stability, yet they clearly hold him subject to their own social and political power. The gambler, in short, is less important to the story as the one man in the town who represents deadly threat than the one man who genuinely lives by risk but at the same time is guided by moral principles.

This is the man the Swede assaults "by chance." For the Swede, the sequence of events that follow his bullying of a man he mistakes for a "dude" seems utterly random. His response to the gambler's knife piercing his body is not pain but "supreme astonishment." To the gambler, on the other hand, the sequence of the Swede's assault, his own violent response, and the consequences he anticipates, though initially random, seem causally related. When he tells the stunned onlookers, "I'll be home waiting" to be arrested (169), he takes full responsibility for his own actions. The Swede experiences order as randomness, the gambler randomness as order. Guilt and innocence are difficult to assign.

But Crane assigns them, contrary not just to Dreiser's amoral naturalism but to the Western myth that also lies behind the story. In Wister's *The Virginian,* violence arises spontaneously from the needs of the community: The Virginian is not guilty of lynching Steve; he would be guilty *not* to. In the final section of Crane's story, however, when the Easterner tells the cowboy months later that "every sin is the result of a collaboration," a seemingly conventional moralism meets the universe of chance and force, but without denying the more deeply ambiguous nature of moral responsibility. Against the cowboy's insistence that the game of High-Five was only "played for fun," the Easterner tells him that Johnnie was indeed cheating. Johnnie is guilty of cheating, the Easterner of silence, the cowboy of provocation, Scully of allowing the events to follow the course they took. The gambler is merely "the apex of a human movement" (170). The effect of this ending is not to absolve the principles in the conflict, the Swede and the gambler, but to implicate the bystanders and the accessories; not to reduce moral ambiguity to conventional moralism, but to retain a sense of responsibility in the face of ambiguity. In Crane's version of the game, his characters both play and are played upon by chance; at some point in the sequence of events, responsibility is assigned.

In his view of the individual as both player and plaything, Crane was consistent with Norris, Dreiser, and London. But against the others' tendency in some of their most representative fiction to proclaim man's heroic powers as a cosmic gamesman only to reduce him at the end to the plaything of mighty forces, Crane tended to move in the opposite direction: from futility toward freedom and responsibility. Crane's surgical ironies, of course, are not as representative of the age's popular voice as Norris's and London's upper-case rhetorical flourishes, with their fundamental uncertainty over man's place in the universe. Sky-assaulting grandeur and microbial insignificance defined the poles of human possibility in the age's most distinctive responses to the universe of force and chance. Sporting rhetoric expressed both collective fantasies of power and collective anxieties over powerlessness, both fascination and outrage in regarding those with actual power. In the incompatible meanings of a single trope, the Progressive Era's ubiquitous "game," longings for transcendence confronted troubling material facts, inherited faith in order and reason grappled with intimations of chaos.

Part III

Twentieth-Century Legacies

A man can be destroyed but not defeated.

Ernest Hemingway, *The Old Man and the Sea* (1952)

He who dies with the most toys wins.

Bumper sticker (c. 1988)

The pervasive sporting rhetoric of the Progressive Era became a cluster of ubiquitous clichés by the 1980s, both generic (the game, playing the game) and particular (playing one's cards, getting into the ring, playing hardball, etc. etc. etc.). But I use the term "cliché" guardedly, with no intention to imply that this language has entirely lost meaning or significance. As sporting metaphors became thoroughly conventional, their values were naturalized to unconscious assumption, but these metaphors often became by the 1980s more *self*-referential than ever; that is, the equation of X with a game sometimes emphasized the "game" more than "X." In both cases, sporting rhetoric continued to bear the weight of myth and ideology, and to read it with full understanding required an awareness of the traditions from which it arose. Although the sporting cowboy, for example, had disappeared into a realm of pure fantasy, in various metamorphoses he now rode the mean streets of national and international politics. If journalists intended mockery in calling Ronald Reagan a "global cowboy," a good number of Reagan's constituents apparently found the image reassuring. "They're cowardly bums," Reagan fumed about the kidnappers of NATO commander General Dozier in December 1981, "They wouldn't have the guts to stand up to anyone individually in any kind of fair contest." If such pronouncements seemed

251

to reveal the poverty of the President's understanding of complex political issues, they also revealed his genius at touching American assumption and desire through his rhetoric.

Sporting cowboys and cavaliers have had a rich presence in the fiction and popular rhetoric of the twentieth century, along with other sportsmen and gamesmen in a variety of guises, players at life and business, and contestants in the more desperate games of human existence itself. The problem for the cultural historian lies not in the poverty of these traditions in this century – their history just an endless noting of cliché after cliché – but in their ubiquity and continuing resonance. How to find pattern in seeming chaos? Although the terrain is too vast for anything but a sketchy topography, the tracks of the nineteenth-century sporting myths can be traced in the twentieth-century cultural landscape through its fiction, and more sketchily yet in public discourse.

The following three chapters will bring the several strands of my cultural history of sporting rhetoric up to the most recent past. Western and Southern writers in the twentieth century have responded to their sporting traditions in very different ways. The Southern myth contributed to one of the richest flowerings in American literature, the so-called Southern Renaissance beginning in the 1920s; the Western story, in contrast, hardened into popular formulas resistant to serious literary consideration. But as the sporting cowboy became a popular hero without roots in any actual history, his code became thoroughly absorbed into the larger culture. I argued in Part I that in the nineteenth century, gamesmanship tended to define a strategy for outsiders to gain power, sportsmanship to appeal (often unwittingly) to aristocratic assumption. The triumphant gamesman celebrated social mobility for the politically powerless; the heroic sportsman reflected the empowered classes' uneasiness over democratic leveling or their need to justify their own power on grounds of merit. The one assumed marginality, in other words, the other centrality within the culture.

I would qualify that distinction now. Cooper's Natty Bumppo and Irving's fur trappers were "outlaws" no less than the wily gamesmen of Southwestern humor. Even the sporting planter of antebellum Southern romances, although the aristocrat of his region, was defined at least implicitly against the normative culture of the threatening or dominant North. It was only in the late nineteenth century that genteel novelists and short story writers sentimentalized all of these figures to the extent that they could be unambiguously celebrated (in dime novels, of course, the frontier gamesman continued to have a problematic relationship to the social order). In other words, the sporting heroes of American popular culture have typically emerged initially as marginal figures; their appropriation and domestication by the social or political center, as we have repeatedly seen, have led to striking contradictions. The emphasis on marginality has grown more conspicuous in the twentieth century, a development I will explore through a variety of texts.

The sporting heroes of American culture in the twentieth century have also continued to represent the possibilities of transcendence. The desperate games of Melville and the naturalists, that challenged liberal pieties in the nineteenth century, became more common in American fiction, expressing what emerged as a distinctive American tragic/heroic sense. The watered-down spiritual *agôn* of nineteenth-century revivalist rhetoric also continued into the new century, with Billy Sunday's life-as-baseball trope yielding most typically to life-as-football. In the 1920s, the *Southern Baptist Student* reprinted two sermonettes that opened with this proposition: "With apologies to Shakespeare, all the world is a football game, and we are the players." The game is played by Christians against anti-Christians, with the Devil as the fullback and Sin as the quarterback on the opposing team, and eternal life as the reward for the home side.[1] The minister with such a text has been sufficiently familiar to be parodied in at least a half-dozen novels, from Sinclair Lewis's *Babbitt* (1922) to Lisa Alther's *Kinflicks* (1976).[2] The marriage of sport, sporting rhetoric, and fundamentalist Christianity has been most striking in the "Jocks for Jesus" movement of the past two decades, with its proselytizing by such groups as Athletes in Action and its endless testimonials to God's determination of athletic success. The shift from justifying sport in the nineteenth century by appeals to religion, to promoting religion by appeals to sport, reveals much about the changing status of both sport and religion in America in little more than a century.[3]

Whereas the fundamentalist sporting metaphor has provoked only ridicule from novelists, the Melvillean spiritual contest has assumed a conspicuous place in twentieth-century American fiction. Melville's rediscovery at the same time that Hemingway and Faulkner published their first fiction meant both that a new generation now read Melville as a contemporary and that his vision influenced other writers. Both Hemingway and Faulkner read *Moby-Dick* and praised it publicly, Hemingway rather condescendingly in *Green Hills of Africa* and Faulkner more extravagantly during his residency at the University of Virginia.[4] Whether through influence or a shared vision, all three writers saw "salvation" as a stake to be won in a contest against "God." It is not difficult to see the great marlin of *The Old Man and the Sea* as a less gargantuan Moby Dick, and to find in the bullfights and hunts in Hemingway's fiction analogues to Ahab's contest with the White Whale in a less heroic world. Direct influence seems more possible in Faulkner's fiction: in his images of a jokester god ("Old Moster," "the cosmic joker," and "the prime maniacal Risibility"); in the metaphor of fate as a stage manager in *Absalom, Absalom!* (Melville used the same figure in the first chapter of *Moby-Dick*); in Ike McCaslin's discarding his compass, rifle, and watch to prepare for his confrontation with Old Ben (as Ahab with very different motivations crushed the quadrant, and scorned lightning rods, compass, and log line to engage the gods on their own terms).

Following Hemingway and Faulkner, in turn, novelists such as Ken Kesey and Norman Mailer continued to find in the figure of desperate sport a compelling vision of humanity's existential predicament. The fiction of all of these novelists raises questions about the relationship of politics to metaphysics, of the consequences, that is, of viewing human struggle as an existential contest for personal selfhood rather than a more material contest for social and political power. The case of black writers from Paul Laurence Dunbar to Richard Wright, Ralph Ellison, and their successors provides a particularly revealing perspective on this question, as they have tied the cruelly sportive Melvillean *agôn* to the particular plight of blacks in racist America.

The other side of the nineteenth-century's metaphysical sporting vision, the view of life as a game of chance, has also been more prominent in the twentieth century. As physical and biological scientists have increasingly acknowledged the role of chance in both animate and inanimate life, artists of all kinds have explored the possibilities of chance composition and "aleatory art."[5] And the esoteric ideas of scientists and artists have been part of the more general cultural embrace of sporting chance which is my primary concern here. From a people who officially denied chance any role at all in human destiny (while nonetheless gambling every day in most fundamental ways), Americans have come openly to take chance for granted. Living through two world wars and a major economic depression, then continuing to live in the shadow of The Bomb in the 1950s, the draft in the sixties, the oil crisis of the early seventies, the AIDS epidemic of the late eighties – to name only the most obvious representations of seemingly random threat – we have absorbed a sense of randomness into our most fundamental assumptions about life's possibilities. And American fiction reflects these new assumptions. The comic-apocalyptic vision of 1960s black humor was rooted in the basic notion that humankind is the sport of chance or of a whimsical deity; such novelists as Thomas Pynchon, Robert Coover, and Jerzy Kosinski explored this idea fully. For these writers, the heroic grandeur of the naturalists' cosmic gamblers had given way to a much more desperate hold on minimal human meaning.

Finally, as the 1980s drew to a close, it was clearer than ever from popular rhetoric that there were two "great games" in everyday American life: politics and business. But these two games were fundamentally different. Whereas politics remained the wholly material game for power, business often retained the transcendent significance with which it was invested in the nineteenth century. The spiritual "game of life" continued to appear in the sermons of liberal Protestant ministers until the 1950s, by which time it was completely absorbed into the therapeutic "game" of the heirs to turn-of-the-century mind-cure prophets. At first a meeting point for psychology and religion, this "game" became a sign of the triumph of psychology *over* religion in the entirely secularized liberal "theology" of postwar America. But this "game" also was not always distinguishable from the entrepreneurial "game" much trumpeted during the Reagan Revolution of the 1980s. Tracing the sporting rhetoric of success reveals profound change within a superficial rhetorical continuity. Heresies of the Gilded Age – unqualified emphasis on playing the game for its own sake, a celebration of gamesmanship rather than sportsmanship, and a recognition of risk and chance as central to the game – became articles of faith in the new entrepreneurial ethic. Moreover, what had been in the nineteenth century essentially a social model of success became entirely individualistic; the ideal shifted from a community of enterprising citizens to lone entrepreneurs, whether in the investment market or in the privacy of the self.

What these multiple narratives suggest, finally, is that once one begins to take the "game" seriously, it seems more and more to touch the bedrock of American culture. Sporting rhetoric seems to reflect a structure of perception and belief that is fundamental to the American way of seeing things. Not just American commitments to personal freedom and competition, but the theoretical classlessness, the lack of tradition, and the constitutional separation of church and state, tend to make individuals believe themselves the arbiters of their own moral universes. In the absence of collectively held absolutes, the "game" provides principles of order and signification. Don DeLillo has described the numerous games, both literal and metaphorical, in his own fiction as his characters' attempts to define rules and boundaries for themselves:

> People whose lives are not clearly shaped or marked off may feel a deep need for rules of some kind. People leading lives of almost total freedom and possibility may secretly crave rules and boundaries, some kind of control in their lives.

Within games, DeLillo adds, "we can look for perfect moments or perfect structures. In my fiction I think this search sometimes turns out to be a cruel delusion."[6]

DeLillo's insight seems borne out by observation. Without question, American social and political behavior is game*like* in many ways: not just our two-party, winner-take-all political system, but relations between advertisers and consumers, employers and employees, government itself and the citizens it governs (as in the paying of taxes). Legal scholars in particular have made this point, writing about how the American adversarial legal system pits prosecution against defense to arrive not at "truth" but at "justice," defined essentially as a fair contest governed by rules that give equal opportunity for victory to both sides.[7] Constructing actions as games may be a fundamental way both to organize the seeming chaos of life and, more problematically, to avoid confronting the moral implications of one's actions by providing immediate and self-justifying outcomes. The television network executives who perceive their task in terms of a "ratings game" do not have to consider the social impact of their programming. Those in the "advertising game" need not judge the value of the products they sell by any public standard; they have only to persuade consumers to buy.

Such generalizations come too easily, of course. In the following chapters I will examine popular sporting rhetoric more concretely, in relation to a handful of basic issues: sportsmanship and gamesmanship, power and powerlessness, metaphysics and politics, celebration and criticism. I will continue to explore the relationship of gender to the language of sport and games, and race will now figure more prominently as a consequence of blacks' finally gaining a voice in both the literature and the public discourse of the mainstream middle-class culture. What will emerge from the next three chapters, I hope, will be a specific sense of continuities and changes in American culture. By continuing to trace the patterns of sporting rhetoric I hope to suggest meaningful ways to read that culture today without reducing its complexity.

Sportsmen and Gamesmen in
Twentieth-Century Fiction

The Western and Southern sporting myths continued to have an important place in twentieth-century American culture, though in different ways. The Southern myth became fully developed in the half-century following the Civil War; in the next half-century and beyond, while it continued to spawn formulaic images in the popular culture, it also contributed to the intellectual and literary "Renaissance" of the 1920s and 1930s. The Western myth, in contrast, did not achieve its full flowering until the first quarter of the new century, after which it generated the country's most popular fictional genre into the 1960s (abetted by countless movies and television series), but it fed no comparable literary or cultural movement. The Western sporting myth also escaped its regional boundaries in the twentieth century. Cooper's Leatherstocking reappeared with minimal change in much of Ernest Hemingway's fiction and in the novels and stories of Hemingway's many imitators. The wily gamesman of the frontier humorists became an urban con man, his possibilities more circumscribed but his strategies for triumph and survival largely unaltered. Washington Irving's fight-or-frolic fur trappers were reincarnated in such figures as Randall Patrick McMurphy in Ken Kesey's *One Flew Over the Cuckoo's Nest*. Bret Harte's soft-hearted gamblers reappeared as Hot Horse Herbie, Last Card Louie, and other racetrack touts and bookies who populated Damon Runyon's Broadway world in the 1930s and 1940s.

The sporting gentlemen of the Southern myth are less easy to detect in transregional guises – confirmation of the fact that "the West" of popular fantasy never was as real a place as the Old South. The Southern myth was created by Southerners through exaggerating, romanticizing, and sanitizing certain elements of actual Southern life. Planters did sport and gamble and live a life of comparative leisure; Confederate soldiers did fight gallantly in a losing cause. The Western myth, on the other hand, was created mostly by Easterners with tourists' understanding of actual Western life. They made heroes of marginal men whose experiences lay on the periphery of frontier development, romanticizing the politically powerless and socially unassimilable. The Southern myth expressed an ideology tied to an actual place and a people's experience. For all its grounding in a supposed Western landscape, the Western myth was more truly an abstraction with no ties to a particular land or people. While Faulkner wrestled with the consequences of both Southern history and Southern myth on the South of his own time, the Western myth in the twentieth century continued its disembodied existence, expressing an endlessly adaptable fantasy of competitive individualism and heroic codes.

Agrarian play and Faulknerian sport

Although sport has not figured in accounts of the "Southern Renaissance" of the 1920s and 1930s, it is possible to read the pressing concerns of this remarkable generation of Southern writers through its sporting rhetoric. The confusion of history and myth that emerged after the Civil War in the writings of John Esten Cooke, Thomas Nelson Page, and others became the legacy of both William Faulkner and the artists and intellectuals who formed the Agrarian movement of the 1930s. An unaltered heroic image of the sporting planter has persisted in the outer circles of American popular culture; Faulkner and the Agrarians placed this figure at the center of their explorations of the South and its lessons for American civilization.

In the work of the Agrarians, the group of reactionary Southerners that included John Crowe Ransom, Allen Tate, Andrew Lytle, Donald Davidson, Robert Penn Warren, and Stark Young, the Southern sporting myth served most explicitly as a critique of modern technocracy. Within the competing strains of Jeffersonian agrarianism and plantation legend in the group's manifesto, *I'll Take My Stand* (1930), a celebration of play appears as part of the latter. Play underlies the ideal not of a hardworking, self-sufficient yeomanry but of a social hierarchy within which leisure figures prominently at every level. "Leisure" appears over and over in the collective introduction to the book and in the individual essays that follow, always to oppose industrialism and the cash nexus, the chief violators of agrarian values. In virtually the same manner in which Southern apologists in the 1850s damned money-minded Yankeedom by contrast to the gracious ease of Southern life, the Agrarians denounced the Yankee legacy in the twentieth century that was now overwhelming the South as well as the North. Modern industrial society, they claimed, blocked human expression and fulfillment in a variety of ways unknown to agrarian societies. In the volume's opening "Statement of Principles," the writers acknowledged a legitimate role for science and technology in the modern world, but only to enable labor to "be performed with leisure and enjoyment." Industrialism renders labor meaningless in itself, valuable only for its rewards – in contrast to agrarian societies where labor "is pursued with intelligence and leisure." The arts, too, are incompatible with industrialism, depending as they do "on a free and disinterested observation of nature that occurs only in leisure." Ransom, Davidson, Lytle, and Young repeated these sentiments in their individual contributions to *I'll Take My Stand*.[1]

Southerners were by no means alone in the Depression in promoting play as an antidote to failed industrialism. Spokesmen from the breadth of the political spectrum addressed the problem, with reactionary Southerners only playing the most conspicuous role in celebrating leisure as the alternative to modern ills. Outside the Agrarian group but still within the South, the journalist Thomas Lomax Hunter – a commonsensical, humorous follower of Mark Twain and Will Rogers, speaking not for an intellectual elite but for the democratic masses – wrote columns in the Richmond *Times-Dispatch* in the early 1930s in which he regretted the passing of the ring tournament ("in romantic mimicry of chivalry's great game") and, most astonishingly, celebrated the "pleasures of unemployment": the "wealth of leisure" enjoyed by the poor man and denied to the "yoke-broken helots of civilization" suffering under "our industrial slavery." In the same year that W. J. Cash in *The Mind of the South* (1941) inaugurated the era of critical Southern self-examination, William Alexander Percy's memoir, *Lanterns on the Levee,* sentimentalized the supposed racial harmony of black and white in the South in a traditional way: in nostalgic reminiscences of crawfishing with a booncompanion named Skillet, the black son of the family cook. Even Cash himself, guiltless of any such sentimentality in his iconoclastic study, found in Southern play the essence of what was genuinely valuable in his region's heritage. Cash laid the South's failure to develop any "complex and intellectual culture" to its "pattern of leisure and hedonistic *drift,*" and he specifically criticized the Agrarians for their elitism, romanticism, and disregard of unpleasant facts. But he nonetheless commended Ransom and his fellow contributors to *I'll Take My Stand* for "puncturing the smugness of progress" by "directing attention to the evils of *laissez-faire* industrialism," and for "recalling that the South must not be too much weaned away from its ancient leisureliness – the assumption that the first end of life is living itself."[2]

The Agrarians provided the focal point for this sentiment, not just in *I'll Take My Stand* but also in their subsequent writings, both fiction like

Stark Young's romance of the Civil War, *So Red the Rose* (1934), and nonfiction like Donald Davidson's study of regionalism, *Attack on Leviathan* (1938).[3] The richest literary contribution to this Agrarian critique came from Caroline Gordon, not one of the twelve who wrote *I'll Take My Stand*, but a Southerner connected to the movement through her marriage to Allen Tate and by a shared perception of the centrality of play to Southern life. Gordon's *Aleck Maury, Sportsman* (1934) would seem an apolitical idyl of sporting pleasures had it not been published in the midst of the Depression by a Southerner linked to the Agrarians. A biographical novel of her father's life-long devotion to field sports, *Aleck Maury* is an unadorned, deceptively simple pastoral narrative, its style too plain for romance, its events too commonplace for mythmaking. But in the context of the Agrarian revolt against industrialism, Gordon expressed concretely through Aleck Maury the ideal of true leisure defined abstractly over and over in the essays of *I'll Take My Stand*.

Aleck Maury is an unexceptional teacher of classics and an amateur angler and huntsman, who by living as fully committed to pure play as is humanly possible takes an implicitly heroic stand against the course of American history. Maury not only devotes more hours to hunting and fishing than to any other activity, he spends most of his nonsporting hours thinking about his last outing or planning his next. He is not *obsessed* with field sports, however, because obsession implies compulsion; rather, he does all this with simple joy. The novel's theme becomes explicit only once. Seeing Maury outfitted for a day's fishing, a hard-working old farmer leaps up from digging post-holes to cry out with furious pride, "I'm sixty years old . . . and I ain't never went a-fishing in my life!" Returning from his stream later in the afternoon, Maury sees the same man still at work. "I'm sixty years old," the sportsman calls back, brandishing a fist, "and I ain't never dug a post-hole in my life."[4] The reader is to decide whose life is more admirable.

Although many in the novel judge Aleck Maury merely lazy and irresponsible, Gordon's portrait of the sportsman does not support their view. Maury's sport has a spiritual quality, not just in his specific sporting code but in his overriding sense that to play is ultimately to open himself to God's grace. When he finds an ideal fishing stream, Maury marvels that "Providence had led me to this perfect sport" (202). Later, after his son dies, the father finds spiritual comfort in a solitary hunt with his favorite dog. And as an old man, retired and widowed, Maury realizes that at last he "might return . . . to the timelessness of childhood," fishing daily, with no sense of competing necessity. "Every day would be a gift from the gods and it would be a man's plain duty to enjoy it" (245). Maury's life is marked by a continual purification, away from slavishness and competitiveness toward absolute play. Play is not mere sport to Maury but a state of holiness.

Gordon's novel is both the purest expression of the Agrarian vision and the purest expression of Southern women's celebration of their regional myth through play rather than contest. Faulkner's fiction from the same period, on the other hand, approaches romantic myth with deep reservations. Although there was no direct link between the Agrarians and Faulkner, in the heroic image of the sportive Confederate cavalryman lies a common interest. In *So Red the Rose,* Stark Young sent his young hero, Duncan Bedford – a reckless "rascal" full of pranks – off to war with the inimitable Jeb Stuart, where Duncan finds merely a larger playground, his letters home sounding "as if they were on a big hunt or running horse-races." In his playful bravado Stuart seems to Mrs. Bedford "about as bad as Duncan is" – mild disapproval badly masking a mother's delight in another winsome Bad Boy. For his first book, a biography of Nathan Bedford Forrest, Andrew Lytle chose a less likely hero than Stuart to immortalize as a playful cavalier. Although Forrest had been a brilliant officer during the war, afterwards as the first Imperial Wizard of the Ku Klux Klan he came to represent a side of Southern life that even popular history eventually repudiated. But in *Bedford Forrest and His Critter Company* (1931), Lytle made his subject a hero of romance by portraying him as both a playful sportsman and a cagey gamesman out of the tradition of frontier humor.[5]

Faulkner was as drawn to such images of the Southern past as any of the Agrarians, but he also saw clearly the less admirable consequences of this Southern character. In a sense, Faulkner restored the ambivalence of the antebellum writers to the sporting myth. Faulkner's own Forrest, his fictional John Sartoris, is a sporting cavalier during the war but a ruthless bigot afterwards; in the conflict between these two images lies Faulkner's sense of the dialectic of Southern history, its glory and its shame. In *Sartoris* (1929), *Light in August* (1932), and *The Unvanquished* (1938), the fight-or-frolic Confederate soldier who emblemized for Young and Lytle the superiority of Southern martial character reappears in several forms: in Jeb Stuart himself, the South's undying hero; in Reverend Hightower's grandfather; and in the two brothers, Bayard and John Sartoris. Stuart appears in *Sartoris,* remembered by Miss Jenny Du Pre as her brother Bayard's commander: a reckless and sportive cavalier who once led a raid, on "dancing mounts," into a Union camp to steal coffee for the breakfast table. Bayard goes his leader one better, racing back into the midst of the now vigilant enemy for anchovies, only to be fatally shot in the back by a cook with a derringer. His brother John survives similar escapades; he once races accidentally into a Yankee camp, single-handedly capturing every last man by pretending his regiment has them surrounded (echoes of Bedford Forrest), then lets them sneak off into the night, unarmed and barely clothed, while he lies in his bedroll smothering his laughter. No nineteenth-century romancer made the sport of war more glorious.

But for Faulkner the sporting myth was destructive as well as joyful, the South's past its curse as well as its glory. Death in quest of anchovies, however sportive in spirit, is pointless. Hightower's obsession with the grandfather whose Civil War raiders were less "men after spoils and glory" than "boys riding the sheer tremendous tidal wave of desperate living" – at once courageous and foolhardy – blights his own life and everything he touches.[6] In *Sartoris* too, the sportive Stuart and Sartoris brothers haunt their ancestors as a violent fate. In Miss Jenny's tellings and retellings of the raid for coffee and anchovies,

> what had been a hairbrained prank of two heedless and reckless boys wild with their own youth had become a gallant and finely tragical focal point to which the history of the race had been raised from out the old miasmic swamps of spiritual sloth by two angels valiantly fallen and strayed, altering the course of human events and purging the souls of men.[7]

The chief listeners to these stories, John Sartoris's twin great-grandsons, Johnny and Bayard III, are driven to live as recklessly as their ancestors, and to die as futilely: Johnny in World War I, needlessly flying into a swarm of German Fokkers just as the first Bayard rode into a Yankee camp for anchovies; young Bayard after the war, dying in an air crash after relentlessly pursuing death for months in speeding cars and planes. In her rage over the waste Miss Jenny thinks of all these foolish Sartoris males as "pawns" in some pointless game:

> But the Player, and the game He plays... He must have a name for His pawns, though. But perhaps Sartoris is the game itself – a game outmoded and played with pawns shaped too late and to an old dead pattern, out of which the Player Himself is a little wearied. (380)

Miss Jenny's fury is only partly warranted; her own enchantment with the sporting Confederate heroes of her youth has helped to drive the equally sportive and reckless Sartorises a half-century later to pointless destruction. The glory of the past that she perpetuates becomes a crushing burden in the present.

In *Absalom, Absalom!* (1936), Faulkner laid the sporting myth of the Lost Cause permanently to rest, when the third-person narrator in a rare intrusive moment declares that the Civil War was lost "not alone because of superior numbers and failing ammunition and stores, but because of generals who should not have been generals, who were generals not through training in contemporary methods or aptitude for learning them, but by the divine right to say 'Go there' conferred upon them by an absolute caste system." As to the heroic sporting moment of cavalier bravado that crystallizes the romance of the Old South in the earlier novels, the narrator goes on to denounce the "obsolete" officers

> who wore plumes and cloaks lined with scarlet at twenty-eight and thirty and thirty-two and captured warships with cavalry charges but no grain nor meat nor bullets, who would whip three separate armies in as many days and then tear down their own fences to cook meat robbed from their own smokehouses, who on one night and with a handful of men would gallantly set fire to and destroy a million dollar garrison of enemy supplies and on the next night be discovered by a neighbor in bed with his wife and be shot to death.[8]

The movement from romance to antiromance in his accounts of the Civil War describes Faulkner's basic strategy in a number of novels dealing with the sporting myth. In *The Unvanquished,* the joyful con games of Granny Millard to requisition Yankee mules and sell them back again and again to the enemy (related in the wonderfully comic manner of the Southwestern humorists) ends abruptly with her murder; and John Sartoris's equally playful raids, retold from *Sartoris,* degenerate after the war into intolerant and arrogant competitiveness that result in his death as well. In *The Hamlet* (1940), the yielding of the old order, represented by men like Will Varner, Pat Stamper, and V. K. Ratliff, to a new order represented by Flem Snopes is portrayed as the defeat of sportsmanship (playing economic games for pleasure as well as profit) by pure games-manship (competing for profit alone). The contrast, that is, rests on an elaborately detailed *aesthetic* critique of economic motives. Also, in the novel's own structure, comic horse swaps and playful contests for a herd of goats or the sale of sewing machines yield to the furious and fatal contest between Houston and Mink Snopes, then to the deadly serious game playing of Flem Snopes for the fate of Frenchman's Bend itself (and in Faulkner's parable, of the entire New South). Flem in turn, in *The Town* (1957) and *The Mansion* (1959), wins contest after contest until he meets his own violent end, the final defeat awaiting even the most skillful of players. And in the stories of *Go Down, Moses* (1942), the comic and romanticized gamesmanship of Uncle Buck and Uncle Buddy McCaslin in "Was" leads to the more biting yet still comic games played by Lucas Beauchamp against Buck and Buddy's descendants in "The Fire and the Hearth," followed in turn by the romantic hunting tale of "The Old People" in which Ike McCaslin wins his manhood through killing his first deer; all of this essentially comic sportiveness culminating in the brilliantly tortured prose of "The Bear," where the tragic implications of race and violence overwhelm the triumphant spirit of the sporting myth. Or almost overwhelm it: Faulkner's genius lay in holding both the myth and its counter-reality in suspension, in undercutting his own romanticism without destroying it altogether. At the end of *Sartoris*, Miss Jenny denounces the sporting recklessness of Sartoris males; at the end of *The Unvanquished*, Bayard II renounces the violent game of Southern honor; in the second-to-last story of *Go Down, Moses*, an Edmonds killing a doe in violation of the sporting code signifies the perpetuation of racial and sexual injustice as well; in the concluding volume of the Snopes trilogy Flem lies dead at the hands of a kinsman he has bested in game after game. But despite all of these defeats and renunciations, the earlier triumphs of magnificent game players retain an impressive power.

Faulkner's profound ambivalence toward Southern history and myth was shared by many other Southern writers, and his fiction provided particular models for expressing it. Faulkner's legacy is most evident in a handful of historical novels by some of the major male writers of his own generation. Southern women's writing lies mostly outside the Faulknerian tradition: the conventional sporting myth in Margaret Mitchell's *Gone with the Wind* (1936), on which she grafted an *un*conventionally strong heroine; the excoriations of Southern sportsmen by Katherine Anne Porter in "Old Mortality" (1939) and "The Old Order" (1944); the conspicuous silence on the matter of the sporting myth in the fiction of Evelyn Scott, Eudora Welty, and Flannery O'Connor. Caroline Gordon alone among these women from the Renaissance generation committed a large and impressive body of writing specifically to the sporting myth, from a dialectical perspective similar to Faulkner's. Though ignoring the subject in her first novel, *Penhally* (1931), and unreservedly celebrating play (though not agonistic sport) in *Aleck Maury, Sportsman*, Gordon addressed the sporting myth more ambiguously in *None Shall Look Back* (1937) and *Green Centuries* (1941). *None Shall Look Back* examines the Southern sporting temperament in the Civil War, where young men bred to a playful kind of bravery through hunting encounter a sterner test of their courage as they face death. In this novel Gordon celebrated Southern heroism but also its costs: the ennobling of individuals that means loss for others and for the entire region when the heroic ones die for honor. An elaborately developed motif juxtaposing hunting with war reflects this ambiguity.[9] In *Green Centuries*, set now in the late eighteenth century, sporting heroism becomes more problematic yet. The historical Daniel Boone appears in the novel, at once the mighty hunter of myth and a shiftless, debt-ridden, shirker of duty in the view of the other settlers. As the novel's protagonist, an admirer of Boone named Orion Outlaw, plays out the consequences of Boone's mode of life, the dreams of the wilderness hunter are pursued at the expense of family and community. In the final pages, his children murdered by Indians and his wife dead from maddened grief, Orion thinks of his life in terms of the constellation for which he was named: "But it seemed that a man had to flee farther each time and leave more behind him and when he got to the new place he looked up and saw Orion fixed upon his burning wheel, always pursuing the bull but never making the kill."[10] Hunters' heroism, as Cooper first claimed, opened up the wilderness but could not sustain the subsequent community. Gordon did not merely debunk the Boones and Orions. She suggested that heroism, however essential to the human spirit, exacted its tragic due. She celebrated the Southern past as an implicit criticism of the less heroic present, but she did so without merely subscribing to the oversimplifications of the available mythology.

Among more recent women writers, Bobbie Ann Mason, Ellen Gilchrist, and Elizabeth Hardwick have dealt briefly or obliquely with the South's sporting mentality; Mason and Gilchrist to deflate it, Hardwick to qualify it as Caroline Gilman first did in her *Recollections of a Southern Matron*.[11] Margaret Walker's *Jubilee* (1966) and Rita Mae Brown's *High Hearts* (1986), novels that engage this subject more fully, similarly suggest the absence of any single "woman's treatment." With its heroine who fights in the Civil War dressed as a man, even defeating her commanding officer in a spectacular horse race, *High Hearts* uneasily mixes nineteenth-century romance and late twentieth-century feminism. *Jubilee,* on the other hand, written by a black woman, gives voice to the silent slaves on whose oppression Southern honor depended. Familiar things look strange from the perspective of the slave quarters. Old Master is a conventional "hunting, fishing political man," but his sport emerges as a means of escape from a bitter, frigid wife, and is made possible by the labor of slaves – the prerogative, that is, of wealthy white males only. Although Christmas for slave as well as master is "always the happiest time of the year," it is celebrated quite differently in the Big House and the Quarters. Black labor in the kitchen makes possible white play in the parlor. For the cooks, "Christmas meant as much hard work as any other time of the year." The blacks' traditional hunt for possum and coon parallels the white folks' Christmas fox hunt, but with pointed ironies. As Walker's heroine puts it, "Marster, he like foxes, but what good is a fox when you can't eat him?" "Pot—hunting," the anathema of sporting gentlemen, is the only "sport" that makes sense to those whose survival is never assured. Class distinctions, not play or provender, lie behind Southern sport in Walker's rendering.[12]

All of these women, whatever their attitudes, addressed the sporting myth essentially from outside it. In contrast, the Faulknerian perspective of profound ambivalence but from within appears in a number of novels by the major male writers of the Southern Renaissance and after. In *The Fathers* (1938), Allen Tate's portrait of the Civil War generation, antithetical philosophies are embodied in the aristocratic planter Major Buchan, for whom "the moves of an intricate game" of Southern honor are the sole protection against the "abyss" of existential nullity; and a disillusioned younger man, the upstart planter George Posey, whose contempt for the sporting code leaves him vulnerable to impulse and every whim of chance. Confronted by the Civil War, the code ultimately provides little protection for Major Buchan and his class from "the abyss," but without it there is none at all. In Tate's novel the outcome of belief is tragedy; of unbelief, nihilism. In *All the King's Men* (1946), Robert Penn Warren assigned similar roles to Judge Irwin and Willie Stark: the Judge, a sportsman of the old tradition whose one lapse from the code precipitates his suicide; Willie, the poor-white gamesman who plays his unscrupulous way to the governor's mansion only to be murdered by one of his victims. A third major figure, the narrator Jack Burden, is alone able to read the moral lesson in these tragedies, giving up his own cynical gamesmanship for moral responsibility at the end. Both of these novels, the one dealing with the Southern past, the other with its present, are saturated with the rhetoric and themes of the sporting myths.[13]

Shelby Foote's *Tournament* (1949) and Andrew Lytle's *The Velvet Horn* (1957) offer two more versions of this same conflict. Foote's Thomas Sutpen-like upstart, Hugh Bart, creates himself as a gentleman by emulating the "hunt and poker and drinking" necessary for acceptance in the planter class, only to discover he has sacrificed his family in doing so. Lytle's Joe Cree, believing life "a fine game" but an ultimately tragic one, courts death as Bayard Sartoris, Quentin Compson, and Judge Irwin did, when he learns his son is another man's bastard. Like Faulkner, Tate, and Warren, Foote and Lytle sustained a dialectical vision: embracing the sportive mentality as a kind of desperate heroism while simultaneously defining its tragic consequences.[14]

These writers, together with Caroline Gordon, represent the richest literary transformation of the Southern sporting myth in the twentieth century. For a popular tradition one looks elsewhere – to football, I would suggest, whose striking prominence in the contemporary South provokes intriguing connections to nineteenth-century mythmaking. To outsiders, football has long seemed to occupy a distinctive place in Southern life, the rabid fans at Alabama, LSU, and other Southern universities having by now become legendary. The South sends a disproportionate number of players to the National Football League.[15] More telling (if less easily documented), the extraordinary importance of the high-school football team to small communities in the South invites a conclusion that the sport has become the chief public arena in the twentieth century for displaying Southern honor. Anecdotal evidence supporting this view appears routinely in the daily sports pages. The most outrageous story of high-school football mania in recent years concerned a coach in Eau Gallie (O Golly?), Florida, who bit off the heads of live frogs and cut his own head with a razor to inspire his young athletes before games. The extreme case reflects on the norm. Dueling disappeared with the Civil War, hunting no longer holds a significant place in the urban South, gambling is done in private. Football seems to substitute as a public spectacle of physical risk and heroic gesture, of violence controlled by a code of ethical behavior. The Old South died at Appomattox but is reborn each autumn Saturday in football stadiums throughout the region.

The best evidence for this connection is offered by Southern novelists. For the historical moment when the nineteenth-century cavalier sportsman became a twentieth-century football player, I would nominate a scene in John Fox, Jr.'s bestseller of 1913, *The Heart of the Hills,* when hillbilly Jason Hawn meets a descendant of Kentucky planters, Gray Pendleton, on a college football field. Jason and Gray have clashed earlier, in a childhood brawl when the young patrician's refusal "to bite, or gouge, or hit him when he was on top" thoroughly puzzled the mountain boy, whose own code says that winning alone counts, by whatever means (the class basis of sportsmanship and gamesmanship are openly declared). Now, Jason Hawn has left the mountains for the university, where he discovers Gray Pendleton is the football captain. Needless to say, Jason barely comprehends the nature of the game, but an invitation to play represents a chance to "outrun and outwrestle his old enemy." The moment of mythic metamorphosis occurs at Jason's first practice, when he finds his opportunity to tackle Gray:

> With a bound Jason was after him, and he knew that even if Gray had wings, he would catch him. With a flying leap he hurled himself on the speeding figure in front of him, he heard Gray's breath go out in a quick gasp under the fierce lock of his arms, and, as they crashed to the ground, Jason for one savage moment wanted to use his teeth on the back of the sunburnt neck under him, but he sprang to his feet, fists clenched and ready for the fight. With another gasp Gray, too, sprang lightly up.
>
> "Good!" he said heartily.
>
> No mortal fist could have filled him with such shame, and Jason stood stock-still and speechless.[16]

Jason learns on the football field what Gray has always known as the son of a Kentucky colonel: the value of sportsmanship and fair play. And in making the connection between the Southern sporting myth and modern football, Fox established a tradition that has flourished in Southern fiction. Faulkner's Labove in *The Hamlet* seems quite possibly a parodic borrowing of Fox's story: a mountain boy who plays furious football on Saturdays at the university to pay for his education, then claims as his reward the cleated shoes in which his grandmother clomps about their cabin.[17] Whether Faulkner read Fox's bestseller as a youth, then picked it from his memory years later for his comic masterpiece, matters less than the fact that a conspicuous number of other Southern novelists have written about football, not just as a game but as an heroic enterprise with a distinctive sense of place. Robert Penn Warren's *All the King's Men* and William Styron's *Lie Down in Darkness* (1951) place football prominently, if briefly, in the Southern landscape, Warren more pointedly portraying Tom Stark, Willie's son, first as a monster created by college football then as a victim of it (dying from a broken neck sustained in a game). Thomas Wolfe's Jim Randolph in *The Web and the Rock* (1939) is the first of many fictional football heroes whose retirement from the game leaves them no reason to live; in this tradition one can also place James Whitehead's *Joiner* (1971), Harry Crews's *A Feast of Snakes* (1976), and Frank Deford's *Everybody's All-American* (1981). The pathetic former athlete has a long history in the wider literature of sport, but he has perhaps a special place in the sporting fiction of the South, where he can represent not only the universal burden of aging but also the South's particular sense of lost glory.

Everybody's All-American has the most explicit ties to the South's heroic sporting traditions. Deford's Gavin Grey (the echo of Gray Pendleton is accidental, I assume) is specifically associated with that premier emblem of Confederate glory, Jeb Stuart. The narrator on one occasion imagines Grey "with Jeb Stuart, riding a great steed to battle, wearing his football uniform, number twenty-five, shoulder pads and all, with the black under his eyes."[18] James Whitehead tied football to history more obliquely. His hero Sonny Joiner, 6'7" and 300 pounds, is lost in an unromantic world when his football career ends, finding only in history books the models of heroic action for which he deems himself chosen. Early in the novel, *Joiner* also offers a wonderful description of football-as-chivalry in the small-town South, the high-school stadium in Bryan, Mississippi, serving in Sonny's words as

cockpit, amphitheater, and bawdy house to all the citizens of Bryan, and on Friday nights I was Saint Henry Suso drinking Christ's blood from all five wounds. I was squire and ogre and I was doing exactly what I had to do – I was a young man well trained to seek the deeds and exploits of war, which are claims to glory.[19]

The presence of a powerful if subterranean connection between football and Southern myth is no more evident than in Crews's *A Feast of Snakes* and Barry Hannah's *The Tennis Handsome* (1983), which by violently parodying this theme acknowledge its potency. In Hannah's novel, a father "turned lopsided and cyclopic by sports mania" brags about the "hustle" of his five-year-old son, who ran out for a pass in the street and was "tackled" by a Buick.[20] Crews's novel pushes such darkly comic possibilities to extremes of absurdity. Joe Lon Mackey, two years earlier the "Boss Snake" of the Mystic (Mississippi) High School Rattlers, is now a wife-and-baby-burdened bootlegger carrying moonshine out to "niggers" not allowed in his store, and wondering (as Jim Randolph, Sonny Joiner, and Gavin Grey before and after him) how his wonderful "wheels with four-five speed for forty yards could have come to this." Joe Lon and Willard Miller, the current Boss Snake, are like two pit bulls or fighting cocks, bristling in each other's presence, edging always toward the ultimate fight to determine male supremacy in Mystic. The grotesque competitiveness and violence in these characters' lives reaches a climax in the annual rattlesnake hunt, a sort of ring tournament for rednecks, where hunters collect the most and the biggest rattlesnakes they can find, to be weighed and measured by the high-school players and dumped in a huge pit in the football field, as the cheerleaders record the results (ah, community ritual!). At the peak of the festivities, Joe Lon, having come to feel his life is utterly meaningless, seizes a shotgun, blows large holes in four people, then is thrown into the snake pit by the enraged hunters. His last feeling, just after shooting his ex-girlfriend's neck away, is peace and contentment: "He felt better than he had ever felt in his life. Christ, it was good to be in control again."[21]

Crews's wicked, perverse comedy and grotesque hyperbole take the Southern sporting tradition as far as one can imagine it going, exploding its fascination with violence and masculine identity. All of these novels are richer when seen in the implicit context of Southern sport that dates from John Pendleton Kennedy and his fellow plantation romancers. Faulkner transformed this tradition into a complex examination of the Southern past and present, substituting for romance a double vision he shared with many of the best writers of the Southern Renaissance. In their furious assaults Hannah and Crews suggest less that the romantic tradition is dead than that it continues to live in assumption. The antebellum romancers created myth out of a social and economic order about which Southerners were ambivalent. The contemporary situation is reversed: Hannah and Crews, as well as Deford and Whitehead to a lesser degree, attacked beliefs that had become commonplace. Between the two extremes stands Faulknerian ambiguity: myth and anti-myth dialectically joined.

Western fiction: from sportsman to gamesman

The Western sporting myths have had an altogether different history in this century, contributing not to a literary "renaissance" but to an ubiquitous popular fantasy of heroic individualism. For this fantasy, Owen Wister's *The Virginian* stands at the apex: the culmination of one century's development of a cultural myth, the *ur*-text of another century's formulaic reproductions of it. Having placed a "game" at the moral center of his novel, Wister bequeathed it to subsequent writers as a crucial element of the Western formula to be adopted, adapted, or rejected. From Rex Beach, Emerson Hough, Zane Grey, and Eugene Manlove Rhodes, to Frederick Faust ("Max Brand") and Ernest Haycox, then to Louis L'Amour and the latest authors of "paperback originals," Western writers have worked a series of variations off the basic sportsmen and gamesmen of the men who preceded Owen Wister in the field. From a myth that wrestled with law and liberty, democratic leveling, territorial expansion, and national identity, the frontier sporting code became an increasingly anachronistic celebration of individual superiority to laws and institutions, a fantasy that denied (without impeding) the consolidation of power and the triumph of bureaucracy.

That code has remained largely consistent for nearly a century now, though not entirely static. The first generation of writers – Beach, Hough, Grey, Rhodes, Frank H. Spearman, Charles Alden Seltzer, Clarence Mulford, William MacLeod Raine, Stewart Edward White – self-consciously developed the formulas that were only beginning to crystallize by the end of the nineteenth century. By the 1930s these formulas had calcified, as the many references to "games" and "playing one's own hand" and holding out a "trump card" sometimes became little more than rhetorical gestures demanded by convention. With the thirties also, the dominance of the romantic, noble cowboy with his traditional sporting code began to yield ground to a hard-boiled gamesman, a more appropriate hero for a nation in psychic as well as economic distress. The heroic sporting cowboy by no means disappeared altogether, returning most spectacularly, for example, in Jack Shaefer's *Shane* in 1949, as fitting an emblem for the 1950s as Ernest Haycox's grim survivors had been in the thirties. One must be careful, however, not to insist on a simple correspondence, particularly in the decades following World War II, between formulaic Western heroes and the culture they might seem to represent. Working in such a highly conventionalized field, writers of pop Westerns have responded to the imperatives of the genre as much as to the cultural values implicit in the formulas. However, continuing popularity must suggest that the formulas still spoke in some way to contemporary concerns.

Popular Western fiction was produced in hardcover, pulps, and later paperbacks, the same writers and stories often appearing in all three forms. Superstar pulp writers like Mulford, Raine, Faust, Haycox, Grey, and Luke Short saw their hastily composed tales transferred from pulp to book (and often to movie), to become popular "classics." Because of its appearance and reappearance, then, in various formats, Western fiction cannot be neatly bracketed by periods. But given these limits on generalization, it is possible to recognize that the pervasiveness of sporting rhetoric is most characteristic of Western fiction in the first quarter of this century. Joe Dextry in Rex Beach's *The Spoilers* (1905) describes the rule of life on the Yukon frontier as a "a square deal an' no questions asked." Red Connors tells his buddy Hopalong Cassidy, in Clarence Mulford's 1910 novel, "Some men'll gamble most any day – you, for instance, in gunplay." Ike Lassiter, the hero of Zane Grey's most famous and popular novel, *Riders of the Purple Sage* (1912), tells the heroine after a little shooting skirmish, "No, Jane, I'm not one to quit when the game grows hot, no more than you. This game, though, is new to me, an' I don't know the moves yet." When Yank Rogers arrives in the California gold country, in Stewart Edward White's *Gold* (1913), he observes, "If we knew how they played this game, it might be all right to go ahead." When someone offers to help the hero in Eugene Manlove Rhodes's *Bransford in Arcadia* (1914), Jeff Bransford responds, "See here, who'd sold you your chips anyway? How'd you get in this game."[22]

The writers in this first generation of formulaic Western novelists shared the values as well as the vernacular of Wister and Alfred Henry Lewis, but in varying degrees.[23] The novels by Beach, Spearman, White, Mulford, and Seltzer considered here are saturated with game images; those by Hough, Grey, and Rhodes invoke the formula more sparingly. But in some way in every novel sporting rhetoric conveys a crucial theme. A particular character, the hero's roughhewn sidekick perhaps – Joe Dextry in *The Spoilers,* for example, or Red Connors in *Hopalong Cassidy* – may spew out a steady stream of game idioms, a device for vernacular characterization at least as old as Cooper's dialect characters, in these cases perhaps specifically indebted to Lewis's Wolfville. Or the writers may use the language of games at climactic moments in the narrative. One hero declares his commitment to a quest, "I'm going to sit in this game and see it out"; another prepares for mortal confrontation, "I'll just play the sheriff isn't in the bunch and build my little bluff according to that pleasing fancy"; a third announces, "I'm just yearning to take a big hand in this game."[24] Sometimes the narrative pace slows to a stop, pausing for a set-piece declamation by a spokesman for the author who waxes philosophical about the stakes in the game. One character in Hough's *54-40 or Fight* (1909) explains to the hero the nature of the dispute between England and the United States over the Oregon Territory:

> It's a race, my boy, a race across this continent. There are two trails –
> one north and one mid-continent. On these paths two nations contend
> in the greatest Marathon of all the world. England or the United States
> – monarchy or republic – aristocracy or humanity? These are some of
> the things which hang on the issue of this contest. (127)

Stewart Edward White's *The Rules of the Game* (1910), as would be expected in a novel with such a title, has not one but several passages of this sort.

The sporting rhetoric of these "classic" pop Westerns served the claims of nationalism, racial superiority, the work ethic, and innumerable other specific values. In all cases, the first generation of twentieth-century Western novelists followed the genteel school of Owen Wister and the magazine writers. Their heroes are gentlemen by nature not birth, who work, fight, and kill (when necessary) by the code of fair play.[25] A number of Western novels make an explicit connection between the frontier and the school playing field, offering cowboy boxers, cowboy football stars, cowboy baseball players.[26] Athletes or not, the heroes in this fiction prefer fair play to cunning, sportsmanship to gamesmanship. Irving's fight-or-frolic motif became conspicuous in twentieth-century Westerns, although gambling, with few exceptions, continued to resist widespread heroic enshrinement.[27] And the mutual adherence to the code by both hero and villain that was essential to *The Virginian* largely disappeared; now, heroes proved their moral superiority by playing fairly against unfair opponents, and the orderliness of the universe was assured by fair play's victory.[28]

A fundamental concern with law and individual freedom continued to mark this Western fiction. The theme first explored by Cooper in *The Pioneers* became a refrain in the novels following *The Virginian,* eventually taking shape in simple formulas: sometimes law versus lawlessness, more often law versus justice or law versus right – all of these frequently translated as law versus the game. At times no conflict exists between the law and the code. In Seltzer's tellingly titled *The Coming of the Law,* for example, the game and the law are on the same side. The sportsman hero who fights with his fists and shakes hands afterward prevents the lynching of a rustler, inverting the scene that focuses the thematic conflict in *The Virginian*. In *Hopalong Cassidy,* frontier "fair play" lays the foundation for later law, whereas in Beach's *The Spoilers* and Rhodes's *Bransford in Arcadia* and *The Proud Sheriff* law and the sporting code more directly conflict. *The Spoilers* in particular is one of those wonderfully confused popular novels, like Jack London's *Burning Daylight* from the same period, that deconstruct themselves to reveal the culture's deeply divided and uncertain attitudes, in this case toward law.

For this first generation of Western writers, "the game" and all its variants were conventional elements in frontier fiction but not yet mere clichés. More than either the nineteenth-century writers or the generations of Western novelists that would follow, these men seem to have used sporting rhetoric self-consciously to express their most important and seriously held ideas. If the nineteenth century marked the formative period of the Western sporting code, the first quarter of the twentieth century marked its triumph as a popular social philosophy. In general, a conflict between nature and civilization no longer mattered; at most the formulaic Western of the new century fed popular nostalgia for an atemporal arcadian past. The patterns of heroic Western behavior were lifted from any significant setting to become an abstraction. The marginal hunters and trappers of Cooper and Irving, the gamblers and cowboys of Bret Harte, dime novelists, and genteel magazinists – all of whom lived beyond the pale of conventional society – were moved to the center of this newly imagined, increasingly imaginary West. Their sporting code became not an ambiguous challenge to the values to which readers' lives were deeply committed, but the center of a fantasy that countered the increasing organization and rationalization of everyday life.

The 1930s saw a shift in this fantasy, as violence became more problematic, the hero's code less pure and genteel. In what might be considered transitional novels, Emerson Hough's *The Covered Wagon* (1922) and Zane Grey's *Code of the West* (1923), for example, sportsmanlike heroes are provoked into no-holds-barred or rough-and-tumble contests by villains who recognize no other code. In pop Westerns of the 1930s, such brutal necessity typically makes sportsmanship itself anachronistic. A new skepticism and cynicism in the modern temper, the onset of the Depression, and a changing audience (more masculine, less genteel) as the pulps replaced the hardcover novel as the primary vehicle for Western writing contributed to the shift toward hard-boiled naturalism in this fiction.

Western fiction became more decidedly masculine, although narrative formulas continued to embrace "masculine" adventure and "feminine" domesticity. The formulaic Western, it is important to remember, began with *The Virginian* as a love story and continued to be a love story through much of its "classic" phase and beyond. Molly and her cowboy marry to conclude *The Virginian;* Lassiter and Jane disappear into an edenic valley at the end of *Riders of the Purple Sage.* Even in such later hard-boiled Westerns as Max Brand's *Destry Rides Again* (1930) and Ernest Haycox's *Trouble Shooter* (1937), the heroes give up violence for marriage. To generalize about the pop Western I would insist not that the formula celebrates code-governed violence but that it sets violence and death against domestic stability, the violence typically portrayed as necessary to assure the latter. The male fantasy embodied in the Western can be summed up in Richard Slotkin's phrase, "regeneration through violence," but this fantasy is made to serve, however contradictorily, a social ideal.

Women's Western writing in the twentieth century, in the few instances when it deals with the sporting myth at all, differs by refusing the conflict altogether or subordinating it more thoroughly to the domestic. Such conspicuous exceptions to the male dominance of pop Westerns as B. M. Bower's novels about the "Happy Family" of the Flying U Ranch and Edna Ferber's *Cimarron* (1930) reveal a distinctively female voice of this sort. Bower (Bertha M. Sinclair) stands virtually alone in the field of Western pulp fiction and series books. Pulps were written primarily by men for men; the alternative to traditional Westerns were the highly domesticated Western-romance pulps, 45 percent of which are said to have been written by women for a readership almost entirely female. Contrary to the story of a lone male battling a hostile environment, Western romances offered, in the words of an unenthusiastic (male) commentator, "soft-core sex with side orders of movie talk, trailside cookbook stuff, and penpal mishmash."[29]

Series Westerns by women have similarly ignored the sporting rhetoric and its accompanying values from male writing. From the early girls' series, Margaret Vandercook's Ranch Girls (1911–24), Frances R. Sterrett's Tales of a Minnesota Girl (1928–32), and so on, to the erotic romance series of the 1980s (Leather and Lace, Indian Ecstasy, Savage Romances), the women's West has simply had different subjects and interests.[30] Bower, then, is a unique figure in male-dominated pop Western fiction, and the West of her Flying U series is distinctly feminized. She cast her cowboys as simple, playful children, sometimes wayward but in innocent ways, always loyal to "the Old Man," their fatherly employer, always chivalrous to the women who have conspicuous roles in their lives. The cowboys respect law and renounce violence, defeating their enemies by clever tricks instead of gunplay. *Chip, of the Flying U* (1904), the initial novel in the series, is, like *The Virginian,* a tale of the stormy courtship of an Eastern lady by a laconic cowboy. Unlike *The Virginian,* however, no violence threatens the marriage. A handful of poker images appear only in relation to the courtship game played by Chip and the Little Doctor. In *Flying U Ranch* (1912), the familiar metaphors of poker and "the game" refer to the pranks by which the Happy Family, with no gun fired, forces the villainous owners of a neighboring ranch to sell their land and flee the territory. Both novels seem quite conscious recastings of Western formulas. From the Wister school Bower borrowed the minor elements of domesticity and playful innocence, but she rejected the major themes of justified violence and personal codes beyond the law. Whereas the heroes in classic Westerns by male writers gunned down their foes in fair fights before they rode off with the heroines, Bower mated them without the distraction of killing.[31]

Ferber's *Cimarron* was no pulp Western but the number-one best seller in 1930, a woman's answer to the best sellers of Zane Grey. The first half of the novel seems an extension of *The Virginian,* emphasizing the conflict between wilderness and society, and between masculine and feminine attitudes toward the frontier, with the novel's sympathies seeming to lie with the freedom-loving male. In a tale of Oklahoma from land rush to statehood, Yancey Cravat is a larger-than-life romantic hero with the sporting spirit of his countless ancestors; while his wife, Sabra, has the strength of a Molly Stark and Molly's revulsion against masculine excess as well. In a novel as full of Western playfulness and sporting codes as anything by Owen Wister or his myriad male successors, the "nightmarish game" of cowboy carousing repels Sabra as much as it delights Yancey. Osage, Oklahoma, is the playground that Wister envisioned: "It was a man's town. The men enjoyed it. They rode, gambled, swore, fought, fished, hunted, drank. The antics of many of them seemed like those of little boys playing robbers' cave under the porch."[32] Sabra and the other women struggle to create order, comfort, and beauty in this rowdy world, with little apparent success.

But the men of Yancey's type prove to be dreamers, the women doers. At a moment halfway through the novel, when a wounded Yancey has to lean on Sabra for support (yet another motif from *The Virginian* handled differently), the power passes from sporting male to civilizing female. When Yancey grows increasingly quixotic and ineffectual, Sabra assumes leadership in both her family and the town. Sabra takes over the editorship of her husband's newspaper, leads civic fights for decency and progress, and is elected to Congress when Oklahoma becomes a state. In the novel's final scene, Yancey breathes his last in Sabra's arms, long broken, now laughed at behind his back, not even an impressive anachronism but a sentimental relic to his fellow townspeople. Sabra, on the other hand, embodies all the vitality of a booming new state. Ferber romanticized both the sporting male and the strong domesticating female – both characterizations undoubtedly contributing to the novel's extraordinary popularity – but she consigned the one to the past while placing the future in the hands of the other.

Ferber, in short, implicitly acknowledged a role for sportive male violence in taming the wilderness, but only as the initial stage in a process to be completed by the civilizing female. Men's formulaic Westerns of the 1930s, on the other hand, froze the West in its wildness and fully confronted its violence; but contrary to the Wister-Grey school, as grim necessity now rather than as glorious sport. The gamesman's code, whose flirting with anarchy had long prevented official sanction, now became dominant. In Max Brand's *Destry Rides Again* and Ernest Haycox's *Trouble Shooter,* as well as E. B. Mann's *Killer's Range* (1933), Luke Short's *The Feud at Single Shot* (1936), and Haycox's *The Wild Bunch* (1943) – all typical novels of the new school – the language and values of the poker table predominate. The rhetoric of "bluffs" and "trump cards" and "tricks" and "long odds" conveys a sense of life as a more desperate affair than Wister or Grey implied, presided over by Chance or Fate more likely than a sporting Umpire.[33] Heroes must soil themselves to survive; some, like Harry Destry, prevail only by luck. The writers of these novels worked against their genre's conventions of triumphant sportsmanship, only to establish new formulas for subsequent writers. In general, sporting rhetoric became less frequent beginning in the 1930s, its ability to sustain important ideas impaired by its conventionality. But also, as the formula itself became clichéd, it was the poker table rather than the fair fight that became dominant, as in Louis L'Amour's *The First Fast Draw* (1959) and *The Quick and the Dead* (1973).[34] The hero's *control,* crucial to the Western myth in all ages, becomes measured considerably more by his response to circumstances than by his ability to determine them.

The *reductio ad absurdum* of the cowboy gamesman would have to be Faro Blake, hero of two dozen-odd "paperback originals" by Zeke Masters in the 1980s, all bearing such titles as *Ace in the Hole, Diamond Flush, Stacked Deck,* and the like. A representative example, *Inside Straight* (1982), offers hard-core Western and soft-core porn, with a "hero" who cheats at cards and beats the villain only when the sheriff kills him from ambush. The villain, not the hero, proposes a fair-play showdown, "according to the Code of the West." After gunning him down from behind, the sheriff chuckles, "That 'Code of the West' crap is fine for some, but you don't get to be an old fart like me by playin' kid games with crazies."[35]

Such novels seem to suggest the exhaustion of possibilities in the Western formula. Masters parodied the classic Western while exaggerating the conventions of the hard-boiled school to a point of equal silliness, signaling less a cultural attitude toward Western themes than the

trivialized familiarity of Western motifs. Although the issues that Westerns traditionally engaged – freedom and law, violence and restraint,
individualism and the common good – have continued as pressing public concerns, the Western formula seems less and less able to probe
them meaningfully. Masters's parodies only reinforce an impression
gained from the disappearance of Westerns from television, their near-
disappearance from movie theaters, and Western fiction's yielding of
much of its market to detective stories, romances, and science fiction.
The decline of the Western as a popular genre shifted the frontier sporting
code to other genres, the code still potent but the West less and less able
to embody it.

The code never sustained a major literary tradition. The dearth of sporting heroes in women's mainstream Western fiction from Willa Cather
to Louise Erdrich is matched by a dearth of sporting heroes in comparable
male writing.[36] Women have mostly been silent on the subject; men have
frequently responded with parody: the burlesques of Nathanael West,
Ishmael Reed, Thomas Berger, and William S. Burroughs, for example,
or the brutal antimyth of E. L. Doctorow's *Welcome to Hard Times*
(1960).[37] For writers living in the West and viewing themselves as Westerners, the myth could not be so easily debunked, but as Wallace Stegner
has pointed out, to engage the myth seriously as a vital part of the Western
past with observable links to the present has proven extremely difficult.[38]
Walter Van Tilburg Clark's *The Ox-Bow Incident* (1940), Edward Abbey's
The Brave Cowboy (1956), Larry McMurtry's *All My Friends Are Going
to Be Strangers* (1972), and Stegner's own *Angle of Repose* (1971) share a
common view that the sporting myth is either fraudulent or irrelevant
to the modern West.

The one figure from the mythic past who has engaged the attention
of serious writers has been the mountain man or fur trapper, whose real
history bears closer resemblance to his mythic incarnations than the cowboy's ever did. In A. B. Guthrie's *The Big Sky* (1947), Frederick
Manfred's *Lord Grizzly* (1954), Don Berry's *Trask* (1960), and Vardis
Fisher's *Mountain Man* (1965), the trapper emerges in a range of portraits
that variously debunk or celebrate the sporting myth. Manfred's Hugh
Glass renounces the "sport" of wilderness survival for Christ-like for-
giveness of his enemies; Guthrie's Boone Caudill glories in the brutal
"fun" and "frolic" of the rendezvous and of physical contests, but only
to reveal his own self-defeating brutality; Berry's Trask first plays "the
great game" at its most heroic then renounces it for the "simple delight"
of nonaggressive existence in the natural world after undergoing a vision
quest. Fisher's Sam Minard, like Boone Caudill, revels in violence, but
in forgoing vengeance against the Crows (giving up not violence but

butchery) he redeems the violence of frontier life in a traditional sporting way.[39]

Whatever the writer's response to the sporting myth, none of these novels connects the legendary Western past with its actual present, even by contrast. The absence of a Faulkner of the West may have more to do with the rarity of Faulkners than the radical discontinuity between Western myth and Western history, but this situation surely has consequences for the kind of novels a Western Faulkner might write. Perhaps no novel illustrates the disconnection of Western myth from history better than Larry McMurtry's *Lonesome Dove* (1985), a popular success that was also hailed by many reviewers as the long-awaited Great Western Novel. McMurtry's *magnum opus* (843 pages) is a richly varied compendium of Western materials, its echoes of *The Virginian* and Bret Harte competing with scenes so brutal as to rival the darkest moments in Doctorow's *Welcome to Hard Times*. The prevailing muse is Harte, whose surface realism overlaid on sentimental romance has long characterized the most successful Western fiction. In *Lonesome Dove,* brutality is restricted to hard-core villains, while the white-hatted side, led by two grizzled ex-Texas Rangers and a good-hearted whore, displays all the virtue, innocence, and fine Western talk of the fabled frontier at its romantic best. The novel takes place at the most Western of times: that historical moment when the old West is beginning to disappear, a time when the two Rangers can walk into a saloon and see fifteen-year-old photographs of themselves hanging on the wall – images of an era when bandits and Indians made men like themselves necessary. Mostly forgotten now, as they are by the saloon's new proprietor, the Rangers are remembered only by a fat old sheriff who complains that "being a lawman these days is mostly a matter of collaring drunks and it does get tiresome."[40]

The two Rangers, Augustus McCrae and Woodrow Call, nonetheless preserve the West's heroic spirit in this tamer age. In the time-honored manner they live beyond law by a higher code, the sporting code of men too big to be regulated. Running a sort of livery stable, they steal cattle and horses to order, usually across the border in Mexico where such theft "stopped being a crime and became a game" (125). Call, a loner and misogynist, follows in the tradition of fight-loving mountain men. After hearing that Call has nearly killed a bully, another of the old Rangers declares with satisfaction, "Well, he's a fighter, the Captain . . . . He'll box 'em if they get him riled." "Box?" one of the young hands who witnessed the fight asks in amazement. "He didn't box. He run over the man with a horse and then near kicked his head off when he had him laying on the ground." "Oh, that's boxing, to the Captain," the Ranger replies (666–7). Gus, on the other hand, is made in the mold of John

Oakhurst, though more genial and talkative, a gambler both at cards and at life. "The best card cheat I ever met," one friend calls him (192); a man who cuts cards with a whore for $50 against a "poke," explaining to her later that sex is "a kind of game" and that she should enjoy it because "games are played for fun" (346). Gus likes fights because "they sharpen the wits" (485), and he delights in almost every other aspect of what he considers "chancy life" (621). When he has to hang a former Ranger, in a scene lifted directly from *The Virginian,* Gus acknowledges that his is a "harsh code" (572); but as the friend accepts the rope with manly grace there can be no doubt that the code is a fair and heroic one. McMurtry attempted the same synthesis at the root of nineteenth-century Western romance: a wedding of gamesmanship to sportsmanship that ignores their darker implications and contradictions.

Lonesome Dove responds more to Western conventions than to an authorial vision of the actual West or a "usable past." Its sharply drawn, engaging characters and page after page of witty dialogue seem written with an eye to Hollywood, where the author was remarkably successful with four previous novels and where *Lonesome Dove* did in fact become a popular and critically praised television miniseries. Writing for a broad audience, McMurtry wisely dressed up the familiar in artful new clothes, reconstituting Bret Harte's blend of grit and romance for a more sophisticated, Western-saturated age. The unchanged presence of the sporting code would seem, then, to say much about its enduring appeal. Individuals today may assert their freedom from law by snorting cocaine or hiding income from the Internal Revenue Service, instead of drinking bootleg gin. Concern over the government's right to tax or grant property rights may give way to disputes over legal intrusions into the family and uneven justice for rich and poor. But the underlying issue remains the same: a persistent desire to view the self as separate from and superior to all institutional arrangements.

McMurtry's transformation of Bret Harte and Owen Wister is actually more complete than this. In traditional Westerns the hero's code typically defies institutional ones, with the fate of a worthy community at stake in the conflict. In *Lonesome Dove* no such competition or stake exists. The fact that former Texas Rangers rustle livestock for a living draws no comment from any moralizing voice. The sporting code of Gus and Call is a personal matter rooted in no social conflict. Moreover, the novel's central action, around which lives are lost and character is tested, is a daunting but pointless trail drive (with a herd of stolen cattle) from Texas to Montana, taken on by Gus and Call for no better reason than the simple sake of doing it. Gus dies at the moment of success, bequeathing to Call an even more pointless quest: to return his body three thousand miles to Texas for burial. Heroic adventure, in other words, approaches play in the purest sense, becoming also an occasion for the *dis*play of noble qualities no longer demanded by the Rangers' settled life.

From one perspective, then, *Lonesome Dove* demonstrates the degree to which the frontier sporting myth, once rooted at least loosely in history, has completely escaped from history. From another, however, one can read in this novel a commentary on the entire Western tradition. Cooper first articulated a hunter's code that was individually heroic but incapable of governing an entire society. Many of Cooper's successors denied this fact, suggesting that the hero's code and social justice were one and the same. In *Lonesome Dove,* McMurtry returned to Cooper's vision, but with the triumph of civilization now a given there is no conflict between code and community. Heroic action and sporting ethics, the novel tells us, are meaningful on personal terms but have no power to affect history or alter the prevailing power arrangements. *Lonesome Dove* in effect romanticizes the political impotence of the individual in America, declaring meaningful living to be simply *play,* without reference to the sources of power in the larger culture. Marginality is its own reward, *Lonesome Dove* a Western for the New Age. From an expression of faith in (or longing for) individual power, the Western myth becomes a fantasy of joyful powerlessness. McMurtry's novel offers a strikingly ironic comment on the myth of pastoral play in the Earthly Garden out of which the American frontier myth emerged more than three centuries ago. A myth of man's beginnings that foreshadowed paradise becomes a dream from the past with no future at all.

Et alia: the myriad games of marginal men

The lone male with his code, though once quintessentially a Western hero, became a pervasive figure in twentieth-century American culture, contained by no regional boundaries. This figure and the sporting rhetoric that describes him have become so commonplace that any attempt to identify patterns might seem foolhardy: the imposition of a grid on randomness. But without presuming to account for the full rhetorical landscape, I would emphasize the theme of heroic marginality as central to literary celebrations of sportsmanship as well as gamesmanship since the 1930s. Natty Bumppo and his offspring have played either of two roles: as the representative of the larger society's values (the sportsman hero whose code reinforces law) or as the solitary individual superior to institutions (the hero whose code is set against law). This second version of a code rooted in aristocratic assumption ironically implies a sense of alienation from the social, political, or economic center. Anxiety about marginality in the United States has not been limited to the truly disadvantaged. From the story of expulsion from the Garden of Eden to

Freud's description of birth trauma, alienation has been understood in the West as fundamental to the human condition. More specifically, whereas immigrants, minorities, the poor (and women more problematically) have been America's truly marginal citizens, a recurring sense of marginality was inevitable for a people in a new land without a history.

The degree of anxiety in America has not been constant, however. Warren Susman has described the common view of the 1930s in particular as a decade of "marginal men," the wanderers, vagabonds, and tramps who "became the subjects of a literature that has emerged as a special legacy from that period."[41] Susman points out that this literature of marginality was actually less admired in the 1930s than a generation later, when the economically marginal tramp of the Depression seemed kin to the philosophically alienated Beat or Jew or gray-flanneled businessman of the 1950s. This continuity, of course, can be extended into the rebellious sixties and malaise-ridden seventies, even into the supposedly complacent but troubled 80s; the periodization of American culture by discontinuous decades is not simply borne out by its literature. To read the content of much American fiction since World War I is to discover no center, only very crowded margins.

Both the gamesman and the sportsman at odds with society – the two figures at times barely distinguishable – illustrate this sense of marginality. The most popular writing about these figures, the hard-boiled detective fiction that began to appear in the 1920s in *Black Mask* magazine, also has the most direct ties to the Western sporting myth (to think of the hard-boiled detective as an urban cowboy has become a truism since critics first began taking this genre seriously). The most distinctive feature of this fiction has been its language, the vernacular of tough guys immune to sentiment, contemptuous of lofty abstractions, accustomed to violence; a concrete, action-oriented language, often pungent, sometimes wonderfully absurd. Consider Raymond Chandler's description of a woman's laughter: "The giggles got louder and ran around the corners of the room like rats behind the wainscoting." Or, more extravagantly, Robert Leslie Bellem's hero describing a quick getaway in a hot car:

> I blooped the sedan up to seventy from a standing start; kicked the everlasting tripes out of it. The yellow-haired Vale cutie shivered against me like a cat coughing lamb-chops; she must have thought she was headed for the pearly gates. Her even little teeth chattered like pennies in a Salvation Army tambourine.[42]

On one level, sporting rhetoric is simply part of this vernacular. Tough guys habitually talk of "games" and "plays" and crooked "deals" – sneeringly, out of the corners of their mouths as it were. The detective reduces the world to objects of his verbal inventiveness, making them less threatening, revealing both self-control and superior intelligence. The detective's language also divorces him *from* the world in certain ways, freeing him from contamination by the ugliness. On another level, however, the language of games used by or about the hero can embody a value system that transcends mere toughness and that links the private eye to the noble heroes of America's past. Hard-boiled sporting rhetoric is both the lingo of the jazzed-up modern city and its underworld, and a vestige of heroic honor.

Dashiell Hammett and Raymond Chandler did not invent the sporting vernacular of hard-boiled detective fiction, but as the most influential writers in this tradition they assured its place in the genre's formulas.[43] Together they presided over the extraordinary popularity of detective novels in the 1930s, when nearly a quarter of all new books were of this type. Susman interprets this fiction as a response to the pervasive threats to the autonomous self from mechanized, organized, rationalized civilization. "A deep current of pessimism in the Thirties about the possible survival of individualism" found an answer in Chandler's "shop-soiled Galahad," Philip Marlowe, and in Hammett's morally more ambiguous heroes, Sam Spade and the Continental Op.[44] Hammett specifically renounced sentiment. "I'm no Galahad," the Op announces in "The Whosis Kid," as he refuses to prevent a young woman's being frisked. "This woman had picked her playmates, and was largely responsible for this angle of their game. If they played rough, she'd have to make the best of it."[45] But the heroes of these stories remain heroic nonetheless.

Hammett and Chandler represent a divided mainstream in hard-boiled detective fiction: Chandler more romantic, Hammett grittier; Chandler's code tending toward traditional sportsmanship, Hammett's more thoroughly toward gamesmanship; Chandler's hero transcendent, Hammett's mired inescapably in the dirt of power and politics. To term Marlowe a transcendent hero would seem to contradict the stories' hard-boiled worldview. In *The Big Sleep* (1939), Marlowe tells his client, "The game I play is not spillikins. . . . I may break a few rules, but I break them in your favor. The client comes first, unless he's crooked. Even then all I do is hand the job back to him and keep my mouth shut."[46] In *The High Window* (1942), Marlowe declines to turn in a mother and son, both murderers, because they have employed him. He has learned the truth; others may determine legal guilt. A major recurring image in both novels is the chess board in Marlowe's flat, on which he plays games and works out problems in solitude. Marlowe plays chess the same way he approaches life: to solve the puzzle, to render the game intelligible. Not to purge the world of evil.

But Chandler's sporting rhetoric also casts Marlowe as a chivalrous knight in a sordid world; he's physically vulnerable but morally impregnable. In *Farewell, My Lovely* (1946), a crooked cop tells him that "a guy can't stay honest if he wants to. . . . You gotta play the game dirty or you don't eat." Marlowe disagrees. As an exasperated admirer tells him later, "Everybody bats you over the head and chokes you and smacks your jaw and fills you with morphine, but you just keep right on hitting between tackle and end until they're all worn out." The football image evokes not just persistence but an honorable sporting code. Surrounded by degenerate wealth, perverse sexuality, corrupt or compromised police – pervasive nastiness in short – Marlowe remains a romantic hero in an antiromantic world. Although his integrity cannot transform the sordidness he uncovers, it is crucial as the sole vestige of honor and virtue.[47]

Chandler was no simple sentimentalist; the central theme of his fiction is the precarious possibility of heroism in a vicious world. Hammett, however, confronted this precariousness more directly; in his world integrity is the most anyone can hope for. The unnamed Op of the Continental Detective Agency – short, fat, and middle-aged – is Everyman with noble intentions but a pragmatic sense of the possible. Criminals dictate the terms of the "game"; the Op can only "make his play" or "play his hand" as best he can. In *The Red Harvest* (1929), the Op and the mobsters use the same gamesman's idioms and similar tactics; by the end the Op has tricked the four chief hoods into killing each other, but control of the town is back in the hands of old Elihu Willson, the autocratic mine owner who initially brought the mobsters to Personville ("Poisonville" by local pronunciation) to break heads in a miners' strike. In *The Maltese Falcon* (1930), Sam Spade may or may not be interested in the falcon for his own gain; what he most certainly wants is control: "This is the city and my game," he tells a client. In *The Glass Key* (1931), Ned Beaumont as number-one gofer for the city "boss" willingly plays the "game" of dirty politics – bribes, fixed elections, manipulated courts, even killings, whatever the game requires. He differs from his corrupt colleagues and employer only by his self-awareness and his relentless pursuit of truth. "Justice" is not even imagined.[48]

The chief threat to both Hammett's and Chandler's heroes is a kind of political and economic power that do not exist in the popular Western. History and heroic myth can meet in hard-boiled detective fiction as they cannot in the Western. From the novels of James M. Cain and Richard Hallas in the 1930s, to those of Mickey Spillane, Ross Macdonald, and John D. MacDonald in the postwar period, to Elmore Leonard's and Robert B. Parker's most recently, the "game" has continued to represent either the politics of the possible or heroic transcendence.[49] In general, this fiction differs from the pop Western formula in a crucial way that reveals distinct worldviews. Despite the noble cowboy's extraordinary virtues, society is ultimately the hero of the Western novel and the chief beneficiary of the individual hero's triumph. From Leatherstocking on, even when the frontiersman's code opposes civilization's law, his code creates the possibility for the law's and society's eventual triumph. At the center of the hard-boiled detective novel, on the other hand, stands the private eye himself as solitary hero, as unreconciled to his social world at the end of the novel as at the beginning, that world still as vile as he first found it. The Western ends in stasis; having established order, the cowboy hero trades his guns for domesticity or rides away from the peace he has made possible. The detective novel ends in tension; the hero is unharmed and partially successful, but corrupt wealth still holds power, Evil is thwarted in only one small case. The central problem facing the detective hero has little to do with either law or violence. The helplessness of the law, not just to solve a specific crime but to regulate society, is axiomatic. Violence likewise is inevitable and necessary, however troubling on occasion. Rather, the chief issue in detective fiction is the individual's ability to retain integrity and control in an irrational, corrupt world. Even in its hard-boiled variants the Western tends toward romance; the hard-boiled mystery is a naturalistic novel with to varying degrees a romantic hero. Although the sporting code itself changes little, its context and implications darken, producing a new male fantasy with equal parts of romance and cynicism.

Alienated from society, the detective hero who either struggles against it or transcends it represents not just a popular genre but the larger post-World War II literary landscape. Heroic marginality is the key. Gamesmen protagonists in such picaresque novels as Saul Bellow's *Adventures of Augie March* (1953) and John Barth's *Sot-Weed Factor* (1960), and in political novels like Robert Penn Warren's *All the King's Men* (1946) and Edwin O'Connor's *The Last Hurrah* (1956), have a closer kinship with the sportsmen heroes of, say, the Hemingway school than is immediately apparent. Bellow's and Barth's marginalized outsiders, Augie March and Henry Burlingame, use the gamesman's tricks to triumph or at least survive in a hostile world. Warren's Willie Stark is a dangerous demagogue, O'Connor's Frank Skeffington a benign patriarch, yet both political bosses gain readers' sympathy to the extent they appear as outsiders without power winning their "games" against those who already have it. In apparent contrast, the numerous Hemingway epigones from Norman Mailer and James Jones to Ken Kesey and William Kennedy have created heroes who perform mighty deeds of physical and moral prowess. Yet Mailer's Croft and Jones's Prewitt, Kesey's McMurphy and Kennedy's Billy Phelan, are deeply alienated from the social structures within which they must act. Their triumphs neither contribute to nor break down these structures but assure only their own personal integrity apart from them. All of these characters, sportsmen and gamesmen alike, are marginal men, their common desire the chief psychic goal of our time: preservation of the autonomous self.

By linking these writers in this way I risk reducing postwar fiction to a single, endlessly reiterated narrative that can be read through its sporting rhetoric. Rather, I wish to suggest that a surprising amount of postwar fiction appropriates traditional sporting rhetoric in a variety of ways, to produce a range of narratives arising from this shared sense of alienation. Barth's Henry Burlingame in *The Sot-Weed Factor* is a shape-shifting illusionist who, by making life a game of Who's Got the Button, becomes an artist and creator of history. Ralph Ellison's Invisible Man, on the other hand, tries out the advice of the mad vet doctor who tells him, "Play the game, but play it your own way," only to reject such games-manship as morally irresponsible. Between these two poles, Bellow's Augie March practices an ambiguous kind of artful gamesmanship, whose model is the many poker games he plays and whose underlying principle is the *"animal ridens"* within him, described on the final page as a joke on both nature and the self.[50]

Postwar gamesmanship thus serves many uses, as does heroic sports-manship. Prewitt's doomed contest with the military bureaucracy in James Jones's *From Here to Eternity* (1951), McMurphy's sacrificial com-petition with the Big Nurse and the Combine she represents in Ken Kesey's *One Flew Over the Cuckoo's Nest* (1962), Ed Gentry's profoundly ambiguous initiation into the rites of athletic manhood in James Dickey's *Deliverance* (1970), the protagonist's moral triumph in William Kennedy's *Billy Phelan's Greatest Game* (1978) (Billy is "a gamester who accepted the rules and played by them, but who also played above them") respond to the traditions I have been describing in different ways. Jones's concern with bureaucracy, Kesey's with gender and institutional power, Dickey's with law and personal codes, Kennedy's with the dignity of the working class, found expression in the basic paradigm of the alienated sportsman's contest with a powerful opponent.[51]

These novelists responded to the sporting myths with varying degrees of self-consciousness. Mailer's open appropriation of Cooper, Melville, Hemingway, and Faulkner is central to *The Naked and the Dead* (1948) and *Why Are We in Vietnam?* (1967). Dickey's *Deliverance* acknowledges its cultural heritage, the narrative of wilderness adventure, in numerous ways. Barth's burlesque of "The Bear" in the interpolated tale of Billy Rumbly in *The Sot-Weed Factor;* Pynchon's parody of wilderness sport in *V.* (1963), where Benny Profane hunts alligators in New York's sewers with a twelve-gauge shotgun; and Thomas McGuane's novel-length par-ody of heroic hunting in *The Sporting Club* (1968) make the sporting myths themselves one of their chief subjects.[52]

Yet for all their differences, the sense of alienation in these novels is consistent. The protagonists in all of them define themselves against society in some way; their struggles and desires are consistently personal and anti-institutional. The gamesman is no more an outsider than the sportsman in this sense; celebrations of sporting prowess and parodies of sporting prowess are equally anti-institutional. The sporting myth of Kesey's *One Flew Over the Cuckoo's Nest,* for example, provides a vocabulary and a heroic model for the individual to resist the technological and institutional power represented by "the Combine." The sporting myth in McGuane's *The Sporting Club,* on the other hand, is itself one of the institutions to be attacked and parodied. In Mailer's *Why Are We in Vietnam?* celebration and parody are not easily distinguished, but the enemy, modern technology, is the same in either case.

I will return to several of these novels in greater detail in the next two chapters, but even this cursory overview suggests that to a considerable degree America's literary heroes over the past half-century have been fundamentally antagonistic to the country's economic and political development. It has not been only "alienated artists" but also popular writers of hard-boiled Westerns and hard-boiled detective stories who have created a literary culture at odds with the country's institutional arrangements. Even the heroic game-playing entrepreneur, a major symbol of the so-called Reagan Revolution of the 1980s and an answer to the cheerless doomsmen of the seventies, was proclaimed to represent not the superiority of current business practices but the endurance of the true capitalist spirit in the face of its institutional obstacles. The sporting myths have always embodied fantasies of personal empowerment. In this century their fundamental theme has shifted from empowerment either within or without the established order toward empowerment wholly without.

8

In the Wake of Moby-Dick

The story of a defiant outsider's contest with a mighty opponent can emphasize either the material or the metaphysical terms of the contest. As we saw in Part II, although Melville published the classic text of metaphysical sport in 1851, it was not until the turn of the twentieth century that the desperate games of defiant mortals against the powers of the universe became conventionalized in American fiction. From 1900 to the end of the 1960s, the heirs of Melville and the naturalists became conspicuous and numerous, reflecting what would seem contradictory collective experiences. The sense of human *diminishment* that I have emphasized – theological and scientific as well as political and economic – made the obstacles to personal success and self-worth seem comparably greater. Yet until the Civil Rights movement, the women's movement, and Vietnam, belief in guiltless American power and invincibility had never been thoroughly undermined by actual American experience. Life's contests, then, would seem more desperate and the stakes higher, but the possibility of winning would nonetheless remain.

As Melville's chief heir, I would nominate William Faulkner, the novelist whose ludic vision is most complex and most central to an astonishingly rich body of fiction, rather than the perhaps more obvious choice, Ernest Hemingway. Together, Hemingway and Faulkner represent the competing impulses toward metaphysics and politics that are fundamental to the American tragic/heroic sense. A Melvillean contest between the individual and the gods is central to the novels of both writers. Hemingway's fiction consistently sets up a transcendent ideal; Faulkner's more thoroughly roots metaphysical struggle in material circumstances. Though viewed by his early contemporaries as a hard-boiled philosopher for whom life meant "winner taking nothing," Hemingway in fact taught the more reassuring lesson that heroic losers take all. Faulkner's sense of life as sporting contest was more complex, dialectical instead of dualistic. In this, too, he was the truer heir to Melville.

Hemingway: the last Puritan

According to a once-commonplace assessment, Hemingway through most of his career was a writer of hard-boiled fiction about physical action in a world bereft of spiritual values. He then supposedly "discovered God" in writing The Old Man and the Sea in the last decade of his life, a turn toward idealism that gained him the Nobel Prize. This popular notion misconstrued early Hemingway, of course. Hemingway was one of the most deeply moralistic novelists who ever wrote in this country; his chief preoccupation, from his first book, In Our Time, to his last, remained the search for spiritual meaning in the contemporary secular world. The God he "discovered" in The Old Man and the Sea was the same God he had found in The Sun Also Rises and the novels that followed: the Opponent in the individual's contest to achieve a meaningful life.

The "religious" writer I have in mind is not the existentialist that many readers have identified behind stories like "A Clean Well-Lighted Place" and in his basic view of the human condition. Contrary to the existentialists' rebellion against all systematic philosophies and unchanging moral orders, Hemingway insisted in novel after novel, story after story, on a single moral system summed up in his well-known sporting code. Although Hemingway's protagonists have to make "existential choices," the correct choice is always the same, deriving from an ethical absolute rather than a multiplicity of situational options. To explore the role of "the game" in Hemingway's fiction is thus to touch on several critical commonplaces: the prevalence of sport, the importance of the code, the distinction between code heroes and "tyro" heroes, the significance of the code for both Hemingway's aesthetic practice and his philosophy of life. My own version of these well-rehearsed matters can claim novelty only in the context in which I place them: the post-Melvillean theology of the desperate game.[1]

From this perspective, Hemingway was closer kin to Michael Wigglesworth and Increase Mather than to Sartre and Camus. In his insistence on an absolute moral order and intolerance of all others, Hemingway was the "last Puritan" among major American novelists. His insiders and outsiders are simply the elect and the damned in different contexts. His code reveals an implicit belief in a "covenant" with an absent God and defines its own "morphology of conversion": a step-by-step path to the sainthood of living and dying well. His novels recount a series of spiritual journeys, of spiritual tests like those described by Jonathan Edwards and other Puritans in their autobiographies. For Hemingway, as for the Puritans, the central fact of life was the spiritual odyssey of a soul in distress.

Hemingway defined his individualist's code primarily in relation to the sports of hunting, fishing, and bullfighting – all arenas for a single sporting ethic. Bullfighting, the sport he discovered first and explored in most detail, can serve as a center from which to view his fiction; hunting and fishing, and to a lesser degree boxing, can be viewed as versions of this same sport.[2] In the three "acts" of the bullfight, as he described them in *Death in the Afternoon* (1932), Hemingway found his model for life. In the first act, or *suerte de varos* (trial of the lances), the picadors worked the bulls; as a symbol, *"suerte"* could imply many things, as Hemingway suggested in defining the word:

> Suerte, f., chance, hazard, lots, fortune, luck, good luck, haphazard; state, condition, fate, doom, destiny, kind, sort; species, manner, mode, way, skillful maneuver; trick, feat, juggle, and piece of ground separated by landmark.[3]

The Spanish word embraces virtually the entire range of meanings linked in American culture to "the game." The bullfight, like life, began in chance, in the drawing of the bull. Whether the bull was monstrous or small, unresponsive or nearly blind, "a bullfighter is not always expected to be good, only to do his best" (91). So too, the lottery of life created unequal individuals, but for Hemingway – as for Melville, the naturalists, the frontier romancers, and the entire tradition of writers who have celebrated the game in its many forms – you played the hand you were dealt.

The second act, the work of the banderillas, was the briefest of the three, merely an interlude before the climactic *faena,* ending in death. It distorts little to say that Hemingway portrayed life itself as an interlude between birth and the final confrontation. For Hemingway, death made the bullfight a tragedy rather than a sport, and thus an appropriate symbol for authentic human living. "We, in games, are not fascinated by death, its nearness and its avoidance," Hemingway wrote in *Death in the After-noon.* "We are fascinated by victory and we replace the avoidance of death by the avoidance of defeat. It is a very nice symbolism but it takes more cojones to be a sportsman when death is a closer party to the game" (22). The death of the bull ended most bullfights, but the possibility of the matador's fatal goring made bullfighting "the only art in which the artist is in danger of death and in which the degree of brilliance in the performance is left to the fighter's honor" (91). The "moment of truth," when the matador, sword in hand, faced the bull, culminated all that preceded it. The bullfight began in chance and ended in death; between that alpha and omega of human life the torrero created his art in the face of final annihilation.

Hemingway's discovery of the bullfight in Spain in the 1920s provided a meaningful symbol for human life in a world without the traditional Christian God or still-potent religious traditions. First in *The Sun Also Rises* (1926), the novel that grew out of his first visit to Spain and the bullfights, then in *For Whom the Bell Tolls* (1940) and *The Old Man and the Sea* (1952), the ethical system implied in the bullfight serves as the novel's moral center. In each case, Hemingway asked the same question: how can one live in the face of . . . ? In *The Sun Also Rises*, in face of the personal crises caused by a world war? In *For Whom the Bell Tolls*, in face of a lost cause in war? In *The Old Man and the Sea*, in face of the limitation and weakness that most generally define human mortality? The bullfight figures literally, and prominently, in *The Sun Also Rises* and *For Whom the Bell Tolls*. In *The Old Man and the Sea*, fishing plays an identical role: The *suerte* of Santiago's hooking a fifteen-hundred pound marlin brings him face to face with death and the challenge of acting honorably in life's tragedy. All of these novels enact the same morality play; only *A Farewell to Arms* strikes a discordant note. Not only does love, not the bullfight or any sporting substitute, provide the moral focus of *A Farewell to Arms*, the sporting code for the only time in Hemingway's fiction is challenged by irony.

In the confrontation between man and bull, or man and marlin, or man and lion (in "The Short Happy Life of Francis Macomber"), Hemingway recreated the tragic *agôn* of Ahab and Moby Dick, but for an age that had to confront human diminishment. It was no longer possible to imagine God incarnated in a mountainous sperm whale, or even to imagine a natural monster as powerful and malignant as Moby Dick. Hemingway created the same paradigm of a man contesting with the powers of the universe, not in the naturalists' world of chance but in Melville's world of fate and will. A fully secular world, however, wrought certain changes. In the first place, Hemingway shifted the emphasis from the contest itself to the rules by which it was waged. In the second place, the paradigmatic contest of man and beast in the novels before *The Old Man and the Sea* serves not as the central conflict but as an ideal against which the more human dilemma is played out. In each case, a protagonist confronts two possible models for living his life: the way of the bullfighter, or the way of some other player of "mere" games. The true way is clear; only the ability of the vulnerable protagonist to model his life successfully after the sportsman-hero's is in doubt.

The moral order in *The Sun Also Rises*, then, is defined by the contrast of Pedro Romero to Robert Cohn; in *For Whom the Bell Tolls*, of Finito to Pablo; in *The Old Man and the Sea*, of Santiago as an old man to the youth he once was. Here lay Hemingway's potential weakness as a moralist, the dilemma on which his entire moral system could easily founder. Romero lives by one sporting code, Cohn by another; by what standard can Romero's code be declared superior? In substituting a sportsman's code for traditional religious moral systems, Hemingway lost the ultimate authority, God, on whom those traditional moralities rested. In the absence of a final Umpire, all games are equal, their meaning entirely self-referential. But clearly Hemingway intended much more; to live by Romero's code is heroic, by Cohn's is shameful. Unlike in Melville's *Moby-Dick* (and as we shall see, even more so in Faulkner's writing), there is no ambiguity in Hemingway's moral vision. Ambiguity arises only in the fiction's meeting with the world of readers, some of whom have rejected his vision as puerile or steeped in anachronistic machismo. Yet there is no better testimony to the potency of the sporting myth within the larger culture than the readiness with which innumerable readers have accepted the validity of the "Hemingway code," rooted as it is only in assumption.

For a suggestive parallel to Hemingway's sporting code in European philosophy, we might consider not the ideas of Sartre or Camus, but those of Hans Vaihinger, whose book on the philosophy of the *Als-Ob*, the "as if," appeared in German in 1911 and in English in 1924. Vaihinger described the "fictions" by which men live, knowing they are false but recognizing their utility in the world. Such fictions, according to Vaihinger, have included not just scientific models of various kinds, but also the ideas of an orderly cosmos, God, immortality, and moral law. Hemingway's code can seem such a fiction: a system of beliefs tenaciously maintained *as if* they were absolutely true. To link Hemingway with Vaihinger, however, raises a crucial question in considering Hemingway's writing: Was the code entirely a "fiction" in Vaihinger's sense; that is, known by its creator (and his characters) to be false? If so, Hemingway's moral universe appears more fragile, his characters' hold on moral values more precarious. Hemingway himself in this reading becomes more truly an existentialist, confronting life at the edge of the abyss. A case might be made for seeing Jake Barnes and Robert Jordan as self-conscious fictionists, and *A Farewell to Arms* is certainly steeped in irony. But in *The Old Man and the Sea,* Santiago, wholly without self-consciousness, lives by the same code that provides meaning for the lives of Jake and Robert. Although one could argue that Hemingway began in doubt and only late in his life laid claim to certainty, I find the moral claims of *The Sun Also Rises* and *For Whom the Bell Tolls* as absolute as Calvinist orthodoxy to the Mathers. Hemingway's novels succeed or fail not as rational arguments but as declarations of faith. The weakness of *To Have and Have Not* and *Across the River and into the Trees* derives in large part from Hemingway's simple failure to compel readers' belief in the same code that operates in the better novels. Harry Morgan and Richard Cantwell play as well as Robert Jordan and Santiago, by the same code in all cases, but even most of Hemingway's admirers simply have not cared.

In his "major" novels, each a version of the same basic parable of the human condition, Hemingway has been more successful in compelling readers' belief. *The Sun Also Rises* is representative. Set against the background of a religious festival, with a main character who wanders in and out of churches searching for spiritual sustenance, *The Sun Also Rises* is a modern morality play: True Player (Romero) stands at one end of the stage, False Player (Cohn) at the other, with Everyman (Jake Barnes) forced to decide whose path to follow. Although the book's opening with Cohn happened, in effect, by accident (when Hemingway cut a long alternative opening, already set in galleys, in response to Fitzgerald's criticism), the novel that we have accentuates the opposition of Cohn and Romero. The world seems chaos in the novel's first section, ruled by the values of the Anti-player and awaiting redemption by the Knight of the True Game. "Robert Cohn was once middleweight boxing champion at Princeton," Jake begins the story, and by the second sentence readers know that something is wrong with this boxer's understanding of himself. "Do not think that I am very much impressed by that as a boxing title, but it meant a lot to Cohn." Robert Cohn plays at amateur sports for mere victories, failing to realize that the game is life, not just an isolated contest to gratify his ego. Jake's introduction goes on:

> He cared nothing for boxing, in fact he disliked it, but he learned it painfully and thoroughly to counteract the feeling of inferiority and shyness he had felt on being treated as a Jew at Princeton. There was a certain comfort in knowing he could knock down anybody who was snooty to him, although, being very shy and a thoroughly nice boy, he never fought except in the gym.

Such innocuous details, presented with heavy irony, foretell all that Cohn does or says as the novel progresses. He has been trained in a sport whose significance does not extend beyond the gymnasium, valuing physical prowess only to avoid facing his more personal weakness. Tellingly a middleweight who boxes like a featherweight, Cohn once has his nose flattened by a more powerful opponent. Most damning, Jake reports having "never met any one of [Cohn's] class who remembered him. They did not even remember that he was a middleweight boxing champion."[4]

Cohn from the outset is presented as an *amateur,* a player of *mere* games, football as well as boxing, bridge and tennis later. Jake reports that recently in New York Cohn played bridge "for higher stakes than he could afford" and with good cards won several hundred dollars (9). The irony of considering such stakes high becomes apparent when a contrasting game is introduced. When Cohn confesses to Jake that he is not "really living" his life, Jake responds, "Nobody ever lives their life all the way up except bull-fighters." With Cohn's rejoinder, "I'm not interested in bull-fighters," the opposition of true and false players is established (10).

The contrast of amateur sports to bullfighting reflects strategies for life. Cohn's desire, if he could do anything he wanted – to play football with what he knows now about handling himself – is a sign of "arrested development" (44). His indifference to winning and losing at tennis reflects his more serious purposelessness as writer and man. "He probably loved to win as much as Lenglen," Jake says (referring to Suzanne Lenglen, the great French player of the 1920s, who Jake implies is more "manly" than Robert Cohn). "On the other hand, he was not angry at being beaten" (45). Cohn's domination by women and lack of control over his sexual affairs is epitomized by the collapse of his tennis game after he falls in love with Brett Ashley. "People beat him who had never had a chance with him. He was very nice about it," Jake says not at all nicely (45). Cohn has been trained for life by women, as he was trained for boxing by his coach. He learned his ideas from H. L. Mencken and his aspirations from romantic novelists, just as he learned to box like a featherweight. He plays at life as if it were a gentlemanly contest in which the stakes are not high enough to warrant any hard feelings.

Cohn as the ultimate amateur is contrasted to a series of professionals: first the black prizefighter whom Jake's friend Bill encounters in Vienna earning a livelihood in a corrupt profession, then the boxers Ledoux and Kid Francis in Paris, whose fight Jake watches while Cohn is out of town "having a very quiet time . . . bathing, playing some golf and much bridge" (81). But Pedro Romero is most truly the Player to Cohn's Antiplayer: serious about his sport, working close to the bull without the tricks of other bullfighters, faking none of the danger. He has "the old thing, the holding of purity of line through the maximum of exposure" (168). With no illusions about his ability, Romero criticizes his own work with neither embarrassment nor boastfulness, talking of it "as something separate from himself" (174). Whereas Cohn is always a satellite attached to some individual or group, Romero is the boy standing "altogether by himself" in a room full of hangers-on (163). So, too, in fighting bulls. Even when he performs before Brett, he does it more "for himself inside" (216). Love destroys Cohn's tennis game; it gives Romero additional motivation to excel in the bullring. Romero fights the difficult bulls competently and the excellent bulls brilliantly, accepting the chance draw of the bull as a given and creating the best possible outcome by his own ability and will.

The antagonistic forces of Sport and Anti-sport directly clash only once, when Cohn and Romero fight in Brett's room. Wearing a polo shirt of "the kind he'd worn at Princeton" (194), Cohn regards the fracas as yet another gentlemanly contest governed by a prep-school code of honor, to be ended by a handshake and "no hard feelings." To Romero it means a test of courage as serious as the bullfight whose end is always death. When Cohn wins the boxing match, Romero becomes the first of Hemingway's heroes who will not be defeated. Refusing the hand-shake, Romero continues to fight even from the floor, nearly uncon-scious. Confronted by a player so committed, Cohn is permanently "ruined" (203).

There is a moment of uncertainty in this morality play, a sudden glimpse into emptiness, when Jake reports with hard-boiled unconcern the pointless death of a Spanish peasant during the running of the bulls: the man gored by a bull who is later killed by Pedro Romero . . . who gives the bull's ear as a trophy to Brett . . . who leaves it in a drawer, ingloriously littered with cigarette butts. *All* pointlessness, it would seem, including Romero's supposedly exemplary performance. But the transcendent sporting code, closer this one time to a necessary fiction than to a moral absolute, is immediately reaffirmed by the account of Romero's bout with Cohn and subsequent wounded brilliance in the ring. The same bull that kills Vicente Girones – farmer, husband, father of two – to no good purpose dies by the sword of Pedro Romero after a veritable "course in bull-fighting" (219). Absurdist comedy is trans-formed into tragic heroism.

In living with the *suerte* of the war wound that has left him impotent, Jake Barnes must choose between the way of Cohn and the way of Romero. Coping well at first and reserving for the nighttime his deepest anguish, Jake becomes a "steer" in Pamplona by sacrificing Romero to Brett, aligning himself with the novel's other "steer," Robert Cohn. When he shakes hands with Cohn after their own fight, as Romero does not, and when he imagines himself carrying a "phantom suitcase" up the stairs afterwards, as he had "felt once coming home from an out-of-town football game" (192–3), Jake's metaphorical association with Cohn's amateur sports is most damning. But the greater game is ongoing, not a matter of discrete victories and defeats. In the novel's understated conclusion, Jake witnesses the corruption of professional sport among the cyclists in San Sebastian, cleanses himself in the ocean waters, then steerishly answers yet another summons from Lady Brett. With Brett in the final scene Jake takes to drinking for oblivion once again, rather than for pleasure as at San Sebastian, but he also, in the novel's famous last

line, implies a cynical self-knowledge that may be a prelude to redemption. Jake saved or not, in either case the terms of moral judgment are
the same.

This basic paradigm of the vulnerable individual having to choose
between true and false sporting codes distinguishes a great deal of Hemingway's fiction, with the code of the transcendent player remaining
constant: unillusioned self-knowledge, self-reliance, self-possession, un-
flinching recognition of limitation and death. In *For Whom the Bell Tolls,*
the exemplary player, Finito de Palencia, remains offstage, present only
in Pilar's memories of him: stories of great fear overcome by greater
courage. Against Finito stands the guerilla leader Pablo, whose character
is revealed through his menial job in the bullring before the war, his
unwillingness to take risks, and his shameful killing of the fascists from
his home town in a grim parody of sport. Robert Jordan chooses the
way of Finito; ignoring his own safety and not misconstruing the meaning of "victory," he goes to his death "like a lion" into the ring.[5] *The
Old Man and the Sea* strips this fable to its barest elements. The false
player against whom Santiago must be measured is Santiago himself,
the younger man who long ago arm-wrestled a black giant from Cien-
fuegos for the title *El Campeon*. To win then required the same strength
and endurance now necessary for wrestling a fifteen hundred-pound
marlin, but competing merely for acclaim is the spurious competition
of a Robert Cohn. Santiago's veneration of Joe Dimaggio is ironic in
this context; the athlete's coping with a painful bone spur for the sake
of a baseball game seems trivial before the extraordinary physical endurance of the old fisherman. The true game is neither baseball nor arm-
wrestling but fishing too far out, "without hope but with resolution."
In this novel the tendency toward abstraction in Hemingway's beliefs is
most apparent. The loss of fifteen hundred pounds of fish flesh is insignificant before Santiago's achievement of matching the marlin's literally
immeasurable grandeur. The novel's theme, "A man can be destroyed
but not defeated," might be glossed: A man can lose all that the world
offers yet still win the greater game.[6]

A Farewell to Arms seems a surprising blasphemy against this Hemingwayesque faith. Frederic Henry's famous outcry near the end of the
novel – "Now Catherine would die. That was what you did. You died.
You did not know what it was about. You never had time to learn. They
threw you in and told you the rules and the first time they caught you
off base they killed you" – sounds simply like a more hard-boiled version
of Hemingway's perennial theme, or half of his theme: the hard challenge
without the hope.[7] But Henry is the least self-aware of Hemingway's
protagonists, his final cynicism unearned, *A Farewell to Arms* the most
ironic of Hemingway's novels. The game here is love, the true player

Catherine Barkley, and the false player her callow lover. Frederic regards love as a game of chess or bridge (26, 30–1); Catherine understands it as a religion (116). Frederic is an "amateur," Catherine a "professional," according to the terms set up in *The Sun Also Rises*. Although Catherine's commitment to an unworthy lover verges on self-annihilation, Frederic fails to commit himself enough.[8] That Frederic has changed little by the final scenes in the Alps is evident in an exchange when Frederic suggests they play chess. "I'd rather play with you," Catherine responds. Frederic: "No. Let's play chess." Catherine: "And afterward we'll play?" Frederick, finally: "Yes" (300). "Play" means very different things to the two lovers.

While Catherine agonizes through a fatal childbirth, Frederic is able to read newspapers and eat his meals, even after their child is stillborn and Catherine lies in critical danger. Frederic's sport-of-the-gods cynicism is wholly unearned, then. In Hemingway's world, had Frederic loved well enough, even Catherine's death could not have invalidated their tragic triumph. *A Farewell to Arms* undercuts Hemingway's more typical morality play most obviously by placing a false player at the center of the novel. But it also inverts Hemingway's basic tendencies as a novelist more fundamentally. Rejecting the metaphysical abstraction of life as sporting contest, the novel offers an alternative center for its values: love, commitment, personal relationships. For the only time in his novels, Hemingway revealed doubt about the "game" that elsewhere embodied his own deepest faith.

Faulkner: sporting at the edge of the abyss

Faulkner's wrestling with Southern history, as discussed in Chapter 7, was part of a wide-ranging meditation on the human condition in both its material facts and its metaphysical possibilities. If Hemingway's spiritual ancestors were Wigglesworth and Mather, Faulkner's more directly was Melville. Both Melville and Faulkner envisioned their protagonists engaged in desperate contests with a cruel but sportive deity, yet they did not ignore the social and political forces that lay behind those contests. Faulkner's moods were more varied than Melville's, the range of possibilities he conceived in life even broader. On the one hand, there is a joyful liberation in his characters' gamesmanship in his "comic" fiction, however futile its eventual outcome. On the other hand, no character in his "tragic" fiction triumphs even so ambiguously as Ahab. Faulkner amplified the ambiguity at the heart of the Melvillean vision. The deterministic forces in Faulkner's world – race, sex, caste, religion, history – cannot be thwarted by an unconquerable though doomed will. Tragic dignity is possible only by entering the contest, but it comes

through acceptance rather than fist-shaking defiance. Faced with inexorable fate, Faulkner's tragic protagonists redeem their lives by *choosing*
their fates, an act signifying more than submission but less than autonomous will – a more problematic version of "conditional necessity."
"Salvation" is harder earned, though more impressive for being earned
at all. At the root of Faulkner's view of the human condition is a sense
of mystery and ultimate uncertainty, from which he derived a precarious
affirmation. The fundamental paradox inherent in viewing life as a game
captures this spirit.

On the surface, Faulkner's fiction seems to move in a general way
from fatalism to affirmation. Bayard's suicide in *Sartoris* (1929), Quentin's
in *The Sound and the Fury* (1929), Joe Christmas' butchering in *Light in
August* (1932), Sutpen's defeat in *Absalom, Absalom!* (1936), all seem to
suggest human lives determined by forces beyond their control. But
beginning in the 1940s, the Snopes trilogy progresses toward justice, *Go
Down, Moses* (1942) ends in reconciliation, *A Fable* (1954) offers a parable
of redemption, *The Reivers* (1962) is pure joy. In the earlier novels,
metaphors of games suggest that humankind is the sport of the gods in
the most fatalistic sense. In *Soldier's Pay* (1926), the characters seem
battered by Chance and Fate – Donald Mahon the most obvious victim
of war's cruel hoax, but Joe Gilligan and Margaret Powers also defenseless
against the whims of circumstance, discovering that happiness simply
"isn't in the cards" for them.[9] In *Sartoris,* men at war are described as
soldiers "caught timelessly in a maze of solitary conflicting preoccupa-
tions, like bumping tops, against an imminent but incomprehensible
nightmare."[10] At the end of that novel, in that striking passage I quoted
in the last chapter, Miss Jenny thinks about the men of her family as
mere pieces in a chess game played by an omnipotent Player, silly and
tragic at the same time. Similarly in *The Sound and the Fury*, in his last
moments before leaving his room at Harvard to drown himself, Quentin
Compson recalls his father's description of the futility of human striving:
every act "a gamble" with loaded dice, man's end a desperate risk of
everything "on a single blind turn of a card" that "is not particularly
important to the dark diceman."[11]

Faulkner named the gods in a variety of ways, always suggesting some
oppressive aspect of a cruel Calvinist Deity. God is "Circumstance" in
Soldier's Pay and *The Sound and the Fury*, "Omnipotence" as well in the
latter novel; in *Light in August,* He appears alternately as "Player," "Opponent," "Chance," "Juggernaut," or "Fate." In *Absalom, Absalom!* He
is the "Creditor"; in *The Wild Palms*, a generic threatening "They"; in
"The Bear," a seemingly fairer but still judgmental "Umpire." Even in
the early comic novels, the God who is a "cosmic joker" ("Old Man"
in *The Wild Palms*), or "the prime maniacal Risibility" (*The Hamlet*) is

no benign deity but a Practical Joker presiding over a world of chance and ultimately futile gamesmanship. It is interesting that these capitalized gods nearly disappear after *Go Down, Moses,* a fact that in itself suggests Faulkner came to view men and women as less god-bullied in his later fiction.

But one can too easily overstate this apparent shift. Fate and Circumstance preside over Faulkner's last, most comically joyful novel, *The Reivers,* Old Moster over *The Mansion,* his previous book. Human agency is never totally absent in his earlier works, fate never absent from the later ones. Faulkner's fiction repeatedly portrays situations of ultimate indeterminacy, leaving readers without answers but with questions: In his meticulous care on the day of his suicide, is Quentin Compson despairing or triumphant? Does Joe Christmas simply surrender to the inescapable forces of race and sex, or does he somehow will the manner of his death? In renouncing his inheritance was Ike McCaslin a saint or a fool? In *Requiem for a Nun,* does Nancy save Temple's baby or merely murder it? These are moments of "fear and trembling," to use Kierkegaard's term, when reason confronts the irrational without possibility of simple resolution. Truth remains ultimately mysterious and unknowable, human character an irreconcilable contradiction. Caddy in *The Sound and the Fury* and Lena in *Light in August* are innocent but promiscuous; Jason III is obsessively rational but less "sane" in some ways than his brothers; Lucas Beauchamp of *Go Down, Moses* is a proud black man whose pride resides in his descent from a white racist monster. In key situations in Faulkner's fiction, the irrational orderliness of a "game" emblemizes this fundamental human paradox.

It is also important not to view Faulkner's fiction simply as metaphysical allegories. The capitalized "gods" in all of the novels must be seen also as emblems of social and political forces, apotheosized to signify their enormous power. Ike McCaslin tries to undo not an abstract deterministic force but the acts of his grandfather and other men from his grandfather's class. Thomas Sutpen defies not an abstraction, the omnipotent "Creditor" (the term is Shreve's), but the power of the privileged class that shunned him as a redneck youth. The "Player" who through Percy Grimm stalks and murders Joe Christmas is the force of bigotry and violence in Grimm's Southern culture. History and metaphysics are inseparable in Faulkner's novels, each grounded in the other.

Faulkner's version of the desperate game was part of a ludic vision that is the most varied and complex in American fiction. In Yoknapatawpha County Faulkner created an entire universe of sporting contest. It begins with a prehistory: the tales of Indians and then the first whites who populated the land before any towns were erected or land hoarded for private ownership. Faulkner adopted a grandly epic though comic mode in these stories, celebrating the gargantuan play of "tall men" as one tale characterizes them. In "Red Leaves," "A Justice," "Lo!" and "A Courtship," red men and white enact elaborate rituals of creative sport. In "Red Leaves," the hunting then killing of a runaway slave becomes a ritualistic race conferring ironic dignity on both pursuers and pursued. In "A Justice," a dispute between an Indian chief and a black slave over possession of the black man's wife is resolved by first a cockfight, then by a contest to climb a high fence. In "Lo!" the chief's nephew wagers against white men in a series of contests for control of the only ford for several miles on the river. And most impressively in "A Courtship," Ikkemotubbe and the white man, David Hogganbeck, vie for an Indian maiden in a series of epic contests: dancing, racing, drinking, eating, and finally running a 130-mile foot race in which both men lose the faithless woman but win the glory of epic heroes.[12]

Faulkner's foundation myth for the white South befits such legendry. Jason Lycurgus Compson wins the square mile of land that eventually becomes the center of Jefferson in either a horse race or a horse trade with Ikemotubbe, the Chickasaw chief (the record is properly uncertain; see the Appendix to *The Sound and the Fury*). The building of a courthouse and the founding of a town are precipitated by the removal of an entire wall of the old jail by escaping bandits – in "a kind of gargantuan and bizarre playfulness" – after which the new town is named Jefferson, not for the third president but for Thomas Jefferson Pettigrew, as a bribe, a clever move in a con game directly out of the frontier tall-tale tradition (*Requiem for a Nun*). The first generation of Yoknapatawpha County's citizens are desperate gamblers and men of ferocious honor like the Compsons and Sartorises, and like Thomas Sutpen, who drinks and gambles and fights with his wild slaves, perhaps even winning their daughters at cards; who pits his human frailty against history and the wilderness, meeting his inevitable doom with "impotent and furious undefeat" (*Absalom, Absalom!*). Others play more outwardly humorous games. Buck and Buddy McCaslin lock their slaves each night in a house with empty windows, out of which the blacks escape before the bolt has even slid into place (like "a game with rules," *The Unvanquished* calls it). In *Go Down, Moses*, Buck chases after Tomey's Turl in a parody of a fox hunt, then plays poker against Hubert Beauchamp with slaves and his brother's bachelorhood at stake ("Was"). The tragic contests of Sartorises and Sutpens define the Faustian reach of the human species; the comic games of Uncle Buck and Uncle Buddy define the merely human attempts to alleviate the tragic injustices tolerated by law. While defeat awaits all these game players, ambiguous triumph lies in the playing itself.

The descendants of the founding giants are doomed never to match the first generation's epic stature, yet also to live with the consequences of its equally epic blindness. Buck and Buddy McCaslin, even before the Civil War, futilely attempt to rectify their father's abominations; in the next generation, Ike continues their efforts with equally noble futility. Bayard III is haunted by Sartoris history, as Quentin III is by that of the Compsons. Thomas Sutpen's defiant contest produces a legacy of death, misery, idiocy, and outrage. This planter class with its exaggerated sense of sporting honor dies out altogether, yielding power to a plague of Snopeses, descendants not of a sporting planter but of a tricky horse trader, and an unscrupulous one at that. In *The Hamlet, The Town,* and *The Mansion,* Faulkner portrayed the economic transformation of the Old South into the New in part as a shift from noble, if self-defeating, sporting honor to triumphant but amoral gamesmanship.

Among Faulkner's novels *The Hamlet* comes closest to an overview of his sporting universe. The novel is largely written in mythopoeic rather than realistic language: Eula, Flem, Ike and his cow, Houston's hound – all loom larger than life. In Faulkner's comic myth, Snopesism supplants the Rabelaisian play spirit of Frenchman's Bend, the primeval village, with the joyless, deadly spirit of commercial gain. The old order is embodied in Will Varner and his "old idle busy cheerful existence"; in the horse trader Pat Stamper, who plays "horses against horses, as a gambler plays cards against cards, for the pleasure of beating a worthy opponent as much as for gain"; in Eula's vanquished suitors, who attack Hoake McCarron only after sending him a formal warning, because "they would have met the profferer of a mortal affronting and injury with their hands bound up in boxing gloves"; in Jack Houston and Lucy Pate, whose bizarre courtship transforms the agonistic sexual relations typical in Faulkner's fiction into a sporting contest in which "points" are won and lost.[13] Against Houston as representative of the old order, Mink Snopes embodies the new. In their dispute over the pasturing of a yearling calf, Houston proposes a contest to Mink to settle their differences: "They would lay the pistol on a fence post and back off one post apiece on each side and count three and run for it" (160). Instead, Mink murders Houston from ambush.

The presiding genius of the older order is V. K. Ratliff, his antithesis not Mink but Flem Snopes. Both are shrewd traders, but Ratliff barters in the spirit of playful sport, whereas Flem schemes only for the power and profits to be won. Ratliff's *presence* in the novel as a vital life force is matched by Flem's essential *absence,* both his actual departures and his disappearance into abstraction (as well as the pervasive imagery of blankness, emptiness, that describes him). Ratliff contests face-to-face, Flem more often through intermediaries, remaining the untouchable manipulator behind the scenes. Ratliff and the old order love contest for its own sake; Flem and the new order see contest only as the means to an end. Flem's triumph over Ratliff concludes the novel and signals the final defeat of the old older. From one perspective, Flem's rise at Will Varner's and then Ratliff's expense merely redistributes the wealth of Frenchman's Bend. What matters, however, is the transformation in the manner of economic exchange. The spirit of play makes barter a social relationship; the spirit of acquisitiveness makes economic transactions acts of exploitation. This shift, Faulkner felt deeply, is what had happened to his own South.

Flem continues to play his unplayful games through *The Town* and *The Mansion*. In *The Town* Ratliff thinks of Flem not as a contestant or even an umpire but as an aloof, almost godlike being who plays a kind of solitaire, "running a little mild game against hisself."[14] He remains virtually invulnerable until the end of *The Mansion,* manipulating the destinies of his family and kin, until Mink murders him in his own study. Ratliff describes the killing in terms of a childhood game, give-me-lief:

> It was a game we played. You would pick out another boy about your own size and you would walk up to him with a switch or maybe even a light stick or a hard green apple or maybe even a rock, depending on how hard a risk you wanted to take, and say to him, "gimme lief," and if he agreed, he would stand still and you would take one cut or one lick at him with the switch or stick, as hard as you picked out, or back off and throw at him once with the green apple or the rock. Then you would stand still and he would take the same switch or stick or apple or rock or anyways another one jest like it, and take one cut or throw at you. That was the rule.[15]

As Ratliff says, "Flem had had his lief fair and square like the rule said, so there wasn't nothing for him to do but jest sit there," as Mink and Linda take their turn. The ending of *The Mansion* can signify grim comeuppance or merely Flem's weariness after having won all there is to win. But it also can suggest redeeming grace in even the most bankrupt soul. In any case, fair play triumphs, whether the fair play of the universe in dragging Flem down, or the fair play of Flem in granting Mink and Linda their due, his implicit acknowledgment at the last that the players of the game are people, not markers.

The Snopes trilogy develops ideas, and their rhetorical representation, that are pervasive in Faulkner's fiction. Contest is central to Faulkner's view of the human condition (yet another type of play, not the subject of this book, is the play of narrative creation: "Let me play now," Shreve says in the well-known line from *Absalom, Absalom!*). In the Yoknapatawpha novels social hierarchy, sexual relations, the relationship of man and nature, even theology are all rooted in contest. Contest itself is morally neutral; the manner of contesting determines its ethical value.

On this basis the Flem Snopeses are distinguished from the V. K. Ratliffs, the Carothers McCaslins from the Uncle Bucks and Uncle Buddys, the Boon Hogganbecks from the Ike McCaslins. Obsessive competitors such as Thomas Sutpen and John Sartoris are redeemed from simple villainy by their sporting spirit, while their coeval, Carothers McCaslin, is left unregenerate because he lacks such a spirit. In sexual relations the element of contest that Faulkner presented as inevitable, even "natural," is not itself dehumanizing. The furious contests among Eula Varner's suitors and between Eula herself and those young men emerge as social rituals of value to the community. Flem Snopes's backroom barter for Eula, on the other hand, is life-denying rather than life-producing. In like manner, Joe Christmas's brutal experiences with women in *Light in August* are altogether different from the relationship of Jack Houston and Lucy Pate or even of Mink Snopes and his amazon bride in *The Hamlet*: the difference lying in the presence or absence of a sporting spirit. The portrayal of the most important human experiences as games ("mere" games, from one perspective) implies a problematic, ironic, paradoxical affirmation of human possibilities. Faulkner's comic frontier gamesmanship is always touched by tragedy, his tragic games always hinting at the ludicrous. But even at their bleakest, Faulkner's novels, by virtue of their sporting spirit, are never simply nihilistic. Play is Faulkner's sign of hope, but hope must always contend with human history.

In four novels that directly confront the precariousness of human possibility – *Sartoris, The Sound and the Fury, Light in August,* and *Absalom, Absalom!* – the central symbol of a desperate contest suggests both the futility of resisting fate and the only chance for redemption. In *Absalom, Absalom!* as Thomas Sutpen emerges from four different viewpoints, his chroniclers agree in seeing him as a defiant sportsman. Rosa Coldfield, the least objective observer but the one who knew Sutpen most intimately, describes his ruthless attempt to carve a dynasty out of the wilderness as a desperate gamble:

> His was the cold alert fury of the gambler who knows that he may lose anyway but that with a second's flagging of the fierce constant will he is sure to: and who keeps suspense from ever quite crystallizing by the sheer fierce manipulation of the cards or dice until the ducts and glands begin to flow again.

Mr. Compson describes for his son the sporting code that Sutpen absorbed as a child in the West Virginia mountains and never relinquished, and that took on a metaphysical as well as social dimension. Quentin Compson shares this perspective of Sutpen when he imagines watching him "drag house and formal gardens violently out of the soundless Nothing and clap them down like cards upon a table beneath the up-palm immobile and pontific, creating the Sutpen's Hundred, the *Be Sutpen's*

Hundred like the oldentime *Be Light.*" Each of these people thinks of
Sutpen as a cosmic contestant or gambler, pitting his courage and shrewd-
ness against all opposition, or playing his cards scornful of that implacable
Opponent who can be defied perhaps but never beaten. Like Melville's
Ahab, Sutpen challenges God himself, the Creditor as Shreve imagines
him, who finally demands his due.[16]

But Sutpen's contest is also grounded in Southern class relations. As
a boy in West Virginia, Sutpen grew up with an egalitarian mountain
code that recognized only two determinants of status: that "measured
by lifting anvils or gouging eyes or how much whisky you could drink
then get up and walk out of the room," and that decided simply by
"whether you were lucky or not lucky" (226). In Tidewater Virginia
young Sutpen discovers a world where caste and race have created an
artificial social hierarchy, but he persists in holding to his simple code
of contest and luck. Perceiving that the contest against the powerful is
not with rifles but with "land and niggers and a fine house to combat
them with" (238), Sutpen commits himself to a grand design he never
relinquishes. He is eventually destroyed by his own need to view the
world solely in terms of simple contest, oblivious to the fact that his
fellow beings have comparable needs to be recognized as human. He can
imagine only "mistakes," not faulty vision, as his dreams are thwarted
while he becomes finally pathetic: clinging to the last shreds of his design,
attempting to beget a male heir on Milly Jones then provoking her
grandfather to murder. But his various chroniclers in the novel refer to
his "bitter though unmaimed defeat," his "impotent and furious undefeat," his "indomitable desperation of undefeat" – rhetorical figures of
paradoxical futility and triumph (161, 184, 189). Even to his death Sutpen
"never did give up" (268), as General Compson tells his son. And dead,
Sutpen becomes "a thousand times more potent and alive" as he haunts
the memory of Rosa Coldfield and the consciousness of Quentin Compson. Monster or tragic Faustus, Sutpen earns a problematic and paradoxical immortality.

A similar sense of paradoxical triumph and defeat permeates *Sartoris,
The Sound and the Fury,* and *Light in August.* In Miss Jenny du Pre's
perception of Sartoris males as mere pawns in an outmoded game, and
in Mr. Compson's view of mankind as the victim of fate's loaded dice,
men and women are pitted against a Player or dark diceman in a contest
they have no chance of winning. But Miss Jenny and Mr. Compson do
not speak with unchallenged authority. Miss Jenny helps perpetuate a
crippling cavalier code. Mr. Compson speaks for pure chance, man a
helpless victim not of fate but of randomness, when in fact his own
paternal failings contribute conspicuously to his family's dissolution.
Bayard Sartoris and Quentin Compson seem more fate-ridden than

Thomas Sutpen – Bayard destined for early meaningless death, Quentin driven by sexual confusion and the weight of a familial history over which he has no control. But like Sutpen, both young men seem to accept the Player's terms, to embrace their destinies rather than meekly submit. Faulkner portrayed Bayard and Quentin as individuals who paradoxically will what they are driven to do. Bayard pursues an early death by courting danger wherever he can find it. Quentin chooses to die properly, even ritualistically, in his own time, not when the dice dictate. Futile, meaningless waste of young lives? Or heroic dignity in the face of overwhelming fate? Faulkner allowed no simple answers. Although Bayard and Quentin share little of Sutpen's personal power, their deaths are moving in ways that the working out of a rigid fatalism could not be. In the image of the desperate game again lies this ultimate sense of mystery and fragile affirmation.

The rhetorical figure of the sporting contest against fate is most explicit in *Light in August,* against a background of other "games" that reflect ironically on this central one. In his petty scheming Lucas Burch plays a trivial version of Joe Christmas's tragic game, seeming to think, as Byron Bunch puts it, that "getting money is a kind of game where there are not any rules at all." Repeatedly frustrated in his efforts to get the sheriff's reward for the arrest of Christmas, Lucas finds himself at the end groping "for some last desperate cast in a game already lost" and feels himself the victim of a malevolently playful God – "an Opponent who could read his moves before he made them and who created spontaneous rules which he and not the Opponent, must follow."[17] In his fanatical bigotry, Doc Hines appears as a perverse Jacob, who "wrestled and . . . strove" with God not for a blessing but for a commission to murder his own grandson (365). Less grim and more pathetic, Reverend Hightower plays a "game" of uncommitted accommodation that evades life (461, 463); for her part, his wife lives out her existence as a "harassed gambler" – losing her wager that marriage will ease her desperation (454). Joanna Burden engages in a different sort of sexual contest with Joe Christmas, a series of trivial games (222, 224) that evolve into a fierce contest of wills and eventual murder.

All of these contests flesh out the world in which Joe Christmas lives and in which he plays out the ultimate Faulknerian game against fate and history. Throughout *Light in August* the "game" represents ritualized Southern behavior, ludicrous or pointless in some manifestations, perverse or destructive in others. Joe Christmas is the victim of much of this game playing: Joanna Burden plays games with him, the sheriff plays games with him ("Like there is a rule to catch me by, and to capture me that way would not be like the rule says" [319, also see 312]), Percy Grimm in the novel's brutal climax plays the most horrifying and most elaborately developed game of all. Grimm, however, is less a contestant in this game than the "pawn" moved about by an omnipotent "Player," a god whose will demands the death and mutilation of Joe Christmas (437–40).[18]

But Joe Christmas is no mere plaything in a deterministic universe. Reluctant to play but forced to play at last, Christmas, rather than the fateful Player or his agent Percy Grimm, orchestrates his own murder. In Faulkner's rendering, the outcome was foreordained from Christmas's earliest childhood, from the moment the dietitian withheld the punishment that five-year-old Joe believed was his due for stealing toothpaste; yet in his final days and hours Joe Christmas paradoxically wills his fate. The question whether Joe Christmas in any way controls his own destiny can be framed by the narrator's reference to "that strength to cling to either defeat or victory, which is the I-Am" (372). Against the opposing evidence of Christmas's doom his actions insist on the more paradoxical of the two possibilities, his clinging to defeat.

Allowing himself to be captured in Mottstown, then running from his captors through the streets of Jefferson certainly aware that escape was impossible, and finally forcing the townspeople to lynch him, Joe Christmas chooses to die as a "nigger," chooses to be lynched by a community that refuses to acknowledge the humanity of the black man. The most haunting element in Joe Christmas's death is not his mutilation but his "peaceful and unfathomable and unbearable eyes" with which he looks upon the scene that *he* has chosen to enact. Joe Christmas is a brutalized victim but also the agent of his own destiny: the same paradoxical mystery that lies behind the sporting vision in Faulkner's other novels. In dying, Joe Christmas achieves an ironic immortality, "soaring into [the townspeople's] memory forever and ever" (440).

Structurally, *Light in August* confirms this fragile affirmation. Following Joe's death and Hightower's remorse, which comes too late, Lena Grove commands the final pages as the narrative ends with a very different image of play. Among the major characters, Lena alone plays no "game." Living in the concrete present, she elicits kindness from others to which a "fallen woman" is not entitled. Lena herself seems less real than abstract. In a novel that uneasily holds on to both history and metaphysics, Lena Grove is as free as Percy Grimm is driven. Between those extremes, Joanna Burden, Lucas Burch, and Gail Hightower in different ways pursue illusions of freedom in games they misapprehend. Hightower in particular is a victim of his fate, playing games that are simply a cover for obsession. Fate, chance, and will equally inform Faulkner's metaphysical universe; race, caste, and freedom his historical one. The dialectical understanding that results from the collision of these forces is summed up in Faulkner's portrait of life as a sporting contest.

Ellison and the black agôn

It becomes necessary once again to sketch with broad strokes. The essential part of this discussion that awaits development is the relationship of Ralph Ellison's *Invisible Man,* and black fiction more generally, to the ideas we have been considering. But I also wish to trace out, however briefly, the figures of the desperate game and the sport of the gods in postwar American fiction. Following Hemingway and Faulkner, the image of humankind as the helpless victim of a cruelly sportive power has become an increasingly familiar expression of one distinctively modern worldview. Shirley Jackson's extraordinarily controversial short story "The Lottery" (1948), in which one citizen in an ordinary New England town is chosen annually by lot to be calmly, chillingly stoned by the rest of the community, seems anything but modern in its echoes of primitive rituals and Puritan scapegoating. But it is also possible to read "The Lottery" as a modernist fable: a story either about the eruption of the irrational into seemingly orderly existence, or about transforming the arbitrariness of life and death into a perversely meaningful public ritual.[19] More conventionally, in the 1930s, playwrights Robert Sherwood and William Saroyan, in *Idiot's Delight* (1936) and *The Time of Your Life* (1939) respectively, imagined man as the sport of a god who plays solitaire (Sherwood), human Destiny as a pinball machine (Saroyan).[20] Post-1960s writers such as Joan Didion (*Play It as It Lays* [1970]), Norman Mailer (*The Executioner's Song* [1979]), and William Burroughs (*The Place of Dead Roads* [1985]) used similar metaphors of men and women as markers in cosmic games of craps or checkers.[21]

Among recent novelists, Jerzy Kosinski has returned most obsessively to this motif. Kosinski's novels, including *Cockpit* (1975), *Blind Date* (1977), *Passion Play* (1979), and *Pinball* (1982), offer variations on a central theme: the possibilities of human meaning in a universe of random force. Kosinski's primary mentor has been the French biologist and philosopher of chance, Jacques Monad, his formative experience a childhood under Nazi terror. Yet Kosinski's sporting metaphors can also be read in an American context. A child's "wheel game" (*Cockpit*), a "game" of indiscriminantly cruel or benign role-playing (*Blind Date*), high-risk polo (*Passion Play*), and pinball (*Pinball*) serve as central images around which the interaction of chance and freedom, both political and metaphysical, is worked out.[22] Politics and metaphysics clash disturbingly in Kosinski's later fiction, where his earlier concern with the victims of random violence gives way to the domination and debasement of others by godlike gamesmen. (One critic has noted that this shift corresponds to Kosinski's own "progression up the ladder of social and economic privilege.")[23]

Tarden in *Cockpit* is the chief example of this tendency, whereas the cruelly sportive hero of *Passion Play* is the most extravagantly romanticized of Kosinski's empowered gamesman, sentimentalized in the manner of bad Hemingway (Col. Cantwell in *Across the River and into the Trees*, for example).

Two postwar literary voices in particular are rooted squarely in the rhetorical tradition of the sport of the gods. Perhaps the most distinctive voice of the 1960s, black humor can be seen as a development of the darkly comic vision of Melville in *The Confidence-Man* and Twain in "The Chronicle of Young Satan." In the comic-apocalyptic novels of Joseph Heller, Kurt Vonnegut, Robert Coover, and Thomas Pynchon, the sportive god is a whimsical deity, his human playthings empowered or powerless in varying degrees. The romantic humanism that concludes *Catch-22* (1961) and Vonnegut's sentimentalizing of his characters' powerlessness make these popular sixties novels very different from Melville's and Twain's bleak fables.[24] In *The Universal Baseball Association, J. Henry Waugh, Prop.* (1968), Coover more complexly envisioned life as a baseball game delicately balanced between strategy and chance, ruled by the rolls of cosmic dice. By the novel's end, the dice-rolling God has disappeared, his creations are uncertain whether he exists or not, and their sense of orderly, meaningful history has been exposed as fraudulent patterns imposed on random events. But they can respond without despair, accepting life for the game it is and just playing it for its own sake.[25] Although Pynchon's *Gravity's Rainbow* (1973) defies any such simple summation, it includes a long meditation on freedom and determinism, expressed in part by a series of images of life as a game of chance that is alternately exhilarating and appalling: Roger Mexico's "play" with the randomness of rocket strikes; the perversely erotic Hansel and Gretel "game" played by Blicero, Gottfried, and Katje as a refuge from the unbearable thought of "the absolute rule of chance"; Slothrop's wondering if what has seemed free or random in his life has in truth been determined by "a fixed roulette wheel."[26]

A more general literary (and artistic) movement rooted to a considerable degree in a sportive view of chance is the entire phenomenon termed postmodernism. Chance became an aesthetic principle in "aleatoric" and "aleamorphic" music (music governed by chance either in its creation or in its performance) beginning with John Cage in the 1950s; in the drip paintings of Jackson Pollock; and in the poetry and fiction of such writers as Jackson Mac Low, William Burroughs, Ronald Sukenick, Raymond Federman, and Gilbert Sorrentino.[27] Such formalist experiments with chance also imply something about the historical world. As one critic has put it, postmodern fiction in general assumes an indeterminate universe governed by "the cosmic role of the dice."[28] Thus the attempts by such novelists as Burroughs and Federman to create either the illusion or the reality of chance composition implicitly declare life, not just art,. to have no determinate author. The tradition of the grandly heroic desperate game is similarly rich in postwar American fiction. Melville, Hemingway, and Faulkner loom conspicuously behind the novels in this tradition: Shelby Foote's *Tournament* (1949) and Andrew Lytle's *The Velvet Horn* (1957) reveal a Faulknerian sense not just of cavalier sport but of metaphysical sport as well; James Jones, Wright Morris, and Ken Kesey wrote novels about the ultimate Hemingwayesque contest; Norman Mailer's fiction repeatedly echoes all three literary precursors. Kesey's *One Flew Over the Cuckoo's Nest* (1962), both novel and film, whose hero in the Hemingway manner is "destroyed but not defeated," was the most popular of these narratives of desperate sporting heroism. These novels can be interestingly viewed in relation to an alternative narrative, most conspicuous in a series of immensely popular films. Against *Cuckoo's Nest* stand dozens of movies – many starring Joe Don Baker, Clint Eastwood, Charles Bronson, Chuck Norris, Arnold Schwartzenegger, or Sylvester Stallone – in which a lone male takes on an impossibly overwhelming opponent, not to lose but to win. This narrative, the "walking tall" plot we might call it, became one of the most distinctive cultural fantasies in post-1960s America. The contest in these movies is decidedly no game but all-out war, with Baker's baseball bat as weapon in *Walking Tall*, the prototypical movie of this type, yielding to the high-tech arsenals of Stallone and Schwartzenegger, who lay waste to entire populations. Although the novels of the business titan in 1900 and the movies of the solitary avenger in 1980 are not entirely comparable cultural products, nor their audiences structurally identical, it is still instructive to recognize the striking difference in these popular masculine fantasies separated by several decades. *Walking Tall, Dirty Harry,* and *Rambo* must have appealed to audiences with considerably more anger and sense of diminution than the readers of *The Octopus* and *The Pit.*

The tragic game of Randall Patrick McMurphy is the minor voice in postwar American popular culture, then, but a nonetheless conspicuous one in American fiction. In several novels the power against which the desperate player must contend is an institution of modern bureaucratic power: the military in Mailer's *The Naked and the Dead* (1948) and Jones's *From Here to Eternity* (1951), "the Combine" in Kesey's *Cuckoo's Nest,* the loggers' union in his *Sometimes a Great Notion* (1964). But metaphysics by no means yields entirely to politics. In *Cuckoo's Nest,* for example, McMurphy's contest, elaborately developed as a series of games, is waged against both the Big Nurse, whose name suggests the Woman as perversely emasculating nurturer, and the Combine she represents; in other words, both psychosexual and sociopolitical oppression. But the Big Nurse and the Combine exist in the novel more as allegorical embodiments of transcendent force than as representatives of actual material power. So, too, in *Sometimes a Great Notion,* where Hank Stamper's contest is not just against his fellow townsmen and their union (the overt politics of these novels is consistently antiliberal) but against the transcendent powers of the universe. Hank's ultimate opponent is symbolized in the powerfully indifferent river that eats away the banks of his land and against which he continually wages "a little grudge match" as he attempts to prevent this erosion. In both novels, the hero's political defeat is insignificant before his transcendent victory.[29]

The uneasy meeting of politics and metaphysics in postwar versions of the desperate game is no more elaborately played out than in the fiction of Norman Mailer, the chief heir to the sporting traditions of Melville, Hemingway, and Faulkner. In Mailer's writings through the 1960s particularly, life is consistently portrayed as unremitting contest, each individual man pitted not just against every other man, but against every woman as well.[30] The sexual antagonism that is relatively covert in earlier American novels of desperate game playing here becomes open, brutal, and pervasive. Life's contest for Mailer is primarily psychosexual. In much of his fiction but most spectacularly in "The Time of Her Time" from *Advertisements for Myself* (1959), in which Sergius O'Shaughnessy uses "the avenger of my crotch" not to seduce but to subdue the women he brings to the "gymnasium" of his Village loft, Mailer envisioned sexual relations as contests in which the slender reserve of man's "vital substance" is crucially at stake.[31] Mailer's fascination with both metaphorical and actual boxing, and with deviance and outlawry, all contributed to this idea that a man's greatest and ever-present challenge is to prove over and over, through triumph in life's desperate games, that he is a man.[32]

Mailer's psychosexual contest is not simply personal, however; it lies at the heart of a Manichean struggle, expressed most explicitly in *An American Dream* (1965) as a contest between God and Satan that God could lose without man's assistance. "The White Negro" (1957), Mailer's celebration of the existential saint as a psychopathic hipster locked in mortal contest against everything that threatens autonomous selfhood, can be taken as his basic "theological" treatise on this subject. For the hipster, life is perpetual contest; to withdraw is to be defeated. "The unstated essence of Hip," Mailer wrote, "its psychopathic brilliance, quivers with the knowledge that new kinds of victories increase one's power for new kinds of perception; and defeats, the wrong kind of defeats, attack the body and imprison one's energy until one is jailed in the prison air of other people's habits, other people's defeats, boredom, quiet desperation, and muted icy self-destroying rage." In what Mailer called his "morality of the bottom," all acts are equally valid if chosen and embraced – "perversion, promiscuity, pimpery, drug-addiction, rape, razor-slashing, bottle-breaking, what-have-you."[33]

With "The White Negro" Mailer defined his stance against bureaucratic, technological, conformist, corporate America, taking a political position somewhere on the "left." In his fiction, however, chiefly "The Time of Her Time" and *An American Dream,* the sexual politics of his leftist hip existentialism proved to be brutally oppressive; and with the onset of the war in Vietnam the contradiction between the politics that he practiced and the philosophy of desperate sport that he espoused became most obvious. *Why Are We in Vietnam?* (1967) is a central text in Mailer's career for this reason. The novel deconstructs Cooper's frontier sporting myth in scenes of orgiastic slaughter of Alaskan wildlife that stand symbolically for the United States' technological ravaging of Southeast Asia. The killers, corporate executives from Texas armed with ridiculously large-caliber rifles and assisted by helicopters, represent the technocrats who conduct the war in Vietnam. But in following Faulkner's model of ritual initiation beyond violence in "The Bear," the novel's narrative logic contradicts Mailer's own well-publicized politics. D. J. Jethroe and his buddy Tex reject meaningless butchery for a more profound, Ike McCaslin-like encounter with the wilderness on its own terms. The lesson they learn is not Ike's renunciation of violence, however, but the salvific possibilities of *personal* violence. "God was a beast, not a man," D. J. discovers in the novel's epiphanic climax, "and God said 'Go out and kill – fulfill my will, go and kill.'"[34] Recalling this experience two years later, on the eve of his entry into the Army, D. J. prepares to carry this message into war.

In *Why Are We in Vietnam?* Mailer declared technological warfare obscene but killing possibly meaningful to individual soldiers. The Vietnamese could scarcely have appreciated the distinction. Mailer's opposition to the war was well established by the time he wrote the novel, but so too was his fascination with the hip existentialist whose acts of personal violence supposedly defied the collective violence of the totalitarian state. *Why Are We in Vietnam?* insists on a fundamental difference between D. J. and his unprincipled, wantonly destructive father, yet in the end the consequences of their acts are indistinguishable. A contradiction lies at the heart of this book, similar to the contradictions in the fiction of Frank Norris and Jack London in an earlier age. Their simpler confusion gives way in Mailer's stunningly written novel to a deeply resonant dialectical impasse, but it is that impasse rather than any reconciliation of Mailer's politics to his personal philosophy that becomes his fundamental commentary on American fantasies of sporting violence.

While pushing elements of the sporting *agôn* to their furthest extreme, Mailer nonetheless remained within the boundaries of the Melville/Hemingway/Faulkner tradition. Ralph Ellison's *Invisible Man* (1952) would seem to belong there, too. Ellison has been as explicit as Mailer in identifying himself with these white writers, specifically naming Hemingway and Faulkner among his literary "ancestors." This assertion appeared in Ellison's public response to Irving Howe, who had charged the author of *Invisible Man* with, in effect, a betrayal of his own blackness. Ellison's answer was unequivocal: Richard Wright was necessarily a racial "relative" but not an "ancestor," by which term Ellison designated those writers he *chose* to be his literary forebears. In the 1960s this seemed to Howe an unacceptable position for a black writer to take, but in explaining the choice of Hemingway, Ellison made a telling observation: "Because all that he wrote – and this is very important – was imbued with a spirit beyond the tragic with which I could feel at home, for it was very close to the feeling of the blues, which are, perhaps, as close as Americans can come to expressing the spirit of tragedy."[35]

Howe and the critics within the Black Arts movement who denounced Ellison for denying his racial heritage thus missed a crucial point. According to Ellison's own testimony, not only did he appropriate the modernist forms created by Joyce and Eliot as a way to translate black folk materials into literary art, he claimed kinship with Hemingway (and Faulkner) as white writers who wrote, ironically, in the idiom of African-American blues. As Henry Louis Gates might say, Ellison's tracing of his literary ancestry was an ingenious act of signifying: rhetorically stealing two of white American fiction's most important figures right from under whitey's nose.

Ellison's comment invites two responses here. On the one hand, it suggests a new perspective on the Melvillean tradition we have been examining, offering a name, the blues, for the American (near-)tragic sense of life expressed as a game that can only be courageously lost. On the other hand, it points to a parallel and overlapping tradition to that Melvillean lineage, a tradition of black writers' metacommentary on the "games" at the center of American white, male, middle-class culture. Blacks are truly the invisible men in the white fiction of sportsmanship and gamesmanship, games of life and desperate games; not, like women and the white underclass, occasional victims but an all-but-total absence. In filling that void black writers have not only named forgotten victims, they have also exposed unexamined assumptions on which the white traditions rest. Against white writers' frequent tendency to suppress politics and history for the sake of imagining a transcendent cosmic "game," black writers have insisted on the inescapably political nature of American life.

Black writing is thus full of "games," the familiar games examined in these chapters, but serving somewhat different functions. Even the most superficial survey of black literary history reveals the importance of game playing in African-American culture. Sportsmanship, of course, has virtually no place there; the code of gentlemen is reserved for those who can make at least minimal claim to privilege. Gamesmanship, on the other hand, has long been recognized as a primary strategy for blacks' survival in racist America. Both black folklore and the rich literary traditions that draw on folkloric sources offer abundant examples of tricksters, con men, conjurers, and hustlers who outwit the more powerful white man or his symbolic representatives in deftly orchestrated "games." Brer Rabbit is the paradigmatic hero, and his representatives have been legion. Within black communities, both real and fictional, signifying, specifying, and playing the dozens are just a few of the deeply meaningful rhetorical games that numerous literary and social historians have found central to African-American life and literature.[36]

A more focused examination of twentieth-century black fiction reveals an additional pattern more directly related to the subject of this chapter. In novels and stories, from Paul Laurence Dunbar's *The Sport of the Gods* (1902) to John Edgar Wideman's Homewood trilogy in the 1980s, black characters are frequently portrayed as futile players of a "game" they cannot win. But these characters do not emerge as tragic Ahabs or near-tragic Santiagos, overmatched opponents of existential reality. Rather, they are victims of concrete, material power, victims not of "God" or "the gods" but of wholly human yet comparatively god*like* white men. Alongside the tradition initiated by Melville's metaphorical construction of Ahab's sporting contest with his Calvinist God, we must place a series of metaphors in African-American fiction: the fixed crap game run by whites in Chester Himes' *If He Hollers Let Him Go* (1946), the doomed contest between a black Pullman waiter and the white Commissary with its ironically termed "black bible" of rules in James Alan McPherson's "A Solo Song: For Doc" (1969), the "scare game" black boys play with an onrushing locomotive in Wideman's *Sent for You Yesterday* (1983). Each of these metaphors suggests the futility rather than transcendence possible for the black man who contests with white "gods."[37]

Several African-American writers have thus distinguished between the creative, tradition-conscious, community-building verbal games blacks play among themselves and the destructive or futile "games" they are forced to play against whites. To interject race into narratives of sporting competition is to force an examination of the assumptions on which such competition, in both kinds of "games," is based. The defiant contestant against white power is doomed to unambiguous defeat, but the successful gamesman of black folklore and fiction, though seemingly a "winner," is no less a problematic figure. As the critic Michael Cooke has pointed out, signifying "makes up for a lack of social power with an exercise of intellectual or critical power." Keith Byerman has offered a similar perspective, arguing that "the folk worldview implicitly assumes that endurance rather than political power is its objective. It insists not on overcoming the enemy so much as outwitting and outliving him." Here lies the dilemma facing the black artist concerned with personal and collective empowerment. The trickster figure in Charles Waddell Chesnutt's conjure tales at the turn of the century, for example, assures his own comfort through outwitting white men without altering in any way the racist power arrangements of his world.[38]

The politics of gamesmanship, in other words, look different when viewed through a racial lens. Sportsmanship, as we saw earlier, is rooted in an aristocratic ethos whereby winning matters less than the manner and style of competing. Privilege and power are assured whatever the outcome. Gamesmanship, on the other hand, is rooted in a democratic ideology whereby winning alone guarantees material rewards and/or power. Against these assumptions, with their images of black characters powerless in their "games" with whites, African-American writers like Dunbar, Himes, and Wideman, as well as Wright, Ellison, Baldwin, and many others, have declared that winning itself is not possible for blacks in racist America. Games within the black community – the verbal repartee of signifying, loud-talking, and the dozens – can be positive expressions of an organic folk tradition. But "games" between black and white are altogether different. The triumphant black gamesman who outwits his white antagonist achieves a personal (psychological) victory without collective (political) consequences.

The various traditions of heroic game playing that I have been describing throughout these chapters have all been concerned with personal empowerment. But these traditions rest on an assumption that the victors can win whatever there is to be won in American society. Blacks and black writers have not been able to make this assumption. Barry Beckham's little known novel, *Runner Mack* (1972), makes this point most graphically in a surreal episode in which the black hero, ironically named Henry Adams, attempts to make a Major League baseball team. At his tryout the young black man is sent to the outfield to demonstrate his defensive abilities:

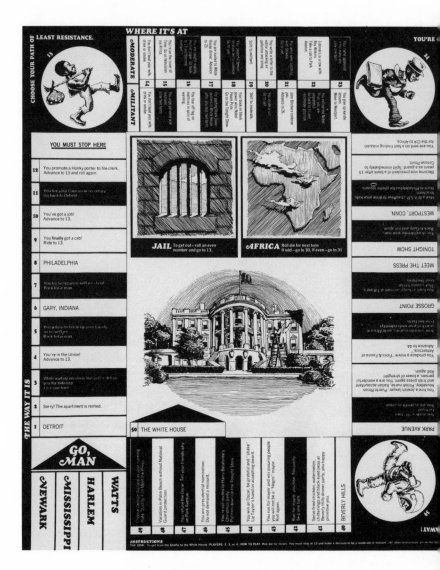

This 1968 board game, a parody of *Monopoly* and the numerous games of success that preceded it, but more intentionally a satire on American political realities, neatly illustrates a major theme in twentieth-century black fiction. Titled *50 EASY STEPS TO THE WHITE HOUSE: A GREAT NEW GAME for discriminating people of all races!*, the game board marks the route "To get from the Ghetto to the White House"; square 49, for example, says, "Choose George Wallace as your running mate. Justify it on Meet the Press." (Designed by Godfrey Cambridge and Robert Cenedella; produced and distributed by Robert Cenedella, Oggi Products, New York, NY. Courtesy of Robert Cenedella)

The first ball was a high, high accelerating fly, and Henry turned to go
back, finally reaching the wall. . . . He knew if he leaped he would still
be four or five feet too short, so he began furiously to scale the wall,
sticking his cleats into the wood – his glove had been thrown away for
the climb – and fingernails grabbing into the tiny cracks. He would slip
a foot and grab again, slip, grab some more, until he had reached the
top of the wall and could climb over it, climb over the metal railing.
Now he saw the ball sailing downward. There was one possibility, he
thought, and balanced himself on the railing, jumped in the air toward
the arc of the ball's flight, and cap in hand, stabbed at the ball. He felt
it break into the cap as he plummeted down toward the grass. Dazed
for an instant from the fall, he got up, raised the cap in his hand to
indicate that he had caught it.[39]

Baseball, the "national game," stands in Beckham's novel for the American Dream in its entirety. Despite exceptional skill and astonishing effort,
Henry of course fails to make the team.

Blacks' inability to win in white America leads to both the anger in
Richard Wright's *Native Son* (1940) and the ambiguous existentialism of
Ellison's *Invisible Man* (1952). Wright's rhetoric of game playing, though
elaborately worked out, is much more straightforward than Ellison's.
The numerous figures of the "game" in *Native Son* consistently point to
whites' absolute power and to their systematic control of the mechanisms
for achieving success. A campaign poster screaming at Bigger Thomas
in the opening pages, "IF YOU BREAK THE LAW YOU CAN'T
WIN," only hints at the insuperable obstacles to a black's winning in
white America. Bigger's game of playing white with his friends is a
parody of possibilities denied to black youths; the Ping-Pong tables do-
nated by the white slumlord symbolize not just the meaninglessness of
white philanthropy but also the pointlessness of black attempts to play
the whites' games. On the possibilities of getting rich, Bigger understands
that "it was all a game and white people knew how to play it." On the
self-serving actions of black leaders, Bigger tells his lawyer Boris Max
that "it's a game and they play it," while Bigger's "got nothing" with
which to play. The power of those who create and govern the game is
clear to Bigger: "They like God," he says of whites.[40]

Through such language Wright described the same conditions that
govern *The Sport of the Gods* and *If He Hollers Let Him Go,* but *Native
Son* insists on a terrible alternative to the impotent despair of Dunbar's
and Himes' protagonists. Having first attempted to conceive his killing
of Mary Dalton as an act that "evened the score" (140), then having seen
himself reduced to the helpless "sport" of his white world (169, 236,
237, 240, 266) – having decided, that is, to play the game, then discovering in doing so he can only be a toy of white games-masters – Bigger

finally renounces the game to embrace murder as literal, wholly non-symbolic self-creation. In a racist world, Wright's novel declares, the "games" of the masters must lead eventually to mutual destruction.

In thus rejecting metaphysics for politics, Wright took a position common to black writers. Not everyone has agreed that resistance is pointless, of course. "The spook who sat by the door" in Sam Greenlee's 1972 novel has a machine gun after all, and he intends to use it. This novel's black conspirators, many of them former athletes, speak of beating whitey at his own "game" – until the end, that is, when they realize that they are not "playing games" but waging war.[41] A telling moment in James Baldwin's *If Beale Street Could Talk* (1974) offers another slant on the metaphysics of game playing. The white man's "game" in Baldwin's novel is, as always, to keep the black man down. But after Fonny Hunt has endured the physical and mental tortures of an unjust imprisonment for several months, Fonny's faithful lover declares, "They beat him up but they didn't beat him."[42] When Hemingway wrote, "A man can be destroyed but not defeated," the passive voice names no opponent; it implies not a school of ravenous sharks but an impersonal cosmic force as the agent of destruction. Baldwin's active voice identifies a material agent if only by the pronoun "they"; blacks like Fonny are not assaulted by abstractions but by white people with their courts and their fists.

So too with Bigger Thomas. Wright's black Everyman is no Ahab or Santiago or Joe Christmas winning an ambiguous victory against the powers of the universe, but the nightmarish extension of racist logic. Boris Max, who seems at first to argue Wright's as well as Bigger's case, fails to understand his own argument. When Max tells Bigger, "You got to fight," his understanding of "fight" is shaped by an assumption that blacks have a chance to win by the rules of the whites' contest – even after he has himself eloquently pleaded that Bigger lives in a world without options. In court Max calls racism a "vicious game" (328). Bigger understands the pointlessness of the game as Max does not. Bigger indeed "fights," but violently rather than sportingly, against the game rather than within it. Bigger cannot win, but he needn't lose; he can kill and he can die.

Ellison's *Invisible Man* in effect seeks an alternative to Wright's apocalyptic vision but without simply romanticizing black self-creation. To be a black American, Ellison has written, is to have "a tragicomic attitude toward the universe."[43] Blacks' double-consciousness of themselves in a white world, as first described by W. E. B. DuBois in *The Souls of Black Folk* (1903), and then reiterated in well-known essays by Ellison and Baldwin, makes possible a heightened kind of seeing: an insight available only to those on society's margins. *Invisible Man* says that there are other kinds of double-consciousness in American race relations as well: blacks' attraction to normative white values that at times are in fact racially oppressive; blacks' perception of whites as godlike in power, monsterlike in their use of power, fool-like in their pursuits of power; whites' perception of blacks as social (or cultural or racial) inferiors yet also as projections of white fantasies, both romantic and nightmarish. All of these elements are present in the novel, and the "game" is one of their chief rhetorical signs.

Ellison in *Invisible Man* was more interested in metaphysics than Wright in *Native Son,* but in asking what a man is and how he is to live in his world, Ellison never ignored the fact that the man was black and his world was white. The "game" once again becomes a site of conflict between various possibilities. In one of the most explicitly ludic novels in American fiction, black or white, the richness of the sporting rhetoric threatens to overwhelm interpretation, but the lines of inquiry that we have been exploring can provide an entry into Ellison's masterpiece.

I would emphasize three primary sporting motifs in the novel. In the most frequent sporting image the invisible man is kept *running:* an echo of the liberal "game of life" that declares life subject to rational control and success available to whoever makes the necessary commitment. In Ellison's version, the invisible man does not *run* but is *kept running*: chasing chimerical dreams, pursuing the prizes in the game of life that the white world holds out to him but will never give him. Dutifully attempting to please first his town fathers, then Bledsoe and Emerson at the college, then his employers at Liberty Paints and the leaders of the Brotherhood, the invisible man in each case discovers that compliance brings no reward. In the most telling instance of the image, he senses at one point, "I seemed to run a foot race against myself." The invisible man nonetheless continues to run, despite disappointment and disillusionment; he runs until he falls into a sewer then finally understands enough to tell himself, "You've run enough, you're through with them at last."[44]

If the world is neither orderly nor fair; it requires an altogether different game. The novel's second ludic motif draws on both black folklore and the Anglo tradition of frontier gamesmanship for a response to the "vast and complicated game" that the invisible man first encounters at the Golden day, "a game whose goal was laughter and whose rules and subtleties I could never grasp" (57). This is the game of both Simon Suggs and Brer Rabbit, the game that takes chaos as the given and rewards imagination and wit. "Play the game, but play it your own way" (118), the mad vet doctor advises him on his bus ride north; although the opponent – "the white folks, authority, the gods, fate, circumstances" (118) – is all-powerful, wit can circumvent power. But the cynical gamesmanship of his grandfather, of Bledsoe, of Rinehart proves as futile as running after life's prizes. The signifying of Peter Wheatstraw, the verbal gamesmanship of black with black, indifferent to the politics of the larger society, establishes kinship and preserves a shared heritage. But earlier when Bledsoe explains how blacks survive in white America, the implications of black gamesmanship are altogether different: "I don't even insist that it was worth it, but now I'm here and I mean to stay – after you win the game, you take the prize and you keep it, protect it; there's nothing else to do" (111). As one critic of this scene has observed, the masking and manipulation by which Bledsoe wins his games "generate no new possibilities; the universe they describe is closed."[45] Such gamesmanship does not liberate but culminates in a riotous and bloody Feast of Fools in Harlem's streets, the tragic flipside of the chaotic celebration at the Golden Day earlier in the novel.

By renouncing both the "game of life" and the stratagems of gamesmanship, Ellison rejected two of the most potent traditions of the American success ethic. In each case, he insisted, winners win nothing. The third ludic motif reinforces this theme by challenging the ultimate symbol of black success in postwar popular culture. This image is announced in the prologue:

> Once I saw a prizefighter boxing a yokel. The fighter was swift and amazingly scientific. His body was one violent flow of rapid rhythmic action. He hit the yokel a hundred times while the yokel held up his arms in stunned surprise. But suddenly the yokel, rolling about in the gale of boxing gloves, struck one blow and knocked science, speed and footwork as cold as a well-digger's posterior. The smart money hit the canvas. The long shot got the nod. The yokel had simply stepped inside of his opponent's sense of time. (7)

The implications of this passage are not immediately obvious. One of the "invisible" black men in Ellison's novel is Joe Louis – not entirely invisible, actually, because he is mentioned twice, the second time at the height of the Harlem riot when "a huge woman in a gingham pinafore," riding a Borden's milk wagon and surrounded by railroad flares, drunkenly, laughingly sings this ditty:

> If it hadn't been for the referee
> Joe Louis woulda killed
> Jim Jefferie
> Free beer!!

We might take this as an instance of Ellison's conflating black American experience in order to contain its entire history within a single generation for the sake of his novel's structural unity. But if we take the passage literally, the singer's mistaking Joe Louis for Jack Johnson, the actual conqueror in 1910 of the "white hope" Jim Jeffries, reflects ironically on the theme of black triumph over white that is celebrated in the stanza. Behind Johnson's and Louis's victories lies the classic literary episode of black physical triumph: the thrashing of the Negro-breaker Covey in Frederick Douglass's autobiography, at the conclusion of which the young slave declares, "*I was a man* now."[46] Such mastery proved more elusive within the supposedly "fair" world of the twentieth-century prizefight ring and, as Ellison's novel insists, within American society. Johnson indeed beat Jeffries but was eventually hounded from the country and denied the customary rewards of the heavyweight championship. Moreover, in its celebration of black triumph the drunken woman's ditty reflects with near tragic irony on the riot in which she takes part: an uprising of the black underclass wholly contained within the black community, wholly inconsequential for the power arrangements in the larger society. The futility of playing the whites' game is reinforced in this scene by the images of Ras the Destroyer "riding like Earle Sand in the fifth at Jamaica" and his followers using baseball bats against policemen armed with guns.

But the dominant motif for this futile contest is boxing. Joe Louis is one of the invisible men in Ellison's novel because he is mentioned only twice but is pervasively present in the novel, always in ironic ways. Writing about race in the late-1940s, Ellison could not have used the image of a prizefighter without evoking for readers Joe Louis. Although the Brown Bomber's greatest victories against Max Schmeling and Billy Conn occurred before the war, following the armistice Louis continued to beat his "bums of the month" until he retired in 1949. Louis's victories in the thirties and forties were causes of celebration throughout black America, on rare occasions escalating into open violence. A riot by blacks in Durham, North Carolina, erupted after Louis first won the heavyweight title; more typically, blacks sitting by their radios, listening to their champion's demolishing of another, usually white, challenger, quietly exulted. Louis's victories symbolized the possibility that they too could win in the white man's world.[47] African-American novelists have added their own testimony to Louis's importance in the black community: Himes's *If He Hollers Let Him Go*, Ernest J. Gaines's *The Autobiography of Miss Jane Pittman* (1971), and Wideman's *Sent for You Yesterday*, for example, all include scenes of black pride fired by Joe Louis's victories. Ellison himself has written that Louis helped teach him how to be black and angry, and how to express his anger.[48]

The boxing images in *Invisible Man*, written during and immediately after the reign of an all-conquering black man, are particularly ironic, then. Suggesting the futility of boxing during an era in which a black man dominated the heavyweight division, Ellison undercut the major symbol of black triumph in white America. The yokel in the passage cited above could only be white; I know of no black from the athletic world described as a yokel, while that figure (also termed "rube" or "hick") is a commonplace in the lore of Anglo sport. To the sporting consciousness of the time, the yokel who, against all odds and justice, beats the man of speed and science, must be an ordinary white man whipping Joe Louis. The meaning is muted but nonetheless clear: Even the most potent of black men cannot win the white man's game.

This boxing motif is played out through the novel as a third futile game the invisible man attempts to play. When the contestants are black and white – Brother Tod Clifton, who "knows how to use his dukes" (331), versus a cop with a gun – black can only lose. When the contestants are both black, the result is *self*-destruction. The "battle royal," in which blindfolded black boys pummel each other for the amusement of their town's white leaders, prefigures several later scenes – the conflicts between college blacks and poor black farmers, between Lucius Brockway and the striking workers at the Liberty Paint Company, among blacks within the Brotherhood and between the blacks of the Brotherhood and the followers of Ras the Exhorter – in all of which the outcome cannot affect the distribution of power in the larger society. In another version, when Bledsoe tells the invisible man in the course of dismissing him from the school, "Your arms are too short to box with me, son" (111), this fundamental irony is compounded. Bledsoe echoes the preacher in James Weldon Johnson's *Autobiography of an Ex-Colored Man* (1912) who thunders to the narrator, "Young man, your arm's too short to box with God!"[49] Speaking in the voice of an invincible *white* "god," Bledsoe is ironically both oppressor and victim: master of the powerless student but blind to the inconsequence of his own circumscribed power as a black man in white America. For his part in this scene, the invisible man appears as a luckless but as yet uncomprehending Jacob in blackface, boxing with a "god" who lacks the power to "bless" him. Later, in yet another version of the boxing motif, when the invisible man enters a building with "a football-locker smell" to deliver his first speech for the Brotherhood, he sees a photograph "of a former prizefight champion, a popular fighter who had lost his sight in the ring" (252) – again, implicitly, an ironic undercutting of Joe Louis's triumphant image. This motif culminates in the wildly comic scene where the invisible man attempts to play Rinehart's game of deceit with Sybil, the white woman drunk on a racist fantasy of rape by a "big black bruiser." "She had me on the ropes," he says at one point in their sexual sparring; "I felt punch drunk, I couldn't deliver and I couldn't be angry either" (393). The tragicomedy of this scene is constructed with equal parts of slapstick and impotence.

Invisible Man rejects all of these games, then seemingly affirms a higher game. "It's 'winner take nothing,' " the protagonist comes to realize (in an explicit echo of Ernest Hemingway); "that is the great truth of our country or of any country. Life is to be lived, not controlled; and humanity is won by continuing to play in face of certain defeat" (435). But even here, Ellison's appropriation of a white literary tradition is not without its ironies. "Winner take nothing," Hemingway said, but the committed players in his fiction win the greatest prize of all: self-created human worth. To the last, Ellison was wary of such metaphysical confidence. In the novel's epilogue, from his underground womb the invisible man declares his imminent rebirth into the "infinite possibilities" of life above ground. But this optimism is complicated by Ellison's implicit view of history. The novel's structure – repetitions of a handful of themes, each restatement yielding more understanding – suggests the likelihood of additional variations rather than open-ended possibility. As numerous critics have noted, *Invisible Man* is in this sense a blues novel: the blues as based on a reiterated lament that is not resolved. Although the invisible man has been progressively stripped of illusions and false identities, there is no clear evidence that he is poised at the end of the novel for unencumbered self-creation. He is still playing a futile game, after all, stealing the electric company's light but not its power. Moreover, everything in the novel declares that personal empowerment cannot be achieved outside the social and political world. Ellison leaves his character poised between defeat and rebirth, his possibilities numerous but by no means infinite as he mistakenly believes, limited not just by his incomplete self-knowledge but by political realities. Ellison rejected Wright's apocalyptic vision, but as a black man with his own double-consciousness he could not simply embrace the color-blind existentialism of the Melvillean tradition.

I will return to the blues in a different context in Chapter 11; for now, Ellison's alternative to the Melvillean *agôn* is consistent with the white American tradition in a more fundamental way. From Butler to Melville, to London, to Hemingway and Faulkner, to Wright and Ellison, to Kosinski and Mailer, a common thread has run: Human fulfillment is not a matter of simply willing it. These writers, in all their diversity, have collectively maintained a philosophically or theologically conservative tradition standing in opposition to the game of life celebrated by ministers, businessmen, and novelists in the liberal mainstream. Black writers' chief contribution to this tradition has been a qualified "No" to those who more grandiloquently have said "No! in thunder": a sharp reminder that the problematic interplay of fate, chance, and will in human lives is grounded in history.

9

The "Great Games" of Politics and Business

Anyone who followed the news media and publishers' booklists in the 1980s would have recognized that the two contenders for the "great game" in the United States were politics and business. *Time* magazine ("the National Poet Laureate," as Robert Coover would have it in *The Public Burning*) ran sixteen covers during the decade with a caption or graphic representing a game. From "Ronnie's Romp! And Now the Real Race Is On" (March 10, 1980) to "Hell-Bent for Gold: The presidential pack races toward Super Tuesday" (February 29, 1988), ten of the sixteen concerned politics, either elections (six) or superpower strategies (four). Three of the remaining six illustrated the "games" of venture-capital investment, pricing airline tickets, and laundering money; the other three – featuring T. Boone Pickens, RJR Nabisco's F. Ross Johnson, and Donald Trump – announced stories about conspicuous players of financial games.[1]

Parallel lists of some recent nonfiction book titles offer similar impressions:

American Politics: Playing the Game	The Game of Business
Playing for Keeps in Washington	Winning the Money Game
Playing to Win	The Game-Players
Playing Politics	Playing the Game
The Presidential Game	The Takeover Game
The Power Game	Board Games
Hardball	Your Career Game

The titles on the left are all about politics, those on the right about business. While *Time,* by nearly a two-to-one margin, seemed to lean toward politics as the great American game, my own impression of the booklists (unsubstantiated by any statistical record) sees a tilt toward

322

business in the 1980s. Let's call it a toss-up. Of considerably greater
interest are the major differences between the two popular versions of
the great game, differences that reveal much about American percep-
tions of both politics and business. In the previous two chapters I traced
twentieth-century sporting motifs chiefly through literary texts; in the
final chapter of this section I want now to focus more closely on the rhetoric of popular journalism.

Let's begin with a passage from a book in each of the two columns
above. In his introduction to *Hardball: How Politics Is Played – Told by
One Who Knows the Game* (1988), Christopher Matthews, a journalist
and former speechwriter (for President Carter) and spokesman (for
Speaker of the House Tip O'Neill), describes the subject of his book:

> Lived to the hilt, a political career is a grand and exuberant experience.
> In the following pages you will enjoy some candid glimpses of how
> well-known figures achieved their ambitions. You will meet some un-
> likely success stories, people who learned the game, played hard and
> won.[2]

"Hardball," as it has been used to describe politics for about two decades,
is an interesting metaphor. Since the 1930s, baseball's dominant image
has been lyrical and pastoral. "Hardball," in contrast, is hard-boiled
baseball, no wimps or sissies (or, by implication, women) allowed. Consider now this very different description from *Your Career Game* (1987)
by Hap Vaughan, identified on the book's back cover as a "Manager for
Training for Corporate Facilities" at Texas Instruments:

> This game is not trivial. This game has rules. This game has tactics and
> strategies. Prizes can be won by all. Your prizes, your success, your
> winnings depend on your understanding the game – your tactics, your
> strategies, but mostly how effectively you use yourself during the
> workday.[3]

The first statement suggests that politics is a game played by the
shrewdest few and watched by the fascinated many – America's premier
spectator sport. Business, on the other hand, is a participatory sport, the
game of success played not just by CEO's but by everyone from the
mail clerk up. While the more heroic "games" of entrepreneurial geniuses
and takeover arts predominated in the media and books during the Reagan years, even the mightiest players of the game were presented as
models for the small investor or ambitious employee. Stakes in the two
games differed also. The game of politics played on the world's stage
has only one stake in Matthews's account: power. Not power to enact
any particular legislation or win support for any specific policy, but
power itself, power in effect for its own sake. The stake in the game of
business, in contrast, the career game that Vaughan outlined, is success

defined as a combination of satisfaction and pay, the twin elements of personal happiness.

Politics is a hard game, according to Matthews, its winners often not very admirable men; but even personally unlikable politicians like Lyndon Johnson and Richard Nixon convey "a Big Casino flavor to their lives that interests even the most disapproving observer" (17). Matthews's account of Washington politics is actually less cynical than he implies: "inside" anecdotes about political strategies that range from savvy, and by most standards ethically sound, actions to slick con games and worse. But the rhetorical packaging as a "game" – as "hardball" to be exact – renders such readerly distinctions irrelevant. The book's lessons apply to any political objective, however small or grandiose; *Hardball* is a book about the getting of power, not its uses. The political game has its rules, steeped in tradition, but these rules are entirely self-reflexive: They maintain the game for its own sake irrespective of any extra-game moral standard. In a revealing aside, while describing politicians' necessary distrust of the press, Matthews refers to John Dean as the man who "had sold out his President" in the Watergate affair. Although by some measures Dean might seem a hero for exposing Richard Nixon's crimes, in a world governed by the rules of sport Dean was no team player. In a popular political history of the seventies and eighties, John Dean would be a traitor, Ollie North a hero.

Whereas politics as *Hardball* describes it has both winners and losers, more of the latter in fact, every career in business can have a successful outcome. Vaughan's book has two themes: "You have personal potential greater than anything you have yet dreamed, and every person creates his or her own success or failure in a company" (v). Vaughan advised readers first of all to learn their companies' games, then design their own in relation to it. That the company's "game plan" might be wrongheaded, and the necessity of "playing" by it be objectionable or stifling, is never acknowledged. Any employee can develop a game plan for fully satisfying personal success within the framework of the company game. Employees are not in competition with each other for higher salaries and a limited number of management slots; at least in the middle or lower ranks "competition is not a significant career factor" (96). To approach one's career as a game makes it both "fun" and more productive (100–1); everyone wins.

As representative writers about their respective "games," Vaughan and Matthews revealed both continuity and change in the rhetorical traditions and their cultural implications that I have been tracing. In the 1980s, gamesmanship lay at the heart of both politics and business as popularly perceived, but with a crucial difference. Political gamesmanship was frankly amoral, although what caused outrage in 1900 was admired in 1988. Or better, not amoral but self-validating; winning the game was good in itself. As an object of criticism, the business games-man, in contrast, was usually described as someone who broke the rules (Ivan Boesky) or played only for greed (Nabisco's Johnson); but in its more typical celebratory form economic gamesmanship had be-come transcendent. The authority to which it appealed for validation was no longer aristocratic assumption or Christian doctrine but the en-trenched structure of the American success ethic – and to some degree the rhetorical tradition of "the game" itself. "The game," that is, evoked less any actual sport that Americans played than the long habit of celebrat-ing business as a "game." And whereas the stake in the game of politics was power, in the game of business it remained America's version of secular "salvation." In this chapter I want to sketch out a history of these rhetorical traditions in the twentieth century and pursue some of the consequences of continuing to perceive politics and business as "games."

The "game" of politics

During the 1988 presidential campaign, the major theme of the media's coverage was not the candidates' proposals but their "handlers' " orchestration of the election. Journalism at times became metajournalism: At the same time that the media were routinely manipulated by campaign strategists, the media's own commentators complained that their cov-erage was being manipulated. The emphasis on *selling* the president that began with the emergence of electoral advertising in the 1950s, and that seemingly reached a peak in the scripted perfection of Ronald Reagan's packaging in 1980 and 1984, became openly the key to political success in the Bush campaign.[4] In a story titled "It's the Year of the Handlers" following the first presidential debate between George Bush and Michael Dukakis, *Time* lamented that the campaign had become "a referendum on gamesmanship, not leadership" (oblivious to the fact that its own rendering of politics as a spectator sport contributed to the problem it deplored); and in an accompanying profile called Bush's campaign man-ager, James Baker, "Master of the Game."[5] Bush's media–created image as an outdoor sportsman, and his pointed use of locker-room language first as vice-presidential and then as presidential candidate, revealed his own or his strategists' awareness of the power of sporting rhetoric with voters. Kenneth Burke has written about "how the dominant group of a society tends to legitimize its power by linking it to a higher principle, through the appropriation of the sacred vocabulary of religion or other important social institutions."[6] As the popular media amply illustrate, political candidates in recent years have consciously attempted to appropriate the metaphors of sport and gamesmanship as the "sacred vocabulary" of the age.

The rhetoric is not new, only the more obvious calculation with which it is used. The language of gamesmanship has been tied to politics in America since the seventeenth century – a carry-over from British colloquialisms no doubt, but also most likely an adaptation to New World political instability. The earliest reference I have found is a contemporary account of Bacon's Rebellion in the 1680s describing how the rebel leader responded to learning that the governor had declared him a traitor: "This strange and unexpected news put him, and some with him shrodely [shrewdly] to there trumps, beleving that a few such deales, or shuffles (call them which you please) might quickly ring the cards, and game too, out of his hand." Another Virginian in 1697 used similar language to describe colonial politics in a letter to a friend:

> Your self will see what a hard Game we have to play[,] the contrary party which is our Opposers, having the best Cards and the trumps to boot especially the Honor. Yet would my Lord Fairfax there [in England], take his turn in Shuffling and Dealing the Cards and his Lordship with the rest see that we are not cheated in our game, I question not but we should gain the Sett, tho' the game is so far plaid.[7]

Such metaphors in colonial America could thrive more easily in the South than in New England, where gaming was more stigmatized as a theological as well as social vice. How extensive this language was in the South, I do not know, but it is clear that by the Jacksonian Era politics and poker had become thoroughly mixed in the popular imagination. Card-playing presidents from Washington to Jackson (then to Harding most conspicuously in the next century), contributed to this image; and the national capitol itself became famous/notorious as the country's gambling capitol. Politics became steeped in the language of "tricks" and "bluffs," "raises" and "calls." John Quincy Adams once called Henry Clay "a gamester in politics as well as cards." A senator from Texas in 1872, objecting on the floor to a call for adjournment after a legislative session not to his liking, declared that "I for one will sit here for the next month. . . . before [the liberal Republicans] shall thus go off with their stacked *deck,* if I may say so without cutting in and breaking their lead." The following year, in the debate over the state of constitutional government in Louisiana, this same Senator Flannagan accused a colleague of having submitted a bill "just as a gambler would an old greasy deck of cards and be ready to turn a jack with it at any time." At the beginning of the next century Teddy Roosevelt offered Americans a "square deal" then in the 1930s FDR proposed a new one. Warren G. Harding explained his nomination in 1920 by declaring, "We drew to a pair of deuces and filled" (in the 1930s, historian Mark Sullivan described Harry Daugherty's manipulation of Harding into the Republican nomination as "*The Game of Games*"). "Dark horse" candidates for years have "thrown their hats in the ring" (originally, to challenge a boxer). Officeholders since the nineteenth century have "stood pat," played their "ace in the hole, "fast shuffled" or "dealt from the bottom of the deck"; have "called bluffs" or had a "card up their sleeves." As early as 1923 a study of the American political system bore the title *The Great Game of Politics*.[8]

The ubiquitous metaphors of political gamesmanship in recent years, then, simply continued a long rhetorical tradition, and novelists have contributed to it as well. Many of the late nineteenth- and early twentieth-century novels of business discussed in Chapter 5 include scenes of political gamesmanship as an inevitable accompaniment to financial gamesmanship. Other muckraking fiction from this period – Will Payne's "The Chairman's Politics," Alfred Henry Lewis's *The Boss* (1903), and I. K. Friedman's *The Radical* (1907), for example – attend more exclusively to political "games." The Irish patriarch of Lewis's novel speaks in the common idiom when he explains to a stubbornly honest candidate for alderman:

> City Government is but a game; so's all government. Shure, it's as if you an' me were playing a game av ca-ards, this politics; your party is your hand, an' Tammany is my hand. In a game of ca-ards, which are ye loyal to, is it your hand or the game? Man, it's your hand av course! By the same token! I am loyal to Tammany Hall.[9]

Robert Penn Warren's Willie Stark in *All the King's Men* (1946) and Edwin O'Connor's Frank Skeffington in *The Last Hurrah* (1956) are later versions of the political boss as gamesman.

It would be difficult to say whether political sporting rhetoric has grown more pervasive in recent years or not, but the metacritical attention several writers are now paying to this rhetoric marks a newly heightened awareness. As a referential metaphor in both fiction and public discourse, the "game" of politics has long implied that politics is something *like* a sporting contest. As a *self*-referential metaphor in critical writing about politics, the "game" raises the question whether the relation has moved beyond metaphor, rhetoric become practice: whether politics sometimes becomes actually a game, its chief purpose winning for its own sake, while policy assumes minor importance.

Journalists have contributed to this rhetorical criticism. Of course, sporting metaphors in political reportage are often no more than stylistic flourishes. A case in point: In three recent volumes about arms-control negotiations by *Time* correspondent Strobe Talbott, *Endgame: The Inside*

D. C. Johnston, "A Foot-Race" (1824). (Print Collection Miriam & Ira D. Wallach Division of the New York Public Library, Astor, Lenox and Tilden Foundations)

Anonymous, "Set to Between Old Hickory and Bully Nick" (1834). (Courtesy, American Antiquarian Society)

The "game" of politics took many forms in the nineteenth century: a foot-race, a game of brag, a boxing match, even baseball.

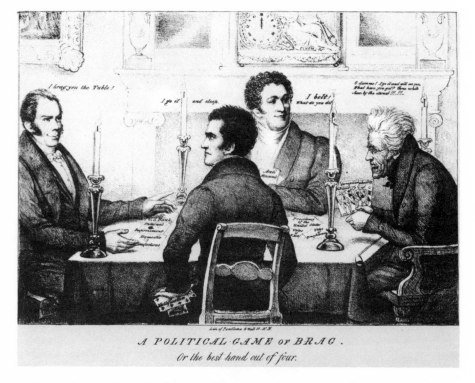

H. R. Robinson, "A Political Game of Brag. Or the Best Hand Out of Four" (1831). (Courtesy, American Antiquarian Society)

Currier & Ives, "The National Game. Three 'Outs' and One 'Run.' Abraham Winning the Ball" (1860). (Courtesy, American Antiquarian Society)

During the muckraking period in political journalism, the "game" appeared decidedly less sporting, as in this cartoon by E. W. Kemble in *Collier's* (December 9, 1905).

Story of Salt II (1979), *Deadly Gambits: The Reagan Administration and the Stalemate in Nuclear Arms Talks* (1984), and *The Master of the Game: Paul Nitze and the Nuclear Peace* (1988), the metaphors in the titles are not developed in the books' analyses. For the political journalist, sporting rhetoric can simply be part of the available idiom associated with the subject. But sometimes it's more than that. *Time*'s concern about the increasing importance of electoral gamesmanship moves closer toward a critique of the political "game" as *game*. And Hedrick Smith's *The Power Game* (1988), first a book that received considerable attention and then a four-part series on public television, moves closer yet. Smith introduced his argument with a series of propositions: that "Americans are a nation of game players"; that "some people treat life itself as a game, to be won or lost, instead of seeing it in terms of a religious ethic or of some overarching system of values"; and that "in Washington, senators and congressmen talk of politics as a game, and of themselves as 'players.' To be a player is to have power or influence on some issue." The crux of Smith's assessment of American politics lay in his claim that in Washington "substance" and "strategem" coexist in policy-making:

> Principles become intertwined with power plays. . . . Politicians are se-rious when they debate about Star Wars, arms control, a fair tax system, protectionism, and welfare reform. But they are no less serious when they devise gambits to throw the other team on the defensive, when they grandstand to milk a hot issue for public relations points and applause.

In short, although playing the "game" had not become a substitute for policy, according to Smith, it took place simultaneously with the making of policy, and thus affected the making. Politicians pursued the interests of "their home team," their constituents, but also "their highly personal interests in the inside power games – turf games, access games, career games, money games, blame games – each of which has an inner logic of its own that often diverts officeholders away from the singleminded pursuit of the best policy."[10]

Smith was critical of several of the ways in which the "game" was played without finally objecting to the fact it was a game. "The power game will never be tidy," he wrote on the last page; the changes he called for would enable the game to serve the commonweal more effectively. The assault on the "game" itself, on the very nature of power when conceived as the object in a game, has come most notably in recent years from women writers, both novelists and feminist intellectuals, particu-larly such rhetorically minded writers as Marilyn French and Mary Daly, who have been specifically concerned with the ways in which language embeds values and beliefs in culture. Sexual politics, rather than political practice in Washington, has been the chief subject of this critique, but the two have been related in feminist thinking. Although French's critical history of patriarchy, for example, is primarily concerned with the "games" by which men have oppressed women, *Beyond Power* (1985) also ties the fate of individual women to the fate of our world. French cited Hannah Arendt's earlier description of superpower rivalry as the latest version of Kipling's "Great Game": "the limitless pursuit of power after power that could roam and lay waste the whole globe with no certain national territorial purpose and hence with no predictable direction." The outcome, French like Arendt feared, might bear out Kipling's view in *Kim:* "When every one is dead the Great Game is finished. Not before."[11]

While this anxiety was implicit in much feminist writing about "games" in the 1970s and 1980s, the politics of personal relations received the major emphasis. In this context the diversity of nineteenth-century women's responses to masculine sporting rhetoric gave way to nearly unanimous rejection. The exceptions included a handful of popular writers of sexy self-help books who celebrated the "game" of love, and some popular romance fiction.[12] In novels with titles like *Playing the Game* and *Dating Games,* the connotations of "game" in Harlequin Romances and similar series can be either positive or negative. Sometimes the heroine learns the folly of her own game-playing, sometimes she cures the hero of this tendency, and sometimes she transforms brutal games of power into tender games of love.[13] The publishers of these novels, written to rigid formulas that are developed through extensive market research, have clearly not determined a consensus among their female audience about love "games."

Among "mainstream" women novelists, on the other hand, and more emphatically yet among feminist intellectuals, there was no division whatever. Sporting rhetoric rarely occupies the center of the fiction by women in the seventies and eighties *that came to seem a distinctive literary movement,* but in novels by Erica Jong, Gail Godwin, Joan Didion, Marge Piercy, Ann Beattie, Gloria Naylor, and several others – writers, that is, whose willingness to identify themselves as feminists, or even as "women novelists," varied considerably – the "game" consistently appears as a rhetorical sign of male oppression. (The major exception is Joyce Carol Oates, an exception to most generalizations about contemporary "women's fiction.").[14] Some of the more self-consciously feminist novelists, Alix Kates Shulman and Marilyn French most notably, subjected masculine sporting rhetoric to a more extensive critique. French's *The Women's Room* (1977) is the exemplary text, extremist yet representative in its indictment of patriarchy through a systematic denunciation of men's "games." In French's novel single women must play the "mating game," married couples the "snarky game" of cocktail-party flirtation. Mira, the central character, seemingly plays the larger game of gender roles successfully – winning a husband, children, clothes, a house; dinner at the club and golf when she wants them, housecleaning by choice not need ("Wasn't that winning?" she wonders aloud) – only to realize, when she learns of her husband's affair, that men make the rules and can change them whenever they want. Women who seem to win the game actually lose at life, because their living is second-hand. But winning is an illusion anyway: "Women lose, always, even extraordinary women."[15]

Appearing eight years after *The Women's Room,* French's *Beyond Power* elaborated her novel's themes into a feminist history of patriarchy from the beginning of human time. "What patriarchy has done," French wrote in a characteristic passage that is developed throughout the volume, "is turn many parts of life into games which interlock with each other (just as gambling, say, interlocks with certain sports) and declared winners those who achieve great wealth and/or power." The "game" is not a metaphor in French's reading of history but the very essence of patriarchal oppression. Patriarchy arose in prehistoric times when males decided they wanted power, leaving females "only two options – to abandon the relation entirely or to play the game." But once one partner has made power the basis of the relationship, whatever the other does "will be turned into part of a contest." Thus, willy-nilly, women have played men's game through the centuries because it has been, quite literally, the only game in town.[16]

Beyond Power appeared as the *Summa* of a radical critique of patriarchal power in which masculine sporting rhetoric was consistently denounced by some of the most prominent feminist writers of the 1970s and 1980s, including Kate Millett, Shulamith Firestone, and Germaine Greer, in similar terms. More self-consciously than Stowe and other nineteenth-century predecessors, feminists attacked both the "games" between men and women and the "games" women were forced to play with each other – women's "sexual competition" for "the prizes at stake in the marriage competition," as Mary Ryan put it.[17] What was only implicit in women's objections to the love game in the nineteenth century became explicit in the seventies and eighties: The object of the game was not pleasure but power; the love game was but the "great game" of politics as played between men and women. Several guides to corporate success for newly liberated women sought to teach their readers how to play men's "games," but they did so as if reluctantly, without the celebratory fervor of entrepreneurial prophets.[18] For radical feminists, on the other hand, to learn such games was itself destructive. In an appropriately titled feminist journal, *No More Fun and Games* (1968–71), Dana Densmore warned that women "willing to play by male rules" were "freaks in female bodies," seduced by the illusion that they will be given a chance to win.[19]

As the most rhetorically self-conscious radical American feminist, Mary Daly joined Marilyn French in pursuing most thoroughly the implications of a "game" of power. Seeking to reinvent English as a woman-centered language, Daly wrote prose that defies paraphrasing but that in its entirety asserts a rhetorical critique of those who in *Gyn/Ecology* (1978) she called the "gynocidal gamesters." This description of the "Patriarchal Pleasure Park" is typical:

> It is the place for the preservation of females who are the "fair game" of the father, that they may be served to these predatory Park Owners, and service them at their pleasure. Patriarchal Paradise is the arena of games, the place where the pleas of women are silenced, where the law is: Please the Patrons. Women who break through the imprisoning walls of the Playboys' Playground are entering the process which is our happening/happiness. This is Paradise beyond the boundaries of "paradise." Since our passage into this process requires making breaks in the walls, it means setting free the fair game, breaking the rules of the games, breaking the names of the games. Breaking through the foreground which is the Playboys' Playground means letting out the bunnies, the bitches, the beavers, the squirrels, the chicks, the pussycats, the cows, the nags, the foxy ladies, the old bats and biddies, so that they can at least begin naming themselves.

The "Fragmenters" preached: "Face the fact that this is a competitive world, in which there is a scarcity of commodities and a scarcity of ideas. Find your own niche and learn to play the game." Against this view of life as a zero-sum game, Daly joined French and numerous other feminists in insisting that women must create a new world beyond games.[20]

Whereas feminists such as Daly and French mounted the widest ranging and most sustained attack on masculine sporting rhetoric, Robert Coover's *The Public Burning* (1977) is the single postwar novel most deeply concerned with the narrower subject of political gamesmanship. Other male novelists, John A. Williams in *The Man Who Cried I Am* (1967) and John Updike in *The Coup* (1978), for example, wrote briefly on the subject: Williams' narrator despairs over the "Ultimate Game" of politics endlessly played with little concern for its real consequences; Updike's Colonel Elleloû speaks of African nations as pawns in a chess match played by the superpowers, "yawning over their brandy" as they pursue "a desultory end game."[21] But where Williams and Updike were brief, Coover was exhaustive; the primary subject of *The Public Burning* is the theatrical and rhetorical nature of American political power. In a literary and cultural history of American sporting rhetoric, *The Public Burning* must take a central place.

In chapters alternating between the voices of Vice President Richard Nixon and a third-person narrator, *The Public Burning* recreates the 1953 execution of Julius and Ethel Rosenberg, the "atomic spies" convicted of selling secrets to the Russians. But it does so from the perspective of the Nixon presidency and fall from grace a generation later, the period when Coover wrote the novel. That is, the Nixon who as vice president in *The Public Burning* speaks obsessively in the language of sport and poker seems closer to the Nixon who as president initiated the practice of telephoning the locker rooms of winning football and baseball teams, who diagrammed special plays for the edification of Washington Redskins' coach George Allen (and for the press and public, of course), and who most conspicuously appropriated the language of "team players" and "game plans" for his executive manner and image. Likewise, the surreal spectacle of electrocutions in Times Square, orchestrated by Cecil B. DeMille, presided over by Betty Crocker, and attended seemingly by all of the public figures of the day, owe more to the wild theater of later events like the 1968 Democratic Convention in Chicago than to the more constrained political hysteria of the Cold War. In more or less conflating the politics of the Cold War and the Vietnam eras, Coover's novel reveals a deep sense that political "sport" in America has had a long history.

Three voices dominate the novel. Nixon – part pratfalling buffoon, part hard-nosed pragmatist, part bumbling *naïf* – speaks incessantly in the idioms of football, baseball, golf, boxing, poker, and chess, a profusion and confusion of metaphors that comprises a political "philosophy" of pure gamesmanship. Besides Nixon, the novel's chief character is Uncle Sam, alternately the incarnation of the national spirit in American presidents and an actual character, part Superman, part "Sam Slick, that wily Yankee Peddler."[22] There actually seems to be more of the ringtailed roarer than the Yankee peddler in Uncle Sam; he speaks in the idiom not of Downeast drollery but of frontier con games and bare-knuckle brawling. And finally, the third-person narrative voice is a stream-of-consciousness flow of political slogans, popular platitudes, advertising jingles, newspapers headlines, scriptural and literary allusions, scatalogical slang: the full rhetorical life of the nation exaggerated and intensified.

The "game" of politics has three realms of meaning in *The Public Burning*. The first derives from Coover's awareness of sporting metaphors' simple presence in postwar political discourse: The novel overflows with references to a dizzying array of sports and games. The second emerges from the first and concerns the uses to which these metaphors are put: on the one hand, the rendering of global politics as a Manichean contest between the forces of darkness and light – the communist Phantom and Uncle Sam himself – with the fate of the planet at stake; on the other, the personal game of acquiring power and then holding it, in large part by convincing the public that the global contest with the Phantom is real and urgent.

The third level emerges in turn from the second: the "game" of making History by imposing pattern on randomness, among the most prominent of those patterns the rendering of the struggle between the Phantom and

Uncle Sam as a sporting contest. Reflecting on the Rosenbergs' trial at one point, Nixon wonders: "Strange the impact of History, the grip it had on us, yet it was nothing but words. Accidental accretions for the most part, leaving most of the story out. We have not yet begun to explore the true power of the Word, I thought. What if we broke all the rules, played games with the evidence, manipulated language itself, made History a partisan ally?" (136). A little later, while working a crossword puzzle (a game of words) in the back of a limousine chauffeured through the congestion of an anti-Rosenberg demonstration, Nixon describes the puzzle as "a kind of matrix, a field of play" (206). History, Coover's novel tells us, is just such a matrix of rhetorics: messianic and apocalyptic, accusatory and hopeful, desperate and boosterish, calculating and inspirational. The "history" of Cold War America is a rhetorical grid laid over events to create patterns, one of which is the pattern of the "game." Given the fact that *The Public Burning* itself is a rhetorical construction, whose subject is history as a rhetorical construction, reviewers who objected to the novel's supposed misuse of "real" history made assumptions about history that Coover did not share. His "history" of the United States in the 1950s, the novel argues, is no less "true" than the one written by journalists and scholars. *The Public Burning* is history about those who make history, not in the sense of performing important acts but in the sense of imposing pattern on events.

"I'm a rhetorician, not a general, and for me that's power," Nixon says (224). And again: "That was what language was for: to transcend the confusions, restore the spirit, recreate the society" (234). One of the politician's needs, as Kenneth Burke has pointed out, is to appropriate "sacred vocabularies." Nixon's and Uncle Sam's chief rival in the competition for sacred vocabularies is the Phantom, and His agents, the Rosenbergs. "The Rosenbergs were Brooklyn Dodger fans," Nixon muses at one point. "Or pretended to be. They talked about it in their letters. Of course, I understood the emotional and political motives, it was rhetorically sound, I'd used much the same techniques myself – but what was wrong with the Rosenbergs' appeal was that it was obvious they didn't know the first thing about baseball" (302). Nixon's evidence? The Rosenbergs loved the Dodgers for having broken the racial barrier when they signed Jackie Robinson. Nixon and Uncle Sam lay claim to the sacred rhetoric of baseball and other sports for altogether different purposes.

Early in the novel Nixon reports his first important meeting with Uncle Sam, a match at the Burning Tree Golf Club (the "Burning Bush," as Nixon thinks of the place where he received the Word). The subjects Uncle Sam teaches the future president on the golf course include "rules for the Community of God, the meaning of the sacred in modern society

and the source of the Phantom's magical strength, the uses of rhetoric
and ritual, and the hierology of free enterprise, football, renewal meetings, five-card stud, motion pictures, war, and the sales pitch" (83).
These are not separate subjects but aspects of a single political philosophy;
and although football and five-card stud are only part of the curriculum,
Coover's novel suggests they touch the center of political power. Uncle
Sam (in his incarnation as President Eisenhower) has discovered golf
only recently; before this

> he'd pretty much limited himself to hunting and fishing, riding, swim-
> ming, war, billiards, and the odd cockfight [the sporting recreations of
> presidents from Washington to Truman] – indeed, the very idea of
> Uncle Sam wasting his time playing idle games would have been un-
> thinkable fifty years ago. But such was the character of our twentieth-
> century revolution: gamesplaying was now the very pulse and purpose
> of the nation (89).

This is the understanding necessary to a career in politics; *The Public
Burning* describes Richard Nixon's political education in these truths.
Commitment ultimately exacts a higher price than mere understanding:
The novel concludes with a grotesque rape by which Uncle Sam incar-
nates himself in future president Richard Nixon.

In the interview from which I took the epigraph for my own book,
Coover discussed the importance of games in a skeptical age, without
belief in ontological meaning, as "a metaphor for a perception of the
way the world works." Those who are cynical manipulate the game for
what they can win from it; those who are not might "expose the game
plan" to reveal its capacity for exploitation.[23] Saying this shortly after
the publication of *The Public Burning,* Coover summed up both an important theme in his own novel and a fundamental strategy of his nov-
elistic practice.

The "game" of success

What *The Public Burning* is to postwar political rhetoric, William
Gaddis's *J R* (1975) is to the rhetoric of business. The novel that William
Gass has called "perhaps the supreme masterpiece of acoustical collage"
is comprised almost entirely of conversations, often interrupted or overheard in fragments, many of them related to the workings of corporate
finance.[24] Criticism of *J R* tends to discuss how financial transactions
function as metaphors representing Gaddis's views on art, love, disorder,
information systems, entropy, and representation itself. They also represent, parodically to be sure, financial transactions – the self-referential
operations of American business. The emblem for this view of finance
as a self-contained, self-justifying system could only be the "game."

JR Vansant, a runny-nosed, semi-articulate sixth grader with a fetish for mail-order catalogues, builds a financial empire without capital by buying and selling large and small businesses over the telephone. Although no one had heard of a "junk bond" in 1975, Gaddis anticipated the takeover mania of the 1980s. The creation of a hugely profitable corporate empire literally out of paper is no more bizarre in Gaddis's satire than on Wall Street a decade later. Perhaps an actual twelve-year-old with only a sixth-grade education and a telephone could not manage this feat in real corporate America; it might take a twenty-five-year-old with an M.B.A. and a computer. For JR Vansant the takeover game is just that, a game. As one critic has written, "Bombarded with the media's get-rich-quick-by-investing-in-America hype, JR takes it into his head to 'play the market' as he would play any other children's game."[25] But JR's "game" closely resembles the "real" financial world, where a corporate executive can talk of the corporate "team," with its subordinate linemen "running interference" for the managers "carrying the ball." "As long as you're in the game you may as well play to win," the executive tells school children on a field trip. JR takes the message to heart. "You can't just play to play," he later says in trying to explain his own business principles, "because the rules are only for if you're playing to win which that's the only rules there are." And again: "I mean where they said if you're playing anyway so you might as well play to win but I mean even when you win you have to keep playing."[26] Gaddis's point, of course, is not that the preadolescent entrepreneur garbles the wisdom of corporate finance, but that he understands too well its self-referential principles.

JR plays out the consequences of taking the business community's sporting rhetoric seriously. The paper with which he builds his financial empire is the play money of his game, yet also the real money of corporate capitalism, yet again only paper at last when his empire crumbles. Along the way he destroys other businesses, personal and corporate fortunes, even lives when he sells toy weapons to an African tribe that is destroyed by enemies with real guns. As Joel Dana Black has written, "The sixth-grade entrepreneur's paramount delusion is that he takes the game he plays to win in complete seriousness, but never with sufficient seriousness, because it always remains for him just a game." But in the end "JR is right: in terms of a conception of absolute truth, there is ultimately no difference between his operation and Wall Street's, between a game and an empire, between fiction and reality."[27]

A fundamental difference between *J R* and *The Public Burning* lies in the fact that despite their comparable rhetorical excessiveness, Coover's novel operates by inflation, Gaddis's by deflation. Coover took the observable fact of gamesmanship in political rhetoric and extrapolated outward to a metaphysics of history that ultimately lay behind it. Gaddis took a very different observable fact – the transcendent assumptions underlying the popular rhetoric of business and success – and punctured them as so many balloons full of . . . laughing gas? Gaddis's gargantuan parody is but a more exhaustive version of a common perspective among recent novelists of business. The "game" of business rhetoric has become so commonplace that it seems no longer capable of eliciting fascination, or even outrage, from serious novelists. But it nonetheless continues to carry a heavy load of cultural assumption.

During *J R's* long gestation following the publication of *The Recognitions* in 1955, Gaddis might well have encountered the 1968 bestseller by "Adam Smith" (George J. W. Goodman), *The Money Game,* the book that seems to have launched the most recent phase of sporting business rhetoric. "I think the market is both a game and a Game," Smith wrote, "i.e., both sport, frolic, fun, and play, and a subject for continuously measurable options." In a troubled time, when disenchantment with American capitalism was running high, Smith's playful exuberance might seem an odd rejoinder. To an embattled society locked in morally charged debate over not just the war in Southeast Asia but capitalism too, Smith offered perhaps surprising comfort: "If it is a game, then we can relieve ourselves of some of the heavy and possibly crippling emotions that individuals carry into investing, because in a game the winning of the stake is clearly defined. Anything else becomes irrelevant." In an ironic move, given the rhetorical traditions on which he drew, the author wanted freedom from "the compulsions of theology." The game, played for its own sake, offered that release. Eighty percent of investors, Smith claimed, were not out to make money:

> The irony is that this is a money game and money is the way we keep score. But the real object of the Game is not money, it is the playing of the Game itself. For the true players, you could take all the trophies away and substitute plastic beads or whales' teeth; as long as there is a way to keep score, they will play.

In denying "the compulsions of theology," Smith merely substituted an alternative religion as earlier writers had less openly done; but his was a religion of play, not work.[28]

Gaddis might also have encountered another best seller, Robert J. Ringer's *Winning Through Intimidation* (No. 1 in 1973, to *The Money Game's* No. 7 in 1968). Offered as a self-help guide for investors in real estate, *Winning Through Intimidation* was more truly an extraordinary "theology" for a cynical post-Vietnam, post-Watergate era. Ringer's place in the cultural history of sporting rhetoric is summed up in this passage describing his "Ice Ball Theory," the notion that it's "ridiculous to take myself too seriously because years from now it wouldn't make any difference anyway" (the sun will burn out, becoming a "frozen ice ball," in fifty billion years):

> It made me look at life as a big game and at business as a sort of huge poker game within that bigger game of life. I thought of the earth as a great poker table upon which the game of business is played, with only a fixed number of chips on the table. Each player gets to participate for an unknown period of time, and the name of the game is for him to see how many of the chips he can pile onto his stack. Of and by themselves, the chips, of course, are of no use to the player, but they *are* a means to an end; the rules of the bigger game of life provide for the exchange of these chips for those things that *help* to create the greatest amount of enjoyment in the player's remaining "thirty years" [a reference to his "Thirty Year Theory"]. You might ask, "If life is just a game, why play so hard to win?" To that I would answer, "Heck, if it *is* only a game, why *not* have some fun and try to win."[29]

If placed next to *Winning Through Intimidation,* is *J R* parody or realism? Ringer's book itself seems a parody of volumes like *The Money Game,* a deconstruction of America's competitive value system that exposes its underlying anarchy and amorality. But *Winning Through Intimidation* did not become a number-one best seller as a parody but as the straight goods. It is a book of its time, the period of disenchantment and withdrawal following the debacle in Vietnam, but it is also a disturbing commentary on the entire tradition in which it resides. In *The Book of Business* (1913), Elbert Hubbard seemed to anticipate Ringer when he wrote that "the habit of continually looking out for Number One is fatal to success."[30] Ringer's next book, after the extraordinary success of *Winning Through Intimidation,* was titled, without irony, *Looking Out for Number One.*

If Gaddis didn't encounter these particular books, he understood well the culture that produced them. Behind them lay most obviously the popular rhetoric of sporting business that since the 1920s had become a distinctive voice of the business community itself. As I noted in Chapter 4, nineteenth-century businessmen did not embrace the sporting rhetoric of the success prophets, and this silence continued into the new century. From its founding in 1913 through the First World War, *Nation's Business,* the monthly journal of the Chamber of Commerce, published no articles with sporting titles. But then in January 1919 appeared "Foreign Trade: The Game Is On" by the president of U.S. Steel, followed by a steady stream of others: "Team Work and Teeming Millions" on the "two-way game" of trading in Asia and South America (July 1920), "Team Play for Prosperity" (December 1923), "Let's Play But Play Our Own

Game" (November 1924), and numerous others. "Knute Rockne Talks Teamwork" (May 1928) discussed commerce, not football. The journal's publisher and editor, Merle Thorpe, contributed editorials on "The Sportsmanship of Business" (December 1928) and "For the Game's Ache" (December 1929), the latter a post-crash salute to the value of hard knocks whether in football or business. A poem by the dean of Boston University's college of business administration in the August 1924 issue gave a laureate's blessing to the official faith, declaring business "A game in which all may play; / Where every move must accord with the rules / And no one his fellow betray."[31] Rhetorical restraint among the spokesmen for business gave way entirely.

Behind *The Money Game* and *Winning Through Intimidation* also lay the many successors to nineteenth-century liberal ministers whose "game of life" had paralleled and complemented the more narrowly commercial game. A number of published sermons, "Playing the Game" (1924) by the dean of Yale's divinity school, "The Game of Life" (1934) by a minister of the social gospel, an entire collection under the title *Play the Game* (1937), used the familiar trope in familiar ways. The chief liberal successor to Horace Bushnell, Henry Ward Beecher, and Lyman Abbott was Harry Emerson Fosdick, whose sermons from the 1920s through the 1940s were widely disseminated over the radio, then in popular books. Pauline sporting metaphors are everywhere in Fosdick's sermons, which may mark the last time this rhetoric could be used to wrestle seriously with crucial issues of Christian living and belief. He drew on St. Paul's figure of the "race" of life to preach a gospel of reassurance but without equating spiritual with merely psychological health. A committed pacifist and social critic, Fosdick rejected the martial but not the agonistic in Christian spirituality. "Life is a difficult game," he insisted in a typical sermon. Living in a world that is afflicted with evil, men and women must understand that "the harder the game, the more strength, fortitude, intelligence and skill" are required. Fosdick even voiced the blasphemy of an earlier age when he declared "every man a gambler" who risks immortal life on the strength of his beliefs.[32]

Following Bushnell, Beecher, and Abbott, Fosdick in turn was followed by Norman Vincent Peale in a genealogy of liberal preachers on sporting salvation. But Peale's books owe more to the "therapeutic ethos" of the mind-cure prophets than to Protestant theology. The interpenetration of theology and psychology that began in the 1890s, and that continued in such books as Florence Shinn's *The Game of Life* (1941), became complete by the 1950s. In an early sermon Fosdick specifically rejected psychologists' equation of "the well-adjusted life" with "salvation itself." Rather, Christians must be "maladjusted to the status quo," Fosdick insisted, at odds with the world's values.[33] A generation later, Peale removed all barriers between peace of mind and spiritual health. Couching his advice in the familiar language of "winning" and of turning "defeat to victory," Peale defined mankind's goal simply as "victorious living": "a happy, satisfying, and worthwhile life" achieved through belief in oneself and in the precepts of Christianity. In perhaps his most revealing phrase, Peale called on his readers to "win victories over defeat": a tautology that implies no competitor, no external obstacle; that simultaneously says nothing and is utterly reassuring.[34] As Donald Meyer has written about Peale's "positive thinking": "The image of the game amounted to Peale's final resolution of the problem of the 'hostility' of the world. It was not truly hostile since it was constructed according to fixed ground rules, and to find yourself in life, to be an identity, to stay alive all your life was simply to give yourself to the rules." "Cheap grace," the theologian Dietrich von Bonhoeffer called it.[35]

Peale-ite books in the 1950s included Floyd Van Keuren's *The Game of Living* (1953), A. L. Hendrickson's *Playing the Game* (1954), and Russell V. DeLong and Mendell Taylor's *The Game of Life* (1954), all of which preached a similar feel-good philosophy through which self-help psychology became truly the liberal theology of the age.[36] Appropriately, if perhaps ironically, the 1950s also marks a major crisis in the "faith" that underlay all these "games" of secular/spiritual/psychological salvation. After the Depression muffled the 1920s' exuberant trumpeting of the game of business, the resurgence of prosperity following the Second World War was not accompanied by untroubled faith in the traditional success ethic. David Riesman's distinction between inner- and other-directed individuals, C. Wright Mill's announcement of "the decline of the free entrepreneur and the rise of the dependent employee," William H. Whyte's identification of the representative American as an "organization man" – a cipher within the bureaucratic structure with scant resemblance to the heroic individualists of the past – all proclaimed a crisis in American capitalism.[37] These much-read intellectuals of the 1950s called attention to a process that had been underway since the 1890s, but which an epoch-ending world war made particularly apparent. The increasing organization and bureaucratization of industrial capitalism had replaced the heroically individualistic entrepreneur with a myriad of mere managers and employees. *Fortune* magazine announced that "the Tycoon is dead"; sociologist Max Lerner termed the shift "The Decline of the Titan."[38] Moreover, within bureaucratic corporate organization, necessary competition among peers for advancement created a new source of anxiety (the "rat race"), and the control of markets by a handful of large corporations induced a fear that no real competition of the traditional sort existed in the factory or marketplace. Whatever competition did exist appeared in advertising, not in pricing or quality. At the beginning of the century muckrakers such as Upton Sinclair worried about the losers in the game; now there emerged increasing anxiety about the unfulfilled winners.

Popular post-World War II fiction can open a window into the anxieties of the age, in part through the novelists' handling of traditional sporting rhetoric. Novelists of the previous generation, including Abraham Cahan, Sinclair Lewis, John Dos Passos, and Nathanael West, tended to reject or ridicule the popular idioms of business "games," as William Gaddis's generation would later do. Lewis's *Babbitt* (1922) in particular stamped the businessman with a label that he did not easily lose: In Lewis's satiric portrait, "playing the game" is the rhetoric of mindless boosterism – of babbittry.[39] But in the 1950s, the sportive businessman became the central figure in a number of searching and earnestly troubled novels. Seriousness returned to business fiction, but a dramatically different seriousness from the fiction of the Progressive Era. Such writers as J. P. Marquand, Sloan Wilson, Cameron Hawley, John Steinbeck, and Louis Auchincloss created no foolish babbitts but anxiety-ridden businessmen for whom the boosterish faith of *Nation's Business* in the 1920s had vanished. Ayn Rand expressed the age's uncertainty in a different way: Her celebration in *Atlas Shrugged* (1957) of those who play "for the biggest stakes in the world" was meant to denounce equally an industrial order dominated by the weak who are unwilling to play and the "looters" whose "game" aimed too low.[40]

Most of the postwar novelists revealed considerably more anxiety than defiance. Marquand in *Point of No Return* (1949) and *Sincerely, Willis Wayde* (1955) created protagonists who are betrayed by their belief in the old rhetoric of business as "the contest for life's prizes" and "the most fascinating game of the world" – empty slogans, these men discover, when they try to apply them to the real world.[41] The "game" in Steinbeck's *The Winter of Our Discontent* (1961) and Auchincloss's *The Embezzler* (1961) is immoral or amoral, but its players are more akin to the pathetic villains of Gilded Age fiction than the gambling titans of the Progressive Era.[42] In different ways these writers found in business a common theme: the disappearance of moral heroism from the contemporary world.

Sloan Wilson's *The Man in the Gray Flannel Suit* and Cameron Hawley's *Cash McCall*, both published in 1955, are the era's exemplary texts in placing the "game" at the center of the issues raised by Riesman, Mills, and Whyte about the emerging postindustrial society. Both novels reassured readers that the apparently radical changes in American life had not invalidated traditional values: that playing the game still offered rewards. But they arrived at this affirmation only after chronicling their heroes' painful struggles. For Tom Rath of *The Man in the Gray Flannel*

Suit, the glorious "race of life" has become merely the "rat race." Although Rath wants the American Dream – wealth, position, power, security – he does not want to sacrifice his family and his personal happiness to its pursuit. He feels the pull of the older Protestant ethic, which tells him, "A man's work should be his pleasure." But there is a new ethic in America in the 1950s, a leisure ethic described by Riesman, Whyte, Mills, and others that insisted work and play were separate, and one worked in order to have time to play. Tom wants balance, or "a sense of proportion," not the all-consuming involvement of the heroic entrepreneur. He also wants to get ahead, but without becoming a "cheap cynical yes-man," an organizational player of the game. *The Man in the Gray Flannel Suit* reconciles these conflicts in a manner that guaranteed its popularity: It lets Tom Rath have everything he wants. When Tom's workaholic boss adopts the younger man as a surrogate son, he accommodates Tom's corporate advancement to his desires for a rich life outside the office. In addition, when Tom wins a rezoning fight in his community, he is freed to develop twenty-three acres of inherited ocean-view property into a housing project that will make him wealthy. By the novel's end he has resisted becoming merely another man in a gray flannel suit without sacrificing any of the rewards for which such men rushed about in "a frantic parade to nowhere." The option of not playing the game had offered a solution to Gilded Age critics of business practices. Sloan Wilson's message was even more reassuring: One could refuse to join the rat race but win the game anyway.[43]

Although *The Man in the Gray Flannel Suit* came to define the 1950s as Twain and Warner's *Gilded Age* did the 1870s, Cameron Hawley's *Cash McCall* is the postwar period's central text for my cultural history of the business "game." Himself a former corporate executive, Hawley addressed the age's anxieties in a very different way from Wilson's: through a rejuvenated nineteenth-century fantasy of heroic game playing that accommodated individual entrepreneurship to the common good. *Cash McCall* celebrates venture capitalism but in a strikingly defensive way – that tension suggesting the mood Hawley apparently assumed in readers. Cash McCall lives to make money: buying and selling businesses, indifferent to whatever products they manufacture or men they employ. And in defiance of the national conscience that seems to think the rich should feel guilty, Cash *enjoys* making money, not for the money's sake but for the sport of it. As he tells an associate: "It's like trout fishing, Gil. It's easy enough to make money – like catching trout with worms – but once you've graduated to dry flies you lose your taste for worm fishing."[44] In a characteristic speech Cash explains why he's untroubled by tax laws that make his money-getting so easy: "I don't make the rules, Gil. I only play the game. I never thought much of the kick-for-point after touchdown, either, but as it's in the rule book, that's the way the game is played." Even with a change in the tax laws, "it'll still be essentially the same game" (164–5).

Were this a muckraker's novel in the Progressive Era, Cash would be exposing here the moral bankruptcy for which he would be punished by novel's end. But Cash McCall is no corrupt Croesus. He wheels and deals in a series of barely legal transactions, governed by a familiar code higher than law: a principle that leads him to pass up any deal that seems "*unsporting*" to him (229). But the novel turns out to be no simple fantasy of sportive heroism. When he buys a small company owned by his lover's father, Cash faces the same moral crisis that many writers at the turn of the century explored in the conflict between woman/home and game. Hawley's very different resolution of the crisis is revealing. As the game becomes more personal, and Cash becomes more aware of the other players in it, he feels driven to defend the system of which he is a part. "*The very foundation of our life is what we call free enterprise,*" he tells his fiancée Lory Austen (Hawley's italics suggesting an acute sense of urgency). "*But now we've come to regard money-getting as a secret vice indulged in by all but never mentioned in the best society*" (427). Despite his absolute assurance that he has acted honorably in beating Lory's less scrupulous father on a deal, Cash is willing to give the company back, out of love for Lory. And for the first time he questions his most basic assumptions. "If there's something wrong with making money," he tells her, "there's something wrong with our whole way of life." The "game" itself is on trial:

> I've kept on telling myself that I was just playing a game. . . . But it isn't a game. It can't be. How can you play a game if you don't know the rules – if there aren't any rules? And what's the point of the game if you can't win – if you have to keep telling yourself that it isn't the winning that matters? (440–1).

Here is American capitalism at crisis in 1955, driven to doubt its professed commitment to open competition and victory to the better man. But unlike in the typical story a half-century earlier, the faithful woman now steps forward not to reassert traditional Christian (antibusiness) values but to restore Cash McCall's faith in his game. "It does matter!" Lory tells Cash. Others depend on him. Not just the big players he deals with but all the little people are affected, the workers for the companies that are bought and sold. Whatever the outcome for the big players, all these others are winners. They have jobs. "I've been so wrapped up in playing the game," Cash tells Lory after hearing her out, "that I never took time enough to figure out where the goal line was – what it meant to win – or even *how* you won" (443). The solution lies, then, not in giving up the game but in realizing that so many others benefit. "When you win," Lory tells him, "they win." And more reassuring yet: "And sometimes even when you don't." Contrary to the muckrakers' claim that the big players win at the little people's expense, Hawley assured readers that the big players alone risk victory and defeat. Whoever wins the deal, the little people win regardless; they continue to work no matter who owns the factory. The crisis of confidence in the capitalist system derives not from the game but from the players' insufficient faith in it.

In restoring the element of transcendence to the business novel, missing since the age of Norris and London, *Cash McCall* is at the same time one of the most enthusiastic and one of the most defensive paeans to sporting business in American fiction. The two impulses are strangely consistent, of course, and particularly revealing about a pervasive mood in the 1950s. In using the word "faith" to describe Hawley's message, I also wish to emphasize the continuing connection between the secular "game" of business and the spiritual "game of life," and their conjunction in the therapeutic "game" of personal fulfillment. Politics may have been the "great game" of those in power, but the business of America continued to be business, and the "game" of business – whether the business of Wall Street or the business of positive thinking – continued to be the path toward "salvation."

The resurgence of this faith in the 1980s, following the apostasy of the sixties and the "malaise" of the seventies, is one of the striking facts of our most recent history. Distinguishing separate decades in this way obscures their continuity, but it does provide a useful context for considering significant changes in the popular perception of capitalism's most fundamental "game." The "game" of spiritual striving has been wholly subsumed by the heirs of Norman Vincent Peale, the "I'm OK, You're OK" school of pop psychologists with their stream of self-help best sellers. Transactional analysis (for example, the popular text *Born to Win* [1971]), Abraham Maslow's concepts of self-actualization and "peak performance," and pop-psych programs like the Erhard Seminars Training (as celebrated by Carl Frederick in *EST – Playing the Game the New Way* [1976]) offer several versions of the same "game" of self-fulfillment.[45] As a perfect paradigm for this game I would nominate a little known contribution to this genre, William G. Nickels's *Win the Happiness Game* (1981). Endorsed by Peale and written by a veteran of *EST*, Lifespring, Insight, and an amazing number of similar programs, *Win the Happiness Game* offers readers a prescription for achieving "the 'no-lose' goal of happiness." The game's objectives are self-knowledge, self-satisfaction, and contentment with life as it is. The book invites readers to sign a "Happiness Contract" at the outset, offers them five rules to govern the game, teaches them warm-up exercises and "happiness skills" and methods for selecting partners in the game, and encourages them to tally their own progress on score cards at the end of each chapter. Most wonderfully, the dust jacket folds out to reveal a gameboard: a "morphology of conversion" that completes the transformation of William Perkins's original nearly four centuries earlier.[46] Nickels's teleological tone in the absence of any mention of God reveals both the complete secularization of "spiritual" success and the clinging to habits of thought rooted in religious traditions. The vagueness about "the game" and its elements that appeared to some degree in earlier writings is fully realized now, making it adaptable to any desire. "Happiness" is the goal, but each player decides what will make him or her happy. The earlier hard race that many would run but not all win has yielded to an easy game winnable by all, requiring no resources but those that every person naturally possesses. This is a feel-good, warm-fuzzy game of life, a generic game of life to go with the generic consumer goods on store shelves, a game for people who live by the code of "Have a good day."

Nickels's "happiness game," Adam Smith's "money game," Hap Vaughan's "career game," and Robert Ringer's real estate "game" shared common assumptions. The amorality of the game and its potential for anarchy have always hovered about the very idea of a *game* of life or business; these writers simply defined the opponents, rules, and stakes in different ways. From Thayer and Marden to Ringer and Nickels, one also sees the shift from producer to consumer virtues as the keys to winning the game. While mastery or power is the object early and late, it is defined in different terms and in different contexts: from punctuality, industry, thrift, deferred gratification, and so on – virtues for mastering one's fate in the public arena; to accumulation, self-satisfaction, self-confidence, present enjoyment – virtues for mastering one's self in solitude. Zebediah Flint's "game" of fiscal management pointed in this direction in 1918. But even that most crassly financial version of the game emphasized a goal of *modest* prosperity and portrayed wise investment in a social context: a partnership between lawyer-mentor and client, a common enterprise shared by numerous investors small and large, an economic order beneficial to everyone of merit. Although Nickels acknowledged the importance of personal relationships – of playing for others as well as self – his social model emphasized individual autonomy respectful of others' autonomy. Relationships were to be more like contracts than personal commitments. Vaughan explained intracorporate relationships in terms of strategies for advancement; Ringer more simply declared everyone else an opponent to be beaten if you can. "The game" always concerned *individual* "salvation" but traditionally implied social benefit as well. Whereas the idea is only implicit in Vaughan's and

The dusk jacket of William Nickels's *Win the Happiness Game* could be turned over to reveal this game board, illustrating the author's prescription for happiness. (Reprinted with the permission of Acropolis Books, Ltd., Washington, D.C. 20009)

Nickels's books, Ringer unapologetically declared the solipsistic nature of success/"salvation" when conceived as a "game."

What these changes might reveal about "late capitalism" as an economic system is less clear than what they reveal about idealized middle-class conceptions of life in America. The most recent effusions about sporting entrepreneurship in the 1980s also reveal less about a shift in the way America did business under Ronald Reagan than about Americans' continued longing to believe in the possibilities of self-generated transcendent success. The latest version of the popular faith was radically different from the nineteenth-century's success ethic that it rhetorically echoed. I would single out three principles that were heresy to the earlier generation: the emphasis on play itself (as in *The Money Game*), the celebration of a now-transcendent ethic of gamesmanship (Michael Maccoby's *The Gamesman*, 1976, is an exemplary text), and a recognition of risk and chance as central to the game.[47]

Amidst the numbing profusion of paeans and guides to sporting entrepreneurship in the 1980s, at whose number the list of titles at the beginning of this chapter barely hints, the emergence of an actual "theology of capitalism" based on these principles is most notable. The high priest was George Gilder, whose *Wealth and Poverty* (1981) became holy scripture in the early Reagan years. Gilder set out to reclaim "the high adventure and redemptive morality of capitalism" – both its play spirit and its religious grounding – in order to restore the entrepreneurial spirit from low repute and bureaucratic smothering, and to reassert the entrepreneur's reality from claims of his disappearance. For too long, Gilder insisted, the country had groaned under the burdens of a most unplayful welfare state; what was needed was no new sociopolitical wisdom but renewed faith in the old (echoes of *Cash McCall*). He reclaimed the spirit of capitalism, however, on terms that nineteenth-century capitalists would have found abhorrent. For Gilder, the entrepreneurial spirit was rooted in *chance,* that *bête noir* of the Carnegies and Mardens. "Lottery is a paramount fact of life," Gilder wrote in *Wealth and Poverty,* "from the moment of biological conception from among millions of sperm. We all begin – in the very DNA . . . of our individual existences – as winners of a sweepstakes against astronomical odds." Gilder moved from that irrefutable point to proclaim a lottery as *natural* to the social, political, and economic realms as well, with capitalism as the system through which providence works its will. Capitalism refuses to interfere with "the real and continuing lotteries of lower-class life" by raising the biological losers to equality with winners. "Capitalism succeeds," Gilder insisted, "because it accommodates chance and thus accords with the reality of the human situation in a fundamentally incomprehensible, but nonetheless providential, universe." To the nineteenth century, the notion of chance threatened the very fact of Providence; to George Gilder in 1981, it was only through chance that providence could work. Gilder argued that "the movement of chance toward order and truth is not assured in any one lifetime. The odds are against each individual in the serial lotteries of his own life. Chance cannot be shown to work except in the long run of the human adventure." What Americans needed, by Gilder's doctrine, was a millenial faith so strong that the miseries of the poor could not shake it.[48]

Gilder's version of life's lottery was echoed by other conservative and neoconservative theorists in the Reagan years. The economists Milton and Rose Friedman explained in *Free to Choose* (1980) how chance compensated for inequality of talents to create true fairness in life. Theologian Michael Novak, in what he explicitly called a theology of democratic capitalism, quoted Thomas Aquinas himself on this matter: "It would be contrary to the meaning of Providence, and to the perfection of things, if there were no chance events." Sociologist Peter Berger added yet another voice, describing life's lottery – what he termed "the relation of the wheel of fortune to the ladder of success" – as the guarantor of material progress and class mobility under democratic capitalism. Most important in Berger's view, the system was fair: "Anyone can throw *some* dice." Moreover, most Americans, Berger insisted, believe "that the present class system does not, *grosso modo,* violate their standards of fair play."[49]

The conversatives' lottery deftly collapsed the lottery of the gene pool and the lottery of social circumstances into a single principle whereby not just intellectual capacity but the unequal opportunities due to gender, race, and class became as natural as red hair or blue eyes – a convenient notion, one needs little cynicism to recognize, for the privileged white males who wrote these books. The entrepreneurial ethos of the 1980s announced not the overturning of the Protestant ethic but its reconstitution for postindustrial America. The celebration of corporate gamesmanship, the rule of chance, and the notion of playing the game for its own sake reflected a world much changed over a century. It was a more precarious world, a world of greater risks and fewer certainties, a world whose hold on moral or ethical principles was tenuous at best. In declaring life a lottery, Gilder proclaimed what was unspeakable among the prophets of the game as recently as the 1950s: The fairness of the game required that most not win, that there be losers as well as winners due to chance and unequal talents. The potential cynicism in this hard nut of conservative thought was nowhere more apparent than in Ringer's *Winning Through Intimidation.*

The popularized "game" of business in the 1980s, for which writers like Gilder provided the underlying "theology," was dominated in the public arena by two figures. On one side stood the entrepreneur, the latest avatar of the sporting businessman: the player of the game for the sheer pleasure of playing as described by "Adam Smith," the gamesman described by Maccoby and Ringer, the gambler described by Gilder. The key to his success lay in his willingness to take risks: not the tortoise of the Mardens and Thayers but an inventive, daring hare. As Carter Henderson described him in *Winners: The Successful Strategies Entrepreneurs Use to Build New Businesses* (1985), the entrepreneur plays "The Greatest Game in Town," for which the author listed "Eight Steps to Riches" – from "conceptualizing your new product or service" to "breaking out into big-time sales and profits" – that are as vague and abstract as the first morphology of conversion developed four centuries ago.

Against the entrepreneur stood the corporate raider and risk arbitrager, or "arb" – the raider launching hostile takeovers, the arb speculating on the outcomes (the investment bankers and lawyers who were also key players in the "takeover game" did not capture the public imagination to a comparable degree). If Lee Iacocca was the hero of the age, T. Boone Pickens, Carl Icahn, and Ivan Boesky (before his inglorious fall) were its mysterious and romantic Robin Hoods. Pickens in particular cast himself in this role, claiming in his autobiography to represent the small shareholders against the self-serving CEOs in the corporations he raided. The raider was to the entrepreneur as the Titan of Norris or Dreiser had been to the more modest captain of industry: gargantuan excess of the age's business values. Nowhere was the spirit of the gambler more celebrated in the 1980s.

Like cornering the market in Progressive Era novels of finance, the "takeover game" became a central image for a highly controversial morality play.[50] Boosterish sporting rhetoric in the early 1980s gave way, increasingly after the insider-trading scandals of 1986–7 and the stock market crash on Black Monday in October 1987, to jeremiads about "casino capitalism." Ivan Boesky was profiled in the *Atlantic* in 1984 as "the biggest risk-taker in the dangerous game of risk arbitrage"; his subsequent downfall and its outward rippling led in the popular press to grave doubts about the takeover game he played.[51] The ironic fact that, in the supposed age of the entrepreneur, takeovers led to more corporate giantism was less troubling to critics than the more concrete economic consequences. Nineteen-eighty-five alone saw 3,000 mergers or takeovers worth 200 billion dollars. A 1.4 trillion dollar corporate debt load, much of it in "junk bonds" to finance such takeovers, raised ominous questions about the economic future. John Kenneth Galbraith caustically observed that "those engaged in the takeover game cite effusively the entrepreneurial spirit that inspires them and the economic and social good that flows therefrom. Such self-serving recitation of cliché should evoke only vulgar sounds."[52]

Even before the Boesky affair and Black Monday the game in the 1980s was never universally applauded. Rather, as in the Progressive Era and the 1950s, it provided one focus for debate about issues of fundamental importance to both the economy and the culture. Defenders of the "takeover game," for example, claimed that the takeover frenzy of the eighties would restore the competitiveness of American industry; critics saw it as a different kind of "game": wheeling and dealing with illusory assets (junk bonds) that will prove no more real than monopoly money when the inevitable recession hits. The actual wealth, in the meantime, will be safely deposited in the accounts of a handful of master gamesmen. Equally disturbing, under the protection of bankruptcy laws, takeover gamesmen whose corporate empires later crumbled emerged with their enormous personal fortunes intact. In an age that celebrated risk as economic salvation, these men risked everybody's money but their own. The entrepreneurial spirit of the 1980s was embodied not only in modern-day Fords and Carnegies but also in the "Mayflower Madam" with her whore house for the rich; in the sixteen-year-old "wonder boy" Barry Minkow, whose manner of building a bogus financial empire seems to have been uncannily anticipated by William Gaddis in *J R;* in drug lords; in Reagan appointees who parlayed public influence into private fortunes; in those both in and out of government who pillaged the Department of Housing and Urban Development and the nation's savings-and-loan institutions. Even traditionally staid investment bankers began playing what one Wall Street insider characterized as "Liar's Poker."[53] Despite the grave forebodings of many observers of these events, others predicted that what would emerge from the rubble of fallen corporations and financial institutions would be an economic order more vital than ever. Depending on one's perspective, the latest version of capitalism's great "game" seemed to reveal either the wonderful adaptability of American capitalism or a desperate endgame by a bankrupt system denying its own demise.

The economic consequences of the takeover game were indeed real and serious, if not easily predictable, but the public debate it generated also produced something independent of those consequences: a narrative of conflicting responses to shifting cultural values. The "game" of success, whether in business or in life, has always expressed not the way life is but the way the spokesmen for middle-class culture have proclaimed or wished it to be. In this context the changes are most revealing. The 1980s cult of entrepreneurship rested on the dream of sudden wealth: the spectacular success of the computer whiz, a millionaire, even billionaire, at age twenty-five. The nineteenth-century success ethic, on the other hand, distrusted sudden wealth because it emphasized ends over means. The modest prosperity or "competence" earned over time was much preferred, its champions emphasizing the moral lessons learned through the gaining of it. The new emphasis on play, gamesmanship, and chance also signified a loss of faith in progress, a world without absolutes, and a repressed uneasiness over the intransigence of inequality. Perhaps most revealing of all, whereas the Progressive Era's success ethic celebrated an economic system that guaranteed personal fulfillment for those who played the game well, the cult of entrepreneurial gamesmanship in the 1980s defined a hero who transcended the constrictions of an oppressively organized and bureaucratic economy. For all their boosterish rhetoric, that is, the latest prophets of "the game" actually revealed little faith in the way the economic order currently operated. Their faith lay either in the opportunities for amassing personal wealth or in the possibility of revitalizing a moribund economy through a new commitment to supposedly traditional values that were not traditional at all. From Andrew Carnegie to T. Boone Pickens the dream of success became utterly transformed, but the metaphor of the game continued to offer rhetorical reassurance in the face of the times' most troubling dilemmas.

Novelists engaged themselves little with capitalism's latest crisis. The sporting rhetoric that fired the self-conscious imaginations of serious novelists in the Progressive Era and at midcentury elicited only satire or burlesque in such novels as Stanley Elkin's *The Franchiser* (1976) and George Lee Walker's *The Chronicles of Doodaw* (1985). Most striking, I am aware of no recent popular novel that is comparable to *Cash McCall* in reaffirming a hard-won faith in sporting entrepreneurship. Arthur Hailey's *The Moneychangers* (1975) offers high-risk game playing as heroic adventure; Paul Eerdman's *The Crash of '79* (1976) counters with an apocalyptic vision of the ruin brought about by financial gamesmen. The corporate gameswoman in Sidney Sheldon's *The Master of the Game* (1982), an unfulfilled but all-successful monster, resembles in some ways a comparable figure from the Progressive Era; but the banality of Sheldon's worn-out plot, developed in numbing prose, falls short of any serious examination of the "games" she plays. Somewhere in the literary space between Sidney Sheldon and William Gaddis, Louis Auchincloss might seem a possible heir to Sloan Wilson and Cameron Hawley. But the gamesman lawyer in *The Diary of a Yuppie* (1986) is simply an exploiter out of the muckrakers' school. In Tom Wolfe's *The Bonfire of the Vanities* (1987), sporting rhetoric has an incidental place at most in his rendering of bond selling on Wall Street; in Joseph Heller's *Something Happened* (1974), none at all. In not one of these recent novels does the metaphor of the game generate a complex examination of the issues at the heart of public discourse in the 1980s.

The absence of a *Cash McCall* of the 1980s itself says something about this moment in our capitalist culture. While the "game" always embodied cultural conflict rather than consensus, the nature of dissent has changed. With the ambiguously exploitative but fascinating financial Titan, turn-of-the-century business novels expressed a profound cultural ambivalence. Similarly, uncertainty was the taking-off point for midcentury popular business novelists, a collective sense of material abundance but anxiety about the spiritual impoverishment that seemed to accompany it. The polar certainties, in contrast, that mark the most recent novels of business, as well as the public discourse about entrepreneurial and takeover games, reveal deeper divisions in middle-class American culture than ever before. As Ronald Reagan's "economic recovery" was achieved at the cost of mind-boggling indebtedness and a widening rift between rich and poor, white and black, earlier generations' ambivalence gave way to shrill affirmation and denial.

At the beginning of 1988, just three years after declaring 1984 "The Year of the Yuppie," *Newsweek* magazine announced that "The 80s Are Over" and "Greed Goes Out of Style."[54] The editors apparently forgot to tell RJR Nabisco's CEO, F. Ross Johnson, whose attempt to take over his own company for enormous profit shocked a great many people both within and without the financial community. Actually, Johnson's ultimately unsuccessful move followed the logic of the "game," whose object has always been individual, not collective, reward. And in gaining for himself fifty-three million dollars by losing, Johnson added a new, deeply ironic wrinkle to the conventional faith that everyone wins just by playing. *Newsweek*'s obituary for greed, of course, was intended to suggest narrative closure for a decade, and for the presidency of the man who presided over it: the kind of pop history that offers a comforting sense of order to readers who might feel lost in the chaos of the everyday. The death of greed was no more real than the birth of the Yuppie three years earlier; the greedy, like the poor, have always been with us. But in raising up, then dismantling, a cultural symbol of acquisitive hedonism, the media did dramatize a questioning of values that touched many more people in the 1980s than the few who had to choose between buying a new BMW and endowing a shelter for the homeless. The rise and fall of the Yuppie and inside trader in the mass media marked the latest act in a long-running morality play, whose performers have always represented the competing impulses toward desire and guilt, selfishness and altruism, that have perennially defined the inner life of American prosperity. But the material foundation of the "game" does change. Looking toward a future burdened by personal, corporate, and national indebtedness, contemplators of the "game" as the 1980s drew to a close felt a new sense of urgency.

Part IV

Holy Play and the Counterculture

And the streets of the city shall be full of boys and girls playing in the streets thereof.

Zechariah 8:5

I can see nothing so proper and holy as unrelaxed play and frolic in this bower God has built us.

Henry Thoreau, *Journal* (1841)

Underlying the entire discussion to this point, as the larger context in which the several narratives of the "game" have emerged, has been a cultural history of American attitudes toward play. As an element of the "game," the spirit of play has become increasingly prominent in American culture; by many accounts, around 1900 America's Century of Work gave way to its Century of Play, although pollsters have disagreed on the extent of the transformation. One survey in 1981 revealed that 63 percent of the sample agreed that "people should place more emphasis on working hard and doing a good job than on what gives them personal satisfaction and pleasure"; another declared the opposite: that a majority of Americans in the 1970s sought and found their fulfillment in leisure rather than labor.[1] The popular media in the seventies and eighties certainly portrayed a middle class more concerned with play than work (and even in the case of the first survey, the 63 percent was a significant decrease from the 75 percent in a comparable poll in 1958). A cultural history of the "game" in the context of a rising leisure culture reveals the adaptation of traditional values of work and striving and deferred gratification to new values of enjoyment and consuming.

355

The specific relationship of play to this protean "game" has been to transform potentially disturbing competition into culture-affirming sport. The spirit of play marks the crucial difference between "game" and "battle": It makes tragic contest ennobling rather than futile, wealth and power the rewards for virtue rather than the spoils of ruthlessness. But "play" itself has its own history as well in the cultural rhetoric I am examining, not as an element in the "game" but as a rejection of it. To put the case simply: If work has defined official cultural values since the seventeenth century, play has defined the spirit of the perennial counterculture. The celebrations of the "game" described in the preceding chapters have idealized work in various ways; the rhetoric of "play" has rejected the cultural preeminence of work to envision utopia.

In the interaction of official culture and counterculture in the nineteenth and twentieth centuries, work has increasingly yielded ground to play, with each victory play becoming redefined by the next generation in more radical form. An overview of this process is neatly suggested by a series of interpretations of the first famous confrontation of culture and counterculture in North America: the conflict over the Maypole of Merry Mount in 1627–8. The original incident concerned not just the collision of Old World pagan pastimes with Puritan austerity, but entirely pragmatic questions of authority and safety for the colonists. Those who danced about the maypole were also trading guns to the Indians. But beginning with Nathaniel Hawthorne's 1835 tale, "The May-pole of Merry Mount," a succession of artists joined historians in subordinating the issue of physical danger to an emphasis on archetypal confrontation between anarchic play and stern duty, whose outcome had momentous consequences for the New World inhabitants.

From the outset, accounts of this conflict between work and play had a theological dimension. The first chroniclers of the event, William Bradford and Nathaniel Morton, portrayed Thomas Morton as a heathen "Lord of Misrule," consorting lasciviously with Indian women, "dancing and frisking together like so many fairies, or furies, rather," maintaining a virtual "School of Atheism." When Thomas Morton published his own account in *New English Canaan* (1637), he defended himself by denying the religious implications. Morton insisted that the revels around the maypole were merely "merriment after the old English custome" and "the harmless mirth made by younge men," their suppression by the Puritans motivated not by righteousness or even self-preservation but merely by envy of the prosperity enjoyed by those at Morton's plantation.[2] Two centuries later, to create his allegory of American beginnings Hawthorne drew chiefly on Nathaniel Morton but modified his partisan view by in effect acknowledging some truth in Thomas Morton's account. In the contest between "jollity and gloom" for the future of an empire, gloom wins out but not in any simple victory of good over evil or repression over freedom. Play proves incapable of sustaining genuine happiness, the arch-Puritan Endicott is eventually softened by "the fair spectacle of early love," and the May King and Queen turn "heavenward" with not "one regretful thought on the vanities of Merry Mount." In Hawthorne's version, play and duty must acknowledge each other's rightful place in human life, but duty's claims must take precedence.[3]

Hawthorne seems to have been the first to break in any way with Bradford's and Nathaniel Morton's Puritan interpretation of the maypole.[4] At midcentury, although such historians as Peter Oliver and John Gorham Palfrey continued to read this episode from an essentially pro-Puritan perspective, consensus was beginning to crumble.[5] From a perspective similar to Hawthorne's, the historian John Lothrop Motley wrote a long romance titled *Merry-Mount* (1849), that equally rejects the Puritans' bigotry and the revelers' excesses, while approving the more temperate positions in both parties.[6] This midcentury moderation began to tilt toward the revelers in Charles Francis Adams' historical revision of 1877, in which Morton becomes a lover of nature and field sports, an unprincipled man surely, who jeopardizes the colonists' safety by trading guns to the Indians, but also the victim of high-handed Puritans with their "sour, narrow-minded dislike of innocent and joyous relaxation."[7] A half-century later, the revision was completed: Morton emerges in William Carlos Williams' *In the American Grain* (1925) and Richard Stokes' verse libretto *Merry Mount* (1932) as an unambiguous countercultural hero.[8] Finally, in the 1960s and 1970s, first Robert Lowell in *Endicott and the Red Cross* (1965), then Richard Slotkin in *Regeneration Through Violence* (1973) and John Seelye in *Prophetic Waters* (1977), reread the allegory of Merry Mount in the context of sixties' radicalism. Writing as America began to escalate its involvement in Vietnam, Lowell minimized the conflict over play to focus on Morton's political rebellion. Slotkin and Seelye, writing in the aftermath of the sixties' playful anarchy, both found in Morton the fountainhead of the American counterculture but differed over the consequences. According to Slotkin, the Puritans "saw the New World as a desert wilderness," while "Morton saw it as a New Arcadia, a land rich in the promise of spiritual and erotic fulfillment and renewal." The revels on Merry Mount were "psychological treason" to the Puritan worldview but implicitly the prototype for psychic liberation. Seelye, on the other hand, returned to the ambivalence of an earlier age, presenting Morton as "an outlaw who personified the lawless plenty of Nature" and whose "renegade revels [were] symbolic of the dark side of New World freedom."[9] In this most recent reading, Merry Mount emblemizes both ecstasy and danger in the spirit of play.

These successive interpretations suggest a pattern in the history of play's place in a countercultural tradition: a dawning concern in the antebellum period over play's suppression, an increasing stress on restoring play to work-centered American life as the nineteenth century wore on, the tentative first radical experiment with play-centered living around World War I, then a widespread countercultural enshrinement of play in the 1960s, and most recently a reassessment of that experience in the seventies and eighties. Throughout this period, "play" has consistently expressed the dreams of a prosperous but unfulfilled middle class, traceable to the original European dream of a garden of earthly play to be found in the New World. We can borrow from the German Marxist philosopher of utopia, Ernst Bloch, a distinction between "night-dreams" and "day-dreams" here. Play as night-dream has been, in Bloch's words, "a journey back into repressed experiences and their associations"; play as day-dream has been an "unrestricted journey forward, through images of what is not yet . . . phantasied into life and into the world."[10] More simply, "play" has expressed both Americans' repressed desires and their longing for utopia.

To these two kinds of dreams we can add a third: play as nightmare. Images of play have also signified the culture's fears about unregenerate human nature, personal irresponsibility, and social chaos. To those men and women receptive to the inroads of play on work-centered American values, the rhetoric of play has pointed to the realm of the ideal. For those threatened or repelled by this cultural shift, "play" has connoted frivolity or anarchy. Proplay sentiments have exalted the possible; antiplay sentiments have condemned what is.

In its deepest implication, the affirmative rhetoric of "play" has also expressed a pattern of countercultural spirituality, defining what amounts to a third religious mainstream at odds with the liberal and conservative traditions represented by their contrasting "games." This countercultural theology is antinomian, mystical, spiritually radical. Through images of holy play a wide range of writers have declared that salvation comes not from dutiful actions according to the rules of an immeasurably superior and distant God, nor from defiance of that God, but through releasing the God already present in every human soul. Such a God plays at His creation; His right worship lies in His creatures' imitation of that divine play.

I am describing here the so-called "theology of play" that did not appear explicitly until the 1960s but that implicitly underlay the two major countercultural eruptions that preceded the Vietnam era: the bohemianism centered in Greenwich Village before and after World War I and the Transcendentalism of Emerson and company in the 1830s and 1840s. Hawthorne's revisionist allegory of the Maypole of Merry Mount

appeared at the historical moment when more radical writers began exploring the possibility that true holiness lay not in earnest striving or
powerless submission to a sovereign God, but in the spontaneous actions
of the innately divine human spirit. Hawthorne did not explicitly answer
Emerson, whose *Nature* appeared a year after "The May-pole of Merry
Mount"; rather, both writers responded in different ways to ideas ger-
minating within American culture that were challenging Protestant doctrine at its deepest roots.

The roots of a countercultural theology of play, that is, ultimately lie
in colonial New England. Despite the wider flourishing of play in the
South than in New England, it was ironically the nature of Puritan
resistance, and the influence of Puritanism in American intellectual life,
that determined later belief in the spiritual possibilities of play. In considering Puritan attitudes toward play, I wish to reconstitute on new
grounds a stereotype that sport historians have striven to disprove in
recent years: the image of the stern, unplayful Puritan (iron-willed Endicott routing the revelers at Merry Mount). H. L. Mencken evoked this
image most memorably when he defined puritanism as "the haunting
fear that someone, somewhere, may be happy."[11] Sport historians have
demonstrated that this popular view, prevalent since early in this century,
distorts the facts. Colonial Puritans and Quakers did indeed legislate
against various sporting practices, but selectively – and not very successfully. In general, bans on sport protected three things: economic
security, the safety of lives and property, and Sabbath observance.[12] The
wasting of time during years of economic insecurity jeopardized the
survival of the colony. Sledding and football within town limits threatened personal injury and destruction of property, while gambling led
too easily to financial ruin. Above all, the Lord's Day was emphatically
to remain the Lord's Day (preservation of the Sabbath remained an issue
well into the twentieth century, professional baseball on Sundays not
becoming legal in Boston until 1929, in Philadelphia and Pittsburgh until
1934). By the eighteenth century, private play on the Sabbath tended to
be approved by the gentry and the theologically liberal, abhorred by
conservatives. Riotous life- and property-threatening play never received
official sanction.[13]

The popular view that Puritans forbade all play is incorrect, then. They
banned certain recreations for particular reasons while officially allowing
it on other occasions. And at least one historian has insisted that Puritan
legislation against popular recreations was ineffective: Both church members and nonmembers played with little inhibition.[14] But if Puritan theology had little effect on sporting behavior in the larger society, it
profoundly influenced the way American social and religious leaders
thought about play. Against the Puritans' relative legal and institutional

tolerance, or simple ineffectiveness, stood their more profound antagonism to play amply evident in ministers' tracts and sermons, both in England and in America. Social practice and official cultural values were dramatically at odds. Whether in the eccentric rantings of Phillip Stubbes in his *Anatomy of Abuses* (1583), or in the more moderate admonitions of Richard Baxter in his *Christian Directory* (1673), play was thoroughly circumscribed in a manner that belied the official tolerance.[15]

The Puritan conscience could wrestle endlessly with the nuances of recreational behavior, for play challenged both the duty to work and the broader duty to account for all one's time. The basic principle was clear, as John Bailey declared it in 1689: "God sent you not into the world as into a Play-house, but a Work-house."[16] But even the Puritans granted play its uses. A series of American divines in the seventeenth and eighteenth centuries, including John Cotton, Increase Mather, Benjamin Colman, and Joseph Seccombe, wrote major treatises with a common orthodoxy. Although laymen's embrace of play increased with religious liberalism, the ministers were virtually unanimous in their misgivings.[17] Whether liberal or conservative, they acknowledged the right, sometimes even the duty, to play (in order to refresh oneself for more productive work), then cautioned the faithful against countless possible abuses of proper play.[18] Cotton and Mather, major figures from the first and second generations, described in detail the differences between lawful and unlawful amusements, with Mather's deeper conservatism manifesting itself only in a shriller tone. The more liberal Colman, a generation later, distinguished "carnal," "civil," and "spiritual mirth" in ways that challenged Mather's position not at all; and Seccombe, preaching in 1739 to genteel sportsmen on an annual fishing party, took the most benign view, but again without altering his predecessors' basic doctrines. Together, these four represent the Puritan legacy to the nineteenth century: a view of play as permissible if not inherently evil (excluding, that is, dice, cards, and certain other noxious amusements), if moderate, if pursued at proper times in proper places, if subordinated to work and devotion, and if serving proper ends. Such circumscribed play was not truly "play" as later generations would define it (joyful activity pursued for its own sake), but play transformed into purposeful activity, or work.

And yet these reservations only hint at the more profound antagonism to play revealed not in self-conscious doctrinal statements but indirectly, in the subtexts of conversion narratives and spiritual autobiographies. It is here in particular that I want to reconstitute Mencken's stereotype on new grounds. In a wide range of such works from the seventeenth to nineteenth centuries, a striking pattern emerges in which play is pitted against piety in a context that makes play, in its deepest implications, not just secondary to work but virtually unholy.

The proto-Puritan spiritual autobiography was the *Confessions* of St. Augustine, who described his sinful youth in terms of disobedience to his parents, "all out of a desire to play: aspiring to be captain in all sports, and to have mine ears tickled with feigned fables, to make them itch the more glowingly."[19] Turning to God meant turning away from this sinful play. Among English Puritans thirteen centuries later, the most famous of spiritual autobiographers was John Bunyan, whose *Grace Abounding* epitomizes the entire genre. In his account Bunyan related "the merciful working of God upon my Soul" that began during a game of cat (a forerunner of baseball):

> But the same day, as I was in the midst of a game of Cat, and having struck it one blow from the hole; just as I was about to strike it the second time, a voice did suddenly dart from Heaven into my Soul, which said, *wilt thou leave thy sins, and go to Heaven? or have thy sins and go to Hell?*[20]

Overwhelmed by recognition of his sinfulness, but fearing that it was too late for repentance, Bunyan returned "desperately to my sport again." But in the following months as he gradually responded to God's offer of grace, he signaled his regeneration by renouncing his sports and "childish vanities," giving them up entirely for service to God.

Scholars have discovered that the spiritual autobiographies of New England Puritans follow a consistent pattern; I would add that in a remarkable number of them this pattern includes an identical turning away from sport and play to God.[21] Thomas Shepard recounted in his autobiography how he "fell from God to loose and lewd company, to lust and pride and gaming and bowling and drinking," before he received God's saving grace. Another first-generation Puritan, John Dane, recalled that as an eight-year-old he "was given much to play and to run out without my fathers consent and againe his command." Roger Clap confessed that he "had such a love to play with children and youth, that I did too often play with them upon the Lord's Day, if I could hide it from my dear relatives." Like Bunyan later, Clap experienced an initial revelation of his own sinfulness while involved in a game. Holding the stakes for his friends as they played on the Sabbath, young Roger heard God's warning that Paul, in holding their cloaks while others stoned Stephen, was as guilty as the murderers. "I then put down that which I had in keeping for them," Clap wrote, "and went away; and God did help me afterwards to delight more in them that feared him."[22]

The journal of the Quaker John Woolman records the resolutions and backslidings of a young man drawn incessantly to "mirth and wantonness" until his eighteenth year, when at last he came to feel God's judgment "like a consuming fire."[23] Another seventeenth-century Quaker, Joseph Pike, remembered his sinfulness this way:

> Beginning to love pastimes, I lost that inward sweetness and peace which I had before enjoyed; and by endeavoring to stifle these secret reproofs, I grew harder, until, from a desire to keep company with other wild boys, I took delight in getting out into the streets to play with them, so that I grew very wanton, although my dear parents endeavored to restrain me.

After his conversion in 1654 John Banks renounced "the time I had spent in wildness and wantonness . . . in vanity, sport, and pastime." David Brainerd repented of being "exceedingly addicted to young Company, or Frolicking (as it is called)." Eleazer Wheelock confessed a youth given "to Sports and Play to the total neglect of the Soul's Salvation."[24]

This pattern is repeated by contemporary accounts of the Great Awakening in the 1730s and 1740s that portray the harvest of young souls in terms of the same turning from play to God. In the major document of the Awakening, Jonathan Edwards's *Faithful Narrative* (1737), the minister describes the youth of Northampton as initially given much to "mirth and jollity, which they called frolics." But then, as God's grace infused them, they "left off their frolicking, and grew observably more decent in their attention on the public worship." At the height of the revival, "even at weddings, which formerly were merely occasions of mirth and jollity, there was now no discourse of anything but the things of religion, and no appearance of any but spiritual mirth."[25] Edwards's account was echoed by other ministers who witnessed or participated in the Awakening. Jonathan Parsons reported that at Lyme in 1744, "Many of the *young* People were greatly reformed: they turned their Meetings for vain Mirth into Meetings for Prayer, Conference and reading Books of Piety." At Somers, Connecticut, "those *Youths* that delighted themselves in Frolicking and Mischief" gave up their amusements, finding "more Pleasure and Satisfaction in serving GOD, than ever they did in the Ways of *Sin* and *Satan*." At New Londonderry, the revivals had to counter "a vain and frothy Lightness," and worse, "very extravagant Follies, as Horse Running, Fiddling and Dancing" that had too often prevailed on social occasions. At Halifax, Massachusetts, the young men and women turned away from "all Frolicking and Carousing, and merry Meetings" to find "more delight in going to a Meeting than ever they did to a Frolick." At Wrentham, the young people had "generally and voluntarily *done* with their *Frolicking* and *merry Meetings*," afterward lamenting the time so wasted. At Bridgewater, they ceased "their youthful Practices of Singing, Dancing, Company-keeping, which before they esteemed lawful Recreations, and took abundance of Pleasure in."[26]

Several accounts of the Second Great Awakening reveal the persistence of this pattern even into the age of Emerson and Thoreau: how the youth in one town who were "much addicted to sinful diversions" turned to God; how in another they "now reflected on their former gayety, vanity, and sinful amusements with bitterness and entire disapprobation"; how in yet another "they gave up their vain amusements" and "crowded to conferences and lectures."[27] As with the spiritual autobiographies, the implication in all of these records is clear: If to turn to God is to turn away from play, then play, by extrapolation, is fundamentally sinful. Although Puritans played and tolerated play within prescribed limits, at a level below explicit articulation they assigned play to satan's domain. Evangelical conservatives most openly and stridently took this position, their strict moralism fed by lower-class antagonism to the leisured gentry.[28] But colonial Protestantism more generally assumed this view to some degree and bequeathed it to the nineteenth century. Puritan theology set play not just against work but against piety. Consequently, for those who would come to reject both the Puritan past and its later incarnations, play could become an expression not just of countercultural values but of an alternative definition of holiness.

In proposing the possible holiness of play, then, Emerson and Thoreau reversed a two-centuries-old pattern of religious thinking, while embracing a different element within Puritanism itself. We must go back to Edwards's mention of "spiritual mirth," and before him to Benjamin Colman's sermon on this subject. In distinguishing necessary "spiritual mirth" from vicious "carnal mirth" and merely permissible "civil mirth," Colman's doctrine was this: "*That there is a Spiritual & Religious Joy, proper to a Saint; his rich Priviledge and his Duty to Aspire after. It is a Joy on* Spiritual Accounts, *Spiritually* Felt; *and Spiritually* Expressed."[29] Colman's sermon thus tied "mirth" (a cognate of play in this period) to what can be considered the antinomian strain within Puritan orthodoxy. Following the Hutchinsonian crisis, Antinomianism survived not just in such sects as Familists, Seekers, Anabaptists, and Quakers, but in the pietistic element essential to orthodox Puritanism. The Quakers' "inner light" and, later, the Shakers' holy dancing and other physical manifestations of religious enthusiasm were but extreme versions of the more common view of saving grace. The infusion of God's grace was understood to be no calm event but a joyful ravishing of the soul. The regenerate saint was to delight in God's grace and to anticipate with joy the ultimate union of his soul with God. Edwards's sermon on "A Divine and Supernatural Light" is perhaps the best known statement of the doctrine, his monumental treatise on *Religious Affections* its fullest elaboration. As late as 1873, the revivalist minister Charles Grandison Finney was preaching this same doctrine of spiritual mirth: the "spiritual cheerfulness" and "joy in the Lord" surpassing any earthly pleasure.[30]

In describing the play of grace in the soul and the play of the soul in grace, Colman and Edwards described Puritan pietism, whose religious roots ultimately lay in the long tradition of mysticism from the pagan Heraclitus to the Christians Teresa of Lisieux and Jacob Boehme, the major Protestant figure in this tradition – for all of whom holiness was not to be striven for but spontaneously experienced. Boehme expressed this idea most explicitly in the language we are concerned with: "As God plays with the time of this outward world, so also should the inward divine man play with the outward in the revealed wonders of God in this world, and... open the Divine Wisdom in all creatures, each according to its property."[31] Thoreau and Emerson (who was influenced by Boehme as well as by his own Puritan ancestors) inherited both this antinomian or mystical tradition and the pattern of thinking that pitted play against work and piety. In their image of the child as a model of spiritual vision, with the child's spontaneous play suggesting an ideal of authentic holiness, the Transcendentalists created the first tentative "theology of play" in America. It is important to see Emerson and Thoreau in dialogue not just with their Puritan ancestors but also with the middle-class culture of their own day. Images of the child at play became pervasive in the literature of sentimentalism, as conservative Calvinism yielded ascendancy to religious liberalism between the 1820s and the Civil War. Although the radical Transcendentalists explored the icon of the playful child with self-conscious attention to its extreme spiritual implications, they also contributed to this popular liberalization of the Protestant mainstream, for which the child at play was a major emblem. Emerson in particular was both a radical cultural innovator in his own day and a primary shaper of the conventional culture of the following generation.

The history of play and the cultural history of "play" run corresponding but distinct courses, then. Americans continued to play through the nineteenth and twentieth centuries, independent of "official" approval or disapproval. Yet cultural sanction affected both the ways men and women viewed their play and their attitudes toward the larger issues of human possibility for which play served as symbol. This cultural history of "play" followed an erratic course, marked most importantly by three major outbreaks of the antinomian play spirit that followed a consistent pattern. The rise of Transcendentalism in the 1830s was the first of three middle-class countercultural movements that declared their rebellion at least partly in the name of play. In each case – with the Concord Transcendentalists of the 1830s and 1840s, the Greenwich Village bohemians around the First World War, and the Beats and then the hippies of the 1950s and 1960s – an initial radicalism was absorbed, conventionalized, and accommodated to a reconstituted mainstream, whose values were in turn assaulted by the next eruption of the counterculture. This process is similar to William Morris's description in a different context: "Men fight and lose the battle, and the thing that they fought for comes in spite of their defeat, and when it comes, turns out not to be what they meant, and other men have to fight for what they meant under another name."[32] In this sense, each countercultural rebellion failed to transform American society as its leaders intended, yet permanently altered that society in unintended ways. Countercultural eruptions have stretched the limits of official attitudes toward play and then been accommodated in a safer form. Thus, the Transcendentalists contributed importantly to the triumph of genteel sentimentalism in the last half of the nineteenth century; pre-World War I political cultural radicalism was absorbed into the ambivalent hedonism of the 1920s; and the spirit of the youth movement of the 1960s fed directly into the human potential movement of the seventies and eighties.

Middle-class American culture over the past century and a half has indeed shifted increasingly away from work to play as the imagined source of happiness and fulfillment; I am chiefly interested here in the rhetoric of play that has accompanied, and to some degree helped shape, that transformation. Images of play throughout this period also reveal certain patterns. One finds, for example, a long tradition of projecting the spirit of play, in both its appealing and its appalling forms, onto a series of cultural others. As I pointed out in Part I, the first Europeans and their colonial descendants projected onto the Caribbean natives both their fears and their desires for a New World garden of play. This habit of mind has continued into the nineteenth and twentieth centuries, in middle-class projections of play onto children, women, blacks, Indians, even lower-class outlaws.

Cultural radicalism in twentieth-century America has been preeminently the result of generational conflict: young people first in the 1910s and 1920s, then in the fifties and sixties, assaulting cultural norms and entrenched taboos, with the middle class at large then appropriating and conventionalizing large elements of the new freedoms. The production of cultural images of play, on the other hand, has been not just by young rebels but by writers spanning the generations. Tracing the rhetoric of play in a wide range of texts not only documents the persistent encroachment of play into the domain of work, where cultural values once exclusively resided, but also records the uncertain, groping, ambiguous responses of an anxious middle class to an historical development that only appears straightforward. Since the 1830s writers have both embraced and rejected the emerging play spirit; those who have embraced it have done so with varying degrees of enthusiasm and ambivalence. The "discovery" of play as an autonomous state in the nineteenth century was simultaneously an awareness of a work/play dualism in American, and human, life. One result of these twin discoveries has been a century and a half of attempts to define a proper balance between work and play – invariably in response to perceived needs to grant play an increasingly important role in human fulfillment. Against this balancing act of social engineering, by which work and play would be assigned to their proper spheres, a handful of cultural visionaries – radical antinomians and mystics from Ralph Waldo Emerson (in certain moods) to Norman O. Brown – have sought to overcome this fragmenting dualism by abolishing work altogether in a utopia of pure play. And against both the defenders of the middle ground and the utopian visionaries of total play, a third group of writers has conceived work and play dialectically rather than dualistically: attempting to theorize (and eventually to realize) an essential wholeness in human life. Among these dialecticians of work and play, finally, I would further distinguish between those whose dialectic holds work and play in unresolved tension and those whose dialectic transcends the union of opposites to envision new forms of "work/play." Needless to say, in all of these cases the relationship of visionary play to social and political actualities has remained problematic.

The following chapters will trace these several rhetorical strands within the overall pattern of countercultural play. The persistent drive toward transcendence has assumed different forms over time. Since the beginning of industrialization in America, play has consistently signified the realm of freedom – for those unhindered in the workplace, that is (a major theme in the writing of progressive women in the nineteenth century, for example, defined work as the realm of freedom for women, leisure as their prison). But if the equation of play with freedom, in this qualified sense, has been constant, the meaning of freedom, and hence of play, has not. The Transcendentalists' explorations of play were unambiguously theological. Following several decades of secularization, the Greenwich Village bohemians substituted psychology and aesthetics for theology in defining ultimacies for human existence, with the result that art and psychological well-being became implicitly "spiritual." Politics seemed at the time to occupy the foreground of 1960s radicalism, but for the post-World War II generation religion also returned, if often in wildly heterodox forms: from the Zen mysticism of the Beats to the spiritual eclecticism of the sixties youth movement to New Age cosmic consciousness. The "theology of play" in whatever form declares salvation by grace, not works; it's a theology not of ethics but of aesthetics, its goal beauty rather than duty. As the contexts of play's meanings have changed, so have the terms of opposition. Play has meant freedom from work, from tyranny (either divine or earthly), from mechanization, from inhibition, from violence, from self-destruction. A cultural history of play includes shifting paradigms of both "freedom from" and "freedom to," as well as an accretion of meanings from period to period; in other words, as always, both change and continuity.

The texts that document this cultural groping toward an ever greater accommodation to the spirit of play are varied: from the essays of Emerson and Thoreau, and the fiction of Nathaniel Hawthorne and a host of sentimental writers at midcentury; to popularizations of Nietzsche and Freud, bohemian manifestoes, popular fiction, and the writings of the Harlem Renaissance in the 1910s and 20s; to the writings of the Beats, widely read intellectuals, leading radicals, and popular novelists of the entire post-World War II era. In these final three chapters I will focus on each of the countercultural moments in turn, to describe these successive cultural transformations from within, through a range of texts in which the rhetoric of play has had a prominent place.

10

Transcendental Play and the Theology of Sentimentalism

The Transcendentalists' theology of play was part of that larger European Romantic movement in which such writers as Schiller and Rousseau set play against Enlightenment rationalism, to create a dualism with which a range of nineteenth-century writers – from Carlyle and Fourier, to Marx, Ruskin, and Morris – grappled with varying degrees of success.[1] This first American theology of play was only implicit, and it expressed one pole in sharply divided Transcendentalist thinking. In the ideas of Ralph Waldo Emerson, Bronson Alcott, Margaret Fuller, Henry Thoreau, and their associates, Puritan heritage confronted radical Romanticism with inevitably complex results; an ideal of holy play competed with a contradictory insistence on purposeful striving. To put the issue in its American religious context, Arminian and antinomian strains clashed within Transcendentalism. The Arminian was manifest in specific efforts at social reform (Thoreau's abolitionism, Fuller's feminism), but also more generally in the overriding emphasis on self-culture. Efforts at self-culture assumed human perfectibility but not human perfection; the Transcendentalists were as earnest as their Puritan forebears in striving after their goals.

The antinomian strain was present in an altogether different cluster of ideas and concerns: neo-Kantian and Coleridgean idealism, the primacy of Reason (intuition) over Understanding (rationality), belief in the Oversoul or common divinity of all creation. One primary expression of this antinomian element was the image of the child as a model of spiritual vision, with spontaneous play as an ideal of authentic holiness. Alcott's belief in the perfect intuition of his young pupils, Emerson's numerous notebook entries on frolicking children, Thoreau's equally numerous images of sporting creatures (both animal and human) all celebrated this ideal. But Alcott also insisted on the careful nurture of the young, Emer-

368

son claimed necessity as well as freedom in human lives, Thoreau was as serious about work as he was eager for play.

The history of Brook Farm offers a concrete instance of the clash of work and play in Transcendentalist ideals. A common view in the late nineteenth century dismissed the Transcendentalists as naive and child-like, their attempt at utopian living a foolish masquerade (Hawthorne's *Blithedale Romance* contributed much to this judgment). One cultural historian who rejects this "equation Transcendentalism equals play" laments scholars' need "to rely heavily for information about the daily life of the community on writers who lay great stress on the fun they had during their time there." But contrary evidence is available. Among the communalists at Brook Farm, Elizabeth Palmer Peabody described their basic principle as *"labor is the germ of all good"*; in the same spirit Orestes Brownson, a sympathetic observer, described Brook Farm as fundamentally "an INDUSTRIAL ESTABLISHMENT."[2] It was the collision of work and play, rather than the dominance of either, that characterized both the Brook Farm experiment (the desire, but failure, to transform work into play) and Transcendentalism generally. The Transcendentalists rebelled against the religion and culture of their day from two opposite perspectives: They countered the prevailing work ethic and rational theology with the spirit of play, but also the superficiality of the new business civilization with more purposeful work. The result was a persistent dualism within Transcendentalism itself.

This dualism has been a major obstacle confronting the attempts of cultural radicals to transform American society over the past century and a half. The problem is social, intellectual, and rhetorical: a matter of actually overcoming the labor/leisure dualism at the heart of industrial capitalism, a matter of envisioning how that dualism might be overcome, and a matter of expressing the relationship of work and play in a rhetorical figure that expresses that vision. My specific concern is with the rhetorical configurations of work and play in the writings of the major Transcendentalists and their successors, but obviously that rhetoric cannot be divorced from the intellectual and social issues it expressed.

Emerson, Thoreau, and the dialectic of work and play

The images of work and play in the writings of Emerson and Thoreau reveal a common concern but significantly different responses to it. Work and play form a dichotomy in the writings of both men, but while Thoreau envisioned a transcendent dialectic in which work and play are transformed by their fusion, Emerson vacillated between competing desires without ever resolving them. Emerson conceived his nascent theology of play during a period when progressive-minded

Americans, troubled by the consequences of industrialization and urbanization, first gave serious consideration to social, psychological, and physical needs for play. Emerson himself did not live playfully. As a child he and his brothers were forbidden to play with the "rude boys" who roamed his neighborhood, and young Waldo never owned a sled. He found pleasure in the outdoors when he attended the Boston Public Latin School, and he was later introduced to rowing by Thoreau, but in general, sobriety rather than playfulness ruled Emerson's life.[3] The *idea* of play, however, ruled at least a part of his thought. If the poles of Emerson's ideas can be identified as "freedom" and "fate," then play expressed his belief in freedom.[4] The early Emerson insisted more on freedom, often extravagantly; the later Emerson made peace with the world, acquiescing to limitation and to things as they were, while clinging to a faith in beneficent necessity and not abandoning altogether his original quest for freedom. Not surprisingly, it is in the early essays that we find rhetorical figures of holy play.

The image of the child at play could have been suggested by any of Emerson's major influences: the mysticism of Swedenborg, Boehme, George Fox, and the neo-Platonists; the philosophy and theology of the Orient; the intuitional philosophy of Kant, by way of Coleridge and Carlyle; the Romantic cult of the child as expressed in Wordsworth's poetry, Alcott's views on education, or the emerging sentimentalism in American culture. Whatever its specific sources, "play" embodied several of the major tenets of Emerson's Transcendentalism. In *Nature* (1836), the movement's originating manifesto, Emerson called on men and women to see and experience the phenomenal world as a child does. As a major case in point, Shakespeare's genius lay in *playing* with the world: Emerson described him as a poet whose "imperial muse tosses the creation like a bauble from hand to hand, and uses it to embody any capricious shade of thought that is uppermost in his mind."[5] In the later essay "The Poet" (1844), Emerson described poetry itself as play, the true poet as a childlike being who plays with the objects of nature as if with his toys.[6] Neither Shakespeare nor poets generally were for Emerson figures of solitary genius; rather, they were types for the genius latent in every person. Man is but "a young child, and his huge globe a toy," Emerson wrote at the beginning of the "Divinity School Address" (1838), where he likened joy in the fullness of life to the state of a child at play:

> The sentiment of virtue is a reverence and delight in the presence of certain divine laws. It perceives that this homely game of life we play, covers, under what seem foolish details, principles that astonish. The child amidst his baubles, is learning the action of light, motion, gravity, muscular force; and in the game of human life, love, fear, justice, appetite, man, and God, interact.[7]

Child's play became Emerson's symbol for freedom: spontaneous, instinctual, indulged for its own sake; denying regulation and limits, existing in a timeless present. In "The Over-Soul," he wrote that "the spirit sports with time." In "History," he asked rhetorically, "Why should we make account of time or magnitude, or of figure: The soul knows them not; and genius, obeying its laws, knows how to play with them as a young child plays with graybeards in churches." All of these images of ontological playfulness extend in specific ways a more general declaration of freedom that Emerson recorded in his journal in 1839:

> My life is a May game, I will live as I like. I defy your strait laced, wary, social ways & modes. Blue is the sky, green the fields & groves, fresh the springs, glad the rivers, & hospitable the splendor of sun & star. I will play my game out. And if any shall ⟨dare⟩ say me Nay, shall come out with swords & staves against me to prick me to death for their foolish laws, – come and welcome. I will not look grave for such a fool's matter. I can not lose my cheer for such trumpery. Life is a May game still.[8]

This was Emerson's closest approach to an explicit theology of play. To play was to "live from within" in the full self-sufficiency of the soul. But even at the height of Emerson's confidence, one hears in this journal entry the troubling hints of an insistent, not-so-playful reality. Emerson could defy the "strait laced, weary, social ways & modes" but not make them go away, and in his later essays he was increasingly unable to ignore them. Fate obscures freedom in these later writings, and even when play appears, it is altered to accommodate a more restrained philosophy. Emerson came to see, in Stephen Whicher's words, "that, for all the increasing affirmation at the bottom of the heart, man would remain, as he had always been, confined to the millround of his fate."[9]

Extending Whicher's argument, David Robinson has described Emerson as having struggled throughout his literary life, with no final unambiguous success, to articulate a monistic resolution to an essentially dualistic understanding of a bipolar universe. Emerson achieved his eventual pragmatic optimism by sacrificing an intensely personal response to living for a detached cosmic view rooted in confidence that everything in life ultimately coheres into a meaningful whole.[10] Robinson has identified "Experience" (1844) as Emerson's key midcareer essay between the greater confidence of "Self-Reliance" and the greater skepticism of "Fate." Written after the death of his son, while Emerson was grieving over his inability to grieve, "Experience" presents images from the earlier essays with altered meaning. Where play once expressed the perfect union of the human individual with nature, it now signifies mere illusion. No longer the poet's bauble, nature now makes of men "her fools and playmates." "We may have the sphere for our cricket–ball, but. . . . direct strokes she never gave us power to make; all our blows glance, all our hits are accident."

In "Experience," the ideal Emerson once expressed as immanent becomes obscured behind impenetrable reality. Play, from an image of intuitive, spontaneous grasping of the ideal, becomes an image of the illusory world in which all humankind is trapped. "The plays of children are nonsense, but very educative nonsense," Emerson wrote, seeming to echo his earlier essays, but children's play is educative now in teaching humanity the insubstantiality of even "the largest and solemnest things." Emerson advised now to live in the world and take it as it is without trying to discover life's higher purposes: "We live amid surfaces, and the true art of life is to skate well on them." A kitten chasing her own tail becomes an emblem not of freedom but of illusion:

> If you could look with her eyes you might see her surrounded with hundreds of figures performing complex dramas, with tragic and comic issues, long conversations, many characters, many ups and downs of fate, – and meantime it is only puss and her tail.

So with the play of man. "How long," Emerson asked rhetorically, "before our masquerade will end its noise of tambourines, laughter and shouting, and we shall find it was a solitary performance?" Play once denied any split between self and other; here Emerson insisted on both "a subject and an object, – it takes so much to make the galvanic circuit complete." Although "Experience" affirms the harmonious design underlying the operations of the cosmos, that harmony remains hidden to mere mortals. Emerson concluded the essay by counseling patience, for "we shall win at last"; but the "winning" of a deferred victory implies the resolution of an agonistic contest, not transcendence to be experienced now by those who joyfully, spontaneously play.[11]

The late essays "Fate" (1860) and "Illusion" (1860) recapitulate these themes. Having surrendered his faith in temporal perfection, Emerson became increasingly Platonic in denying the substance of the physical universe, leaving perfection to the ideal world imperfectly reflected by it. "What if you shall come to discern that the play and playground of all this pompous history are radiations from yourself, and that the sun borrows his beams?" he asked in "Illusions." In these essays the full and free play of spirit and matter have become the *mere* play of illusion and subjectivity. "Whatever games are played with us, we must play no games with ourselves," he wrote, "but deal in our privacy with the last honesty and truth."[12] The illusory nature of human life should cause no despair; final rest awaits its conclusion. But the value of that life in itself, as play is valued for itself, is diminished. A law of progress rather than a celebration of the perpetual present determines what ultimately matters in human existence.

The possibilities for a theology of play, then, lay only in the earlier, more extravagantly confident Emerson. Even then it is not fully articulated, and it simply ignores the realm of necessity confronted in the later essays. The celebration of play exists alongside an emphasis on duty and self-culture, the two halves of Emerson's thought never truly reconciled. Emerson's dualism – Undulation, or Polarity, he called it in "The American Scholar" – was shared by Bronson Alcott as well, who believed more fully than Emerson in the sanctity and intuitive wisdom of children, but who also thought of infancy as the ideal period for the improvement of character, of childhood as the stage for moral instruction.[13] Margaret Fuller addressed these issues only indirectly. Although in an essay in *The Dial* she celebrated the myriad amusements available in wintertime Boston, this piece stands apart from her more characteristically earnest writing in the causes of literary independence and feminism.[14] Among the Transcendentalists who addressed the possibilities of play, Thoreau alone articulated a transcendent dialectic.

Oddly enough, Thoreau shared with Emerson an unplayful childhood. As a boy he refused to play games with the other children, preferring to watch from the sidelines. A classmate at the Concord Academy remembered him as a youth "not given to play or to fellowship with boys." As an adult, however, Thoreau became passionate about solitary sport: hunting and fishing, hiking, drifting in his hand-built rowboat on ponds. As Emerson's friend he was also a playmate to the older man's children, making tops, whistles, boats, and popguns for young Waldo. He delighted in children generally, taking the young people of Concord walking and huckleberrying, telling them stories, playing the flute, entertaining them with juggling tricks. Emerson remembered Thoreau as "the only man of leisure in his town," a man who "lived extempore from hour to hour, like the birds and the angels."[15] At the same time, Thoreau cared little for holiday festivities, and was sternly demanding of those who accompanied him on excursions. Ellery Channing, his companion on many rambles and boat outings, left a portrait of a man earnest even in play:

> His whole figure had an active earnestness, as if he had no moment to waste. The clenched hand betokened purpose. In walking, he made a short cut if he could, and when sitting in the shade or by the wallside seemed merely the clearer to look forward into the next piece of activity. Even in the boat he had a wary, transitory air, his eyes on the outlook, – perhaps there might be ducks, or the Blondin turtle, or an otter, or sparrow.[16]

In short, Thoreau was a most unplayful playful man, that paradox characterizing his books and essays as well as his life. What I would call Thoreau's dialectic of *earnest play* appears most concretely in his etymology of the word "saunterer" with which the essay "Walking" (1862) opens. The word derives, Thoreau claimed:

> from idle people who roved about the country, in the Middle Ages, and asked charity, under pretense of going *"à la Sainte Terre,"* to the Holy Land, till the children exclaimed, "There goes a *Sainte-Terrer,"* a Saunterer, – a Holy-Lander. They who never go to the Holy Land in their walks, as they pretend, are indeed mere idlers and vagabonds; but they who go there are saunterers in the good sense, such as I mean.

Thoreau seems to have anticipated Ellery Channing's portrait. "Every walk is a sort of crusade," Thoreau wrote, although today "we are but faint-hearted crusaders." We simply return to our point of departure when we should rather walk "in the spirit of undying adventure." Only a free man can walk, can become a "Walker Errant." "No wealth can buy the requisite leisure, freedom, and independence which are the capital in this profession. It comes only by the grace of God." Walking is not just recreation, but re-creation of the spirit.[17]

"Walking" appeared a month after Thoreau died, a final testament to a faith perhaps not so serenely maintained in his life as the essay implies, but nonetheless a summary of a central motif in his writings. To saunter is to wander purposefully, to be idly intent, to playfully work or workfully play. And the terrain over which a sojourner strolls is a "holy land." The poles of Thoreau's dialectic sometimes appear separately. In his journals, for example, appear innumerable images of natural play: of two ducks "merrily dabbling in their favorite basin," of "the king of days" who "plays at bo-peep round the world's corner," of Jack Frost "playing singular freaks" with the landscape. Ice cracking in winter seems the "merry gambols" of pond sprites; a sail boat in summer seems a "bauble of the heavens and the earth" and a playmate of the breezes; "the young fry that leap in ponds" seem evidence that "joy is the condition of life."[18] These images culminate in the joyous declaration of December 1841 that I have used as an epigraph to Part IV:

> I can see nothing so proper and holy as unrelaxed play and frolic in this bower God has built us – The suspicion of sin never comes to this thought –
> Oh if men felt this they would never build temples even of marble or diamond, but it would be sacrilege and prophane – but disport themselves forever in this paradise.[19]

In these early journal entries, Thoreau was clearly conscious of the philosophical resonance of his images of play. During this same period, he wrote about the gods revealing themselves not to "sedate and musing gentlemen" but to "the buffoon in the midst of his antics"; and he distinguished "diversion," which merely recoups energies drained by work, from "amusement," which is play for its own sake.[20] In declaring later the same year, then, that the earth was a "bower" built by God for man's "play and frolic," Thoreau clearly intended the spiritual implications. Play in God's bower was holy: no image of future immortal bliss but a description of holiness now, on earth. To play was to surrender to impulse, to wed one's own nature to external Nature in perfect union.

But in the same pages of his journal Thoreau the Puritan also wrote that "to be a man is to do a man's work – Always our resource is to endeavor." And elsewhere: "I find my life growing slovenly when it does not exercise a constant supervision over itself." And again: "Of all the duties in life it is hardest to be in earnest."[21] Heroism, discipline, earnestness, and labor are recurring themes in the journals for the early 1840s, a cluster of ideas antithetical to play. Like Emerson, Thoreau revealed a divided consciousness, a commitment to both earnest striving and spontaneous enjoyment. And in his own life the world may have eventually defeated his desire to play. Sherman Paul has argued that Thoreau's journals after 1850 reveal the "desperation of the spiritual seeker who has lost his communion."[22] But in his published writings, from the early essays on natural history to the posthumous essays and books, images of joyful play never disappear, and in the later work particularly Thoreau succeeded in fusing his contradictory desires into rhetorical figures of earnest play.

Thoreau's early essays, "Natural History of Massachusetts" (1842) and "A Winter Walk" (1843), contain numerous images of play in nature, often taken directly from the journals. The "young fry that leap in ponds," the "gambols" of foxes, the "brisk and playful" squirrels and rabbits, and the "frolic gambols" of the shapes created by snow on walls and fences all suggest that nature is indeed the bower of God in which men and women, too, are called to play.[23] In his later works – both the books *A Week on the Concord and Merrimack Rivers* (1849), *The Maine Woods* (1864), and *Cape Cod* (1865), and the essays "Autumnal Tints" (1862) and "Life Without Principle" (1863) – this celebration of play persists, but as one element in a dialectic that rhetorically transcends simpler dualism. In *A Week,* I would point to the figure of the angler on the Concord River, whose "fishing was not a sport, nor solely a means of subsistence, but a sort of solemn sacrament and withdrawal from the world"; and to a description of sailing on the river as a fusion of opposites: thin and full, noiseless and noisy, labored and leisurely, driven and waiting. In *The Maine Woods,* the comparable image appears in Thoreau's call for national preserves or "forests, not to hold the king's game merely, but to hold and preserve the king himself also, the lord of creation, – not for idle sport or food, but for inspiration and our own true recreation." In *Cape Cod,* a more ambiguous meditation on fishing as both frivolous and serious fits this pattern; in "Autumnal Tints," the play of light through the leaves of a scarlet oak becomes another symbol of transcending the assumed duality of matter and spirit; in "Life Without Principle," a celebration of work done not for money but "for love of it" offers yet another example.[24] In all of these instances, Thoreau's ideal declares "earnestness" superior to "frivolity," but earnestness is a quality of Thoreau's sense of play, not its antithesis.

It was inevitably in *Walden* (1854), his masterpiece, that Thoreau developed his dialectic most fully. The lived experience behind *Walden* also grounded Thoreau's Transcendentalist ideals in the material world, in a way that Emerson's never were. It is dangerous to claim any one image-pattern in *Walden* as the preeminent one, but certainly a case can be made that the book's philosophy centers on a vision of authentic life as earnest play. Thoreau seems to have denied such a paradoxical possibility in the very first chapter, where he insisted that students "should not *play* life, or *study* it merely, while the community supports them at this expensive game, but earnestly *live* it from beginning to end."[25] It is no mere semantic trickery, however, to point out that "play" here connotes frivolous pretending, while "live" implies what *Walden* as a whole suggests is earnest play. Thoreau both damned the commercial culture of his day and proposed an alternative manner of living. Play offered a key to both intentions. Thoreau felt that life in midcentury America distracted men from what was important, consumed them with mere busyness, enslaved them with its material enticements, oppressed them with despair. In the paragraph that includes *Walden's* most quoted line – "The mass of men lead lives of quiet desperation" – appears this statement as well: "A stereotyped but unconscious despair is concealed even under what are called the games and amusements of mankind. There is no play in them, for this comes after work" (8). Thoreau's solution to this cultural dualism for physical man was to transform labor into play; for spiritual man, to transform moral striving into holy sport.

The philosophy of *Walden* in both of these dimensions is rooted in the paradox that work must be play. "To maintain one's self on this earth is not a hardship but a pastime," he insisted, "if we will live simply and wisely" (70). Near the end of the chapter "Where I Lived, and What I Lived For," Thoreau wrote, "Children, who play life, discern its true law and relations more clearly than men, who fail to live it worthily, but who think that they are wise by experience, that is by failure" (96). Later, as he leaves Baker Farm, Thoreau as narrator addresses his readers directly:

Rise free from care before the dawn, and seek adventures. Let the noon find thee by other lakes, and night overtake thee every where at home. There are no larger fields than these, no worthier games than may here be played. Grow wild according to thy nature, like these sedges and brakes, which will never become English hay. Let the thunder rumble; what if it threaten ruin to farmers' crops? This is not its errand to thee. Take shelter under the cloud, while they flee to carts and sheds. Let not to get a living be thy trade, but thy sport. (207)

It is essential to notice that Thoreau did not merely define play in opposition to work, so as to deny purposefulness to life. Thoreau refused to subscribe to the work/play dualism that dominated thinking on the subject in the nineteenth century. Partial readings of *Walden* can reveal either a playful or an earnest Thoreau. While the unplayful voice may be contemptuous of business, it insists on meaningful labor. It rejects society's version of success but is earnest in pursuit of spiritual perfection. It is suspicious of reformers yet reports Thoreau's own defiant stand on the poll tax. It rejects ceaseless activity for contemplation, not sport. But a reading of the whole must see this moral earnestness as never separated from Thoreau's playfulness.

Thoreau expressed his dialectic of earnest play through symbol rather than argument. In "Higher Laws," for example, he defended hunting and fishing against "the objection of the score of humanity":

When some of my friends have asked me anxiously about their boys, whether they should let them hunt, I answered, yes – remembering that it was one of the best parts of my education, – *make* them hunters, though sportsmen only at first, if possible, mighty hunters at last, so that they shall not find game large enough for them in this or any vegetable wilderness, – hunters as well as fishers of men. (212)

The metaphysical angling of *A Week* becomes more exlicit in the following paragraph:

The Governor and his council faintly remember the pond, for they went a-fishing there when they were boys; but now they are too old and dignified to go a-fishing, and so they know it no more forever. Yet even they expect to go to heaven at last. If the legislature regards it, it is chiefly to regulate the number of hooks to be used there; but they know nothing about the hook of hooks with which to angle for the pond itself. (213)

Although Thoreau's own attraction/repulsion in regard to actual hunting continued throughout the 1850s, in his journals he repeatedly expressed the affirmative side of that ambivalence in images of metaphysical sport. "Now I go a-fishing and a-hunting everyday," he wrote in January 1853, "but omit the fish and the game, which are the least important." And a year later: "Are there not hunters who seek something higher than foxes, with judgments more discriminating than the senses of fox-hounds, who rally to nobler music than that of the hunting-horn?" And in March 1859 he wrote of "setting my traps in solitude, and baiting them as well as I know how, that I may catch life and light."[26] He expressed the same ideas in *Walden*.

The consummate image of Thoreau's theology of play in *Walden* comes in "Spring," both the season of rebirth and the emblem of that renewal man must experience continually if life is to have meaning. The image of a sportive hawk is more potent here than comparable images of frolicking foxes and playful rabbits in earlier essays, because the context is immeasurably richer. The hawk's flight suggests the joy and freedom that can liberate men, even in a world of work and necessity:

> It was the most ethereal flight I had ever witnessed. It did not simply flutter like a butterfly, nor soar like the larger hawks, but it sported with proud reliance in the fields of air; mounting again and again with its strange chuckle, it repeated its free and beautiful fall, turning over and over like a kite, and then recovering from its lofty tumbling, as if it had never set its foot on *terra firma*. It appeared to have no companion in the universe, – sporting there alone, – and to need none but the morning and the ether with which it played. (316–7)

Not just such images as this, but the entirety of *Walden* celebrates the ideal of what Hugo Rahner a century later would call the "grave-merry" man. Rahner could have been glossing *Walden* when he described his own ideal:

> I am trying to make plain that such a man is really always two men in one: he is a man with an easy gaiety of spirit, one might say a man of spiritual elegance, a man who feels himself to be living in invincible security; but he is also a man of tragedy, a man of laughter and tears, a man, indeed, of gentle irony, for he sees through the tragically ridiculous masks of the game of life and has taken the measure of the cramping boundaries of our earthly existence.[27]

Thoreau's model was a little rougher, more angular, more Yankee than Rahner's portrait, but otherwise their spirit was the same. If anything, Thoreau affirmed the value of *this* life more than Rahner did. Thoreau, like Rahner, was able to conceive life as play in a way that did not deny limitation, constraint, necessity. Thoreau's imaginative fusion, then, should be seen as an alternative to Emerson's dualism. Emerson more accurately reflected the dilemma facing American culture; Thoreau's dialectic anticipated the repeated efforts of both writers and cultural rebels in future generations to transcend that dualism.

Hawthorne and sentimental fiction

The Concord group was small, its "movement" short-lived, but its influence on American middle-class culture deep and far-reaching. In this as in many other things it prefigured the later cultural revolutionaries of play, the bohemians of the 1910s and the Beats of the 1950s. The cultural response to the radical challenge of Emerson's celebration of play in the 1830s also prefigured the later eruptions and then tamings of the spiritually and politically anarchic play spirit. From the 1830s to the end of the century, American culture increasingly granted play a significant role in human life, undermining the traditional work ethic as it did so. This change did not take place through a gradual step-by-step process, however, but through a much messier, less certain, more groping accommodation to ideas and feelings not well understood.

Horace Bushnell's essay "Work and Play" suggests how the Transcendentalists' antinomian notion of play was modified and absorbed in a safer form by the cultural mainstream. Originally presented as a Phi Beta Kappa lecture at Harvard in 1848, "Work and Play" was not published until 1864, when it provided the title for a collection of Bushnell's writings. Those dates are significant: In 1848 Bushnell's ideas would have seemed considerably more daring than in 1864 when he offered them to the public at large. Bushnell was a Congregationalist minister, trained at Yale in Edwardsean orthodoxy and the author of a treatise, *Nature and the Supernatural* (1858), whose explicit purpose was to refute Transcendentalist heresy. But Bushnell has nonetheless been described as "the theologian who best gathered in the Transcendental harvest"; that is, who brought the more radical propositions of Emerson and his circle into the Protestant mainstream.[28] His discussion of play offers a specific instance of that process.

Defining "work" simply as "activity *for* an end" and play as "activity *as* an end," Bushnell declared that man was created to play, but that he had to work in order to reach that promised end. Bushnell thus acknowledged the essential dualism central to work-centered American culture, but by giving work an external purpose he implicitly, perhaps even unwittingly, challenged its preeminence. Bushnell was careful to assert that he had no intention to "denigrate thus from the dignity of work"; he claimed, in fact, to "dignify it the more, that I represent it as the preparative to a state so exalted." But the essay's implications say otherwise. Bushnell also tacitly denigrated the importance of spiritual striving when he declared that religion "in its very nature and life" was "a form of play." Worldly play infuses genius, humor, poetry, and creativity. Spiritual play is impulsive and inspired rather than driven, joyful rather than disciplined; it is the highest state of mankind, an anticipation of eternal blessedness.[29]

Bushnell's essay appeared in ten editions between 1864 and 1910. And he incorporated these same ideas into his vastly influential *Views of Christian Nurture* (1847; rev. 1864), the book that made him virtually "the patron saint of the religious education movement."[30] In both works, although Bushnell granted play more importance than any major American theologian had given it till now, he stopped far short of declaring life entirely an Emersonian "May game." For Bushnell play was not holy in itself but became holy as the activity of one who has already been saved; its sanctity lay more in its foreshadowing image of heavenly blessedness than in its earthly manifestations. And play could easily become excessive. "But it is not the whole life, even to a child, to be indulged in play," he warned in *Christian Nurture*. "There is such a thing as order, no less than such a thing as liberty; and the process of adjustment between these two contending powers, begins at a very early date."[31] Bushnell's compromise was not a Thoreauvian dialectic but what would become the culture's conventional dualism: a golden mean by which life is work and play, each in moderation, each in its proper times and places.

Bushnell thus stands at the forefront of midcentury liberal clergymen, a group that includes Henry Ward Beecher, Edward Everett Hale, and the rest of the muscular Christian team, who made play safe for Protestant theology. The 1850s and 1860s marked the capitulation of theological conservatism to its liberal counterforce: the moment at which an increasing liberalism in the Protestant mainstream overtook the ruling conservatism to dominate the religious views of later generations. The changing attitudes toward play in the popular fiction of this period offer an even better glimpse into the uneasy and contested responses of middle-class American culture to this transformation. In the image of the child at play in sentimental fiction, the modern reader can observe the culture wrestling with the old and new theologies, declaring finally for liberalism but in a form that denied its most radical implications.

The rhetorical terms of the conflict were "playfulness" versus "earnestness" – words and ideas innocuous today but potent in antebellum America. Given the traditional Calvinist belief in infant depravity, paeans to childish playfulness expressed the ascendant liberalism, whereas earnestness embodied the lingering conservatism. For a conservative model of the ideal child, we can look back to Jonathan Edwards's account of four-year-old Phebe Bartlett in his *Faithful Narrative* of the Great Awakening. Edwards found little Phebe a remarkable case of the infant saint: a child whose uncanny sobriety, incessant praying, and preoccupation with religious matters offered evidence that even the very young could experience God's saving grace. Above all, Phebe was "earnest," an adjective that recurs over and over in Edwards's account. Eighteenth-century Americans considered children naturally inclined to play; an earnest child was an *un*natural child, one whom God's saving grace had raised above unregenerate humanity.[32]

Edwards's Phebe can serve as a model for innumerable fictional children in the first half of the following century, from Margaretta in a novel by that name in 1807 to Harriet Beecher Stowe's Little Eva in 1852 and countless other young heroines in the popular domestic novels of the so-called feminine fifties. The fiction written before 1820 when liberal religious ideas began to figure prominently in American literature, offers virtually no alternative view of the child. In the anonymously published *Margaretta; or, The Intricacies of the Heart,* evidence of the heroine's remarkable virtue is noticeable in childhood by "a singularity of character" that "distinguished her from her little associates":

> When they would be at their gambols and plays, she would seldom join in their amusements; and though amidst all the alluring temptations of juvenile mirth, and laughing hilarity, she would either sit musing as a philosopher, or spend her leisure hours in reading.[33]

Either earnest striving or pious resignation (as in the fortune's-football school) characterizes this early fiction, to be occasionally challenged only by an incipient sentimentalism.

By the 1820s this sentimentalism began eating away at orthodoxy. The emergence of fiction written expressly for children, for their amusement as well as edification, itself signified a shift toward child-centeredness and religious liberalization. But the 1820s also marked the appearance of a new image of the child in fiction for adults. As one historian of American childhood has written, fiction *about* children was much more liberal than fiction *for* children.[34] A gap began to emerge between ideas about actual children and the image of the child as a cultural icon (a distinction that Bushnell later confused when his advice on regulating children's play became tangled with his reflections on "play" as a metaphor for perfect holiness). Against conservative resistance, liberal theorizers about child-rearing increasingly granted play a place in the child's life, but without implying that a child's spontaneous activities were in any way holy. In fiction, on the other hand, child's play took on more profound connotations.

In the 1820s, religious liberals such as Lydia Maria Child and Catherine Sedgwick created images of the child less constrained by orthodoxy. Scenes in their novels of the "bewitching sports of childhood" and "healthful sporting children" by evoking childhood innocence symbolized natural human goodness. In Child's *Hobomok* (1824) and Sedgwick's *Hope Leslie* (1827), the child is not just a young person but a symbolic alternative to the novels' brooding Puritans.[35] Although these authors did not grapple openly with the question of depravity or innocence, in portraying the play of children they implicitly took a stand: To idealize children at play implied the goodness of human nature.

By the 1850s, in such domestic bestsellers as *The Wide, Wide World, Uncle Tom's Cabin, The Lamplighter,* and *Ruth Hall,* suspicion of infant depravity seems overwhelmed by a batallion of youthful heroines more angelic than human. In novel after novel, children are portrayed not only as innocent and virtuous but as the means of salvation for the more mature, and thus less pure, adults around them. Within this fiction, however, lies a more interesting theological conflict that has been lost to us, centering on the rhetorical figures of playfulness and earnestness. The two possibilities can be exemplified by Harriet Beecher Stowe's *Uncle Tom's Cabin* (1852) and another best seller of the day, Sylvester Judd's *Margaret* (1845; rev. 1857). Scenes of Christian domestic harmony in *Uncle Tom's Cabin* typically include children at play, whether Tom's and Chloe's little scamps tumbling over each other under the table while Mamma makes dinner, or the "frolicsome juveniles" of Mrs. Bird, "effervescing in all those modes of untold gambol and mischief that have astonished mothers ever since the flood."[36] Such frolicking babes are part of a cluster of images centering on the hearth, the primary symbol of all that is good in this world, the symbolic center not just of *Uncle Tom's Cabin* but of domestic fiction generally. However, when Stowe focused on play more directly, in pairing Little Eva with Topsy, she linked play to the unregenerate, earnestness to the holy.

Stowe's narrator describes Topsy, the black imp who foreshadows the literary portraits of playful black primitives in the 1920s, as wholly given over to play:

> Her talent for every species of drollery, grimace, and mimicry, – for dancing, tumbling, climbing, singing, whistling, imitating every sound that hit her fancy, – seemed inexhaustible. In her play-hours, she invariably had every child in the establishment at her heels, open-mouthed with admiration and wonder, – not excepting Miss Eva, who appeared to be fascinated by her wild diablerie, as a dove is sometimes charmed by a glittering serpent. (289)

Although Topsy is not as wicked as she believes, neither is she capable of true virtue until Eva redeems her. To Topsy's play, Eva is all earnestness. When we first meet her, Eva seems capable of both qualities: She is described as a "busy, tripping" creature, notable for both a "dreamy earnestness of expression" and "an airy and innocent playfulness" that "seemed to flicker like the shadow of summer leaves over her childish face" (175–6). But "dreamy earnestness" soon overwhelms "innocent playfulness." Eva is the offspring of Edwards's Phebe, no more evident than on a certain Sunday when her father invites her to "stay at home and play with me." "Thank you, papa," Eva responds, "but I'd rather go to church" (214–15). "Earnest" and "earnestness" become the most frequent descriptions of her demeanor as the moral burden of slavery grows heavier on her. As she prepares for death and the holy duty of redemption to which she has been called, Eva gives up her play altogether. "She still loved to play with Topsy, and the various colored children," the narrator reports, "but she now seemed rather a spectator than an actor of their plays." As she stands apart, watching the others, delighting in their sport, "a shadow would seem to pass across her face," as she would think suddenly of God and the souls of her unconverted loved ones (309). On her deathbed, in the scene that moved millions of readers to tears and became one of the most popular tableaux of the nineteenth-century stage, Eva turns Topsy to earnestness as she turns her father to God. Play in the novel signifies an innocent but unregenerate state of nature; earnestness signifies supernatural innocence and grace.

Given the facts that Stowe was the daughter of a Congregationalist minister and the wife and sister of others – and was herself a strongly intellectual woman who, because of her sex, was denied the pulpit and had to channel her theological views into her fiction – the clash of sentimental child worship with orthodox religious views in her work is not surprising. Sylvester Judd, on the other hand, was a Unitarian minister with Transcendentalist leanings. Equally unsurprising, his novel *Margaret* offers the most one-sided celebration of play in any of these sentimental novels.

Margaret apparently grew from Judd's observing a young girl, perhaps his sister Pin, "frolicking in the freedom and glee of youth." Their ensuing conversation convinced him of human innocence – and led to his own "Conversion from Calvinism," as he described it in his first published work.[37] In Judd's novel, Margaret is from her first appearance that same frolicsome child sporting with the woodsy creatures in perfect communion with nature. To her conservative religious community Margaret is damned; to her they are estranged from God. In defiance of the larger community that worships by repression, Margaret's father proposes an alternative: "Let us praise God in the dance, praise him with the stringed instrument. Let us, as David did, dance before the Lord." Judd's novel envisions a utopia founded on just such a dancing before the Lord. When, as a married woman, Margaret and her husband found a new church on Mons Christi, childlike sports and games define the substance of their Christian life. The new church institutes twelve festival days to augment the more secular May Day celebrations, all of which are occasions for worshipping God through sport, games, and amusements. In a letter to a friend at the end of the novel, Margaret in her perfect contentment calls herself "a child" with "a child's feelings. I lie on the grass and frisk, a mere baby in God's universe."[38]

Margaret embodies uncritical Antinomianism, *Uncle Tom's Cabin* a more conservative orthodoxy at odds with its own liberal sentimentalism. In the image of the child in 1850s fiction one sees a culture torn between the conservative past and an increasingly liberal present, with the drag of tradition generally holding out. In Caroline Lee Hentz's *Eoline, or Magnolia Vale* (1852), the play of young girls successfully challenges their elders' Calvinism. Similarly, scenes of a mother and her child at play in Fanny Fern's *Ruth Hall* (1855) and of an edenic frontier garden of play in Caroline A. Soule's *The Pet of the Settlement* (1860) reveal the authors' liberalism.[39] But the image of Edwards's earnest Phebe hovers over most of the decade's most popular domestic novels. Susan Warner's Ellen in *The Wide, Wide World* (1850) has "that singular mixture of gravity and sweetness that is never seen but where religion and discipline have done their work well." At various times in the novel she refuses to play on the Sabbath and maintains her pious sobriety against the complaints of her worldly guardians. Gerty of Maria S. Cummins's *The Lamplighter* (1853) is another of these painfully earnest heroines who learn that "it is through suffering only we are made perfect."[40]

A number of novels – Mary Jane Holmes's *Tempest and Sunshine* (1854), Catharine Sedgwick's *Married or Single?* (1857), Ann S. Stephens's *Mary Derwent* (1858), and A. D. T. Whitney's *The Gayworthys* (1865), for example – center on a contrast between playful and earnest sisters, in each case earnestness signifying human feeling and piety, playfulness only frivolity or heedlessness. "God has made us for something better than playfellows to each other," a minister tells Mary Derwent.[41] The playful sister in *Tempest and Sunshine, Married or Single?* and *The Gayworthys* undergoes a "sobering down," as Whitney put it – a pattern repeated by the heroines in Hentz's 1854 novel, *The Planter's Northern Bride* (the playfulness in her earlier *Eoline* had been suitably moderate), Marion Harland's *Alone* (1854), and Cummins's *Mabel Vaughan* (1858). This last novel opens with a particularly detailed exemple of the type, a long scene which turns from sentimental glorying in childish play to a sober lesson on "chasing the butterflies of folly" at the expense of learning "life's great lesson."[42]

What is most interesting in this scene from *Mabel Vaughan* is the tension between the idyllic joy of the children's play (smiled upon with great pleasure by Mabel's guardian) and the moral lesson that defies it. In all of this fiction, the sentimental emblem of the playing child confronted a theological tradition not yet ready to embrace that symbol's implications. Sentimentalism seems to have been less a mirror of theological transformation than a force behind that change. By preferring earnestness to play, the majority of these writers declared their sentimental child worship without embracing the claim for natural innocence at its root. Like Edwards's Phebe, the earnest heroines of *The Wide, Wide World, Uncle Tom's Cabin,* and *Mabel Vaughan* are unnatural children elected by a sovereign Lord not just for their own salvation but for saving others. In their utter sobriety these angel-children are symbols that bear no relation to actual childhood as understood in the mid-nineteenth century. Sylvester Judd's playful child, on the other hand, whose portrait denies the reality of evil and limitation altogether, is equally symbolic, equally detached from the age's understanding of infancy and childhood. Both are sentimental icons but radically different ones, revealing both the tensions within nineteenth-century sentimentalism and a religious mainstream in transition.

Nathaniel Hawthorne's romances of the 1850s can be viewed as his skeptical responses to this sentimental tradition, as well as to the Transcendentalism of his sometimes neighbors, Emerson and Thoreau. Hawthorne consistently embraced the conventional dualism of the day, tending more toward the conservatism of Stowe's *Uncle Tom's Cabin* than to the liberalism of Judd's *Margaret.* But in his final published romance, the deeply ambivalent, nearly incoherent *Marble Faun,* Hawthorne moved beyond the dualism of his earlier fiction to express a dialectic of tragic play – not a transcendent dialectic like Thoreau's, however, but a more conservative version in which work and play are held in irreconcilable tension.

"The Paradise of Children," one of the juvenile fictions included in *A Wonder-Book for Boys and Girls* (1852), can serve as our touchstone Hawthornian text, a more explicit version of the theme in "The May-pole of Merry Mount." In "The Paradise of Children," Hawthorne rendered the legend of Pandora as a myth of the Fortunate Fall: a story of a paradise of play that is forfeited but replaced with something better. In the paradise of children in Hawthorne's story there is "no labor to be done, no tasks to be studied; nothing but sports and dances, and sweet voices of children talking, or carolling like birds, or gushing out in merry laughter, throughout the livelong day." Pettish Pandora is nonetheless discontented, because a life of perpetual play quickly loses its enchantment. The children "could not be forever playing at hide-and-seek among the flower-shrubs, or at blindman's buff with garlands over their eyes, or at whatever other games had been found out, while Mother Earth was in her babyhood. When life is all sport, toil is the real play." Pandora destroys the play-paradise when with a playmate she opens a forbidden box, letting loose "the whole family of earthly Troubles." But enticed

The frontispiece to Nathaniel Hawthorne's "Paradise of Children" illustrates, in the lesser figures framing the central tableau, the iconic
representation of playful children that was emerging as a powerful
cultural symbol. The classical iconography, although tied directly to
Hawthorne's legend, was no less appropriate for the numerous symbolic
children in midcentury sentimental fiction. (Courtesy of Special Collections, Arizona State University Library)

by a sweet voice, the two children open the box a second time, releasing
"a sunny and smiling little personage" named Hope, who "fluttered
sportively over the children's heads," promising "something very good
and beautiful that is to be given [them], hereafter."[43]

The vision underlying Hawthorne's transparent allegory for children's
understanding is central to his major romances as well. In Hawthorne's
fictional universe "play" connotes the state of childhood and prelapsarian
innocence, but life demands something more. In *The Scarlet Letter* (1850),
Pearl's play in the forest signifies her unregenerate innocence; only by

acknowledging sin and sorrow does she become fully human and capable of redemption. In *The House of the Seven Gables* (1851), Phoebe's playfulness enlivens the dreary Pyncheon household, but as Phoebe matures into womanhood she leaves her play behind her. In *The Blithedale Romance* (1852), play is least empowering, as Priscilla's sportiveness is but a sign of her ethereal weakness. Only in *The Marble Faun* (1860), when Donatello's prelapsarian playfulness is wed to Miriam's tragic sense, does Hawthorne's fiction claim play for a serious engagement with life.

The rejection of sentimental play in the first three romances is embodied in varied contexts. Theological ideas lie closest to the surface in *The Scarlet Letter,* where Pearl appears to represent the same ideal of physical and spiritual play that Emerson envisioned in his most hopeful moments. Pearl's characteristic behavior is "to caper and dance," often at inappropriate times, in direct contrast to the Puritan children, of whom the narrator says, "What passed for play with those sombre little urchins" seems barely play at all.[44] But while the Puritans are excessively earnest, Pearl represents an equally unacceptable opposing extreme. In her play Pearl embodies Hawthorne's mistrust of human nature unredeemed by spiritual and tragic consciousness.

When Pearl makes a playmate of her own reflection in a glassy pool, she signifies her isolation from the human community (168). When she makes "sport" of killing jellyfish and pelting birds with rocks, she signifies the innocent cruelty of the natural state (177–8). When she becomes "the playmate" of the forest creatures, sharing their "kindred wildness," she signifies not the natural holiness of Judd's Margaret but the disorderly impulses of an animal condition (204–5). And when Dimmesdale's anguished cry from the scaffold at midnight – sounding "as if a company of devils, detecting so much misery and terror in it, had made a plaything of the sound" – is answered by Pearl's "light, airy, childish laugh," a kinship is established between Pearl's unredeemed nature and Dimmesdale's fallen state (148, 152). Throughout the novel, play with its connotations of spontaneity, vivacity, and communion with nature, but also of wildness, disorder, and even demonism, stands counter to an equally complex image of Puritanism: sobriety, dullness, and bigotry on the one hand, order, law, and sanctity on the other.

As in "The May-pole of Merry Mount" and "The Paradise of Children," Hawthorne reconciled these opposites in the novel's final dramatic scene, to the disadvantage of play. Pearl's redemption is foreshadowed in Chapter 15, when with unaccustomed "earnestness" she inquires about the scarlet "A" on her mother's breast; this brief moment of earnestness passing when Hester, for the first time, betrays the emblem with a lie. Play and earnestness meet at last in the concluding chapters, in multiple images of metaphoric as well as actual reconciliation. Election Day seems to Pearl "a play-day for the whole world"; even the somber Puritans for once "smiled, grimly, perhaps, but widely too" in the midst of the traditional wrestling-matches, bouts at quarter-staff, and exhibitions with the buckler and broadsword (231). And just as Puritan severity is tempered by a freer spirit of play on this day, so Pearl is at last humanized when she kisses her father on the scaffold, the tears of "the wild infant" serving as her "pledge that she would grow up amid human joy and sorrow, nor for ever do battle with the world, but be a woman in it" (256). Pearl's airy laugh is silenced, her wild antics stilled, and Hawthorne seems to have rejected the idea that holiness has anything to do with the play of spontaneous innocence.

The House of the Seven Gables and The Blithedale Romance restate this theme in less interesting ways. Phoebe in The House of the Seven Gables initially creates order and vitality through the "gush and play of her spirit," her labor expressing "the easy and flexible charm of play"; but as the novel progresses she grows less playful in direct proportion to her womanly maturity. Moreover, when Clifford Pyncheon, a supposedly mature adult, is identified with a similar pattern of play imagery, this prolongation of "baby-play" marks his ineffectuality in the social world. In the novel's most impressive scene, when Clifford blows bubbles from an upper window that float down to the street, they burst feebly against the more substantial reality of Judge Pyncheon. Later, when Clifford attempts to flee with Hepzibah, he is drawn to the ball games of laughing young people on the train. But his courage falters; play, the novel tells us, is for youth, not for adults who must take control of their lives. Phoebe, like Pearl, gives up her play to join the world as a woman in it; Clifford remains a child, excluded from any effectual role in the world at all.[45]

Although The Blithedale Romance situates play in its most interesting social context, Hawthorne's recreation of Brook Farm, Priscilla is the least substantial of all his sentimental heroines. "Blithedale" by its very naming is a Valley of Play, where the attempt by a handful of high-minded men and women from the leisure class to remake society through "the spiritualization of labor" degenerates into a Feast of Fools, a wild masquerade that echoes the excesses of Merry Mount. In this context, Priscilla's playfulness – her fondness for "playing with the other girls out-of-doors," her habit of spontaneously racing and skipping as she walks with her friends – suggests none of the empowering qualities of Phoebe's play in the early chapters of the previous novel, only Clifford's impotence. In her "simple, careless, childish flow of spirits" Priscilla seems, to Coverdale, "like a butterfly, at play in a flickering bit of sunshine, and mistaking it for a broad and eternal summer." Priscilla is all weakness, Hollingsworth excessive force; Coverdale is insufficiently serious but not truly playful, while Zenobia is prone to both excesses. No happy reconciliation draws the dualistic extremes toward a final middle ground as in the previous narratives. The marriage of Priscilla and Hollingsworth at the story's end seems but a reciprocal punishment.[46]

The Marble Faun (1860), then, offers a remarkable contrast to Hawthorne's customary position. From 1835 to 1852 (from "Merry Mount" to *Blithedale*) Hawthorne reiterated a basic theme: attraction to play, then recoil and refusal. But the profoundly disturbing impact of Rome on Hawthorne's imagination, its seductive appeal despite his deep abhorrence, seems to have altered this long-held position. Although *The Marble Faun* is yet another allegory of the Fall, its meaning has changed in significant ways. Once again, images of play suggest freedom and innocence, but Hawthorne's usual association of play with limited human development is complicated here. Play commands an importance it has never been granted, as a mode of courageous human freedom in the face of life's essential tragedy. Rather than collapse the extremes into a conventional middle ground, or settle on one or the other, *The Marble Faun* holds both play and tragic consciousness in an unresolved dialectical tension – confronting the cultural dualism without a sentimental resolution.

Initially, Donatello seems simply the most archetypal of Hawthorne's childlike innocents. His youthfulness represents the childhood of the race, his innocence the innocence of humanity before the Fall. Incessantly called "playful" or "sportive," Donatello represents man in his Golden Age playing at life in perfect harmony with nature before sin drove him from paradise. In her speculations about Donatello's likeness to the Faun of Praxiteles, Miriam speaks to Donatello about "those happy times when your race used to dwell in the Arcadian woods, playing hide-and-seek with the nymphs in grottos and nooks of shrubbery."[47] And in the three key early chapters that take place in the Borghese gardens, Donatello runs races with himself, dances through the woods, and offers his love to Miriam as "a toy." Usually sober Miriam for once joins in his races, the two of them playing

> together like children, or creatures of immortal youth; for (so much had they flung aside the somber habitudes of daily life) they seemed born to be sportive forever, and endowed with eternal mirthfulness instead of any deeper joy. It was a glimpse far backward into Arcadian life, or, further still, into the Golden Age, before mankind was burthened with sin and sorrow, and before pleasure had been darkened with those shadows that bring it into high relief, and make it Happiness. (83–4)

At this point it appears that Hawthorne had written "The Paradise of Children" for adults, making more explicitly mythic the ideas about play in his earlier fiction. The reader, then, awaits Donatello's fall into sober maturity. But in *The Marble Faun,* by linking the fate of Donatello to that of the dark and fallen Miriam, Hawthorne for the first time refused the conventional melioration of extremes. By murdering Miriam's tormentor, Donatello does indeed lose his edenic playfulness. As the narrator describes him afterwards, "Hitherto . . . even while [Donatello] was standing perfectly still, there had been a kind of possible gambol indicated in his aspect. It was quite gone now" (180). When Kenyon visits Donatello at his rural estate in Tuscany, the fallen faun's stories of his playful youth are but poignant reminders of the innocence he has now forfeited. With Donatello's fall, the play spirit seems to have disappeared from his life.

But Miriam's presence in the novel suggests a purpose for play in a fallen world. In the scene in the Borghese garden Miriam's sporting with Donatello was uncharacteristic of her:

> Naturally, it is true, she was the more inclined to melancholy, yet fully capable of that high frolic of the spirits which richly compensates for many gloomy hours; if her soul was apt to lurk in the darkness of a cavern, she could sport madly in the sunshine before the cavern's mouth. (83)

Hawthorne's image of sporting in the mouth of the cavern resembles others we have considered in different contexts: the violent contests of fur trappers and doomed Southern sportsmen, the desperate games of Ahab, Magnus Derrick, Thomas Sutpen, and their literary kin. But to sport in the mouth of the cavern is to play, not to contest. This image rejects the competitive, instrumental nature of these other games, but without rejecting altogether the agonistic element of life. The rhetorical figure of sporting in the mouth of the cavern clings to play, but to play in a tragic context: to play that accepts necessity, fallenness, death.

Hawthorne seems closest to Melville in *The Marble Faun*. The "Grand Armada" chapter in *Moby-Dick* offers a comparable image: the sportiveness of the mating and suckling whales in the midst of brutal, murderous struggle. Ishmael, naturally, derives an allegory from the scene, observing how "even so, amid the tornadoed Atlantic of my being, do I myself for ever centrally disport in mute calm."[48] Much of Melville's other fiction follows an overall pattern more melodramatically dualistic than dialectical in portraying play and its antithesis. Tommo's delight in the playfulness of the Typee natives turns to horror when he discovers their cannibalism; Pierre Glendinning's youthful frolic in Saddle Meadows turns to despair and madness once his illusions are shattered; even the whole of *Moby-Dick* turns from the playfulness of the opening comic chapters to the tragic unraveling of Ahab's mad quest. For Melville, "play" tended to signify the illusion of security in a very uncertain world; in assigning play entirely to youth in *Typee* and *Pierre,* Melville in effect pushed a cultural convention to its furthest extreme. But in *Moby-Dick* he also worked against the overall movement of the novel with the dialectical counterpoint of such scenes as the "Grand Armada."

Hawthorne expressed the same dialectical vision with Miriam and Donatello. As in his earlier romances, play must confront a darkly intransigent reality, but for the first time Hawthorne granted it potent value in the face of that reality. By refusing to make Miriam yet another Phoebe, Donatello another Clifford, Hawthorne for once granted spiritual wisdom to those who can "play" in the face of existential sorrow. That he did so consciously is evident in the narrator's extended lament on the theme that "mankind are getting so far beyond the childhood of their race, that they scorn to be happy any longer." By our obsession with purpose, "we go all wrong, by too strenuous a resolution to go all right" (239). Play offers not just relief from work and sorrow but a response to them. "There is a Wisdom that looks grave," the narrator tells us, "and sneers at merriment; and again a deeper Wisdom that stoops to be gay as often as occasion serves, and oftenest avails itself of shallow and trifling grounds of mirth; because, if we wait for more substantial ones, we seldom can be gay at all" (437). More succinctly, "The sport of mankind, like its deepest earnest, is a battle" (439). "There is a wisdom that is woe," Melville wrote in "The Try-Works" chapter of *Moby-Dick,* in language Hawthorne seems to have echoed; "but there is a woe that is madness. And there is a Catskill eagle in some souls that can alike dive down into the blackest gorges, and soar out of them again and become invisible in sunny spaces."

There is no transcendence implied in Hawthorne's image. Thoreau's figures of earnest play transformed both work and play as society knew them. Hawthorne's dialectic, on the other hand, maintains "sport" and "the cavern" as separate realities but refuses to allow the one to be swallowed by the other. *The Marble Faun* concludes at the Carnival (most fitting backdrop), where, in their final playful act before resigning themselves to prison or exile, Miriam and Donatello poignantly sport in the mouth of the cavern. Unlike sober Kenyon, on the one hand, "a care-stricken mortal [who] has no business abroad, when the rest of mankind are at high carnival" (445); and unlike the unnamed celebrants who play nonsensically, on the other; Miriam and Donatello sport in full consciousness of life's essential tragedy. Hilda, the character who most closely resembles Hawthorne's earlier heroines, matures into compassionate womanhood through an awareness of sin, much as Pearl in particular before her. But while Pearl ceases to play, Hilda is described by Kenyon at the carnival as "sporting in good faith, and with a kind of seriousness" (370) in echoes of the language that describes Miriam and Donatello. Hawthorne's version of the Fortunate Fall now depends on the play spirit as the principle of human freedom within a fated universe. Miriam and Donatello do not give up their play as Pearl and Phoebe did, but cling to it as strongly as possible without denying the pain and sorrow that life inevitably inflicts on them. Sporting in the sunshine before the cavern's mouth may be "mad," Hawthorne implied, but it is the madness of spiritual courage and a deeper wisdom.

Good girls, bad boys, Mark Twain, and the secularization of play

By the 1870s, two things happened to the image of the child in American fiction: Play triumphed over earnestness to express the values of a newly dominant liberalism, and the context became fully secularized – childhood play no longer raised theological questions. In the decades following the Civil War, middle-class American culture absorbed Romantic radicalism, accommodating the new concern with play to traditional work values without openly embracing play's deeper implications. The rise of organized sport can be viewed in this context. The years following the Civil War saw not just the wholesale reconstitution of American colleges and universities as sponsors of athletic teams but a proliferation of sporting activities throughout society. America's first leisure class identified itself through its country clubs and yachting clubs. Churches recruited one of Satan's chief lieutenants, Public Amusement, to become its own most powerful ally against the temptations of the modern city. As the century waned, municipal governments as well as liberal reformers found in regulated play a primary solution to the problems created by the new urban reality. About the same time, in the 1880s and after, psychologists and anthropologists discovered the necessity of play as a developmental experience in the childhood of both the individual and the race. And with Theodore Roosevelt in the White House during the first decade of the twentieth century, sport enjoyed sanction from the highest authority in the land.

But the play so cherished in these various developments was a very unplayful sort. The period between the Civil War and World War I saw the first official endorsement of the play spirit in America, yet the *organization* of play that resulted throughout society expressed an ideology with little of play's essence. Organization under any guise is fundamentally antiplay. The new interest in teams, leagues, associations, rankings and championships, statistics and records created a variety of objectives beyond the activity itself. The prophets of intercollegiate sport endorsed not play but character building, and churches built gymnasiums to counteract temptation. The wealthy played, at least in part, in order to prove that they had the time and money to do so; employers and reformers promoted working-class play for the sake of better work and less crime. Social scientists proclaimed the *necessity* of play to every healthy organism, whether individual or collective. Other researchers explored play's function in creating culture.

Collectively, the many advocates of play embraced the cultural dualism that the Transcendentalists had sought to transcend: a balanced life of work and play (with play in service to work), or the "symmetrical development" of a tripartite self – mind, body, and will or spirit. Pursuit of the elusive balance infused discussions of work and leisure, the concern over "nervousness" or "neurasthenia" as a national disease in the 1870s and 1880s, nearly every effort at social reform.[49] Even in its separate sphere play could not remain untouched by the instrumental bias of the age. The official recognition of play insisted on its *utility* in a variety of ways, no more clearly than in the so-called play movement beginning in the 1880s. Unlike the managerial classes, large elements of both the nativist and the immigrant working classes had long found their own cultural values in leisure rather than labor – in the streets, on the ballfield, at the prize ring, in the dance hall, preeminently in the saloon.[50] In addition, as recent social and labor historians have argued, preindustrial work habits, which retained large elements of play within work itself, survived among factory workers in resistance to the demands of the new industrial order for efficiency.[51] Both the "vice" and the potential anarchy of working-class play were threatening to middle-class morality and desires for a well-regulated society.

As Taylorites attempted to maximize the efficiency of labor, other reformers were insisting on the development of "organized" or "directed" play. The play movement constituted a shift from play as an individual activity to play in the service of community interest, organized by the community. The movement ultimately attempted, as its contemporary historian noted in what he intended as praise, "to bring about the social utilization of all leisure through the provision of opportunities for participation by all ages of people in behavior that is both personally developmental and socially constructive."[52] It goes without saying that the engineers of lower-class leisure were far from totally successful. Their degrees of success and failure are complex matters, a thorough understanding of which would contribute much to the current debates over "mass culture" and domination. But successful or not, their understanding of play was antagonistic to play's essential spirit.

Once again, the rhetoric of American fiction can offer a glimpse "inside" the social history of play. Postbellum novels reveal not a consciously articulated theory of play but the sense of play in the imagination of the genteel culture. The *absence* of play from certain kinds of novels is itself revealing. Play, for example, is largely irrelevant to the utopian fiction that proliferated between 1865 and 1917, particularly after the success of Edward Bellamy's *Looking Backward* in 1888.[53] The utopias in this fiction are "reconstructive" rather than "escapist," concerned, that is, with imagining a rationally ordered society rather than a paradise of pleasure.[54] Such writers as Edward Everett Hale, William Dean Howells, and Ignatius Donnelly, as well as Bellamy granted leisure some importance in their ideal worlds, but utopian writers were primarily concerned with meaningful work.[55] If a burden, the duty of work was to be shared by all; if a pleasure, work rather than play was to be life's chief source of satisfaction. In more than twenty utopias, only T. Wharton Collens's *Eden of Labor* (1876) – despite its title – envisioned a utopia of play: a prelapsarian garden where Adam shares in "the joyous gambols of his children."[56] Even in this exception, the natural world celebrated as a garden of play cannot provide the superior happiness only the supernatural can give. For Collens, the genuine ideal had to be a Christian utopia.

A character in Mary E. Bradley's utopian novel *Mizora: A Prophecy* (1889) would seem to speak for the majority viewpoint when she declares, "Nature has taught us the duty of work."[57] But as a woman, Bradley also spoke in a distinctly gendered voice. The other body of fiction in which play is conspicuously absent is a significant range of women's novels. Whereas play embodied a countercultural desire for work-oriented men in the nineteenth century, work embodied the reformist desire of play-burdened women. Although less than 5 percent of the female population could have been identified as genuinely leisured in the Gilded Age (another 10 percent perhaps had a single servant), persistent assumptions about gender defined the woman's "sphere" in terms of play and leisure. Although the Victorian "lady" was rarely as idle as either her admirers or her detractors claimed, as Ann Douglas has written, "Leisure, whether hypothetical or actual, was increasingly treated as the most interesting and significant thing about her; her function was obscured and intended to be so." Mary Abigail Dodge in *Woman's Worth and Worthlessness* (1872) expressed a prevalent viewpoint when she proclaimed woman "divinely designed" for a "state of repose, ease, leisure."[58]

Resisting these ideas, such prominent women writers as Lydia Maria Child, Louisa May Alcott, Elizabeth Stuart Phelps, and Julia Ward Howe criticized the idle woman in essays and books. The foremost American feminist at the end of the century, Charlotte Perkins Gilman, denounced the relegation of women to a world of play while at the same time so restricting feminine play that it offered none of the rewards available in masculine sport.[59] In this same spirit, several of the most prominent women novelists of the period took up the cause of liberating labor. For signs of a profound cultural shift, one can compare the mid- to late-nineteenth-century fiction of Louisa May Alcott, Harriet Beecher Stowe, Kate Chopin, Edith Wharton, and Gilman herself to Hannah Foster's *The Coquette* from the 1790s. Whereas Eliza Wharton in *The Coquette* is publicly damned for her "natural disposition for gaiety," the heroines of numerous later novels by these women struggle to assert their desire to work, against a society that insists they play. Alcott's succinctly titled *Work* (1873) offers a series of chapters illustrating the rewards of a useful life and the emptiness of an idle one, while the heroine of Stowe's *My Wife and I* (1871) and *We and Our Neighbors* (1873) leaves behind the frivolity of gay society for the more rewarding duties of domestic economy. The theme explored in both of Stowe's novels appeared in an essay she wrote in the mid-sixties, in which she insisted that there was "some task, some burden, some cross each one must carry; and there must be something done in every true and worthy life, not as amusement, but as duty, – not as play but as earnest work."[60] To fail to heed this fact, or worse, to be denied the ability to heed it, can lead to tragedy: Chopin's heroine in *The Awakening* (1899) and Wharton's in *The House of Mirth* (1905) are both victims of a leisure culture that places women, in Wharton's words, in "bondage to other people's pleasures."[61] In Gilman's famous story "The Yellow Wallpaper" (1892), a woman goes mad when she is confined in a room that for past tenants was a "nursery first and then playroom and gymnasium" – emblems of the condition of childlike play to which supposedly privileged women were bound. The woman's diagnosed "nervousness" was endlessly discussed in this period, by such doctors as Gilman's own, S. Weir Mitchell, as a psychological and emotional illness whose cure lay in rest and recreation. Through her story Gilman answered that play was the disease, women its victims, work its cure.[62]

Progressive women writers' rejection of play must be qualified, however, because class is a crucial factor here. While work could define the realm of freedom for upper-middle- and upper-class women, leisure served that function for women of the working classes, at least to a limited extent, as it did for working-class men.[63] Against the novels of oppressive urban leisure stand many stories of oppressive rural labor, one of the distinctive themes of New England local-color writing, for example. We saw that the writing about the West and the South is deeply imbued by an implicitly countercultural play spirit. Much of the regional writing of New England, on the other hand, emphasizes the drudgery of daily existence, the scant opportunities for play. Such writers as Rose Terry Cooke, Alice Brown, and Mary Wilkins Freeman wrote numerous stories portraying wives ground down by endless unrewarding domestic labor. When play is celebrated, as in Sarah Orne Jewett's *The Country of the Pointed Firs* (1896), it is the rare outburst of the traditional, ritual play of the Bowden reunion, whose wellsprings are patriotism, friendship, and kinship – wholly different from the "petty excitements of every day that belong to cities."[64]

Work and play thus figure interestingly in the intersection of class and gender in late nineteenth-century fiction. For a sense of the culture's dream life, however, its less calculated responses to contending values, the popular juvenile fiction of the day and the adult fiction in which juveniles prominently figure provide a richer resource. Here, one can see the culture's less conscious absorption of the radical challenge posed by play. Here also, one can see a fundamentally theological culture transformed into a fully secular one. The years immediately following the Civil War mark a transitional moment in our cultural history. As representative texts, Henry Ward Beecher's *Norwood* (1868) and Harriet Beecher Stowe's *Oldtown Folks* (1869) address the implications of play in the theological context of Hawthorne and the sentimentalists; Louisa May Alcott's *Little Women* (1868–69) and Thomas Bailey Aldrich's *The Story of a Bad Boy* (1870) deal with similar themes in the spirit of the new secular age. Overriding this difference in orientation is a basic similarity in worldview: an acceptance of play but relegation of it to the status of lesser element in a fundamental dualism. In all of these novels the celebration of childhood play is a projection of adult desire, but in a form that is utterly safe.

Norwood and *Oldtown Folks* are remarkable novels for their documentation of a culture in transition. Both novels are set in small New England towns, with casts of characters that represent the full spectrum of their region's religious viewpoints. In *Norwood,* a liberal doctor and a conservative parson, a Southern gentleman and a Yankee farmer, a worldly judge and an ascetic housekeeper, all watch the heroine grow from playful child to mature woman as a spiritual ideal. In a strikingly similar way, Stowe's Oldtown and its environs are home to Arminians, Calvinists, Episcopalians, and skeptics, with a heroine even more playful than Beecher's, and a Rip Van Winkle-like "village do-nothing," Sam Lawson, who challenges all the common assumptions about work and worth. Sin and innocence, salvation and damnation lie at the center of both novels – structured in part on the dualism of work and play.

Both novels recount the liberalization of New England theology – with Beecher's simple approval and Stowe's deeper ambivalence. Beecher's Rose Wentworth and Stowe's Tina Percival are similar icons of sentimental play (each revealed in the seemingly inevitable scene of woodland sport that appeared earlier in Judd's *Margaret* and Hawthorne's *Scarlet*

Letter), their playfulness a sign of spiritual as well as physical health. But both heroines also grow into mature womanhood. And in both novels, this characterization of the heroine is set in the context not just of New England local color but of a revisionary history that insists on the moderate playfulness of the maligned Puritans – a rhetorical strategy for claiming an ideal past as guide to contemporary life. According to the novels' narrators, the lack of festival days and public amusements in Puritan New England had legitimate political purposes and was offset by an abundance of what Stowe's speaker calls "sober, well-considered merriment." The narrator of *Norwood* hails work, but as the instrument that "shall drive out Drudgery and bring in Leisure." More elaborately, the narrator of *Oldtown Folks* looks back to a time in preindustrial New England when work and play were together the substance of life, not discordant activities relegated to separate days and hours. The long description of the splendid and general "mirth" of a New England Thanksgiving with its meeting-house proclamation, joyous busyness in preparation, generosity to the less fortunate, and culminating feast and dance presided over by a beaming minister and his lady reveals most concretely the interpenetration of work, play, and religion in New England village life just after the Revolution, emphatically (if only implicitly) unlike the situation in Stowe's America in 1869.[65]

The two novels are remarkably similar, then, but Stowe did not tuck in all her theological corners as neatly as her brother did. In *Norwood* the narrator consistently seeks a middle ground between Puritan seriousness and its complete rejection, as he follows Rose Wentworth's growth into responsible womanhood, most notable when she becomes a nurse during the Civil War. In the same spirit, a stereotypical Southern planter comes not only to appreciate a society in which labor is honorable rather than servile, but also to discover that Norwood has its own New England brand of play: a nutting expedition to "shouts of merriment" and incessant "pranks and mirth" attended even by Parson Buell (341–43). Play, in other words, is modified by work, work by play. *Oldtown Folks,* on the other hand, is more truly "dialogic" or multi-vocal, its disparate voices not simply resolved into a single dominant one. In the manner of much domestic fiction, playful Tina and earnest Esther are in fact drawn toward a conventional middle ground in the novel's closing chapters. Having reached womanhood, Tina's continuing beyond youth "to make a frolic of life" makes her "fair game" for a man who pursues romance as amusement (510–11). Only the blow of discovering her husband's infamy can transform Tina at last: It drives "her soul inward, from the earthly upon the spiritual and immortal," raising "her into a higher plane" (587, 591). In a complementary way, Esther's solemn temperament is lightened by love.

But against such conventional rejection of extremes, Sam Lawson, a character who hovers on the periphery of the story as the village's anarchic play spirit – more interested in playing the fiddle at husking and quilting frolics than in supporting his long-suffering wife and six children – remains unchanged, and unchastened, at the novel's end. And in a separate plot, convening Calvinist ministers praised for their "jocund mirthfulness" (454) represent a kind of Thoreauvian dialectic of earnest play. Both work and play receive their due in *Oldtown Folks;* the novel tends toward confirming the necessity of moral earnestness, yet the voice of playful enjoyment is neither silenced nor fully compromised. In short, both *Norwood* and *Oldtown Folks* accommodate play to emerging liberal religious values, but Stowe's novel retains a richer sense of conflict within the cultural transformation. *Norwood* more thoroughly domesticates play, both theologically and socially, a strategy crucial to the genteel culture of the postbellum period.

The shift from an essentially conservative theology in *Uncle Tom's Cabin* to the liberalism of *Oldtown Folks* reflects not just Stowe's personal religious odyssey but the larger cultural shift in which her fiction played a part. In like manner, the turn from a religious emphasis in *Oldtown Folks* to the merely social world of *My Wife and I* just two years later reflects another aspect of that larger cultural change. While the Little Evas of 1850s domestic fiction were symbols of theological principles, the Jo Marches and Tom Sawyers of the Gilded Age were more simply the boys and girls that their creators and readers had once been, refracted through nostalgia. In their play they were also idealized figures on whom middle-class America projected its desires and fantasies, but without jeopardizing its ultimate commitment to work. In the sports and games of juvenile protagonists, that is, one can see the radicalism of the Transcendentalists fully absorbed into a reconstituted and wholly secular middle-class culture.

Alcott's *Little Women* and Aldrich's *Story of a Bad Boy* are the prototypical novels of the new era. *Little Women* in particular is a transitional novel, its two parts seeming to be nearly different books. The controlling metaphor of Part One is a *game* of Pilgrim's Progress that amounts to earnest moral striving.[66] But the simpler spirit of play also pervades the girls' lives: the frolics of parlor theatricals at Christmas, a New Year's Eve dance, snowballing and indoor games in winter, picnics and garden romps in spring and summer. Play has its limits, however. When the girls complain at one point about their hard tasks, Mrs. March proposes an experiment: all play and no work for a full week – "Fun for ever, and no grubbage," as Jo enthusiastically puts it. In a reprise of Hawthorne's "Paradise for Children," after a single day of delight the girls grow increasingly weary of their leisure. "Have regular hours for work and play," their mother tells them when the experiment has ended, and life will "become a beautiful success, in spite of poverty."[67]

Part One of *Little Women* thus insists on the conventional dualism in a children's story. Part Two, on the other hand, is a novel about girls entering womanhood and making their way in a masculine world. Here, as in the novels by women mentioned earlier, play becomes frivolity, work the essence of female worth. Jo announces the theme when she declares to a friend, "We are man and woman now, with sober work to do, for play-time is over, and we must give up frolicking" (546). As a *woman's* novel, *Little Women* thus rejects the cultural projection of play onto femininity; as a *girl's* novel, it endorses the conventional relegation of play to childhood, work to maturity. In this, *Little Women* was followed by such juvenile classics as Margaret Sidney's *Five Little Peppers and How They Grew* (1880), Kate Douglas Wiggins's *Rebecca of Sunnybrook Farm* (1903), and Gene Stratton Porter's *Laddie* (1913) – all of which celebrate work and play as the two halves of the ideal life, assigning play to childhood on natural rather than supernatural grounds.[68]

Thomas Bailey Aldrich's *Story of a Bad Boy* initiated a parallel tradition in boys' fiction celebrating the same cultural values: an absorption of the liberal play spirit in apparent blindness to its deeper implications. From Aldrich's *Bad Boy,* Charles Dudley Warner's *Being a Boy* (1878), and William Dean Howells's *A Boy's Town* (1890), three classics of the era, emerges a composite portrait of the sporting boy in the genteel imagination, in which boyhood appears as an edenic state with play its essence. The theological implications of earlier fiction linger lightly in the boys' chafing at Sabbath restrictions, but overwhelmingly play has been naturalized for a secular age.[69] In all three books childhood, most simply, is the time for play. Aldrich's Tom Bailey delights in baseball, outdoor excursions, and winter sports, including the grandly heroic snow war on Slatter's Hill that became the novel's most famous set piece. Warner's boy loves fishing best, though he also enjoys sledding and snowball fights, parties and innocent pranks. Most fully, Howells's entire book defines childhood by the variety of its play, most of the chapters focusing on particular types of amusement: river sports, school sports, circuses and shows, highdays and holidays, and so on, including what would seem a gratuitous chapter on "Plays and Pastimes."

But working against this casual acceptance of play – unthinkable even a generation earlier, it is important to remember – a persistent work ethic clings to these novels. *The Story of a Bad Boy* ends with Tom's departure for college, leaving not just his home behind but childhood and play as well. The fictional Tom Bailey writes his memoir from the perspective of one who has grown into a "hard, worldly" man, "fighting the fight of life" (156). Warner never does decide which is more wonderful, work or play, alternately praising one or the other, in this inconsistency reflecting his culture's uncertainty. Even Howells's most thoroughly playful boy begins work in a printing office at age ten. The theme of all three books, finally, is that play defines the essence of childhood, to be put aside for life's labors with maturity. But there is more at stake than a simple declaration of life's progressive stages. The celebration of boyhood play expresses a longing that the acquiescence into adult responsibility cannot disguise: a potent fantasy at odds with conventional values.

In different ways, John Habberton's *Helen's Babies* (1876), B. P. Shillaber's *Ike Partington* (1878), Hamlin Garland's *Boy Life on the Prairie* (1899), and Booth Tarkington's *Penrod* (1914) promote these same themes. In the last decades of the nineteenth century, play displaced earnestness as the sentimental ideal, but in a naturalized form, with all its formerly dangerous implications submerged. One generation's radicalism became the next generation's convention. Overtly, the authors of boy fiction satirized conventional manners through their heroes' rascally, sportive behavior; covertly, they embraced the genteel world at which they poked fun. In celebrating childhood play these genteel authors also defied the ruthless commercialism from which they felt estranged, yet they embraced its dominant values in their boys' ultimate turn from play to work. The calm of the novels' surfaces masks an unacknowledged uneasiness characteristic of the time.

No one wrestled more relentlessly with these conflicting allegiances than Mark Twain. Twain's imagination dwelt, at times obsessively, on play and childhood throughout a lifetime in both conventional and unconventional ways.[70] Twain began writing about children by spoofing the Sunday-School-tract portraits of Good Boys and Bad Boys ("The Story of the Bad Little Boy" [1865] and "The Story of the Good Little Boy" [1870]), but his own novel in the Bad Boy tradition, *The Adventures of Tom Sawyer* (1876), immortalized a merely different sentimental stereotype. In such later books as *The Prince and the Pauper* (1881) and *Personal Recollections of Joan of Arc* (1896), as well as his *Autobiography* and, in life, his late attraction to prepubescent "Angel Fish," Twain continued to sentimentalize the conventional image of childhood in genteel culture. At other times in Twain's writing play represents something far more potent: the possibility of total freedom and transcendence on the one hand, or the futility of human action on the other. The narrator atop a stage coach in *Roughing It* (1872), thrilled by "gladness and the wild sense of freedom"; the narrator of *A Tramp Abroad* (1880), rafting down the Neckar River in "a deep and tranquil ecstasy"; Huck and Jim on the raft in *Huckleberry Finn* (1885), floating in perfect freedom; Huck and Jim and Tom in *Tom Sawyer Abroad* (1894), sailing in a balloon through the air, where "it was so still and sunshiny and lovely, and plenty to eat, and plenty of sleep, and strange things to see, and no nagging and no pestering, and no good people, and just holiday all the time" – all represent the playful freedom that Twain always longed for.[71] In starkest contrast, the carelessly cruel play of Satan in "The Chronicle of Young Satan" and the pointless play of his human playmates epitomize Twain's darkest fear that life had no meaning.

I have discussed two Twains in separate chapters, this and Chapter 6. My terms of inquiry, "sport of the gods" and "play," can thus stand for the unreconciled aspects of Samuel Clemens's twain-ness, a literary truism addressed by critics in numerous other contexts. But it is also important to acknowledge the range of possibilities within each aspect, in this case the merely sentimental and the more radical possibilities in Twain's playful humanism. Freedom and determinism were sometimes at stake in Twain's treatment of play, as they had been for antebellum writers; at other times Twain merely succumbed to convention, however artful some of his conventional stories. For all its superiority to Aldrich's *Story of a Bad Boy* and others of the type, *Tom Sawyer* is merely Twain's major contribution not just to a specific literary convention of boy's stories but to the conventional work/play dualism in genteel fiction. In *Tom Sawyer,* play triumphs over everything that would oppose it: work, adulthood, constraint, even reality. Tom not only lives a life of nearly uninterrupted play, he induces the adult population of St. Petersburg to collaborate with him "in creating the illusion that the world is ultimately given over to play."[72] But while Tom's play is creative, the adults appear merely foolish, though nothing intrinsic otherwise distinguishes the two kinds. Play is for children, the novel insists. Tom's play is safe, conventional, with no hint of anarchy, no defiance of respectable society, not even much, at last, of true freedom.

The narrator defines play explicitly, for the only time in Twain's fiction, in the famous whitewashing scene early in *Tom Sawyer*: "Work consists of whatever a body is *obliged* to do. . . . Play consists of whatever a body is not obliged to do."[73] By this standard, ironically, most of Tom's play in the novel is not truly playful. When Tom, Huck, and Joe sneak off to Jackson's Island, Tom and Joe must endure loneliness, pangs of conscience, and nausea from Huck's tobacco long after they have wearied of their adventure but feel compelled to remain. Tom, quite simply, is no cultural revolutionary but a conventional citizen of St. Petersburg, a "sanctioned rebel" as one critic has termed him.[74] Although one might argue that for the only time in his fiction Twain in *Tom Sawyer* imagined a world of perfect peace and freedom, he did so entirely on the terms established by Aldrich and other genteel writers, and by simply evading adult reality. *Tom Sawyer* neither comes to terms with the fallen world (*à la* Hawthorne in *The Marble Faun*), nor comprehends work and limitation within the sphere of play (*à la* Thoreau).

The Prince and the Pauper and *Joan of Arc*, Twain's most "respectable" novels, are equally conventional in their treatment of play. In the earlier of the two, Prince Edward's attraction to Tom Canty's life of rough sports and rustic pastimes confirms the conventional golden mean in an uninspired way (all work and no play make Edward a dull prince). Twain's Joan of Arc in the later book is a more interesting figure: In her dancing about the Faery Tree of her village, the playmate of spirits as well as people, Joan becomes a sort of fifteenth-century Little Eva in a secularized world. "All through her childhood," her biographer and playmate Louis de Conte reports, "and up to the middle of her fourteenth year, Joan had been the most light-hearted creature and the merriest in the village, with a hop-skip-and-jump gait and a happy and catching laugh." But like Eva before her, Joan is called to more serious business: the saving of France rather than souls. Her manner accordingly becomes "grave," her motto in war, "Work! work! and God will work with us!" Twain's narrator carries on like a fifteenth-century Orison Swett Marden: "For in war she never knew what indolence was. And whoever will take that motto and live by it will be likely to succeed. There's many a way to win in this world, but none of them is worth much without good hard work back of it." Joan's earnestness follows her into battle with the English and eventually to the stake.[75]

Despite its conventionality, the Faery Tree of Domremy is another version of that potent symbol in Twain's imagination, another in that series of paradisaic images of play that began in life with the Quarles farm and reappeared in most of his books. Only in *Huckleberry Finn*, however, with Huck and Jim on a raft floating down the Mississippi, did Twain find a symbol that could bear the psychological burden he placed on it.[76] In *Tom Sawyer, The Prince and the Pauper,* and *Joan of Arc,* Twain subscribed to the conventional sentimentalizing of childhood play, reserving adulthood for seriousness and work. In *Huckleberry Finn,* on the other hand, Twain challenged such conventions, but here he was defeated by an inability to wed his fantasy of freedom to his sense of necessity and limitation. Dualism persists in the novel, but fixed on unresolved opposition rather than directed toward the usual golden mean. *Huckleberry Finn* most directly dramatizes the competing impulses toward convention and anarchy in Twain's psyche, and in Twain's culture as well.

The conflicting principles of freedom and constraint are represented by Huck and Tom. Whereas in the fantasy world of his own novel Tom's play seems innocent, in the adult reality of slavery, greed, cruelty, and deception that define the Mississippi Valley of *Huckleberry Finn,* his play is cruel and coercive. Viewing life from a hogshead, Huck is unbound by convention. Viewing life from Aunt Polly's parlor or *The Arabian Nights,* Tom is bound by both middle-class values and the dictates of fictional romance. In the boys' play early in the novel, these differences are only intimated. In the St. Petersburg chapters Huck defers as Tom proposes they tie Jim to a tree "for fun" and "play something on him," then joins Tom in playing pirates and robbers with the rest of the gang.[77] When Huck eventually loses patience, insisting that swords are only lath and broomsticks, A-rabs and elephants only a Sunday School outing, he seems deficient in imagination, unable to play. Only when Huck runs off with Jim does the truer distinction between the two boys begin to emerge. Tom's play is make-believe, sometimes with cruel consequences for the victims who do not share his fantasies. Huck, on the other hand, accepts the world as it is but seeks to play within it, in defiance of society's demands and values. Huck wants total freedom within the world; Tom wants merely to ignore the world as it is.

The various episodes in *Huckleberry Finn* develop this opposition. Huck is truly free – at play – only when alone with Jim on the raft. During the few brief days of idyllic interlude on the River, between the Grangerford-Shepherdson feud and the arrival of the King and Duke, Huck's harmony with both himself and his environment is complete. Time slips by, "so quiet and smooth and lovely," as Huck and Jim lie naked and drift, without anxiety, without conflict, without compulsion (156). Huck's utter contentment and his lack of loneliness are sharply contrasted to the uneasiness of the boys on Jackson's Island in *Tom Sawyer.* Huck's life on the river is uncoerced leisure. But there is a shore world on either side where play is powerless, and even on the raft Huck is capable of cruelty until he sheds Tom's influence. In the first third of the novel, whenever Huck invokes Tom's name in devising a scheme, disaster follows. In the next third, as Tom disappears in spirit as well as name, Huck must now confront the cruel "games" that dominate and demean the lives of the adult population: the fatal game-playing of the Shepherdsons and Grangerfords, the predatory con games of the King and Duke, the vicious games played by the vagrant citizens of Bricksville that progress from the torture of dogs to a pointless murder. All are crueler, more consequential versions of Tom Sawyer's false play: refusals to see the world as it is, "playing" at life in a way that denies reality. Huck deals with people as they are, not as figments of his imagination, but the shore offers him no possibility for his truer kind of play. On the raft, Huck is powerful as well as free, playing his life in defiance of social norms. On shore, Huck is powerless either to prevent the evil he sees or to guarantee his own freedom.

The famous moral crisis of Chapter 31 – and the equally famous critical controversy over the final third of the novel – illuminate Twain's problem in finding a meeting place between play and the world. Had Huck been alone on the raft, he would still have had to come to shore at some point, just as the child someday has to become an adult (the specter of Pap Finn constantly reminds us of this fact). Moreover, the oft-cited description of the rafting idyl has a revealing parallel earlier in the novel: Huck's comment in Chapter VI on his life with Pap after being kidnapped from the Widow's house. "It was kind of lazy and jolly," Huck says, in language that could easily describe the delights of rafting, "laying off comfortable all day, smoking and fishing, and no books nor study." With Jim, Huck experiences idyllic brotherhood; with Pap, the pleasures of unconstrained cussing. As play, the one is not "good," the other "bad"; play has no moral conscience. Play on the raft is threatened by the shore world; play as Pap's prisoner is threatened by drunken cowhidings. But even more fundamentally, as the novel develops, Huck's play is threatened by Jim. Not just a corrupt society but human relations themselves are inimical to sustained play, a truth not invalidated by the brief idyl of Huck and Jim on the raft. As his lessons in compassion and responsibility from Jim give Huck new dignity, this moral growth also destroys the freedom of his play. Play is anarchic; it has nothing to do with either a "sound heart" or a "deformed conscience," as these moral options are developed in the novel, but represents a third possibility: neither sentimentalism nor corrupted Calvinism but antinomian holiness with its inherent social anarchy. Huck's famous declaration, "All right, then, I'll *go* to hell," signifies moral growth but also loss of freedom. He defies society but in the name of love and responsibility, not of play. He declares his engagement with, not his freedom within, the world.

Twain the anarchic individualist and Twain the indignant moralist were not compatible. Libertarianism and determinism, freedom and necessity, childhood and adulthood, the raft and the shore refused to meet in his fiction. The novel that seems to have been born out of a longing for the freedom of childhood play became instead a moral fable. In bringing back Tom Sawyer to preside over the final section, Twain violated not only the moral heroism Huck achieved at the cost of his play spirit, but Huck's play spirit as well. Huck and Tom "play" out the remainder of the novel, but in the manner of *Tom Sawyer,* not of Huck on the raft. As a passive, reluctant, even guilt-ridden accomplice, Huck watches Tom transform the Phelps farm and surrounding countryside into the same play world Tom enjoyed in St. Petersburg in the earlier novel. The great escape rests on make-believe: on pretending that Jim is still a slave, not a free man by Miss Watson's dying decree. This time, Twain cheated the reader, too, by withholding this crucial, and preposterous, bit of information. But what was he to do? True play had proven self-sufficient only in isolation, helpless before social evil, deficient in moral responsibility, and impossible to sustain. Twain seems to have chosen the only way out: exit laughing.

Huckleberry Finn was both Twain's noblest attempt and grandest failure to imagine a life truly rooted in play. It is a most Emersonian novel, as James L. Johnson has argued in another context: dreaming of freedom without denying fate but failing to embrace the two in a coherent vision.[78] In his later fiction, as Twain continued to dream of playful childhood freedom, these dreams either became more conventional, as in *The Prince and the Pauper* and *Joan of Arc,* or turned to nightmare. In *A Connecticut Yankee,* Hank Morgan plays with sixth-century English society as Tom Sawyer played with nineteenth-century St. Petersburg, but with appalling consequences. Twain could not decide whether King Arthur's knights were lovable, playful children or cruel oppressors and obstacles to progress, portraying them as both at different times. The gross, sensual, cruel lords of Hank's initial experiences in Camelot resemble little the boyish comrades later in the novel who play baseball in their armor and arrive by bicycle in the nick of time to save the Boss. Out of the real world they are playful children; in the world they are enemies to reform. So, too, with Hank. When the novel ignores its social and political context Hank is an enchanting player. When the world returns, Hank becomes an earnest Yankee obsessed with "progress" and corrupted by his game-playing. The "darling fifty-two" boys who merrily assist Hank in destroying 30,000 Englishmen are the most chilling evidence of Twain's inability to sustain a vision of play in a world of necessity. And he restaged this nightmare vision over and over: self-mockingly in "The Private History of a Campaign that Failed" (1885), where boys playing soldier blunder on the harsh reality of war; ironically in the perverse play of Tom Driscoll and Chambers as children in *Pudd'nhead Wilson* (1894); most bleakly in several of the dream manuscripts of the last years – "The Enchanted Sea-Wilderness" (1896), "Which Was the Dream?" (1897), "The Great Dark" (1898) – that begin in play and end in horror. "The Chronicle of Young Satan" capped a transformation of the child from player to play*thing,* while imagining a childlike deity as a capriciously cruel player with human lives. Both sides of the nightmare are realized here: total surrender of freedom on the one hand, the complete perversion of the empowered play spirit on the other.

Twain dreamed of freedom but despaired of achieving it. Only in *Huckleberry Finn,* and only momentarily there, did he embody his dream in an adequate symbol, but his inability to solve his personal or the culture's dualism defeated him there as well. Twain's contemporaries more safely celebrated play at a distance – projecting it onto a childhood to be outgrown and left behind for work. Their clichés invited the irony of Stephen Crane as well as Twain (particularly in Crane's Whilomville stories), but their domestication of what had once been a potent and problematic image easily survived the debunkers.[79] By the twentieth century, Americans were playing as never before while still officially clinging to the older values of work and duty. To a degree not fully acknowledged yet, play challenged these values most profoundly, but the conventional accommodation ignored its contradictions. It would be left to succeeding generations of young rebels to renew the assault on the culture's sanctioned values in the name of play.

11

Play and the Counterculture in the 1920s

Sometime on or about September 7, 1909, to echo Virginia Woolf, the spirit of antinomian play arose from genteel entombment to be reborn in a new countercultural rebellion. Give or take a few years. On that day, Sigmund Freud delivered his first lecture on the new science of psychoanalysis at Clark University in Worcester, Massachusetts, his only visit to the United States. In 1909 also, Friedrich Nietzsche's *The Birth of Tragedy* was translated into English, appearing in the same year as James Huneker's discussion of Nietzsche in *Egoists: A Book of Supermen,* and following by a year H. L. Mencken's initial American book-length study of the "mad" German philosopher. By 1913, Oscar Levy's eighteen-volume English translation of Nietzsche's works had been completed; A. A. Brill had translated Freud's *Interpretation of Dreams,* which became one of his two most influential works in America in the 1920s; Van Wyck Brooks had launched his campaign against "puritanism" in his first book, *The Wine of the Puritans* (1908); Gertrude Stein had written *Melanctha* (1909), the first major American novel of black primitivism in this century; Randolph Bourne had described the redemptive power of "Youth" in the *Atlantic Monthly* (1912) and in a volume of essays, *Youth and Life* (1913); and the Armory Show in New York had introduced European modernism to the American art world. In each of these events contributing to the disruptive and rejuvenating intellectual currents of the day, the spirit of play was an important theme.

Nietzsche, Freud, and the playground of bohemia

The resurgence of an American radical play spirit was, of course, part of a much larger movement. In Europe during and after World War I, dadaists and surrealists, for example, less cautiously explored the boundaries of play in their ravaged land. The American play spirit more specifically assaulted late-Victorian cultural conservatism, ironically by acting out one of its unexamined assumptions. The cult of the child had made childhood a sentimental ideal. The youth cult of the years before and after the First World War saw those sentimentalized young people step forward in the flesh now, no longer figments of literary imagination, to denounce the older generation for the very sentimentality and prudery that had given youth its cultural potency. "Youth" was less innocent now: no Bad Boys and Good Girls playing at pirates or sporting with woodsy creatures, but disillusioned young adults who had fled small towns and been through psychoanalysis, attempting to sport at life in order to free themselves from sexual repression and to liberate their world from mechanization. In this real world, the play of Tina Percival and Tom Sawyer became more troubled and troubling; carefree sport gave way to rebellious and desperate play.

The chief enemy was "puritanism." In manifesto, essay, and book – from Van Wyck Brooks' *America's Coming-of-Age* (1915) and Randolph Bourne's "The Puritan's Will to Power" (1917); to Waldo Frank's *Our America* (1919), Harry O'Higgins's *The American Mind in Action* (1920), and Harold Stearns's *America and the Young Intellectual* (1921); to H. L. Mencken's series of *Prejudices* and William Carlos Williams's *In the American Grain* (1925) – young rebels equated "puritanism" with any kind of repression, bigotry, or prudishness.[1] Speaking, he claimed, for American youth generally, Stearns declared the nation's culture antipathetic to the vitality of the younger generation, ruled instead "by the anaemic, the feminine, and the fearful." "Puritanism" thwarted all desire "to laugh and play and be gay," allowing only "subterraneous" outlets for the play spirit, or worse, perverse or destructive ones: the "game" of business and money-making; more darkly, lynching and violence; most trivially, "gum-chewing, rocking-chair ecstasy, and 'jazz.' " "Pitiful substitutes," Stearns called these attempts at play, "yet proof, too, that all vitality has not quite been vacuum-cleaned out of us by the moralists."[2] Here is neatly encapsulated what proved to be the dilemma of the entire bohemian counterculture: a rebellion against the mainstream culture in the name of play, but uneasiness, doubt, and even revulsion against the playful nature of its own rebellion. By identifying "puritanism" as the enemy, young turks like Stearns implied that the context for their rebellion was vaguely spiritual as well as social, psychological, and cultural. If "puritanism" most explicitly meant sexual repression, it tacitly included a larger philosophical perspective through which the entire world was viewed. Thus as the counterforce to puritanism, "play" acquired the same vaguely spiritual connotations: suggesting the possibilities of redemption in a secular world.

The actors in the rebellion were "Young Intellectuals," as they styled themselves in the 1910s, their chief muses Nietzsche and Freud, their manner bohemianism of various sorts, their emblems dance, music, art, and sexual freedom. All of these were embodied in their rhetoric of play. The keywords in their manifestoes composed a litany that recast the Transcendentalists' play spirit in terms of modern psychology: "released personality," "expression of self," "emotion," "intuition," "liberation," "experiment," "freedom," "rebellion."[3] Nietzsche ruled the teens, Freud the twenties, although the Young Intellectuals' Nietzsche and Freud were often no closer to the originals than their idea of puritanism to the religion of Winthrop and the Mathers. Nietzsche's American followers included Mencken, Bourne, Brooks, and William James; Emma Goldman, Max Eastman, Walter Lippmann, and John Reed; John Dewey and Josiah Royce; Isadora Duncan and Rockwell Kent; Jack London, Theodore Dreiser, Upton Sinclair, Floyd Dell, and Eugene O'Neill.[4] More than two dozen books on Nietzsche's thought, several dozen chapters or sections of books, more than four hundred essays or reviews, and five doctoral dissertations appeared in the United States by 1925.[5] Nietzsche was praised and damned for things he never said.[6] To his admirers, who included reactionaries like Mencken and revolutionaries like Goldman and Reed, his message was variously understood: to some, individualism; to others, iconoclasm; to others yet, a vision of a rejuvenated civilization. Chiefly he seemed to offer an impassioned Nay to all that was dead in Western civilization and an equally impassioned Yea to life itself. Nietzsche's best-known works in the 1910s – The Birth of Tragedy (trans. 1909), Beyond Good and Evil (1907), and particularly Thus Spoke Zarathustra (1899) – preached to his American readers a philosophy of playfulness. In Zarathustra, Nietzsche wrote of man's highest state as that of a child and dancer, of the only true God as one "who would dance." The sense of exhilaration in Nietzsche's writing elicited from one of his commentators an image suggestive of Miriam and Donatello sporting in the mouth of the cavern: "It is as the tightrope dancer living dangerously on a line strung between precipices and eternal snows that Nietzsche is so much of a 'wonder, a beauty, and a terror.' "[7] H. L. Mencken, perhaps his most influential American interpreter in this period, reduced the Nietzschean philosophy to a pair of essentials: "Two things are wanted by the true man: danger and play."[8]

Nietzsche's influence waned in the 1920s, partly because of his perceived contribution to German militarism, partly because the young turks became more conventional, partly because Nietzsche's battle had been won: A Dionysian play spirit of a sort ruled middle-class life in the twenties. Its presiding genius was Freud now rather than Nietzsche, an equally distorted Freud derived less from Freud himself than from explicators like Max Eastman, Walter Lippmann, and others, or through discussions with A. A. Brill and other Freudians at bohemian soirées.[9] Although psychology did not become "a national mania" until the twenties, more than two hundred books on Freud's theories were published in the teens when he became a craze among intellectuals, "like the Turkey Trot or the Tango."[10] Freud's twofold message seemed clear and simple: 1) man's instinctual quest for pleasure was frustrated by society's demands, and 2) psychological health lay only in uninhibited expression of the libido. Translation: A healthy life lies in unhindered erotic play. In *Civilization and Its Discontents* (trans. 1930), Freud would explore the necessity of repression for society's sake, but already he had discussed the individual's need for repression as protection from the painful results of instinct given free reign.[11] The Young Intellectuals and their kin were deaf to that caveat.

What Concord was to the first American counterculture, Greenwich Village was to this later one. And Greenwich Village, by the accounts of some of its most famous inhabitants, was essentially a "playground." Floyd Dell, the "Prince" of the Village, wrote in 1916 of "the gaiety, the daring, the talk, the laughter, the love, the effervescent youth" of the Village. As a spokesman for the Villagers, Dell cast their playfulness as a spirit of defiance and nonconformity. "The romantic impression prevails," he said, "that nobody in Greenwich Village does any work. This is not strictly true. But the Village does play, and with such gay and riotous abandon that it is no wonder if sober middle-class people disapprove." The sentiment here is identical to that of Emerson nearly a century earlier, perceiving life as a May game in defiance of his countrymen's deadening busyness. After its heyday had passed, Dell wrote nostalgically of the Village as "a place known to all the world as the happy playground of artists and writers," a place where alienated intellectuals shared "the joys of comradeship and play and mere childish fun."[12] A later historian characterized the Village in its golden age simply as "The Playground of Utopia."[13]

The language of play expressed bohemian values particularly in relation to the arts and to sexual mores. At the center of Village life lay the quest for sexual fulfillment, for freedom of the Freudian libido from puritanical repression. Villagers spoke and wrote of sex as "play," and of the ideal woman not as a wife or potential mother but as a "playfellow."[14] In like spirit, they most admired those expressions in dance, music, and literature that gave free play to the passions and instincts, that seemed spontaneous and intuitive rather than crafted: Isadora Duncan's modern dance rather than classical ballet, jazz and ragtime rather than stately symphonies, the experiments of modernism in fiction and poetry rather than conventional realism. In *America's Coming-of-Age,* Van Wyck Brooks identified a "free, disinterested, athletic sense of play" as the essential spirit of any culture, lamenting that such a spirit in culturally impoverished America was found only in business.[15]

This motif of redemptive play runs through much of the young rebels' most characteristic writing. The Pagan (1916–19) and Playboy (1919–24), little magazines committed to bohemian values, are cases in point. The Pagan called itself "A Magazine for Eudaemonists" – men and women for whom personal happiness was the greatest good – while Playboy announced its own birth "from the womb of JOY." The Pagan published fantasies of wildly dancing nymphs and the god Pan playing his pipes in the rain, and poems on such themes as "The Pagan Soul": "born for laughter and the bright / Gold sun of morning, and white fire at night / . . . born for music and gay mirth / A mad glad soul sent jubilant to earth."[16] Playboy greeted readers in one issue, "I tell you one must still have chaos in one to give birth to a dancing star." It celebrated the liberating spirit of Isadora Duncan's dancing, the new trend toward spontaneity in dramatics, and the joys of the carnival. It published drawings and stories by three- and five-year-olds – a reprise of the nineteenth century's belief in the natural genius of children – and it numbered among the great "Playboys" of history King Solomon, Jesus, Blake, Whitman, Lawrence, and Nietzsche.[17]

No consensus on these matters emerged from the Young Intellectuals and Village bohemians. Whereas Louis Untermeyer praised Isadora Duncan in the Seven Arts, Margaret Anderson debunked her pretentiousness in the Little Review; Hiram Kelly Moderwell found "something Nietzschean" in jazz, "in its implicit philosophy that all the world's a dance," but H. L. Mencken attacked jazz for its "monotonous rhythms" and "puerile tunes."[18] Aesthetic questions about music and dance ultimately raised the issue of modern civilization and its future, with a commitment to play suggesting an alternative to rational progress. Primitivists like Moderwell and Carl Van Vechten found in jazz an expression of anarchic joy that deeply threatened other music critics. In her Intimate Memories, Mabel Dodge Luhan described the lascivious "cavortings" of a Negro dancer at the first of her famous "Evenings" with a squeamishness not shared by Van Vechten, who "rocked with laughter" and "clapped his pretty hands."[19] Although Van Vechten's enthusiasm sent many others besides himself uptown to Harlem in the twenties to hear what seemed the jungle rhythms of a music rooted in anarchy and spontaneity, others balked at endorsing such a spirit. Clive Bell, an English critic much read and admired in the United States, dismissed jazz as unintellectual. Gilbert Seldes and Paul Rosenfeld, the foremost American music critics of the period, praised the innovative rhythms of jazz but found them best used by the more disciplined and cerebral white composers and conductors.

The cover of the final issue of *Playboy* (1924) captures well the desires for risk and play that defined much of the spirit of the bohemian counterculture. (Reprinted by permission of Harcourt Brace Jovanovich, Inc.)

Rosenfeld praised Aaron Copeland, in whose music "the characteristic jazz polyrhythms have been conquered for musical art"; while Seldes, after celebrating jazz as America's "characteristic expression," embodying "all there is of gaiety and liveliness and rhythmic power in our lives," cautioned, "I do *not* think that the negro . . . is our salvation." Having claimed Irving Berlin, George Gershwin, Jerome Kern, and particularly Paul Whiteman to be the great jazz *artists,* Seldes concluded, "I say the negro is not our salvation because with all my feeling for what he instinctively offers, for his desirable indifference to our set of conventions about emotional decency, I am on the side of civilization."[20]

Dance raised the same issues in similar terms. The language of play ("gaiety," "liveliness") could suggest either freedom or anarchy. "Dance" itself became a cognate for "play" in much of this writing. Untermeyer's essay in the Seven Arts discussed the origins of dance in religion, impulse, and joy; its suppression by Christianity because of its supposed lewdness; and its recent rescue by Isadora Duncan, who uncovered the human body and restored dance's original freedom. Duncan challenged audiences less with her modernist aesthetics than with the metaphysics of her dancing. In her own writing she claimed her dance as a "spiritual expression," a revolt against puritanism in the spirit of her great predecessors: Beethoven, Wagner, and preeminently Nietzsche, whom she considered "the first dancing philosopher." She founded a school on the principle that dance originated in the soul, and she proposed that mankind could liberate itself if only it would dance. "I danced from the moment I learned to stand on my feet," she wrote in her autobiography. "I have danced all my life. Man, all humanity, the whole world must dance. This was and always will be. It is in vain that people interfere with this and do not want to understand a natural need given us by nature."[21]

Although Duncan stopped short of calling life itself a dance, others did not. The Hindu scholar Ananda Coomaraswamy's The Dance of Shiva (1918) was warmly welcomed by reviewers in Broom and the Little Review as the expression of an Oriental philosophy of harmony and unity that could be the ideal for transforming Western civilization.[22] Havelock Ellis's The Dance of Life (1923) gave the same ideas a Western cast. Better known as the author of the multi-volumed Studies in the Psychology of Sex, one of the age's chief contributions to sexual freedom, Ellis more directly played the philosopher in The Dance of Life. Dancing is not just one of the two essential arts (together with building), Ellis wrote, it is also "the supreme symbol of spiritual life," the underlying principle in both human existence and the workings of the universe. Thinking, writing, religion, and morals are all arts to be danced in the spirit of playful enjoyment, and in opposition to dogmatism, rigid standards, the obsession with measurement – all those tendencies of modern civilization to place limits on the vital spirit. Most men and women are trapped in narrow channels of organization, unable to see the infinite variety of life to be played.[23]

In expressive dance, in jazz, in sexual freedom, the bohemian spirit sought to transform American life in the name of play. And more fully than their predecessors in the nineteenth century, bohemians tried to put their ideas into practice. Their own records reveal their failure. The

uneasy relationship between abstraction and material reality that has re-
curred throughout these chapters emerges once again as an important
theme. The bohemians' sexual dilemma is wonderfully illustrated by
Hutchins Hapgood's anonymously published memoir, *The Story of a
Lover* (1919), another of those documents that neatly encapsulate the
cultural contradictions of an age. As a founding member of the Provincetown Players, one of the era's foremost journalists of radical politics
and bohemian mores, and a major prophet of free love, Hapgood was
particularly qualified to speak for the bohemian view of sexuality. What
his memoir reveals is desire at odds with itself. The book is deeply
informed by a new psychological version of the traditional work/play
dualism: the "play" of light, lyrical sensuality set against the soul's longing for "intimate seriousness." A recurrent motif of erotic play confronts
a second symbolic pattern: The lovers, Hapgood and his wife, are em-
barked on a Pilgrim's Progress of spiritual striving. For a brief moment
three-quarters of the way through the book an equilibrium is reached.
In Italy, the memoirist and his lover/wife indulge in "that satisfying
mixture of work and play – where work is play and play is work." But
even in the fullness of the moment its dissolution is immanent: Passion,
rues Hapgood, always "ends in an unpremeditated, intense situation
which destroys both work and play."[24]

In *The Story of a Lover,* play and work – "amorous play" and "the
deeper need of the soul" – define a polarized consciousness with real
consequences: an open marriage whose affairs end in hurt and jealousy,
a lover whose commitment to playful sexual dalliance clashes with his
belief that only profound knowledge is worth pursuing. Moreover, the
Pilgrim and the player turn out to suggest not compatible halves of life
but conflicting and mutually defeating impulses that underly the same
actions. In the closing chapters Hapgood's frustration derives not from
fitful fluctuations between play and seriousness in his relationships, but
from erotic play's failure to be both frolicsome and spiritual. Hapgood
emerges as a kind of Barnacle Bill, the would-be Transcendental Sailor:
a man who both lusts for women with gargantuan appetite and defines
woman's soul as "a spiritual abode of deep rebellion against man's conventional moralities and laws" (172). He wants to touch not bodies but
souls, seeking "life's essence" rather than a mere spurt of pleasure. The
antipuritanical bohemian, in other words, remains emphatically a puritan, projecting onto Woman (the capitalized "Her" by which he apo-
theosizes his wife) both erotic abandon and spiritual knowledge. His
women fail him, of course, less by their jealousies than by their seeming
to withhold their deepest spiritual being. As the memoirist finds himself
unable to satisfy his many mistresses because he remains bound to "Her"
as a slave to his master, "She" grows maternal and platonic in her love

– accepting without desiring "my metaphysical needs, my sexual straining towards the universe's oblivion" (196). Doomed to live in a world that thwarts metaphysical diddling, the Man Who Would Be Lover must remain forever "passionately unsatisfied" (197).

While it is impossible today to grant Hapgood's personal crisis the high seriousness with which he invested it, it is important to realize that on its lower frequencies *The Story of a Lover* spoke for its age. A convulsive desire to play at life confronted resistance rooted deep in the middle-class conscience. What Hapgood portrayed as Life's betrayal of the spirit others less pretentiously described as the social and political failures of bohemian play. In assessing "The Fall of Greenwich Village," Floyd Dell wrote in 1926 of the Village becoming "a side-show for tourists, a peep-show for vulgarians, a commercial exhibit of tawdry Bohemianism." The men and women who had fled to the Village "for peace from the victorious hosts of a huge robber-civilization too ready to enslave them to its dull tasks" found bourgeois America following them to the Village "to be shown how to play." But the Villagers in turn discovered in themselves "certain bourgeois traits – the desire for, say, a house in the country, and children, and a settled life – for one becomes tired even of freedom."[25] Dell himself, once "a symbol for uninhibited sexual love," married, then came to write defenses of traditional marriage.[26] Ten years after celebrating the playground of Greenwich Village, Dell wrote in *Intellectual Vagabondage* (1926) about the coupling of "playfellows" in the Village as an evasion of love and commitment. Both defending his generation of intellectuals and acknowledging their failures, Dell saluted the "blithe resurgence of the Play spirit, which is one of the finest elements of young idealism," but lamented that it had expressed itself in a too restricted sphere. There was "no desire to play with machinery"; "no desire to engage in what might be the great game of politics, nor any protest against the depressing rules with which that game has been spoiled for free men." The idealists, he wrote, proved themselves at last to be "unenterprising children . . . content with little toys":

> Their play is not the beginning, but the renunication of endeavor. It is a prolonged holiday from life. Its essence is a breezy and hearty triviality. And just as their work has become a playful thing in this sense, so has their love. Both have been cut off from tragic issues.[27]

Dell and Hapgood in different ways described the same failure to escape or transcend the work/play dualism. The collapse of the prewar counterculture in the 1920s resulted in part from the fact that, just as the Transcendentalists had imperfectly joined play and earnest striving, the bohemian play spirit, essentially personal and aesthetic, was an uneasy partner of the collective and activist political radicalism of the day. Cultural and political radicalism were joined in the teens; the socialist editors of *The Masses,* Max Eastman and Floyd Dell, for example, were also major spokesmen for cultural liberation. But personal freedom and political change became separate causes in the 1920s, as the First World War and the Bolshevik revolution forced commitments that separated cultural from political radicals.[28] A deeper problem lay in the fact that the young rebels were simply too much a part of the bourgeois culture against which they revolted. Their commitment to the radical freedom of play confronted their desires for the conventional securities of middle-class life.

But ironically, the countercultural revolt of the 1910s bore fruit in the twenties as middle-class America absorbed the no longer radical play spirit. Psychology became "a national mania"; psychoanalysis was converted "into parlor small talk."[29] Most pervasively, play and leisure were essential to the emerging consumer culture. Desire in America had long been defined in terms of play; now advertising became the science of stimulating and directing desire. As historians of Madison Avenue have argued, advertising and consumption in the 1920s were perceived explicitly as a counterforce "against Puritanism."[30] Bohemian radicals thus ironically served as a vanguard for a new capitalist order they sought to oppose. Commercial entertainment, popular songs ("Hot Lips," "Baby Face," "I Need Lovin'," "Burning Kisses"), popular movies (*The Shiek, Up in Mabel's Room, Her Purchase Price, A Shocking Night*), and popular dances (the Charleston, the Black Bottom, slow fox trots to sensual jazz) conventionalized a playful eroticism that daring bohemians just a few years before had promoted as cultural rebellion.

Sport was another arena in which play could be safely embraced in the 1920s. During the decade that has been called America's "Golden Age of Sport," college football survived its "ugly decades" from earlier in the century, baseball its Black Sox scandal of 1919, professional boxing its taint by the heavyweight championship of black and swaggering Jack Johnson – all of these sports to flourish as national passions. The new arts of promotion produced the first million-dollar boxing gates and transformed a host of athletes, Jack Dempsey, Babe Ruth, Red Grange, Bill Tilden, Bobby Jones, Man o' War, into the first generation of sporting celebrities for the new era of mass spectator sport.[31] Ring Lardner's sometimes genial, often trenchant ironies that dominated the 1910s gave way to his friend Grantland Rice's unrestrained mythopoeia as the characteristic voice of sports journalism. (It was Rice who named Notre Dame's Four Horsemen in 1924 and who penned the immortal lines about the Great Scorer not caring "that you won or lost – but how you played the game.") As sport increasingly became entertainment for spectators more than activity for participants, debunking was out, hero worship in.

Not in daily journalism but in more considered commentary, the perceived relationship of sport to play also changed. A generation earlier, sport was championed for the upper classes, in college football, as the proving ground for Anglo-Saxon "manliness"; for the rest, in the organized play movement, as a school for model citizenship. In the 1920s, sport also began to be praised for its preservation of an imperiled play spirit. No consensus on this matter emerged, of course. Lardner himself, in a contribution to Harold Stearns's symposium, *Civilization in the United States* (1922), denounced the mania for spectator sports as not just an invitation to passivity but an elevation of play above work. Writing in another of the decade's encyclopedic assessments of modern civilization, Stuart Chase shared Lardner's concern over spectatorial inaction but declared play "a profound expression of personal impulse and desire." In the machine age, Chase argued, play was more crucial to the human spirit than it had ever been, but ironically and tragically the industrial revolution, which had created both the need and the opportunities for play, degraded mankind's experiences at play by standardizing and commercializing them. A writer in *The Independent* in 1924 declared that America had entered an Age of Play. Lardner agreed and was horrified; Chase regretted that this was only apparently true.[32]

Popular fiction reflected the same uncertainty about sport. Lardner, the decade's chief writer about games, both indoor and outdoor ones, described a world devoid of play: of bridge games in which husbands and wives barely contain their contempt for each other; of golf matches at the country club in which the wealthy cheat whether anything is at stake or not; of prizefights and professional baseball games in which the spirit of play is maintained only as the sheerest fraud perpetrated by promoters and sportswriters.[33] F. Scott Fitzgerald in *The Great Gatsby* (1925) and Warner Fabian in *Flaming Youth* (1923) portrayed the college football star as a monster or oaf; a more positive image appeared in Fitzgerald's earlier novel, *This Side of Paradise* (1920), and in Percy Marks's *The Plastic Age* (1925) and *The Unwilling God* (1929). In the latter novel, a professor tells the hero, "I believe in work, but I believe in play, too." Education and football are both important; living must be play as well as labor.[34] *The Unwilling God,* that is, embraced the late-nineteenth-century's ideal of the balanced life and its assigning of play to youth, work to adulthood. Traditional dualism ruled.

Both the lack of consensus over the value of sport and the conventional wisdom of Marks's narrator reflect the fate of the newly energized spirit of play in the larger culture of the 1920s. The new age followed the pattern of the previous century: a challenge to the dominant work ethic in the name of play, followed not just by a general absorption of that radical play spirit by the larger middle class, but also by a recoiling from its most threatening consequences. The traditional culture of work was not transformed into a new culture of consumption without deep-rooted anxiety. The Jazz Age danced, smoked, drank, and petted, but the new moral license took on a desperate quality, a compulsion toward unwanted sexual affairs, an artificial resistance to the stability of conventional marriage that many in fact desired. The decade's popular fiction reveals two narratives written over and over, compulsively it would seem. One is the story of playful rebellion ending in disillusionment with play; the other is an exploration of erotically playful black life as an alternative to repressive, "puritanical" white civilization. The first concerns the psychology of the individual self; the second, the metapsychology of the Western world. Both reveal the culture's anxiety as it attempted to come to terms with a newly insistent desire to play.

Fitzgerald and the tale of disillusioned play

F. Scott Fitzgerald's *This Side of Paradise* (1920) can stand as the protonovel of disillusioned play in the twenties. Floyd Dell's *Moon-Calf* (1920) tells the same tale, as it chronicles the frustrations of Felix Fay, who finds that the "kissable" girls available for "play" remain forever separate from the intellectual girls suitable for serious relationships. But Fitzgerald's novel is the one that seemed to contemporary readers most clearly to announce the spirit of a new era. At the time, *This Side of Paradise* was a daring novel, full of the most notorious practices of the younger generation: smoking, drinking, petting, and frank discussion (in snappy dialogue) of all these matters. It was a novel that could reassure as well as shock, however, ultimately conventional and highly moral, its disillusionment with conventional mores matched by its disillusionment with the rebellious alternative. The striking fact about the sensational fiction of the Jazz Age is its fundamental conservatism. As the rebellious hedonism of bohemians in the teens became the ambivalently accepted practices of middle-class America in the twenties, the popular fiction of flaming youth expressed the troubled response of the respectable middle class to the latest eruption of the anarchic, now typically erotic, play spirit.

This Side of Paradise professes to illustrate the transformation of Amory Blaine from a "romantic egotist" to a true "personage." The romantic and egotistical Amory dreams in his youth of glory on football fields and battlefields, later declares Princeton "the pleasantest country club in America," and feels toward the World War that interrupts the education of his generation only a "sporting interest in the German dash for Paris."[35]

In other words, Amory's deepest desires and basic responses to life are both described as a whole-hearted commitment to play. Life for Amory is an either/or dualism – the work of the classroom or the play of his social life – between which he makes a clear choice. His sophomore year at Princeton is a "carnival" of "colorful ramblings" and "gambling fever" (80, 82): all play and no work that nearly gets him expelled. Mostly he plays at love with a series of young women – "games" of lines and poses, conventionalized phrases and inviolable rules. But play, or more precisely, the women who embody the erotic spirit of play for Amory, ultimately betrays him. Amory's disgust with his life of play is prefigured in an Oscar Wildean scene when, hallucinating during one of his "Dionysian" revels, he confronts the devil himself, or perhaps the devil in himself. Once believed to be liberating, play becomes a descent into the abyss.

The crisis comes through Rosalind, the decade's prototypical flapper. In a series of scenes breathlessly rendered by stage directions and theatrical dialogue, Fitzgerald crystalized for twenties youth the bohemian notion of lovers as playfellows. Rosalind smokes, drinks, kisses, and wears cosmetics, believes in "*carpe diem* for herself and *laissez-faire* for others," and dances before a mirror in a perfect image of narcissistic play. In the jazziest, snappiest dialogue yet to appear in American fiction, Rosalind plays out a game of flirtation and courtship with an only partly willing Amory, grown cynical now by having served in the War:

> HE: Well – Rosalind, Rosalind, don't argue – kiss me again.
> SHE: (*Quite chilly now*) No – I have no desire to kiss you.
> HE: (*Openly taken aback*) You wanted to kiss me a minute ago.
> SHE: This is now.
> HE: I'd better go.
> SHE: I suppose so.
> *(He goes toward the door.)*
> SHE: Oh!
> *(He turns.)*
> SHE: (*Laughing*) Score – Home Team: One Hundred – Opponents: Zero.
> *(He starts back.)*
> SHE: (*Quickly*) Rain – no game.
> *(He goes out.)* (177)

This scene is repeated almost verbatim a few pages later as Rosalind "plays" with one of Amory's rivals (181).

Young America ate this up. Readers were to believe that Amory and Rosalind truly loved each other as equals in the game, but that they could not sustain their love in the face of the tawdrier reality of Amory's poverty. More truly, in a move that would be repeated over and over in the 1920s, Fitzgerald projected onto the woman the longings of his own gender for erotic play, as an earlier generation projected its utopian play spirit onto children, then denounced her for embodying that very play spirit. When Rosalind marries Ryder Dawson, a young man with wealth but otherwise inferior to Amory in every way, our hero, crushed, falls into cynicism and boredom, feels contempt for business (but not for money), and is uncertain whether he will ever be able to love again. Life becomes to him "a damned muddle . . . a football game with every one off-side and the referee gotten rid of – every one claiming the referee would have been on his side" (265). In his disillusionment Amory imagines himself an artist and intellectual, a "spiritually unmarried man" bound by no convention or tradition, forever pursuing the new. "One thing I know," he says near the end of the novel. "If living isn't a seeking for the grail it may be a damned amusing game" (278). Where play had formerly expressed life's possibilities, "game" now implies its utter meaninglessness. But Amory seems as unamused, and unamusing, as anyone could possible be. In a world with "all Gods dead, all wars fought, all faiths in man shaken" (282), Amory faces an undefined future, armed only with his painfully earned self-knowledge.

It is difficult today to take the disillusioned "personage" any more seriously than the "romantic egotist," but writing out of his own inchoate longings and frustrations, Fitzgerald tapped the longings and frustrations of young middle-class Americans in the twenties. A number of the most popular novels in the decade followed a pattern remarkably similar to the one Fitzgerald employed in *This Side of Paradise*. Sinclair Lewis's *Babbitt* (1922) tells the story of a businessman's temporary fling at bohemian play, then his abrupt and chastened return to the safety of family and boosterish friends. Joseph Hergesheimer's *Cytherea* (1922) recounts a passionate rebellion against marriage and convention that ends in total disillusionment. Warner Fabian's *Flaming Youth* (1923) tells a similar tale of daring rebellion against conventional mores, the "teasing games" and skinny-dipping "games," and "indoor sport" of marital infidelity – "the game of passion" in all its forms – in order to damn not to celebrate erotic play and in the end renounces it for romantic marriage.[36] In Percy Marks's *The Plastic Age* (1925), the hero flirts with sexual freedom before stopping in shocked dismay still short of carnal knowledge. All of these novels could have shared a single title: *Spent Frenzy*. Even Hemingway's *The Sun Also Rises* (1926), seemingly far removed in sensibility as well as geography, follows this pattern.

The books that most shocked the moralists in the twenties were ultimately quite chaste and moral. Although much of their appeal lay in their exposé of Dionysian youthful revels, their refusal to embrace that Dionysian spirit must have been equally crucial to their popularity. The last paragraph of Owen Johnson's *The Wasted Generation* (1921) epitomizes the spirit of all these novels. "In each of us is the choice between rebellion and acceptance of life," the hero declares. "Rebel against life and destroy ourselves with a beating of the wings against the bars of circumstance, – or meet it with a deliberate, difficult acceptance." David Littledale opts for the latter, despite the cost: "Youth, too often, must be burned out, like a fever."[37] The other spokesmen for "flaming youth" agreed that this sacrifice must be made.

"Play" in this fiction, as always, expresses a fantasy of freedom but also the dangers of anarchy. More striking, these novels by men seem to suggest a profound male anxiety about women, or perhaps about sexuality itself. If popular fiction can serve as an index, the sexual revolution that made the "new woman" no longer the guarantor of propriety and purity, as her mother and grandmother had been, but now the "playfellow" of men with the equal right to sexual pleasure implied by that term, deeply disturbed American males. The best selling novels by American women in the 1920s that deal either openly or implicitly with women's new freedoms and the age's changing sexual mores – Dorothy Canfield's *The Brimming Cup* (1921), Gertrude Atherton's *Black Oxen* (1923), Anne Douglas Sedgwick's *The Little French Girl* (1924), Anita Loos' *Gentlemen Prefer Blondes* (1925), and Viña Delmar's *Bad Girl* (1928) – have little in common with this male-authored tale.

To these can be added Edith Hull's *The Shiek* (1921), Margaret Kennedy's *The Constant Nymph* (1924), and Elinor Glyn's *"It"* (1927), novels by Englishwomen that became American best sellers (*"It"* and *The Shiek* were also extraordinarily popular movies, in the case of *"It"* the movie preceding the novelization). These books by women deal with the theme of sexuality in a variety of ways, most of them morally conservative, but none of them includes characters who are hysterically repelled by sex or a dangerous male. *The Brimming Cup* reconstitutes a domestic ideal in the face of the Freudian challenge, specifically rejecting sex as play. In *Bad Girl,* a working-class girl's sexual fall leads to marriage and motherhood, not to wild abandon or despair. *The Little French Girl* sets English restraint against the "pagan gaiety" of the French, opting for the former. Among the Englishwomen's novels, *The Shiek* is a bourgeois fantasy of domesticated rape; in Glyn's novel two strong people with that indefinable "It" play a long love game that culminates in marriage; in *The Constant Nymph* a young woman transcends her family's chaotic bohemian existence only to die tragically when betrayed by a ruthless, self-centered lover. In *Black Oxen,* the novel that most directly confronted the age's obsession with youth and sexual desire, a miraculously rejuvenated woman chooses political power over "that old game of prowling sex" as played by a young reporter and his bohemian friends. Within this range of treatments, several of the novels characterize sexuality as "play," in some cases positively, in others negatively. But none of them projects sexual play onto a single gender, none of them recoils from sexuality itself.[38]

In the novels by men, sexual play and Dionysian rebellion are both more enticing and more frightening. Sinclair Lewis's George Babbitt yearns for escape from the deadening demands of work and family, but the mandatory leisure activities of his class (baseball and golf) offer no real pleasure, and his occasional fishing trips to the Maine woods cannot sustain him. When he finally dares to join The Bunch, the bohemian hedonists he has half envied, half despised, he discovers, however, that the very things that stifled him gave him security. The wild side is thrilling but also terrifying. Moreover, The Bunch in their own way are as oppressive as his booster crowd – ironically forcing on him "the exceedingly weary demands of their life of pleasure and freedom."[39] The lure of Tanis Judique as an erotic playfellow leads him to the edge of the abyss, from which he flees back to the safety of home, wife, office, and club. Lewis satirized boosters no more strongly than bohemians, who in their compulsive pleasure-seeking are just babbitts who dance.

In *Cytherea,* Joseph Hergesheimer wrote a more solemn tale of middle-class desperation, of men and women trapped in a wearying round of work and forced gaiety. The cocktail parties that transform a "crass reality" into something "glittering" are but anodynes for boredom. "People danced at stated times, in not crowded rooms, because life was pedestrian; they were sick of walking in an ugly meaningless clamor and wanted to move to music, to wear pearl studs and fragile slippers and floating chiffons." Everywhere in the middle-class suburb of Eastlake there is a "mad effort at escape," but escape proves impossible. Lee Randon, a respectable married man, runs off to Cuba with an equally respectable married woman, only to see her die. But the reality of sexual passion has already defeated them before the final catastrophe. In Cuba they find the heart of darkness in a shockingly obscene, totally Dionysian world, "the nakedness of passion everywhere surcharging the surface of life." Between Cuba and Eastlake there seems to be no compromise.[40]

This same pattern is replayed in *Flaming Youth* and *The Plastic Age.* All of these male novels recoil from erotic "play." *This Side of Paradise, Flaming Youth,* and *The Plastic Age* – and to some degree *Babbitt* – also specifically blame the woman for passion gone awry. "Warner Fabian" (Samuel Hopkins Adams) prefaced *Flaming Youth* with an extraordinary dedication that could have been written by either Fitzgerald or Marks as well:

> To the woman of the period thus set forth, restless, seductive, greedy, discontented, craving sensation, unrestrained, a little morbid, more than a little selfish, intelligent, uneducated, sybaritic, following blind instincts, and perverse fancies, slack of mind as she is trim of body,

neurotic and vigorous, a worshipper of tinsel gods at perfumed altars, fit mate for the hurried, reckless and cynical man of the age, predestined mother of – what manner of being?: To Her I dedicate this study of herself.

Fitzgerald's Amory Blaine is betrayed by a series of faithless flappers; Marks's Hugh Carver of *The Plastic Age,* a "nice boy" from Merrytown, nearly loses his virginity to a "fast" girl drunk on alcohol and lust. The social construction of gender through the centuries had at times declared women insatiably lustful, at others denied their sexual passion altogether. Victorian American officially claimed the latter. Many male writers in the 1920s, at the very moment when sexuality was seemingly receiving more "scientific" than superstitious scrutiny, retreated to a dark-age fear of the woman as succubus. To what degree these writers spoke for their male readers is impossible to know for certain, but their novels reveal a nearly hysterical revulsion from the liberated "playfellow" that a moral revolution had created.

Fitzgerald's fiction offers an extended case study. In stories and novels after *This Side of Paradise,* Fitzgerald returned repeatedly to this fear of women, more often yet to the overriding theme of disillusioned play. His short stories in the twenties reveal a range of attitudes toward play. In *Flappers and Philosophers* (1921), "The Ice Palace" sets Southern playfulness against Northern sobriety, symbolized in the coldly beautiful but also lifeless, and life-taking, ice palace. In *Tales of the Jazz Age* (1922), "O Russet Witch" sets the dullness of work and marriage against the enchanting image of a beautiful woman who dances on tables in cafes, embodying perpetual youth and irresponsibility. In *All the Sad Young Men* (1926), the man who insists in "Gretchen's Forty Winks" that play must balance work in life suffers a complete breakdown; work, and work alone, brings success and gives real pleasure. Numerous other stories in these volumes celebrate or reject play, long for or regret it. Fitzgerald's novels, on the other hand, more consistently tell a single story: of youthful play disillusioned over time, usually through a woman's heartlessness.

Work and play obsessed Fitzgerald in his fiction because they obsessed him in his life: He never successfully reconciled his competing desires to write and to revel. The dualistic thinking that had long prevented a cultural ideal of human wholeness defeated Fitzgerald in particularly telling ways. And because his personal dilemma faced the nation as well, Fitzgerald became all but officially the laureate of the Jazz Age. The heroes of his novels fail to reconcile their needs to work and to play; desire is always defeated by intransigent reality. In *The Beautiful and Damned* (1922), although Anthony and Gloria Patch succeed in playing at life in a world that demands work, their success becomes ironic failure, play an unfulfilling state. When they meet, Anthony is committed to doing nothing, willing to inherit his grandfather's thirty millions but not to submit to any of the unsatisfying work with which such fortunes are earned. In Gloria he finds his ideal playmate, a woman who prefers men to be "gracefully lazy" and who is herself a beautiful child playing at life. At one point when their love is fresh, the narrator describes how "Anthony lay awake and played with every minute of the day like a child playing in turn with each one of a pile of long-wanted Christmas toys."[41] To Anthony in love the whole world seems transformed into a paradise of play:

> From the night into his high-walled room there came, persistently, that evanescent and dissolving sound – something the city was tossing up and calling back again, like a child playing with a ball. In Harlem, the Bronx, Grammercy Park, and along the water-fronts, in little parlors or on pebble-strewn, moon-flooded roofs, a thousand lovers were making this sound, crying little fragments of it into the air. All the city was playing this sound out there in the blue summer dark, throwing it up and calling it back, promising that, in a little while, life would be beautiful as a story, promising happiness – and by that promise giving it. It gave love hope in its own survival. (149–50)

For her part, Gloria describes this period in her diary as "blowing bubbles – that's what we're doing, Anthony and me. And we blew such beautiful ones to-day, and they'll explode and then we'll blow more and more, I guess – bubbles just as big and just as beautiful, until all the soap and water is used up" (147).

For Anthony and Gloria, the bubble bursts as surely as time passes and youth fades, like Clifford's bubbles breaking harmlessly against Jaffrey Pyncheon's solidity in *The House of the Seven Gables*. After a honeymoon in the West, they settle into a life of bachanals, dances, iceskating parties, and football games. Anthony briefly tries to work, but rejects the bond business as "fruitless circumambient striving toward an incomprehensible goal" (229–30). Next he fails as a writer. Gloria sleeps clutching a child's doll to her bosom, symbol of the youth to which she frantically clings. They fight and grow estranged, Anthony enlists for the war – "no child's play" his captain tells him, but "a man's game" (335) – but leaves the army disgraced. They have affairs; they host and attend endless parties that bring no joy, only desperation, futility, mutual recriminations, and gradual impoverishment. Echoing Hawthorne in "The Paradise of Children" and anticipating Floyd Dell's lament for the fall of Greenwich Village, the narrator summarizes their plight: "There was nothing, it seemed, that grew stale so soon as pleasure" (418). They refuse to believe what their friend Maury realizes in remembering his own childhood: "The playtime was so short!" (254). Anthony believes himself heroic in refusing all compromise with work, but the novel says otherwise. In a late scene, broken in health and mind now, Amory childishly plays with his stamps exactly as he had done as a boy. Play has only betrayed him.

Jay Gatsby and Dick Diver meet similar fates. Although the image of Gatsby, refracted through Nick Carroway's narration, remains insubstantial to the end of the novel, through the moonlight haze appears a man who attempts to freeze the playtime of youth, to perpetuate a moment of perfect romance until he can reassemble the principal actors, himself and Daisy Buchanan, to restage the past. The parties at Gatsby's mansion seem to Nick part "amusement park," part romantic fantasy with men and women coming and going "like moths among the whisperings and the champagne and the stars."[42] In a cynical world that repeatedly violates the human play spirit – in which brutal Tom Buchanan muscles his way through life in search of some "irrecoverable football game," and the golfer Jordan Baker cheats at her sport, and the bookie Meyer Wolfsheim toys with an entire nation's faith by fixing the World Series – Gatsby achieves a very Fitzgeraldian greatness by clinging to his illusion, his fantasy of play.

But the other three live while Gatsby dies, and even before the final catastrophe Gatsby's dream has proven too fragile to survive the dreaming. When he first realizes that Daisy can once again be his – when he kisses her "and forever wed[s] his unutterable visions to her perishable breath" – Gatsby himself knows that "his mind [will] never romp again like the mind of God" (112). From that moment, tawdry reality increasingly intrudes into Gatsby's world: the evasions and secret meetings, Tom's jealousy, Daisy's uncertainty, all leading up to the sordid events that cause his pointless death. In *The Great Gatsby* as in neither of the earlier novels, Fitzgerald achieved some aesthetic distance from his personal obsessions, not only making Gatsby seem possibly heroic and tragic rather than merely silly or pitiful, but also wedding his hero's quest not just to the age's dilemma but to the nation's mythos: to the sense of wonder out of which the New World had been born and from which it had fallen ever since. Fitzgerald imagined no Fortunate Fall, however, as Hawthorne had done. Not just Gatsby, but Tom, Daisy, Jordan, even Nick all long for some irrecoverable innocence from the past, some youthful playtime before the real world intruded. The focus on *play* in these contexts is more oblique than in the other novels, but play pervades the book as a haunting dream.

In the midst of the Depression, Fitzgerald looked back on the 1920s as a time when "effort *per se* had no dignity against the mere bounty of those days," when work was known only by a "depreciatory word": Every "successful programme became a racket – I was in the literary racket." From Fitzgerald's perspective in the thirties, the previous decade was a "children's party taken over by the elders," a time when Americans danced at the edge of an abyss oblivious to the danger.[43] The novel Fitzgerald wrote in the thirties, *Tender Is the Night* (1934), and the one he left unfinished at his death in 1940, *The Last Tycoon*, seem written from within this abyss – from the perspective of one looking back on an age that betrayed its citizens by telling them that life was play. In *The Beautiful and Damned* and *The Great Gatsby*, Fitzgerald's heroes play defiantly but discover too late that the world demands something different of them. In *Tender Is the Night* and *The Last Tycoon*, the main characters seek fulfillment entirely in work. Monroe Stahr in *The Last Tycoon* no longer plays tennis or baseball but only works – all day, late at night, and on weekends. He says quite simply, "I enjoy working most." According to his doctor this obsession is unhealthy, a "drug" and a "poison" and a "perversion of the life force" that animated Stahr in the twenties. Now, the party's over and work is an unhealthy substitute. But it's all Stahr has.[44]

In *Tender Is the Night,* on the other hand, work alone offers salvation to Dick Diver, but he is a victim of the Jazz Age *Zeitgeist* that demands he play. Contrasting images of the hero at play early and late in the novel reveal most concretely the depth of Dick's fall. The book opens with Dick on the French Riviera in 1925, appearing to a romantic and impressionable Rosemary Hoyt to be "giving a quiet little performance" for the amusement of his wife and a small group of friends. Dick seems to Rosemary the vital spirit energizing a perfectly harmonious private world, the little group of individuals "in the plot," distinctly separate from the tourists who look on with envious disdain. A little later, thinking of the pleasure these chosen few must have, Rosemary envies "them their fun, imagining a life of leisure unlike her own." The Divers and their circle of friends seem to live in a perfect paradise of play.[45]

Near the end of the novel, after both his affair with Rosemary and his marriage to Nicole have ended, Dick is again at the beach but seen through Nicole's eyes this time, attempting another little performance. Now, however, all grace and control have disappeared. Nicole remarks how Dick always fumbled now at "stunts he had once done with ease," and how "this summer, for the first time, he avoided high diving" (282). To his own annoyance and the increasing embarrassment of those watching, Dick fails three times at "his lifting trick" while riding an aquaplane behind a speed boat, tumbling awkwardly into the sea with each effort. "He had done the thing with ease only two years ago" (284).

Dick's deterioration revealed in this scene is not just physical but spiritual; his unease and lack of control are matters of mind and heart as well as body. His playful mastery in the earlier scene, however, is partly a figment of Rosemary's romanticism. She is unaware of the "desperate bargain with the gods" by which the Divers achieve their illusion of playful harmony (21). In envying them their fun, Rosemary "thought of it as resting, without realizing that the Divers were as far from relaxing as she was herself" (99). Since his marriage to Nicole, Dick in fact has tried to salvage his own life not through play but through meaningful work – to avoid the self-destruction of his friend Abe North, and not to fall victim to either of the women who depend on him. In Fitzgerald's novels generally, play represents both life's finest possibilities and its gravest dangers. In *Tender Is the Night* it offers only threat without promise. The work that Amory Blaine and Anthony Patch scorn becomes Dick Diver's only hope for salvation; women, particularly Nicole, are the chief obstacle to attaining it.

In *Save Me the Waltz* (1932), Zelda Fitzgerald's fictionalizing of her life with Scott, the roles are reversed; Alabama Knight, the Zelda (or Nicole) of the novel, is the one who seeks the salvation of work. Having spent the early years of their marriage in wild gaiety, as the Patches do in *The Beautiful and Damned,* Alabama and David go off to the Continent, together with the sixty thousand other Americans who are "wandering over the face of Europe in a game of hare without hounds." But David has his art while Alabama is meant merely to play. Boredom and restlessness follow, then a near affair with a French aviator, until finally she resolves, despite her age, to become a ballerina – to *work* through dancing for "that peace which she imagined went only in surety of one's self." Learning to discipline her body is not play but contest: seeming to Alabama "like playing a desperate game with herself." Despite David's petty hindrances, Alabama persists, speaking incessantly of her *work,* of the *sweat* it takes to learn to dance; insisting it is not a "circus," not for "fun," not to be done in a drawing room but on stage, for an audience. In an ironic anti-Hemingwayesque image, Alabama is described at one point as working "till she felt like a gored horse in the bullring, dropping its entrails."[46]

Scott's contrasting view of their marriage is represented in the relationship of the Divers. Dick sacrifices his ambition to be the best psychiatrist there is by "playing truant from the clinic" in order to care for Nicole (213). In a striking image midway through the novel, Dick pursues a troubled Nicole to a local carnival, looking everywhere, then circling a "merry-go-round[,] keeping up with it till he realized he was running beside it, staring always at the same horse" (189). Here is Fitzgerald's emblem of the futile play of wealthy expatriates that distracts Dick from his life's work. As Dick becomes totally unproductive, a hired eunuch to Nicole's wealthy family, Nicole vampirically absorbs his strength. Her independence at the end of the novel marks Dick's ironic triumph as a clinician – achieved at the cost of any larger success in his profession. Zelda ended *Save Me the Waltz* with Alabama finally defeated in her attempt to be a dancer; *Tender Is the Night* ends with Dick disappearing into the anonymity of small-town America. Through their fiction the Fitzgeralds blamed each other for squandered success. Scott never had envisioned an escape from the dualism of work and play, but by the thirties he lost all faith in play's redemptive power. To both Fitzgeralds by the thirties, work alone could bring salvation; they only disagreed over who prevented whom from achieving it.

Whites and blacks and the blues

The repeated story of disillusioned play reveals the longings of middle-class America (male only?) confronting its fears about the consequences of those desires – a conflict between freedom and security, pleasure and achievement, traditional values and the demands of a changing world. Ambivalence about play became one focus for many anxieties wrought by modernity: the increasing fragmentation of life into labor and leisure, the loss of connection between public and private selves, the shift from producing to consuming as the means to fulfillment. From the middle of the nineteenth century, play increasingly encroached on work as the imagined source of happiness, but the transformation was slow and uncertain. The fact that the popular male novelists of the 1920s were engrossed by the play spirit but balked at embracing it suggests the incompleteness of the cultural transformation and the uneasiness it aroused.

Writers in the 1920s told another story as well, complementary in theme if not in content. Instead of projecting onto women the enticing and dangerous spirit of play, many white writers projected it onto blacks, the racial rather than sexual other. The primitivism of Rousseau, Chateaubriand, and other Romantics, which found one outlet in nineteenth-century America in Western writing, then a more purified genteel expression in the children's novels of the century's later decades, flourished afresh in the years on either side of World War I as part of an international movement. In modern art, it appeared in the work of Klee, Miro, Kandinsky, Dufy, Chagall, Dubuffet, Picasso, and others.[47] In American culture after the war it contributed to the vogue of the Negro and the Harlem Renaissance. The positive racial stereotype in the nineteenth century – Black Sam in *Uncle Tom's Cabin* (rather than Tom himself, who is utterly earnest), *Huck Finn's* Jim, the entire minstrel tradition – frequently cast blacks as playful children. In the age of Freud they became figures of uninhibited desire. As early as 1909, Gertrude Stein in *Melanctha* typed the white and black races as respectively constrained and free. "The wide abandoned laughter that makes the warm broad glow of negro sunshine" is a refrain in her novella. In the 1910s, Vachel Lindsay wrote many poems imbued with this primitivist play, his most famous, "The Congo" (1914), celebrating the abandon of "Wild crap-shooters with a whoop and a call" who "Danced the juba in their gambling-hall." In Willa Cather's *My Ántonía* (1918), the black pianist Blind D'Arnaut's barbarous but wonderful playing complements the novel's central emphasis on the play of immigrant country girls, whose dancing and sexuality provide the dominant counterpoint to the "evasions and negations" of the Nebraskan townspeople.[48]

Twenties primitivism found similar expression in Oliver LaFarge's Pulitzer Prize-winning novel, *Laughing Boy* (1929), in which Indians' dancing, gambling, and racing contrasts with the death-dealing decadence of white Americans. But in the 1920s it was chiefly blacks who represented freedom and spontaneity in the white imagination. In the primitivist novels that flourished in the twenties, the stakes were higher than in the fiction of erotic desire. The novels of flaming youth were preoccupied with personal relations; the primitivists weighed the future of the West itself in the balance. The spirit of play in novels about black life represented an alternative to centuries of Western progress. Recall, for example, Gilbert Seldes preferring Paul Whiteman to black jazz masters because, as he put it, "I am on the side of civilization." Although novelists in the twenties who wrote of blacks' spontaneous, intuitive, playful attitudes toward life did not have to declare their allegiances so openly, in all of these novels Western civilization was implicitly at stake.

By projecting onto blacks their anarchic desires, white writers (and readers) could indulge their longing without directly confronting the consequences. Novelists did in fiction what many whites were doing literally in the 1920s: slumming uptown in black cabarets like Connie's and the Cotton Club (where black patrons were not admitted), listening to black jazz, watching black dance, becoming intoxicated with black rhythms before returning to the security of comfortable middle-class existence. In the same way, "downtown" writers slummed uptown in a fictional Harlem, as Easterners like Washington Irving had slummed in the West in the 1830s and 1840s; though now, in the 1920s, novelists were titillated by savagery in the guise of Eros, not of Nature. In a sense, the primitivist writers could view the Dionysian spirit from a safer distance than the novelists of bourgeois mores could enjoy. Because their subject was exotic and alien, they could register both their fascination and their repulsion with little psychic risk. No white person seriously could have preferred to be black in the racist twenties. Blacks at play, like the tiny heroines of 1850s fiction, were an abstraction rather than models to be emulated.

Carl Van Vechten's *Nigger Heaven* (1926) was the most famous and

"Cake Walk"

"The Stomp"

"Charleston"

"Dancing the Blues"

The caricatures of black life by Miguel Covarrubias, appearing in the 1920s in such popular magazines as *Vanity Fair*, captured both the simpler and the more complex images of black playfulness. "Cake Walk," "The Stomp," and "Charleston" suggest all grace and gaiety, as white novelists typically portrayed black experience; the oddly contorted figure and grimace of "Dancing the Blues," on the other hand, are considerably closer to the literary portraits by black writers such as Langston Hughes, Claude McKay, and Zora Neale Hurston. (From *Negro Drawings* by Miguel Covarrubias. Copyright 1927 by Alfred A. Knopf, Inc. and renewed 1955 by Miguel Covarrubias. Reprinted by permission of Alfred A. Knopf, Inc.)

notorious of the primitivist novels, but it followed after many others. A chapter of E. E. Cummings' *The Enormous Room* (1922) portrays Jean Le Nègre as a playful, childlike black man who dances with joy in prison, beguiles himself with games, sings and shows off and plays practical jokes, in contrast to the dreary regimentation of the prison that symbolizes modern life. Waldo Frank in *Holiday* (1923), DuBose Heyward in *Porgy* (1925), Sherwood Anderson in *Dark Laughter* (1925), and Julia Peterkin in *Scarlet Sister Mary* (1928) explored black life in similar ways as an alternative to existence in the machine age – with the play spirit always defining the blacks' difference from whites.

The writers' responses to black life varied, from what seemed at the time Van Vechten's brutal "realism" to Anderson's dreamy romanticism. *Nigger Heaven* rings with "the tormented howling of the brass, the barbaric beating of the drum" in black nightclubs, its black characters ranging from prim to savage but with the emphasis on passion and violence, sensuality and despair, thwarted ambition and degradation.[49] Seemingly intended as a tragedy, the novel appeared to most readers of the twenties, particularly to black intellectuals, as a titillating glimpse at black degeneracy, despite Van Vechten's reputation as a patron of black artists. In *Scarlet Sister Mary* (winner of the Pulitzer Prize the year before *Laughing Boy*), Julia Peterkin, a Southerner, offered a less sensational portrait, this one of rural black life in South Carolina, with characters again ranging from the licentious to the puritanical but dominated by a heroine given entirely to joyful erotic play. Although by bearing many children to different fathers Sister Mary outrages the pious members of her community, she embodies a life force on which nearly everyone draws. Mary "laughed and played through most of her fifteen years," the narrator says early in the novel, and she doesn't change with age. She has the ability to make even washing clothes "a frolic instead of drudgery." Sister Mary loves dancing more than she loves the church, accepting its banishment as a fair price for her pleasure.[50]

This is the image that predominated: black sexual freedom and playfulness in contrast to a repressed white world. The contrast is only implicit in *Scarlet Sister Mary;* Heyward, Frank, and Anderson made it the central theme of their novels. In Heyward's *Porgy,* the black citizens of Catfish Row parading once a year through the streets of Charleston provoke the narrator's comparison:

> For its one brief moment out of the year the pageant had lasted. Out of its fetters of civilization this people had risen, suddenly, amazingly. Exotic as the Congo, and still able to abandon themselves utterly to the wild joy of fantastic play, they had taken the reticent, old Anglo-Saxon town and stamped their mood swiftly and indelibly into its heart.

There they passed, leaving behind them a wistful envy among those who had watched them go, – those whom the ages had rendered old and wise.[51]

In Frank's *Holiday* and Anderson's *Dark Laughter* the contrast runs deeper, in parallel narratives or motifs. *Holiday* opens at dusk in Nazareth, a small Southern community on the Gulf of Mexico, with alternating scenes in the white church and Niggertown. While blacks sing in the sensuous twilight, a white preacher exhorts his congregation to live upright lives. In one part of town a black girl, flirting, "slips away, her voice in laughter drawing a silver riband above the brown dance of her body"; across the color line live "*white folks wanting, white folks shutting down, white world hungering and a cold hard hate, a hating poison from its hungering love.*" Niggertown is movement and life: "Babies jet their savage lambent cries into the womb of silence. Boys shout cadences of play. Girls make calls over dishes that paint soft throats." Main Street is stasis and death: "Young men stand in the storeways. They are lean and motionless. Their heads upon their necks do not turn. Their faces do not speak. Their words are ejaculations of a static sense. Thought and sentiment and passion dwell fixed within a moveless pivot of their souls."[52]

Frank's lyrical Freudianism focuses on black John Cloud and white Virginia Hade, on the repression of white sexuality by a sterile religiosity and the oppression of black freedom by white racism. John feels choked, dreaming to breathe free. Virginia longs for a different kind of freedom she senses is natural in black life. When John and Virginia finally meet, racism defeats their chance of finding what they seek in each other. The "holiday" of the title is not a festive celebration by playful blacks, but John Cloud's lynching for a rape that never happened: an outpouring of repressed white passion into inevitable brutality.

These white writers obviously did not write with a single voice. Peterkin's novel sympathetically portrays black rural life; *Nigger Heaven* peeps at an exotic sideshow; *Porgy* falls somewhere in between. Only Waldo Frank of these four writers treated racism as a major fact in black lives. But it was Sherwood Anderson who most explicitly put modern civilization at stake through a confrontation with the black play spirit. In *Dark Laughter*, Anderson in effect translated Havelock Ellis's *Dance of Life* into fiction: The narrative sets the sensual dark laughter of blacks against the sterility of white business and social conventions, with the theme of the novel summed up in a refrain: "Dance life! Awake and dance!"[53] A lyrical evocation of the playful black eroticism that the white protagonist encounters in sultry New Orleans gives the novel its thematic center. A prose poem extending over nine pages, this passage offers, against a shrill counterpoint of white obsession with "progress" and "earnestness," a sequence of images of languorous, playful sensuality. Bruce Dudley observes blacks "standing laughing – coming by the back door – with shuffling feet, a laugh – a dance in the body." He sees "niggers on the docks, niggers in the city streets, niggers laughing. A slow dance always going on." He watches a young black man and woman making love, seeming like "young colts playing in the pasture." Everywhere he witnesses a "dance of bodies, a slow dance" (74–82).

Bruce has left wife and work to float aimlessly down the Mississippi to New Orleans, only to return to Old Harbor, Indiana, and a factory job – searching for something, he's not sure what, but something expressed in the dark laughter of blacks. "The dance of life!" he thinks to himself. "Don't stop. Don't go back. Dance the dance out to the end" (92). Eventually Bruce meets Aline, the wife of the factory owner, to become first her gardener then her lover. Aline has hungered to break out of the feminine counterpart to Bruce's masculine sterility, the petty conventions of the social world. She has traveled to Europe, coming close to the wild abandon of sensual passion only once, on hearing a friend's account of the orgiastic Quat'z Arts Ball in Paris. Desperate for such sexual awakening, Aline has instead married the aptly named Fred Gray, the quintessence of repression.

Dark Laughter verges on allegory, its theme the Western world *in extremis*. The narrative voice repeatedly calls for remaking Western art and values. It praises handcraft over manufacture, gardening over running a factory. It mocks the "silly American painters" (77) who chase Gauguin to the South Seas while ignoring their own blacks at home; and scorns Southern white songwriters who fill themselves with Keats and Shelley instead of listening to black music for inspiration. It honors the aboriginal Indians of the Midwest, who "danced there, made feasts there . . . threw poems about like seeds on a wind" (113). And it wonders whether white men's progress hasn't "cost them more than they had gained" (108). As representatives of their class and race, when Bruce and Aline finally break through their reticence to make love, then leave Old Harbor for an uncertain future, they act out a larger cultural longing. The novel ends with "the high shrill laughter" of a black woman, while Fred Gray, alone and abandoned, sits "upright and rigid in bed." Fred's repression, unfortunately, is more convincing than Bruce and Aline's escape into erotic play. The lovers' flight falls into the long American tradition of "lighting out for the territory," and just as Cooper could not keep Natty Bumppo in Templeton, nor Twain return Huck to St. Petersburg, Anderson apparently could not imagine how Bruce and Aline could live freely in Oak Harbor. All of these primitivist novels project play and repression onto a racial dualism that precludes any possibility of dialectical transcendence.

The objects of those projections were subjects of their own history. They also wrote poems and novels in which this black primitivism plays a part. The major trend in black literary and cultural studies in the 1980s emphasized the folk traditions underlying African-American literature. By this reading the "renaissance" of the 1920s was no rebirth but rather a continuation of black self-confidence and self-expression that began early in the century, when W. E. B. DuBois, Paul Laurence Dunbar, Charles Waddell Chesnutt, and others began to explore in their writings what DuBois termed "the souls of black folk." Although the crisis in white intellectual and artistic worlds over what seemed a failed civilization stimulated, supported, and helped shape this black cultural awakening, its primary impulses derived from the black race's own folklife.[54]

To ignore white influence entirely would overcompensate for earlier denials of black self-creation. Black writers' varied responses to the primitivist stereotype reflect a range of positions within African-American literary and intellectual circles in the 1920s and 1930s, as well as the complex interplay of black artist and white patronage. As one critic has put it, the writers of the New Negro movement were caught between "the well-meaning but pernicious influence of whites encouraging them to emphasize the exotic aspects of Harlem life" and the "misguided counsel of the black elite criticizing them for literary pandering and for not using their talents to portray the intellectual and social purity of the race."[55] Black artists of the 1920s had to choose first of all between folk culture and bourgeois culture as sources for their fiction; if they embraced the folk traditions, they also had to choose between realistic and romantic approaches to them. By making these choices, novelists of the Harlem Renaissance explored a range of themes and styles: from the urban realism of Nella Larsen and Jessie Fauset to the folk realism of Langston Hughes and Countee Cullen; from the romanticism of Jean Toomer, Claude McKay, and Zora Neale Hurston to the racial satires of Rudolph Fisher, George Schuyler, and Wallace Thurman. Black primitivism, in both its urban and its rural moods, was but one subject among many; I emphasize it here because it touched most directly on the decade's cultural fantasy of play.

The primitivism of Negrophiles like Van Vechten not only represented potentially restrictive desires of white audiences and publishers, it also offered, more positively, a way to celebrate blackness. However, to embrace the primitive as authentic self-portraiture not only risked displeasing the "uplifters" of the race, it placed blacks outside the pale of Western civilization. The stakes were high, and the lines were sharply drawn. Uplifters like DuBois, Benjamin Brawley, and William Stanley Braithwaite opposed champions of the New Negro like Wallace Thurman and Alain Locke. Thurman's short-lived journal *Fire!!* took a position toward black folk culture radically different from that in *The Crisis* and *Opportunity,* the official publications of the NAACP and the Urban League respectively. Following the notoriety of Van Vechten's *Nigger Heaven* in 1926, pressure on black writers to explore Negro primitivism increased. But writers like Hughes and McKay more consciously rebelled against the uplifters of their own race than imitated the stereotypes of white fantasists.

Among those who sought their inspiration, their subjects, and their themes in the common experience of African-American life, the primitivist idealization of black play offered ambiguous possibilities. For black artists to reject the dominant popular image of their race risked losing patrons, publishers, and an audience (Charotte Osgood Mason, for example, the wealthy white patron of Langston Hughes, Zora Neale Hurston, and others, became displeased with Hughes when his writing turned political). Moreover, for black artists to claim for the Negro a natural impulse to play risked implying their race was essentially uncivilized. An emphasis on the instinctual, anti-bourgeois nature of black culture simply inverted the racist stereotypes of Thomas Dixon and other white supremacists from the dark days before World War I.[56] The question of jazz raised this dilemma. As a black creation, jazz was an object of black pride, but danger lay in accepting it as the soul of black folk. In an essay on jazz in Alain Locke's *The New Negro* (1925), J. A. Rogers began by affirming that "jazz isn't music merely" but "a spirit that can express itself in almost anything. . . . a joyous revolt from convention, custom, authority, boredom, even sorrow – from everything that would confine the soul of man and hinder its riding free on the air." Jazz was "the revolt of the emotions against repression," "hilarity expressing itself through pandemonium"; it was "always impromptu, for the sheer joy of it" – in other words, the antithesis of all that was culturally defined as white and puritanical. But if black jazz was emotional rather than cerebral music, a black critic celebrated it at great risk. While claiming the true home of jazz to be the seamy black cabaret, Rogers joined white critics in granting that Paul Whiteman and other white orchestra leaders had demonstrated "the finer possibilities of jazz music." Rogers and other blacks had as much at stake in civilization as Gilbert Seldes did.[57]

According to one historian of the Harlem Renaissance, Langston Hughes was the only important black writer of the day to embrace jazz as serious music.[58] Through such poems as "Jazzonia" Hughes has also been credited with introducing jazz into poetry.[59] Hughes is most important here not as the first but as the central figure among renaissance artists of a blues vision that embodied a distinctive black alternative to the white fantasy of primitivist play. In his famous definition of the blues, Ralph Ellison called it "an impulse to keep the painful details and episodes of a brutal experience alive in one's aching consciousness, to finger its jagged grain, and to transcend it, not by the consolation of philosophy but by squeezing from it a near-tragic, near-comic lyricism."[60] In the language of recent literary theory, Houston Baker has described the blues as a "mediational site where familiar antinomies are resolved (or dissolved) in the office of adequate cultural understanding."[61] In the terms of my own inquiry, the blues entails a celebration of tragic existence, a dialectic of playful tragedy or tragic play.

The blues by any of these definitions is not simply a theme or subject matter in African-American culture but, again in Ellison's words, "part of a total way of life, and a major expression of an attitude toward life" that celebrates "man's ability to deal with chaos."[62] The rhetoric of play in black literature, then, is a linguistic sign for an entire worldview, a metaphysics of black existence. And this sign is pervasive in the fiction and poetry of Langston Hughes, Claude McKay, Zora Neale Hurston, and other renaissance writers who embraced a complex Negro primitivism as a key to black life. Where Sherwood Anderson heard only dark laughter, Langston Hughes heard "the tune / That laughs and cries at the same time" ("Jazz Band in a Parisian Cabaret"). Where Julia Peterkin saw only black playfulness without pain, Claude McKay saw "wine-flushed bold eyed boys, and even girls" devouring a beautiful black cabaret dancer whose "self was not in that strange place" ("The Harlem Dancer"). In general, where white primitivists of the 1920s found dualism – either between white repression and black impulse or between the tragedy and the lyricism of black life – black primitivists found a blues dialectic.

Sadness, the hustler with a tragicomic outlook on life in Paul Laurence Dunbar's *The Sport of the Gods* (1902), has been called "the first blues figure in the Afro-American novel."[63] James Weldon Johnson's *The Autobiography of an Ex-Colored Man* (1912), a more immediate precursor text to the Harlem Renaissance (reprinted in 1927 at its height), centers on the tensions between ragtime and the European classical tradition, between black heritage and the material rewards of life in the white world. Jean Toomer's *Cane* (1923), frequently cited as the first novel of the actual renaissance, celebrates the primitive sensuality of black rural life (not, however, by setting black against white as in the novels by Frank and Anderson, but by setting woman against man and peasant against bourgeois – typologies of gender and class, not race). And Rudolf Fisher's *The Walls of Jericho* (1928), in the midst of its largely satirical treatment of race and class, sounds a blues note when one character, a notorious high-stepper, tells a squeamish white patroness, "Some folks laugh to keep from crying."[64]

But it was Hughes, McKay, and Hurston who most pointedly developed the blues dialectic out of an African-American rhetoric of play. We can take Hughes's *Not Without Laughter* (1930) as our representative text, a conventional coming-of-age story given a distinctive voice by its immersion in the blues. Growing up in a small Kansas town, the black boy Sandy is subject to the influences of the elders who raise him: a loving, self-sacrificing grandmother; two aunts, one painfully respectable and class-conscious, the other rebellious and bitter; a conscientious but passive mother and a mostly absent, blues-singing father, who was "cut out for playing." Sandy is constantly faced with alternatives: his grandmother's Christianity or the male culture of the pool hall, Aunt Tempy's proprieties or Aunt Harriett's profane ragtime and blues, the revival or the carnival that come to town at the same time. As he discovers his own identity and forms his values, Sandy comes to accept or reject no possibility entirely.

Through this cast of characters, a contrapuntal structure, and a series of rhetorical figures, Hughes thus developed the novel's blues vision. Chapter VI, "Work," describes what blacks give to white folks; Chapter VIII, "Dance," describes what blacks claim for themselves. Other juxtaposed scenes create similar oppositions. In several images within these scenes, play and its opposites come together. At the dance, for example, the dancers' feet go "down through the floor into the earth . . . down into the center of things" as the band plays "the heart out of loneliness." At the pool hall, as he witnesses the lying contests that grow increasingly belligerent and lewd, Sandy learns that for even the poorest of blacks, "no matter how hard life might be, it was not without laughter." And in the novel's thematic climax, Sandy thinks of all the people who have touched his life as a "band of dancers." His dicty uncle has complained to him that black people were poor "because they were dancers, jazzers, clowns." Sandy understands instead that "the other way around would be better: dancers because of their poverty; singers because they suffered; laughing all the time because they must forget." His people seem to Sandy "black dancers – captured in a white world," but "dancers of the spirit, too. Each black dreamer a captured dancer of the spirit."[65]

It is Hughes's refusal of simple choices, his denial of closure, his both/ and dialectic rather than either/or dualism that distinguishes *Not Without Laughter* from, say, Anderson's *Dark Laughter*. And this dialectical embrace of play and sorrow characterizes the fiction of such other writers of the Harlem Renaissance as McKay and Hurston. In two of McKay's novels, *Home to Harlem* (1928) and *Banjo* (1929), and in Hurston's *Their Eyes Were Watching God* (1937), I would single out a scene in each, a blues moment, that expresses the vision of the entire novel, with strik-

ingly similar language in all three. In *Home to Harlem,* a long passage
near the end describes the "primitive, voluptuous rhythm" of jazz dancers
as an emblem of both the joy and the tragedy of life:

> Haunting rhythm, mingling of naive wistfulness and charming gayety,
> now sheering over into mad, riotous joy, now, like a jungle mask,
> strange, unfamiliar, disturbing, now plunging headlong into the far,
> dim depths of profundity and rising as suddenly with a simple, childish
> grin. And the white visitors laugh. They see the grin only. Here are
> none of the well-patterned, well-made emotions of the respectable
> world. A laugh might finish in a sob. A moan end in hilarity. That
> gorilla type wriggling there with his hands so strangely hugging his
> mate, may strangle her tonight. But he has no thought of that now.
> He loves the warm wriggle and is lost in it. Simple, raw emotions and
> real. They may frighten and repel refined souls, because they are too
> intensely real, just as a simple savage stands dismayed before nice emo-
> tions that he instantly perceives are false.[66]

In *Banjo,* a parallel passage shifts the emphasis to a fuller celebration of
the joy blacks create from life, not by denying pain but by accepting and
playing it. The tune that Banjo and his fellow musicians play, "Shake
That Thing," becomes another metaphor for black existence:

> Shake to the loud music of life, playing to the primeval round of life.
> Rough rhythm of darkly-carnal life. Strong surging flux of profound
> currents forced into shallow channels. Play that thing! One movement
> of the thousand movements of the eternal life-flow. Shake that thing!
> In the face of the shadow of Death. Treacherous hand of murderous
> Death, lurking in similar alleys, where the shadows of life dance, never-
> theless, to the music of life. Death over there! Life over here! Shake
> down Death and forget his commerce, his purpose, his haunting pres-
> ence in a great shaking orgy. Dance down the Death of these days, the
> Death of these ways in shaking that thing. Jungle jazzing, Orient wrig-
> gling, civilized stepping. Shake that thing! Sweet dancing thing of prim-
> itive joy, perverse pleasure, prostitute ways, many-colored variations
> of the rhythm, savage, barbaric, refined – eternal rhythm of the mys-
> terious, magical, magnificent – the dance divine of life. . . . Oh, Shake
> That Thing![67]

And in *Their Eyes Were Watching God,* finally, Hurston described rural
black life on "the muck" – the rich mud of the Florida Everglades where
poor blacks harvest beans by day and throw their money after liquor,
dice, and music by night – in briefer but comparable terms:

> All night now the jooks clanged and clamored. Pianos living three
> lifetimes in one. Blues made and used right on the spot. Dancing,
> fighting, singing, crying, laughing, winning and losing love every hour.
> Work all day for money, fight all night for love.[68]

Among the striking elements in these passages, the blues images in the novels by Hughes, McKay, and Hurston, in contrast to the long anti-nomian tradition I have been tracing, are of *communal* play, not the play of the solitary self.

To note the similarities of these scenes is not to reduce the three novels to variations of a single theme. The blues is not an element in such novels, nor merely a theme or motif; it is finally a metaphysic as Ellison has described it, an explanation of life and death. The blues entails an understanding of human possibility – possibility for black humans in particular, in twentieth-century white America. Another of McKay's novels, *Banana Bottom* (1933), set among the peasants of Jamaica, moves further from the sometimes brutal realism of *Home to Harlem* toward pure pastoral, yet retains a similar dialectical sense of work and play, joy and endurance. The significant differences among these novels by writers of the Harlem Renaissance (McKay's and Hurston's romantic primitiv-ism, Hughes's greater realism) is less important here than their common alternative to the simpler sense of black play in the novels by Frank, Van Vechten, and Anderson.

As a metaphysic, however, the blues presents its own challenge to the African-American writer who wishes to be true to black experi-ence. It can be no accident that McKay's most lyrical celebration of black life is set in rural Jamaica, where the social and political struc-tures of Western civilization have not yet triumphed. Equally telling, the Harlem novels of the renaissance writers tend to focus on the black metropolis almost as if it were not surrounded by a larger white society. What is most conspicuously missing from all of this fiction is overt politics. As Ellison has written, "The blues are not primarily concerned with civil rights or obvious political protest; they are an art form and thus a transcendence of those conditions created within the Negro community by the denial of social justice."[69] I have intermit-tently traced the relationship of "transcendence" to the rhetoric of play in American culture. Ellison's language reminds us that "tran-scendence" has different connotations for those at the center and those at the margins of that culture. "No matter how strictly Negroes are segregated socially and politically," Ellison has written in another es-say, "on the level of the imagination their ability to achieve freedom is limited only by their individual aspiration, insight, energy and will."[70] Seemingly as counterpoint, Michael G. Cooke has pointed out that "black American culture before this century couched itself in the blues and in signifying, because by their obliquity, those forms enabled the culture to exist without demanding, indeed without pro-voking recognition (since recognition was likely to be hostile)." And Keith Byerman has denied transcendence altogether. "History," writes

Byerman, "with the suffering and joy it brings, cannot, in the folk worldview, be transcended; it must be lived through."[71]

This disagreement suggests a tension between the metaphysics and the politics of the blues, which in turn parallels the cultural/political dichotomy in bohemian radicalism – and in the entire tradition of countercultural play that I am tracing from the 1830s to the 1980s through its rhetoric. The conflict is more acute when it involves an oppressed underclass, but it is crucial not to oversimplify it. The blues embodies simultaneous assertion and acceptance: neither passive, powerless victimization nor violent rebellion, but a more complex engagement with white power through self-determined black identity. What Cooke calls the "obliquity" of the blues describes the nature of this engagement. While the blues is conservative in the sense that it accepts the impossibility of changing the world, it does not merely acquiesce. The blues confronts oppression by indirection and blocks the internalization of oppression by, in effect, declaring that even oppression can be *played*. Taking unreason rather than reason as life's basic principle, creativity (playfulness) as the necessary response, the blues implies that politics itself is the product of an illusion that rational control is possible. The blues is ultimately political as well as existential, because the existence of a racist society is always implied. Or, to put the case another way, the blues cannot even be imagined without the implied oppressive context. This oblique politics, then, marks a major distinction between white and black versions of countercultural play in the 1920s. For Emerson and Thoreau, Hawthorne and Twain, the entire tradition I have been examining, the tragic limitation which play opposes is embodied in personal or human finitude. For black writers like Hughes, McKay, and Hurston, tragic limitation is more pressingly embodied, if only indirectly, in the politics of a racist society.

In this chapter and in Chapter 8 I have structured my discussions of black fiction around two subjects that touch directly on my examination of sporting rhetoric in American culture, but in doing so I have also approached the center of African-American culture as it has been described in the major studies by literary critics in recent years. And while the themes of victimization and resistance, discussed in Chapter 8 in terms of a contest between black men and white "gods," have had a long presence in African-American literary history, the tradition that increasingly has been defined by critics as the major voice of black American literature is the one rooted in folk culture and transformed into art, most notably by the writers of the Harlem Renaissance, by Ralph Ellison, and by the most recent generation of black artists in the 1970s and 1980s. (The two traditions are complementary: The protest novel says blacks can't win; the blues novel offers the alternative to futile contesting. Many protest novels are blues novels as well.) From this generative folk culture individual critics have identified a range of master terms – signifying, specifying, call-and-response, the blues – or addressed folk materials more eclectically. But within this seeming diversity the common emphasis on a black oral tradition, rooted in an essentially playful spirit, is pronounced.[72]

Thus the blues dialectic in the fiction of the Harlem Renaissance ought to be seen not just as a minor strain in the mainstream middle-class American tradition but also as a major strain in black writing. Later "blues novels" identified by black critics include not just Ellison's *Invisible Man* as the classic text but also fiction by James Baldwin, John A. Williams, Ishmael Reed, Ernest J. Gaines, Albert Murray, Toni Cade Bambara, Alice Walker, Toni Morrison, Gayl Jones, John Edgar Wideman, Leon Forrest, and Clarence Major. In much of this fiction the distinctive African-American rhetoric of play from the Harlem Renaissance continues to have a prominent place. Jes Grew in Reed's *Mumbo Jumbo* (1972) is the African-American spirit of play itself. A victim of white injustice in Baldwin's *If Beale Street Could Talk* (1974) learns to face the worst, "even taunt it, play with it, dare." An activist in Bambara's *The Salt Eaters* (1980), caught between the competing needs of the spiritual and the political, learns at last "to keep on dancing." Wideman's *Sent for You Yesterday* (1983) concludes in an evocation of jazz, blues, and the voices of past and present, with the old generation teaching the new "to stand, to walk . . . to dance."[73]

In the context of American culture in the 1920s and 1930s, then, the blues dialectic is significant as a rhetorically successful alternative to cultural dualism, expressing a vision of human wholeness that continued to elude most white writers. It is surely one of the major ironies of American cultural history that such a dialectic emerged as a distinctive vision from within America's most oppressed minority. But in addition, in the context of the black writers' own racial heritage, the blues dialectic that thrived in the twenties became one of this generation's chief legacies to future writers in the African-American grain.

12

From Beats and Hippies to
the New Age

The pattern of eruption and containment, resulting in an expanded accommodation to play in middle-class culture, was replayed once more in the third quarter of the twentieth century. The difference this time was that the playful counterculture of the 1960s youth movement, no longer the creation of a coterie of artists and intellectuals, came close to overwhelming the entire society. At the time, the rebellion of hippies and yippies and diggers and druggies seemed an unprecedented aberration in a stable and rational culture, when in fact it was but the most recent and most intense convulsion in a process that had been fitfully underway for more than a century. As Americans in the twentieth century turned increasingly from labor to leisure for both personal fulfillment and collective prosperity, the fundamental dualism wrought by industrialism began to turn inside out. Middle-class men and women became less likely to play in order to work more efficiently, than to work for the time and money to play. As work's century gave way to play's century, social critics became concerned not with finding a legitimate role for recreation, but with salvaging what was valuable from the disappearing work ethic.

"The sixties" was less a revolution than a culmination, not the final result of course, but an extreme expression of the countercultural impulse born with the emergence of industrial capitalism. The Transcendentalists waged a revolution mostly of ideas, the pre- and post-World War I bohemians a more social but still intellectual one. The counterculture of the 1960s had its thinker-heroes, too, but its manifestations were mostly played out in the social arena: an assault on the senses and feelings rather than the minds of fellow citizens.

To leap ahead to the explosion of "play power" in the 1960s, and its grounding in the more limited cultural rebellion of the previous decade, is not to imply that between 1930 and 1950 play disappeared from American consciousness. A recommitment to work emerged from the prolonged political debate in the 1930s over the appropriate length of the workweek, its outcome a New Deal affirmation of the forty-hour standard.[1] But as Warren Susman has argued, the usual differentiation in cultural values between twenties hedonism and thirties political engagement ignores a more significant continuity.[2] The 1930s was the decade of swing bands and Busby Berkeley musicals, the golden age of the movies and the "democratization of sport," to use Frederick Lewis Allen's term. Public works agencies built bathing beaches, playgrounds, and national parks; private golf clubs suffered, but municipal courses boomed; a skiing craze, a spectacular increase in the popularity of softball and other nonelite games, and a widespread relaxation of laws against gambling marked the years of the Depression. The thirties was also a decade of fads: of Monopoly, dance marathons, roller derbies, six-day bicycle races, flagpole-sitting and goldfish-swallowing contests. In part, these were frantic efforts to escape the dreariness of Depression America; in part, parodies of the traditional American success ethic. But as Susman points out, they also, strangely, were efforts "to maintain and reinforce essential values, to keep alive a sense of hope."[3]

As to the supposed anti-hedonism of the social vanguard, Susman argues that the left-leaning politics of the thirties did not run very deep, that it was more populist than communist, more personal and psychological than collective and political. As anxiety over the state of Western civilization continued into the 1930s, "play" emerged as a rhetorical emblem of "culture," in opposition to "civilization," which was rational, bureaucratic, industrial, urban – everything that thwarted the human spirit. To some degree it seems appropriate to think of the concern with play and culture as the alternative to radical politics. Interest in alternative cultures produced Stuart Chase's bestselling *Mexico: A Study of Two Cultures* (1931), in which the lifeways of the "machineless men" of Mexico were contrasted to those that prevailed north of the border. In the Indian villages to the south, Chase wrote, local government is "a form of play," abundant fiestas release "the spirit of play . . . on a vast and authentic scale," and the people "take their fun as they take their food, part and parcel of their organic life."[4] Comparable interest in the indigenous culture(s) of the United States produced Constance Rourke's 1931 study of American humor (subtitled "The Roots of American Culture") and lay behind the decade's many excavations of American popular culture and folklore.

Not interest in, but concern about American culture led to the Southern Agrarian movement; to the philosopher George Santayana's *The Last Puritan* (1936), another surprising bestseller of the decade that tied culture to the human play spirit; and to numerous studies, both popular and academic, of leisure.[5] This sociology of leisure continued in a direct line from the late-nineteenth-century play movement, but considerably expanded now. ·A bibliographer of leisure studies recorded only seventy-two books and articles in the first two decades of the twentieth century, then 199 in the 1920s, and 431 in the 1930s.[6] Not lack of leisure but leisure itself became the chief problem – to be diagnosed, analyzed, and treated.[7] Earnest Calkins began his *Care and Feeding of Hobby Horses* (1934) by asking readers, "What are you going to do with your leisure?" Jay B. Nash posed a more ominous question: "Can we be trusted with leisure?"[8] Concern over play came from both left and right, if such terms are even appropriate at a time when "liberalism" abandoned laissez-faire economics for a New Deal for the masses. A better term to describe the prophets of play in the thirties would be "antimodernist." Liberals like Lewis Mumford and Chase and conservatives like the Southern Agrarians and Santayana shared a common fear that mechanization would kill the vital play spirit necessary for fully human existence.[9]

Between 1930 and 1950, then, play did not disappear from cultural consciousness, but its implications actively engaged intellectuals more than the middle class generally, and certainly no consensus emerged about the relative importance of work and play. The renewed prosperity and superficial complacency following World War II raised anxiety about play to a higher pitch, still without bursting through the boundaries of normal cultural discourse. Postindustrial America, the consumer culture, the culture of abundance, the affluent society – whatever America was in the 1950s, it wasn't the America of the nineteenth century, and both ordinary citizens and intellectuals groped to come to terms with the new realities. A bestselling novel like *The Man in the Gray Flannel Suit*, disparaged by elite critics almost as enthusiastically as it was enjoyed by "middlebrow" readers, addressed the same issues that engaged David Riesman and Daniel Bell, C. Wright Mills and William Whyte. The degradation of work, the barrenness of "mass culture," the pressure to conform to sterile values and behavior concerned all of these writers. And so did what they perceived as the absence of a genuine play spirit in American life. These writers and many others set the stage for the countercultural explosion of the 1960s in the name of play.

The Beats and American culture in the 1950s

As with "the twenties" and "the thirties," the popular separation of the post-World War II era into discrete decades, each with its distinctive *Zeitgeist*, again ignores a fundamental continuity. The common understanding of the sixties as a rebellion against the placid fifties, followed by retrenchment in the seventies, is partially true, but the entire postwar period was also marked by a prolonged search for cultural values to replace or bolster a disintegrating work ethic. The "leisure problem" of the fifties that engaged numerous intellectuals yielded to a debate over the value of a playful counterculture in the sixties, then another over the self-centered hedonism and "narcissism" of the seventies. At root lay the same issues: the presence or absence of a play spirit in American culture, the nature of that spirit, and the prospects for personal and cultural regeneration through play.

The 1950s saw a resumption of developments related to play that a World War had interrupted. Professional baseball and boxing recovered the momentum lost briefly in wartime; professional basketball and football began to emerge as spectator sports to rival them. Advertising entered its "golden years," as the arts of selling utopia (the Good Life) and salvation (self-realization) became increasingly sophisticated and effective.[10] And of course television, the medium that transformed both sport and advertising and was in turn shaped to their requirements, quickly became the primary focus of American leisure. The 1950s was also the decade of Jean Piaget's *Play, Dreams and Imitation in Childhood* (1951), of *Playboy* magazine (1953) and Nelson N. Foote's "Sex as Play" (1954), of Gregory P. Stone's study of American sport as "Play and Dis-Play" (1955), of anthropologist Gregory Bateson's "Theory of Play and Fantasy" (1955), of the translation of Huizinga's *Homo Ludens* into English (1955) – a decade, that is, not just when people played in new and old ways but when play itself was "discovered" on an unprecedented scale.

As one aspect of this discovery, the leisure "problem" of the 1930s approached a crisis. The degradation of work – attested to by Riesman in *The Lonely Crowd* (1950), by Mills in *White Collar* (1951), by Whyte in *The Organizational Man* (1956), by Bell in *The End of Ideology* (1960) – seemed matched by an equal degradation of play in mass leisure. Declaring that hope for autonomous individuality lay in play not work, Riesman judged Americans inept at play, having forgotten how to fantasize and be spontaneous (his view was more hopeful in *Individualism Reconsidered* [1954]). Mills described contemporary leisure as "the amusement of hollow people," incapable of satisfying them "as old middle-class frolics and jollification may have done." According to Mills, leisure offered men and women only diversion "from the restless grind of their work by the absorbing grind of passive enjoyment of glamour and thrills." Whyte described the supplanting of the Protestant ethic by a social ethic that counseled a bland sort of relaxation and adjustment to the system. Bell insisted that play could have no zest as long as work remained drudgery – the solution lay in returning spontaneity and freedom to the workplace, not in creating more leisure.[11]

To these books that dominated intellectual discussion in the fifties can be added the work of leisure "experts" – sociologists like Charles Bright-bill, Max Kaplan, Nels Anderson, Sebastian de Grazia, and the contrib-utors to a special issue of *The Annals of the American Academy of Political and Social Science* on "Recreation in the Age of Automation" (1957), who wrote extensively of leisure's ills and proper uses.[12] De Grazia's *Of Time, Work, and Leisure* (1962) can be taken as the culmination of these writings on play: a paean to the aristocratic leisure societies of the ancient and premodern world and a lament for the absence of "true leisure" in the present. One of the new leisure experts went so far as to call for trained "recreationists" who would "disseminate the doctrine that the enjoyment of leisure is an end in itself, and that recreation skills should be com-pulsorily taught"! Such ideas contributed to what Martha Wolfenstein in 1955 called a "fun morality," by which "having fun" became virtually obligatory – diffusing impulse into harmless activities in order to preserve "unacknowledged and unrecognized the tradition of puritanism."[13]

It is in this context that I wish to consider the advent of the Beats. When Allen Ginsberg's "Howl" appeared in bookstores in 1956 – pro-voking the most famous obscenity trial since the banning of *Ulysses* – to be followed a year later by Jack Kerouac's novel of restless youth, *On the Road,* a startlingly new sensibility seemed to have burst onto the American scene. Ginsberg's "angelheaded hipsters" and Kerouac's "Holy Goof," Dean Moriarty, struck even those intellectuals who proudly de-fined themselves "against the American grain" as an invasion of bar-barians threatening the very survival of "culture" as they knew it. What strikes one looking back from the perspective of three decades is some-thing very different: the extent to which the Beats not only laid the foundation for the upheavals of the sixties but also expressed, in an exaggerated form to be sure, the fantasies and anxieties that pervaded the American middle class, including these intellectual critics, in the 1950s.

Kerouac, Ginsburg, and the rest of the Beats proclaimed themselves the prophets of a new sensibility: "hot" or "cool," but "hip" not "square" in either case; both a Great Refusal to conformity and a wild Yea to spontaneity, impulse, freedom, and "kicks." For all their conspicuous iconoclasm, the Beats' hip/square dichotomy tied them to what was conventional in the American middle-class imagination: the persistent dualism that frustrated searches for transcendence. Two accounts of the 1950s currently compete for consensus: the view that emphasizes general confidence and complacency, and the view that emphasizes deep anxiety beneath the surface contentment. By the first account, Riesman et al. were cranky intellectuals complaining that the masses had "let them down," the Beats a disaffected vanguard for the next decade's radical-ism.[14] By the second, not just Riesman and company but the Beats as

well spoke for a more general uneasiness that grew inevitably into widespread rebelliousness. The figure of "play" throughout 1950s culture
suggests the latter case. The Beats were not a revolutionary underclass
but the alienated children of the leisure society: generally middle class
and well educated, rebelling not against the overt oppression of an au-
thoritarian work ethic but against the more subtle coercions and repres-
sions of a leisure culture. Like the middle-class rebels of earlier
generations, the Beats projected their desires onto cultural others: onto
the black hipster in particular, whose voice was jazz; onto ethnic and
class outsiders of various kinds; onto Neal Cassady specifically, the working-class Westerner who became a chief participant in and primary icon
for the movement as a whole.

Although the Beats' most familiar voice is heard in the poetry of
Ginsberg, Ferlinghetti, Snyder, and others, it is to their fiction that I
look for their distinctive rhetoric of play. And what appears most striking
from the vantage point of a later generation is the similarity of the Beats'
longing for a world of play to a persistent fantasy in much of the fiction
in the decade's acknowledged mainstream. The major Beat novels – John
Clellon Holmes's *Go* (1952), Kerouac's *On the Road,* Alexander Trocchi's
Cain's Book (1960), and Henry Miller's *Tropic of Cancer* (published in
Paris in 1934 but not in the United States until 1961) – indulge less
reservedly in the anarchic possibilities of play, but otherwise their similarity to the fiction of such writers as Saul Bellow, John Cheever, and
particularly J. D. Salinger is striking.

The image from the literary past that constantly echoes in Beat writing
is Miriam and Donatello sporting in the mouth of the cavern. "Beat"
implied both beaten-down and beatific, the potential dialectic that remains an unresolved dualism in *Go* and *On the Road.* Near the end of
Go Holmes's narrator characterizes his generation as "children of the
night; everywhere wild, everywhere lost, everywhere loveless, faithless,
homeless." But against this "beaten down" quality of life, the "beatific"
plays a counterpoint – in the spirit of "go" as a manifesto of joy, movement, spontaneity, unreflective affirmation; and in the jazz that for
Holmes's self-determined outcasts is "something rebellious and nameless
that spoke for them. . . . more than music . . . an attitude toward life." At
the Go Hole, a jazz club on Times Square, they experience a vision of
all America "as a monstrous danceland."[15]

In *On the Road,* the book that became THE Beat novel and holy
scripture for countless young people in the late fifties and sixties, this
same dualism is expressed through the relationship of Sal Paradise and
Dean Moriarty, although in Moriarty the spirit of anarchic play asserts
itself more forcefully. Whether as Hart Kennedy in *Go,* Dean Moriarty
in *On the Road,* or himself driving the bus for Ken Kesey's Merry Prank-

sters in the following decade, Neal Cassady evoked the same images: constant motion, radiant enthusiasm, supercharged energy – the counterculture's spirit of play. In the fragments of his autobiography published as *The First Third* in 1971, Cassady contributed to this image with his own recollections of his childhood, when he first discovered "the sheer ecstatic escape of great rounds of play."[16]

From the opening paragraph of *On the Road* Cassady/Moriarty is a life force. "I first met Dean not long after my wife and I split up," says Sal in the first sentence, describing his "feeling that everything was dead." Then: "With the coming of Dean Moriarty began the part of my life you would call my life on the road." Dean "comes," that is, as a fertility god to a wasteland, bringing "life" with him. As is always true of prophets and demigods, Dean's past is "shrouded in mystery." He is "excited with life," crying out to everything he sees, "Yes! That's right! Wow! Man! Phew!" Sal describes "a kind of holy lightning . . . flashing from his excitement and his visions." Dean seems clothed by "the Natural Tailor of Natural Joy," bringing his "wild yea-saying outburst of American joy" to a dead world. He's "a Western kinsman of the sun," through whom Sal can "hear a new call and see a new horizon."

But in these opening pages Kerouac also laid the foundation for another motif: Dean as madman as well as saint, Dionysian in life-threatening as well as life-giving ways. And from the beginning Sal is Dean's critic as well as his partner. Sal (Kerouac's self-portrait) describes himself as "a lout compared" to Dean and Carlo Marx (Ginsberg), who "danced down the streets like dingledodies" while Sal "shambled after." Sal "shambles after" Dean through the entire novel. Dean is pure libido, the pleasure principle, the antinomian play spirit; Sal is his acolyte but also his betrayer: repeatedly drawn back to work and the reality principle. At the end of this first chapter Sal foretells "Dean's eventual rejection of me as a buddy," but the rejection is really Sal's – or Kerouac's – unwillingness, finally, to commit himself to the anarchic play spirit.[17]

The rest of the novel plays out the ambivalence of this opening chapter: four frantic cross-country journeys in which Sal meets Dean, dances briefly in the streets with him in search of the ecstatic "IT," is abandoned, then returns to the safety of his aunt's house and the serious work of his writing. Several scenes of sport – a footrace that leaves Sal with "a mad vision of Dean running through all of life" (154), a basketball game of frantic exuberance, an impromptu and creative game of catch, a softball game played by a multi-racial gang of kids – all emphasize the joy of play over mere rivalry. But in the end Sal cannot commit himself to Dean Moriarty's play spirit. Sal is *with* Dean on their wild adventures, but apart from him, too, watching, doubting, ambivalent about the carefree spirit that acknowledges no goal beyond the moment. In the novel's final scene, Sal abandons Dean for home, work, and another woman, embracing in effect the entire middle-class world whose life-lessness they had repeatedly fled. Perhaps this ending was necessary to the novel's cult of readers, who longed for the joyful play of life on the road, but for whom fantasy and middle-class security were irreconcilably opposed.

The ambivalence of *Go* and *On the Road* is the same ambivalence we saw in Hawthorne's romances before *The Marble Faun,* in the nineteenth-century fiction of bad boys who grow up to be sober citizens, in the novels of flaming youth chastened by near calamity. Play in all of this fiction means freedom but also anarchy, against the dreariness but also the security of the world it defies. In "beaten down" and "beatific" Kerouac and others thus reinscribed a familiar cultural dualism. In terms of "play," the Beats' trivialized popular image as "beatniks" emphasized the irresponsibility of their play – neither beaten down nor beatific, but silly. In their own writings, the extreme of unrestrained playful abandon does not appear at all, becoming a major voice only in the 1960s. At the other pole, Norman Mailer in "The White Negro" (1957) and particularly William Burroughs in *Naked Lunch* (1962 in the U.S.) and other novels explored the dark side of the Beat sensibility (Mailer more as fellow traveler than as card-carrying member). In blending black primitivism with his Reichian philosophy of sex, Mailer heard dark laughter where Sherwood Anderson dared not listen: in "the infinite variations of joy, lust, languor, growl, cramp, pinch, scream and despair of [the black man's] orgasm." More disturbingly, what Burroughs in *Nova Express* called "The Orgasm Death Gimmick" – "the orgasm of a hanged man when the neck snaps" – is a central symbol in his fiction that pushes "play" into regions of the unthinkable. One critic has described this motif as "some urban recreation of *The Bacchae,* mingling the blood rites of Thessalian maenads with homosexual cannibalism."[18] (The dark pos-sibilities of play burst through fantasy to public horror in 1958, when nineteen-year-old Charlie Starkweather, with his fourteen-year-old girl-friend, Caril Fugate, killed ten people then declared, "i'm not sorry for what i did cause for the first time me and caril had more fun.")[19]

The most characteristic Beat writing rejected extremes. But while *Go* and *On the Road* are trapped in their authors' divided consciousness, Alexander Trocchi's *Cain's Book* and Henry Miller's *Tropic of Cancer* join the handful of novels that have escaped their culture's deeply embedded dualism for a more truly dialectical vision. A Scot who lived in New York for three years while writing his novel, Trocchi followed Holmes and Kerouac in celebrating jazz as "the most vigorous and yea-saying protest of *homo ludens* in the modern world." Jazz is the music of the outsider; inside society, "man is forgetting how to play." But Trocchi fused this emblem of joy to play's darker possibilities, following Burroughs in using the junkie as the prototype of *Homo ludens,* his emblem of rebellion. Through his chemical fix the junkie enters "a play region, surprising, fertile, and unmoral," a region – echoing Miriam and Donatello – "at the edge of the gallow's leap."[20]

Tropic of Cancer, included here because its initial American publication in 1961 made it a novel of the period and because of its affinity with and influence on the Beat sensibility, has a similar vision. The fictional "Henry Miller" of the novel lives in a world of cockroaches, whores, and filth, but as he says of his early days in Paris, he continues "dancing the streets on an empty belly." Though the human race may be doomed, Miller nonetheless proclaims, "Let the dead eat the dead," while "us living ones dance about the ruin of the crater, a last expiring dance. But a dance!" Both Miller and Trocchi (whom Miller influenced) were Emersonians in singling out the artist as the dancer who can remake civilization; who can, in Miller's quite un-Emersonian words, restore life to the "pooped out" world, creating "a world that produces ecstasy and not dry farts."[21] More like Hawthorne than Emerson, Trocchi and Miller also declared that one could "play" in the face of the existential abyss. Miller's scatalogical vision would seem to share little with Hawthorne's prickly morality, but Miller's was simply a more radical affirmation of Hawthorne's vision in *The Marble Faun:* more "radical" because the abyss had yawned wider in the twentieth century but also because, unlike Miriam and Donatello who understand that they must eventually give up their sport to meet a fallen world on its terms, Miller insisted that one could dance indefinitely on the crater's rim.

For all their desire to shock readers out of their complacency, Holmes, Kerouac, Trocchi, Miller, and even Mailer (though not Burroughs) translated into fiction not an aberrant vision but the fears and longings of their age, a dream shared by more "respectable" and supposedly representative writers of the 1950s. In *Invisible Man* (1952), Ralph Ellison imagined the freedom of play, the *spiel* of the trickster that was possible "outside history"; in *The Sot-Weed Factor* (1960), John Barth imagined the playful freedom of tricksters who can create history. An anarchic impulse to defy convention, to shun tradition and responsibility, to play at life rather than work at it, runs through this and much more fifties male fiction as an antidote to wife-home-suburbs, the Cold War, Eisenhower conservatism, and gray flannel suits. The decade saw Saul Bellow's most play-centered novels, first *Augie March* (1953), then *Henderson the Rain King* (1959) with its dream of recovering humankind's animal nature, both playful and powerful, a state of being, not becoming. John Steinbeck followed up *Cannery Row* (1945) with *Sweet Thursday* (1954), both idyls of sentimental play among Monterey's outcasts. Wright Morris contrasted a spiritless present to a more heroic but also more playful past in two novels, *The Huge Season* (1954) and *The Field of Vision* (1956). In the earlier book, a chipmunk literally dancing before the jaws of a cat creates a Hawthornian symbol for the spirit lacking in the human world; in a crucial scene in the latter, children's antics at a playground seem the sole vestige of passionate living in the world.[22] In John Cheever's *The Wapshot Chronicle* (1957), the world of play, of fishing and sailing specifically, is more simply a refuge for woman-bullied Wapshot males from an emasculating existence. Closer to anarchy, in J. P. Donleavy's *The Ginger Man* (1958), Sebastian Dangerfield devotes himself entirely to "women, drink and general chaos . . . and this crazy dancing in the street," as a friend puts it, to a life of play heedless of future, career, or other people (especially women).[23]

Although none of these novels was tied to the Beat movement, a common desire connects them. A longing for play, imagined as freedom, escape, and at times a kind of holiness, runs through this fiction. In the 1950s, play continued to define the realm of dream and desire for the American middle class, but usually without the threatening overtones of the erotic play in the 1920s. The Beats most unlikely partner in their longing for play was J. D. Salinger, in his hold on impassioned readers surely one of the postwar years' quintessential writers, and a writer for whom play and holiness were most clearly linked. In "Seymour: An Introduction" (1959), Buddy Glass disparages "Dharma Bums" and "the Beat and the Sloppy and the Petulant," who "look down their thoroughly unenlightened noses at this splendid planet."[24] But Buddy's creator nonetheless shared with the despised Beats a fundamental belief in the sanctity of play, in Salinger's case, play as the essence of the most romantic celebration of childhood since the 1850s. Holden Caulfield's dream of being the "catcher in the rye," the guardian of "all these little kids playing some game in this big field of rye and all" who prevents their falling over the edge of the cliff, seems to have been Salinger's dream as well: a dream that longs to deny the cavern before which humankind desires to sport. Over that cliff lies adulthood and sexual awareness; back in the field of rye Hawthorne's paradise of children remains intact. Salinger shared the Beats' sense of alienation from modern America but responded differently: Whereas the Beats envisioned playing in defiance of life's bitterness, Salinger divided life into a childhood of prelapsarian play and a sadly fallen adult reality.

Salinger indulged this nostalgia most fully in his various stories about the Glass family, that tribe of precocious children grown to troubled adults who cling to the wisdom of their youth. All of the Glass children are "players" of one sort or another: Franny and Zooey are professional actors; Walt and Boo Boo were wonderful dancers when they were younger; Buddy dances and plays various games; Waker, the priest, was an expert juggler as a youngster, and "family rumor" reports that he was once chastened for tossing the Eucharistic wafer to his communicants' waiting lips "in a lovely arc over his left shoulder." Seymour, the principal sibling, is also the principal player, the one who as a boy had been carried on a vaudevillean's bicycle about the stage, then later, as an adult, confided to his father that "he wasn't sure if he had ever got off Joe Jackson's beautiful bicycle."[25] In the sequence of stories as Salinger wrote them, from "A Perfect Day for Bananafish" (1948), to "Raise High the Roofbeam, Carpenters" (1955), to "Seymour: An Introduction" (1959), Seymour grows progressively younger: from the man committing suicide, to the younger man marrying, to the child in Buddy's memory. In different sections of the final story Buddy remembers Seymour, on the one hand, as a "God-knower" and a "saint," on the other, as "Athlete and Gamesman." The two modes of being join when Buddy calls Seymour "the Aesthete as Athlete," for Seymour expressed his saintliness through his play. Unlike the other kids, the unenlightened mortals of the Glass children's world, for Seymour sport was always play, not contest. He played Ping-Pong ferociously and joyfully, "without a particle of interest in the score." When he had a good hand at cards, he could never put on a poker face but grinned "like an Easter Bunny with a whole basketful of eggs." He was "a lemon at four out of five outdoor sports" only because he cared nothing for winning. "At soccer or hockey," for example, as Buddy recalls, "Seymour had a way, singularly unendearing to his teammates, of charging downfield – often brilliantly – then stalling to give the opposing goalie time to set himself in an impregnable position." In those games at which he excelled – stoopball, curb marbles, and pool – he was always guilty of "Formlessness" and idiosyncratic technique that made his success seem unearned. But *earning,* trying, working to win are perversions of true play. Seymour coached Buddy to "try not aiming so much": to play a sort of Zen marbles, the shooter and the shot becoming one. Buddy concludes his long recollection of Seymour's sporting spirit with a sudden shift from sport to spirituality. "Seymour once said," Buddy reports in attempting to sum up the lesson of those childhood games, "that all we do our whole lives is go from one little piece of Holy Ground to the next." The world was Seymour's church and play his truest worship.[26]

The enemies of play in Salinger's fictional world are maturity, sex, work, war, competition, and the rhetorical "game of life" that rules the world of adults. "Life *is* a game, boy," one of Holden Caulfield's teachers tells him. "Life *is* a game that one plays according to the rules." "Yes, sir," Holden pretends to agree, but then to himself: "Game my ass. Some game. If you get on the side where all the hot-shots are, then it's a game, all right – I'll admit that. But if you get on the *other* side, where there aren't any hot-shots, then what's a game about it? Nothing. No game."[27] This rhetorical opposition of "play" to "game" is also pervasive in John Clellon Holmes's *Go,* where "games" refer to social or intellectual posing or interpersonal pettiness.[28] For the following decade's counterculture, this dichotomy summed up an entire social philosophy. In the same way, play for Salinger meant the surrender of the ego to natural holiness, not mastery of the material world but denial of it.

For all their differences, whether apparent or real, Salinger and the Beats met on common ground in setting "play" against conformity to the "phony" or "square" world of fifties America. Acknowledged or not, they had common roots in the Transcendentalism of Emerson and Thoreau, and common concerns about the quality of life in postwar America. Salinger also shared with Kerouac and Holmes, as with Morris, Cheever, and the Bellow who wrote *Henderson the Rain King,* an inability to conceive an actual world transformed by play. Play remained in the realm of memory or desire, everywhere obstructed by a most unplayful reality. But a generation raised on the dream of the fifties would attempt to live it out in the following years.

Politics and play in the 1960s

The continuity belied by popular conceptions of the conservative fifties and the radical sixties emerges clearly in a pattern bridging the fiction of both decades: a recurring motif of what might be termed an "oasis of play." Holden Caulfield's dream of being the "catcher in the rye" seems in retrospect to have expressed a pervasive American fantasy in the decades since World War II. This motif, harking back to Huck Finn's brief idyl on the raft, runs through novel after novel: a pastoral moment in the midst of a crushing or anxiety-producing reality, a brief atemporal experience of innocent joy repeatedly described as play. Between Huck and Holden there were Thomas Wolfe's nostalgic evocations of rural splendor in the youthful ballplaying of Nebraska Crane, and Jack Burden's recollections in Warren's *All the King's Men* of childhood afternoons at the swimming hole with his friends. After Holden there was Charles Eitel in Mailer's *The Deer Park* (1955), watching surfers on the beach one golden day, one beautiful girl in particular who seems "so confident of her body and the sport of being alive" – a sport at which neither Eitel nor anyone else in the novel is very adept. More ironically, there was Humbert Humbert in Nabokov's *Lolita* (1958) recalling a park where nymphets frolick, as he wishes they could "play around me forever." There was Conner in John Updike's *Poorhouse Fair* (1958), dreaming an erotic and beatific vision of "men and women, lightly clad, playing on the brilliant sand of a seashore, children's games." And Harry Angstrom in Updike's *Rabbit, Run* (1960), dwelling on the perfect moment of his youth, a practice game against tiny Oriole High when everything he throws at the basket drops in and he knows, he *knows*, he "can do anything."[29]

With the new decade came more of the same: the family fishing camp where Binx Bolling in Walker Percy's *The Moviegoer* (1961) finds the peace and vitality missing from his flattened-out life; the fishing trip in Ken Kesey's *One Flew Over the Cuckoo's Nest* (1962), when the inmates break free for an afternoon of joyful play at sea; the game of "Chinese handball" in Paul Goodman's *Making Do* (1963), played by Irish, black, Jewish, and Spanish kids who share an hour of exuberance in the midst of the impersonal city; the boyhood yo-yo tricks remembered by the narrator of Frank Conroy's *Stop-Time* (1967), by which he transcended the "paralyzing sloppiness of life," seeming as he executed one supremely difficult move to stop time itself. Perhaps the most beatific vision in all these novels occurs in Philip Roth's *Portnoy's Complaint* (1969), when Alexander Portnoy recalls the centerfield of his boyhood as an island of peace:

> Just standing nice and calm – nothing trembling, everything serene – standing there in the sunshine (as though in the middle of an empty field, or passing the time on the street corner), standing without a care in the world in the sunshine, like my king of kings, the Lord my God, The Duke Himself [the Dodgers' Snider].

"Oh, how unlike my home it is to be in centerfield," Portnoy sighs.[30]

This pervasive dream of play spanning the quarter century following World War II also reveals how much America changed between the 1920s and the 1950s: play no longer recoiled from or always projected onto the cultural other, no longer threatening in any way but reveled in as the truest expression of innocent human desire. By the 1960s, as much of the decade's most representative fiction attests, play displaced work altogether as the visionary ideal. Much of what has come to seem the decade's distinctive fiction – the novels and stories of Heller, Vonnegut, Brautigan, Nabokov, Pynchon, Reed, Barthelme, Coover, Barth – are less *about* play than themselves playful books, self-referential excursions into what Barth called "the funhouse" of language. In a 1976 essay, Tony Tanner described the " 'carnivalization' of consciousness and speech" that distinguished recent American fiction – a conjunction of play, game, and ritual in "an enactment of life freeing itself from old rigidifying forms." Other critics have defined postmodern fiction in general as essentially the literature of play.[31]

This playfulness is more politically grounded in the black humor of Heller, Vonnegut, Terry Southern, and others. What I considered in Chapter 8 as a contemporary version of the "sport of the gods" can also be seen as yet another updating of Hawthorne's *Marble Faun:* the anti-heroes of sixties fiction sporting at life in the face of apocalypse. A distinction between fiction *as* play and fiction *about* play would be too facile, however. Self-referential aesthetic play cannot avoid reflecting the outer world, while the authors of such fiction also implicitly present themselves as models for *Homo ludens,* the playful creator of his own universe. In this sense, playing with texts and playing at the barricades were related attempts to remake the world. The celebration of play documented in these chapters ultimately constitutes a vision of life in which the aesthetic and the moral are one and the same. Whatever the specific definition of play, it rests on a conviction, first articulated for modern times in Schiller's *Aesthetic Education of Man,* that the beautiful *is* the good. In this light, the innovative writers of the 1960s who sub-stituted for "reality" the free play of their imaginations were engaged in a rebellion comparable to that of the young rebels who were seeking to transform themselves or their world through play. We have here two attempts at the same cultural revolution, both of them ultimately choosing aesthetics over politics.

Among those writers who more thoroughly grounded their play in social contexts, Peter Matthiessen, Robert Coover, and Thomas Pynchon did so with particular self-conscious awareness of the implications of "play." Written before the countercultural explosion of the late sixties, Matthiessen's *At Play in the Fields of the Lord* (1965) seems both to an-ticipate that event and to prejudge its shallowness. "Playing in the fields of the Lord" is no act of self-realization but the very opposite: liberation through annihilation of the self. This is what Lewis Moon, an embittered college-educated Cheyenne Indian, learns when he transcends the ulti-mate dualism at the heart of Western civilization – that between self and nature – by surrendering utterly to the Brazilian jungle.[32] With a similar drive toward ultimate meanings, Coover's *Universal Baseball Association* (1968) declares play not the way to antinomian salvation but a radical affirmation of the phenomenal world as all there is – against not just the casual hedonism of the time but Western metaphysics and Western his-toriography as well.[33] And Pynchon's *Gravity's Rainbow* (though pub-lished in 1973 an *encyclopedic* "sixties novel") both captures and deflates the period's ludic impulse in its myriad manifestations. While the rocket arcs toward apocalypse on the final page, the novel's characters engage in a dizzying array of games: some creative, most destructive, all ulti-mately futile. Pynchon's is a darker comic version of Henry Miller's dance at the rim of the crater: emphasizing not the transcendence possible through play but the world's final engulfment by the abyss. Moments of playful freedom do occur, and the novel's sympathies lie with the outcast, the Preterite, the marginal – the representatives of countercultural alienation. But *Gravity's Rainbow* also parodies the counterculture's spiritual questing in the "game" of "Holy-Center Approaching" and its utopian vision of innocent play in the episode of the *Zwölfkinder*. And in the end the novel offers no vision of cultural or personal transformation; the rocket will complete its rainbow arc to land on the movie house in which we all sit, waiting.[34]

In ways too various to acknowledge here, sixties fiction both reflected and contributed to the cultural transformation that underlay the more conspicuous social upheaval in the name of play. As a final example, we can consider the fiction of sport itself, which underwent a transformation during this period reflecting the newly heightened valuation of play. Generally, where the writers of the 1910s and 1920s tended to criticize the individual athlete for not adapting to the team's or community's requirements, writers of the fifties and sixties tended to damn society for failing the nonconformist athlete. More specifically, the image of baseball, which for Mark Twain had seemed "the very symbol, the outward and visible expression of the drive and push and rush and struggle of the raging, tearing, booming nineteenth century," became identified, from the 1930s on (most notably beginning with Thomas Wolfe), with the pastoral impulse: baseball as garden in a land of machines, baseball as "the summer game." The football novel of the sixties invariably pitted a hero's love of the game for its own sake against management's insistence on regimenting his life both on and off the field. And the basketball novel of this decade and the seventies went further in rejecting social norms: featuring brilliant, free-lancing athletes burdened by discipline- and pattern-obsessed coaches, players who live by irrational "touch" and coaches who'll die for control. Two constants run through the novels dealing with all three sports: a new preoccupation with the work/play dichotomy, and a shift from earlier in the century when writers of sports fiction valued athletic work to an almost unanimous insistence that what was meaningful in sport was its endangered spirit of play.[35]

The basketball player boogeying to a different beat, then soaring above the rim while his earth-bound coach grits his teeth in impotent rage, makes a particularly apt emblem for what was different as well as the same in the 1960s: the same desire to play but a more rebellious, anarchic manner of playing. While Americans dreamed of ecstatic play in the fifties, they attempted to live it in the sixties – not just the anti-heroes of black comedy but an entire generation of young people dancing before the cavern of the Vietnam War. Many of the major voices heard in these chapters contributed directly to this play spirit: the Transcendentalists, particularly Thoreau, who became as one disapproving member of the older generation put it, "the patron saint of the hippie cult"; Nietzsche and Freud, or, more accurately, the worldviews they represented; Riesman, Mills, and the entire fifties sociology of alienation; Salinger, Kerouac, and the rest of its literary accompaniment.[36] Neal Cassady and Allen Ginsberg personally embodied the continuity of Beat and hippie sensibilities, Ginsberg's fifties rage yielding to sixties ecstasy (Kerouac, on the other hand, died repentant in 1969, an admirer of William F. Buckley and reviler of hippies). Wilhelm Reich (play as orgasm) and Paul Goodman (play as anarchic freedom) were influential as well.

The major prophets of the counterculture's play spirit were Norman O. Brown and Herbert Marcuse. For both Marcuse and Brown play opposed repression as the chief obstacle to human fulfillment, but they confronted the problem in crucially different ways. Brown's *Life Against Death* (1959) and *Love's Body* (1966) fall squarely in the mystical antinomian tradition, seeking to abolish repression and sublimation altogether in a state of pure play, described by Brown as "activity governed by the pleasure-principle." Marcuse, on the other hand, first in *Eros and Civilization* (1955), then in several essays in the sixties, distinguished *basic* from *surplus* repression, acknowledging the necessity of the first but declaring the possible disappearance of the other once economic scarcity has been eliminated. Unlike Brown, then, Marcuse envisioned life as a dialectical work/play that transcended basic repression without denying its necessity.[37] Though Marcuse looked to Marx and Freud, his spiritual precursor in American culture was Henry Thoreau.

The distinctions between Brown's and Marcuse's utopian visions were largely lost on young readers who saw both writers more simply teaching the radical freedom possible through play. The counterculture of the 1960s from the perspective of this study was a massive eruption of the anarchic play spirit, manifesting itself throughout the era's cultural radicalism: in "turning on" to drugs, in festivals of love, in communal or "tribal" living experiments. A number of the decade's gurus preached in the language of play. Timothy Leary invited his disciples to tune in to "the dance" of cosmic energy, to experience through LSD "the playful acrobatics of the free intellect." Ken Kesey and the Merry Pranksters pioneered "the trip," the psychedelic rock concert, the arts of spontaneity and costume. Allen Ginsberg, Abbie Hoffman, and Jerry Rubin promoted revolution as *fun*.[38] What jazz was for the Beats, and to some degree for earlier Negrophile bohemians, rock 'n' roll was for the newest counterculture, providing not just the anthems of its rebellion but the sounds of its dreaming. In what are certainly two of the most distinctive notes in sixties rock, the music of apocalypse and the music of good times – "The Eve of Destruction," say, and "Groovin' " – can be heard the musical equivalent for the sometimes compatible but fundamentally contrary impulses toward politics and play.

As was true for the Transcendentalists and the Greenwich Village bohemians, the desire to play defined only one side of 1960s rebelliousness. Politics defined the other. Many of the disputes that divided radicals – between the Old and the New Left, between factions within the New Left, between politicos and hippies, between political radicalism and cultural radicalism most generally – can be viewed as unresolved disagreements over the revolutionary possibilities of play. As was clear to observers even as the events were unfolding, play and politics defined a dualism on which the revolution eventually foundered.

Like the bohemians and politicos of pre-World War I Greenwich Village, activists and countercultural rebels were not distinct groups in the 1960s: Radicals had their countercultural values, hippies their political stance. But as primary strategies for bringing about a revolution the two approaches are easily distinguishable. One can identify two histories of the decade: on the one hand, the Freedom Bus rides, the Free Speech Movement at Berkeley, race riots, antiwar marches, the clenched fists of Tommie Smith and John Carlos at the Mexico City Olympics, the organization of SDS, SNCC, the Black Panthers, and NOW; on the other, the busrides not of freedom fighters but of Merry Pranksters in 1964, the Gathering of the Tribes at Golden Gate Park in San Francisco for the first Human Be-In in January 1967, the "summer of love" in San Francisco and invasion of Haight Ashbury by hippies in 1967, the assembling of 400,000 young people to drop acid and listen to rock music at Woodstock in 1969.

Politics and play mingled most obviously in the marches on the Pentagon, demonstrations on campuses, and disruptions of the 1968 Democratic convention in Chicago. But they mixed uneasily. Leaders of the New Left warred over the nature of the strategies to be used in Chicago: organized political protest or anarchic festival. In *The Armies of the Night* (1968), Norman Mailer described the October 1967 march on the Pentagon as a sometimes paradoxical compound of politics and play. And in his book on the Merry Pranksters, Tom Wolfe described an earlier emblematic moment: when Ken Kesey arrived in Berkeley for Vietnam Day in 1965 with the Pranksters' Day-Glo bus rigged out like an armed fortress, to berate the protesting students for playing the Pentagon's "game." The effect on the rally was deadening. "The only thing the martial spirit can't stand," Wolfe commented, was "a put-on, a prank, a shuck, a goose in the anus." In 1969, countercultural theologian Harvey Cox bemoaned the "unnecessary gap in today's world between the world-changers and the life-celebrators." Cox wanted more "festival

"Play Power": Jerry Rubin arrives in Washington for his appearance
before the House Un-American Activities Committee dressed as Santa
Claus — and surrounded by the media. (AP/World Wide Photos)

radicals" – productive activists who were also players at life. But this
joining did not ultimately occur; the visions of pranksters and politicos
proved incompatible.[39]

The attempt to join play and politics centered in the "Yippies."
Whereas "hippies" renounced politics altogether for play, Yippies attempted to confront straight America at the barricades with "play
power," as the British journalist Richard Neville called it – with "the
politics of play." Not just in America, but in England and most spectacularly in the student uprisings in France, play defined a dual strategy
for creating the revolution and defying the traditional socialists of the
Old Left. Abbie Hoffman and Jerry Rubin were the chief American
proponents of play power. Hoffman in *Revolution for the Hell of It* (1968)
and *Woodstock Nation* (1969) declared the "politics of ecstasy"; Rubin in
Do It (1970) insisted, "If it's not fun dont do it." Yippies exorcised the
Pentagon in October 1967, scattered money in front of the Stock Exchange, appeared at HUAC hearings dressed as Santa Claus or Paul
Revere, nominated a pig for president in Chicago in 1968. Their target
was as much the old leftist politics as the corporate state. "They do
socialism, we blow pot in the grass," Hoffman wrote of the Old Left in
Revolution for the Hell of It, "they do imperialism, we go swimming, they

do racism, we do flowers for everybody and clean up the room." The chief difference was clear:

> Fun. I think fun and leisure are great. I don't like the concept of a movement built on sacrifice, dedication, responsibility, anger, frustration and guilt.... nobody listens to politically relevant statements.... When I say fun, I mean an experience so intense that you actualize your full potential. You become LIFE. LIFE IS FUN. Political irrelevance is more effective than political relevance.

Theodore Roszak described such strategies as "revolutionary carnivals."[40]

For all the disruptions it caused, the politics of play proved more culturally than politically liberating. The cultural failure of the political revolution in the 1960s was matched by the political failure of the cultural rebellion. The lack of consensus over organization, play, or violence as revolutionary tactic undermined political radicalism, as cultural radicalism also self-destructed in paradoxical yet predictable ways. For one thing, play's anarchic potential always threatened: While Timothy Leary led flower children toward playful enlightenment, Charles Manson led his children on bloody rampage; ecstatic rides on LSD sometimes became bad trips or o.d.'s; a journalist at Woodstock discovered not the frenzied communal orgy out of which the press created a myth, but a grimly silent affair attended by atomized individuals.[41] Even when more successful, play was undermined from within. As in previous generations, the rebels against middle-class American life were themselves from the middle class, sharing in both its habits and its desires. Having declared their opposition to society's pervasive "games," hippies replicated these hierarchical and patriarchal "games" in their own alternative communities.[42] Most ironically, as an insider wrote in 1970, the revolutionary potential of the counterculture was subverted in part by its appeal to a broad base of the American middle class. Through the inevitable processes of the consumer society, countercultural cult figures became media superstars and hippie millionaires. At the same time, "hippie entrepreneurs" commercialized the emblems of rebellion, and mass advertisers appropriated countercultural style for the consumer culture. The potentially anarchic playfulness of the disaffected young became incorporated into new middle-class lifestyles.[43]

The roots of play's ultimate failure as revolution can be examined more thoroughly through the writings of its chief theorist, Herbert Marcuse, and the quintessential contemporary account of the subject, Tom Wolfe's *Electric Kool-Aid Acid Test*. Marcuse began in the 1930s with an orthodox Marxist privileging of work over play, writing in a 1933 essay, for

example, that one could not even speak of "life as play."[44] But beginning
with *Eros and Civilization* in 1955, and continuing in such later books as
An Essay on Liberation (1969), *Five Lectures* (1970), and *Counterrevolution
and Revolt* (1972), Marcuse looked to play as the key to both personal
and political freedom. In *Eros and Civilization*, Marcuse envisioned the
possibility that human existence could be "play rather than toil," once
conditions of abundance had eliminated economic scarcity. After his
pessimism in *One-Dimensional Man* (1964) was alleviated by the events
of the mid-sixties, Marcuse returned to this theme in his most hopeful
writings, "The End of Utopia" (1967; published in *Five Lectures*) and *An
Essay on Liberation*. But by *Counterrevolution and Revolt*, written as the
youth movement deteriorated, Marcuse had become acutely aware of its
own failures.

Marcuse's vision of human possibility remained consistent from the
fifties to the seventies. As I briefly mentioned earlier, by distinguishing
between "basic repression" and "surplus repression" (leading to non-
repressive or repressive sublimation, respectively), Marcuse theorized
what he described in *An Essay on Liberation* as "the possibility of freedom
within the realm of necessity." Surplus repression was necessary only
for domination, basic repression for civilization itself. But under conditions of abundance, Marcuse argued, not only could surplus repression
be overthrown, the basic repression essential to civilization could be freely
chosen, its debilitating tensions eliminated. Marcuse, that is, rejected
both Norman O. Brown's belief in the possibility of pure play and the
abolition of all repression, and the conventional Freudian insistence on
a realm of necessity opposed to free play. Basic repression would not be
erased but transcended: freedom within necessity, work as play.[45] Marcuse thus rejected not only the separation of work from play but the
embrace of work *and* play as a nontranscendent dialectic. In *Counterrevolution and Revolt*, Marcuse lashed out at what he called "the obscene
symbiosis of opposites" by which "pleasure and horror, calm and violence, gratification and destruction, beauty and ugliness" are equally
accepted.[46] In other words, as if responding directly to the cultural history
I have been tracing, Marcuse rejected the Hawthornian dialectic (work
and play unreconciled), while theorizing a Thoreauvian dialectic through
which the work/play dichotomy could be transcended.

But Marcuse came to realize that his theory must remain visionary for
now. The failure of play power to overthrow authority in either Europe
or America led in *Counterrevolution and Revolt* to a reconsideration of its
political potential. Having in *An Essay on Liberation* endorsed playful
radicalism against "the *esprit de sérieux*" of oldstyle socialists, Marcuse
declared in *Counterrevolution and Revolt* that "the liberating laughter of
Yippies . . . may help tear the ideological veil but leaves intact the struc-

ture behind the veil."[47] As early as 1955 Marcuse had forewarned that countercultural play would fail as politics: that "one can practice non-repressiveness within the framework of the established society"; that "the gimmicks of dress and undress" and "the wilder paraphernalia of the hot or cool life" create a style of protest that "turns into a vehicle of stabilization and even conformity, because it not only leaves the roots of the evil untouched, but also testifies to the personal liberties that are practicable within the framework of general oppression."[48]

Despite Marcuse's temporary hopefulness, rebellion in the 1960s became an illustration of this "repressive de-sublimation." In *Counterrevolution and Revolt* Marcuse reiterated that both personal and political rebellion were necessary, that social revolution could not be achieved without private liberation. But he also insisted on "the distinction between self-indulgence and liberation, between clownery and irony." The counterculture of the 1960s failed to ground itself in a *"dialectic of liberation,"* becoming instead an inverted mirror image of the culture it sought to subvert. "Where the protest assumes features which are those of the Establishment itself, of the frustration and repression released by it," revolt becomes counterrevolution.[49]

Tom Wolfe implicitly predicted this outcome in 1968, when the counterculture was at its zenith, its long-term success still conceivable. In *The Electric Kool-Aid Acid Test,* politics and play – with countercultural play defined as fundamentally spiritual – emerge as an irreconcilable dualism on which the quest of the 1960s prototypical cultural rebels, Ken Kesey and his Merry Pranksters, eventually founders. In Wolfe's telling, the Pranksters' escapades complete the adventure begun a decade earlier by the Beats, signaled when Kesey meets Jack Kerouac in New York early in the book, a speechless moment during which no benediction is given but the baton is silently passed. Kerouac and Kesey shared the same copilot, Neal Cassady, similar athletic backgrounds, the same impulse to *go;* but Kesey was going where all but angels feared to tread: into the inner space of psychedelia to become a god.

In presenting the Merry Pranksters' quest as essentially spiritual, Wolfe joined several other writers, both in the decade and afterward, who viewed the entire counterculture as a search for spiritual fulfillment unavailable in the mainstream culture.[50] The most overtly spiritual outgrowth of this search was the emergence of an explicit theology of play, the culmination of ideas forming in America since the age of Emerson. The concern over the new leisure in the 1950s led to Robert Lee's *Religion and Leisure in America* (1964), while books like Dom Aelred Graham's *Zen Catholicism* (1963) and particularly Alan Watts' *Psychotherapy East and West* (1961) and *Beyond Theology* (1964) attempted to join Eastern and Western spirituality through common beliefs in holy play (a post-humous collection of Watts' lectures was published in 1982 under the title *Play to Live*).[51] Then, at the height of the upheavals of the late sixties, Harvey Cox's *The Feast of Fools,* Robert E. Neale's *In Praise of Play,* Sam Keen's *To a Dancing God,* and David Miller's *Gods and Games* all appeared in 1969 and 1970. This same period also saw Hugo Rahner's *Man at Play* (1967) and Jürgen Moltmann's *Theology of Play* (1972) translated into English. Although these writers disagreed over certain ideas – most significantly over the familiar question whether play could comprehend the totality of human existence or must come to terms with its dualistic or dialectical other – they agreed in their basic doctrine: Christianity had become burdened with an excess of earnestness, a predilection for the ascetic over the celebrative; true holiness, on the contrary, lay in play-fulness, in festivity and fantasy in Cox's terms, in adventure as Neale put it, in frolic or dancing before the dancing God.[52]

Although the Merry Pranksters seemed to most observers intent on considerably more earthly delights, Wolfe saw them as prophets of the theology of play. Key refrains run through the book: the group's engagement in a prolonged "carnival," one of their central experiences as "dancing ecstasy."[53] Most simply, the Pranksters – stoned on LSD, ricocheting about the country in their Day-Glo bus, tootling the multitudes, staging their acid tests up and down the West Coast to the rocking sound of the Grateful Dead and the flickering phantasms of strobe-lighted dancers – are, as Wolfe put it, "at play" (263). LSD, they discover, re-creates an experience formerly available only to primitive men, children, and mystics (all among the earlier avatars of the holy player in American culture). On LSD, the Pranksters cartwheeling in the muck of a lake or flinging kelp outside their bus as they "played like very children" (191) achieve a higher, holier state denied those from the straight world who stare upon them with uncomprehending mistrust. Theirs is the dance of those who recognize the god in everyone – the "ecstasy of the All-one . . . all become divine vessels in union" (274).

As mystic cults arise by opposition, this holy play stands against society's "games." As Wolfe listens to the Pranksters talk, it seems to him that the "straight world outside . . . is made up of millions of people involved, trapped, in games they aren't even aware of." There are "cops-and-robbers games," "the justice game," "political games," "games of status, sex, and money," "the eternal game of middle-class intellectuals" – all the various "non-games of life." Even antiwar protestors merely play the oppressors' "games."[54] The Pranksters are on a spiritual mission, not a political foray. They have reconstituted the wisdom of mystic sages for a psychedelic counterculture, searching for an "adventure in living," for a life in which every day is a happening. They believe in synchronicity, surrender to the moment, bridging the "lags" between perception and response – immersion of the self in the timelessness of perfect play.

The Pranksters see allegories everywhere, especially in their own experiences in sixties America. Wolfe agreed, rendering the Day-Glo odyssey of Kesey's band as an allegory of the larger middle-class countercultural rebellion. The Pranksters were a specific historical phenomenon: the apostles of the mad god LSD to the youthful multitudes, the creators of acid rock, multi-media light-and-sound shows, and a manner of living that became centered in San Francisco's Haight-Ashbury district then spread to mini-Haights throughout America. But to Wolfe they were also one side of a cultural dualism: the spirit of play questing for transcendence, at odds with the spirit of politics working for a more material revolution.

Conflicts abound in the book: Pranksters versus politicos, acid heads versus Kesey who desires to move "beyond acid." But the conflict that most engaged Wolfe's interest, and the one that is most revealing about the countercultural potential in play, is the conflict among the Pranksters themselves. Despite their opposition to society's "games," the Pranksters unwittingly play their own. Everyone is either "on the bus" or "off the bus," in the inner or the outer circle of Prankster faithful. Although there is supposed to be no hierarchy among the Pranksters – "no games" – a hierarchy and "the old personality game" nonetheless intrude (332). Most troubling, there are two Keseys, Wolfe decided early on, "Kesey the Prankster and Kesey the organizer" (93). While the first plays, the second controls, directs, and organizes the play. Kesey "wanted [the Pranksters] to do their thing and be Pranksters, but he wanted them to be deadly competent, too" – as in being ready at all times to catch a red rubber ball when someone tosses it. Kesey also devises a game called "Power," the winner to have "thirty minutes of absolute power in which your word was law and everyone had to do what you wanted. Very allegorical, this game," Wolfe noted (117).

Allegorical indeed, but how to read it? The devil Control haunts this Garden of Eden. "The trip," as Wolfe put it, "had been liberation and captivity all at the same time" (343). In seeking to release the god in everyone, Kesey perhaps inevitably succumbs to the ultimate temptation to remain the chief god among lesser deities. Kesey revels in coming as a "Prophet" to the young Unitarians at Asilomar, a neo-Emersonian defying a new century's corpse-cold religious liberalism. Although Kesey denies this self-glorifying role, Wolfe denied the denial. Wolfe also touched on the deeper paradox of holy play as mystical religion. How does the mystic with his private vision, he wondered, share that vision with his followers without violating its personal, irrational nature? Kesey falls into the trap of mystic-become-teacher, appearing as a tripped-out version of a recreation director of the 1910s, insisting on compulsory play for the good of young souls.

In the book Kesey understands at least part of the problem, envisioning a movement "beyond acid" as the only way to keep creating, to maintain the dynamism, to continue the play by finding new ways to play. The resistance of a suspicious "head" community committed to acid becomes less important in defeating this desire than Kesey's own inability to imagine what in fact might lie "beyond." In a most allegorical rendering of the Pranksters' end, Wolfe suggested the inevitable implosion of pure play. Delivering the eulogy at his own funeral, Kesey tells his followers, "For a year we've been in the Garden of Eden. Acid opened the door to it. It was the Garden of Eden and Innocence and a ball" (395–6). But the ball's over. First at their "graduation," then at a party afterward, the Pranksters wire the music only to their own headphones, so that no one else can hear it. As outsiders look on with puzzlement or anger, the Pranksters draw in closely around Kesey, in tighter and tighter circles; they draw in, draw in, draw in, and . . . poof! . . . they disappear. The Merry Pranksters disband to go their separate ways.

John Updike and the new age

If Tom Wolfe's *Electric Kool-Aid Acid Test* can stand in my narrative as the quintessential account of "the sixties," Tom Robbins's *Even Cowgirls Get the Blues* (1976) would seem to play that role for the decade that followed: a comic fairy tale for hippies-turned-yuppies. All of the elements of a "sixties novel" are there. Its heroine drops out to hitchhike her way to freedom, in tune with "the rhythms of the universe" (meeting Jack Kerouac himself in an Iowa cornfield, where her sexuality frightens him – the King is dead, long live the Queen). An Oriental guru called the Chink declares life "essentially playful" and humankind's chief need "the freedom to play freely in the universe." Several more cultural others – interred Japanese during World War II, an Indian tribe, a community of women at a Western ranch – also appear, in every case to represent the spirit of play in a deadly and deadening world.[55] But this "sixties" cast settles on a "seventies" solution to the world's ills. The Chink declares that those who live in the Western world must change "as individuals, of course; not in organized groups" (234) – a theme played out in the novel's plot. After the utopian experiment of the cowgirls at the Rubber Rose Ranch has ended in near-apocalypse, the most militant feminist among them comes to realize that "playfulness ceases to serve a serious purpose when it takes itself too seriously" (343). The cowgirls disperse to pursue personal interests – some to college, some to the rodeo circuit, others to "different lifestyles," a few remaining at the ranch – each to play at life in her own way. Abandoning the collective for the personal, they must fight only one enemy, "the tyranny of a dull mind" (342). As one of the cowgirls puts it: "There's a whole universe of things to play with" (348).

I can imagine certain reviews: the New Ager praises Robbins for celebrating the continuation of cultural radicalism into the quest for self-actualization; the neoconservative and the leftist both damn the book as an epitome of "me decade" cultural narcissism, only disagreeing over the desired alternative. In the sustained cultural debate of the seventies and eighties, the central text of which was Christopher Lasch's *The Culture of Narcissism* (1979), it is possible to follow the process by which the countercultural play spirit was absorbed and conventionalized, rejected and celebrated one more time. Either as text or subtext, "play" had an important place in the debate over cultural narcissism. Liberals and conservatives, radicals and reactionaries were nearly unanimous in assessing the contours of American culture from the 1880s to the 1980s: Older values of hard work, self-denial, producing goods, and public service had given way to consumerism on a scale unimagined by even capitalism's most ardent champions in the nineteenth century, accompanied by a preoccupation with the self and its fulfillment in lieu of collective enterprises. Having agreed on the diagnosis, however, the cultural critics disagreed loudly over the proposed cure. Or whether there even was a sickness that required curing.

At the heart of the cultural debate was a common assumption that play had replaced work as Americans' primary source of fulfillment. This was the legacy of the 1960s: radical countercultural play absorbed into the cultural mainstream. In the post-Vietnam era, play became the essence of consumer culture: the implicit message of every beer commercial, car commercial, soda-pop commercial, credit-card commercial. Play had undergone a complete transformation: from the source of a cultural critique in the nineteenth century to the essence of American "mass culture" in the 1970s. At stake in the debate, then, was the success or failure of American capitalism as an economic and cultural system, the prospects for democratic culture in an age of consumption, and the course Americans should pursue into the future. The leisure society required new thinking about an old problem. After more than a century of struggling to come to terms with play in relation to work, Americans now had to come to terms with work in relation to play. This cultural dialogue in its many voices played out once more the pattern of the 1850s and the 1920s. In the denunciations of narcissistic playful hedonism one sees the familiar recoiling from the dangerous consequences of the radical play spirit through which a previous generation challenged the status quo.

For the defense, in the various celebrations of the spirit of play, whether in the name of self-actualization or in the cause of capitalist renewal, one sees the absorption by the cultural mainstream of the earlier generation's anarchic playfulness, made safe now and rendered serviceable to competing cultural values.

What is most striking about the latest cultural debates, suggesting a fundamental confusion rather than certainty as the hallmark of the New Age, is the meaninglessness of old political labels for the opposing sides in the debate. The critics of play in the seventies and eighties included self-proclaimed radicals and neoconservatives. Its champions of play numbered not just questers for planetary consciousness but prophets of the entrepreneurial ethic. In placing the entire proplay faction under the umbrella of the "New Age," I include many writers who would undoubtedly prefer to see themselves standing apart. But a common belief in the personally liberating power of the play spirit joins such concepts as the self-actualizing psychology of Abraham Maslow, the ecstatic theology of Matthew Fox (an obscure Catholic priest made famous when he was silenced by the Vatican), and the concept of "flow" developed by Mihaly Csikszentmihalyi, to the more openly New Age ideas of Charles Reich, Marilyn Ferguson, Jean Houston, the "New Physicists," and others.[56]

The breadth of the New Age movement would have shocked those Americans who thought of it only as a handful of crackpots who believed in magic crystals. New Agers had virtually their own publisher, J. P. Tarcher, and a *Catalogue* of source materials whose eight chapters ranged from channeling and chakras to business and investing.[57] A new edition of Marilyn Ferguson's *The Aquarian Conspiracy* in 1987 (500,000 copies already in print) included a foreword by futurist John Naisbitt, who wrote of the enthusiasm of business people for this "handbook of the New Age." When Ferguson wrote about a society grounded in "playfulness," "a sense of flow" and "risk-taking," she spoke for the prophets of corporate revitalization as well as the explorers of cosmic consciousness.[58] The New Age movement, despite the outlandishness on its fringe, was emphatically middle-class, even conventional, in collapsing the traditional success ethic and the countercultural spirit that once opposed it, into a single vision of life as play. In some versions – most crudely represented by Robert Ringer – success was frankly material but nonetheless ultimately "spiritual." In other versions – those defined through self-actualization, for example – success was psychological, but psychology had become the liberal theology of the age. In many versions, including the more exotic manifestations such as the commune at Rashneeshpuram in eastern Oregon and the attention-getting cults devoted to extraterrestrial communication, the means of salvation was described in the language of play.[59] A metaphysics of play underlay the entire New Age vocabulary of "synergism" and "synchronicity," telepathy and clairvoyance, whole-brain thinking and "psychosynthesis," out-of-body experiences and the Gaia hypothesis. Through concepts like "peak performance" the traditional success ethic was most explicitly redefined in terms of play. Through the psychology of self-actualization the playful spirit of the earlier counterculture was most explicitly redefined in terms of personal success.

Insofar as New Age writers addressed politics, they did so by casting their visions in the American libertarian mold: seeking to transform society through changing individual selves. They were deeply committed to environmental issues but not to collective political action. The communal spirit of the 1960s youth movement, that made it ambiguously political as well as countercultural, gave way to a new version of antinomian spirituality, the persistent belief in America that salvation is a matter of the solitary self discovering its god. In short, once again, the threatening countercultural impulse of one generation was emptied of political content and absorbed into the cultural mainstream.

The sharpest critics of American culture in the seventies and eighties were a handful of radicals and neoconservatives, the two groups as difficult to distinguish as the "liberals" and "conservatives" who trumpeted salvation and success. The neoconservative Daniel Bell explored the fundamental contradiction of capitalism as a conflict between the continuing demand for "a Protestant ethic in the area of production – that is, in the realm of work" – and "a demand for pleasure and play in the area of consumption." The self-professed radical Christopher Lasch was as critical as Bell of the new cultural elite which identified itself "not with the work ethic and the responsibility of wealth but with an ethic of leisure, hedonism, and self-fulfillment." Both Lasch and Bell, as well as Irving Kristol, Richard Sennett, and Irving Louis Horowitz, shared a common desire to solve the work/play dualism without abandoning work entirely for the sake of play.[60] In *The Fall of Public Man* (1976), Sennett urged divorcing "the cultural meaning of play from the current celebration of play as a revolutionary principle" that "identifies play with spontaneity," in order to recover a sense of play as children experience it: rule-governed, serious, directed to both personal pleasure and communal sociability.[61] For Sennett, as for Lasch, the principle opposed to such genuine play was "narcissism," their term for New Age consciousness. Likewise for both Sennett and Lasch, the alternative kind of play – rule-governed and communal rather than spontaneous and personal – was a dialectical "game." In *The Minimal Self* (1984), Lasch derived his model for this "game" from Aristotle's conception of practical reason, specifically the "contests of oratorical skill and physical prowess" championed by Aristotle by which work became play.[62]

What goes around comes around: The "game" desired by radicals Sennett and Lasch was strikingly similar to the "game" celebrated by late nineteenth-century prophets of capitalism and reconstituted in the 1980s entrepreneurial ethic. And the ideal of narcissistic New Agers, whose ascendancy Sennett and Lasch decried, proved not wholly unlike their own. Where dualism once predominated, that is, the New Agers' rhetorical formulation of work and play tended to be dialectical. The playful entrepreneur was to revitalize the country's moribund forces of production. Maslow's concept of "peak performance" rested on the premise that the most successful people were those for whom work was play. Jean Houston wrote in one book that "some of the best human experiences happen when work and play are one," in another of "bliss-plus-knowledge" as the desired ideal. Annie Gottlieb described "the ability to play together as well as be serious, to grow up and be childlike at the same time" as "a distinguishing mark of the tribe" of former sixties rebels that was now coming into its full powers. A decade after his *Making of a Counter Culture,* Theodore Roszak in *Person/Planet* (1978) continued to disparage the narrowly competitive "game or race" appropriate to an economy of scarcity, claiming that postindustrial society made possible both creative (playful) work and more fulfilling play. Futurist Alvin Toffler prophesied a Third Wave in the Western world in which "the old distinction between work and leisure falls apart," and a "balance between work and play" becomes possible.[63]

New Agers had to salvage work for their primary commitment to play; their critics had to salvage play for their commitment to work. But to sort out too neatly the "liberal," "conservative," "neo-conservative," and "radical" voices in addressing this issue would misrepresent what was more truly a cacophany. Both work and play were necessary, all of these writers continued to insist, but to what degrees and in what specific forms remained a pressing question without clear answers. Through the language of play, New Agers expressed confidence that transformation was in their grasp; their critics more skeptically intimated what a better future might be.

The novels of John Updike document in particular detail the social transformation underlying the debate over play in postwar America. Updike joined the latest critical chorus most openly in his novel *S.* (1988), a burlesque of New Age consciousness in which a Rashneesh-like guru, who preaches a "playful fatalism" and seduces female disciples with invitations to "cosmic play," turns out to be a Jewish-Armenian-

470   HOLY PLAY AND THE COUNTERCULTURE

American con man from Watertown, Massachusetts, who was first "en-lightened" by reading Salinger, Ginsberg, and Alan Watts in the late sixties. In a stroke, Updike thus punctured a quarter-century of spiritual questing as if an overinflated balloon.[64]

S. was also Updike's latest installment in a long-running dialogue with Nathaniel Hawthorne, developed explicitly in a trio of novels (*The Witches of Eastwick* [1984] and *Roger's Version* [1986] in addition to *S.*) and in his essays ("On Hawthorne's Mind" and "Hawthorne's Creed").[65] Updike's kinship with Hawthorne lay in part in a common worldview rooted in a residual theological orthodoxy (for Hawthorne, his ancestral Puritanism; for Updike, the early influence of Karl Barth), against which skepticism and secular doubt exerted constant pressure. In addition, both writers pressed their skepticism on the intellectual and cultural currents of the day: in Hawthorne's case, on both the Transcendentalism of the Concord circle and the larger culture of sentimentalism; for Updike, on the ever expanding leisure culture.

Within the context of this larger literary relationship, Updike's novels from the 1950s to the 1980s include a series of Hawthornian responses to the possibilities of spiritual play. Just as Hawthorne consistently re-treated from a radical affirmation of holy innocence potentially embodied in his figures of play, so Updike repeatedly opposed the excesses of his own culture, though in his case toward either work or play. Like Haw-thorne's, Updike's treatment of work and play often collapses under the weight of an unresolvable dualism, but at its most satisfying it achieves the same nontranscendent dialectic that informs *The Marble Faun*. Liberty and duty on the social level, freedom and necessity on the metaphysical plane, define the poles of Updike's as well as Hawthorne's thought.

Updike's novels reveal a continuing quarrel with American culture for its alternating suppression of and overindulgence in play. Thus, in *Rabbit, Run* (1960), Updike affirmed the antinomian play spirit at a time of deadening conformity; in *Couples* (1968), looking back on the Kennedy years from the vantage point of the Vietnam era, he chronicled the period when a rejuvenated play spirit was crushed by cultural as well as social and political tragedy; and in *Rabbit Redux* (1971), he recoiled with un-disguised squeamishness from the excesses of the new playful counter-culture. In what amounts to a second cycle, in *A Month of Sundays* (1975), written during a period of retreat and retrenchment, Updike reaffirmed the now endangered play spirit, then lamented its continuing absence in *Rabbit Is Rich* (1981), only to satirize in *S.* the newly conspicuous, New Age play spirit of the 1980s.

The three Rabbit novels provide a convenient overview of the Up-dikean dialectic, *Couples* and *A Month of Sundays* (in addition to *Rabbit,*

Run) the most direct probing of the spiritual possibilities of play. At the center of the Rabbit novels is an unexceptional man of his times, first an unemployed peddlar of kitchen utensils, then an unemployed printer, and finally a family-employed seller of new and used cars. Harry Angstrom is a man on whom society imprints its concerns and values, less a mirror than a reflex. In his innermost heart he also harbors his middle-class male world's deepest fantasies, its longings for freedom that must compete with accommodations to duty. In *Rabbit, Run,* Harry is an antinomian dimly awaiting his inner light, following the dictates of his own heart whether it tells him to run from responsibility or to stay. In the novel's pervasive basketball imagery Rabbit's morality is a matter of "touch": The instinctive feel of his hands for the basketball mirrors the intuitive, spontaneous nature of both his spiritual quest and his moral choices. As a high-school player Harry was the star, the gunner, the showboat – the hero who shot but didn't play defense, who scored many points but never fouled. As a twenty-six-year-old *ex*-basketball star, Rabbit finds his touch occasionally, but it just as often deserts him. So, too, as son, husband, father, lover, his instinctive allegiance to playful freedom rather than duty creates pain as well as pleasure for others, death (his daughter drowned, a possible abortion) as well as life.

In the novel's clearest affirmation of possible transcendence, the metaphor shifts from basketball to golf. After flailing at his golf ball through several holes while groping to explain his mystical sense that somewhere out there in the universe some perfect Truth awaits his discovery, Rabbit just once raises his clubhead "very simply" and swings with unforced natural grace through the ball. "The sound has a hollowness, a singleness he hasn't heard before." As Harry watches it, the ball "recedes along a line straight as a ruler-edge"; just as Rabbit expects it to die, it seems to take a "final leap . . . a last bite of space before vanishing in falling." "That's *it!*" he cries to Reverend Eccles in joy and wonder. "That's it."[66]

But such experiences are momentary, and in the novel's third sporting motif, Rabbit's *running* is simultaneously creative and destructive. Harry remains defiantly true to his own inner light, running not toward anything, nor merely away from life, but finally for the sake of running – for the play of his own instincts. "He runs. Ah: runs," the novel ends. In his spiritual freedom he achieves a kind of mystical saintliness but at great social cost.

In *Rabbit Redux,* Harry's instincts wholly betray him. In the context of the late sixties, when American youth collectively played out Rabbit's role from the earlier novel, Updike drew back in revulsion. Jill, the flower child who represents the spirit of the counterculture, describes that spirit in familiar terms:

"The point is ecstasy," she says. "Energy. Anything that is good is ecstasy. The world is what God made and it doesn't stink of money, it's never tired, too much or too little, it's always exactly full. The second after an earthquake, the stones are calm. Everywhere is *play*."

But play can no longer sustain Rabbit, nor the world in which he lives. Updike retained the basketball metaphor from the first novel, but Rabbit's shooting touch has utterly deserted him now, while the game has been usurped almost entirely by blacks, whose inner life fascinates Rabbit but remains impenetrably mysterious. Reflecting on his earlier "inner light trip," Rabbit decides now that "all I did was bruise my surroundings." "Revolution," he adds, "or whatever, is just a way of saying a mess is fun. Well, it *is* fun, for a while, as long as somebody else has laid in the supplies. A mess is a luxury." The mess Rabbit leaves at the end of this novel includes a dead girl, an innocent black fugitive, a neglected son, and his own inner deterioration.[67]

With *Rabbit Is Rich* Updike reclaimed some of the dialectical tension from *Rabbit, Run,* but Rabbit's contentment as a Toyota dealer and country club member has been achieved at the expense of that spirit that once made him somehow special. Rabbit's game is golf now, but the game that once gave him a glimpse of godliness has become a country club recreation. Most simply, Rabbit has forgotten how to play, or, to be more accurate, has given up the transcendent possibilities of a playful spirit for the safer rewards of middle-class security. In a scene that ironically mirrors the earlier one in *Rabbit, Run,* Harry again finds himself on the golf course, this time at his city's second-best country club, playing with successful but not too successful businessmen like himself. Rabbit is a weekly golfer now, playing avidly but "without getting much better at it." Still the perfectionist in small ways, "he cannot make himself take a divot," with the result that he consistently hits the ball thin. "His practice swing is always smooth and long," but each time he faces the ball, "anxiety and hurry enter in." Golf has become "more like work" for Harry Angstrom as he settles into middle age, "pleasant work but work, a matter of approximations in the realm of the imperfect, with nothing breaking through but normal healthy happiness."[68] Later in the novel, flying back home from a Caribbean vacation to family responsibility – South to North, reversing the direction he once dreamed to fly – Harry passes over golf courses where people play all winter, "swinging easy" (427). Rabbit has given up such easy swinging. Established in a new house, secure in his business, responsible for his family, Harry in the novel's final scene accepts a new granddaughter as "his. Another nail in his coffin. His." In *Rabbit, Run,* he had clung to his spiritual freedom at great social cost. In *Rabbit Is Rich,* social responsibility and "normal healthy happiness" require his spiritual impoverishment.

Couples and *A Month of Sundays* fill in the cultural gaps between episodes of Harry Angstrom's representative life. *Couples,* Updike's most direct and detailed meditation on the postwar play spirit, reveals neither abiding faith in play's possibilities nor outrage over its excesses, but pain over its loss after the national carnival of the early 1960s. The "couples" of the title are ten married pairs living in Tarbox, Massachusetts, whose lives are governed by a "calendrical wheel" of parties and games.[69] Weekends are given to basketball and beach-going, tennis and touch football, lasting until depressing Sunday evenings "without a game" (73). Then comes "Monday and the long week when they must perform again their impersonations of working men, of stockbrokers and dentists and engineers, of mothers and housekeepers, of adults who are not the world's guests but its hosts" (74). The rhythm of the year recapitulates the weekly pattern, as the summer "of many games" gives way to "an autumn of responsibility, of sobered mutuality and duty" (236). And the age recapitulates the year: John Kennedy's assassination shatters "the *fun* in being an American." It "fucks up our party," as the resident games-master, Freddy Thorne, puts it (294).

Play seems to stand here for mindless frivolity, Updike to have rejected it entirely for a proper sense of responsibility; but *Couples* is more complex than that. The landscape of Tarbox is dominated by a Congregational church and an adjoining baseball diamond: emblems less of competing values than of a single belief, a conjunction of religion and play, with play defined fundamentally as sex (a constellation that appears in much of Updike's fiction). "People are the only thing people have left since God packed up," Freddy Thorne says. "By people I mean sex. Fucking" (145). For Piet Hanema and Foxy Whitman, the sexual play that serves as a substitute religion for the couples of Tarbox is grounded in a more genuine religious sense. Piet in particular, raised in the puritanical Dutch Reformed Church, clings to his faith in a God who damns as well as saves, to belief in conscience and guilt as well as ecstasy. In his affair with Foxy Whitman, Piet feels that "they have been let into God's playroom." But Foxy is pregnant with her husband's baby; when the child is born, Piet feels that to continue their affair would be wrong, that "the time had come to return the toys to their boxes, and put the chairs back against the wall" (323).

No equilibrium between play and responsibility seems possible in *Couples.* Earlier in the novel, both the personal and historical found their balanced moment on a day in October 1962, when Piet and a friend play golf while President Kennedy squares off with Khruschev over missiles in Cuba. Between swings they glance skyward, looking for the Russian bombers whose anticipated arrival has kept other golfers away. With clear Hawthornian echoes, Piet joyfully plays "each hole on the edge of an imaginary cliff" (224), awaiting the end. But the dialectical moment dissolves when no bombers appear. Afterward, hearing the Russians have capitulated, Piet is dismayed to realize "that they must go on, all of them." Kennedy's assassination follows, as does Piet's fall from grace when his adultery is discovered. Unlike *The Marble Faun,* which ends at the Carnival, *Couples* leads readers back into the world that remains after the carnival ends. In the winter following Kennedy's assassination, "parties all but cease" (456), as divorce, estrangement, and death turn the couples from play to earnestness. For Piet and Foxy, one last meeting, a new pregnancy, an abortion, and final exposure break up two marriages and cut Piet adrift from everyone and everything in Tarbox. When the Congregational church burns down, unprotected by God, Piet at last feels freed from his guilt; but by marrying Foxy and accepting the "official order and regular hours" (458) of marriage, he also loses the freedom of play.

In *Couples,* the search for a work/play dialectic collapses into dualism. And in this *Couples* can stand for most of Updike's fiction that assesses the state of play in postwar American life. Only in *Rabbit, Run* in 1960 and *A Month of Sundays* in 1975 did Updike sustain a dialectical vision of play. Reaffirming the value of spiritual play, but without denying tragic limitation, *A Month of Sundays* thus assumes a more significant place in my reading of Updike's fiction than in most accounts. *Couples'* conjunction of religion, play, and sex is repeated in *A Month of Sundays,* but here erotic, salvific play is neither defeated nor denied. And it is pointedly distinguished from the feel-good religion of post-sixties liberalism. Railing against the "limp-wristed theology" of liberals, the novel's monologuist Reverend Tom Marshfield insists on a neo-orthodox tragic sense of life; but in a fallen world play is necessary in ways the liberals cannot imagine: as the sport by which human beings affirm their existence in the mouth of the Hawthornian cavern.[70]

Banished to the western desert for his sexual indiscretions with the church organist, Marshfield reflects on his affair in the language of erotic play. "We played in each other like children in puddles," he recalls in the major passage of this sort, and he meditates on the connotations of that sexual play:

> Play. There was that, in daylight, laughing, after a marriage bed of nighttime solemnity and spilt religion, spilt usually at the wrong angle, at the moment when the cup had been withdrawn. What fun my forgotten old body turned out to be – the toy I should have been given for Christmas, instead of the jack-in-the-box, or the little trapeze artist between his squeezable sticks, or the Lionel locomotive entering and re-entering his papier-mâché tunnel. Thank you, playmate, for such a light-hearted snowy morning, your own body more baubled than a

Christmas tree, with more vistas to it than within a kaleidoscope. In
holiday truth my wonder did seem to rebound upon you, merry, merry,
and make you chime. (35)

Marshfield sounds here suspiciously like his liberal minister father, who
has told him once that "the Lord holds us entitled to a little *plaisir*" (126).
But Marshfield's understanding is emphatically dialectical, in the Barth-
ian/Hawthornian sense. Following this meditation on "play," the next
paragraph turns to "play, and pain": first the seeming pain of moans and
cries during intercourse, then the real pain of infidelity and departure.
The proper response, Updike's adulterous minister insists, is not to abandon play but to cling to it fully mindful of all its consequences.

To Marshfield, all of life teaches this lesson, illustrated in *A Month of
Sundays* by a series of ludic scenes and metaphors. On the golf course
where Marshfield spends his afternoons, the joy of "swinging with a
nice clicking freedom from tee to green" is followed by the pain of
missing three short putts (18–19). A later transcendent golfing moment,
like Harry's in *Rabbit, Run*, passes when Marshfield's next swing, equally
unthinking and effortless, slices the ball into the rough. "Even a half-hit
demands a shoulder-turn," he concludes (181–2). Here is one of Updike's
favorite parables, appearing first in *Rabbit, Run*, repeated here and in
Rabbit Is Rich. In an essay from this period Updike described golf as "the
most mysterious, the least earthbound [sport], the one wherein the wall
between us and the supernatural is rubbed thinnest."[71] In the recurring
parable represented by golf in his fiction, play is freedom, but freedom
brings dread. The Paradise of Play is momentary; work, a "shoulder-
turn," cannot be ignored. Transcendence is possible but only temporarily; joy is but the other face of sorrow.

As in *Rabbit, Run*, the dialectic of joyful play and sorrowful necessity
in *A Month of Sundays* is sustained to the end. The desert in which
Marshfield sojourns becomes itself a metaphor for this vision: Known
to Americans as Death Valley, it was called by the Spanish explorers *La
Palma de la Mano de Dios*, the Palm of God's Hand. All humankind, the
novel says, lives in this "desert," in both God's palm and the valley of
death. Noting the astonishing life of the desert, Marshfield draws the
appropriate lesson: "Let us be grateful *here*, and here rejoice" (166). So
Updike concluded in 1975. But as doubt and anxiety seemed to give way
to antinomian certitude in the public temper, in the novels following *A
Month of Sundays*, the dialectic broke down. From Updike's view, a
moment of equilibrium in American culture collapsed once again into
groping and doubt.

Updikean skepticism seems the appropriate note for conclusion. Underlying the latest debate over contemporary American culture and its

future has been an ongoing preoccupation with American promise and American failure. The middle-class utopian experiments of communitarians in the 1840s, bohemians in the 1910s, and hippies in the 1960s all failed to bring about the millenium, but the dream lives on. It is a dream at odds with the official American Dream of success, which has seemed to many a mere "game" of money-getting or product-buying. But it is a reprise of that older American dream: the vision of a New World garden of play that first sent many Europeans to these shores. In the persistence of that dream, and continually impelled by economic change, American middle-class culture for a century and a half has lurched toward a future increasingly defined by play instead of work.

Epilogue

The rise of the sports metaphor in American life is among the most significant cultural developments of our age. The ubiquity of the metaphor may now have reached the point where sports is *the* metaphor for what we mean by American life.

Stanley Aronowitz, Foreword to *Choosing Sides* (1979)

Wild Crone-centering creation is vigorous play/work which is utterly Other than the ritualized rigor mortis of gamesmanship exhibited in phallocratic plays and works.

Mary Daly, *Gyn/Ecology* (1978)

As my inquiry has ranged widely over American writing – from Western and Southern fiction to business novels and success literature, from the distinctive literature of women and blacks to representative texts from the white male literary "mainstream" – it has dealt with the same salient facts of American social, economic, spiritual, and political life. Whether to criticize, justify, or celebrate these realities (as "games"), or to envision transforming them (as "play"), whether to do this obliquely (as in the Western and Southern writing), or directly (as in the literature of politics and success), America's sporting rhetoric in all its variety ultimately has been concerned with status and power and opportunity, both material and spiritual, within the American system of industrial capitalism. Without cross-cultural evidence it is impossible to know how distinctive this American sporting rhetoric is (to know, that is, whether such texts as Hesse's *Magister Ludi*, Kawabata's *The Master of Go*, the several versions of *The Rules of the Game* by Pirandello, Renoir, and Monteiro, and so

477

on reflect rich vernaculars with comparable significance in other national cultures). Certainly the British have a long tradition of celebrating their "great games." Recently Greil Marcus has traced a "secret history of the twentieth century" that amounts in part to a "secret history" of the anarchic play spirit in the Western (preponderantly French) world.[1] And play as *maya,* or illusion, is central to certain Oriental philosophies. But the "game" has had a particularly important place in the United States, serving particular American needs. In the absence of tradition, American society has been more completely dependent on laws, on gamelike rules of behavior against which other gamelike codes of personal belief can be formulated. In both our relative classlessness and our egalitarian assumptions in the face of the facts of class; in our greater social mobility and our preoccupation with personal opportunity; in our passion for competition and persistent faith in its ultimate fairness – in all of these elements that have always seemed characteristically American – lie sources for a belief that life is essentially a "game" on a playfield that may or may not be level.

The rhetoric of sport and play records middle-class Americans' uncertain, anxious responses to fundamental yet changing facts of national life. Metaphors of "play" and "game" have challenged dominant cultural values but also validated them, transforming them into forms both more heroic and more consistent with changing human desires. Play has been the realm of fantasy, dream, hope, longing; work the realm of duty, commitment, and responsibility. Civilization requires work; culture depends on play as well. In America, the spirit of play has been evoked to defy work but also to revitalize and humanize it. Americans have used images of "play" and "game" to describe the pettiest acts of self-promotion and the grandest states of cosmic harmony. We have celebrated or railed against the "games" of stock gamblers, and we have struggled for more than a century to envision human life free from the constraining dualism of work and play. To reach some sort of conclusion without being merely reductive, three broad observations seem appropriate: that the longings and anxieties represented by America's sporting rhetoric are perennial ones; yet that they are not constant, and that the desire to play, and to transform work into a "game," has increased dramatically over the past century and a half; and, finally, that to be in a position to envision fulfillment from play has depended to a considerable degree on one's material conditions.

Somewhere behind the "play" and "games" of American vernacular have lain the actual sports that generate many of these metaphors, and it stands to reason that the meanings of these sports have also changed over time. In professional football and baseball in the 1970s and 1980s, for example, one can see a significant shift toward the values of self-fulfillment against the demands of the team. Free agency, ballooning salaries, product endorsements, jock memoirs, up-close-and-personal media profiles, even the various on-field, look-at-me antics of homerun trots and end-zone dances – all the elements and consequences of the mediated culture of celebrity – are signs that sport has increasingly become an arena for self-actualization rather than male-bonding, team effort, or even, as critics often charge, win-at-all-costs. This shift has been abetted by judicial decisions, as court after court has settled major lawsuits in favor of individual players against the rights of ownership. (Earlier decisions granting unique antitrust exemptions to baseball owners and ignoring football owners' monopolistic practices were motivated, I suspect, less by a commitment to owners' property rights than by a belief that "the game" is a vital public possession, and therefore more important than any of its individual contributors.) Although sport remains a metaphor for life in America, "life" is different in 1990 from what it was in 1950 or 1900. To be sure, individual pressures on the ideology of "the team" have never been absent, nor have team values been entirely superseded by the latest forces of personal interest. And sport's relationship to work and play has always been profoundly ambiguous – and troubling because of the ambiguity. Individual/team and work/play dialectics remain at the center of our major sports, but shifts in those dialectics can be detected, shifts that have both contributed to and reflected the culture of self-actualization.

The subjects of all these chapters – codes of sportsmanship and gamesmanship, "games" of love and politics and business, the "race" for salvation and the desperate contest against a sportive "god," the play of desire and the play of holiness in the fields of the Lord – are but several manifestations of this cultural shift, as registered in the texts of American writers. I hope that these chapters have convincingly demonstrated not just the indisputable presence and significance of sporting rhetoric in American writing over the past century and a half, but also the more arguable patterns that I have detected in this rhetoric. I have assumed throughout this study that a cultural history aware of gender, race, and class, and of diversity within the "dominant" culture as well, while eschewing simple consensus can nonetheless reveal a coherent narrative of the successive issues that have seemed most pressing. My own interpretation of that narrative, of course, has been shaped by whatever I have learned both from books and from the times in which I have lived. In successive revisions, for example, I found it necessary to account for Ivan Boesky's emergence as a popular hero and subsequent fall from grace, for new waves of political and financial sporting rhetoric, for the sudden turn from exuberance to doubt on Wall Street with the stock market crash of 1987 and the insider-trading scandals, for a steady accretion of New Age literature (my campus bookstore now has a special section for New Age writing). In every case, however, the latest efflorescence of "play" and "game" confirmed the larger cultural patterns I had already detected.

But if the patterns I have described are indisputable in my view, the questions I have raised about them are more open to debate. My claims about the specific meanings of sporting rhetoric for groups within and outside the cultural mainstream; my definition of that mainstream; my accounts of the relationship of such cultural expressions to social and economic institutions and to political power; my interpretations of dualism and dialectics, transcendence and materiality, metaphysics and politics; and the implications of all of these distinctions inevitably fall short of settling the question of what play and sporting rhetoric have "meant" in American culture. At the very least I hope I have provoked further discussion of what seems to me an exceptionally rich and untapped subject.

Other studies of this subject may well be underway, for my own book contributes to a wide-ranging academic interest in play since the 1960s. Clifford Geertz's "deep play," Victor Turner's "liminality," Mikhail Bakhtin's "carnival," and Jacques Derrida's "free play of signifiers" are but four of the most prominent theoretical models for studying play in a variety of disciplines. All of these concepts are as grounded in their historical moment as was the playful primitivism of the 1920s; if they are familiar mostly within the academy, they have nonetheless participated in the larger cultural shift toward finding value in play. The most sustained intellectual engagement with play today appears in the writings of a handful of "Freudo-Marxists" and numerous feminists. While Marcuse's legacy remains largely unclaimed in contemporary American Marxism, a few psychoanalytic neo-Marxists and political neo-Freudians, for whom Freud and Marx configure not only the personal and the collective but also play and work, have continued to pursue Marcuse's vision of utopia.[2] French neo-Marxists in the 1950s and afterwards – the Lettrists, followed by the Situationists and the Arguments group – have been more receptive than their Anglo-American counterparts to neo-Marxist revisionism in the name of play (French intellectuals have a long history of serious engagement with play, from Fourier and then the Paris Communards in the nineteenth century, to the dadaists and surrealists in the 1920s, to the poststructuralists in the 1970s).[3] On this side of the Atlantic, a few signs of resistance to the traditional "left melancholy" of Western Marxism have emerged: a reconsideration of orthodox concepts like "utopia" and "unalienated labor," for example, and the recent interest in working-class leisure. But for the most part, Marcuse's more radical challenge to Marxist orthodoxy has not been taken up. Fredric

Jameson, as a representative case, wrote admiringly of Marcuse in *Marxism and Form* in 1971, only to dismiss him ten years later in *The Political Unconscious* as a spokesman for the wrong-headed tradition in radical politics, that ignores collective action in favor of a "Utopia of libidinal gratification."[4]

The feminist embrace of "play" in the seventies and eighties has been far more prominent, primarily in two contexts: in debates over sexuality and in a radical feminist utopian vision. What unites these different concerns is their common emphasis on articulating and realizing women's desires, freed from patriarchal oppression. The rhetoric of play in these two contexts has tended to come from different groups within feminism: the interest in sexual "play" from materialist feminists, the vision of utopian "play" from radical essentialists. "Play" can embody a number of radical feminist ideas: nonseparation from nature, rejection of domination, celebration of the female body and of intuition and feeling. Those whose goal is an androgynous or gender-free society rather than a woman-centered one, and whose commitment is to pursuing social and political goals rather than to defining a female alternative to male power, have in general been less concerned with play.

The issue of sexuality, specifically heterosexuality, has become deeply divisive within feminism, the dilemma arising from an awareness, as Carole Vance has described it, that "sexuality is simultaneously a domain of restriction, repression and danger as well as a domain of exploration, pleasure, and agency."[5] For many feminists, heterosexuality is by its very nature oppressive; insofar as a woman serves male pleasure, she reenacts patriarchy's fundamental violation of female identity, no matter what pleasure she may herself experience. But against this position, other feminists have argued that the post-sixties sexual revolution has in fact been a women's revolution, and from this prosex perspective sexual liberation has been frequently imagined as the freeing of desire in sexual "play." In different ways, Jessica Benjamin, Muriel Dimen, and Barbara Ehrenreich (writing with Elizabeth Hess and Gloria Jacobs) have all claimed women's right, as Dimen put it, "to play sexually" as a major achievement of the feminist movement.[6]

The setting of "play" (or "pleasure") against power also lies at the foundation of a full-scale gender-based worldview, whose adherents have been variously identified as "cultural," "romantic," "essentialist," or "radical" feminists (French feminists who celebrate *jouissance* as the essence of women's distinctive nature represent a similar position).[7] The American feminists to whom I refer have embraced their culturally defined historical "otherness" as a radically affirmative self-definition. In the nineteenth century, Stowe, Alcott, Gilman, and others struggled to free women from relegation to a sphere of play. In 1963, Betty Friedan in *The Feminine Mystique* launched the most recent woman's movement in effect by taking up the same cause, when she reported that leisured women were desperately unfulfilled. In the face of this long history of progressive women's resistance to their cultural definition through play, leisure, and consumerism, in the 1970s and 1980s radical feminists began declaring women's essential being to lie in play. At its most extreme, as in Marilyn French's *Beyond Power* (1985), the radical feminist worldview emerged as a three-part history of humankind as a Manichean battle between Female Good (play) and Male Evil (power): a prehistory of play in the garden of the Mother Goddess, a history dominated by the evil of masculine power, and a future that will eventually belong to feminist play.[8]

Among the adherents to this radical feminist position has been a group of writers, including Mary Daly, Carol Christ, Starhawk, and numerous others, who have in effect claimed the theology of play for a distinctive female spirituality. Play is central to the goddess religion and witchcraft that some of these writers have proclaimed against patriarchal religious traditions, but also to feminist theologies closer to the Judaeo-Christian mainstream. For its linguistic playfulness and self-conscious articulation of a theology of play, Daly's *Gyn/Egology* (1978) is the *Summa* of this literature.[9] The politics of this feminist spirituality bears interesting relationships to the blues dialectic of black writers but also to the New Age movement to which it is sometimes linked (New Agers are generally "feminist" in their views of both ecological harmony and personal relations). Against the radically antinomian tradition of holy play (a basic element in New Age emphasis on self-fulfillment) feminist spirituality, like the blues dialectic of black writers since the 1920s, is fundamentally communal, a vision of sisterhood harmoniously playing out individual and collective desires. But unlike the black writers, and like the New Agers, radical feminists have characteristically abandoned politics for metaphysics, while wholeheartedly embracing their essential "otherness" in ways that most black writers have refused. Once again, middle-class white women's more ambiguous political and social position – marginalized by gender but not by race or class – is reflected in their rhetoric of play.

Like the Freudo-Marxists, these feminist theorists represent an intellectual movement without a popular base, as feminism in the 1980s lost ground in the larger culture. The extraordinary body of women's fiction in the seventies and eighties, however, offers evidence that play has been appropriated in distinctive ways by women more generally. In novels like Alix Kates Shulman's *The Memoirs of an Ex-Prom Queen* (1972), Gail Godwin's *The Odd Woman* (1974), Marilyn French's *The Women's Room* (1977), and Louise Erdrich's *Love Medicine* (1984), scenes and images of innocent play define an alternative, if only momentary, to oppressive masculine "games."[10] Such writers as Kate Millett in *Flying* (1974), Toni Morrison in *Song of Solomon* (1977), and Erica Jong in *Fear of Flying* (1973) and its two sequels have used the motif of liberated "flying" in ways that make it equivalent to "play." More striking yet is the treatment of play in women's utopian fiction of the 1970s: such novels as Thea Alexander's *2150 A.D.* (1971), Ursula Le Guin's *The Dispossessed* (1974), Joanna Russ's *The Female Man* (1975), Mary Staton's *From the Legend of Biel* (1975), Dorothy Bryant's *The Kin of Ata Are Waiting for You* (1976), and Marge Piercy's *Woman on the Edge of Time* (1976). In these novels play stands variously opposed to rigidity, control, alienation from one's true self; to rationality; to competition and violence; to oppressive earnestness and work; to power and domination. Four of these novels (only Alexander's and Bryant's excluded) specifically reject dehumanizing "games"; play stands instead for the "dance" of enlightenment (Staton and Bryant), or for communal celebration (Russ and Piercy). The anarchic playfulness of Russ's Whileaway represents the fullest expression of this feminist vision.[11]

Christopher Lasch included radical feminists among the cultural narcissists he criticized, but the sharpest attack has come from within feminism itself: from materialist or socialist feminists who deplore the ahistorical and idealist polarization of masculinity and femininity; the construction of an essentialist, monolithic, and unchanging male power "out there" and of an essentialist woman's nature in opposition; and the inability of radical feminists to describe a course of social and political action by which their utopia could be attained.[12] The champions of a uniquely feminine play spirit have been antinomians preaching sisterhood through personal awakening to the divine femininity within; their materialist critics have proposed instead a feminism of works, not grace.

For all their radicalism, then, these feminists expressed a familiar fantasy of freedom through play. The possibly disturbing underside of this fantasy was suggested a century ago by Dostoyevsky's Grand Inquisitor, whose utopian vision of a world without freedom, but grounded in the illusion of freedom, reserved a crucial place for play. "We shall set them to work," the Inquisitor says of the people in this world, "but in their leisure hours we shall make their life like a child's game with children's songs and innocent dance."[13] Here, seemingly, is a prophetic vision of the consumer culture, in which men and women will be kept in the condition of children constantly pursuing the pleasures of the moment. The challenge to those who would envision human possibility through play has always been to articulate a serious playfulness that engages the world as it is rather than denies or masks its troubling aspects. Radical feminists have in fact addressed this problem by imagining new possibilities of work/play, as in Mary Daly's call for women's "ludic cere-bration which is both work and play."[14] What Lasch called "narcissism" and diagnosed as the nation's most serious illness many feminists saw as humankind's only chance at liberation, or even survival. The breakdown of boundaries between the self and its world, envisioned as play both by Lasch (negatively) and by radical feminists (positively), would mean the loss of the self as exploiter, these feminists argued, and the discovery of a new self that coexists harmoniously with all other life.

This vision awaits a social movement. The problem has remained constant since the 1830s: the inability to ground American social reality in a more satisfying integration of work and play. But the terms change, as do the prospects for success. In relation to earlier phases of American culture, our contemporary "postmodernism" is distinctly the culture of play: of play with conventional forms in the arts, of play with the prod-ucts of our economic prosperity in everyday life. Yet while American culture has become markedly more playful, critics of that culture have continued to decry the absence of true freedom or creativity. Postmodern consumer culture, they argue, converts play into the engine of insatiable consumption, which drives the economy without leading to personal fulfillment. But if it is true that a people can only realize what they first imagine, then there is hope in the fact that writers have become more sophisticated and self-conscious in addressing the persistent dualism. As we look to the future, the history of American sporting rhetoric might predict another eruption of countercultural play, out of the convulsive discontent of a materially satisfied but spiritually unfulfilled middle class. But whether this pattern will be repeated, or play's century will end as scarcity rather than abundance reshapes both our desires and our attempts to realize them, only the coming years will tell.

Notes

After the initial citation in the Notes, subsequent references are included parenthetically in the text.

Preface

1. George Lakoff and Mark Johnson, *Metaphors We Live By* (Chicago: University of Chicago Press, 1980).
2. Robert A. Palmatier and Harold L. Ray, *Sports Talk: A Dictionary of Sports Metaphors* (New York and Westport, CT: Greenwood, 1989).

Prologue

1. Owen Wister, *The Virginian: A Horseman of the Plains* (New York: Macmillan, 1902), 1–2, 15–42, 66.
2. For a discussion of this subject, see Christian K. Messenger, *Sport and the Spirit of Play in American Fiction: Hawthorne to Faulkner* (New York: Columbia University Press, 1982), 143–6.
3. See Richard Harding Davis, *A Year from a Reporter's Note-Book* (New York: Harper and Brothers, 1897), 193; *The Notes of a War Correspondent* (New York: Scribner's, 1911), 142, 146; *With the French in France and Salonika* (New York: Scribner's 1916), 41; and *The Cuban and Porto Rican Campaigns* (New York: Scribner's 1898), 151–3 (this last one quoted in Messenger, *Sport and the Spirit of Play*, 144). For Davis's fictional representations of his sporting code, see, for example, *Soldiers of Fortune* (New York: Scribner's 1897), *The King's Jackal* (New York: Scribner's, 1898), and *Captain Macklin* (New York: Scribner's, 1902).
4. Alfred Henry Lewis, *The Boss, and How He Came to Rule New York* (1903; Ridgewood, NJ: Gregg Press, 1967), 58; I. K. Friedman, *The Radical* (1907; New York: Johnson Reprint, 1971), 298.
5. See J. A. Mangan, *Athleticism in the Victorian and Edwardian Public School: The Emergence and Consolidation of an Educational Ideology* (Cambridge: Cambridge University Press, 1981) and *The Games-Ethic and Imperialism: Aspects of the Diffusion of an Ideal* (Harmondsworth: Allen Lane/Penguin, 1986); and Colin Veitch, " 'Play Up! and Win the War': Football, the Nation and

the First World War 1914–1915," *Journal of Contemporary History* 20 (1985), 363–78.

6. See E. D. Cope, "The Effeminisation of Man," *Open Court,* 26 October 1893, 3847; Josephine Conger-Kaneko, "The 'Effeminization' of the United States," *World's Work* 12 (May 1906), 7521–4; and G. Stanley Hall, "Feminization in School and Home," *World's Work* 16 (May 1908), 10237–44.

7. See Christopher P. Wilson, *The Labor of Words: Literary Professionalism in the Progressive Era* (Athens: University of Georgia Press, 1985).

8. See Frank Norris, "The Decline of the Magazine Short Story," San Francisco *Wave,* 30 January 1897, 3; "Why Women Should Write the Best Novels: And Why They Don't," *Boston Evening Transcript,* 13 November 1901, 20; and "Novelists of the Future: The Training They Need," *Boston Evening Transcript,* 27 November 1901, 14. All are reprinted in Donald Pizer, ed., *The Literary Criticism of Frank Norris* (Austin: University of Texas Press, 1964). See also Pizer's commentary throughout this volume, and Grant C. Knight, *The Strenuous Age in American Literature* (Chapel Hill: University of North Carolina Press, 1954).

9. Edith Wharton, *The House of Mirth* (New York: Charles Scribner's Sons, 1905), 136, 234.

10. Frances Trollope, *Domestic Manners of the Americans* (1832; London: George Routledge and Sons, 1927), 59; Alexis de Tocqueville, *Democracy in America,* ed. J. P. Mayer (Garden City, NY: Doubleday & Company, 1969), 609, 610.

11. James Bryce, "America Revisited: The Changes of a Quarter-Century," *Outlook* 79 (1905), 738–9. Quoted in William R. Hogan, "Sin and Sports," in *Motivations in Play, Games and Sports,* ed. Ralph Slovenko and James A. Knight (Springfield, IL: Charles C. Thomas, 1967), 133. Hogan's essay provided a useful bibliography for the later discussion of muscular Christianity.

12. Bruce Haley, *The Healthy Body and Victorian Culture* (Cambridge, MA: Harvard University Press, 1978), 123–4; Sir Charles Tennyson, "They Taught the World to Play," *Victorian Studies* 2 (March 1959), 211.

13. The history of English sport in the nineteenth century has been exceptionally well documented by a large body of scholarship. In particular see Haley, *The Healthy Body and Victorian Culture;* Peter C. McIntosh, *Physical Education in England Since 1800,* rev. ed. (London: Bell, 1968); Peter Bailey, *Leisure and Class in Victorian England: Rational Recreation and the Contest for Control, 1830–1884* (Toronto: University of Toronto Press, 1978); and Mangan, *Athleticism in the Victorian and Edwardian Public School.* For the incidents of British officers rushing to war as to a public-school football match, see Veitch, " 'Play up! and Win the War.' "

14. For a history of the rise of intercollegiate sport, see Ronald A. Smith, *Sports & Freedom: The Rise of Big-Time College Athletics* (New York: Oxford University Press, 1988). Smith's account emphasizes the struggle over control of sport, rather than the cultural context. See also the general histories of American sport: John Rickards Betts, *America's Sporting Heritage: 1850–1950* (Reading, MA and Menlo Park, CA: Addison-Wesley, 1974); John A. Lucas and

NOTES TO PP. 11–13

Ronald A. Smith, *Saga of American Sport* (Philadelphia: Lea & Febiger, 1978); Betty Spears and Richard A. Swanson, *History of Sport and Physical Activity in the United States* (Dubuque, Iowa: Wm. C. Brown, 1978); and Benjamin G. Rader, *American Sports: From the Age of Folk Games to the Age of Spectators* (Englewood Cliffs, NJ: Prentice-Hall, 1983). On the relation of sport to health reform, see James C. Whorton, *Crusaders for Fitness: The History of American Health Reformers* (Princeton, NJ: Princeton University Press, 1982); Harvey Green, *Fit for America: Health, Fitness, Sport, and American Society* (New York: Pantheon Books, 1986); Roberta J. Park, "The Attitudes of Leading New England Transcendentalists Toward Healthful Exercise, Active Recreation and Proper Care of the Body: 1830–1860," *Journal of Sport History* 4 (Spring 1977), 34–50; and Patricia Vertinsky, "Sexual Equality and the Legacy of Catharine Beecher," *Journal of Sport History* 6 (Spring 1979), 38–49.

15. See Frederic W. Sawyer, *A Plea for Amusements* (New York: D. Appleton, 1847); Edward Everett Hale, *Public Amusement for Poor and Rich* (Boston: Phillips, Sampson, 1857); and Edwin Sidney Williams, *Christian Amusements* (Saint Paul, MN: Davidson Hall, 1866).

16. "Amusements," *New Englander* 9 (August 1851), 358.

17. "Amusements," *New Englander* 26 (July 1867), 400.

18. For Beecher, see for example his *Star Papers; or Experiences of Art and Nature* (New York: J. C. Derby, 1855) and "Health and Education," reprinted in *Eyes and Ears* (Boston: Ticknor and Fields, 1862). Higginson's essays included "Saints, and Their Bodies," *Atlantic Monthly* 1 (March 1858), 582–95; "Physical Courage," *Atlantic Monthly* 2 (November 1858), 728–37; "A Letter to a Dyspeptic," *Atlantic Monthly* 3 (April 1859), 465–74; "The Murder of the Innocents," *Atlantic Monthly* 4 (September 1859), 345–56; "Gymnastics," *Atlantic Monthly* 7 (January 1861), 51–61; "The Health of Our Girls," *Atlantic Monthly* 9 (June 1862), 722–31; all were reprinted in *Out-Door Papers* (Boston: Ticknor and Fields, 1863). For Tyler, see *The Brawnville Papers: Being Memorials of the Brawnville Athletic Club* (Boston: Fields, Osgood, 1869). And for Murray, the least remembered of these men, see the essay by David Strauss, "Toward a Consumer Culture: 'Adirondack Murray' and the Wilderness Vacation," *American Quarterly* 39 (Summer 1987), 252–69, and the works by Murray that Strauss discusses.

19. N. S. Shaler, "The Athletic Problem in Education," *Atlantic Monthly* 63 (January 1889), 79–88.

20. See, for example, Alexander Johnston, "The American Game of Foot-Ball," *Century* 34 (October 1887), 888–98; Frederick Evans, Jun., "The Football Championship," *Harper's Weekly*, 10 December 1887, 903; and Walter Camp, "The American Game of Foot-Ball," *Harper's Weekly*, 10 November 1888.

21. Walter Camp, "Team Play in Foot-Ball," *Harper's Weekly*, 19 November 1892, 1115; see also "The American Game of Foot-Ball"; "A Day's Foot-Ball Practice at Yale," *Harper's Weekly*, 24 November 1888, 890; and "Football of 1893. Its Lessons and Its Results," *Harper's Weekly*, 3 February 1894, 117–18.

22. For a succinct overview of this subject, see John Hammond Moore, "Foot-

ball's Ugly Decades, 1893–1913," *Smithsonian Journal of History* 2 (Fall 1967), 49–68.

23. Whitney wrote a regular column on "Amateur Sport" in *Harper's Weekly* from 14 February 1890 to 30 December 1899; Eliot's reports were reprinted in the *Harvard Graduates' Magazine* for the years 1894 to 1900.

24. Act V, scene i, line 67 and scene ii, line 118. The editors of the major editions agree in glossing "fair play" as the code of chivalry.

25. See also Roger Ascham, *Toxocophilus* (1545), Sir Humphrey Gilbert, *Queen Elizabeth's Academy, a Book of Precedence* (1564), Richard Mulcaster, *Positions* (1581), and Henry Peacham, *The Compleat Gentleman* (1622).

26. Note, for example, the appeals to "fair play" in a range of political essays: "Fair Play," *Harper's Weekly*, 24 January 1863, 50 (on the Civil War); T. W. Higginson, "Fair Play the Best Policy," *Atlantic Monthly* 15 (May 1865), 622–31 (on the freed slaves); George Truman Kercheval, "Fair Play for the Indian," *North American Review* 152 (February 1892), 250–3; and Samuel M. Jones, *The New Right: A Plea for Fair Play Through a More Just Social Order* (New York: Eastern Book Concern, 1899).

27. Amos Alonzo Stagg and Wesley Winans Stout, *Touchdown!* (New York: Longmans, Green, 1927), 130–1, 57–8.

28. Thorstein Veblen, *The Theory of the Leisure Class* (1899; New York: Macmillan, 1911), 253–5, 261, 274.

29. John Dizikes, *Sportsmen and Gamesmen* (Boston: Houghton Mifflin, 1981), 39.

30. See Ida Tarbell, *The History of Standard Oil,* 2 vols. (New York: McClure, Phillips, 1904), II, 292; Alfred Henry Lewis, "Owners of America," *Cosmopolitan* 45 (1908), 259; Bolton Hall, *The Game of Life* (New York: A. Wessels, 1902); Veblen, *Theory of the Leisure Class,* passim; William James, *The Will to Believe and Other Essays in Popular Philosophy,* bound with *Human Immortality: Two Supposed Objections to the Doctrine* (New York: Dover, 1956), 213.

31. Quoted in Howard Mumford Jones, *The Age of Energy: Varieties of American Experience, 1865–1915* (New York: Viking Press, 1971), 391.

32. See Poultney Bigelow, "Theodore Roosevelt, President and Sportsman," *Collier's Weekly,* 31 May 1902, 10; William Allen White, "Theodore Roosevelt," *McClure's* 18 (November 1901), 41; Henry Beach Needham, "Roosevelt To-Day," *Collier's Weekly,* 7 May 1910, 14.

33. William Allen White, *The Autobiography of William Allen White* (New York: Macmillan, 1946), 348; Charles A. Beard and Mary R. Beard, *The Rise of American Civilization,* 2 vols. (New York: Macmillan, 1927), II, 423; Jones, *The Age of Energy,* 411.

34. Theodore Roosevelt, "Expansion and Peace," quoted in Richard Slotkin, "Nostalgia and Progress: Theodore Roosevelt's Myth of the Frontier," *American Quarterly* 33 (Winter 1981), 634.

35. Theodore Roosevelt, "The Value of an Athletic Training," *Harper's Weekly,* 23 December 1893, 1236; "The American Boy," in *The Works of Theodore Roosevelt,* National Edition, 20 vols. (New York: Scribner's 1926), XIII, 401.

36. Theodore Roosevelt, "Character and Success," in *Works*, XIII, 383, 384; "Athletics, Scholarship, and Public Service," in *Works*, XIII, 560.
37. "The American Boy," 401; "Athletics, Scholarship, and Public Service," 560.
38. Theodore Roosevelt, "Professionalism in Sports," in *Works*, XIII, 587.
39. The Wister-Roosevelt relationship is detailed in Wister's own memoir, *Roosevelt: The Story of a Friendship, 1880–1919* (NY: Macmillan, 1930); and in Forrest G. Robinson, "The Roosevelt-Wister Connection: Some Notes on the West and the Uses of History," *Western American Literature* 14 (Summer 1979), 95–114.
40. Edmund Morris, *The Rise of Theodore Roosevelt* (New York: Coward, McCann & Geoghegan, 1979), 330.
41. Theodore Roosevelt, *Hunting Trips of a Ranchman: Sketches of Sport on the Northern Cattle Plains* (New York: G. P. Putnam's Sons, 1885), 140, 28. See also *Ranch Life and the Hunting-Trail* (1888; New York: Century, 1911); and *The Wilderness Hunter* (1893; New York: G. P. Putnam's Sons, 1909); in which Roosevelt elaborated on these same ideas.
42. Theodore Roosevelt, *The Winning of the West*, 2 vols., in *Works*, VIII, 100. Subsequent paranthetical references to volumes I or II in the text refer to volumes VIII and IX in the *Works*).
43. Jones, *Age of Energy*, 411.
44. Consider in this context the fact that Roosevelt himself once tried to enlist in a vigilante group in the Dakotas, but was rejected as too socially prominent for a secret society. See Morris, *Rise of Theodore Roosevelt*, 278.
45. Roosevelt, *The Wilderness Hunter*, 448.
46. Morris, *Rise of Theodore Roosevelt*, 285–6.
47. Theodore Roosevelt, "Kidd's 'Social Evolution,' " *North American Review* 161 (1895), 96–7, 98, 105–6, 108.
48. Harbaugh, *Power and Responsibility*, 355.

Part I

1. Edmundo O'Gorman, *The Invention of America: An Inquiry into the Historical Nature of the New World and the Meaning of Its History* (1961; Westport, CT: Greenwood, 1972).
2. See Hugh Honour, *The New Golden Land: European Images of America from the Discoveries to the Present Time* (New York: Pantheon Books, 1975); A. Bartlett Giamatti, *The Earthly Paradise and the Renaissance Epic* (Princeton, NJ: Princeton University Press, 1966); Harry Levin, *The Myth of the Golden Age in the Renaissance* (Bloomington: Indiana University Press, 1969); and Loren Baritz, "The Idea of the West," *American Historical Review* 66 (April 1961), 618–40.
3. Quoted in Levin, *The Myth of the Golden Age*, 60. Martyr's *De Novo Orbe* appeared originally in Italian in 1515.
4. Barlow is quoted in Levin, 66; for a facsimile of Hariot's *Briefe and True Report of the New Found Land of Virginia*, see *Virginia: Four Personal Narratives*

(New York: Arno Press, 1972). Drayton's poem is quoted in Honour, *The New Golden Land*, 27.

5. Smith's accounts of Virginia and New England were first written in 1612 and 1616 respectively, then collected in his *General Historie* in 1624. See John Smith, *The General Historie of Virginia, New England & the Summer Isles*, 2 vols. (New York: Macmillan, 1907), I, 172; I, 64; and II, 33–5. For Bradford's comment, see William Bradford, *History of Plymouth Plantation, 1606–1646*, ed. William T. Davis (New York: Charles Scribner's Sons, 1908), 96.

6. Robert Beverley, *The History and Present State of Virginia*, ed. Louis B. Wright (Chapel Hill: University of North Carolina Press, 1947), 156, 319.

7. Michael Wigglesworth, *The Day of Doom* (1662), quoted in Henry Nash Smith, *Virgin Land: The American West as Symbol and Myth* (Cambridge, MA: Harvard University Press, 1950), 4.

8. See David Bertelson, *The Lazy South* (New York: Oxford University Press, 1967). The pastoral tradition has received much scholarly attention. See Louis B. Wright, *The Colonial Search for a Southern Eden* (University: University of Alabama Press, 1953); Lewis P. Simpson, *The Dispossessed Garden: Pastoral and History in Southern Literature* (Athens: University of Georgia Press, 1975); Lucinda Hardwick MacKethan, *The Dream of Arcady: Place and Time in Southern Literature* (Baton Rouge: Louisiana State University Press, 1980); and Smith, *Virgin Land*, Chapter XIII, "The South and the Myth of the Garden." For well-known contemporary accounts of Southern backwoods slothfulness, see William Byrd's description of "Lubberland" in *The History of the Dividing Line*, in *The Prose Works of William Byrd of Westover*, ed. Louis B. Wright (Cambridge, MA: Belknap Press of Harvard University Press, 1966), 204; and Charles Woodmason, *The Carolina Backcountry on the Eve of the Revolution*, ed. Richard T. Hooker (Chapel Hill: University of North Carolina Press, 1953), 52.

9. Elliott J. Gorn, " 'Gouge and Bite, Pull Hair and Scratch': The Social Significance of Fighting in the Southern Backcountry," *American Historical Review* 90 (February 1985), 37–8.

10. For a discussion of the broader differences between New England and the Southern colonies, see T. H. Breen, *Puritans and Adventurers: Change and Persistence in Early America* (New York: Oxford University Press, 1980), particularly Chapter Six, 107–27.

11. See C. Vann Woodward, *American Counterpoint: Slavery and Racism in the North-South Dialogue* (Boston: Little, Brown, 1971), Chapter One ("The Southern Ethic in a Puritan World"). Whether Protestantism and capitalism suppressed or rechanneled the play element in Western cultures can be endlessly debated. My study suggests the latter.

Chapter 1

1. Anthropologists of sport offer particularly interesting perspectives on this subject. See, for example, John M. Roberts, Malcolm J. Arth, and Robert R. Bush, "Games in Culture," *American Anthropologist* 61 (1959), 597–605; John M. Roberts and Brian Sutton-Smith, "Cross-Cultural Correlates of

Games of Chance," *Behavior Science Notes* 1 (1966), 131–44; and, of course, Clifford Geertz, "Deep Play: Notes on the Balinese Cockfight," *Daedalus* 101 (Winter 1972), 1–37.

2. On backwoods fighting, see Elliott J. Gorn, " 'Gouge and Bite, Pull Hair and Scratch': The Social Significance of Fighting in the Southern Back-country," *American Historical Review* 90 (February 1985), 18–43. On the rendezvous, see virtually any history of the trappers or the fur trade; for particularly detailed accounts, see LeRoy R. Hafen, ed., *Ruxton of the Rockies* (Norman: University of Oklahoma Press, 1950), 23–31; and George Eisen, "Amusements & Pastimes of the Fur Hunters in the Rockies," *Journal of the West* 22 (January 1983), 37–43.

3. See, for example, Josiah Gregg, *Commerce of the Prairies; or, The Journal of a Santa Fe Trader,* in *Early Western Travels, 1748–1846,* ed. Reuben Gold Thwaites, 32 vols. (Cleveland, OH: Arthur H. Clark, 1904–07), XX, 32–7; Rufus B. Sage, *Scenes in the Rocky Mountains,* in *The Far West and the Rockies Historical Series, 1820–1875,* ed. LeRoy R. Hafen and Ann W. Hafen, 15 vols. (Glendale, CA: Arthur H. Clark, 1954–61), V, 129–30; Elisha Douglas Perkins, *Gold Rush Diary: Being the Journal of Elisha Douglas Perkins on the Overland Trail in the Spring and Summer of 1849,* ed. Thomas D. Clark (Lexington: University of Kentucky Press, 1967), 165; and the numerous accounts reported in Robert K. DeArment, *Knights of the Green Cloth: The Saga of the Frontier Gamblers* (Norman: University of Oklahoma Press, 1982); and John M. Findlay, *People of Chance: Gambling in American Society from Jamestown to Las Vegas* (New York: Oxford University Press, 1986).

4. Hector St. John de Crevecoeur, *Letters from an American Farmer* (New York: Fox, Duffield, 1904), 66–70.

5. For a discussion of the popularizing of the "hunters of Kentucky" following Jackson's victory at New Orleans, see John William Ward, *Andrew Jackson: Symbol for an Age* (New York: Oxford University Press, 1955).

6. James Fenimore Cooper, *The Pioneers, or the Sources of the Susquehanna,* ed. James Franklin Beard (Albany: State University of New York Press, 1980), 202.

7. On the development of law as a tool of the powerful, see Morton J. Horwitz, *The Transformation of American Law, 1780–1860* (Cambridge, MA: Harvard University Press, 1977).

8. This is also Hemingway's code as summarized by Scott Donaldson in *By Force of Will: The Life and Art of Ernest Hemingway* (New York: Viking Press, 1977), 78.

9. See George D. Wolf, *The Fair Play Settlers of the West Branch Valley, 1769–1784: A Study of Frontier Ethnography* (Harrisburg: The Pennsylvania Historical and Museum Commission, 1969), 99, 46.

10. Quoted in Richard Slotkin, *The Fatal Environment: The Myth of the Frontier in the Age of Industrialism, 1800–1890* (New York: Atheneum, 1985), 60.

11. James Fenimore Cooper, *The Last of the Mohicans; or, A Narrative of 1757* (Boston: Houghton, Mifflin, 1898), 274.

12. James Fenimore Cooper, *The Pathfinder, or The Inland Sea,* ed. Richard Dilworth Rust (Albany: State University of New York Press, 1981), 73. For

other sporting language in this novel, see pp. 30, 69, 82. And in *The Last of the Mohicans*, 78, 79, 160, 217, 246, 249. Only *The Prairie* (1827) is without significant sporting metaphors.

13. All the quotations in this scene are from chapter seven of *The Deerslayer or, The First War-Path*, ed. James Franklin Beard (Albany: State University of New York Press, 1987).

14. Philip Fisher, *Hard Facts: Setting and Form in the American Novel* (New York: Oxford University Press, 1985), 42. Fisher's brilliant interpretation of the novel lies behind my own discussion here.

15. For Cooperesque sporting characters and scenes, see, for example, James Kirke Paulding, *Westward Ho! A Tale*, 2 vols. (New York: J. & J. Harper, 1832), I, 68, 81; Washington Irving, *A Tour on the Prairies*, ed. Dahlia Kirby Terrell, in *The Complete Works of Washington Irving*, 29 vols. (Madison and Boston: University of Wisconsin and Twayne Publishers, 1969–81), XXII, 56, 79; and C. F. Hoffman, *Wild Scenes in the Forest and Prairie*, 2 vols. (1839; Upper Saddle River, NJ: Gregg Press, 1970), I, 116–17.

16. For a discussion of these forces, see Carrol Smith-Rosenberg's discussion of the Crockett myth in *Disorderly Conduct: Visions of Gender in Victorian America* (New York: Alfred A. Knopf, 1985). What Smith-Rosenberg says about the Crockett myth can be extended to Southwestern humor more generally.

17. See Karen Haltunnen, *Confidence Men and Painted Women: A Study of Middle-Class Culture in America, 1830–1870* (New Haven, CT: Yale University Press, 1982). I have substituted "gamesman" for Haltunnen's "confidence man" without distorting her argument, I believe.

18. See David S. Reynolds, *Beneath the American Renaissance: The Subversive Imagination in the Age of Emerson and Melville* (New York: Alfred A. Knopf, 1988); and George Lippard, *The Monks of Monk Hall* (New York: Odyssey Press, 1970).

19. See William Gilmore Simms, *Guy Rivers: A Tale of Georgia*, rev. ed. (Chicago and New York: Belford, Clarke, 1886); also, Charles W. Webber, *Old Hicks the Guide* (1848; Upper Saddle River, NJ: Gregg Press, 1970); and Emerson Bennet, *Mike Fink: A Legend of the Ohio*, rev. ed. (1852; Upper Saddle River, NJ: Gregg Press, 1970).

20. Joseph G. Baldwin, *The Flush Times of Alabama and Mississippi* (1853; New York: Sagamore Press, 1957), 167.

21. See T. B. Thorpe, "Bob Herring, the Arkansas Bear Hunter," in *A Quarter Race in Kentucky and Other Tales*, ed. William T. Porter (1847; New York: AMS Press, 1973), 130–45; Charles F. M. Noland, "Pete Whetstone's Bear Hunt," in *Humor of the Old Southwest*, ed. Hennig Cohen and William B. Dillingham, 2nd ed. (Athens: University of Georgia Press, 1975), 109–10; Henry Clay Lewis, "The Indefatigable Bear-Hunter," in *Humor of the Old Southwest*, 346–65; and John S. Robb, "Smoking a Grizzly," in *Polly Pea-blossom's Wedding; and Other Tales*, ed. T. A. Burke (Philadelphia: T. B. Peterson, 1856), 110–13. For representative *Crockett Almanacs*, see *Davy Crockett's Almanack of Wild Sports in the West, Life in the Backwoods, & Sketches of Texas* (1837; San Marino, CA: Huntington Library, 1971); and Michael A. Lofaro, ed., *The Tall Tales of Davy Crockett: The Second Nashville Series*

of *Crockett Almanacs, 1839–1841* (Knoxville: University of Tennessee Press, 1987).

22. Alexander B. McNutt, "Chunkey's Fight with the Panthers," in *The Big Bear of Arkansas and Other Tales,* ed. William T. Porter (1845; New York: AMS Press, 1973), 137–38.

23. A. B. Longstreet, *Georgia Scenes* (1835; New York: Sagamore Press, 1957), 14–21.

24. "The Way 'Lige' Shaddock 'Scared Up a Jack,' " in *The Big Bear of Arkansas,* 175–77. For tales of the duped innocent, see T. W. Lane's "The Thimble Game" and the anonymous "War's Yure Hoss?" both in *Polly Peablossom's Wedding,* 28–40, 41–43.

25. Johnson Jones Hooper, *Adventures of Captain Simon Suggs* (Chapel Hill: University of North Carolina Press, 1969). See also Thomas A. Burke, "A Losing Game of Poker," in *Polly Peablossom's Wedding,* 44–8; and "Old Tuttle's Last Quarter Race," in *A Quarter Race in Kentucky,* 117–21.

26. George Washington Harris, *Sut Lovingood's Yarns,* ed. M. Thomas Inge (New Haven, CT: College and University Press, 1966), 183, 283. Sut's callousness works both ways: His similar experience with an enraged bull leads a bystander to offer "*ten* tu one on the bull, an' iseters [oysters] fur the wun what takes the bet" (111–12).

27. Washington Irving, *The Life and Voyages of Christopher Columbus,* ed. John Harmon McElroy, in *Complete Works,* XI, 120, 230, 212, 293.

28. Numerous accounts of the rendezvous are extant. For particularly detailed examples, see LeRoy R. Hafen, ed., *Ruxton of the Rockies* (Norman: University of Oklahoma Press, 1950), 23–31; and George Eisen, "Amusements & Pastimes of the Fur Hunters in the Rockies," *Journal of the West* 22 (January 1983), 37–43.

29. Washington Irving, *The Adventures of Captain Bonneville,* ed. Robert A. Rees and Alan Sandy, in *Complete Works,* XVI, 108.

30. Appendix to another edition of *Captain Bonneville,* ed. Edgeley W. Todd (Norman: University of Oklahoma Press, 1961), 385.

31. Caroline M. Kirkland, *A New Home – Who'll Follow? Glimpses of Western Life,* ed. William S. Osborne (New Haven, CT: College and University Press, 1965), 57–62.

32. Caroline M. Kirkland, *Western Clearings* (1845; New York: Garrett Press, 1969), 27–8.

33. Annette Kolodny, *The Land Before Her: Fantasy and Experience of the American Frontiers, 1630–1860* (Chapel Hill: University of North Carolina Press, 1984), xii–xv.

34. Mrs. Mary Austin Holley, *Texas: Observations, Historical, Geographical and Descriptive* (1833; New York: Arno Press, 1973), 43; Eliza W. Farnham, *Life in Prairie Land* (1846; New York: Arno Press, 1972), 177, 198.

35. Mrs. Caroline A. Soule, *The Pet of the Settlement: A Story of Prairie Land* (Boston: A. Tompkins, 1860), 18–19. The central theme of *Mabel Vaughan* is the redemptive power of work, in the face of the temptations of frontier sport. See Maria S. Cummins, *Mabel Vaughan* (Boston: Crosby, Nichols, 1858). In other recastings of the sporting myth, the title character in Ann S.

Stephens' *Mary Derwent* tames the savagery of warring Indians with gentle saintliness, not a long rifle; while in *Clovernook Sketches* a young man who arrives at a farmhouse with gun in hand and dead birds hanging from a string stays to mend fences, make sugar, and marry the daughter. See Ann S. Stephens, *Mary Derwent* (Philadelphia: T. B. Peterson and Brothers, 1958); and Alice Cary, "About the Tompkinses," in *Clovernook Sketches and Other Stories,* ed. Judith Fetterley (New Brunswick, NJ: Rutgers University Press, 1987).

36. Hoffman, *Wild Scenes in the Forest and Prairie*, 32–3.

37. James Hall, *Tales of the Border* (1835; Upper Saddle River, NJ: Literature House, 1970), 34.

38. See "To Leadville," *Atlantic* 43 (1879), 567–79. For the several towns named Fair Play, see George R. Stewart, *Names on the Land: A Historical Account of Place-Naming in the United States*, rev. ed. (Boston: Houghton, Mifflin, 1958), 296–7; and Erwin G. Gudde, *California Place Names: The Origin and Etymology of Current Geographical Names*, 3rd ed. (Berkeley and Los Angeles: University of California Press 1969), 106.

39. Louis Legrand, M. D., "The Hunter's Vow," *Beadle's Dime Novels*, no. 66 (1864), 14; Frederick Whittaker, "The Mustang-Hunters; or, The Beautiful Amazon of the Hidden Valley," *Beadle's Dime Novels*, no. 226 (1871), 44; Maj. Max Martine, "Old Bear-Paw, the Trapper King; or, The Love of a Blackfoot Queen," *Beadle's Dime Novels*, no. 385 (1873), 54; Ned Buntline, "Old Sib Cone, the Mountain Trapper," *Beadle's New Dime Novels*, no. 35 (24 March 1876), 29; and Frederick Whittaker, "Boone, the Hunter; or, The Backwoods Belle," *Beadle's Dime Novels*, no. 278 (25 March 1873), 22–3.

40. Ned Taylor, "Ted Strong's Nerve; or, Wild West Sport at Black Mountain," *The Young Rough Riders Weekly*, no. 8 (11 June 1904), 18.

41. W. J. Hamilton, "Big Foot, the Guide; or, The Surveyors," *Beadle's Dime Novels*, no. 103 (1866), 45–6.

42. See James L. Bowen, "The Red Rider; or, The White Queen of the Apaches," *Beadle's Dime Novels*, no. 184 (1869), 84; Edward L. Wheeler, "Deadwood Dick, the Prince of the Road; or, The Black Rider of the Black Hills," *Beadle's Half-Dime Library*, no. 1 (15 October 1877), 82; Edward Willett, "The Roving Sport; or, The Pride of Chuckaluck Camp," *Beadle's Half-Dime Library*, no. 311 (10 July 1883), 7; and Lieut. A. K. Sims, "Captain Cactus, the Chaparral Cock; or, Josh Peppermint's Ten Strike," *Beadle's Half-Dime Library*, no. 546 (10 January 1888), 7. Numerous other examples appear in the dime novels surveyed.

43. Captain Mayne Reid, "The Helpless Hand: A Tale of Backwoods Retribution," *Beadle's Dime Novels*, no. 141 (1868), 48; Buntline, "Old Sib Cone," 10, 81; Wheeler, "Deadwood Dick," 78; W. J. Hamilton, "Mad Tom Western, the Texas Ranger; or, The Queen of the Prairie," *Beadle's Half-Dime Library*, no. 72 (1878), 11; Badger, "Hurricane Bill," 6; Jos. E. Badger, "Mustang Sam, the King of the Plains," *Beadle's Half-Dime Library*, no. 119 (4 November 1879), 6; Willett, "The Roving Sport," 11.

44. Colonel Prentiss Ingraham, "Adventures of Buffalo Bill from Boyhood to Manhood," *Beadle's Boys' Library of Sport, Story and Adventure*, no. 1 (14

December 1881), in *Eight Dime Novels,* ed. E. J. Bleiler (New York: Dover, 1974), 104; "Frank James on the Trail," *Morrison's Sensational Series,* no. 46 (1 July 1882), in *Eight Dime Novels,* 37; Edward L. Wheeler, "Deadwood Dick's Leadville Lay; or, Bristol and Bucket's Boom," *Beadle's Half-Dime Library,* no. 606 (5 March 1889), 10; Willett, "The Roving Sport," 9.

45. See Philip Ashton Rollins, *The Cowboy: His Characteristics, His Equipment, and His Part in the Development of the West* (New York: Charles Scribner's Sons, 1922), 79–80.

46. See Col. Prentiss Ingraham, "Buck Taylor, 'King of the Cowboys' or, The Raiders and the Rangers," *Beadle's Half-Dime Library,* no. 497 (1 February 1887).

47. Pat F. Garrett, *The Authentic Life of Billy, the Kid,* ed. J. C. Dykes (Norman: University of Oklahoma Press, 1954), 152–53. It is Dykes, in his introduction, who identifies the two voices of Upson and Garrett.

48. Michael Denning, *Mechanic Accents: Dime Novels and Working-Class Culture in America* (New York: Verso, 1987), 45–6. Denning essentially revises earlier emphasis on the extended audience that downplayed the primacy of a working-class audience. See Jones, *Dime Novel Westerns,* 14; Albert Johannsen, *The House of Beadle and Adams and Its Dime and Nickel Novels: The Story of a Vanished Literature,* 2 vols. (Norman: University of Oklahoma Press, 1950), I, 9.

49. On the magazinists' alienation from the forces transforming America in the late nineteenth century (immigration, urbanization, industrialization, and so on), see John Tomsich, *The Genteel Endeavor: American Culture and Politics in the Gilded Age* (Stanford, CA: Stanford University Press, 1971).

50. See J. Ross Browne, "A Peep at Washoe," *Harper's Monthly* 22 (1861), 145–62, 289–305.

51. [G. W. Nichols], "Wild Bill," *Harper's Monthly* 34 (February 1867), 273–85.

52. For the newspaper accounts, see Nyle H. Miller and Joseph W. Snell, *Why the West Was Wild* (Topeka: Kansas Historical Society, 1965), 176–82, 189, 228; for two dime-novel representations of Hickok's life, see Col. Prentiss Ingraham, "Wild Bill, the Pistol Dead Shot; or, Dagger Don's Double," *Beadle's New York Dime Library,* no. 168 (11 January 1882); and Dangerfield Burr, "Wild Bill's Trump Card; or, The Indian Heiress," *Beadle's New York Dime Library,* no. 175 (1 March 1882). A similar disparity appears in dime-novel and magazine versions of Kit Carson's life. See Richard Slotkin, *The Fatal Environment: The Myth of the Frontier in the Age of Industrialization 1800–1890* (New York: Atheneum, 1985), 203–6.

53. Bret Harte, "The Luck of Roaring Camp," in *Argonaut Edition of the Works of Bret Harte,* 25 vols. (New York: P. F. Collier, 1899), 6–7.

54. "Luck," in *Works,* VII, 4, 10; and "Tennessee's Partner," in *Works,* VII, 59, 61, 63, 65.

55. Bret Harte, "The Outcasts of Poker Flat," in *Works,* VII, 20–21, 33, 36. See also "Brown of Calaveras," "The Convalescence of Jack Hamlin," and "A Passage in the Life of Mr. John Oakhurst."

56. See, for example, "The Great Prize Fight," in *Mark Twain's San Francisco,* ed. Bernard Taper (New York: McGraw-Hill, 1963), 21–2; the portrait of

Slade and the account of Buck Fanshawe's funeral in *Roughing It;* the ritual fight and "The Professor's Yarn" in chapters 3 and 36 of *Life on the Mississippi;* and the escapades of the King and Duke in *Huckleberry Finn.* Twain's colleague on the *Territorial Enterprise,* William Wright ("Dan de Quille") burlesqued the staples of Western folklore in similar ways. See, for example, the excerpts from Wright's *The Big Bonanza* reprinted in *Mark Twain's Frontier,* ed. James E. Camp and X. J. Kennedy (New York: Holt, Rinehart and Winston, 1963). Crane's Western stories and sketches are collected in *The Western Writings of Stephen Crane,* ed. Frank Bergon (New York: New American Library, 1979). For a representative anti-mythic Western tale by Bierce, see "The Famous Gilson Bequest," in *In the Midst of Life: Tales of Soldiers and Civilians* (New York: Boni, 1909).

57. Wm. M. Baker, "The Red Hand," *Atlantic* 27 (February 1871), 221–31, and "Red Reminiscences of the Southwest," *Atlantic* 29 (June 1872), 657–73; and Louis C. Bradford, "Among the Cow-Boys," *Lippincott's* 27 (June 1881), 565, 571.

58. Ernest Ingersoll, "The Camp of the Carbonates," *Scribner's* 19 (March 1879), 801–24. For another strikingly inconsistent account, see Henry King, "Over Sunday in New Sharon," *Scribner's* 19 (March 1880), 768–75.

59. Mrs. Orrin James, "Rob Ruskin, the Prairie Rover; or, The Forest Maid," *Beadle's Dime Novels,* no. 154, 7 July 1868, 9. See also Ann S. Stephens, "Maeleska; the Indian Wife of the White Hunter," *Beadle's Dime Novels,* no. 1, 9 June 1860; Mrs. M. V. Victor, "The Gold Hunters; A Romance of Pike's Peak and New York," *Beadle's Dime Novels,* no. 49, 10 January 1863; Mrs. M. V. Victor, "The Two Hunters; or, The Canyon Camp," *Beadle's Dime Novels,* no. 81, 30 May 1865; and Mrs. Orrin James, "The Border Rivals; or, The Mill-Flume Mystery," *Beadle's Dime Novels,* no. 162, October 1868.

60. See Frances Fuller Victor, *The River of the West* (1870; Oakland, CA: Brooks-Sterling, 1974), particularly, 51–2, 169, 218, 296, 300.

61. See Henry Nash Smith, *Virgin Land: The American West as Symbol and Myth* (Cambridge, MA: Harvard University Press, 1950), Ch. X, "The Dime Novel Heroine." All quotations that follow are from Smith's citations. See also Reynolds, *Beneath the American Renaissance,* 346–7.

62. For the stories of these famous gamblers and dealers, see Robert K. De Arment, *Knights of the Green Cloth* (Norman: University of Oklahoma Press, 1982), Chs. 9–12 ("Queens").

63. Alice McGowan, "A Successful Round-Up," *Overland Monthly,* n.s. 40 (November 1902), 458–9, 460, 462.

64. See Mary A. Denison, "Dick Truch's Wife," *Frank Leslie's Popular Monthly* 33 (January 1892), 97–101; Elia W. Peattie, "In Husking Time," *Harper's Weekly,* 15 October 1892, 993–4; Bessie B. Croffut, "The Sheriff of Canon City," *Frank Leslie's Popular Monthly* 35 (May 1893), 8–23; Nellie Mackubin, "Texas," *Century* 47 (December 1893), 294–300; Mackubin, "Rosita," *Atlantic Monthly* 75 (June 1895), 769–76; and Olive F. Canby, "Haggerty's Wooing," *Harper's Weekly,* 3 October 1896, 986.

65. See Elia W. Peattie, "The Three Johns," *Harper's Weekly,* 26 December 1891, 1037–9; Lillian Bell, "The Heart of Brier Rose," *Harper's Weekly,* 18 April

1891, 281–2; Claire Potter, "A New Mexican Episode," *Frank Leslie's Popular Monthly* 40 (November 1895), 612–16; and Nellie Mackubin, "A Coward," *Century* (1886), 201–7; "His Honor," *Atlantic Monthly* 74 (October 1894), 463–70; "A Public Confession," *Atlantic Monthly* 77 (March 1896), 367–73; and "The Love Story of a Selfish Woman," *Atlantic Monthly* 83 (May 1899), 691–7.

66. The few specific "games" one does find in Western magazine fiction by women serve entirely different purposes. In "A-Playin' of Old Sledge at the Settlement," Mary Noailles Murfree ("Charles Egbert Craddock") redeemed the scandalous morals of cardplaying mountaineers by having the winner of a rival's entire property return his spoils, despite having already lost his woman to him. Lizzie W. Champney, in "Father Acacio's Little Game," made religion, not wealth, the stake in a children's game devised by a Spanish missionary to teach the catechism to young Indians. Mary Hallock Foote's "The Led-Horse Claim" described a boundary dispute between two companies of miners as a "game," but only to convey its foolishness. See Charles Egbert Craddock, "A-Playin' of Old Sledge at the Settlement," *Atlantic Monthly* 52 (October 1883), 544–57; Lizzie W. Champney, "Father Acacio's Little Game," *Scribner's Magazine* 2 (August 1887), 252–6; and Mary Hallock Foote, "The Led-Horse Claim: A Romance of a Mining Camp," serialized in six installments in the *Century* 25 (1882–83). The one exception I have found, Harriet Prescott Spofford's "A Last Card," uses a plot right out of Bret Harte: fatalistic miners trapped by winter snows, playing cards to pass the time until they die. See *Harper's Weekly*, 26 June 1875, 578–9.

67. Alfred Henry Lewis, *Wolfville* (1897; New York: Grosset & Dunlap, n.d.), 107; Frederic Remington, "A Failure of Justice," *Harper's* 100 (January 1900), 271. And see O. Henry's stories "Hearts and Crosses," "Telemachus, Friend," "The Handbook of Hymen," and "Cupid à la Carte" in *Heart of the West* (New York: McClure's, 1907).

68. Hayden Carruth, "The Cash Capital of Sunset City," *Century* 45 (April 1893), 838–43; Anna Fuller, "An Amateur Gamble," *Scribner's* 14 (July 1893), 83–90; J. Frederic Thorne, "The Game at Bull Gap," *Frank Leslie's Popular Monthly* 45 (January 1898), 51–4.

69. See, for example, Wolcott LeClear Beard, "Rouge-et-Noir," *Scribner's* 22 (November 1897), 569–75; and Frederic Remington, "Sun-Down LeFlare's Money," *Harper's* 97 (September 1898), 195–9; as well as Remington's novel, *John Ermine of the Yellowstone* (1902; Ridgewood, NJ: Gregg Press, 1968), 118ff.

70. John Baumann's "Experiences of a Cow-Boy," *Lippincott's* 38 (September 1886), 313–14, and Roosevelt's *Ranch Life and the Hunting-Trail* (1888; New York: Century, 1911), 55–6, celebrate the sporting cowboy in the late 1880s.

71. See, for example, John M. Osborn, " 'Only the Master Shall Praise,' " *Century* 59 (January 1900), 327–35; Charles Warren, "How the Law Came to Jenkins Creek," *McClure's* 16 (November 1900), 77–86; Hamlin Garland, "Delmar of Pima," *McClure's* 18 (February 1902), 340–8; Frank Norris, "The Passing of Cock-Eye Blacklock," *Century* (July 1902), 385–91; and O. Henry, "Hearts and Crosses," "Telemachus, Friend," "The Handbook of Hymen,"

and "Cupid à la Carte," in *Heart of the West* (New York: McClure's, 1907). These stories appeared in a variety of magazines – *Everybody's, Munsey's, McClure's,* and others – between 1902 and 1907.

72. Frederic Remington, "A Rodeo at Los Ojos," *Harper's* 88 (March 1894), 523–4. For other sporting sketches, see "Coursing Rabbits on the Plains" (*Outing,* May 1887), "A Peccary Hunt in Northern Mexico" (*Harper's Weekly,* 1 December 1888), "Stubble and Slough in Dakota" (*Harper's,* August 1894), "Bear-Chasing in the Rocky Mountains" (*Harper's,* July 1895), "The Blue Quail of the Cactus" (*Harper's,* October 1896), and "The Trouble Brothers: Bill and the Wolf" (*Harper's,* November 1899). In addition, Remington's sketches of military athletics in the East ("Troop A Athletics" [*Harper's Weekly,* 3 March 1894] and "Squadron A's Games" [*Harper's Weekly,* 28 March 1896]) bridge the gap between East and West through the twin devices of military and sporting valor, and his account of English military sports ("Athletics at Aldershot" [*Harper's Weekly,* 10 September 1892]) ties Britain's fitness for racial supremacy in an age of moral cowardice to its military-athletic spirit – with a clear message for his own countrymen. All of these are reprinted in *The Collected Writings of Frederic Remington,* ed. Peggy and Harold Samuels (Garden City, NY: Doubleday and Company, 1979).

73. Owen Wister, *Lin McLean* (1898; Upper Saddle River, NJ: Gregg Press, 1970), 1. I cite the book rather than the magazine publications (the six stories in the volume appeared individually in *Harper's* between 1892 and 1897).

74. Owen Wister, "The Evolution of the Cow-Puncher," *Harper's* 91 (1895), 608.

75. The seven Wolfville volumes are *Wolfville* (1897), *Sandburrs* (1900), *Wolfville Days* (1902), *Wolfville Nights* (1902), *The Black Lion Inn* (1903), *Wolfville Folks* (1908), and *Faro Nell and Her Friends* (1913).

76. Alfred Henry Lewis, *Wolfville* (1897; New York: Grosset & Dunlap, n.d.), 6.

77. Alfred Henry Lewis, *Wolfville Days* (1902; New York: Grosset & Dunlap, n.d.), 224.

Chapter 2

1. For my discussion of honor I rely primarily on Bertram Wyatt-Brown, *Southern Honor: Ethics and Behavior in the Old South* (New York: Oxford University Press, 1982); but I also draw on Orlando Patterson, *Slavery and Social Death: A Comparative Study* (Cambridge, MA: Harvard University Press, 1982); Julian Pitt-Rivers, "Honor," in *International Encyclopedia of the Social Sciences,* ed. David L. Sills, 18 vols. (New York: Macmillan and the Free Press, 1968), VI, 503–11; Elliott J. Gorn, " 'Gouge and Bite, Pull Hair and Scratch': The Significance of Fighting in the Southern Backcountry," *American Historical Review* 90 (February 1985), 18–43; Daniel Boorstin, *The Americans: The National Experience* (New York: Random House, 1965); William R. Taylor, *Cavalier and Yankee: The Old South and American National*

Character (New York: Braziller, 1961); and Dickson D. Bruce, *Violence and Culture in the Antebellum South* (Austin: University of Texas Press, 1979).

2. Wyatt-Brown claims in effect that honor preceded slavery, while Patterson and Boorstin argue that slavery was fundamental to Southern honor.

3. For discussions of the relation of sport to class, see Louis B. Wright, *The First Gentlemen of Virginia: Intellectual Qualities of the Early Colonial Ruling Class* (1940; Charlottesville, VA: Dominion Books, 1964); Jane Carson, *Colonial Virginians at Play* (Williamsburg, VA: Colonial Williamsburg, 1965); T. H. Breen, *Puritans and Adventurers: Change and Persistence in Early America* (New York: Oxford University Press, 1980); and Nancy L. Struna, "The Formalization of Sport and the Formation of an Elite: The Chesapeake Gentry, 1650–1720s," *Journal of Sport History* 13 (Winter 1986), 212–34.

4. C. Vann Woodward, *American Counterpoint: Slavery and Racism in the North-South Dialogue* (Boston: Little, Brown, 1971), 16. See also David Bertleson, *The Lazy South* (New York: Oxford University Press, 1967); and Eugene Genovese, *The World the Slaveholders Made: Two Essays in Interpretation* (New York: Pantheon Books, 1969).

5. Rhys Isaac, *The Transformation of Virginia, 1740–1790* (Chapel Hill: University of North Carolina Press, 1982), 99. A dissenting view is offered by Struna, who claims that the sporting gentry *were* governed by a code of fairness. See "The Formalization of Sport and the Formation of an Elite." Struna's more benign account has not yet supplanted that of Breen and Isaac, however. On planters' brutal fighting, see Gorn, " 'Gouge and Bite.' "

6. See Wiliam Byrd of Virginia, *The London Diary (1717–1721) and Writings,* ed. Louis B. Wright and Marian Tinling (New York: Arno Press, 1972); Jack P. Green, ed., *The Diary of Colonel Landon Carter of Sabine Hall, 1752–1778,* 2 vols. (Charlottesville: University of Virginia Press, 1965); Louis Morton, *Robert Carter of Nomini Hall: A Virginia Tobacco Planter of the Eighteenth Century* (Williamsburg, VA: Colonial Williamsburg, 1941); and Donald Jackson, ed., *The Diaries of George Washington,* 6 vols. (Charlottesville: University of Virginia Press, 1976–9). Breen, Isaac, and Wyatt-Brown, as well as Carson in *Colonial Virginians at Play,* discuss and interpret the extravagance of colonial betting. Struna in "The Formalization of Sport" again casts the dissenting vote.

7. Breen, *Puritans and Adventurers,* 151–62.

8. Wyatt-Brown, 327–49.

9. See Bruce, *Violence and Culture,* 196–201.

10. Wyatt-Brown, *Southern Honor,* 331–9.

11. Pitt-Rivers, "Honor," 508.

12. My chief sources on the plantation romance are Francis Pendleton Gaines, *The Southern Plantation: A Study in the Development and Accuracy of a Tradition* (1924; Gloucester, MA: Peter Smith, 1962); J. V. Ridgely, *Nineteenth-Century Southern Literature* (Lexington: University Press of Kentucky, 1980); Taylor, *Cavalier and Yankee;* Richard Devon Watson, Jr., *The Cavalier in Virginia Fiction* (Baton Rouge: Louisiana State University Press, 1985); and Mary Ann Wimsatt, "Antebellum Fiction," and Lucinda H. MacKethan, "Plantation

Fiction, 1865–1900," in *The History of Southern Literature*, ed. Louis D. Rubin et al. (Baton Rouge: Louisiana State University Press, 1985).

13. [Isaac E. Holmes], *Recreations of George Taletell, F.Y.C.* (Charleston, SC: Duke & Browne, 1822), 30; George Tucker, *The Valley of Shenandoah; or, Memoirs of the Graysons* (1824; Chapel Hill: University of North Carolina Pree, 1970), *passim*.

14. John Pendleton Kennedy, *Swallow Barn, or A Sojourn in the Old Dominion* (New York: Hafner, 1971), 23, 88. This is a reprint of the second edition of 1851.

15. See Patterson, *Slavery and Social Death:* 80–96. In *Swallow Barn*, the slaves are consistently childlike.

16. Charles E. Whitehead, *Wild Sports in the South; or, The Camp-Fires of the Everglades* (New York: Derby & Jackson, 1860), 176.

17. William Elliott, *Carolina Sports by Land & Water* (1846; New York: Arno Press, 1967), 107.

18. Nathaniel Beverley Tucker, *George Balcomb* (New York, 1836), I, 224; quoted in Bertelson, *The Lazy South*, 188.

19. Nathaniel Beverley Tucker, *The Partisan Leader* (1836; Upper Saddle River, NJ: Gregg Press, 1968), 250, 253, 204.

20. William A. Caruthers, *The Cavaliers of Virginia, or the Recluse of Jamestown: An Historical Romance of the Old Dominion* (1834–5; Ridgewood, NJ: Gregg Press, 1968), 4.

21. John Esten Cooke, *The Virginia Comedians; or, Old Days in the Old Dominion*, 2 vols. (1854; Ridgewood, NJ: Gregg Press, 1968), *passim*.

22. My chief sources for the discussion that follows are Wyatt-Brown, *Southern Honor*, Part Two, "Family and Gender Behavior"; and Anne Firor Scott, *The Southern Lady: From Pedestal to Politics, 1830–1930* (Chicago: University of Chicago Press, 1970). For a more detailed study of individual works by seven Southern women, see Anne Goodwyn Jones, *Tomorrow Is Another Day: The Woman Writer in the South, 1859–1936* (Baton Rouge: Louisiana State University Press, 1981).

23. Wyatt-Brown, *Southern Honor*, 227.

24. "On Duelling," Methodist Episcopal Church Tract Society, vol. iv, no. 105 (c. 1840), 3–4.

25. [Eliza Ann Dupuy], *The Planter's Daughter: A Tale of Louisiana* (Philadelphia: T. B. Peterson and Brothers, 1858), 18, 56.

26. [Caroline Howard Gilman], *Recollections of a Southern Matron* (1837; New York: G. P. Putnam, 1852), 129, 243, 207–8, 212.

27. For Dupuy's full-scale attack on gambling "games," see *The Planter's Daughter*, 19, 20, 37–8, 56, 91, 122, 260; as well as the account of Victor's downfall.

28. Marion Harland, *Alone* (New York: J. C. Derby, 1854), 95. "Marion Harland" was the pseudonym of Mary Virginia Terhune.

29. Caroline Lee Hentz, *Marcus Warland; or, The Long Moss Spring. A Tale of the South* (Philadelphia: T. B. Peterson, 1852), 41.

30. See William A. Caruthers, *The Knights of the Horseshoe* [the title of many later editions] (1845; New York: A. L. Burt, n.d.), 318 and *passim*; and John

Pendleton Kennedy, *Horse-Shoe Robinson: A Tale of the Tory Ascendancy*, ed. Ernest E. Leisy (New York: Hafner, 1962), 73–5, 194, and *passim*.

31. In his other fiction Simms explored related themes. See, for example, *Guy Rivers* (1834) and *The Yemassee* (1835), the first of his border and colonial romances respectively. I emphasize the Revolutionary romances because they are tied most directly to Southern identity.

32. This overview of Simms's fiction is derived primarily from J. V. Ridgely, *William Gilmore Simms* (New York: Twayne, 1962).

33. See William Gilmore Simms, *Mellichampe: A Legend of the Santee*, Caxton Edition (Chicago, New York, and San Francisco: Belford, Clarke, 1889), 58; and *The Scout; or, The Black Riders of Congaree* (1854; Ridgewood, NJ: Gregg Press, 1968), 126.

34. William Gilmore Simms, *The Partisan: A Tale of the Revolution*, 2 vols. (1835; Ridgewood, NJ: Gregg Press, 1968), II, 79–83.

35. Simms, *Mellichampe*, 153–4; *Katharine Walton; or, The Rebel of Dorchester*, rev. ed. (Chicago and New York: Belford, Clarke, 1888), 167; *The Forayers; or, The Raid of the Dog-Days*, Caxton Edition (Chicago, New York, and San Francisco: Belford, Clarke, 1889), 506.

36. William Gilmore Simms, *Eutaw: A Sequel to The Forayers; or, The Raid of the Dog Days*, rev. ed. (1885; New York: AMS Press, 1970), 118–23. In *Eutaw*, Simms also reiterated his identification of war with game, chiefly in a chapter titled "Games of Peace and War," but in images throughout the novel as well. See, for example, 341, 354, 355.

37. D. R. Hundley, *Social Relations in Our Southern States* (New York: Henry B. Price, 1860), 30–1, 34, 35, 40–1, 43.

38. See Bertelson, *The Lazy South*, 190–1.

39. George Fitzhugh, *Sociology for the South, or the Failure of Free Society* (1854; New York: Burt Franklin, n.d.), 38.

40. Scott, *The Southern Lady*, 106ff.

41. Thomas Nelson Page, preface to *The Old South: Essays Social and Political*, in *The Works of Thomas Nelson Page*, 18 vols. (New York: Charles Scribner's Sons, 1906–12), XII, vii.

42. John Esten Cooke, *Virginia: A History of the People* (1883; Boston: Houghton, Mifflin, 1897), 370, 373, 364, 479.

43. See George W. Bagby, *The Old Virginia Gentleman and Other Sketches*, ed. Thomas Nelson Page (New York: Charles Scribner's Sons, 1910), 7, 9, 10–1, 26 (in his introduction Page acknowledged Bagby's influence and called "The Old Virginia Gentleman" "to my mind the most charming picture of American life ever drawn"); R. Q. Mallard, *Plantation Life Before Emancipation* (Richmond, VA: Whittet & Shepperson, 1892), 28; Walter Hines Page, "The Rebuilding of Old Commonwealths," reprinted in *The School That Built a Town* (New York: Harper & Brothers, 1952), 85, 87; and Philip Alexander Bruce, *Social Life of Virginia in the Seventeenth Century* (1907; Williamstown, MA: Corner House, 1968), 177.

44. John Esten Cooke, *Surry of Eagle's Nest, or The Memoirs of a Staff Officer Serving in Virginia* (1866; New York: G. W. Dillingham, 1894), 10–1.

45. See Esther J. Crooks and Ruth W. Crooks, *The Ring Tournament in the United States* (Richmond, VA: Garrett and Massie, 1936). After declining interest early in the twentieth century, the ring tournament underwent a revival in the 1930s, in the midst of the Depression.

46. Francis Fontaine, *Etowah. A Romance of the Confederacy* (Atlanta, GA: Francis Fontaine, 1887); Maurice Thompson, *His Second Campaign* (Boston: James R. Osgood, 1883), 126–7; and John Fox, Jr., *The Knight of the Cumberland,* bound with *The Kentuckians* (New York: Charles Scribner's Sons, 1909), 242.

47. For anti-gambling sentiments, see George Cary Eggleston's *A Man of Honor,* William Baker's *Colonel Dunwoddie,* Page's *Red Rock,* Thomas Dixon's *The Clansman,* Fox's *The Kentuckians,* and John W. Moore's *The Heirs of St. Kilda.* For attacks on dueling, see *St. Kilda* and Thompson's *His Second Campaign* and *A Tallahassee Girl.* The hero of Page's "Marse Chan" declines to fire at one opponent, then nearly participates in another duel, but for his lady's honor (the daughter of the man he had spared earlier). F. Hopkinson Smith's *Colonel Carter of Cartersville* renders the duel comically, but in such a way that Southern honor emerges superior to Yankee practicality.

48. Paul H. Buck has described, for example, how Northern periodicals such as *Scribner's, Lippincott's, Harper's,* and the *Atlantic* "discovered" Southern writers in the 1870s and 1880s. *Scribner's* was first to do so, but in promoting a common America the magazine's editors allowed "no truckling to the contentious partisan." See Paul H. Buck, *The Road to Reunion, 1865–1900* (1937; New York: Vintage Books, 1959), 229–30.

49. See George Cary Eggleston, *A Rebel's Recollections* (1875; Bloomington: Indiana University Press, 1959), 28; [William Mumford Baker], *Colonel Dunwoddie, Millionaire: A Story of To-Day* (New York: Harper & Brothers, 1878), 65; and Thomas Nelson Page, *Red Rock: A Chronicle of Reconstruction* (1898; Ridgewood, NJ: Gregg Press, 1967), 578.

50. See Fontaine, *Etowah,* Chapter Two; John W. Moore, *The Heirs of St. Kilda: A Story of the Southern Past* (Raleigh, NC: Edwards, Broughton, 1881), 88–9, 281.

51. Mrs. Burton Harrison, *Flower de Hundred: The Story of a Virginia Plantation* (1890; New York: Century, 1899), 13–16, 19, 45, 131.

52. Mrs. Burton Harrison, *A Son of the Old Dominion* (Boston and New York: Lamson, Wolffe, 1897), 28, 11, 49, 181–2.

53. See Mary Tucker Magill, *The Holcombes: A Story of Virginia Home-Life* (Philadelphia: J. B. Lippincott, 1871), 159, 101–3; and M. G. McClelland, *Broadoaks* (St. Paul, MN: Price-McGill, 1893), 157, 82.

54. Mark Twain, *Adventures of Huckleberry Finn* (1885; Berkeley and Los Angeles: University of California Press, 1985), 142–55. Twain also parodied dueling in his early sketch "Journalism in Tennessee" (1869) and English chivalry in *A Connecticut Yankee in King Arthur's Court* (1889), less as an assault on British tradition than on the fascination with chivalry that marked America in his own time, particularly the South. And in *Life on the Mississippi* (1883), he made his famous, outrageous claim that Walter Scott, the chief popularizer of the chivalric tradition in nineteenth-century America, was responsible for

the Civil War. For a full discussion of these matters, see Arthur G. Pettit, *Mark Twain and the South* (Lexington: University Press of Kentucky, 1974).

55. George W. Cable, *The Grandissimes: A Story of Creole Life* (New York: Charles Scribner's Sons, 1880), 29, 35, 38–9.

56. Ellen Glasgow, *The Battle-Ground* (New York: Doubleday, Page, 1902), 48.

57. August J. Evans, *St. Elmo* (1866; New York: Grosset & Dunlap, n.d.), 56, 82, 95.

58. See E.D.E.N. Southworth, *The Hidden Hand; or, Capitola the Mad-Cap* (New York: G. W. Dillingham, 1888), 444–67.

59. For Pelham, see 378, 383, 388; for Farley, 379, 380, 412; for Jackson, 184, 202, 224; for Ashby, 154, 164, 203, 217.

60. See Emory M. Thomas, *Bold Dragoon: The Life of J. E. B. Stuart* (New York: Harper & Row, 1986).

61. John Esten Cooke, *Mohun; or, The Last Days of Lee and His Paladins* (1869; Ridgewood, NJ: Gregg Press, 1968), 20, 70–1, 74, 99.

62. See John Esten Cooke, *The Wearing of the Gray; Being Personal Portraits, Scenes and Adventures of the War* (New York: S. B. Treat, 1867), 174–90. This is Cooke's account of Stuart's famous "ride around McClellan."

63. See Eggleston, *Recollections of a Rebel*, 116, 120, 123, 124.

64. Thomas Dixon, Jr., *The Clansman: An Historical Romance of the Ku Klux Klan* (1905; Ridgewood, NJ: Gregg Press, 1967), 8.

65. See Grace King, *New Orleans: The Place and the People* (1895; New York: Macmillan, 1912), 293–7; and Susan Dabney Smedes, *A Southern Planter* (1887; New York: James Pott, 1892).

66. Mary Johnston, *To Have and To Hold* (Boston and New York: Houghton Mifflin, 1900) *passim*. Sporting rhetoric is abundant.

67. Mary Johnston, *The Long Roll* (Boston and New York: Houghton Mifflin, 1911), 43, 63, 193.

Chapter 3

1. Henry James, *The Bostonians* (New York: Macmillan, 1886), 13, 23, 187.

2. John Mack Faragher, *Women and Men on the Overland Trail* (New Haven, CT: Yale University Press, 1979), 14.

3. In addition to Faragher's book, see Christiane Fischer, *Let Them Speak for Themselves: Women in the American West* (Hamden, CT: Archon, 1977); Julie Roy Jeffrey, *Frontier Women: The Trans-Mississippi West, 1840–1880* (New York: Hill and Wang, 1978); Joanna L. Stratton, *Pioneer Women: Voices from the Kansas Frontier* (New York: Simon and Schuster, 1981); Lillian Schlissel, *Women's Diaries of the Westward Journey* (New York: Schocken, 1982); and Sandra L. Myres, *Westering Women and the Frontier Experience, 1800–1915* (Albuquerque: University of New Mexico Press, 1982).

4. Schlissel, *Women's Diaries*, 15–16.

5. See the reminiscence of an army wife on a frontier outpost in Fischer, *Let Them Speak*, 131; Myre's discussion of "play-parties" in *Westering Women*, 175ff.; and Stratton's account of the importance of social life on the Kansas frontier in *Pioneer Women*, 129ff.

6. Quoted in Faragher, *Women and Men,* 99.
7. See Philip Fisher, *Hard Facts: Setting and Form in the American Novel* (New York: Oxford University Press, 1985), Chapter 1.
8. See Mary P. Ryan, *Womanhood in America: From Colonial Times to the Present* (New York: New Viewpoints, 1975); Barbara Welter, *Dimity Convictions: The American Woman in the Nineteenth Century* (Athens: Ohio University Press, 1976); Nancy F. Cott, *The Bonds of Womanhood: "Women's Sphere" in New England, 1780–1835* (New Haven, CT: Yale University Press, 1977); Linda K. Kerber, *Women of the Republic: Intellect and Ideology in Revolutionary America* (Chapel Hill: University of North Carolina Press, 1980); Carroll Smith-Rosenberg, *Disorderly Conduct: Visions of Gender in Victorian America* (New York: Alfred A. Knopf, 1985); and Glenna Matthews, *"Just a Housewife": The Rise and Fall of Domesticity in America* (New York: Oxford University Press, 1987).
9. See Welter, *Dimity Convictions,* for a reprint of the essay first published in 1966. More recent feminist history has not rejected Welter's ideas but expanded on them.
10. *Dimity Convictions,* 21.
11. See Frances Cogan, *The All-American Girl: The Ideal of Real Womanhood in Mid-Nineteenth-Century America* (Athens: University of Georgia Press, 1989).
12. [Catharine M. Sedgwick], *Married or Single?* 2 vols. (New York: Harper & Brothers, 1857), I, vi.
13. "Sports of Love," *Godey's Lady's Book* 2 (June 1831), 281.
14. "Sporting with Female Affections," *Godey's Lady's Book* 2 (January 1831), 26.
15. On the love game, see Molly Myerowitz, *Ovid's Games of Love* (Detroit, MI: Wayne State University Press, 1985); John Jay Parry's introduction to his translation of *The Art of Courtly Love* by Andreas Capellanus (New York: Columbia University Press, 1941); David Lloyd Stevenson, *The Love-Game Comedy* (1946; New York: AMS Press, 1966); and Kenneth N. McKee, *The Theater of Marivaux* (New York: Washington Square, 1958). On the "love chase," see Marcell Thiébaux, *The Stag of Love: The Chase in Medieval Literature* (Ithaca, NY: Cornell University Press, 1974); and Michael M. B. Allen, "The Chase: The Development of a Renaissance Theme," *Comparative Literature* 20 (1968), 301–12.
16. Samuel Richardson, *Clarissa, or the History of a Young Lady,* ed. John Angus Burrell (New York: Modern Library, 1950), 223, 236–7, 308, 376.
17. Mrs. Hannah Foster, *The Coquette,* bound with William Hill Brown, *The Power of Sympathy,* ed. William S. Osborne (New Haven, CT: College & University Press, 1970), 145, 176, 246.
18. On the decline of seduction, see Nina Baym, *Woman's Fiction: A Guide to Novels by and about Women in America, 1820–1870* (Ithaca, NY: Cornell University Press, 1978), 25–6; on the fiction of seduction in story papers see David S. Reynolds, *Beneath the American Renaissance: The Subversive Imagination in the Age of Emerson and Melville* (New York: Alfred A. Knopf, 1988).
19. See Welter, *Dimity Convictions,* 6.
20. Vivian Gornick and Barbara K. Moran, ed. *Women in Sexist Society: Studies*

in Power and Powerlessness (New York: Basic Books, 1971), editors' introduction, xiv.

21. For criticism of males, see Trevors, "Male Coquetry," *Godey's Lady's Book* 19 (1839), 71; and Mary Davenant, "Il s'amuse; or, The Gentleman Flirt," *Godey's* 28 (1844), 288; for a sampling of the more numerous cautionary tales directed to women, see Penny Patch, "Ellen, the Coquette," serialized in vol. 37 (1848); P. Holley, "History of a Flirtation," 39 (1849), 313–19; Alice B. Neal, "The Coquette," 42 (1851), 149–53; and Mrs. E. F. Ellet, "The Fate of a Flirt in Olden Time," 43 (1851), 13ff.

22. Sara Claxton, "A Fateful Game; or, Wedded and Parted," *Waverly Library,* no. 162, 19 December 1882; Sara Claxton, "A Thorny Path; or, Playing to Win," *Waverly Library,* no. 215, 25 December 1883; and Arabella Southworth, "A Desperate Game; or, For Love's Own Sake," *Waverly Library* (octavo edition), no. 91, 16 February 1886. These were reprints of British stories.

23. Byam, *Woman's Fiction,* 12.

24. Quoted in Mary Kelley, *Private Woman, Public Stage: Literary Domesticity in Nineteenth-Century America* (New York: Oxford University Press, 1984), 268.

25. Other English novels include Annie Thomas, *Playing for High Stakes* (New York: Harper & Brothers, 1867) and Mrs. Alexander, *A Winning Hazard* (1896; New York: A. L. Burt, n.d.). A few critics have called attention to the "games" in novels by British women. For a discussion of games in Jane Austen's *Pride and Prejudice* and *Mansfield Park,* see Nancy Morrow, *Dreadful Games: The Play of Desire in the Nineteenth-Century Novel* (Kent, OH: Kent State University Press, 1988), 36–8; on "the game of the marriage 'market' " in *Jane Eyre,* see Sandra M. Gilbert and Susan Gubar, *The Madwoman in the Attic: The Woman Writer and the Nineteenth-Century Literary Imagination* (New Haven, CT: Yale University Press, 1979), 350; and on the relationship between Gwendolen Harleth's gambling and her orientation to life in George Eliot's *Daniel Deronda,* see Patricia Meyer Spacks, *The Female Imagination* (New York: Alfred A. Knopf, 1975), 51.

26. See Reynolds' discussion of contemporary opinion on this matter, in *Beneath the American Renaissance.*

27. See Ruth Weiman, *Playing the Game* (New York: Cupples & Leon, 1910); and Ruth Comfort Mitchell, *Play the Game* (New York: D. Appleton, 1921).

28. See Mary Jane Holmes, *Tempest and Sunshine,* bound with Maria Susanna Cummins, *The Lamplighter,* ed. Donald A. Koch (New York: Odyssey Press, 1968), 156–7; and Madelene Yale Wynne, "A Game of Solitaire," *Atlantic Monthly* 80 (November 1897), 685–94.

29. See Reynolds, *Beneath the American Renaissance.*

30. Harriet Beecher Stowe, *My Wife and I: or, Harry Henderson's History* (New York: J. B. Ford, 1871), 222, 351. See also *We and Our Neighbors* (New York: J. B. Ford, 1873), 28, 32.

31. Harriet Beecher Stowe, *Pink and White Tyranny: A Society Novel* (Boston: Roberts Brothers, 1871), 2, 8, 10, 47, 49, 304ff., and passim.

32. See Harriet Beecher Stowe, *Uncle Tom's Cabin* (1852; New York: Library of America, 1982), 470.

33. Stowe, *My Wife and I*, 343–4.
34. Louisa May Alcott, "The King of Clubs and the Queen of Hearts," in *On Picket Duty and Other Tales* (1864; New York: Garrett Press, 1969), 46–8.
35. Madelaine Stern, ed., *The Unknown Thrillers of Louisa May Alcott* (New York: William Morrow, 1975), 114, 131, 1137.
36. *Unknown Thrillers*, 19, 75, 93, 104.
37. Both passages are quoted in Stern's introduction to *The Unknown Thrillers*, xxvi–xxvii.
38. Dee Garrison, "Immoral Fiction in the Late Victorian Library," in *Victorian America*, ed. Daniel Walker Howe (Philadelphia: University of Pennsylvania Press, 1976), 142–3.
39. E.D.E.N. Southworth, *Fair Play; or, The Test of the Lone Isle* (Philadelphia: T. B. Peterson, 1868).
40. See Baym, *Woman's Fiction*, 125.
41. E.D.E.N. Southworth, *The Hidden Hand; or, Capitola's Mad-Cap* (New York: G. W. Dillingham, 1888), pp. 136–7, 144.
42. Baym, *Woman's Fiction*, Chapter 5; Elaine Showalter, *A Literature of Their Own: British Women Novelists from Brontë to Lessing* (Princeton, NJ: Princeton University Press, 1977), Chapter VI.
43. Dorothy Dix, "Summer Flirtation," in *New Orleans Daily Picayune* (1899), reprinted in the Norton Critical Edition of *The Awakening*, ed. Margaret Culley (New York: W. W. Norton, 1976), 131.
44. Spacks, *The Female Imagination*, 51.
45. Kate Chopin, *The Awakening*, ed. Culley, 28–9.
46. Edith Wharton, *The House of Mirth* (New York: Charles Scribner's Sons, 1905), 234.
47. Edith Wharton, *A Backward Glance* (New York: D. Appleton-Century, 1934), 207.
48. Wharton, *A Backward Glance*, 46.
49. The "game" has a prominent role in this later novel. See Edith Wharton, *The Custom of the Country* (New York: Charles Scribner's Sons, 1913), 222, 230–1, 287.
50. Frank Norris, *Blix*, bd. with *Moran of the Lady Letty* (Garden City, NY: Doubleday, Doran, 1928), 20; William Dean Howells, *A Hazard of New Fortunes*, in *Selected Edition of W. D. Howells*, 32 vols. (Bloomington: Indiana University Press, 1968–83), XVI, 243; Theodore Dreiser, *Sister Carrie* (New York: Doubleday, Page, 1900), 219, 225, 251, 254, 259. From this same period, see also Henry Kitchell Webster, *The Banker and the Bear: The Story of Corner in Lard* (1900; Upper Saddle River, NJ: Gregg Press, 1968), 28, 29; and Jack London, *Burning Daylight* (1910; New York: Regent Press, n.d.), 249, 300.
51. F. W. Dupee, *Henry James: His Life and Writings*, quoted in Ann Douglas, *The Feminization of American Culture* (New York: Alfred A. Knopf, 1977), 266.
52. Alfred Habegger, *Gender, Fantasy, and Realism in American Literature* (New York: Columbia University Press, 1982).
53. Henry James, *The American* (Boston: Houghton Mifflin, 1877), 29.
54. For discussions of this theme see Alfred Habegger, "Reciprocity and the

Market Place in *The Wings of the Dove* and *What Maisie Knew*," *Nineteenth-Century Fiction* 25 (March 1971), 455–73; and two essays by Peggy Mc-Cormack: "The Semiotics of Economic Language in James's Fiction," *American Literature* 58 (1986), 540–55; and "Exchange Economy in Henry James's *The Awkward Age*," *University of Mississippi Studies in English* (1984–87), 182–202.

55. Henry James, *The Europeans: A Sketch* (Boston: Houghton Mifflin, 1882), 79. The actual quotation is a comment by Eugenia's maid: "What fish did she expect to land out of these very stagnant waters? The game was evidently a deep one."

56. Henry James, *The Spoils of Poynton*, New York Edition, 26 vols. (New York: Charles Scribner's Sons, 1907–17), X, 127. The first half of this short novel uses a half-dozen major images of battle to establish the relationships among contenders for the "spoils"; the second half then shifts to game images. Fleda's "double game" involves her competing loyalties to Mrs. Gareth and Owen, while not compromising her own sense of honor. The other players are less scrupulous.

57. In a novel chiefly interested in what Maisie comes to know, her dawning awareness is signaled when she first glimpses the nature of this game, coming to realize that her situation has become "a question of sides." She finds herself in a game "very much like puss-in-the-corner, and she could only wonder if the distribution of parties would lead to a rushing to and fro and a changing of places." See Henry James, *What Maisie Knew*, New York Edition, XI, 14, 94–5. There are at least a dozen and a half significant game images in the novel, several of them elaborate.

58. In this short novel, old Juliana Bordereau is pictured wearing a green eyeshade such as gamblers wear – a clear emblem of her superior skill in the "game" for her dead lover's papers. She is also described as a cat sporting with the weaker male as her mouse. See Henry James, "The Aspern Papers," New York Edition, XII, 11, 73–4, 94.

59. Habegger, *Gender, Fantasy, and Realism*, 254.

60. Henry James, *The Portrait of a Lady*, 2 vols. (Boston and New York: Houghton Mifflin, 1881), II, 273; *The Ambassadors*, New York Edition, XXI, 76; *The Wings of the Dove*, New York Edition, XX, 5, 21, 24; and 255, 347. A more bluntly sexual game develops between Kate and Densher as well. When Densher comes at last to realize the full extent of Kate's plan, he sees "himself master in the conflict" with Kate (XX, 231), and extracts from her a promise to give herself to him sexually. Later, when Densher declares to Kate, "We've played our dreadful game, and we've lost" (XX, 347), he proposes that they square themselves by marrying. Now *Kate* feels "an advantage with his passion" (XX, 350), a reversal of the temporary dominance Densher enjoyed. Power, not passion, is chiefly at stake.

61. A few more examples of this diversity: Meddling outsiders, from Mrs. Tristram to Aunt Penniman to Fanny Assingham, play their games of match-making and social manipulation; in *The Ambassadors*, the process of discovery itself is the chief game Strether plays, while he also feels committed to a code of fair play toward all the parties involved as he executes his ambas-

sadorship ("The larger game," as Strether describes it, includes not just Chad and Madame de Vionnet, but himself, the Pococks, and the Newsomes back home). See *The Ambassadors*, XXII, 72; also XXI, 9, 140, 151, 164, 167, 176, 177, 185, 193; XXII, 11, 14, 43, 126, 215, 218, 297. For alternative discussions of the games in *The American, The Portrait of a Lady, The Wings of the Dove,* and *The Golden Bowl,* see Morrow, *Dreadful Games.*

62. All in New York Edition: *The Awkward Age,* IX, xx and xxiii; *The Wings of the Dove,* XIX, xxii; *The Golden Bowl,* XXIII, vi.

63. Henry James, *The Golden Bowl,* New York Edition, XXIII, 64, 281. See also XXIII, 398.

Part II

1. St. Augustine, *Earlier Writings,* ed. H. S. Burleigh, in *The Library of Christian Classics,* ed. John Baillie, et al., 26 vols. (Philadelphia: Westminster Press, 1953–69), VI, 393. See also, Origen, *On Prayer,* ed. John Ernest Leonard Oulton and Henry Chadwick, *Library of Christian Classics,* II 321; Nemesius of Emesa, *On the Nature of Man,* ed. William Telfer, in *Library of Christian Classics,* IV, 449; Bernard of Clairvaux, *On the Love of God,* ed. Ray C. Petry, in *Library of Christian Classics,* XIII, 58–9; and John Nicolas Lenker, ed., *Sermons of Martin Luther,* 8 vols. (Grand Rapids, MI: Baker Book House, 1983), VII, 93–103. A curious footnote should be added. The chief spiritual athlete from the Old Testament was Job, but through an interesting reincarnation. The biblical Job was the patient bearer of unfair burdens, his story showing that, although God does not always act justly, we must accept His judgments. The post-biblical figure in the *Testament of Job* (first century BC), of Didymos the Blind in the fourth century, of the *Suda,* a Byzantine lexicon from the tenth, and of other commentaries became Job the Wrestler, "a spiritual athlete who wins glory by his contests." See Michael Poliakoff, "Jacob, Job, and Other Wrestlers: Reception of Greek Athletics by Jews and Christians in Antiquity," *Journal of Sport History* 11 (Summer 1984), 48–65.

2. *Republic,* X, 604; quoted in Bayard Rankin, "The History of Probability and the Changing Concept of the Individual," *Journal of the History of Ideas* 27 (1966), 489. And Boethius, *The Consolation of Philosophy,* trans. Richard Green (Indianapolis, IN: Bobbs-Merrill, 1962), 24.

3. See Howard R. Patch, *The Goddess Fortuna in Medieval Literature* (1927; New York: Octagon Books, 1974), 81–2; Michael Olmert, "Chaucer's Little Lotteries: The Literary Use of a Medieval Game," *Arete: The Journal of Sport Literature* 2 (Fall 1984), 171–82; and Shakespeare's *Lear,* IV, i, 37. In *A Midsummer Night's Dream* the same motif appears comically in Puck's sporting with the mismatched couples in the forest (see III, iii, 352).

4. See Num. 26: 55; 1 Sam. 10: 20–1; 1 Chr. 24: 5, 25: 8, 26: 13; Lev. 16: 7–10; Acts 1: 26.

5. John Cotton, *A Practical Commentary, or an Exposition with Observations, Reasons, and Uses upon the First Epistle of John* (London: Thomas Parkhurst, 1656), 126–7.

6. See Increase Mather, *Testimony Against Prophane Customs, Namely Health*

Drinking, Dicing, Cards, Christmas-Keeping, New Year's Gifts, Cock-scaling, Saints' Days, etc. (1687; Charlottesville: University of Virginia Press, 1953); *Diary of Cotton Mather*, 2 vols. (New York: Frederick Ungar, n.d.), II, 66–7 and II, 491; Eli Hyde, *A Sermon; in which the Doctrine of the Lot, is stated, and Applied to Lotteries, Gambling and Card-Playing, for Amusement* (Oxford, NY: John B. Johnson, 1812); and John Richards, *Discourses on Gambling* (Hanover, NH: D. Kimball & Sons, 1852), 6.

7. See Francis Quarles, *The Complete Works in Prose and Verse*, 3 vols. (Edinburgh: Edinburgh University Press, 1880), II, 233; and George Wither, *A Collection of Emblems, Ancient and Moderne* (Columbia: University of South Carolina Press, 1975), 16. For these references I am indebted to Heiner Gillmeister, "Ballspielgedicte des Spätmittelalters und der Renaissance," in *Sport und Literatur*, ed. Nanda Fischer (Clausthal-Zellerbach, West Germany: Deutsche Vereinigung für Sportwissenschaft, 1986), 100–25. Gillmeister discusses other examples of a similar nature from the Dutch and French. For discussions of ludic motifs in medieval literature, see V. A. Kolve, *The Play Called Corpus Christi* (Stanford, CA: Stanford University Press, 1966); and Caroline L. Dinshaw, "Dice Games and Other Games in *Le Jeu de Saint Nicholas*," *PMLA* 95 (October 1980), 802–11.

8. Jaroslev Pelikan and Helmut T. Lehman, ed., *Luther's Works*, 55 vols. (St. Louis, MO and Philadelphia: Concordia Publishing House and Fortress Press, 1955–76), VI, 125–34. Christian mysticism has known a curiously similar sporting motif: the *Ludus Amoris* God plays with the desirous soul, a game of hide and seek in which God reveals himself then withdraws. See Evelyn Underhill, *Mysticism: A Study in the Nature and Development of Man's Spiritual Consciousness* (1911; New York: E. P. Dutton, 1961), 227–8, 286, 383.

9. Samuel Mather, *The Figures or Types of the Old Testament*, ed. Mason I. Lowance, Jr. (New York: Johnson Reprint, 1969), 86.

10. Thomas Shepard, *God's Plot: The Paradoxes of Puritan Piety, Being the Autobiography & Journal of Thomas Shepard*, ed. Michael McGiffert (Amherst: University of Massachusetts Press, 1972), 40; John Williams, *The Redeemed Captive*, ed. Edward W. Clark (Amherst: University of Massachusetts Press, 1976), 44.

11. See "The Diary of Michael Wigglesworth," ed. Edmund S. Morgan, *Publications of the Colonial Society of Massachusetts* 35 (1942–6), 345, 346, 359–60.

12. Increase Mather, *The Autobiography of Increase Mather*, ed. M. G. Hall, *Publications of the American Antiquarian Society* 71 (October 1961), 341–2.

13. Urian Oakes, *The Unconquerable, All-Conquering, & more-then-Conquering Souldier* (Cambridge, MA: Samuel Green, 1674), 11; Joshua Moodey, *Souldiery Spiritualized* (Cambridge, MA: Samual Green, 1674), 7. See also, Joseph Belcher, *The Worst Enemy Conquered: A Brief Discourse on the Methods and Motives to Pursue A Victory over those Habits of Sin, Which War Against the Soul* (Boston: Bartholomew Green and John Allen, 1698); and Samuel Danforth, *The Duty of Believers to oppose the Growth of the Kingdom of SIN PRESSED* (Boston: John Allen, 1708). For background on the artillery sermons, see James A. Levernier, *Souldiery Spiritualized: Seven Sermons Preached*

Before the Artillery Companies of New England, 1674–1774 (Delmar, NY: Scholars' Facsimiles & Reprints, 1979).

14. Moodey, *Souldiery Spiritualized*, 9; Danforth, *The Duty of Believers*, 16; and "An Exhortation...," in *The Wall and the Garden: Selected Election Sermons 1670–1775*, ed. A. W. Plumstead (Minneapolis: University of Minnesota Press, 1968), 170.

15. Nathaniel Walter, *The Character of a Christian Hero* (Boston: J. Draper, 1746). For a mid-nineteenth-century discussion of Paul's life that makes the identical three-part division, see Edward N. Kirk, "Paul's Review of His Life," in *Discourses Doctrinal and Practical* (Boston: American Tract Society, 1860), 199–214. And for other Puritan uses of the Pauline sporting metaphors, see Thomas Shepard, *The Sincere Convert* (London: Thomas Pine, 1640); *Diary of Cotton Mather*, 2 vols. (New York: Frederick Ungar, n.d.), I, 43; and Jonathan Edwards, *Religious Affections*, ed. John E. Smith (New Haven, CT: Yale University Press, 1959), 100.

Chapter 4

1. Washington Gladden, *Live and Learn* (New York: Macmillan, 1914), 118.

2. Zebediah Flint, *Playing the Game* (New York: Fiscal Service Corporation, 1918), 7.

3. My overview of colonial religious history is drawn from many sources, most notably Sydney E. Ahlstrom's introduction to *Theology in America: The Major Protestant Voices from Puritanism to Neo-Orthodoxy* (Indianapolis, IN: Bobbs-Merrill, 1967), 23–107; Perry Miller, *The New England Mind: The Seventeenth Century* (1939; Boston: Beacon, 1961) and *The New England Mind: From Colony to Province* (1953; Boston: Beacon, 1961); Norman Pettit, *The Heart Prepared: Grace and Conversion in Puritan Spiritual Life* (New Haven, CT: Yale University Press, 1966); Edmund S. Morgan, *Visible Saints: The History of a Puritan Idea* (New York: New York University Press, 1963); Conrad Wright, *The Beginnings of Unitarianism in America* (Boston: Starr King Press, 1955); and Alan Heimert, *Religion and the American Mind: From the Great Awakening to the Revolution* (Cambridge, MA: Harvard University Press, 1966). On the later transformations of evangelicalism, see William G. McLoughlin, Jr., *Modern Revivalism: Charles Grandison Finney to Billy Graham* (New York: Ronald Press, 1959); William R. Hutchison, *The Modernist Impulse in American Protestantism* (Cambridge, MA: Harvard University Press, 1976); and Ferenc Morton Szasz, *The Divided Mind of Protestant America, 1800–1930* (University: University of Alabama Press, 1982).

4. Max Weber, *The Protestant Ethic and the Spirit of Capitalism*, trans. Talcott Parsons (1930; New York: Charles Scribner's Sons, 1956), 182.

5. Benjamin Colman, *The Government and Improvement of Mirth According to the Laws of Christianity* (Boston: B. Green, 1707), 76.

6. Cotton Mather, *A Christian at His Calling: Two Brief Discourses, One Directing a Christian in his General Calling; Another Directing him on his Personal Calling* (Boston: B. Green, 1701), 37.

7. In *The History of the Kingdom of Basaruah* (1715), for example, a Calvinist

allegory of man's fall and redemption, Joseph Morgan portrayed covenant theology as a business contract by which an accountant God absolved man of his debt, through his Son's restoration of the delinquent revenues to the celestial treasury. See Joseph Morgan, *The History of the Kingdom of Basaruah* (Cambridge, MA: Harvard University Press, 1946).

8. For a discussion of the morphology of conversion, see Morgan, *Visible Saints*. For examples of the morphology, see William Perkins, *A Treatise Tending unto a Declaration Whether a Man Be in the Estate of Damnation or in the Estate of Grace,* in *The Works of William Perkins,* ed. Ian Breward (1592; Appleford, Abingdon, Berkshire: Sutton Courtenay Press, 1970); Perkins, *A Golden Chaine,* in *Works;* William Ames, *Conscience with the Power and Cases Thereof* (1639; Amsterdam: Theatrum Orbis Terrarum and Walter J. Johnson, 1975); and Arthur Hildersam, *Lectures Upon the Fourth of John* (London: George Miller, 1629).

9. For records of confessions, see, for example, Thomas Shepard, *Confessions,* ed. George Selement and Bruce C. Woolley (Boston: Colonial Society of Massachusetts, 1981); and Michael Wigglesworth, "Diary," ed. Edmund S. Morgan (Boston: Colonial Society of Massachusetts, 1951). For representative spiritual autobiographies, see Donald E. Stanford, "Edward Taylor's 'Spiritual Relation,' " *American Literature* 35 (January 1964), 467–5; and Jonathan Edwards, "Personal Narrative," in *The Norton Anthology of American Literature,* ed. Ronald Gottesman, et al., 2 vols. (New York: W. W. Norton, 1979), I, 207–19; and for discussions of the genre see Sacvan Bercovitch, *The Puritan Origins of the American Self* (New Haven, CT: Yale University Press, 1975) and Daniel B. Shea, *Spiritual Autobiography in Early America* (Princeton, NJ: Princeton University Press, 1968). For captivity narratives that follow this pattern, see Mary Rowlandson, "A Narrative of the Captivity and Restoration of Mrs. Mary Rowlandson," in *Narratives of the Indian Wars, 1675–99,* ed. Charles H. Lincoln (New York: Charles Scribner's Sons, 1913), as well as the others in Lincoln's collection; Richard Van De Beets, ed., *Held Captive by Indians: Selected Narratives, 1642–1836* (Knoxville: University of Tennessee Press, 1984); and famous individual ones such as Jonathan Dickinson's *God's Protecting Providence* (Philadelphia: Reinier Janson, 1699) and John Williams' *The Redeemed Captive,* ed. Edward W. Clark (Amherst: University of Massachusetts Press, 1976).

10. See Joseph Campbell, *The Hero with a Thousand Faces* (New York: Pantheon, 1949).

11. See E. R. B. Whitehouse, *Table Games of Georgian and Victorian Days* (London: Peter Garnett, 1951); David Wallace Adams and Victor Edmonds, "Making Your Move: The Educational Significance of the American Board Game, 1832 to 1904," *History of Education Quarterly* 17 (Winter 1977), 359–83; Katherine Morrison McClinton, *Antiques of American Childhood* (New York: Clarkson N. Potter, 1970); and Joseph J. Schroeder, Jr., *The Wonderful World of Toys, Games & Dolls* (Chicago: Follett, 1971).

12. Benjamin Franklin, *The Autobiography of Benjamin Franklin* (New Haven, CT: Yale University Press, 1964), 164.

13. *Diary of Cotton Mather,* 2 vols. (New York: Frederick Ungar, n.d.), II, 144.

This entry is dated 23 December 1711. The model for all such instructional games was found in John Locke's writings on education.

14. Benjamin Franklin, "Morals of Chess," in *The Works of Benjamin Franklin*, 10 vols., ed. Jared Sparks (Boston: Hilliard, Gray, 1837–40), II, 188.

15. Sacvan Bercovitch, *The Puritan Origins of the American Self* (New Haven, CT: Yale University Press, 1975), 136.

16. My sampling of this literature includes Dorus Clarke, *Lectures to Young People of Manufacturing Villages* (Boston: Perkins and Marvin, 1836); [John Frost], *The Young Merchant* (Philadelphia: R. W. Pomeroy, 1839); John Todd, *The Foundations of Success* (Gettysburg, PA: H. C. Neinstedt, 1844); Henry Ward Beecher, *Lectures to Young Men, on Various Important Subjects* (1844; Salem, MA: J. P. Jewett, 1846); William A. Alcott, *The Young Man's Guide*, rev. ed. (Boston: T. R. Martin, 1850); Wm. Howard Van Doren, *Mercantile Morals; or, Thoughts for Young Men Entering Mercantile Life* (New York: Charles Scribner, 1852); William Arnot, *The Race for Riches, and Some of the Pits into Which the Runners Fall* (Philadelphia: Lippincott, Grambo, 1853); Edwin T. Freedley, *Practical Treatise on Business* (1853; New York: Arno Press, 1973); Freeman Hunt, *Worth and Wealth: A Collection of Maxims, Morals and Miscellanies for Merchants and Men of Business* (New York: Stringer and Townsend, 1857); and T. S. Arthur, *Advice to Young Men on Their Duties and Conduct in Life* (Philadelphia: J. W. Bradley, 1860).

17. Daniel Eddy, *The Young Man's Friend* (New York: Hurst & Company, 1865), 58. The differences between the two editions are discussed in Joseph F. Kett, *Rites of Passage: Adolescence in America, 1790 to the Present* (New York: Basic Books, 1977), 94, 163.

18. Hunt *Worth and Wealth*, 150–1.

19. Karen Haltunnen, *Confidence Men and Painted Women: A Study of Middle-Class Culture in America, 1830–1870* (New Haven, CT: Yale University Press, 1982), 20.

20. Hunt, *Worth and Wealth*, 49, 72, 252, 256, 396–7.

21. Louis B. Wright, "Franklin's Legacy to the Gilded Age," *Virginia Quarterly Review* 22 (1946), 274.

22. T. L. Haines, *Worth and Wealth; or, The Art of Getting, Saving and Using Money* (Chicago: Haines Brothers, 1883), 40, 105, and *passim.*

23. Haines, 663; see also Freedley, *Practical Treatise on Business,* 206.

24. See, for example, Horace Bushnell, "Our Best Weapons Gotten by Conquest" (1848) and "Death a Leveller of Distinction" (1850) in *The Spirit in Man: Sermons and Selections* (New York: Charles Scribner's Sons, 1903); and "How to Be a Christian in Trade" and "Our Advantage in Being Finite," both from 1876, in *Sermons on Living Subjects* (1876; New York: Charles Scribner's Sons, 1905).

25. See Henry Ward Beecher, "The Past and the Future," "Scope and Functions of a Christian Life," and "The Conflicts of Life," all in *The Original Plymouth Pulpit,* 10 vols. (Boston and Chicago: Pilgrim Press, 1869–73), II, 91–108; VIII, 127–46; and IX, 91–106.

26. Beecher's muscular Christianity is also evident in his essays on outdoor life, many of them collected in his *Star Papers.*

27. Lyman Abbott, "Christ's Secret of Happiness," *Outlook,* 22 September 1906, 235–37; and 29 September 1906, 268–70.

28. See, for example, Lyman Abbott, *Signs of Promise: Sermons Preached in Plymouth Pulpit, Brooklyn, 1887–9* (New York: Fords, Howard, & Hulbert, 1889), 55–7, 123, 294; and *Inspiration for Daily Living: Selections from the Writings of Lyman Abbott, D.D.* (Boston and Chicago: Pilgrim Press, 1919), 3, 79, 333. These volumes also include several examples of Abbott's martial metaphors.

29. Lyman Abbott, *The Life and Letters of Paul the Apostle* (Boston and New York: Houghton, Mifflin, 1898), 317; and "The Christian Life," in *The Life That Really Is* (New York: Wilbur B. Ketcham, 1899), 33.

30. Washington Gladden, *Plain Thoughts on the Art of Living: Designed for Young Men and Women* (Philadelphia: Henry T. Coates, 1868), 121, 127, 133.

31. For an echo of the earlier volume, see Washington Gladden, *Straight Shots at Young Men* (New York: Thomas Y. Crowell, 1900), 17–27.

32. See W. H. H. Murray, *Words Fitly Spoken: Selections from the Pulpit Utterances of W. H. H. Murray* (Boston: Lea and Shepard, 1873), 76; Wilbur F. Crafts, *Successful Men of To-Day and What They Say of Success* (1883; New York: Arno Press, 1973), 32; in the 10 volumes of Phillips Brooks' collected *Sermons* (New York: E. P. Dutton, 1910): "The Pillar in God's Temple" and "The Symmetry of Life" (vol. II), "The Battle of Life," "The Mystery of Iniquity," and "Whole Views of Life" (vol. VI), and "The Spiritual Struggle" (vol. IX); and William Lawrence, "The Relation of Wealth to Morals," *World's Work* 1 (1900–01), 286–92.

33. Richard Weiss, *The American Myth of Success: From Horatio Alger to Norman Vincent Peale* (New York: Basic Books, 1969), 98.

34. William Matthews, *Getting on in the World; or, Hints on Success in Life* (1872; Chicago: S. C. Griggs, 1878), 347. See also, James D. Mills, *The Art of Money Making; or, The Road to Fortune: A Universal Guide for Honest Success* (St. Louis and Boston: International, 1874); and John T. Dale, *The Secret of Success, or Finger Posts on the Highway of Life* (New York and Chicago: Fleming H. Revell, 1889).

35. William M. Thayer, *Tact, Push, and Principle* (1880; Boston: James H. Earle, 1888), 34, 143. This is the twenty-seventh edition in just eight years.

36. William Thayer, *Success and Its Achievers* (New York: Hurst & Company, 1893), 98.

37. For contemporary portraits of game-playing plutocrats, see, for example, Otto H. Hahn's admiring portrait of Edward Henry Harriman, in *Memoirs of Three Railroad Pioneers,* ed. Stuart Bruckey (New York: Arno Press, 1981), 2–5, 30–1; and the more typically negative portraits such as those in Alfred Henry Lewis, "Owners of America," *Cosmopolitan* 45 (1908), 259; Thorstein Veblen, *The Theory of the Leisure Class* (New York: Macmillan, 1911), 28; and Ida Tarbell, *The History of the Standard Oil Company,* 2 vols. (New York: McClure, Phillips, 1904), II, 292. In *The Theory of Business Enterprise* (1904), Veblen referred sardonically to the "gaming slang" with which businessmen described their transactions, reducing serious business to a mere sport. Henry Demarest Lloyd, in *Wealth Against Commonwealth* (1894), recognized that the language of games failed to differentiate honorable from dishonorable con-

tests. Echoing St. Paul in ways the prophets of business never did, Lloyd wrote: "It is a race to the bad, and the winners are the worst." See Thorstein Veblen, *The Theory of Business Enterprise* (New York: Charles Scribner's Sons, 1904), 33; Henry Demarest Lloyd, *Wealth Against Commonwealth* (Englewood Cliffs, NJ: Prentice-Hall, 1963), 159, 169, 163. The popular historian Frederick Lewis Allen characterized business in the Gilded Age as a "sort of endless game" in which "the standards of fair play were low." See Frederick Lewis Allen, *The Lords of Creation* (New York: Harper & Brothers, 1935), 4–5, 7. In their autobiographies, Henry Ford and John D. Rockefeller, on the other hand, explicitly distanced themselves from sporting rhetoric. See Henry Ford, *My Life and Work* (Garden City, NY: Garden City Publishing Company, 1922), 20, 58, 274; John D. Rockefeller, *Random Reminiscences of Men and Events* (1909; Garden City, NY: Doubleday, Doran, 1933), 133, 144.

38. See Theodore Dreiser, "Life Stories of Successful Men – No. 10," *Success* 1 (October 1898), reprinted in *Selected Magazine Articles of Theodore Dreiser* (Madison, NJ: Fairleigh Dickinson University Press, 1985), 120–9.

39. Andrew Carnegie, *The Gospel of Wealth and Other Essays* (1886; New York: Century, 1901), 64.

40. Andrew Carnegie, *The Empire of Business* (New York: Doubleday, Page, 1902), pp. 5, 88, 106, 110, 192, 207, 224.

41. T. J. Jackson Lears, "From Salvation to Self-Realization: Advertising and the Therapeutic Roots of the Consumer Culture, 1880–1930," in *The Culture of Consumption: Critical Essays in American History, 1880–1980,* ed. Richard Wrightman Fox and T. J. Jackson Lears (New York: Pantheon, 1983), 10.

42. On New Thought, see Weiss, *The American Myth of Success;* and Donald Meyer, *The Positive Thinkers: Religion as Pop Psychology from Mary Baker Eddy to Oral Roberts,* 2nd ed. (New York: Pantheon, 1980).

43. Elbert Hubbard, *The Book of Business* (East Aurora, NY: Roycrofters, 1913), 85–6.

44. Freedley, *Practical Treatise on Business,* 32; Henry Hardwicke, *The Art of Rising in the World* (New York: Useful Knowledge, 1896), x.

45. Erastus Wiman, *Chances of Success: Episodes and Observations in the Life of a Busy Man* (New York: American News Company, 1893), 284–5; Hardwicke, *The Art of Rising in the World,* xv.

46. Orison Swett Marden, *Pushing to the Front; or, Success Under Difficulties* (1894; New York: Success Company, 1897), 93, 192, 198, 235, 238, 306, 360.

47. Orison Swett Marden, *Little Visits with Great Americans, or Success Ideals and How to Attain Them* (New York: Success Company, 1905), 10–11.

48. Edward Chase Kirkland, *Dream and Thought in the Business Community, 1860–1900,* (Ithaca, NY: Cornell University Press, 1956), 8.

49. The literature on this period is vast. See, for example, Sean Dennis Cashman, *America in the Gilded Age: From the Death of Lincoln to the Rise of Theodore Roosevelt* (New York: New York University Press, 1984); Thomas S. Cochran and William Miller, *The Age of Enterprise: A Social History of Industrial America* (New York: Macmillan, 1942); Peter Conn, *The Divided Mind: Ideology and Imagination in America, 1898–1917* (Cambridge: Cambridge Uni-

versity Press, 1983); John Chamberlain, *The Enterprising Americans: A Business History of the United States*, new ed. (New York: Harper & Row, 1974); Kirkland, *Dream and Thought in the Business Community*; Richard Hofstadter, ed., *The Progressive Movement, 1900–1915* (Englewood Cliffs, NJ: Prentice-Hall, 1963); Robert H. Wiebe, *The Search for Order, 1877–1920* (New York: Hill and Wang, 1967); and Irvin G. Wyllie, *The Self-Made Man in America: The Myth of Rags to Riches* (New Brunswick, NJ: Rutgers University Press, 1954).

50. See, in particular, T. J. Jackson Lears, *No Place of Grace: Antimodernism and the Transformation of American Culture, 1880–1920* (New York: Pantheon, 1981), my chief source for the following discussion.

51. Robert C. Bannister, *Social Darwinism: Science and Myth in Anglo-American Social Thought* (Philadelphia: Temple University Press, 1979), 9.

52. Orison Swett Marden, *The Exceptional Employee* (New York: Crowell, 1913), x.

53. Steven R. Ross, *Workers on the Edge: Work, Leisure, and Politics in Industrializing Cincinnati, 1788–1890* (New York: Columbia University Press, 1985), xvi.

54. Hubbard, *The Book of Business*, 89.

55. See Ford, *My Life and Work*, 7; Carnegie, *The Empire of Business*, 7, 38. Success preachers such as Haines concurred; see *Worth and Wealth*, 34. A writer in *Century* magazine in 1884 discussed business gambling as one of the three dangers that most threatened society (together with intemperance and divorce). See "Business Gambling," *Century* 28 (1884), 629–30.

56. Daniel T. Rodgers, *The Work Ethic in Industrial America, 1850–1920* (Chicago: University of Chicago Press, 1978), 126.

Chapter 5

1. I make this claim on the basis of only a half-dozen Alger novels, but discussions of Alger's fiction by cultural historians suggest that the "game" was not consistent with his worldview.

2. Russel Nye, *The Unembarrassed Muse: The Popular Arts in America* (New York: Dial, 1970), 73–4.

3. Burt L. Standish [Patten's pseudonym], "Frank Merriwell on the Road; or, The All-Star Combination," *Tip Top Weekly*, no. 130, 8 October 1898, 5.

4. Standish, "Frank Merriwell in the Market; or, The Wolves of Wall Street," *Tip Top Weekly*, no. 611, 28 December 1907, 2.

5. Henry James, *The American* (Boston: Houghton Mifflin, 1877), 29.

6. See Theodore P. Greene, *America's Heroes: The Changing Model of Success in American Magazines* (New York: Oxford University Press, 1970).

7. Elizabeth Stuart Phelps, *The Silent Partner* (1871; Ridgewood, NJ: Gregg Press, 1967), 69, 245. Ellison's *Invisible Man* will be discussed in Chapter 8.

8. See Mark Twain and Charles Dudley Warner, *The Gilded Age*, in *Mark Twain's Works*, 25 vols. (New York: Harper & Brothers, 1899), X, 94, 97, 135, 149, 274, 330; XI, 91, 129, 139.

9. For representative game images in this fiction, see Robert Grant, *An Average Man* (Boston: James R. Osgood, 1884), 1; Maurice Thompson, *A Banker*

516 NOTES TO PP. 199–206

of Bankersville (1886; New York: Street & Smith, 1900), 96, 321–22; Amanda M. Douglas, *Hope Mills; or, Between Friend and Sweetheart* (Boston: Lee and Shepard, 1879), 260; C. M. Cornwall [Mary Abigail Roe], *Free, Yet Forging Their Own Chains* (New York: Dodd, Mead, 1876), 27, 63, 104, 132, 133, 196, 257, 286, 303; Rebecca Harding Davis, *John Andross* (New York: Orange Judd, 1874), 98; and [Ellen Kirk Warner], *Queen Money* (Boston: Ticknor, 1888), 187, 501–02, 503.

10. Josiah G. Holland, *Sevenoaks, A Story of To-Day* (1875; Upper Saddle River, NJ: Gregg Press, 1968), 147, 233, 432, 443, 455.

11. Walter Been Michaels, *The Gold Standard and the Logic of Naturalism: American Literature at the Turn of the Century* (Berkeley and Los Angeles: University of California Press, 1987), 40.

12. William Dean Howells, *The Rise of Silas Lapham*, in *Selected Edition of W. D. Howells*, 32 vols. (Bloomington: Indiana University Press, 1968–83), XII, 17, 142, 298, 312, 324.

13. William Dean Howells, *A Hazard of New Fortunes*, in *Selected Edition*, XVI, 13, 11, 335, 342, 375, 409, 484.

14. Letter, 1888, quoted in Robert Shulman, *Social Criticism and Nineteenth-Century Fictions* (Columbia: University of Missouri Press, 1987), 241.

15. See Charles Dudley Warner, *That Fortune: A Novel* (1899; Upper Saddle River, NJ: Literature House, 1970), 358; Robert Herrick, *The Man Who Wins* (New York: Charles Scribner's Sons, 1897), 122.

16. Herbert G. Gutman, *Work, Culture, and Society in Industrializing America: Essays in American Working-Class and Social History* (New York: Alfred A. Knopf, 1976).

17. See Greene, *America's Heroes*, which helped shape the following discussion.

18. Greene, 177–201.

19. "The Great Game," *Saturday Evening Post*, 30 June 1902, 2; Edwin Lefevre, "The Wall Street Game," *Saturday Evening Post*, 31 December 1904, 1–2.

20. Quoted in June Howard, *Form and History in American Literary Naturalism* (Chapel Hill: University of North Carolina Press, 1985), 74.

21. Edwin Lefevre, "The American Gambling Spirit," *Harper's Weekly*, 2 May 1903, 702–5. Lefevre is the same writer who wrote the more equivocal article on "the Wall Street Game" in the *Saturday Evening Post* a few months later – a fact that confirms a sense that confusion and uncertainty rather than clear consensus marked the age.

22. Lears, "From Salvation to Self-Realization," 10.

23. Upton Sinclair, *The Moneychangers* (New York: B. W. Dodge, 1908), 298; see also Frederic C. Howe, *The Confessions of a Monopolist* (1906; Upper Saddle River, NJ: Gregg Press, 1968), 111, 155.

24. See David Graham Phillips, *The Master-Rogue: The Confessions of a Croesus* (1903; Ridgewood, NJ: Gregg Press, 1968); Robert Herrick, *The Memoirs of an American Citizen* (1905; Cambridge, MA: Belknap Press of Harvard University Press, 1963); Thomas W. Lawson, *Friday, the 13th* (New York: Doubleday, Page, 1907); and William Allen White, *A Certain Rich Man* (New York: Macmillan, 1909).

25. See Will Payne, *On Fortune's Road: Stories of Business* (Chicago: A. C. McClurg, 1902).
26. Samuel Merwin, *The Short-Line War* (1899; Ridgewood, NJ: Gregg Press, 1967), 74.
27. Henry Kitchell Webster, *The Banker and the Bear: The Story of a Corner in Lard* (1900; Upper Saddle River, NJ: Gregg Press, 1968), 76, 339.
28. See Margaret Deland, *The Iron Woman* (New York: Harper & Brothers, 1911); and Edna Ferber's *Roast Beef, Medium: The Business Adventures of Emma McChesney* (New York: Frederick A. Stokes, 1913); *Personality Plus* (New York: Frederick A. Stokes, 1914); and *Emma McChesney & Co.* (New York: Frederick A. Stokes, 1915).
29. Frank Norris, *The Octopus* (New York: Doubleday, Page, 1901), 297–8, 319.
30. Frank Norris, *The Pit* (New York: Doubleday, Page, 1903), 86–7.
31. For an account of Dreiser's association with *Success,* see John F. Huth, Jr., "Theodore Dreiser, Success Monger," *Colophon,* n.s. 3 (Winter 1938), 120–33; and "Dreiser and Success: An Additional Note," *Colophon,* n.s. 3 (Summer 1938), 406–10. For examples of his writing for *Success,* see *Theodore Dreiser: A Selection of Uncollected Prose,* ed. Donald Pizer (Detroit, MI: Wayne State University Press, 1977); and Yoshinobu Hakutani, ed., *Selected Magazine Articles of Theodore Dreiser* (Rutherford, NJ: Fairleigh Dickinson University Press, 1985).
32. Theodore Dreiser, *The Financier* (New York: Harper & Brothers, 1912), 190.
33. Metaphors of the "game" abound in the novel. For references to business and political "games," see Theodore Dreiser, *The Titan* (New York: John Lane, 1914), 2, 25, 94, 95, 179, 298, 299, 330, 331, 378, 403, 416, 439, 483, 487, 517, 523, 531, 532, 548. For social and sexual "games," see 31, 60, 73, 105, 106, 447, 458, 460, 492, 499.
34. See Donald Pizer, ed., *Critical Essays on Theodore Dreiser* (Boston: G. K. Hall, 1981), x.

Chapter 6

1. Henry Ward Beecher, *The Original Plymouth Pulpit,* 10 vols. (Boston and Chicago: Pilgrim Press, 1869–73), II, 66–7.
2. Cynthia Griffin Wolff, *Emily Dickinson* (New York: Alfred A. Knopf, 1986), 88–9.
3. See Charles Grandison Finney, *Lectures on Revivals of Religion* (1835), ed. William G. McLoughlin (Cambridge, MA: Belknap Press of Harvard University Press, 1960), 59; P. C. Headley, ed., *The Reaper and the Harvest* (New York: Funk & Wagnalls, 1884), 26, 41; Heman Humphries, *Revival Sketches and Manual* (New York: American Tract Society, 1859), 341.
4. Richard Rabinowitz, *The Spiritual Self in Everyday Life: The Transformation of Personal Religious Experience in Nineteenth-Century New England* (Boston: Northeastern University Press, 1989).
5. See D. L. Moody, *Prevailing Prayer: What Hinders It?* (Chicago: F. H. Revell, 1884).
6. On the "battle" of life, see D. L. Moody, *The Overcoming Life and Other*

Sermons (New York and Chicago: Fleming H. Revell, 1896). For other sermons that lay out Moody's views on God and salvation, see *Glad Tidings. Comprising Sermons and Prayer-Meeting Talks Delivered at the N.Y. Hippodrome* (New York: E. B. Treat, 1876); *The Way to God and How to Find It* (Chicago and New York: Fleming H. Revell, 1884); and *Select Sermons* (Chicago and New York: Fleming H. Revell, 1897).

7. See Reverend "Billy" Sunday, *Burning Truths from Billy's Bat* (Philadelphia: Diamond Publishing Company, 1914), *passim;* and William T. Ellis, *"Billy" Sunday: The Man and His Message* (n.p.: L. T. Meyers, 1914), *passim.*

8. For the view of early American novels that follows, see Herbert Ross Brown, *The Sentimental Novel in America, 1789–1860* (Durham, NC: Duke University Press, 1940); and Henri Petter, *The Early American Novel* (Columbus: Ohio State University Press, 1971).

9. I. Mitchell, *The Asylum; or, Alonzo and Melissa* (Poughkeepsie, NY: J. Nelson, 1811), 132.

10. For an account of this transformation, see David S. Reynolds, *Faith in Fiction: The Emergence of Religious Literature in America* (Cambridge, MA: Harvard University Press, 1981).

11. James Butler, *Fortune's Foot-ball; or the Adventures of Mercutio*, 2 vols. (Harrisburg, PA: J. Wyeth, 1797–8).

12. William Hill Brown, *The Power of Sympathy; or, the Triumph of Nature* (1789; New Haven, CT: College & University Press, 1970), 95; *The History of Constantius and Pulchera; or, Virtue Rewarded* (1796; Exeter: W. C. & S. Hardy, Sawyer & Meder, 1831), 84; Charles Brockden Brown, *Arthur Mervyn; or, Memoirs of the Year 1793*, 2 vols. (1799–1800; Philadelphia: David McKay, 1887), I, 180; and *Edgar Huntly; or, Memoirs of a Sleepwalker* (1799; Philadelphia: David McKay, 1887), 81; and Royall Tyler, *The Algerine Captive; or, The Life and Adventures of Doctor Updike Underhill: Six Years a Prisoner Among the Algerines* (1797; New Haven, CT: College & University Press, 1970), 43, 222.

13. See George Lippard, *The Monks of Monk Hall* (New York: Odyssey Press, 1970), 416, 422 (the novel's original title was *The Quaker City; or, The Monks of Monk Hall*); Bret Harte, "The Outcasts of Poker Flat," in the *Argonaut Edition of the Works of Bret Harte,* 25 vols. (New York: P. F. Collier, 1899), VII, 20–1; A. D. T. Whitney, *Odd or Even?* (Boston: Houghton, Mifflin, 1881), 190; and Maurice Thompson, *A Banker of Bankersville* (1886; New York: Street & Smith, 1900), 267.

14. Herman Melville, *Moby-Dick or The Whale* (Evanston and Chicago: Northwestern University Press and The Newberry Library, 1988), 171.

15. Herman Melville, *Pierre; or, The Ambiguities* (Evanston and Chicago: Northwestern University Press and The Newberry Library, 1971), 182; "The Encantadas," in *The Piazza Tales and Other Prose Pieces, 1839–1860* (Evanston and Chicago: Northwestern University Press and The Newberry Library, 1987), 156.

16. Herman Melville, *The Confidence-Man: His Masquerade* (Evanston and Chicago: Northwestern University Press and The Newberry Library, 1984), 222, 55.

17. Melville annotated the story of Jacob at Peniel in his bible and used it in the poem "Art" as well. See Nathalia Wright, *Melville's Use of the Bible* (Durham, NC: Duke University Press, 1949), 10, 26.

18. Henry Wadsworth Longfellow, "The Song of Hiawatha," in *Longfellow's Works,* 11 vols. (Boston and New York: Houghton Mifflin, 1904), II, 159–68.

19. Merrell R. Davis and William H. Gilman, ed., *The Letters of Herman Melville* (New Haven, CT: Yale University Press, 1960), 124–5.

20. Herman Melville, *White-Jacket; or, The World in a Man of War* (Evanston and Chicago: Northwestern University Press and The Newberry Library, 1970), 105, 107, 110.

21. For the relevant passages that suggest the desperate game in *Pierre,* see 65–6, 182, 347.

22. See, for example, Edwin Fussell, *Frontier: American Literature and the American West* (Princeton, NJ: Princeton University Press, 1965).

23. For discussions of Melville and Calvinism, see William Braswell, *Melville's Religious Thought* (Durham, NC: Duke University Press, 1943); Lawrance Thompson, *Melville's Quarrel with God* (Princeton, NJ: Princeton University Press, 1952); Thomas Werge, "*Moby-Dick* and the Calvinist Tradition," *Studies in the Novel* 1 (1969), 484–506; T. Walter Herbert, Jr., *Moby-Dick and Calvinism: A World Dismantled* (New Brunswick, NJ: Rutgers University Press, 1977); and William H. Shurr, *Rappaccini's Children: American Writers in a Calvinist World* (Lexington: University Press of Kentucky, 1981).

24. Melville's most like-minded contemporary among American writers was Emily Dickinson, the age's other unread genius. Cynthia Griffin Wolff, Dickinson's recent biographer, has argued that Jacob's wrestle with the Lord was the central theme in both the life and the work of this "poet-pugilist." See Wolff, *Emily Dickinson,* 260–365.

25. See James L. Johnson, *Mark Twain and the Limits of Power: Emerson's God in Ruins* (Knoxville: University of Tennessee Press, 1982).

26. Mark Twain, *The Gilded Age,* in *Mark Twain's Works,* 25 vols. (New York: Harper & Brothers, 1899), XI, 259.

27. Mark Twain, *A Connecticut Yankee in King Arthur's Court,* ed. Bernard L. Stein (Berkeley and Los Angeles: University of California Press, 1983), 58, 233–5, 328, 392.

28. Mark Twain, *The Mysterious Stranger,* ed. William M. Gibson (Berkeley and Los Angeles: University of California Press, 1970), 115.

29. Ronald E. Martin, *American Literature and the Universe of Force* (Durham, NC: Duke University Press, 1981), xi.

30. Alexis de Tocqueville, *Democracy in America,* trans. George Lawrence, ed. J. P. Mayer (Garden City, NY: Anchor, 1969), 552–3.

31. James Bryce, *The American Commonwealth,* 2 vols. (New York: Macmillan, 1893–4), II, 661–2.

32. Henry B. Chafetz, *Play the Devil: A History of Gambling in the United States from 1492 to 1955* (New York: Clarkson N. Potter, 1960), 20–1. The details and anecdotes that follow come from Chafetz; Robert K. DeArment, *Knights of the Green Cloth: The Saga of the Frontier Gamblers* (Norman: University of

Oklahoma Press, 1982); and *The Gamblers,* by the editors of Time-Life Books (Alexandria, VA: Time-Life, 1978).

33. Chafetz, 361. See also John Dizikes, *Sportsmen and Gamesmen* (Boston: Houghton-Mifflin, 1981), 360; Edward Pessen, *Jacksonian America: Society, Personality, and Politics* (Homewood, IL: Dorsey Press, 1969), 14ff; and Daniel Boorstin, *The Americans: The National Experience* (New York: Random House, 1965), 103ff.

34. For the Adamses' excoriations of the gambling Gould, see Charles Francis Adams, Jr. and Henry Adams, *Chapters of Erie* (1886; Ithaca, NY: Great Seal Books, 1956), 2, 102, 104; the popular biography is [John Stuart Ogilvie], *Life and Death of Jay Gould and How He Made His Millions* (1892; New York: Arno Press, 1981). See 68, 152.

35. See, for example, Charles S. Peirce, *Chance, Love, and Logic: Philosophical Essays,* ed. Morris R. Cohen (1923; New York: Peter Smith, 1949). And on Peirce's "tychism," see Ian Hacking, "Nineteenth Century Cracks in the Concept of Determinism," *Journal of the History of Ideas* 44 (1983), 455.

36. Thorstein Veblen, *The Theory of the Leisure Class: An Economic Study of Institutions* (1899; New York: Macmillan, 1911), 277.

37. See Henry Adams, *The Education of Henry Adams: An Autobiography,* (1906; Boston and New York: Houghton Mifflin, 1918), 501; and William James, "The Dilemma of Determinism," in *The Will to Believe and Other Essays in Popular Philosophy,* bound with *Human Immortality: Two Supposed Objections to the Doctrine* (New York: Dover Publications, 1956), 181. James's essay was first published in 1884, the book in 1897. In a book titled *The Game of Life* in 1902, the writer Bolton Hall, a progressive critic of capitalist practices, used the same image in a less optimistic context, characterizing men and women as chess pieces in a game, unaware that they merely worked out some predetermined grand design that was not necessarily providential. See *The Game of Life* (New York: A. Wessels, 1902), 163–4.

38. See Louise Bryant, *The Game: A Morality Play,* in *Provincetown Plays: First Series* (New York: Frank Shay, 1916).

39. Frank Norris, *McTeague: A Story of San Francisco* (1899; Garden City, NY: Doubleday, Doran, 1928), 78.

40. Jack London, *A Daughter of the Snows* (Philadelphia: J. B. Lippincott, 1902), 58.

41. See, for example, "A Goboto Night" (1912) and "Shorty Dreams" (1912), both reprinted in *Sporting Blood: Selections from Jack London's Greatest Sports Writing,* ed. Howard Lachtman (Novato, CA: Presidio Press, 1981). Other writers frankly imitated these tales. See, for example, Lincoln Colcord's "The Game of Life and Death," in *The Game of Life and Death: Stories of the Sea* (1914; Freeport, NY: Books for Libraries, 1970), 1–30.

42. Jack London, *The Call of the Wild* (1903; New York: Macmillan, 1924), 39, 41 and 76 (two references to "fairplay"), 18.

43. Jack London, *The Sea-Wolf* (New York: Century, 1904), 132.

44. Jack London, *Burning Daylight* (1910; New York: Regent Press, n.d.), 6.

45. Martin, *American Literature and the Universe of Force,* 195.

46. Theodore Dreiser, *The Financier* (New York: Harper & Brothers, 1912), 409–10.

47. Recent criticism of Dreiser's fiction has repeatedly emphasized the workings of desire. See Rachel Bowlby, *Just Looking: Consumer Culture in Dreiser, Gissing, and Zola* (New York: Methuen, 1985); June Howard, *Form and History in American Literary Naturalism* (Chapel Hill: University of North Carolina Press, 1985); Philip Fisher, *Hard Facts: Setting and Form in the American Novel* (New York: Oxford University Press, 1985); and Walter Benn Michaels, *The Gold Standard and the Logic of Naturalism: American Literature at the Turn of the Century* (Berkeley and Los Angeles: University of California Press, 1987).

48. Theodore Dreiser, *Jennie Gerhardt* (New York: Harper & Brothers, 1911), 401.

49. Howard, *Form and History*, 49.

50. Theodore Dreiser, *Sister Carrie* (New York: Doubleday, Page, 1900), 83.

51. See Michaels' essay, "Action and Accident: Photography and Writing," in *The Gold Standard and the Logic of Naturalism*.

52. Edwin H. Cady, *Stephen Crane* (New York: Twayne, 1962), 101–02.

53. For a more detailed discussion of sport in *The Red Badge,* see Christian Messenger, *Sport and the Spirit of Play in American Fiction: Hawthorne to Faulkner* (New York: Columbia University Press, 1981), 143–6.

54. Stephen Crane, "The Monster," in *The University Edition of the Works of Stephen Crane,* 10 vols. (Charlottesville: University of Virginia Press, 1969–75), VII, 27.

55. Crane, "The Five White Mice," in *The University Edition,* V, 50. Michaels discusses this story in *The Gold Standard and the Logic of Naturalism,* emphasizing only the denial of chance.

56. Crane, "The Blue Hotel," in *The University Edition,* V, 142–3.

Part III

1. Quoted in William R. Hogan, "Sin and Sports," in *Motivations in Play, Games and Sports,* ed. Ralph Slovenko and James A. Knight (Springfield, IL: Charles C. Thomas, 1967), 136–7.

2. See Sinclair Lewis, *Babbitt* (New York: Harcourt, Brace, 1922), 98–9; and *Elmer Gantry* (New York: Harcourt, Brace, 1927), 45; Ring Lardner (with George S. Kaufman), *June Moon* (New York: Charles Scribner's Sons, 1930), 63; *Lose with a Smile* (New York: Charles Scribner's Sons, 1933), 79; and *The Real Dope* (Indianapolis, IN: Bobbs-Merrill, 1919), 56, 69–73, 80–1, 99; Thomas Wolfe, *The Web and the Rock* (New York: Sun Dial Press, 1940), 199–200; and Lisa Alther, *Kinflicks* (New York: Alfred A. Knopf, 1976), 39ff.

3. The relations of sport and fundamentalist Christianity are discussed by Frank Deford in "Religion in Sport," a three-part series in *Sports Illustrated,* April 19, April 26, and May 3, 1976. For recent books of athletes' testimonials, see Rick Arndt, *Winning with Christ* (St. Louis, MO: Concorida Publishing House, 1982); Dallas Groten, *Winning Isn't Always 1st Place* (Minneapolis,

MN: Bethany House, 1983); and Vincent Bove, *And on the Eighth Day God Created the Yankees* (Plainfield, NJ: Logos International, 1981) and *Playing His Game* (South Plainfield, NJ: Bridge Publishing, 1984).

4. See Ernest Hemingway, *Green Hills of Africa* (New York: Charles Scribner's Sons, 1935), 20; Frederick L. Gwynn and Joseph L. Blotner, ed., *Faulkner in the University* (Charlottesville: University of Virginia Press, 1959), 15, 50, 243.

5. On the physical sciences, see Gerald Holton, "Introduction: Einstein and the Shaping of Our Imagination," in *Albert Einstein: Historical and Cultural Perspectives,* ed. Gerald Holton and Yehuda Elkana (Princeton, NJ: Princeton University Press, 1982), vii–xxxii; James Gleick, *Chaos: Making of a New Science* (New York: Viking, 1987); and Paul Feyerabend, *Against Method: Outline of an Anarchistic Theory of Knowledge* (London: NLB, 1975). On the biological sciences, see John Beatty, "Chance and Natural Selection," *Philosophy of Science* 51 (June 1984), 183–211; Jeffrey S. Wicken, "Chance, Necessity, and Purpose: Toward a Philosophy of Evolution," *Zygon* 16 (December 1981), 303–22; and Kenneth G. Denbigh, "Time and Chance," *Diogenes* no. 89 (Spring 1975), 1–20. The image of a game has even crept into highly intellectual discussions of these matters; see, for example, A. R. Peacocke, "Chance and the Life Game," *Zygon* 14 (December 1979), 301–22; Jacques Monod, *Chance and Necessity: An Essay on the Natural Philosophy of Modern Biology,* trans. Austryn Wainhouse (New York: Alfred A. Knopf, 1971); and Manfred Eigen and Ruthild Winkler, *Laws of the Game: How the Principles of Nature Govern Chance,* trans. Robert and Rita Kimber (New York: Alfred A. Knopf, 1981).

6. Interview in *Anything Can Happen: Interviews with Contemporary American Novelists* (Urbana and Chicago: University of Illinois Press, 1983), 81.

7. See, for example, Barbara Babcock, "Fair Play: Evidence Favorable to an Accused and Effective Assistance of Counsel," *Stanford Law Review* 34 (1982), 1133–82; Arthur Allen Leff, "Law and," *Yale Law Journal* 87 (April 1978), 989–1011; and William J. Brennan, Jr., "The Criminal Prosecution: Sporting Event or Quest for Truth?" *Washington University Law Quarterly* 1963 (1963), 279–95.

Chapter 7

1. Twelve Southerners, *I'll Take My Stand* (1930; New York: Harper & Row, 1962), xxii, xxv, xxix; and see in the individual essays John Crowe Ransom, "Reconstructed but Unregenerate," 12, 13; Stark Young, "Not in Memoriam, but in Defense," 350; Andrew Nelson Lytle, "The Hind Tit," 202, 212, 229–34; Donald Davidson, "A Mirror for Artists," 34–5.

2. See Thomas Lomax Hunter, *Columns from the Cavalier* (Richmond, VA: Dietz Press, 1935), 96–9, 123–26; William Alexander Percy, *Lanterns on the Levee: Recollections of a Planter's Son* (New York: Alfred A. Knopf, 1941), 46, 49; and W. J. Cash, *The Mind of the South* (New York: Alfred A. Knopf, 1941), 95, 150, 384.

3. See Stark Young, *So Red the Rose* (New York: Charles Scribner's Sons,

1934); and Donald Davidson, *The Attack on Leviathan: Regionalism and Nationalism in the United States* (1938; Gloucester, MA: Peter Smith, 1962), particularly Chapter Four, "Still Rebels, Still Yankees," 131–54.

4. Caroline Gordon, *Aleck Maury, Sportsman* (1934; Carbondale and Edwardsville: Southern Illinois University Press, 1980), 211, 215.
5. See Young, *So Red the Rose,* 49, 225; and Andrew Nelson Lytle, *Bedford Forrest and His Critter Company* (New York: Minton, Balch, 1931), particularly the incident when Forrest bluffs a Colonel Streight in a game of military poker (173–6). Lytle's treatment of the scene recalls the humorous 1866 account by Charles Henry Smith in *Bill Arp, So Called, A Side Show of the Southern Side of the War* (1866; Upper Saddle River, NJ: Literature House, 1970), 39.
6. William Faulkner, *Light in August* (New York: Harrison Smith and Robert Haas, 1932), 458.
7. William Faulkner, *Sartoris* (1929; New York: Harcourt, Brace, 1951), 9.
8. William Faulkner, *Absalom, Absalom!* (New York: Random House, 1936), 345–6.
9. For the hunting/soldiering motif, see Caroline Gordon, *None Shall Look Back* (New York: Charles Scribner's Sons, 1937), 78, 81, 234, 242, 245, 251, 367.
10. Caroline Gordon, *Green Centuries* (New York: Charles Scribner's Sons, 1941), 469.
11. See Bobbie Ann Mason, "Shiloh," in *Shiloh and Other Stories* (New York: Harper & Row, 1982); Ellen Gilchrist, "Rich," in *In the Land of Dreamy Dreams* (Boston: Little Brown, 1981); and Elizabeth Hardwick, *Sleepless Nights* (New York: Random House, 1979), 91.
12. Margaret Walker, *Jubilee* (Boston: Houghton, Mifflin, 1966), 102, 137, 141, 138.
13. See Allen Tate, *The Fathers* (1938; Chicago: Swallow Press, 1974), 43–4, 167, 185; and Robert Penn Warren, *All the King's Men* (New York: Harcourt, Brace, 1946), 52, 90, 106–7, 147, 352, 359–60, 367, 377, 439.
14. See Shelby Foote, *Tournament* (New York: Dial Press, 1949), xviii, 93, 204; and Andrew Lytle, *The Velvet Horn* (New York: McDowell, Obolensky, 1957), 17, 362.
15. If we include Texas in the South, a study in 1974 revealed that five Southern states, Mississippi, Louisiana, Texas, Alabama, and Georgia, led in the per capita production of players for the NFL. See John F. Rooney, *A Geography of American Sport* (Reading, MA: Addison-Wesley, 1974), 134. In *Myth, Media, and the Southern Mind* (Fayetteville: University of Arkansas Press, 1985), Stephen A. Smith gives brief attention to sport's particular appeal in the South. See 108–110.
16. John Fox, Jr., *The Heart of the Hills* (1913; New York: A. L. Burt, n.d.), pp. 25, 199.
17. For a more detailed discussion of Labove, see Christian Messenger, *Sport and the Spirit of Play: Hawthorne to Faulkner* (New York: Columbia University Press, 1981), 218–24. Messenger discusses Labove in the context of the school-sports tradition.
18. Frank Deford, *Everybody's All-American* (New York: Viking Press, 1981), 9.

The narrator, Donald McClure, grows up to be a Southern historian and biographer of Stuart, beginning several chapters with scenes from Stuart's wartime exploits out of John Esten Cooke.

19. James Whitehead, *Joiner* (New York: Alfred A. Knopf, 1971), 24, 34.
20. Barry Hannah, *The Tennis Handsome* (New York: Alfred A. Knopf, 1983), 7.
21. Harry Crews, *A Feast of Snakes* (New York: Atheneum, 1976), 18, 176.
22. Rex Beach, *The Spoilers* (New York: Harper & Brothers, 1905), 10; Clarence E. Mulford, *Hopalong Cassidy* (1910; New York: Grosset & Dunlap, n.d.), 89; Zane Grey, *Riders of the Purple Sage* (1912; New York: Pocket Books, 1980), 189; Stewart Edward White, *Gold* (Garden City, NY: Doubleday, Page, 1913), 149; Eugene Manlove Rhodes, *Bransford in Arcadia* (1914; Norman: University of Oklahoma Press, 1975), 175.
23. In addition to the novels just cited, see, for example, Frank H. Spearman, *Whispering Smith* (New York: Charles Scribner's Sons, 1906); Emerson Hough, *54–40 or Fight* (1909; New York: A. L. Burt, n.d.) and *The Covered Wagon* (New York: D. Appleton, 1922); Stewart Edward White, *The Rules of the Game* (1910; New York: Grosset & Dunlap, n.d.); William MacLeod Raine, *A Texas Ranger* (1911; New York: Grosset & Dunlap, n.d.); Charles Alden Seltzer, *The Coming of the Law* (1912; New York: A. L. Burt, n.d.); Zane Grey, *The U. P. Trail* (1918; New York: Grosset & Dunlap, n.d.), *The Code of the West* (1923; New York: Grosset & Dunlap, n.d.) and *"Nevada": A Romance of the West* (1928; New York: Grosset & Dunlap, n.d.); Eugene Manlove Rhodes, *Stepsons of Light* (1921; Norman: University of Oklahoma Press, 1969) and *The Proud Sheriff* (1935; Norman: University of Oklahoma Press, 1968).
24. Raine, *A Texas Ranger*, 20; Rhodes, *Bransford in Arcadia*, 131; Seltzer, *The Coming of the Law*, 260.
25. See, for example, *Gold*, 11; *Hopalong Cassidy*, 43; *A Texas Ranger*, 174, 233, 317.
26. See White, *The Rules of the Game;* Larry Evans, *Winner Take All* (New York: H. K. Fly, 1920); Seltzer, *The Coming of the Law;* and Brand, *The Gambler.* In addition to his Westerns, Zane Grey wrote three volumes of baseball stories (*The Short-Stop* [1909], *The Young Pitcher* [1911], and *The Red-Headed Outfield and Other Baseball Stories* [1920]), while Rhodes's cowboys in *Stepsons of Light* actually play baseball. From the opposite perspective, baseball in particular has connections to the Western myth (as football does to the Southern). The classic baseball novel of recent decades – Bernard Malamud's *The Natural* (1952), Mark Harris's *The Southpaw* (1953), and W. P. Kinsella's *Shoeless Joe* (1982), for example – has been in some ways an urban Western.
27. See *The Spoilers*, 2; *The Coming of the Law*, 69; *Gold*, 190; and *The Covered Wagon*, 163.
28. In the novels by Spearman, Mulford, Raine, Grey, and Rhodes, the hero's willingness to grant an adversary an "even break" absolves him of any crime or moral lapse. Sometimes, as in the case of *Hopalong Cassidy*, this fairness marked the superiority of the Anglo-Saxon to the scurrilous foreign-born,

a Mexican in this case. More routinely, it simply distinguished the hero from his bushwhacking enemies.

29. John A. Dinan, *The Pulp Western: A Popular History of the Western Fiction Magazine in America* (San Bernardino, CA: Borgo Press, 1983), 34.

30. See Bernard A. Drew, Martin H. Greenberg, and Charles B. Waugh, *Western Series and Sequels: A Reference Guide* (New York: Garland, 1986).

31. See B. M. Bower, *Chip, of the Flying U* (1904; New York: G. W. Dillingham, 1906), 128–9, 157, 161–2, 227–8, 262; and *Flying U Ranch* (1912; New York: Grosset & Dunlap, n.d.), 238, 251.

32. Edna Ferber, *Cimarron* (Garden City, NY: Doubleday, Doran, 1930), 126, 164.

33. For examples of this rhetoric in particularly significant contexts, see Max Brand, *Destry Rides Again* (1930; New York: Pocket Books, 1980), 97, 189, 203–4; Ernest Haycox, *Trouble Shooter* (1937; New York: New American Library, 1975), 144, 11, 197–9; E. B. Mann, *Killers' Range* (1933; New York: Triangle Books, 1943), 231–2; Luke Short, *The Feud at Single Shot* (1936; New York: Bantam, 1976), 162; and Ernest Haycox, *The Wild Bunch* (1943; New York: New American Library, 1979), 46.

34. See Louis L'Amour, *The First Fast Draw* (New York: Bantam, 1959), 129; *The Quick and the Dead* (New York: Bantam, 1973), 7.

35. Zeke Masters, *Inside Straight* (New York: Pocket Books, 1982), 170–1. Another hero in a series of racy paperback originals, Chance Sharpe, is a gambler but in the sportsman's tradition, declaring his code, "whether at cards or dealing with his fellow men," to be "as simple as the words *fair play*." See Clay Tanner, *Chance* (New York: Avon, 1986), 27. As always, generalizations must acknowledge exceptions.

36. For a discussion of the fiction by women who wrote of the plains, see Carol Fairbanks, *Prairie Women: Images in American and Canadian Fiction* (New Haven, CT: Yale University Press, 1986). A seeming exception, Elizabeth Madox Roberts's *The Great Meadow*, embraces elements of the male myth but foregrounds a complementary women's role in the winning of the West. See *The Great Meadow* (New York: Viking, 1930).

37. See Reed's absurdist *Yellow Back Radio Broke-Down* (1969) and West's Earle Shoop, the Hollywood cowboy in *The Day of the Locust* (1939) poaching quail in a parody of Western sport, and his Pike County Man in *A Cool Million* (1934), a parody of the rip-snortin', ringtailed roarin' frontiersman. The narrator of Berger's *Little Big Man* reports his father's hilarious views on Western "sport" (New York: Dial Press, 1964, 2), and Burroughs' *The Place of Dead Roads* (1983) offers surreal burlesque of many elements in the tradition. Doctorow exploded the sporting myth altogether in scenes of unalloyed viciousness redeemed by no play at all, either fair or foul. Sporting rhetoric and its values are conspicuous only in their absence.

38. See Wallace Stegner, "History, Myth, and the Western Writer," in *The Sound of Mountain Water* (Garden City, NY: Doubleday, 1969).

39. See Frederick Manfred, *Lord Grizzly* (1954; New York: Gregg Press, 1980), 86; A. B. Guthrie, *The Big Sky* (New York: William Sloane Associates,

1949), *passim* (the novel is rich in sporting motifs); Don Berry, *Trask* (New York: Viking, 1960), esp. 8, 81–2, 85, 273, 368–9, 373; Vardis Fisher, *Mountain Man: A Novel of Male and Female in the Early American West* (Boise, ID: Opal Laurel Holmes, 1965), 6, 12, 220–1, 232.

40. Larry McMurtry, *Lonesome Dove* (New York: Simon and Schuster, 1985), 326.

41. Warren I. Susman, *Culture as History: The Transformation of American Society in the Twentieth Century* (New York: Pantheon, 1984), 171.

42. Raymond Chandler, *The Big Sleep* (1939; New York: Vintage Books, 1976), 61; Robert Leslie Bellem, "Death's Passport," in *The Pulps,* ed. Tony Goodstone (New York: Chelsea House, 1970), 119. For a sampling of Bellem's Hollywood Dan Turner stories, see John Wooley, ed., *Robert Leslie Bellem's Dan Turner, Hollywood Detective* (Bowling Green, OH: Bowling Green University Popular Press, 1983).

43. For some of their predecessors, see *The Hard-Boiled Detective: Stories from Black Mask Magazine, 1920–1951,* ed. Herbert Ruhm (New York: Vintage Books, 1977).

44. Susman, *Culture as History,* 168.

45. Raymond Chandler, *The High Window* (1942; New York: Vintage Books, 1976), 161; Dashiell Hammett, "The Whosis Kid," in *The Continental Op,* ed. Steven Marcus (1974; New York: Vintage Books, 1975), 225.

46. Chandler, *The Big Sleep,* 199.

47. Raymond Chandler, *Farewell, My Lovely* (1946; New York: Vintage Books, 1976), 196, 246.

48. See *The Red Harvest* (1929; New York: Vintage Books, 1972); *The Maltese Falcon* (1930; New York: Vintage Books, 1972); and *The Glass Key* (1931; New York: Vintage Books, 1972).

49. For a representative selection of novels in which sporting rhetoric figures, see James M. Cain, *The Postman Always Rings Twice* (1934), and *Double Indemnity* (1943); Richard Hallas [Eric Mowbray Knight], *You Play the Black and the Red Comes Up* (1938); Mickey Spillane, *I, the Jury* (1947); Ross Macdonald, *The Drowning Pool* (1950) and *The Blue Hammer* (1976); John D. MacDonald, *Bright Orange for the Shroud* (1965); Robert B. Parker, *Mortal Stakes* (1975), and virtually all of his novels; and Elmore Leonard, *Bandits* (1987). Of these writers, Spillane and Parker used sporting rhetoric most liberally.

50. See John Barth, *The Sot-Weed Factor* (Garden City, NY: Doubleday & Company, 1960), 18–19, 181; Ralph Ellison, *Invisible Man* (New York: Random House, 1952), 118; Saul Bellow, *The Adventures of Augie March* (New York: Viking, 1953), 536.

51. All of these novels are richly textured with sporting rhetoric and actual sport. See James Jones, *From Here to Eternity* (New York: Charles Scribner's Sons, 1951); Ken Kesey, *One Flew Over the Cuckoo's Nest* (New York: Viking, 1962); James Dickey, *Deliverance* (Boston: Houghton Mifflin, 1970); and William Kennedy, *Billy Phelan's Greatest Game* (1978; New York: Penguin, 1983). The quotation from *Billy Phelan* is from 200.

52. See Barth, *The Sot-Weed Factor,* 641–2; Thomas Pynchon, *V.* (Philadel-

phia: J. B. Lippincott, 1963), 111–23; and Thomas McGuane, *The Sporting Club* (New York: Simon and Schuster, 1968).

Chapter 8

1. Larry E. Grimes, in *The Religious Design of Hemingway's Early Fiction* (Ann Arbor, MI: UMI Research Press, 1985), similarly connects the game to Hemingway's religious outlook, but our two versions of this matter are extremely different. Grimes connects play (Huizinga) with the sacred (Otto, Eliade), does not distinguish play from game, and argues that winning and losing are not important in Hemingway's scheme. In general, Grimes argues for an existentialist reading of Hemingway's religious play; in particular, he reads *The Sun Also Rises* and *A Farewell to Arms* in radically different ways from mine. See also Christian Messenger's discussion of ritual sport in Hemingway's novels, in *Sport and the Spirit of Play: Hawthorne to Faulkner* (New York: Columbia University Press, 1981), Chapter 10.

2. For a discussion that focuses on fishing, see Gregory S. Sojka, *Ernest Hemingway: The Angler as Artist* (New York: Peter Lang, 1985).

3. Ernest Hemingway, *Death in the Afternoon* (New York: Charles Scribner's Sons, 1932), 96.

4. For the development of Cohn's amateur code, see Ernest Hemingway, *The Sun Also Rises* (New York: Charles Scribner's Sons, 1926), 3–4.

5. See Ernest Hemingway, *For Whom the Bell Tolls* (New York: Charles Scribner's Sons, 1940), 103ff., 183ff., 383, 405.

6. Ernest Hemingway, *The Old Man and the Sea* (New York: Charles Scribner's Sons, 1952), 103. The earlier quotation is from 102.

7. Ernest Hemingway, *A Farewell to Arms* (New York: Charles Scribner's Sons, 1929), 327.

8. See Sandra Spanier's similar Catherine-centered reading in "Catherine Barkley and the Hemingway Code: Ritual and Survival in *A Farewell to Arms*," in *Modern Critical Interpretations: "A Farewell to Arms,"* ed. Harold Bloom (New York: Chelsea House, 1987), 131–48.

9. William Faulkner, *Soldier's Pay* (New York: Liveright, 1926), 307.

10. William Faulkner, *Sartoris* (New York: Harcourt, Brace, 1929), 320.

11. William Faulkner, *The Sound and the Fury,* bound with *As I Lay Dying* (New York: Modern Library, 1946), 196.

12. All of these stories appear in Faulkner's *Collected Stories* (New York: Random House, 1950).

13. William Faulkner, *The Hamlet* (New York: Random House, 1940), 59, 30, 138, 211–12. John T. Matthews, in *The Play of Faulkner's Language* (Ithaca, NY: Cornell University Press, 1982), argues that the world of play in *The Hamlet* reveals "the foundation of human ethics as arbitrary and uncentered" (164). I am claiming rather that play is centered in Southern myth and tradition, to whose power Flem is immune. As the title of Matthews's book suggests, he is chiefly interested in different matters than the ones I discuss, aesthetics rather than ethics.

14. William Faulkner, *The Town* (New York: Random House, 1957), 347–8.

15. William Faulkner, *The Mansion* (New York: Random House, 1959), 430. References to the game between Flem and Mink, and Flem and Linda, occur on 69, 98, and 370.

16. William Faulkner, *Absalom, Absalom!* (New York: Random House, 1936), 160–1, 165, 226ff., 8.

17. William Faulkner, *Light in August* (New York: Harrison Smith & Robert Haas, 1932), 90, 400, 414.

18. The fact that this devastating scene is described in game images has seemed to many readers to trivialize the human lives involved. See Wyndham Lewis, *Men Without Art* (1934; New York: Russell & Russell, 1964), 42–64; Irving Howe, *William Faulkner: A Critical Study* (1952; New York: Vintage, 1962), 145–6; and Alfred Kazin, "The Stillness of *Light in August*," in *Faulkner: A Collection of Critical Essays,* ed. Robert Penn Warren (Englewood Cliffs, NJ: Prentice-Hall, 1966), 159.

19. See Shirley Jackson: "The Lottery," *The New Yorker,* 26 June 1948, 25–8.

20. Robert E. Sherwood, *Idiot's Delight* and William Saroyan, *The Time of Your Life,* both in *Famous American Plays of the 1930s,* ed. Harold Clurman (New York: Dell, 1959), 253, 389. For these references I am indebted to Warren Susman, *Culture as History: The Transformation of American Society in the Twentieth Century* (New York: Pantheon, 1984), 163.

21. See Joan Didion, *Play It as It Lays* (New York: Farrar, Straus & Giroux, 1970), 214; Norman Mailer, *The Executioner's Song* (Boston: Little, Brown, 1979), 359, 690; William S. Burroughs, *The Place of Dead Roads* (London: John Calder, 1983), 11.

22. See Jerzy Kosinski, *Cockpit* (Boston: Houghton Mifflin, 1975), 148; *Blind Date* (Boston: Houghton Mifflin, 1977), 213; *Passion Play* (New York: St. Martin's Press, 1979), 33, 271, and *passim*; and *Pinball* (New York: Bantam, 1982), 279, 287.

23. Geoffrey Green, "The Nightmarish Quest of Jerzy Kosinski," in *The Anxious Subject: Nightmares and Daymares in Literature and Film,* ed. Moshe Lazar (Malibu, CA: Undena, 1983), 53.

24. For the novels' sporting metaphors, see Joseph Heller, *Catch-22* (New York: Simon and Schuster, 1961), 178; Kurt Vonnegut, Jr., *Cat's Cradle* (New York: Delacorte/Seymour Lawrence, 1963), 116–17; *Slaughterhouse-Five, or The Children's Crusade* (New York: Delacorte/Seymour Lawrence, 1969), 140; *Breakfast of Champions, or Goodbye Blue Monday* (New York: Delacorte/Seymour Lawrence, 1973), 254–63; and *Slapstick, or Lonesome No More* (New York: Delacorte/Seymour Lawrence, 1976), 230.

25. See Robert Coover, *The Universal Baseball Association, J. Henry Waugh, Prop.* (New York: Random House, 1968).

26. Thomas Pynchon, *Gravity's Rainbow* (New York: Viking Press, 1973), 56, 96, 209.

27. On aleatory music and art, see Michael Nyman, *Experimental Music: Cage and Beyond* (New York: Schirmer Books, 1974); Peter Gena, "Freedom in experimental music: the New York revolution," *Triquarterly* no. 52 (Fall 1981), 223–43; Alan Tormey, "Indeterminacy and Identity in Art," *Monist* 58 (1974), 203–15; and George Brecht, "Chance-Imagery," in *Esthetics Contemporary,* ed.

Richard Kostelanetz (Buffalo, NY: Prometheus Books, 1978), 116–27. On aleatory poetry and fiction, see Jackson Mac Low, "The Poetics of Chance & the Politics of Simultaneous Spontaneity, or the Sacred Heart of Jesus (Revised and Abridged)," in *Talking Poetics from Naropa Institute,* ed. Anne Waldman and Marilyn Webb (Boulder, CO: Shambhala, 1978), 171–92; Frank Kermode, *Continuities* (London: Routledge & Kegan Paul, 1968), 10–27; and Marjorie Perloff, *The Poetics of Indeterminacy: Rimbaud to Cage* (Princeton, NJ: Princeton University Press, 1981). The best known aleatoric novels are non-American: Julio Cortázar's *Hopscotch* and Marc Saporta's *Composition No. 1,* for example, but American writers have also contributed to this attempt to erase the determinate author. See William S. Burroughs's "cut-up" experiments in *The Soft Machine* (1961; New York: Grove, 1966); *The Ticket That Exploded* (1962; New York: Grove, 1967); and *Nova Express* (New York: Grove, 1964); as well as Ronald Sukenick, *The Death of the Novel and Other Stories* (New York: Dial Press, 1969); Raymond Federman, *Double or Nothing: a real fictitious discourse* (Chicago: Swallow Press, 1971); and Gilbert Sorrentino, *Mulligan Stew* (New York: Grove Press, 1979). For an excellent essay on this subject, see John Kuehl, "The Ludic Impulse of Recent American Fiction," *Journal of Narrative Technique* 16 (Fall 1986), 167–78.

28. Allen Thiher, *Words in Reflection: Modern Language Theory and Postmodern Fiction* (Chicago: University of Chicago Press, 1984), 157.

29. Ken Kesey, *Sometimes a Great Notion* (New York: Viking, 1964), 109. Both of Kesey's novels, as well as Jones's and Morris's *The Huge Season* (1954) are rich in the sporting rhetoric and themes of the desperate game.

30. For several versions of this contest, see the pervasive sporting imagery in *The Naked and the Dead* (New York: Rinehart, 1948); *Advertisements for Myself* (New York: G. P. Putnam's Sons, 1959), 20, 349; *The Presidential Papers* (New York: G. P. Putnam's Sons, 1963), 269; *The Armies of the Night* (New York: New American Library, 1968), 206, 211.

31. For the sporting imagery in "Time of Her Time," see *Advertisements,* 490, 492, 503. It was these ideas that brought down the wrath of Kate Millett, Germaine Greer, Mary Ellmann, and other feminists on a strangely puzzled Mailer in the early seventies, and his additionally self-indicting response in *The Prisoner of Sex* (1971).

32. See for example Mailer's self-characterizations of himself as a pugilist-writer in *Advertisements for Myself,* 22; and in *Pieces and Pontifications* (Boston: Little, Brown, 1922), 161. For his most notable writing on professional boxing, see "Ten Thousand Words a Minute," in *Presidential Papers;* "King of the Hill," in *Existential Errands* (Boston: Little, Brown, 1972); and *The Fight* (Boston: Little, Brown, 1975).

33. Norman Mailer, "The White Negro," in *Advertisements for Myself,* 339, 348.

34. Norman Mailer, *Why Are We in Vietnam?* (New York: G. P. Putnam's Sons, 1967), 203.

35. See Ralph Ellison, *Shadow and Act* (New York: Random House, 1964), 140.

36. See Robert B. Stepto, *From Behind the Veil: A Study of Afro-American Narrative* (Urbana and Chicago: University of Illinois Press, 1979); Michael G. Cooke, *Afro-American Literature in the Twentieth Century: The Achievement of Inti-*

macy (New Haven, CT: Yale University Press, 1984); Keith E. Byerman, *Fingering the Jagged Grain: Tradition and Form in Recent Black Fiction* (Athens: University of Georgia Press, 1985); Bernard W. Bell, *The Afro-American Novel and Its Tradition* (Amherst: University of Massachusetts Press, 1987); and Henry Louis Gates, Jr., *The Signifying Monkey: A Theory of Afro-American Literary Criticism* (New York: Oxford University Press, 1988).

37. See Chester Himes, *If He Hollers Let Him Go* (Garden City, NY: Doubleday & Company, 1946), 45; James Alan McPherson, *Hue and Cry* (Boston: Little, Brown, 1969); John Edgar Wideman, *Sent for You Yesterday* (New York: Avon, 1983), 18 and *passim*.

38. Cooke, *Afro-American Literature in the Twentieth Century*, 26; Byerman, *Fingering the Jagged Grain*, 105. See Chestnutt's stories in *The Conjure Woman* (1899) and Cooke's brief discussion of them.

39. Barry Beckham, *Runner Mack* (New York: Morrow, 1972), 85.

40. Richard Wright, *Native Son* (New York: Harper & Brothers, 1940), 11, 15, 250–1, 299.

41. Sam Greenlee, *The Spook Who Sat by the Door* (1969; NY: Bantam, 1970), 189, 235, 246.

42. James Baldwin, *If Beale Street Could Talk* (New York: Dial, 1974), 125, 196.

43. Ellison, *Shadow and Act*, 136–7.

44. Ralph Ellison, *Invisible Man* (New York: Random House, 1952), 287, 429.

45. Byerman, *Fingering the Jagged Grain*, 24.

46. Frederick Douglass, *Life and Times of Frederick Douglass Written by Himself*, new rev. ed. (Boston: DeWolfe & Fiske, 1892), 177.

47. See, for example, the discussion of Louis in Jeffrey T. Sammons, *Beyond the Ring: The Role of Boxing in American Society* (Urbana and Chicago: University of Illinois Press, 1988). Ellison's use of boxing, and the place of boxing more generally in black intellectual life, is the subject of a book-in-progress by Gerald Early, who delivered a paper on this subject, "The Black Intellectual and the Sport of Prizefighting," at the 1987 convention of the American Studies Association.

48. Ellison, *Shadow and Act*, 141.

49. James Weldon Johnson, *The Autobiography of an Ex-Colored Man*, in *Three Negro Classics* (New York: Avon, 1965), 491.

Chapter 9

1. The complete list: "Ronnie's Romp! And Now the Real Race Is On," 10 March 1980; "The Jackpot Stakes: Where the Election Will Be Won," 13 October 1980: "The PAC Men: Turning Cash into Votes," 25 October 1982 (the graphics represent the Pac Man video game); "Nuclear Poker: The Stakes Get Higher and Higher," 31 January 1983; "Arms Control: Making the Wrong Moves?" 18 April 1983 (the image is chess); "Now It's A Race," 12 March 1984 (a chariot race); "Gromyko Comes Calling: High Stakes in U.S.-Soviet Relations," 1 October 1984; "A Real Race?" 22 October 1984 (a horse race); "The Takeover Game: Corporate Raider T. Boone Pickens," 4 March

1985; "Fare Games," 13 January 1986 (on the airlines); "American Best," 16 June 1986 (a special issue featuring nine cover stories, one of which was "How to Play the Venture Capital Game"); "Star War Games: The Stakes Go Up," 23 June 1986; "Hell-Bent for Gold: The presidential pack races toward Super Tuesday," 29 February 1988 (skiing – concurrent with the Winter Olympics); "A Game of Greed," 5 December 1988 (on Johnson); "Trump," 16 January 1989 ("Flaunting it is the game, and TRUMP is the name"); and "Money Laundering: The trillion-dollar shell game," 18 December 1989.

2. Christopher Matthews, *Hardball: How Politics Is Played – Told by One Who Knows the Game* (New York: Summit, 1988), 11.

3. Hap Vaughan, *Your Career Game* (New York: John Wiley & Sons, 1987), 40.

4. See Philip Gold, *Advertising, Politics, and American Culture: From Salesmanship to Therapy* (New York: Paragon House, 1987), 139–57.

5. "It's the Year of the Handlers," *Time,* 3 October 1988, 18–25. (Among the contributors to this article was a reporter named Dan Goodgame.) See also Joan Didion's essay, "Insider Baseball," in the *New York Review of Books,* 27 October 1988, 19–30. When James Baker became Bush's Secretary of State, *Time* continued to represent him as a preeminent player of political "games." A cover story about Baker in the issue for 13 February 1989, was titled "Playing for the Edge."

6. Burke is discussed in these terms by Arun Mukherjee in *The Gospel of Wealth in the American Novel: The Rhetoric of Dreiser and Some of His Contemporaries* (Totowa, NJ: Barnes & Noble, 1987), 5.

7. *The History of Bacon's and Ingram's Rebellion,* in *Narratives of the Insurrections, 1675–1690,* ed. Andrew Charles McLean (New York: Charles Scribner's Sons, 1915), 57; William Fizhugh to Captain Roger Jones, quoted in T. H. Breen, *Puritans and Adventurers: Change and Persistence in Early America* (New York: Oxford University Press, 1980), 258, n. 29.

8. For the Flannagan references, see *The Congressional Globe,* 1 June 1872, 4147; and 27 February 1873, 1887. Both are quoted in Richard H. Thornton, *The American Glossary,* 3 vols. (Philadelphia and New York: J. B. Lippincott and Frederick Ungar, 1912 and 1962), III, 109. Sullivan's chapter appears in *Our Times: The United States, 1900–1925,* 6 vols. (New York: Charles Scribner's Sons, 1926–35), VI, 52–66. For the other references, see William Safire, *The New Language of Politics: A Dictionary of Catchwords, Slogans & Political Usage,* rev. ed. (New York: Collier Books, 1972), *passim.* And see Frank R. Kent, *The Great Game of Politics* (Garden City, NY: Doubleday, Doran, 1923).

9. Alfred Henry Lewis, *The Boss, and How He Came to Rule New York* (1903; Ridgewood, NJ: Gregg, 1967), 58. See also, Will Payne, "The Chairman's Politics," in *On Fortune's Road: Stories of Business* (Chicago: A. L. McClurg, 1902); and I. K. Friedman, *The Radical* (1907; New York: Johnson Reprints, 1971).

10. Hedrick Smith, *The Power Game: How Washington Really Works* (New York: Random House, 1988), xiii–xvi.

11. Marilyn French, *Beyond Power: On Women, Men, and Morals* (New York:

Summit, 1985), 355. French quotes Hannah Arendt's *Origins of Totalitarianism.*

12. See Helen Gurley Brown, *Sex and the Office* (1964); "J," *The Sensuous Woman* (1969); and Marabel Morgan, *The Total Woman* (1973) – all popular nonfiction books that celebrate sex as joyful sport.

13. A single trip to my local used book store in mid-1987 yielded the following examples (among several hundred romances): Amii Lorin, *The Game Is Played* (Dell, 1981), Brooke Hastings, *Winner Take All* (Silhouette, 1981), Meredith Kingston, *Passion's Games* (Berkeley, 1982), Natalie Stone, *Double Play* (Dell, 1983), Shirley Hart, *Play to Win* (Dell, 1984), Cathie Linz, *Winner Takes All* (Dell, 1984), Serena Galt, *Double Game* (Silhouette, 1984), Elissa Curry, *Dating Games* (Berkeley, 1984), Emma Carcy, *Don't Play Games* (Harlequin, 1985), Penny Jordan, *Rules of the Game* (Harlequin, 1985), Charlotte Lamb, *Love Games* (Harlequin, 1985), Monica Barrie, *Lovegames* (Silhouette, 1985), Kate Walker, *Game of Hazard* (Harlequin, 1986), Kathleen Korbel, *Playing the Game* (Silhouette, 1986), Kay Thorne, *Win or Lose* (Harlequin, 1986), Rosemary Hammon, *Loser Take All* (Harlequin, 1986), and Sandra Marton, *A Game of Deceit* (Harlequin, 1987).

14. For examples see Erica Jong, *Fear of Flying: A Novel* (New York: Holt, Rinehart and Winston, 1973), 15, 277, 280, 295; Diane Johnson, *The Shadow Knows* (New York: Alfred A. Knopf, 1974), 65; Gail Godwin, *The Odd Woman* (New York: Alfred A. Knopf, 1974), 81; Mary Gordon, *Final Payments* (New York: Random House, 1978), 92; Joan Didion, *A Book of Common Prayer* (New York: Simon and Schuster, 1979), 264; Marge Piercy, *Vida* (New York: Summit, 1979), 230, 346; Ann Beattie, *Falling in Place* (New York: Random House, 1980), 310–11; Anne Tyler, *Dinner at the Homesick Restaurant* (New York: Alfred A. Knopf, 1982), 151–52; and Gloria Naylor, *The Women of Brewster Place* (New York: Viking, 1982), 59, 71. For an example of a *woman's* exploitative game playing in Oates' fiction, see *them* (New York: Vanguard, 1969), 410.

15. Marilyn French, *The Women's Room* (New York: Summit, 1977), 34, 108, 207, 198. Alix Kates Shulman's *Memoirs of an Ex-Prom Queen* (New York: Alfred A. Knopf, 1972) is another openly feminist novel that develops the metaphor of oppressive masculine game playing.

16. French, *Beyond Power*, 355, 332–33.

17. Mary P. Ryan, *Womanhood in America: From Colonial Times to the Present* (New York: New Viewpoints, 1975), 293, 295. See also Susan Brownmiller, *Femininity* (New York: Linden Press/Simon and Schuster, 1984), 14. On destructive "games" between the sexes, see Shulamith Firestone, *The Dialectic of Sex: The Case for Feminist Revolution* (New York: William Morrow, 1970), 160; Kate Millett, *Sexual Politics* (Garden City, NY: Doubleday, 1970), 326–7; Germaine Greer, *The Female Eunuch* (New York: McGraw-Hill, 1971), 155, 226; Jessie Bernard, *The Sex Game* (Englewood Cliffs, NJ: Prentice-Hall, 1976), 305–8; Barbara Ehrenreich and Deirdre English, *For Her Own Good: 150 Years of the Experts' Advice to Women* (Garden City, NY: Anchor/Doubleday, 1978), 243, 276, 278.

18. See, for example, Betty Harragan, *Games Mother Never Taught You: Corporate*

Gamesmanship for Women (1977; New York: Warner Books, 1978) and *Knowing the Score: Play-by-Play Directions for Women on the Job* (New York: St. Martin's Press, 1983); Florence Seaman and Anne Lorimer, *Winning at Work: A Book for Women* (Philadelphia: Running Press, 1979); and Sherry Chastain, *Winning the Salary Game: Salary Negotiations for Women* (New York: John Wiley, 1980).

19. See Dana Densmore, "The Slave's Stake in the Home," *No More Fun and Games,* no. 2 (February 1969), 14–20.

20. Mary Daly, *Gyn/Ecology: The Metaethics of Radical Feminism* (Boston: Beacon, 1978), 32, 7, 421.

21. John A. Williams, *The Man Who Cried I Am* (Boston: Little, Brown, 1967), 166, 312; John Updike, *The Coup* (New York: Alfred A. Knopf, 1978), 23.

22. Robert Coover, *The Public Burning* (New York: Viking, 1977), 6.

23. Tom LeClair and Larry McCaffery, *Anything Can Happen: Interviews with Contemporary American Novelists* (Urbana and Chicago: University of Illinois Press, 1983), 72.

24. William Gass, "Authors' Authors," *New York Times Book Review,* 5 December 1976.

25. Joel Dana Black, "The Paper Empires and Empirical Fictions of William Gaddis," in *In Recognition of William Gaddis,* ed. John Kuehl and Steven Moore (Syracuse, NY: Syracuse University Press, 1984), 162–3. Black's essay preempts my own argument almost entirely.

26. William Gaddis, *J R* (New York: Alfred A. Knopf, 1975), 106–7, 301, 647.

27. Black, "The Paper Empire," 163, 167.

28. "Adam Smith," *The Money Game* (New York: Random House, 1968), 10, 13, 14.

29. Robert J. Ringer, *Winning Through Intimidation* (New York: Funk & Wagnalls, 1973), 22–4.

30. Elbert Hubbard, *The Book of Business* (East Aurora, NY: Roycrofters, 1913), 91.

31. Everett W. Lord, "Business Is Business: The Inspired Version," *Nation's Business,* August 1924, 24. This is a rewriting of a poem by Berton Braley with the same title (and with the same sporting theme) in *Nation's Business,* (January 1917), 34–5. In like spirit, Edward Earl Purinton's "Big Ideas from Big Business" in the *Independent* (1921) characterized business as "the finest game." See George E. Mowry, ed., *The Twenties: Fords, Flappers & Fanatics* (Englewood Cliffs, NJ: Prentice-Hall, 1963), 4. For other sporting articles from *Nation's Business* in the 1920s, see the seven-part series by "the father of the trusts," on "The Fun I've Had in Business" (April–November 1924), "The Truth About Grain Gambling," (June–July 1924), "The Fight for Fair Play in Chicago" (February 1925), "The Shippers Are Sitting in the Game" (March 1926), "Team Play and Progress" (September 1926), "The Philosophy of Fair Play" (June 1926), "Hurdles on the Trade Tracks" (December 1926), a short story "Teamwork of the Mighty" (July 1928), "The Race for the Guest" (June 1928) on the competition among hotels, "You Can't Win in the Grandstand" (June 1928) on the need for businessmen's involvement in politics, "Teamwork Helps Illinois Farmers" (October 1928), "Teamwork

Builds North Dakota" (February 1929), and "Fair Play in Business" (August 1929).

32. Harry Emerson Fosdick, "How to Stand Up and Take It," in *Living Under Tension: Sermons on Christianity Today* (New York: Harper & Brothers, 1941), 101, 96; and "Every Man a Gambler," in *The Power to See It Through: Sermons on Christianity Today* (New York: Harper & Brothers, 1935). For other sermons on the "game," see "The Hope of the World in Its Minorities," "Christianity at Home in Chaos," "Is Our Christianity Appealing to Our Softness or Our Strength," "Six Ways to Tell Right from Wrong," and "Getting Out of Us the Best That Is in Us," all in *The Hope of the World: Twenty-five Sermons on Christianity Today* (New York: Harper & Brothers, 1933); "The Revolt Against Irreligion," in *The Secret of Victorious Living: Sermons on Christianity Today* (New York: Harper & Brothers, 1934); "The Mainsprings of Human Motive," in *The Power to See It Through;* "Why Worship?" and "Six Paradoxes Concerning Trouble," in *Successful Christian Living: Sermons on Christianity Today* (New York: Harper & Brothers, 1937); and "Are We Part of the Problem or of the Answer?" in *On Being Fit to Live With: Sermons on Christianity Today* (New York: Harper & Brothers, 1946).

33. Fosdick, "Six Ways to Tell Right from Wrong," in *The Hope of the World.*

34. Norman Vincent Peale, *The Power of Positive Thinking* (1952; Englewood Cliffs, NJ: Prentice-Hall, 1969), *passim; The Art of Real Happiness* (New York: Prentice-Hall, 1950), 5. For more of the same, see *A Guide to Confident Living* (New York: Prentice-Hall, 1948) and *You Can Win* (Garden City, NY: Garden City Publishing Company, 1949).

35. Donald Meyer, *The Positive Thinkers: Religion as Pop Psychology from Mary Baker Eddy to Oral Roberts* (New York: Pantheon, 1980), 284. Bonhoeffer is quoted in Meyer on 290.

36. See Florence Scovel Shinn, *The Game of Life and How to Play It* (Brooklyn, NY: Gerald J. Rickard, 1941); Floyd Van Keuren, *The Game of Living: A Personal Philosophy for Our Times* (New York: Charles Scribner's Sons, 1953); A. L. Hendrickson, *Playing the Game of Life* (Washington, DC: Review and Herald, 1954); Russell V. DeLong and Mendell Taylor, *The Game of Life: Specifications for Character Engineering* (Grand Rapids, MI: Wm. B. Eerdmans, 1954).

37. David Riesman, *The Lonely Crowd: A Study of the Changing American Character* (New Haven, CT: Yale University Press, 1950); C. Wright Mills, *White Collar: The American Middle Class* (New York: Oxford University Press, 1951), xii; and William H. Whyte, Jr., *The Organization Man* (New York: Simon and Schuster, 1956).

38. Max Lerner, *America as a Civilization: Life and Thought in the United States Today* (New York: Simon and Schuster, 1957), 274–84. Lerner quotes *Fortune* magazine.

39. See Sinclair Lewis, *Babbitt* (New York: Harcourt, Brace and Company, 1922), 23, 46, 49, 64–5, 84, 120, 186; and also *Main Street* (New York: Harcourt, Brace and Howe, 1920), 285. West followed Lewis in treating the "game" parodically. See Nathanael West, *A Cool Million,* in *The Complete*

Works of Nathanael West (New York: Farrar, Straus & Giroux, 1957), 255. Cahan and Dos Passos, on the other hand, were harshly critical. See Abraham Cahan, *The Rise of David Levinsky* (1917; New York: Harper & Row, 1960), 239, 322, 323, 332; and John Dos Passos, *Nineteen Nineteen* (1932; Boston: Houghton Mifflin, 1946), 387–8.

40. Ayn Rand, *Atlas Shrugged* (New York: Random House, 1957), 1109–10.

41. John P. Marquand, *Point of No Return* (Boston: Little, Brown, 1949), 204; and *Sincerely, Willis Wayde* (Boston: Little, Brown, 1955), 320.

42. See John Steinbeck, *The Winter of Our Discontent* (New York: Viking, 1961), 134, 154, 214; and Louis Auchincloss, *The Embezzler* (Boston: Houghton Mifflin, 1960), 5, 31, 81, 106, 129.

43. Sloan Wilson, *The Man in the Gray Flannel Suit* (New York: Simon and Schuster, 1955), 6, 256, 224, 300.

44. Cameron Hawley, *Cash McCall* (Boston: Houghton Mifflin, 1955), 164.

45. See Muriel James and Dorothy Jongeward, *Born to Win: Transactional Analysis with Gestalt Experiments* (Reading, MA: Addison-Wesley, 1971); and Carl Frederick, *EST: Playing the Game the New Way* (New York: Dell, 1976). Charles Garfield's two books, *Peak Performance* (1984) and *Peak Performers* (1986), deal with athletes and businessmen respectively, their common qualities suggesting the relationship of entrepreneurial to athletic success.

46. See William G. Nickels, *Win the Happiness Game* (Washington, DC: Acropolis Books, 1981).

47. See Michael Maccoby, *The Gamesman: The New Corporate Leaders* (New York: Simon and Schuster, 1976).

48. George Gilder, *Wealth and Poverty* (New York: Basic Books, 1981), x, 253, 266.

49. Milton and Rose Friedman, *Free to Choose: A Personal Statement* (New York: Harcourt Brace Jovanovich, 1980), 137–9; Michael Novak, *The Spirit of Democratic Capitalism* (New York: American Enterprise Institute/Simon & Schuster, 1982), 71; Peter L. Berger, *The Capitalist Revolution: Fifty Propositions About Prosperity, Equality & Liberty* (New York: Basic Books, 1986), 232n, 26, 62.

50. See *Time*'s cover story about Pickens and "The Takeover Game" cited at the beginning of the chapter; as well as Robert Slater, *The Titans of Takeover* (Englewood Cliffs, NJ: Prentice-Hall, 1987); Robert Sobel, *The New Game on Wall Street* (New York: Wiley & Sons, 1987); and John Brooks, *The Takeover Game* (New York: Truman Talley/E. P. Dutton, 1987).

51. See Connie Bruck, "My Master Is My Purse," *Atlantic*, December 1984; and *Time*, 1 December 1986, 48.

52. John Kenneth Galbraith, "From Stupidity to Cupidity," *New York Review of Books*, 15. For a critical account of the Western financial system since the 1960s, in the terms of my subject, see Susan Strange, *Casino Capitalism* (Oxford: Basis Blackwell, 1986).

53. See Michael Lewis, *Liar's Poker: Rising Through the Wreckage on Wall Street* (New York: W. W. Norton, 1989).

54. "The 80's Are Over," *Newsweek*, 4 January 1988; "The Year of the Yuppie," *Newsweek*, 31 December 1984.

Part IV

1. The first is reported by Herbert McClosky and John Zaller in *The American Ethos: Public Attitudes Toward Capitalism and Democracy,* a Twentieth Century Fund Report (Cambridge, MA: Harvard University Press, 1984), 106; the other by Daniel Yankelovich in *New Rules: Searching for Self-Fulfillment in a World Turned Upside Down* (New York: Random House, 1981), 9.
2. William Bradford, *Of Plymouth Plantation,* ed. Samuel Eliot Morison (New York: Alfred A. Knopf, 1952), 205; Nathaniel Morton, *New Englands Memoriall,* ed. Howard J. Hall (New York: Scholars' Facsimile Reprints, 1937), 69–70; Thomas Morton, *New English Canaan* (New York: Da Capo Press, 1969), 132, 135, 137.
3. Nathaniel Hawthorne, "The May-pole of Merry Mount," in *The Centenary Edition of the Works of Nathaniel Hawthorne,* 14 vols. (Columbus: Ohio State University Press, 1962–80), IX, 54, 67.
4. See, for example, Daniel Neal, *The History of New-England* (1720); Thomas Prince, *Annals of New England* (1754); William Hubbard, *A General History of New England* (1815); and Joseph Felt, *The Annals of Salem* (1827). For discussions of the various historical and fictional accounts of Merry Mount, see John P. McWilliams, Jr., "Fictions of Merry Mount," *American Quarterly* 29 (1977), 3–30; and Michael J. Colacurcio, *The Province of Piety: Moral History in Hawthorne's Early Tales* (Cambridge, MA: Harvard University Press, 1984). I am particularly indebted to McWilliams for discovering the versions by Motley and Stokes briefly discussed here.
5. See Peter Oliver, *The Puritan Commonwealth* (Boston: Little, Brown, 1856), 37–9; and John Gorham Palfrey, *History of New England,* 5 vols. (1865; New York: AMS Press, 1966), I, 231–2.
6. [John Lothrop Motley], *Merry-Mount; A Romance of the Massachusetts Colony,* 2 vols. (Boston and Cambridge: James Munroe, 1849), I, 161, 164, 187.
7. Charles Francis Adams, "The May-Pole of Merrymount," *Atlantic* 39 (May 1877), 557–67, and (June 1877), 686–97. The quotation is from page 565. These essays reappeared in Adams' *Three Episodes of Massachusetts History,* 2 vols. (Boston and New York: Houghton, Mifflin, 1892).
8. William Carlos Williams, *In the American Grain* (1925; New York: New Directions, 1933), 75–80; Richard L. Stokes, *Merry Mount: A Dramatic Poem for Music in Three Acts of Six Scenes* (New York: Farrar & Rinehart, 1932).
9. Robert Lowell, *Old Glory* (New York: Farrar, Straus & Giroux, 1965); Richard Slotkin, *Regeneration Through Violence: The Mythology of the American Frontier, 1600–1860* (Middletown, CT: Wesleyan University Press, 1973) 58–65; and John Seelye, *Prophetic Waters: The River in Early American Life and Literature* (New York: Oxford University Press, 1977), 166, 169.
10. See Ernst Bloch, *A Philosophy of the Future,* trans. John Cumming (New York: Herder and Herder, 1970), 86–7.
11. Quoted by Charles A. Fecher, *Mencken: A Study of his Thought* (New York: Alfred A. Knopf, 1978), 12.

12. Nancy L. Struna, "The Cultural Significance of Sport in the Colonial Chesapeake and Massachusetts," Ph.D. diss., University of Maryland, 1979, 39. See also Struna's "Puritans and Sport: The Irretrievable Tide of Change," *Journal of Sport History* 4 (Spring 1977), 1–21; J. T. Jable, "Pennsylvania's Early Blue Laws: A Quaker Experiment in the Suppression of Sport and Amusements, 1682–1740," *Journal of Sport History* 1 (Fall 1974), 107–21; and the only book-length study, Hans-Peter Wagner, *Puritan Attitudes Towards Recreation in Early Seventeenth-Century New England* (Frankfurt: Verlag Peter Lang, 1982).

13. See Rhys Isaacs, "Evangelical Revolt: The Nature of the Baptists' Challenge to the Traditional Order in Virginia, 1765 to 1775," *William and Mary Quarterly* 31 (1974), 345–68; on Sunday baseball, see Steven A. Riess, *Touching Base: Professional Baseball in American Culture in the Progressive Era* (Westport, CT: Greenwood Press, 1980), 137.

14. See Wagner, *Puritan Attitudes Towards Recreation*, whose thesis, announced on the first page, concerns "the gap between Puritan ideas and seventeenth-century New England reality."

15. See Phillip Stubbes, *The Anatomy of Abuses*, ed. F. J. Furnivall, 2 parts (London: N. Trubner, 1877–82), 149, 173–84; and Richard Baxter, *A Christian Directory: or, a Body of Practical Divinity, and Cases of Conscience*, 5 vols. (London: Richard Edwards, 1825), II, 613–16. Baxter listed no less than eighteen requirements for any sport to be lawful.

16. John Bailey, *Man's Chief End to Glorifie God*, 64; quoted in Perry Miller, *The New England Mind: The Seventeenth Century* (1939; Boston: Beacon Press, 1961), 44.

17. See Philip Greven, *The Protestant Temperament: Patterns of Child-Rearing, Religious Experience, and the Self in Early America* (New York: Alfred A. Knopf, 1977).

18. See John Cotton, *A Practical Commentary, or an Exposition with Observations, Reasons, and Uses upon the First Epistle of John* (London: Thomas Parkhurst, 1656), 126–7; Increase Mather, *Testimony Against Prophane Customs* (1687; Charlottesville: University of Virginia Press, 1953); Benjamin Colman, *The Government and Improvement of Mirth According to the Laws of Christianity* (Boston: B. Green, 1707); and Joseph Seccombe, *A Discourse Utter'd in Part at Ammauskeeg-Falls in the Fishing-Season 1739* (rpt. Barre, MA: Barre Publishers, 1971).

19. St. Augustine, *Confessions*, 2 vols. (Cambridge, MA: Harvard University Press, 1960), 31. This is the translation of William Watts in 1631, the one which seventeenth-century Puritans would have known.

20. John Bunyan, *Grace Abounding to the Chief of Sinners*, ed. Roger Sharrock (Oxford, England: Clarendon Press, 1962), 10.

21. See Daniel B. Shea, Jr., *Spiritual Autobiography in Early America* (Princeton, NJ: Princeton University Press, 1968).

22. Thomas Shepard, *God's Plot: The Paradoxes of Puritan Piety, Being the Autobiography & Journal of Thomas Shepard*, ed. Michael McGiffert (Amherst: University of Massachusetts Press, 1972), 40–1; Dane quoted in Shea, *Spir-*

itual Autobiography, 128; Roger Clap, *Roger Clap's Memoirs, with Account of the Voyage of the "Mary and John," 1630* (Seattle, WA: Piggott-Washington, 1929?), p. 20. Originally published by Thomas Prince in 1731.

23. John Woolman, *The Journal and Major Essays of John Woolman,* ed. Phillips P. Mouton (New York: Oxford University Press, 1971), 25–7.

24. Pike, Banks, Brainerd, and Wheelock all quoted in Greven, *The Protestant Temperament,* 56–8.

25. Jonathan Edwards, *A Faithful Narrative of the Surprizing Work of God,* ed. C. C. Goen, in *The Works of Jonathan Edwards,* 6 vols. (New Haven, CT: Yale University Press, 1957–1980), IV, 146–7.

26. Jonathan Parsons, "Account of the Revival at Lyme," in *The Great Awakening: Documents Illustrating the Crisis and Its Consequences,* ed. Alan Heimert and Perry Miller (Indianapolis, IN: Bobbs-Merrill, 1967), 37; see also 39, 99; Samuel Blair, *A Short and Faithful Narrative of the Late Remarkable Revival of Religion in the Congregation of New-Londonderry, and Other Parts of Pennsylvania* (1944), in *The Great Awakening: Documents on the Revival of Religion, 1740–1745,* ed. Richard L. Bushman (New York: Atheneum, 1970), 72. The other four all in Thomas Prince, Jr., ed., *The Christian History Containing Accounts of the Revival and Propagation of Religion in Great Britain & America,* quoted in Ross W. Beales, Jr., "In Search of the Historical Child: Miniature Adulthood and Youth in Colonial New England," *American Quarterly* 27 (1975), 396.

27. See the accounts by Reverends Timothy M. Cooley, Joseph Washburn, and Ira Hunt in Heman Humphrey, *Revival Sketches and Manual* (New York: American Tract Society, 1859), 139–43, 143–5, 156–8. Humphrey's chronicle of revivalism in America includes others of a similar nature: Reverend John B. Preston: "Thirty-five young men and women, the most of whom but one year ago were wholly devoted to sinful amusements, now sit with us around the table of the Lord" (172–3); Reverend Thomas Marques: "Those who formerly delighted in carnal company, merry jests, profane songs, and foolish and vain conversation, now seek the company of them who fear God, and delight in holy exercises and spiritual communion" (193); Reverend Dr. Porter: " . . . and others who had drowned every thought of religion in giddy mirth, now bending their knees together in supplication" (232–3). The dates of these accounts range from 1795 to 1821, nearly, that is, to Emerson's time and the emergence of play as radical holiness.

28. See, for example, Isaacs, "Evangelical Revolt."

29. Colman, *The Government and Improvement of Mirth,* 100–18.

30. See Charles G. Finney, "A More Excellent Way," *Independent* 25 (1873), 229–30.

31. Quoted in Howard H. Brinton, *The Mystic Will: Based on a Study of the Philosophy of Jacob Boehme* (New York: Macmillan, 1930), 218. For discussions of the mystical play tradition, see Hugo Rahner, *Man at Play* (New York: Herder and Herder, 1967); and David L. Miller, *Gods and Games: Toward a Theology of Play* (New York: World, 1970).

32. William Morris, "A Dream of John Ball" (1886), used as an epigraph by

James Miller in his *"Democracy Is in the Streets": From Port Huron to the Siege of Chicago* (New York: Simon and Schuster, 1987).

Chapter 10

1. For a discussion of the European debate on this subject, see Alasdair Clayre, *Work and Play: Ideas and Experience of Work and Leisure* (New York: Harper & Row, 1974).
2. Elizabeth Palmer Peabody, "Plan of the West Roxbury Community," and Orestes A. Brownson, "Brook Farm," both reprinted in *The Brook Farm Book: A Collection of First-Hand Accounts of the Community,* ed. Joel Myerson (New York: Garland, 1987), 15, 26. The scholar I quote and whose discussion guides my own is Richard Francis, "The Ideology of Brook Farm," in *Critical Essays on American Transcendentalism,* ed. Philip F. Gura and Joel Myerson (Boston: G. K. Hall, 1982), 573, 570. In *American Reformers, 1815–1860* (New York: Hill and Wang, 1978), Ronald G. Walters also weighs the Transcendentalists' "frivolous side" at Brook Farm against their "serious self-development" (51–52). The studies by both Francis and Walters are shaped by their authors' own equation of play with frivolity.
3. See Gay Wilson Allen, *Waldo Emerson: A Biography* (New York: Viking, 1981), 10, 25, 383, and *passim.*
4. In developing Emerson's views on play I follow the argument of Stephen Whicher in *Freedom and Fate: An Inner Life of Ralph Waldo Emerson* (Philadelphia: University of Pennsylvania Press, 1953), as extended and reconceived by my friend and colleague, David Robinson. Robinson's reading of early Emerson is found in *Apostle of Culture: Emerson as Preacher and Lecturer* (Philadelphia: University of Pennsylvania Press, 1982); he is currently working on a second volume on later Emerson, our discussions of which have helped me considerably in my approach to Emerson's writings on play.
5. Ralph Waldo Emerson, "Nature," in *The Collected Works of Ralph Waldo Emerson,* 3 vols. (Cambridge, MA: Belknap Press of Harvard University Press, 1971–83), 31–2. Following Emerson, Jones Very also wrote about Shakespeare's "playful and childlike spirit." See Perry Miller, ed., *The Transcendentalists* (Cambridge, MA: Harvard University Press, 1977), 347.
6. *Works,* III, 17.
7. *Works,* I, 76–7.
8. *Works,* II, 162; II, 8; *The Journals and Miscellaneous Notebooks of Ralph Waldo Emerson,* 14 vols. (Cambridge, MA: Belknap Press of Harvard University Press, 1960–78), VII, 208.
9. Whicher, *Freedom and Fate,* 109.
10. See Robinson, *Apostle of Culture.*
11. *Works,* III, 29–30, 34, 46, 48–9.
12. *The Complete Works of Ralph Waldo Emerson,* 12 vols. (Boston and New York: Houghton, Mifflin, 1904), VI, 318.
13. Alcott as both educator and father gave play an important place in child-rearing, but it always had to be *useful* – his play was entirely instrumental.

See *The Journals of Bronson Alcott,* ed. Odell Shepard (Boston: Little, Brown, 1938), 55, 57; Dorothy McCuskey, *Bronson Alcott, Teacher* (New York: Macmillan, 1940); and Charles Strickland, "A Transcendentalist Father: The Child-Rearing Practices of Bronson Alcott," *Perspectives in American History* 3 (1969), 5–73.

14. [Margaret Fuller], "Entertainments of the Past Winter," *The Dial* 3 (July 1842), 46–72.

15. Walter Harding, *The Days of Henry Thoreau* (1965; New York: Dover, 1982), 18, 30, 31, 128–9, 155, 292–3, 322. The Emerson quotation is from "Historic Notes of Life and Letters in New England," in *Complete Works,* X, 356.

16. Ellery Channing, *Thoreau, the Poet-Naturalist,* quoted in Harding, *The Days of Henry Thoreau,* pp. 173–4.

17. [Henry D. Thoreau], "Walking," *Atlantic Monthly* 9 (June 1862), 657–8.

18. Henry D. Thoreau, *The Writings of Henry D. Thoreau,* 8 vols. (Princeton, NJ: Princeton University Press, 1971–81), VIII, 8 (27 October 1837); 13 (17 November 1837); 18 (15 December 1837); 59 (15 December 1838); 145 (30 June 1840); 167 (July & August 1840).

19. *Writings,* VIII, 350.

20. *Writings,* VIII, 231 (24 January 1841); 276 (27 February 1841).

21. *Writings,* VIII, 146 (1 July 1840); 295 (30 March 1841); 321 (18 August 1841).

22. Sherman Paul, *The Shores of America: Thoreau's Inward Exploration* (Urbana: University of Illinois Press, 1958), 57, 256.

23. See [Henry D. Thoreau], "Natural History of Massachusetts," *Dial* 3 (July 1842), 21, 30–1; and "A Winter Walk," *Dial* 4 (October 1843), 211, 216, 225.

24. See Henry D. Thoreau, *A Week on the Concord and Merrimack Rivers,* in *Writings,* VII, 25, 360; *The Maine Woods,* in *Writings,* II, 156; *Cape Cod,* in *The Writings of Henry David Thoreau,* 11 vols. (Boston and New York: Houghton Mifflin, 1899), IV, 217–19; "Autumnal Tints," *Atlantic Monthly* 10 (October 1862), 397; and "Life Without Principle," *Atlantic Monthly* 12 (October 1863), 490.

25. Henry D. Thoreau, *Walden, or Life in the Woods,* in *Writings,* I, 51.

26. *Journals,* 26 January 1853, 1 January 1854, 25 March 1859; all quoted and discussed in Thomas L. Altherr, " 'Chaplain to the Hunters': Henry David Thoreau's Ambivalence Toward Hunting," *American Literature* 56 (October 1984), 355, 359.

27. Hugo Rahner, *Man at Play* (New York: Herder and Herder), 27.

28. Sydney Ahlstrom, ed., *Theology in America: The Major Protestant Voices from Puritanism to Neo-Orthodoxy* (Indianapolis, IN: Bobbs-Merrill, 1967), 62.

29. Horace Bushnell, "Work and Play," in *Work and Play; or, Literary Varieties* (New York: Charles Scribner, 1864), 18, 29.

30. Ahlstrom, *Theology in America,* 64.

31. Horace Bushnell, *Christian Nurture* (New Haven, CT: Yale University Press, 1953), 291–2, 298, 299.

32. Jonathan Edwards, *A Faithful Narrative of the Surprizing Work of God,* ed. C. C. Goen, in *The Works of Jonathan Edwards,* 6 vols. (New Haven, CT: Yale University Press, 1957–80), 199.

33. *Margaretta; or, The Intricacies of the Heart* (Philadelphia: Samuel F. Bradford, 1807), 32–3.

34. Bernard Wishy, *The Child and the Republic: The Dawn of Modern American Child Nurture* (Philadelphia: University of Pennsylvania Press, 1968), 54–55. See also, Anne Scott MacLeod, *Children's Fiction and American Culture, 1820–1860* (Hamden, CT: Archon Books, 1975), 9. My chief guide to religion in early nineteenth-century fiction is David S. Reynolds, *Faith in Fiction: The Emergence of Religious Literature in America* (Cambridge, MA: Harvard University Press, 1981).

35. [Lydia Maria Child], *Hobomok, A Tale of Early Times* (Boston: Cummings, Hilliard, 1824), 171; [Catherine M. Sedgwick], *Hope Leslie; or, Early Times in the Massachusetts* (New York: White, Gallaher and White, 1827), 103. The same Puritan antiplayfulness is criticized in Eliza Buckminster's later novel, *Naomi; or, Boston, Two Hundred Years Ago* (Boston: Crosby and Nichols, 1848); as well as in Hawthorne's *The Scarlet Letter,* of course.

36. Harriet Beecher Stowe, *Uncle Tom's Cabin; or, Life Among the Lowly* (New York: Library of America, 1982), 39, 98.

37. Francis D. Dedmond, *Sylvester Judd* (Boston: Twayne, 1980), 63–4.

38. [Sylvester Judd], *Margaret: A Tale of the Real and Ideal, Blight and Bloom; Including Sketches of a Place Not Before Described, Called Mons Christi,* rev. ed. 2 vols. (Boston: Phillips, Sampson, 1857), I, 25, 89; II, 236.

39. See Caroline Lee Hentz, *Eoline, or the Magnolia Vale: A Novel* (1852; Freeport, NY: Books for Libraries, 1971), 33; Fanny Fern (Sarah Payson Willis), *Ruth Hall: A Domestic Tale of the Present Time* (New York: Mason Brothers, 1855), 69–70; and Caroline A. Soule, *The Pet of the Settlement: A Story of Prairie-Land* (Boston: A. Tompkins, 1860), 92.

40. Susan Warner, *The Wide, Wide World* (1850; New York: Lovell, Coryell, n.d.), 581; Maria S. Cummins, *The Lamplighter; or, An Orphan Girl's Struggles and Triumphs* (1853; New York: Grosset & Dunlap, n.d.), 286. See also Martha Finley, *Elsie Dinsmore* (1868; New York: Arno Press, 1974).

41. Ann. S. Stephens, *Mary Derwent* (Philadelphia: T. B. Peterson and Brothers, 1858), 24. See also Mary Jane Holmes, *Tempest and Sunshine, or Life in Kentucky* (New York: D. Appleton, 1854); [Catharine M. Sedgwick], *Married or Single?* (New York: Harper & Brothers, 1857); and Mrs. A. D. T. Whitney, *The Gayworthys: A Story of Threads and Thrums* (Boston: Loring, 1865).

42. [Maria S. Cummins], *Mabel Vaughan* (Boston: Crosby, Nichols, 1858), 5–8. See also Marion Harland (Mary Virginia Terhune), *Alone* (New York: J. C. Derby, 1854); and Caroline Lee Hentz, *The Planter's Northern Bride* (Philadelphia: T. B. Peterson, 1854).

43. Nathaniel Hawthorne, *A Wonder-Book,* in *The Centenary Edition of the Works of Nathaniel Hawthorne,* 16 vols. (Columbus: Ohio State University Press, 1962–85), VII, 66, 70, 77, 80–1.

44. Nathaniel Hawthorne, *The Scarlet Letter,* in *Centenary Edition,* I, 102–3. On play in *The Scarlet Letter,* see Mark M. Hennelly, Jr., "*The Scarlet Letter:* 'A Play-Day for the Whole World?' " *New England Quarterly* 61 (1988), 530–54.

45. Nathaniel Hawthorne, *The House of the Seven Gables,* in *Centenary Edition,* II, 145. 82. 138, 149.
46. Nathaniel Hawthorne, *The Blithedale Romance,* in *Centenary Edition,* III, 73–75.
47. Nathaniel Hawthorne, *The Marble Faun,* in *Centenary Edition,* IV, 42.
48. Herman Melville, *Moby-Dick or The Whale* (Evanston and Chicago: Northwestern University Press and the Newberry Library, 1988), 389. In contrast to this scene, later in the novel the crew of the *Bachelor,* its hold full to bursting with precious oil after uncommon luck on the whaling grounds, profess not to believe in Moby Dick at all, but play about the deck in "lively revelry," blissfully ignorant of the world's woes (495). Melville distinguished here between play as innocence and ignorance and play as joy in the face of life's tragedies. The novel leaves no doubt which is the higher state of play.
49. There is a growing body of scholarship on this general subject, in addition to a great deal of primary material. My summary has been guided by Daniel T. Rodgers, *The Work Ethic in Industrial America, 1850–1920* (Chicago: University of Chicago Press, 1978); Roy Rosenzweig, *Eight Hours for What We Will: Workers and Leisure in an Industrial City, 1870–1920* (New York: Cambridge University Press, 1983); Dominick Cavallo, *Muscles and Morals: Organized Playgrounds and Urban Reform, 1880–1920* (Philadelphia: University of Pennsylvania Press, 1981); Donald Meyer, *The Positive Thinkers: Religion as Pop Psychology from Mary Baker Eddy to Oral Roberts,* 2nd ed. (New York: Pantheon Books, 1980); Bernard Mergen, "The Discovery of Child's Play," Chapter 4 of *Play and Playthings: A Reference Guide* (Westport, CT: Greenwood, 1982); T. J. Jackson Lears, "From Salvation to Self-Realization: Advertising and the Therapeutic Roots of the Consumer Culture, 1880–1930," in *The Culture of Consumption: Critical Essays in American History, 1880–1980,* ed. Richard Wrightman Fox and T. J. Jackson Lears (New York: Pantheon Books, 1983). Among the primary materials, see particularly, Jacob Abbott's *Gentle Measures in the Management of the Young* (1871), for a striking contrast to the earlier literature on childrearing; William Wells Newell's *Games and Songs of American Children* (1883), Rollin Lynde Hartt's *The People at Play: Excursions in the Humor and Philosophy of Popular Amusements* (1909), and Michael M. Davis's *The Exploitation of Pleasure* (1910), for the new interest in America's recreational heritage; George M. Beard's *American Nervousness* (1881) and Annie Payson Call's *Power Through Repose* (1891), for two of the most famous and representative of the medical and mind-cure treatises promoting the gospel of relaxation; and G. Stanley Hall's *Adolescence* (1905), Benjamin Atkins's *Out of the Cradle into the World of Self Education Through Play* (1895), Alexander F. Chamberlain's *The Child: A Study of the Evolution of Man* (1900), and Karl Groos's *The Play of Man* (trans. 1908) for early and important works by social scientists.
50. See Elliott J. Gorn, *The Manly Art: Bare-Knuckle Prize Fighting in America* (Ithaca, NY: Cornell University Press, 1986); Paul Boyer, *Urban Masses and Moral Order in America, 1820–1920* (Cambridge, MA: Harvard University Press, 1978); Cary Goodman, *Choosing Sides: Playground and Street Life on the Lower East Side* (New York: Schocken, 1979); Francis G. Couvares, *The*

Remaking of Pittsburgh: Class and Culture in an Industrializing City, 1877–1919
(Albany: State University of New York Press, 1984); and Rosenzweig, *Eight
Hours for What We Will*.

51. See Herbert G. Gutman, *Work, Culture, and Society in Industrializing America*
(New York: Alfred A. Knopf, 1976), 19ff.

52. Clarence Rainwater, *The Play Movement in the United States: A Study of
Community Recreation* (Chicago: University of Chicago Press, 1922), 331. See
also Howard S. Braucher, "Play and Social Progress," *The Annals of the
American Academy of Social Science* 35 (March 1910), 109–17; and Joseph Lee,
"American Play Tradition and Our Relation to It," *The Playground*, 7 (July
1913), 148–59.

53. My discussion of utopian fiction is informed by Charles J. Rooney's *Dreams
and Visions: A Study of American Utopias, 1865–1917* (Westport, CT: Greenwood Press, 1985).

54. For this distinction, see Gorman Beauchamp, "The Dream of Cockaigne:
Some Motives for the Utopias of Escape," *Centennial Review* 25 (1981),
343–62.

55. See Edward Everett Hale, *Sybaris and Other Homes* (1869), William Dean
Howells, *A Traveler from Altruria* (1894), Ignatius Donnelly, *Caesar's Column*
(1891), and Edward Bellamy, *Looking Backward* (1888). For other utopias
that include some concern for leisure, see also Calvin Blanchard, *The Art of
Real Pleasure* (1864), Solomon Schindler, *Young West* (1894), Albert Cha-
vannes, *The Future Commonwealth* (1892), Alexander Craig, *Ionia* (1898),
Milan C. Edson, *Solaris Farm* (1900), Bradford Peck, *The World a Department
Store* (1900), William Alexander Taylor, *Intermere* (1901), and Charles Wil-
liam Wooldridge, *Perfecting the Earth* (1902). For a selection of utopias that
ignore play and recreation altogether, see David A. Moore, *The Age of
Progress* (1856), J. W. Roberts, *Looking Within* (1893), W. W. Saterlee, *Look-
ing Backward and What I Saw* (1890), Frank Rosewater, *'96: A Romance of
Utopia* (1894), Charles W. Caryl, *New Era* (1897), William Stanley Child,
The Legal Revolution of 1902 (1898), Thomas McGrady, *Beyond the Black
Ocean* (1901), W. S. Harris, *Life in a Thousand Worlds* (1905), and W. O.
Henry, *Equitania* (1914). The novels by Bellamy, Howells, and Donnelly
were published in many editions. All of the others were reprinted by the
Arno Press and the New York Times in 1971. Women's utopias, with the
late exception of Charlotte Perkins Gilman's *Herland* (1915), were equally
uninterested in play. See Carol Farley, ed., *Daring to Dream: Utopian Stories
by United States Women, 1836–1919* (New York: Pandora Press, 1984).

56. T. Wharton Collens, *Eden of Labor; or, the Christian Utopia* (1876; New York:
Arno Press and the New York Times, 1971), 17.

57. Mary E. Bradley, *Mizora: A Prophecy* (1889; New York: Gregg, 1975), 28.

58. Ann Douglas, *The Feminization of American Culture* (New York: Alfred A.
Knopf, 1977), 55; Dodge quoted in Rodgers, *The Work Ethic in Industrial
America*, 186. Chapter 7 of Rodgers's book is an excellent discussion of this
entire issue.

59. See Charlotte Perkins Gilman, *Women and Economics: A Study of Economic
Relations Between Men and Women as a Factor in Social Evolution* (1898), ed.

Carl N. Degler (New York: Harper & Row, 1966), 307–09; and Patricia Vertinsky, "Feminist Charlotte Perkins Gilman's Pursuit of Health and Physical Fitness as a Strategy for Emancipation," *Journal of Sport History* 16 (Spring 1989), 5–26.

60. Quoted in Rodgers, *The Work Ethic in Industrial America*, 185–6.

61. Edith Wharton, *The House of Mirth* (New York: Charles Scribner's Sons, 1905), 46.

62. Charlotte Perkins Gilman, *The Yellow Wallpaper* (1892; Old Westbury, NY: Feminist Press, 1973), 12.

63. For a discussion of working-class women's leisure in the late nineteenth century, see Kathy Peiss, *Cheap Amusements: Working Women and Leisure in Turn-of-the-Century America* (Philadelphia: Temple University Press, 1986), especially the Introduction where Peiss distinguishes women's from men's leisure within the working classes and considers its possibilities for liberating women.

64. Sarah Orne Jewett, *The Country of the Pointed Firs* (Boston and New York: Houghton Mifflin, 1896), 157. For representative stories of women's drudgery, see Rose Terry Cooke's "Mrs. Flint's Married Experience," Alice Brown's "A Sea Change," and Mary Wilkins Freeman's "The Revolt of 'Mother.' "

65. Harriet Beecher Stowe, *Oldtown Folks* (Boston: Houghton, Mifflin, 1869), 326ff.; Henry Ward Beecher, *Norwood; or, Village Life in New England* (New York: Charles Scribner, 1868), 158.

66. It is instructive to compare the "Pilgrim's Progress" game of *Little Women* to the "Glad Game" of Eleanor Porter's *Pollyana* (1913). In these two juvenile classics spanning half a century of secularization, the March girls' game of moral striving becomes Pollyana's game of feeling good about life.

67. Louisa M. Alcott, *Little Women* (1868–69; New York: Modern Library, 1983), 18, 132, 148.

68. Polly in *The Five Little Peppers* is playful without ever engaging in actual play, her cheerful work creating a delightful life for her family despite extreme poverty. Wiggins's sportive Rebecca brings a stern old aunt to life, while Rebecca herself grows more disciplined and serious. Porter's Little Sister resembles Pearl and Judd's Margaret, but her play in nature lacks any theological resonance.

69. See Thomas Bailey Aldrich, *The Story of a Bad Boy* (1870; Chicago: Goldsmith, n.d.), 67; Charles Dudley Warner, *Being a Boy* (1878; Boston and New York: Houghton Mifflin, 1905), 43; and W. D. Howells, *A Boy's Town* (New York: Harper & Brothers, 1890), 13, 14.

70. See Albert E. Stone, *The Innocent Eye: Childhood in Mark Twain's Imagination* (1961; New York: Archon, 1970); Susan K. Harris, *Mark Twain's Escape from Time: A Study of Patterns and Images* (Columbia: University of Missouri Press, 1982); and James L. Johnson, *Mark Twain and the Limits of Power: Emerson's God in Ruins* (Knoxville: University of Tennessee Press, 1982).

71. Mark Twain, *Roughing It* (Berkeley and Los Angeles: University of California Press, 1972), 66; *A Tramp Abroad*, in *The Writings of Mark Twain*, 25 vols.

(New York: Harper & Brothers, 1899), III, 124; *Tom Sawyer Abroad* (Berkeley and Los Angeles: University of California Press, 1980), 48–9.

72. James M. Cox, *Mark Twain: The Fate of Humor* (Princeton, NJ: Princeton University Press, 1966), 140. My discussion of *Tom Sawyer* merely recapitulates Cox's argument. See also Forrest G. Robinson, "Social Play and Bad Faith in *The Adventures of Tom Sawyer*," *Nineteenth-Century Fiction* 39 (1984–5), 1–24.

73. Mark Twain, *The Adventures of Tom Sawyer* (Berkeley and Los Angeles: University of California Press, 1980), 16.

74. See Judith Fetterly, "The Sanctioned Rebel," *Studies in the Novel* 3 (Fall 1971), 293–304.

75. Mark Twain, *Personal Recollections of Joan of Arc by the Sieur Louis de Conte*, in *Writings*, XVII, 79, 338.

76. For an alternative reading of the novel *sub specie ludi*, see Bruce Michelson, "Huck and the Games of the World," *American Literary Realism* 13 (1980), 108–21.

77. Mark Twain, *Adventures of Huckleberry Finn* (Berkeley and Los Angeles: University of California Press, 1985), 7.

78. See Johnson, *Mark Twain and the Limits of Power*.

79. See particularly "The Fight" and "The Trial, Execution, and Burial of Homer Phelps" in which Crane took on the Bad-Boy school, and "The Monster," in which a complex series of games reveals the racism, cruelty, and social pretension of adults as well as children. For Crane, child nature was human nature in embryo, his adults but grown-up versions of their pettily vicious and convention-ridden offspring. See Stephen Crane, *Tales of Whilomville*, in *The Works of Stephen Crane*, 10 vols. (Charlottesville: University Press of Virginia, 1969–76), VII. For a discussion of "The Monster," see Robert A. Morace, "Games, Play, and Entertainments in Stephen Crane's 'The Monster,' " *Studies in American Fiction* 9 (Spring 1981), 65–81.

Chapter 11

1. See Daniel Aaron, *Writers on the Left: Episodes in American Literary Communism* (New York: Harcourt, Brace & Jovanovich, 1961), 8.

2. Harold Stearns, *America and the Young Intellectual* (1921; Westport, CT: Greenwood Press, 1973), 68–9.

3. Aaron, *Writers on the Left*, 7–8.

4. My chief source on Nietzsche's influence in America is Melvin Drimmer, "Nietzsche in American Thought, 1895–1925," Ph.D. diss., University of Rochester, 1965.

5. See Drimmer's checklist, 668–727, a more complete list than that in Herbert W. Reichert and Karl Schlechta, ed., *International Nietzsche Bibliography* (Chapel Hill: University of North Carolina Press, 1960), 5–25.

6. See Bryan Strong, "Images of Nietzsche in America, 1900–1970," *South Atlantic Quarterly* 70 (Spring 1971), 573–94. For admiring views of Nietzsche, see H. L. Mencken, *The Philosophy of Friedrich Nietzsche*, 3rd ed. (1913; Port

Washington, NY: Kennikat Press, 1967) – by the third edition Nietzsche's works were available in Levy's eighteen-volume translation; James Huneker, *Egoists: A Book of Supermen* (New York: Charles Scribner's Sons, 1909), 236–68; and Otto Heller, *Prophets of Dissent: Essays on Maeterlinck, Strindberg, Nietzsche, and Tolstoy* (New York: Alfred A. Knopf, 1918), 109–57. For a representative assault on Nietzsche, see Paul Carus, *Nietzsche and Other Exponents of Individualism* (Chicago: Open Court, 1914).

7. John Neville Figgis, *The Will to Freedom; or, The Gospel of Nietzsche and the Gospel of Christ* (New York: Charles Scribner's Sons, 1917), 263.

8. Mencken, *The Philosophy of Friedrich Nietzsche,* 187.

9. On Freud's popularization in America, see Hendrik M. Ruitenbeek, *Freud in America* (New York: Macmillan, 1966); William E. Leuchtenburg, *The Perils of Prosperity, 1914–32* (Chicago: University of Chicago Press, 1958), Chapter IX; and Frederick J. Hoffman, *Freudianism and the Literary Mind,* 2nd ed. (Baton Rouge: Louisiana State University Press, 1957).

10. Leuchtenburg, *The Perils of Prosperity,* 164; Hoffman, *Freudianism and the Literary Mind,* 58; Oscar Cargill, *Intellectual America: Ideas on the March* (New York: Macmillan, 1941), 601; Henry F. May, *The End of Innocence: A Study of the First Years of Our Own Time* (1959; Chicago: Quadrangle, 1964), 219.

11. Hoffman, *Freudianism and the Literary Mind,* 30.

12. Floyd Dell, "Out of the World" (1916), in *Looking at Life* (New York: Alfred A. Knopf, 1924), 67; *Love in Greenwich Village* (New York: George H. Doran, 1926), 22, 33.

13. Robert E. Humphrey, *Children of Fantasy: The First Rebels of Greenwich Village* (New York: John Wiley & Sons, 1978), Chapter 7. See also Malcolm Cowley, *Exile's Return: A Literary Saga of the Nineteen-Twenties,* rev. ed. (New York: Viking, 1956), 66ff.

14. See, for example, George Cram Cook's letter to Mollie Price, quoted in Humphrey, p. 95; and Floyd Dell, *Intellectual Vagabondage: An Apology for the Intelligentsia* (New York: George H. Doran, 1926), 161.

15. See Van Wyck Brooks, *America's Coming-of-Age* (New York: B. W. Huebsch, 1915), 136–7, 34.

16. *The Pagan* 1 (1916), 32; 2 (September 1917), 22; 3 (June 1919), 11–12.

17. *Playboy,* nos. 1–3, 7 (1919, 1923).

18. Louis Untermeyer, "The Dance," *Seven Arts* 1 (November 1916), 79–81; Margaret Anderson, "Isadora Duncan's Misfortune," *Little Review* 3 (April 1917), 5–7; Hiram Kelly Moderwell, with Charles L. Buchanan, "Two Views of Ragtime," *Seven Arts* 2 (1917), 370; H. L. Mencken, "Music and Sin," in Louis Cheslock, *H. L. Mencken on Music* (New York: Alfred A. Knopf, 1961), 186–88.

19. Mabel Dodge Luhan, *Movers and Shakers* (New York: Harcourt, Brace, 1936), 80.

20. Clive Bell, *Since Cezanne* (London: Chatto and Windus, 1922), 216–18; Paul Rosenfeld, *Modern Tendencies in Music,* in *Fundamentals of Musical Art,* ed. Edward Dickinson, 20 vols. (New York: Caxton Institute, 1926–28), XVIII, 105; and Gilbert Seldes, *The Seven Lively Arts* (New York: Harper & Brothers, 1924), 83–98.

21. Isadora Duncan, *My Life* (New York: Boni & Liveright, 1927), 168, 341, and *passim*.
22. *Broom* 2 (April 1922), 89–93; *Little Review* 5 (January 1919), 65.
23. Havelock Ellis, *The Dance of Life* (Boston and New York: Houghton Mifflin, 1923), *passim*.
24. [Hutchins Hapgood], *The Story of a Lover* (New York: Boni & Liveright, 1919), 66, 72–3, 150.
25. Dell, *Love in Greenwich Village,* 296–303.
26. Dale Kramer, *Chicago Renaissance: The Literary Life of the Midwest, 1900–1930* (New York: Appleton-Century, 1966), 13.
27. Dell, *Intellectual Vagabondage,* 187–8.
28. See Irwin Marcus, "The Interaction Between Political and Cultural Radicalism: The Greenwich Village Revolt, 1910–1920," in *Cultural Politics: Radical Movements in Modern History,* ed. Jerold M. Starr (New York: Praeger, 1985), 51–78.
29. Leuchtenburg, *The Perils of Prosperity,* 164, 168–70; Ruitenbeek, *Freud and America,* 74.
30. Stuart Ewen and Elizabeth Ewen, *Channels of Desire: Mass Images and the Shaping of American Consciousness* (New York: McGraw-Hill, 1982), 57.
31. There is no major study of sport in the 1920s, but see the chapters in John Rickards Betts, *America's Sporting Heritage: 1850–1950* (Reading, MA: Addison-Wesley, 1974); or any other standard history.
32. Ring W. Lardner, "Sport and Play," in *Civilization in the United States: An Inquiry by Thirty Americans,* ed. Harold Stearns (New York: Harcourt, Brace, 1922), 458. Stuart Chase, "Play," in *Whither Mankind? A Panorama of Modern Civilization,* ed. Charles A. Beard (New York: Longmans, Green, 1928), 332–4; Robert L. Duffus, "The Age of Play," *The Independent,* 20 December 1924, 539; reprinted in *The Twenties: Fords, Flappers & Fanatics,* ed. George E. Mowry (Englewood Cliffs, NJ: Prentice-Hall, 1963), 44–6.
33. See, for example, "Contract," "The Golden Honeymoon," and "Who Dealt?"; "Mr. Frisbie" and "A Caddie's Diary"; "Champion," "My Roomy," and "A Frame-Up." All were collected in *Round Up* (New York: Charles Scribner's Sons, 1929), after previous publication.
34. Percy Marks, *The Unwilling God* (New York: Harper & Brothers, 1929), 337.
35. F. Scott Fitzgerald, *This Side of Paradise* (New York: Charles Scribner's Sons, 1920), 36, 55.
36. Warner Fabian, *Flaming Youth* (New York: Macaulay, 1923), 69, 99, 109, 155, 177, 187, and *passim*. "Warner Fabian" was the pseudonym of journalist Samuel Hopkins Adams.
37. Owen Johnson, *The Wasted Generation* (Boston: Little, Brown, 1921), 343.
38. See Dorothy Canfield, *The Brimming Cup* (New York: Harcourt, Brace, 1921), 355–7; Gertrude Atherton, *Black Oxen* (New York: Boni and Liveright, 1923), 172 and *passim;* Anne Douglas Sedgwick, *The Little French Girl* (Boston and New York: Houghton Mifflin, 1924), 138; Margaret Kennedy, *The Constant Nymph* (Garden City, NY: Doubleday, Page, 1924);

Elinor Glyn, "*It*" (New York: Macaulay, 1927), *passim;* and Viña Delmar, *Bad Girl* (New York: Harcourt, Brace, 1928).

39. Sinclair Lewis, *Babbitt* (New York: Harcourt, Brace, 1922), 338.

40. Joseph Hergesheimer, *Cytherea* (New York: Alfred A. Knopf, 1922), 47, 63, 336.

41. F. Scott Fitzgerald, *The Beautiful and Damned* (New York: Charles Scribner's Sons, 1922), 127.

42. F. Scott Fitzgerald, *The Great Gatsby* (New York: Charles Scribner's Sons, 1925), 39, 41.

43. F. Scott Fitzgerald, *The Crack Up,* ed. Edmund Wilson (1945; New York: New Directions, 1956), 30, 15.

44. F. Scott Fitzgerald, *The Last Tycoon* (New York: Charles Scribner's Sons, 1941), 79, 108.

45. F. Scott Fitzgerald, *Tender Is the Night* (New York: Charles Scribner's Sons, 1934), 6, 99.

46. Zelda Fitzgerald, *Save Me the Waltz* (1932; London: Grey Walls Press, 1953), 133, 161, 162, 199.

47. See Robert Goldwater, *Primitivism in Modern Art,* rev. ed. (New York: Vintage Books, 1967).

48. Gertrude Stein, *Three Lives* (New York: Grafton Press, 1909), 297; Vachel Lindsay, *The Congo and Other Poems* (New York: Macmillan, 1914), 5; Willa Cather, *My Antonia* (1918; Boston: Houghton Mifflin, 1961), 189, 370.

49. Carl Van Vechten, *Nigger Heaven* (New York: Alfred A. Knopf, 1926), 12.

50. Julia Peterkin, *Scarlet Sister Mary* (1928; New York: Grosset & Dunlap, n.d.), 14, 15.

51. DuBose Heyward, *Porgy* (1925; New York: Grosset & Dunlap, n.d.), 114–15.

52. Waldo Frank, *Holiday* (New York: Boni and Liveright, 1923), 9, 13, 29, 38, 40.

53. Sherwood Anderson, *Dark Laughter* (New York: Boni & Liveright, 1925), 65.

54. See Chidi Ikonné, *From DuBois to Van Vechten: The Early New Negro Literature, 1903–1926* (Westport, CT: Greenwood, 1981) in particular for this reading. Recent black scholars such as Ikonné and Houston Baker have sought to counter the emphasis on white influence in earlier studies. See Nathan Irvin Huggins, *Harlem Renaissance* (New York: Oxford University Press, 1971); David Levering Lewis, *When Harlem Was in Vogue* (New York: Alfred A. Knopf, 1981); and Houston A. Baker, Jr., *Modernism and the Harlem Renaissance* (Chicago: University of Chicago Press, 1987).

55. Bernard W. Bell, *The Afro-American Novel and Its Tradition* (Amherst: University of Massachusetts Press, 1987), 113.

56. Charles T. Davis makes this point as a major criticism of the Harlem Renaissance. See *Black is the Color of the Cosmos: Essays on Afro-American Literature and Culture, 1942–1981,* ed. Henry Louis Gates, Jr. (New York: Garland, 1982), 73.

57. J. A. Rogers, "Jazz at Home," in *The New Negro: An Interpretation,* ed. Alain

Locke (New York: Albert and Charles Boni, 1925), 216–24. Some of Hughes's poems that were inspired by jazz also appeared in *The New Negro*.

58. Huggins, *Harlem Renaissance*, 9–10.
59. Bell, *The Afro-American Novel*, 130.
60. Ralph Ellison, *Shadow and Act* (New York: Random House, 1964), 78.
61. Houston A. Baker, Jr., *Blues, Ideology, and Afro-American Literature: A Vernacular Theory* (Chicago: University of Chicago Press, 1984), 6.
62. Ellison, *Shadow and Act*, 257.
63. Bell, *The Afro-American Novel*, 71.
64. Rudolph Fisher, *The Walls of Jericho* (1928; New York: Arno, 1969), 134.
65. Langston Hughes, *Not Without Laughter* (New York: Alfred A. Knopf, 1930), 32, 101–2, 267, 313.
66. Claude McKay, *Home to Harlem* (1928; Chatham, NJ: Chatham Bookseller, 1973), 337–8.
67. Claude McKay, *Banjo* (New York: Harper & Brothers, 1929), 57–58.
68. Zora Neale Hurston, *Their Eyes Were Watching God* (1937; Urbana and Chicago: University of Illinois Press, 1978), 196–7.
69. Ellison, *Shadow and Act*, 257.
70. Ellison, *Shadow and Act*, 116.
71. Michael G. Cooke, *Afro-American Literature in the Twentieth Century: The Achievement of Intimacy* (New Haven, CT: Yale University Press, 1984), 21–2; Keith E. Byerman, *Fingering the Jagged Grain: Tradition and Form in Recent Black Fiction* (Athens: University of Georgia Press, 1985), 169.
72. The references are to: for signifying, Henry Louis Gates, *The Signifying Monkey: A Theory of Afro-American Literary Criticism* (New York: Oxford University Press, 1988); for specifying, Susan Willis, *Specifying: Black Women Writers, the American Experience* (Madison: University of Wisconsin Press, 1987); for call-and-response, John F. Callahan, *In the African-American Grain: The Pursuit of Voice in Twentieth-Century Black Fiction* (Urbana and Chicago: University of Illinois Press, 1988); for the blues, Baker, *Blues, Ideology, and Afro-American Literature* and *Modernism and the Harlem Renaissance;* and for more eclectic folk materials, Bell, *The Afro-American Novel and Its Tradition;* Cooke, *Afro-American Literature in the Twentieth Century;* and Byerman, *Fingering the Jagged Grain.*
73. See Ishmael Reed, *Mumbo Jumbo* (Garden City, NY: Doubleday, 1972); James Baldwin, *If Beale Street Could Talk* (New York: Dial, 1974), 192; Toni Cade Bambara, *The Salt Eaters* (New York: Random House, 1980), 264; John Edgar Wideman, *Sent for You Yesterday* (New York: Avon, 1983), 208.

Chapter 12

1. See Benjamin Kline Hunnicutt, *Work Without End: Abandoning Shorter Hours for the Right to Work* (Philadelphia: Temple University Press, 1988).
2. The discussion that follows is indebted to Chapter 9 ("The Culture of the Thirties") in Susman's *Culture as History: The Transformation of American Society in the Twentieth Century* (New York: Pantheon Books, 1984).

3. See Frederick Lewis Allen, *Since Yesterday: The Nineteen-Thirties in America* (New York: Harper & Brothers, 1940), 147–54; and Susman 162.

4. Stuart Chase, *Mexico: A Study of Two Cultures* (New York: Macmillan, 1931), 205–6.

5. George Santayana, *The Last Puritan: A Memoir in the Form of a Novel* (New York: Charles Scribner's Sons, 1936). For Santayana's earlier meditations on the aesthetics of play, see "Philosophy in the Bleachers," in *George Santayana's America: Essays on Literature and Culture,* ed. James Bellowe (Urbana: University of Illinois Press, 1967), 121–30; "Athletic Ode," in *The Complete Poems of George Santayana,* ed. William G. Holzberger (Lewisburg, PA: Bucknell University Press, 1979), 148; and *The Sense of Beauty, Being the Outlines of Aesthetic Theory* (1896; New York: Charles Scribner's Sons, 1910).

6. See Eric Larrabee and Rolf Meyersohn, eds., *Mass Leisure* (Glencoe, IL: Free Press, 1958), 391–406.

7. A partial list: Clifford Cook Furnas, *America's Tomorrow: An Informal Excursion into the Era of the Two-Hour Working Day* (1931); Lawrence Pearsall Jacks, *Education Through Recreation* (1932); Jay B. Nash, *Spectatoritis* (1932); Arthur Olaus Dahlberg, *Jobs, Machines, and Capitalism* (1932); Gove Hambidge, *Time to Live: Adventures in the Use of Leisure* (1933); Jesse Frederick Stuart, *Americans at Play* (1933); George Lundborg, Mirra Komarovsky, and Mary Alice McInerny, *Leisure* (1934); Harry Allen Overstreet, *A Guide to Civilized Leisure* (1934); Arthur Newton Pack, *The Challenge of Leisure* (1934); Earnest Calkins, *The Care and Feeding of Hobby Horses* (1934); Austin Fox Riggs, *Play: Recreation in a Balanced Life* (1935); Marjorie Latta Greenlie, *The Arts of Leisure* (1935).

8. Earnest Calkins, *The Care and Feeding of Hobby Horses* (New York: Leisure League of American, 1934), 1; Jay B. Nash, *Spectatoritis* (New York: Holston House, 1932), 1.

9. See Mumford's denunciation of modern sport as "one of the mass duties of the machine age," in *Technics and Civilization* (New York: Harcourt, Brace, 1934), 303–7.

10. See Philip Gold, *Advertising, Politics, and American Culture: From Salesmanship to Therapy* (New York: Paragon House, 1987).

11. David Riesman, *The Lonely Crowd: A Study of the Changing American Character* (New Haven, CT: Yale University Press, 1950), especially chapters 15–17; C. Wright Mills, *White Collar: The American Middle Class* (New York: Oxford University Press, 1951), 238; William H. Whyte, Jr., *The Organization Man* (New York: Simon and Schuster, 1956), 233; and Daniel Bell, *The End of Ideology* (Glencoe, IL: Free Press, 1960), 249–51. See also Erich Fromm, *The Sane Society* (New York: Holt, Rinehart and Winston, 1955), 136–7; Paul Goodman, *Growing Up Absurd: Problems of Youth in the Organized System* (New York: Random House, 1960), 38; Lewis Mumford, *The Conduct of Life* (New York: Harcourt, Brace, 1951), 35, 221, 134; and Riesman's later essay, "Leisure and Work in Post-Industrial Society," in *Mass Leisure,* ed. Eric Larrabee and Rolf Meyersohn (Glencoe, IL: Free Press, 1958), 367–8.

12. See, for example, Max Kaplan, *Leisure in America: A Social Inquiry* (New York: John Wiley & Sons, 1960); Charles Brightbill, *Man and Leisure* (En-

glewood Cliffs, NJ: Prentice-Hall, 1961), also among others; Nels Anderson, *Work and Leisure* (New York: The Free Press of Glencoe, 1961); August Hecksler, *The Public Happiness* (New York: Atheneum, 1962); Walter Kerr, *The Decline of Pleasure* (New York: Simon and Schuster, 1962); Sebastian De Grazia, *Of Time, Work, and Leisure* (New York: Twentieth Century Fund, 1962); and *The Annals of the American Academy of Political and Social Science* 313 (September 1957).

13. James C. Charlesworth, "A Bold Program for Recreation," *The Annals of the American Academy of Political and Social Science* 313 (September 1957), 141–7; Martha Wolfenstein, "Fun Morality: Analysis of Recent American Child-Training Literature," in *Childhood in Contemporary Cultures,* ed. Margaret Mead and Wolfenstein (Chicago: University of Chicago Press, 1955), 175.

14. William L. O'Neill, *American High: The Years of Confidence, 1945–1960* (New York: Free Press, 1986), 23–4.

15. John Clellon Holmes, *Go* (1952; Mamaroneck, NY: Paul P. Appel, 1977), 310, 161.

16. Neal Cassady, *The First Third & Other Writings* (San Francisco: City Lights Books, 1971), 42–3.

17. Jack Kerouac, *On the Road* (New York: Viking Press, 1957), 3–11.

18. See Norman Mailer, "The White Negro," in *Advertisements for Myself* (New York: Putnam's, 1959), 341; and Harold Beaver, *The Great American Masquerade* (Totowa, NJ: Barnes & Noble, 1985), 207.

19. Quoted in Greil Marcus, *Lipstick Traces: A Secret History of the Twentieth Century* (Cambridge, MA: Harvard University Press, 1989), 266.

20. Alexander Trocchi, *Cain's Book* (New York: Grove Press, 1960), 11, 41, 246.

21. Henry Miller, *Tropic of Cancer* (New York: Grove Press, 1961), 15, 249, 257.

22. Wright Morris, *The Huge Season* (New York: Viking Press, 1954), 168; *The Field of Vision* (1956; Lincoln: University of Nebraska Press, 1974), 197.

23. J. P. Donleavy, *The Ginger Man,* rev. ed. (New York: McDowell, Obolensky, 1958), 222.

24. J. D. Salinger, *Raise High the Roofbeam, Carpenters and Seymour: An Introduction* (Boston: Little, Brown, 1959), 114.

25. Salinger, "Seymour: An Introduction," 169–74.

26. "Seymour," 226–48.

27. J. D. Salinger, *Catcher in the Rye* (Boston: Little, Brown, 1951), 9.

28. See Holmes, *Go,* 17, 20, 40, 113, 158, 159.

29. Norman Mailer, *The Deer Park* (New York: G. P. Putnam's Sons, 1955), 42; Vladimir Nabokov, *Lolita* (New York: G. P. Putnam's Sons, 1958), 23; John Updike, *The Poorhouse Fair* (New York: Alfred A. Knopf, 1958), 124; and *Rabbit, Run* (New York: Alfred A. Knopf, 1960), 65.

30. Walker Percy, *The Moviegoer* (New York: Alfred A. Knopf, 1962), Chapter 3; Ken Kesey, *One Flew Over the Cuckoo's Nest* (New York: Viking Press, 1962), 212ff.; Paul Goodman, *Making Do* (New York: Macmillan, 1963), 145–51; Frank Conroy, *Stop-Time* (New York: Viking Press, 1967), Chapter 8; Philip Roth, *Portnoy's Complaint* (New York: Random House, 1969), 68–9. For the discovery of Conroy's novel I am indebted to an unpublished

paper by Timothy Dow Adams, " 'A Momentary Stay Against Confusion': Games as a Metaphor of Self in Frank Conroy's *Stop-Time*," presented at the annual convention of the Modern Language Association, December 1978.

31. Tony Tanner, "Games American Writers Play," *Salmagundi* 35 (1976), 115. See also Robert Detweiler, "Games and Play in Modern American Fiction," *Contemporary Literature* 17 (1976), 44–62. On postmodern play, see Allen Thiher, *Words in Reflection: Modern Language Theory and Postmodern Fiction* (Chicago: University of Chicago Press, 1984), Chapter 6 ("Play"); Eugene Goodheart, *The Skeptic Disposition in Contemporary Criticism* (Princeton, NJ: Princeton University Press, 1984), Chapter 7 ("Literature as Play"); John Kuehl, "The Ludic Impulse in Recent American Fiction," *Journal of Narrative Technique* 16 (Fall 1986), 167–78; Christopher Nash, *World-Games: The Tradition of Anti-Realist Revolt* (New York: Methuen, 1987); and Robert Newsom, *A Likely Story: Probability and Play in Fiction* (New Brunswick, NJ: Rutgers University Press, 1988).

32. See Peter Matthiessen, *At Play in the Fields of the Lord* (New York: Random House, 1965).

33. See Robert Coover, *The Universal Baseball Association, Inc., J. Henry Waugh, Prop.* (New York: Random House, 1968).

34. Thomas Pynchon, *Gravity's Rainbow* (New York: Viking, 1973), *passim*.

35. For the pastoral in postwar baseball fiction one can look at almost any baseball novel of the past four decades. See, for example, Bernard Malamud's *The Natural* and Mark Harris's Henry Wiggin novels for particularly good examples from the 50s. For representative football novels, see Robert Daley's *Only a Game* (1967), Gary Cartwright's *The Hundred-Yard War* (1968), Peter Gent's *North Dallas Forty* (1973), and Jack Olsen's *Alphabet Jackson* (1974). And for basketball fictions consider Jeremy Larner's *Drive, He Said* (1964), Lawrence Shainberg's *One on One* (1970), and Charles Rosen's *A Mile Above the Rim* (1976).

36. Lucie Scott Brown, "The Peter Pan of American Literature," *The CEA Critic* 32 (January 1970), 13.

37. See Norman O. Brown, *Life Against Death: The Psychoanalytic Meaning of History* (Middletown, CT: Wesleyan University Press, 1959), 32–33; and Herbert Marcuse, *Eros and Civilization: An Inquiry into Freud* (Boston: Beacon Press, 1955), 187. Marcuse's distinction between basic and surplus repression is clarified and explored by Gad Horowitz in *Repression: Basic and Surplus Repression in Psychoanalytic Theory: Freud, Reich, and Marcuse* (Toronto: University of Toronto Press, 1977).

38. See Timothy Leary, Ralph Metzner, and Richard Alpert, *The Psychedelic Experience: A Manual Based on the Tibetan Book of the Dead* (Hyde Park, NY: University Books, 1964), 65, 69; Tom Wolfe's account of the Pranksters in *The Electric Kool-Aid Acid Test;* Allen Ginsberg, "Demonstration as Spectacle, as Example, as Communication," *Berkeley Barb,* 19 November 1965; "Free" [Abbie Hoffman], *Revolution for the Hell of It* (New York: Dial Press, 1968); and Jerry Rubin, *Do It: Scenarios of the Revolution* (New York: Simon and Schuster, 1970).

39. See Norman Mailer, *The Armies of the Night: History as a Novel, The Novel*

as History (New York: New American Library, 1968); Tom Wolfe, *The Electric Kool-Aid Acid Test* (New York: Farrar, Straus and Giroux, 1968), 224; and Harvey Cox, *The Feast of Fools: A Theological Essay on Festivity and Fantasy* (Cambridge, MA: Harvard University Press, 1969), viii. For other early discussions of this conflict, see two essays by Barbara G. Myerhoff: "The Revolution as Trip: Symbol and Paradox," *Annals of the American Academy of Political and Social Science* 395 (May 1971), 105-16; and "Organization and Ecstasy: Deliberate and Accidental Communitas among Huichol Indians and American Youth," in *Symbol and Politics in Communal Ideology: Cases and Questions,* ed. Sally Falk Moore and Barbara G. Myerhoff (Ithaca, NY: Cornell University Press, 1975), 33-67. And for reassessments on similar terms, see Todd Gitlin, *The Sixties: Years of Hope, Days of Rage* (New York: Bantam, 1987); and Jerold M. Starr, "Cultural Politics in the 1960s," in *Cultural Politics: Radical Movements in Modern History,* ed. Jerold M. Starr (New York: Praeger, 1985), 295-333.

40. See Richard Neville, *Play Power* (London: Jonathan Cape, 1970); Rubin, *Do It,* 85; Hoffman, *Revolution for the Hell of It,* 59, 36, 61-2, and *Woodstock Nation: A Talk-Rock Album* (New York: Random House, 1969); and Theodore Roszak, *The Making of a Counter Culture: Reflections on the Technocratic Society and Its Youthful Opposition* (Garden City, NY: Doubleday & Company, 1969), 153-4.

41. For the discussion of Woodstock, see Bruce Cook, *The Beat Generation: The Tumultuous '50s Movement and Its Impact on Today* (New York: Charles Scribner's Sons, 1971). Recent anniversary reminiscences of Woodstock have tended to celebrate its play spirit.

42. For the rejection of "games," see for example George Metefsky, "Right On, Culture Freeks!" in *Hip Culture: Essays on Its Revolutionary Potential* (New York: Times Change Press, 1970), 6; for the mirroring of these "games" in the counterculture, see Lewis Yablonski, *The Hippie Trip* (New York: Pegasus, 1968), 329-33.

43. See Metefsky, "Right On, Culture Freeks!" 15-18; and Gold, *Advertising, Politics, and American Culture,* 72.

44. Herbert Marcuse, "On the Philosophical Foundations of the Concept of Labor in Economics," *Telos* 16 (Summer 1973), 16. The translation of this early essay in 1973 is a most curious event, given the extraordinarily different views on work and play that Marcuse had developed by this time.

45. See Horowitz, *Repression: Basic and Surplus Repression in Psychoanalytic Theory.* Marcuse addressed his objections to Brown in "Love Mystified: A Critique of Norman O. Brown," in *Negations: Essays in Critical Theory,* with translations by Jeremy J. Shapiro (Boston: Beacon Press, 1965).

46. Marcuse, *Counterrevolution and Revolt* (Boston: Beacon Press, 1972), 129-30.

47. Herbert Marcuse, *An Essay on Liberation* (Boston: Beacon Press, 1969), 25-6; *Counterrevolution and Revolt,* 132.

48. Marcuse, *Eros and Civilization,* ix.

49. Marcuse, *Counterrevolution and Revolt,* 48-51.

50. See Peter L. Berger, *A Rumor of Angels: Modern Society and the Rediscovery of*

the Supernatural (Garden City, NY: Doubleday & Company, 1969); Frank Musgrove, *Ecstasy and Holiness: Counter Culture and the Open Society* (Bloomington: Indiana University Press, 1974); and Charles Y. Glock and Robert N. Bellah, eds., *The New Religious Consciousness* (Berkeley and Los Angeles: University of California Press, 1976).

51. See Robert Lee, *Religion and Leisure in America: A Study in Four Dimensions* (New York: Abingdon Press, 1964); Dom Aelred Graham, *Zen Catholicism: A Suggestion* (New York: Harcourt, Brace & World, 1963); also Alan Watts, *Psychotherapy East and West* (New York: Random House, 1961); *Beyond Theology: The Art of Godmanship* (New York: Pantheon, 1964); and *Play to Live: Selected Seminars* (South Bend, IN, 1982).

52. See Harvey Cox, *The Feast of Fools: A Theological Essay on Festivity and Fantasy* (Cambridge, MA: Harvard University Press, 1969); Robert E. Neale, *In Praise of Play: Toward a Psychology of Religion* (New York: Harper & Row, 1969); Sam Keen, *To a Dancing God* (New York: Harper & Row, 1970); Barry Wood, *The Magnificent Frolic* (Philadelphia: Westminster, 1970); David L. Miller, *Gods and Games: Toward a Theology of Play* (New York: World, 1970); Hugo Rahner, *Man at Play* (New York: Herder and Herder, 1967); and Jürgen Moltmann, *Theology of Play,* trans. Reinhard Ulrich (New York: Harper & Row, 1972).

53. Wolfe, *Electric Kool-Aid Acid Test,* 26, 202, 263, 353, 356, 357, 360, 392; and 239, 242, 261, 263, 271, 367, 393.

54. *Acid Test,* 318. There are more than two dozen references to society's "games."

55. Tom Robbins, *Even Cowgirls Get the Blues* (Boston: Houghton Mifflin, 1976), 47, 87, 227.

56. For glimpses into an astonishingly large body of writing, see Abraham Maslow, *Toward a Psychology of Being,* 2nd. ed. (Princeton, NJ: D. Van Nostrand, 1968); Charles A. Reich, *The Greening of America* (New York: Random House, 1970); Matthew Fox, *Whee! We, Wee, All the Way Home: A Guide to the New Sensual Spirituality* (Wilmington, NC: Consortium, 1976) and *The Coming of the Cosmic Christ: The Healing of Mother Earth and the Birth of a Global Renaissance* (San Francisco: Harper & Row, 1989); Mihaly Csikszentmihalyi, *Beyond Boredom and Anxiety: The Experience of Play in Work and Games* (San Francisco: Jossey-Bass, 1975); Marilyn Ferguson, *The Aquarian Conspiracy: Personal and Social Transformation in the 1980s* (Los Angeles: J. P. Tarcher, 1980); Jean Houston, *Lifeforce: The Psycho-Historical Recovery of the Self* (New York: Delacorte, 1980); and Gary Zukav, *The Dancing Wu Li Masters: An Overview of the New Physics* (New York: William Morrow, 1979). Others that emphasize spiritual transcendence include James P. Carse, *Finite and Infinite Games: A Vision of Life as Play and Possibility* (New York: Free Press, 1986); David Toolan, *Facing West from California's Shores: A Jesuit's Journey into New Age Consciousness* (New York: Crossroad, 1987); Gertrud Mueller Nelson, *To Dance with God: Family Ritual and Community Celebration* (New York: Paulist Press, 1986).

57. *The New Age Catalogue: Access to Information and Sources* (New York: Doubleday, 1988). Tarcher's list in 1988, in addition to the books by Ferguson

and Houston, included W. Brugh Joy's *Joy's Way* (1979), George Leonard's *The End of Sex* (1983), Peter Russell's *The Global Brain* (1983), Rick Fields' *Chop Wood, Carry Water* (1984), John White's *What Is Enlightenment?* (1984), and Neil Fiore's, *The Now Habit: A Strategic Program for Overcoming Procrastination and Enjoying Guilt-Free Play* (1988) – all of which explored the possibilities of play.

58. Ferguson, *The Aquarian Conspiracy*, 116, 345. Naisbitt's Foreword appears in the 1987 edition, published also by Tarcher.

59. See Kate Strelley, *The Ultimate Game: The Rise and Fall of Bagwan Shree Rajneesh* (San Francisco: Harper & Row, 1987).

60. See Daniel Bell, *The Cultural Contradictions of Capitalism* (New York: Basic Books, 1976), 75; Christopher Lasch, *The Culture of Narcissism: American Life in an Age of Diminishing Expectations* (New York: W. W. Norton, 1979), 221; Lasch, *The Minimal Self: Psychic Survival in Troubled Times* (New York: W. W. Norton, 1984), 247; Irving Kristol, *Two Cheers for Capitalism* (New York: Basic Books, 1976), 252; Richard Sennet, *The Fall of Public Man* (New York: Alfred A. Knopf, 1977), 315ff.; Irving Louis Horowitz, *Ideology and Utopia in the United States, 1956–1976* (New York: Oxford University Press, 1977), 122.

61. Sennett, *The Fall of Public Man*, 315.

62. Lasch, *The Minimal Self*, 221n, 253–4.

63. Maslow's concept of the "peak performance," developed in books like *Toward a Psychology of Being*, was taken up by Charles A. Garfield (among numerous others) in *Peak Performance* (Los Angeles: J. P. Tarcher, 1984) and *Peak Performers* (New York: William Morrow, 1986). See also Robert Masters and Jean Houston, *Mind Games* (New York: Delta, 1972), 6; Jean Houston, *The Possible Human: A Course in Enhancing Your Physical, Mental, and Creative Abilities* (Los Angeles, J. P. Tarcher, 1982), 192; Annie Gottlieb, *Do You Believe in Magic?: The Second Coming of the Sixties Generation* (New York: Times Books, 1987), 300, Theodore Roszak, *Person/Planet: The Creative Disintegration of Industrial Society* (Garden City, NY: Anchor Press, Doubleday, 1978), 108, 232; and Alvin Toffler, *The Third Wave* (1980; New York: Bantam, 1981), 277, 391.

64. John Updike, *S.* (New York: Alfred A. Knopf, 1988), 151, 180.

65. For the essays, see "On Hawthorne's Mind," *New York Review of Books*, 19 March 1981; and "Hawthorne's Creed," in *Hugging the Shore: Essays and Criticism* (New York: Knopf, 1983). The fullest discussion of what has become a critical commonplace appears in Samuel Chase Coale, *In Hawthorne's Shadow: American Romance from Melville to Mailer* (Lexington: University Press of Kentucky, 1985).

66. John Updike, *Rabbit, Run* (New York: Alfred A. Knopf, 1960), 126–34.

67. John Updike, *Rabbit Redux* (New York: Alfred A. Knopf, 1971), 159, 172.

68. John Updike, *Rabbit Is Rich* (New York: Alfred A. Knopf, 1981), 50, 178–9.

69. John Updike, *Couples* (New York: Alfred A. Knopf, 1968), 108.

70. John Updike, *A Month of Sundays* (New York: Alfred A. Knopf, 1975), 13.

71. John Updike, *Picked-Up Pieces* (New York: Alfred A. Knopf, 1975), 98.

Epilogue

1. See Greil Marcus, *Lipstick Traces: A Secret History of the Twentieth Century* (Cambridge, MA: Harvard University Press, 1989).
2. Among the works of Freudo-Marxists have been Bruce Brown, *Marx, Freud, and the Critique of Everyday Life: Toward a Permanent Cultural Revolution* (New York: Monthly Review Press, 1973); Francis Hearn, "Toward a Critical Theory of Play," *Telos* 30 (Winter 1976–77), 145–60; Lawrence M. Hinman, "Marx's Theory of Play, Leisure and Unalienated *Praxis*," *Philosophy and Social Criticism* 5 (1977), 193–228; Douglas Kellner, *Herbert Marcuse and the Crisis of Marxism* (Berkeley and Los Angeles: University of California Press, 1984). The Marxian Freudians include Russell Jacoby, *Social Amnesia: A Critique of Contemporary Psychology from Adler to Laing* (Boston: Beacon Press, 1975); and Gad Horowitz, *Repression: Basic and Surplus Repression in Psychoanalytic Theory: Freud, Reich, and Marcuse* (Toronto: University of Toronto Press, 1977).
3. Marcus, *Lipstick Traces;* see for example, Christopher Gray, ed. and trans., *Leaving the 20th Century: The Incomplete Work of the Situationist International* (London: Free Fall Publications, 1974); Richard Gombin, *The Origins of Modern Leftism,* trans. Michael K. Perl (Harmondsworth, Middlesex, England: Penguin Books, 1975); Kostas Axelos, *Alienation, Praxis, and Technē in the Thought of Karl Marx,* trans. Ronald Bruzina (Austin: University of Texas Press, 1976); Henri Lefebvre, *Everyday Life in the Modern World,* trans. Sacha Rabinovitch (London: Allen Lane/ Penguin Press, 1971); and the special edition of *Yale French Studies* (no. 73, 1987), particularly the essay by Edward Ball, "The Great Sideshow of the Situationist International," 21–37. For discussions of play and European Marxism, see Mark Poster, *Existential Marxism in Postwar France: From Sartre to Althusser* (Princeton, NJ: Princeton University Press, 1975); John M. Hoberman, *Sport and Political Ideology* (Austin: University of Texas Press, 1984); Allen Guttman, *From Ritual to Record: The Nature of Modern Sports* (New York: Columbia University Press, 1978) and his introduction to his translation of Bero Rigauer, *Sport and Work* (New York: Columbia University Press, 1981).
4. Fredric Jameson, *The Political Unconscious: Narrative as a Socially Symbolic Act* (Ithaca, NY: Cornell University Press, 1981), 73.
5. Carole S. Vance, ed., *Pleasure and Danger: Exploring Female Sexuality* (Boston: Routledge & Kegan Paul, 1984), 1.
6. See Jessica Benjamin, "A Desire of One's Own: Psychoanalytic Feminism and Intersubjective Space," in *Feminist Studies/Critical Studies,* ed. Teresa de Lauretis (Bloomington: Indiana University Press, 1986), 78–101; Barbara Ehrenreich, Elizabeth Hess, and Gloria Jacobs, *Re-making Love: The Feminization of Sex* (Garden City, NY: Anchor Press/Doubleday, 1986); and Muriel Dimen, *Surviving Sexual Contradictions: A Startling and Different Look at a Day in the Life of a Contemporary Professional Woman* (New York: Macmillan, 1986), 181–6. For early feminist champions of sexual play, see Shulamith Firestone, *The Dialectic of Sex* (New York: William Morrow, 1970), 215–8; Germaine Greer, *The Female Eunuch* (New York: McGraw-Hill,

1971), 324, 328. Recent discussions of Lesbian eroticism have also contributed
to the feminist concept of sexual play. See, for example, Audre Lorde, *Uses
of the Erotic: The Erotic as Power* (Trumansburg, NY: Out & Out Books,
1978); and *Coming to Power: Writings and Graphics on Lesbian S/M* (Boston,
MA: Alyson Publications, 1981).

7. For discussions of French feminisms, their differences from American feminism, and the concept of *jouissance*, see Virginia Thorndike Hules, "A Topography of Difference," in Elissa D. Gelfand and Virginia Thorndike Hules,
*French Feminist Criticism: Women, Language, and Literature: An Annotated Bib-
liography* (New York: Garland, 1985), xv–lii; the introduction by Elaine
Marks and Isabelle de Courtivron to *New French Feminisms: An Anthology*
(Amherst: University of Massachusetts Press, 1980), 28–38; and Ann Rosalind Jones, "Writing the body: toward an understanding of *l'écriture fémi-
nine*," in *Feminist Criticism and Social Change: Sex, Class and Race in Literature
and Culture*, ed. Judith Newton and Deborah Rosenfelt (New York: Methuen, 1985), 86–101.

8. See Marilyn French, *Beyond Power: On Women, Men and Morals* (New York:
Summit Books, 1985). For feminist accounts of the matrilineal prehistory,
see also Elizabeth Gould Davis, *The First Sex* (New York: G. P. Putnam's
Sons, 1971); Merlin Stone, *When God Created Woman* (New York: Harcourt
Brace Jovanovich, 1978); Kim Chernin, *Reinventing Eve: Modern Woman in
Search of Herself* (New York: Times Books, 1987); and Riane Eisler, *The
Chalice and the Blade: Our History, Our Future* (San Francisco, CA: Harper &
Row, 1987).

9. See Mary Daly, *Gyn/Ecology: The Metaethics of Radical Feminism* (Boston:
Beacon Press, 1978); as well as Sheila D. Collins, *A Different Heaven and
Earth* (Valley Forge, PA: Judson Press, 1974); Starhawk, *The Spiral Dance:
A Rebirth of the Ancient Religion of the Great Goddess* (San Francisco, CA:
Harper & Row, 1979); Amanda Porterfield, *Feminine Spirituality in America:
From Sarah Edwards to Martha Graham* (Philadelphia: Temple University
Press, 1980); Charlene Spretnak, ed., *The Politics of Women's Spirituality:
Essays on the Rise of Spiritual Power Within the Feminist Movement* (Garden
City, NY: Anchor, 1982); Beverly Wildung Harrison, "Human Sexuality
and Mutuality," in *Christian Feminism: Visions of a New Humanity*, ed. Judith
L. Weidman (San Francisco, CA: Harper & Row, 1984); Carol P. Christ,
Laughter of Aphrodite: Reflections on a Journey to the Goddess (San Francisco:
Harper & Row, 1987); Christin Lore Weber, *WomanChrist: A New Vision of
Feminist Spirituality* (San Francisco: Harper & Row, 1987); and Anne E. Car,
Transforming Grace: Christian Tradition and Women's Experience (San Francisco:
Harper & Row, 1988).

10. Alix Kates Shulman, *The Memoirs of an Ex-Prom Queen* (New York: Alfred
A. Knopf, 1972), 35; Gail Godwin, *The Odd Woman* (New York: Alfred A.
Knopf, 1974), 99; Marilyn French, *The Women's Room* (New York: Summit,
1977), 318–19; Louise Erdrich, *Love Medicine* (New York: Holt, Rinehart &
Winston, 1984), 220.

11. See Thea Alexander, *2150 A.D.* (Tempe, AZ: Macro Books, 1971); Ursula
Le Guin, *The Dispossessed* (New York: Harper & Row, 1974); Mary Staton,

From the Legend of Biel (New York: Ace Books, 1975); Joanna Russ, *The Female Man* (1975; Boston: G. K. Hall, 1977); Dorothy Bryant, *The Kin of Ata Are Waiting for You* (San Francisco, CA: Moon Books, 1976); Marge Piercy, *Woman on the Edge of Time* (New York: Alfred A. Knopf, 1976). For discussions of women's utopian fiction, see Carol Pearson, "Women's Fantasies and Feminist Utopias," *Frontiers: A Journal of Women Studies* 2 (1977), 50–61; Marleen Barr and Nicholas D. Smith, eds., *Women and Utopia: Critical Interpretations* (Lanham, MD: University Press of America, 1983); and Natalie M. Rosinsky, *Feminist Futures: Contemporary Women's Speculative Fiction* (Ann Arbor, MI: UMI Research Press, 1984).

12. See, for example, Judith Newton and Deborah Rosenfelt's introduction to *Feminist Criticism and Social Change,* xvii; and Alice Echols, "The New Feminism of Yin and Yang," in *Powers of Desire: The Politics of Sexuality,* ed. Ann Snitow, Christine Stansell, and Sharon Thompson (New York: Monthly Review Press, 1983), 439–59.

13. Fyodor Dostoyevsky, *The Brothers Karamazov,* trans. Constance Garnett (New York: Random House, 1933), 268.

14. Daly, *Gyn/Ecology,* 386. See also LeGuin, *The Dispossessed,* 100; Collins, *A Different Heaven and Earth,* 26; Rosemary Radford Reuther, *Sexism and God-Talk: Toward a Feminist Theology* (Boston: Beacon Press, 1983), 254; and French, *Beyond Power,* 509, 539.

Index

CAMBRIDGE STUDIES IN AMERICAN LITERATURE
AND CULTURE

Editor

Albert Gelpi, Stanford University

★Now available in hardcover and paperback

★Published in hardcover and paperback